Tokyo

"All you've got to do is decide to go and the hardest part is over.

So go!"

TONY WHEELER, COFOUNDER – LONELY PLANET

THIS EDITION WRITTEN AND RESEARCHED BY

Rebecca Milner, Simon Richmond

Contents

Plan Your Trip 4

Explore Tokyo 50

Understand Tokyo 209

Survival Guide 241

Tokyo Maps 274

GREG ELMS / GETTY IMAGES ©

DAMIEN SIMONIS / GETTY IMAGES ©

(left) **Tokyo National Museum p155** Buddha statue

(above) **Manga p221** Billboard art in Ginza

(right) **Display at Meiji-jingū p115** Sake containers

GARY CONNER / GETTY IMAGES ©

Welcome to Tokyo

Yoking past and future, Tokyo dazzles with its traditional culture and passion for everything new.

Sci-Fi Cityscapes

Tokyo's neon-lit streetscapes still look like a sci-fi film set – and that's a vision of the city from the 1980s. Tokyo has been building ever since, pushing the boundaries of what's possible on densely populated, earthquake-prone land, adding ever taller, sleeker structures. Come see the utopian mega-malls, the edgy designer boutiques from Japan's award-winning architects, and the world's tallest tower – Tokyo Sky Tree – a twisting spire that draws on ancient building techniques. Stand atop one of Tokyo's skyscrapers and look out over the city at night to see it blinking like the control panel of a starship, stretching all the way to the horizon.

The Shogun's City

Tokyo may be forever reaching into the future but you can still see traces of the shogun's capital on the kabuki stage, at a sumo tournament or under the cherry blossoms. It's a modern city built on old patterns, and in the shadows of skyscrapers you can find anachronistic wooden shanty bars and quiet alleys, raucous traditional festivals and lantern-lit *yakitori* (grilled chicken) stands. In older neighbourhoods you can shop for handicrafts made just as they have been for centuries, or wander down cobblestone lanes where geisha once trod.

Eat Your Heart Out

Yes, Tokyo has more Michelin stars than any other city. Yes, Japanese cuisine has been added to the Unesco Intangible Cultural Heritage list. But that's not what makes dining in Tokyo such an amazing experience. What really counts is the city's long-standing artisan culture. You can splash out on the best sushi of your life, made by one of the city's legendary chefs using the freshest ingredients from Tsukiji Market that day. You can also spend ¥800 on a bowl of noodles made with the same care and exacting attention to detail, from a recipe honed through decades of experience.

Fashion & Pop Culture

From giant robots to saucer-eyed school girls to a certain, ubiquitous kitty, Japanese pop culture is a phenomenon that has reached far around the world. Tokyo is the country's pop culture laboratory, where new trends grow legs. Come see the latest looks bubbling out of the backstreets of Harajuku, the hottest pop stars projected on the giant video screens in Shibuya, or the newest anime and manga flying off the shelves in Akihabara. Or just pop 'round to the nearest convenience store to pick up treats in wacky flavours emblazoned with cute characters.

Why I Love Tokyo

By Rebecca Milner

I've lived in Tokyo for over a decade now and am continuously surprised – sometimes on a daily basis – by something new. Such is the joy of living in a city that prides itself on constant renewal and reinvention; it seriously never gets old. Tokyo has everything you can ask of a city, and has it in spades: a rich, cosmopolitan dining scene, more cafes and bars than you could visit in a lifetime, fantastic public transportation and grassy parks – plus it's clean and safe. Really, what's not to love?

For more about our authors, see p296.

Above: Koishikawa Kōrakuen (p140)

Tokyo's Top 16

Shinjuku Nightlife *(p133)*

1 Shinjuku is the biggest, brashest nightlife district in the land of the rising neon sun. There is truly something for everyone here, from the anachronistic shanty bars of Golden Gai, a favourite haunt of writers and artists; to the camp dance bars of Tokyo's gay quarter, Shinjuku-nichōme; to the more risque cabarets of Kabukichō. There are sky-high lounges, all-night karaoke parlours, jazz dens and *izakaya* (Japanese pub-eateries) stacked several storeys high. The options are dizzying, the lights spellbinding and the whole show continues past dawn.

BELOW LEFT: KABUKICHŌ (P127)

Shinjuku & West Tokyo

Tsukiji Market *(p67)*

2 The world's biggest seafood market moves an astounding 2000 tonnes of seafood a day. You can see all manner of fascinating creatures here, but it is the *maguro* (bluefin tuna) that has emerged as the star. Get up at dawn and you can see these prized fish auctioned off to the highest bidder. Tsukiji Market is one of Tokyo's unique sights, and a rare peek into the working life of the city. Follow up your visit with sushi for breakfast in the market.

BELOW: BLUEFIN TUNA

Ginza & Tsukiji

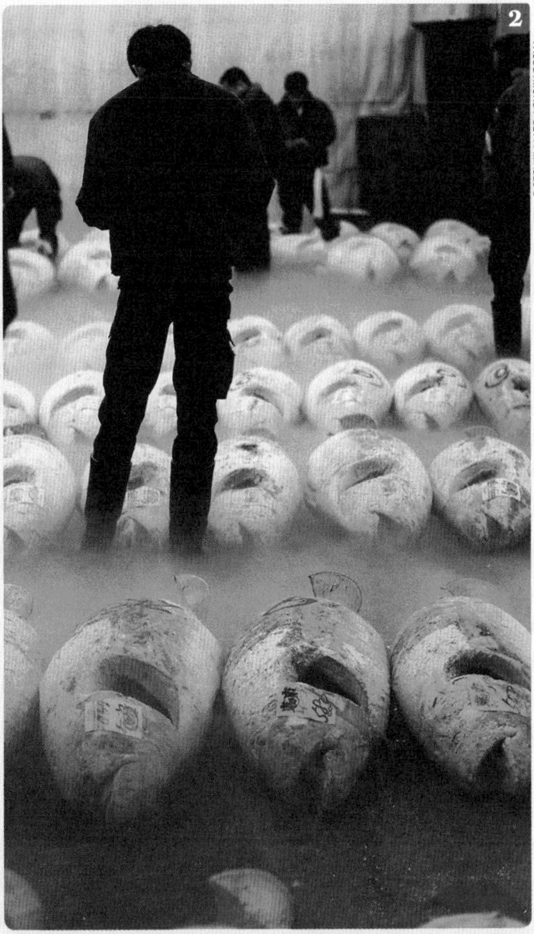

2

3

4

Tokyo Cityscape *(p168)*

3 There's nothing quite like gazing out over the Tokyo cityscape from a few hundred metres in the air. From this vantage point, the city is endless, stretching all the way to the horizon (where, if you're lucky, you might spot Mt Fuji). By night, Tokyo appears truly beautiful, as if the sky were inverted, with the glittering stars below. Tokyo Sky Tree is the city's newest spot for city views – and the tallest, with observatories at 350m and 450m. Standing at this height is a thrilling experience.

Asakusa & Sumida River

Meiji-jingū *(p115)*

4 Tokyo's largest and most famous Shintō shrine feels a world away from the city. It's reached via a long, rambling forest path marked by towering *torii* (gates). The grounds are vast, enveloping the classic wooden shrine buildings and a landscaped garden in a thick coat of green. Meiji-jingū is a place of worship and a memorial to Emperor Meiji, but it's also a place for traditional festivals and rituals. If you're lucky you may even catch a wedding procession, with the bride and groom in traditional dress.

Harajuku & Aoyama

Shopping in Harajuku *(p123)*

5 Harajuku is the gathering point for Tokyo's eccentric fashion tribes. Along Takeshita-dōri, an alley that feels like a bazaar, it's teens in kooky, colourful outfits. Omote-sandō, a broad boulevard with wide sidewalks and high-end designer boutiques, draws high-end divas. The backstreets of Harajuku (known as Ura-Hara) is Tokyo's street fashion laboratory; here's where you'll find the trendsetters, the peacocks and inspiration by the truck load. Simply put: for shopping (and people-watching) there's no better spot in Tokyo than Harajuku.

ABOVE: TAKESHITA-DŌRI (P116)

Harajuku & Aoyama

Dining Out *(p32)*

6 When it comes to Tokyo superlatives, the city's eating scene takes the cake. Wherever you are in the city you're rarely 500m from a good, if not great, restaurant. The best part is that you can get to-die-for food at all budget levels, from seasonal sushi tasting courses prepared by master chefs, all the way down to a steaming bowl of late-night noodles. Tokyoites love dining out; join them, and delight in the sheer variety of flavours the city has to offer. BELOW: SUSHI (P35)

Eating

Roppongi Art Triangle *(p79)*

7 The opening of three high-profile art museums since 2003 has turned Roppongi, once known exclusively for its nightlife, into a polished gem. The area nicknamed 'Roppongi Art Triangle' includes the Mori Art Museum, a showcase for contemporary art perched atop a skyscraper; the minimalist Suntory Museum of Art, dedicated to the decorative arts; and the National Art Center, Tokyo, which hosts blockbuster shows inside a curving glass structure. Within the triangle there are several smaller museums and galleries too. RIGHT: NATIONAL ART CENTER, TOKYO (P79)

Roppongi & Around

Ōedo Onsen Monogatari *(p180)*

8 Don't let Tokyo's slick surface and countless beguiling diversions fool you; underneath the city it's pure, bubbling primordial pleasure. Ōedo Onsen Monogatari pumps natural hot-spring water from 1440m below Tokyo Bay into its many bathing pools, which include both indoor and outdoor baths (called *rotemburo*). But it's not just about bathing: Ōedo Onsen Monogatari bills itself as an 'onsen theme park' – a fantastically Japanese concept – and includes a Disneyland-style version of an Edo-era town with games and food stalls.

Odaiba & Tokyo Bay

Mt Fuji *(p192)*

9 On a clear day, the perfect, snow-capped cone of Japan's national symbol, Mt Fuji, is visible in the distance – putting all of Tokyo's artificial monuments to shame. You can hunt for views from the observatories and restaurants that top many of the city's highest buildings. Or head to the mountains west of Tokyo for a better look. Even better yet, join the thousands of pilgrims who climb the sacred peak each summer. Watching the sunrise from the top is a profound, once-in-a-lifetime experience.

Day Trips

Sensō-ji *(p166)*

10 The spiritual home of Tokyo's ancestors, this Buddhist temple was founded over one thousand years before Tokyo got its start. Today it retains an alluring, lively atmosphere redolent of Edo (old Tokyo) and the merchant quarters of yesteryear. The colourful Nakamise-dōri arcade approaching the temple complex overflows with sweet treats and tacky souvenirs. The main plaza holds a five-storey pagoda and a smoking cauldron of incense. Altogether, Sensō-ji is a heady mix of secular and sacred, and one of Tokyo's most iconic sights.

Asakusa & Sumida River

Sumo in Ryōgoku *(p175)*

11 The purifying salt sails into the air. The two giants leap up and crash into each other. A flurry of slapping and heaving ensues. Who will shove the other out of the sacred ring and move up in the ranks? From the ancient rituals to the thrill of the quick bouts, sumo is a fascinating spectacle. Tournaments take place in Tokyo three times a year; outside of tournament season you can catch an early morning practice session at one of the stables where wrestlers live and train. BOTTOM RIGHT: SUMO WRESTLING AT RYŌGOKU KOKUGIKAN (P175)

Asakusa & Sumida River

10

12

13

Cherry Blossoms in Yoyogi-kōen *(p24)*

12 Come spring, thousands of cherry trees around the city burst into white and pink flowers. If Tokyoites have one moment to let their hair down en masse, this is it. They gather in parks and along river banks for cherry-blossom-viewing parties called *hanami*. Grassy Yoyogi-kōen is where you'll find some of the most spirited and elaborate bacchanals – complete with barbecues and turntables. Many revellers stay long past dark for *yozakura* (night-time cherry blossoms).

Harajuku & Aoyama

Akihabara Pop Culture *(p147)*

13 Venture into the belly of the pop culture beast that is Akihabara, the centre of Tokyo's *otaku* (geek) subculture. You don't have to obsess about manga or anime to enjoy this quirky neighbourhood: as *otaku* culture gains more and more influence on the culture at large, 'Akiba' is drawing more visitors who don't fit the stereotype. With its neon-bright electronics stores, retro arcades and *cosplay* (costume play) cafe waitresses, it's equal parts sensory overload, cultural mind-bender and just plain fun.

LEFT: ANIME FIGURE

Akihabara & Around

Kabuki-za *(p70)*

14 Dramatic, intensely visual kabuki is Japan's most recognised art form. Kabuki developed in Tokyo, then known as Edo, during the 18th and 19th centuries, and an afternoon at the theatre has been a favourite local pastime ever since. Descendants of the great actors of the day still grace Tokyo stages, drawing devoted fans. Kabuki-za is Tokyo's premier kabuki theatre. Established in 1889, the theatre was renovated in 2013. The new structure, designed by Japanese architect Kuma Kengo, has a showy traditional facade and flourishes of scarlet and gold throughout.

Ginza & Tsukiji

Tokyo National Museum *(p155)*

15 This is the world's largest collection of Japanese art, home to gorgeous silken kimono, atmospheric ink scroll paintings, earthy tea-ceremony pottery and glistening samurai swords. Even better: it's totally manageable in a morning and organised into easy-to-grasp, thoughtful exhibitions. The Tokyo National Museum also includes the enchanting Gallery of Hōryū-ji Treasures, a hall filled with dozens of spot-lit Buddha statues dating from the 7th century, as well as art and artefacts that span the Asian continent. RIGHT: WOODBLOCK PRINT AT TOKYO NATIONAL MUSEUM

Ueno & Yanaka

Shibuya Crossing *(p103)*

16 This is the Tokyo you've dreamed about and seen in movies: the frenetic pace, the mind-boggling crowds, the twinkling neon lights and the giant video screens beaming larger-than-life celebrities over the streets. At Shibuya's famous 'scramble' crossing, all of this comes together every time the light changes. It's an awesome sight. Come on a Friday or Saturday night and you'll find the whole scene turned up to 11, when fleets of fashionable young things embark upon a night out on the town.

Shibuya & Shimo-Kitazawa

What's New

Marunouchi Makeover

The formerly drab business district of Marunouchi has undergone a complete overhaul. The latest new building to go up, KITTE, includes a fascinating new museum, Intermediateque. The nine-year undertaking to restore the neighbourhood's signature hub, Tokyo Station, to its pre-WWII glory – domes and all – was completed in 2013. Meanwhile, neighbouring Nihombashi is undergoing a similar facelift, starting with the new Coredo Muromachi complex. (p55)

Toranomon Hills

Following in the footsteps of Roppongi Hills, Toranomon Hills is the city's newest work-live-and-play complex. It opened in 2014, along the new, tree-lined boulevard, Shin-Tora-dōri; the Andaz Tokyo hotel is here. (p81)

Kanda Renaissance

New developments in unused buildings include mAAch ecute (p152), a cluster of shops and hangouts in an old train station, and 3331 Arts Chiyoda (p149), an artsy hub in a former school.

Kabuki's New Home

After three years under a cloak of scaffolding, Ginza's Kabuki-za reopened in 2013. The new theatre, designed by Kuma Kengo, brings modern luxury to the traditional kabuki experience. (p70)

Tsukiji Market Moving

Like it or not, Tsukiji Market is on course to move to a new home on Tokyo Bay in late 2016. Only a short time remains to see this classic Tokyo sight in its present form. (p67)

More Flights in to Haneda

Haneda Airport (p243) opened its international terminal in 2010 and since 2014 has added daytime flights – meaning you can now fly into Tokyo's more convenient airport without arriving at a crazy hour. (p243)

Standing Restaurants

Tokyo's newest dining craze is restaurants without chairs. Why? Because they're cheaper to run and thus cheaper for diners. Dine on *kaiseki* (Japanese haute cuisine) at *izakaya* (Japanese pub-eatery) prices.

Craft Beer

Tokyo's craft-beer scene is coming of age. Not only are more bars around town serving small-batch brews, but the beers themselves are getting tastier and tastier.

Better Wi-Fi

Travellers can now connect to free wi-fi networks (p249) in the city's subway stations. With maps and other online resources at your fingertips, Tokyo will be much easier to navigate.

More Duty Free

Shoppers rejoice: more and more Tokyo shops have signed on to offer foreign travellers duty-free shopping. Look for the tax-free logo in shop windows.

For more recommendations and reviews, see **lonelyplanet.com/tokyo**

Need to Know

For more information, see Survival Guide (p241)

Currency

Japanese yen (¥)

Language

Japanese

Visas

Generally not required for stays of up to 90 days.

Money

Post offices and some convenience stores have international ATMs. Credit cards are accepted at major establishments, though it's best to keep cash on hand.

Mobile Phones

Rent SIM cards (for unlocked smartphones only) and prepaid or pay-as-you-go mobile phones at the airport. Shop around for a deal that meets your needs (data or calls).

Time

Japan Standard Time (GMT/UTC plus nine hours)

Tourist Information

Tokyo Tourist Information Center (東京観光情報センター; ☎5321-3077; www.gotokyo.org; 1st fl, Tokyo Metropolitan Government bldg 1, 2-8-1 Nishi-Shinjuku, Shinjuku-ku; ⏰9.30am-6.30pm; Ⓢ Ōedo line to Tochōmae, exit A4) has English-language information and publications.

Daily Costs

Budget: less than ¥8000

- Dorm bed: ¥2800
- Free sights such as temples and markets
- Bowl of noodles: ¥800
- Back-row seats for kabuki: ¥1500

Midrange: ¥8000–20,000

- Double room at a business hotel: ¥12,000
- Museum entry: ¥1000
- Dinner for two at an *izakaya* (Japanese pub-eatery): ¥6000
- Mezzanine seats for kabuki: ¥5000

Top End: more than ¥20,000

- Double room in a 4-star hotel: ¥35,000
- Sushi-tasting menu: ¥15,000
- Box seats for kabuki: ¥20,000
- Taxi ride back to the hotel: ¥3000

Advance Planning

Two months before Book tickets for the Ghibli Museum; make reservations for any high-end restaurants.

One month before Book tickets online for sumo, kabuki and Giants games, and a spot on the Imperial Palace tour; scan web listings for festivals and events.

As soon as you arrive Get tickets for shows from a Pia ticket counter; look for free copies of Metropolis and Time Out Tokyo magazines at airports and hotels.

Useful Websites

Lonely Planet (www.lonelyplanet.com/tokyo) Destination information, hotel bookings, traveller forum and more.

Go Tokyo (www.gotokyo.org) The city's official website includes information on sights, events and suggested itineraries.

Time Out Tokyo (www.timeout.jp) Arts and entertainment listings.

Tokyo Food Page (www.bento.com) City-wide restaurant coverage.

WHEN TO GO

Spring and autumn are the best times to visit. Mid-June to mid-July is the rainy season; August is hot and humid, but is also the month for summer festivals.

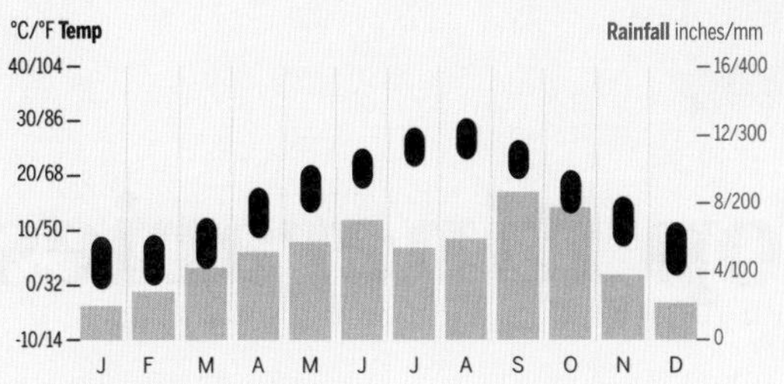

Arriving in Tokyo

Narita Airport Express train or highway bus to central Tokyo is around ¥3000 (one to two hours). Both run frequently 6am to 10.30pm; pick up tickets at the booths inside the terminal. Taxis cost about ¥30,000.

Haneda Airport Train or bus to central Tokyo costs ¥400 to ¥1200 (30 to 45 minutes). Both run frequently 5.30am to midnight. Taxis, your only option for before-dawn arrivals, cost between ¥4000 and ¥10,000 depending on the destination.

Tokyo Station Connect from the *shinkansen* (bullet train) terminal here to the JR Yamanote line or the subway to destinations around central Tokyo.

For much more on **arrival**, see p242

Getting Around

- **Subway** The quickest and easiest way to get around central Tokyo. Runs 5am to midnight.
- **Train** Japan Railways (JR) Yamanote (loop) and Chūō-Sōbu (central) lines hit major stations. Run from 5am to midnight.
- **Taxi** The only transport option that runs all night; unless you're stuck, taxis only make economical sense for groups of four.
- **Cycling** A fun way to get around, though traffic can be intense. Rentals available; some hostels and ryokan lend bikes.
- **Walking** Subway stations are close in the city centre; save a little cash by walking if you only need to go one stop.

For much more on **getting around**, see p244

Sleeping

Tokyo accommodation runs the gamut from cheap dorm rooms to luxury hotels. Business hotels, though rather institutional, fall squarely in between. While boutique hotels haven't really taken off here, ryokan (traditional inns with Japanese-style bedding) fill the need for small, well-tended sleeping spaces; you can find these at any point on the price scale. Even for hostels, it's wise to book in advance – even if it's just the day before – as walk-ins can fluster staff. Many hotels offer cheaper rates if you book for two weeks or a month in advance.

Useful Websites

- **Jalan** (www.jalan.net) Japanese discount accommodation site.
- **Japanican** (www.japanican.com) Accommodation site for foreign travellers, run by Japan's largest travel agency.
- **Lonely Planet** (www.lonelyplanet.com/japan/tokyo/hotels) Compare prices, check availability and book accommodation.

For much more on **sleeping**, see p195

WHAT TO PACK

Tokyo hotels can be tiny, so it's wise to bring as small a suitcase as possible. Remember that you may be taking your shoes on and off a lot, so it helps to have ones that don't need lacing up. Casual clothes are fine, but you'll feel out of place if you're dressed as if you're heading to the gym. Tokyoites themselves are notoriously fashion conscious, though generally forgiving towards foreign tourists.

Top Itineraries

Day One

Harajuku & Aoyama (p113)

Start the day in Harajuku with a visit to **Meiji-jingū**, Tokyo's signature Shintō shrine. Next stroll down **Takeshita-dōri**, the famous teen fashion bazaar. Work (and shop) your way through the back streets of Harajuku, and then head to **Omote-sandō** to see the jaw-dropping contemporary architecture along this stylish boulevard.

Lunch Go for dumplings at local fave Harajuku Gyōza-rō (p117).

Shibuya & Shimo-Kitazawa (p101)

Head down to Shibuya (you can walk) and continue your schooling in Tokyo pop culture by wandering the lanes of this youthful neighbourhood. Don't miss **Shibuya Center-gai**, the main drag, and the mural, **Myth of Tomorrow**, in the train station. Stick around Shibuya until dusk to see **Shibuya Crossing** all lit up.

Dinner Grab skewers of *yakitori* in atmospheric Omoide-yokochō (p129).

Shinjuku & West Tokyo (p125)

Take the train to Shinjuku and immerse yourself in the swarming crowds and neon lights of this notorious nightlife district. The **Tokyo Metropolitan Government Building** observatories stay open until 10pm, for free night views. From around 9pm the shanty bars of **Golden Gai** come to life; take your pick from the quirky offerings and finish up with a time-honoured Tokyo tradition: a late night bowl of noodles at **Nagi**.

Day Two

Ginza & Tsukiji (p65)

Skip breakfast and head directly to **Tsukiji Market**. Spend the morning exploring the cobblestone lanes of the inner market and the bustling stalls of the outer market. You'll have to get there by 4am to get a spot at the tuna auction, otherwise, the inner market opens to the public at 9am.

Lunch Seafood at Tsukiji Market of course! Try Daiwa Sushi (p71).

Ginza & Tsukiji (p65)

From Tsukiji, it's an easy walk to the landscape garden **Hama-rikyū Onshi-Teien**, where you can stop for tea in the teahouse **Nakajima no Ochaya**. Continue up to Ginza, home to stately department stores, art galleries and luxury boutiques. Go as far as Hibiya, to see the edge of the **Imperial Palace**, with its moats and keeps. Then head over to **Kabuki-za**, where you can get seats to watch a single act of kabuki for just ¥1500 (the last act starts around 5.30pm or 6pm).

Dinner Go for contemporary (and affordable) *kaiseki* at Maru (p71).

Marunouchi & Nihombashi (p54)

Walk up Namiki-dōri, home to high-end hostess bars, and pretty, tree-lined Naka-dōri to Marunouchi. Call it a night with drinks at **So Tired**; the terrace overlooks the recently renovated **Tokyo Station**.

MAREMAGNUM / GETTY IMAGES ©

Asakusa-jinja (p167)

TORNE UTTENAI / GETTY IMAGES ©

Hama-rikyū Onshi-Teien (p69)

Day Three

Ueno & Yanaka (p153)

Spend the morning exploring the many attractions of **Ueno-kōen**, home to the **Tokyo National Museum**, centuries-old temples and shrines and Tokyo's biggest zoo. Then take a stroll through the old-fashioned, open-air market, **Ameya-yokochō** and the historical neighbourhood of Yanaka; in the latter you'll find art galleries and studios.

Lunch Get a course of seasonal skewers at historic Hantei (p162).

Asakusa & Sumida River (p164)

Catch the subway for Asakusa to visit the temple complex **Sensō-ji**, the shrine **Asakusa-jinja** and the maze of old-world alleys that surround these sights. There are lots of shops selling traditional crafts and foodstuffs around here, too. Don't miss the temple complex all lit up from dusk.

Dinner Fill up on steaming *oden* at 100-year-old Otafuku (p172).

Asakusa & Sumida River (p164)

Buses run along Kototoi-dōri directly to **Tokyo Sky Tree**. Head up this spindly tower for the night view to end all night views. Or instead, get a view of the illuminated tower and the snaking Sumida-gawa (and a beer) from the **Asahi Sky Room**. Then take the subway to Ryōgoku for more beer: **Popeye** boasts Tokyo's largest selection of Japanese craft brews.

Day Four

Odaiba & Tokyo Bay (p176)

Make this morning a relaxing one and get your onsen on at **Ōedo Onsen Monogatari**, the somewhat kitschy 'onsen theme park' on Tokyo Bay. Then take the Yurikamome line, which skirts through the skyscrapers of downtown, followed by the subway up to Kanda.

Lunch Go for *rāmen* at Kikanbō (p150) or *soba* at Kanda Yabu Soba (p150).

Akihabara & Around (p147)

Walk up from Kanda, stopping at **mAAch ecute**, a shopping centre in an old train station filled with craft and gourmet food shops. Then spend a couple of hours exploring the sensory overload that is **Akihabara Electric Town**. Play retro video games at **Super Potato Retro-kan** and stop for coffee at maid cafe **@Home Cafe**. It's worth taking a detour to see the artisan bazaar **2K540 Aki-Oka Artisan** under the train tracks.

Dinner Get the *izakaya* experience at Jōmon (p84) or Gonpachi (p84).

Roppongi & Around (p77)

Check out **Roppongi Hills**, the first of Tokyo's new breed of live-work-and-play megamalls. On the top floor of a tower here is the excellent **Mori Art Museum**, which stays open until 10pm. Then head out into the wilds of Roppongi's infamous nightlife. Make sure to get in a round of karaoke.

If You Like...

Shintō Shrines

Meiji-jingū Tokyo's grandest Shintō shrine, set in a wooded grove. (p115)

Tōshō-gū Incredibly ornate mausoleum complex for the shogun Tokugawa Ieyasu in Nikkō. (p182)

Yasukuni-jinja Beautiful and controversial shrine to Japan's war dead. (p140)

Nogi-jinja Atmospheric shrine with a dark history. (p80)

Buddhist Temples

Sensō-ji Tokyo's most famous Buddhist temple and the epicentre of old-world Asakusa. (p166)

Daibutsu Kamakura's giant Buddha statue, on the grounds of the temple Kōtoku-in. (p190)

Sengaku-ji This Sōtō Zen temple is the final resting place of the famous 47 *rōnin* (masterless samurai). (p93)

Zōjō-ji The very rare main gate of this Pure Land Buddhist temple dates to 1605. (p80)

Museums

Tokyo National Museum Home to the world's largest collection of Japanese art. (p155)

Hakone Open-Air Museum Impressive collection of 20th-century sculpture in the hills of Hakone. (p186)

Intermediateque Experimental museum drawing on the holdings of the University of Tokyo. (p58)

Nezu Museum Asian antiques in a striking contemporary building. (p116)

Kabuki display at Edo-Tokyo Museum (p170)

Contemporary Art

Mori Art Museum Sky-high galleries that host travelling shows by top Japanese and foreign artists. (p79)

3331 Arts Chiyoda Playful arts hub in an old high school. (p149)

SCAI the Bathhouse Cutting-edge art gallery in a centuries-old public bathhouse. (p161)

Musée Tomo Gorgeous contemporary ceramics from master artists. (p81)

Mizuma Art Gallery Leader in the 'neo-*nihonga*' (contemporary Japanese-style painting) movement. (p140)

Crafts

Japan Folk Crafts Museum Exhibitions highlighting the beauty of everyday objects. (p105)

Crafts Gallery Ceramics, lacquerware and more. (p58)

History

Edo-Tokyo Museum Tells the story of how a fishing village evolved into a sprawling, modern metropolis. (p170)

National Shōwa Memorial Museum Learn what life was like for ordinary Tokyoites during WWII. (p140)

Daimyo Clock Museum Eccentric feudal-era timepieces. (p161)

Shitamachi Museum Recreation of a wooden, Edo-era tenement neighbourhood. (p158)

Traditional Gardens

Rikugi-en Stunning landscape garden evoking scenes from classical literature. (p139)

Hama-rikyū Onshi-teien An ancient shogunal hunting ground, now a vast garden with skyscraper views. (p69)

Koishikawa Kōrakuen Built by the Tokugawa clan, this garden is one of Tokyo's finest. (p140)

Imperial Palace East Garden Part of the Imperial Palace grounds, with the ruins of Edo Castle. (p57)

Parks

Ueno-kōen Tokyo's oldest park with museums, temples, woodsy paths and waterlilies. (p158)

Shinjuku-gyoen Home to 1500 cherry trees and a tropical greenhouse. (p127)

Yoyogi-kōen A big grassy expanse and a popular weekend gathering spot. (p116)

Inokashira-kōen Strolling paths and a central pond where you can rent pedal boats. (p129)

People Watching

Akihabara See *cosplay* kids on Sundays along Chūō-dōri. (p148)

Yoyogi-kōen With people living in tight quarters, dancers and musicians head to the park to practice. (p116)

Omote-sandō The city's de facto catwalk draws fashionistas from all over the world. (p116)

Ginza Head out in the twilight hours and catch high-end hostesses in kimono. (p66)

Takeshita-dōri Tokyo's teen fashion bazaar brims with quirky looks. (p116)

City Views

Tokyo Sky Tree Dizzying views from the lookouts on this tower, the world's tallest. (p168)

Tokyo Metropolitan Government Offices The 45th-floor observation decks in this marvel by Tange Kenzō are free. (p127)

New York Bar One of many luxury hotel cocktail bars with stunning night views. (p135)

Tokyo Bay Take a cruise on a *yakatabune* (pleasure boat) and see the shoreline from the bay. (p178)

For more top Tokyo spots, see the following:

- Eating (p32)
- Drinking & Nightlife (p41)
- Entertainment (p44)
- Shopping (p46)

Markets

Tsukiji Market Feast your eyes on the bounty of the sea at this pantheon of fishmongers. (p67)

Ameya-yokochō Tokyo's last open-air market dates to the tumultuous days after WWII. (p158)

Harmonica-yokochō Classic low-ceiling, lantern-lit covered market. (p129)

Ōedo Antique Market Hunt for antique treasures at this monthly gathering. (p59)

Offbeat Attractions

Meguro Parasitological Museum Internal creepy-crawlies on display. (p92)

Ikebukuro Earthquake Hall The simulation room here mimics a real earthquake. (p141)

Beer Museum Yebisu A concise history of beer in Japan. (p92)

Super Potato Retro-kan Arcade with only vintage machines. (p152)

Month by Month

TOP EVENTS

Hatsu-mōde, January

Cherry Blossoms, April

Sanja Matsuri, May

Sumida-gawa Fireworks, July

Kōenji Awa Odori, August

January

Tokyo comes to a virtual halt for Shōgatsu, the first three days of the new year set aside for family and rest; most places close and many residents return to their home towns.

Hatsu-mōde

Hatsu-mōde, the first shrine visit of the new year, starts just after midnight on 1 January and continues to about 6 January. Meiji-jingū (p115) is the most popular spot in Tokyo; it can get very, very crowded, but that's part of the experience.

Greeting the Emperor

On the morning of 2 January, the emperor and imperial family make a brief – and rare – public appearance in an inner courtyard of the Imperial Palace (p56); the same ceremonial greeting is also held on 23 December, the emperor's birthday.

Coming-of-Age Day

The second Monday of January is *seijin-no-hi*, the collective birthday for all who have turned 20 (the age of majority) in the past year; young women don gorgeous kimonos for ceremonies at Shintō shrines.

February

February is the coldest month, though it rarely snows. Winter days are crisp and clear – the best time of year to spot Mt Fuji in the distance.

Setsubun

The first day of spring is 3 February in the traditional lunar calendar, a shift once believed to bode evil. As a precaution, people visit Buddhist temples to toss tiny sacks of roasted beans while shouting, *'Oni wa soto! Fuku wa uchi!'* ('Devil out! Fortune in!').

Plum Blossoms

Plum *(ume)* blossoms, which appear towards the end of the month, are the first sign that winter is ending. Popular viewing spots include Koishikawa Kōrakuen (p140) and Yushima Tenjin (p159).

March

Hina Matsuri

On and around 3 March (also known as Girls' Day), public spaces and homes are decorated with *o-hina-sama* (princess) dolls in traditional royal dress.

Tokyo International Anime Fair

In late March, Tokyo International Anime Fair (www.tokyoanime.jp/en) has events and exhibitions for industry insiders and fans alike.

April

Warmer weather and blooming cherry trees make this quite simply the best month to be in Tokyo.

Cherry Blossoms

From late March through the start of April, the city's parks and riversides turn pink and Tokyoites toast spring in spirited parties, called *hanami*, under the blossoms. Ueno-kōen (p158) is the most famous spot, but grassy Yoyogi-kōen (p116) and Shinjuku-gyoen (p127) are more conducive to picnicking.

Buddha's Birthday

In honour of the Buddha's birthday on 8 April, Hana Matsuri (flower festival) celebrations take place at temples. Look for the parade of children in Asakusa, pulling a white papier-mâché elephant.

Tokyo Rainbow Pride

In late April, Japan's LGBT community comes together for the country's biggest pride event, some years followed by a parade (http://en.tokyorainbowpride.com/). It's not London or Sydney, but a spirited affair just the same.

May

There's a string of national holidays at the beginning of May, known as Golden Week, when much of the country travels. Festivals and warm days make this an excellent time to visit.

Children's Day

On 5 May, also known as *otoko-no-hi* (Boys' Day), families fly *koinobori* (colourful banners in the shape of a carp), a symbol of strength and courage.

Kanda Matsuri

This is one of Tokyo's big three festivals, with a parade of *mikoshi* (portable shrines) around Kanda Myōjin (p149). It's held on the weekend closest to 15 May on odd-numbered years (next up 2017).

Design Festa

Weekend-long Design Festa, held at Tokyo Big Sight in mid-May, is Asia's largest art festival, featuring performances and thousands of exhibitors. Also in November.

Sanja Matsuri

Arguably the grandest Tokyo *matsuri* (festival) of all, this three-day festival, held over the third weekend of May, attracts around 1.5 million spectators to Asakusa-jinja (p167). The highlight is the rowdy parade of *mikoshi* carried by men and women in traditional dress.

June

Early June is lovely, though by the end of the month *tsuyu* (the rainy season) sets in.

Sannō Matsuri

For a week in mid-June Hie-jinja (p81) puts on this major festival, with music, dancing and a procession of *mikoshi*. The parade takes place only every other year, next in 2016.

July

When the rainy season passes in mid- to late July, suddenly it's summer – the season for lively street fairs and *hanabi taikai* (fireworks shows).

Tanabata

On 7 July, the stars Vega and Altar (stand-ins for a princess and cowherd who are in love) meet across the Milky Way. Children tie strips of coloured paper bearing wishes around bamboo branches; look for decorations at youthful hang-outs such as Harajuku and Shibuya.

Mitama Matsuri

Yasukuni-jinja (p140) celebrates O-bon early: from 13 to 16 July, the shrine holds a festival of remembrance for the dead with 30,000 illuminated *bonbori* (paper lanterns).

Ueno Summer Festival

From mid-July to mid-August various events, including markets and music performances, take place at Ueno-kōen (p158).

Lantern Festivals

Toro nagashi is a photogenic summer tradition, connected to O-bon, where candle-lit paper lanterns are floated down rivers. They take place from mid-July to mid-August; two big ones take place at Chidori-ga-fuchi, along the Imperial Palace moat, and at Sumida-kōen in Asakusa.

Sumida-gawa Fireworks

The grandest of the summer firework shows, held the last Saturday in July, features 20,000 pyrotechnic wonders. Head to Asakusa early in the day to score a good seat. Check events listings for other firework displays around town.

August

This is the height of Japan's sticky, hot

summer; school holidays mean sights may be crowded.

O-bon

Three days in mid-August are set aside to honour the dead, when their spirits are said to return to the earth. Graves are swept, offerings are made and *bon-odori* (folk dances) take place. Many Tokyo residents return to their home towns; some shops may close too.

Fukagawa Hachiman Matsuri

During this spirited festival at Tomioka Hachiman-gū (p171), spectators throw water over the *mikoshi* carriers along the route. It's held in a big way only every three years; next up in 2017.

Kōenji Awa Odori

This is the most famous of Tokyo's *awa odori* (dance festivals for O-bon), with 12,000 participants in traditional costumes dancing their way through the streets of Kōenji. Kōenji Awa Odori takes place over the last weekend in August.

Asakusa Samba Carnival

On the last Saturday in August, Tokyo's Nikkei Brazilian community and local samba clubs turn Kaminarimon-dōri into one big party for the Asakusa Samba Carnival.

September

Days are still warm, hot even – though the odd typhoon rolls through this time of year.

(Top) Display at Tori-no-ichi

(Bottom) Young women celebrate *seijin-no-hi* (coming-of-age day), Meiji-jingū (p115)

GARY CONNER / GETTY IMAGES ©

SHENYANG'S / GETTY IMAGES ©

Moon Viewing

Full moons in September and October call for *tsukimi*, moon-viewing gatherings. People eat *tsukimi dango* – *mochi* (pounded rice dumplings), which are round like the moon.

Tokyo Game Show

Get your geek on when the Computer Entertainment Suppliers Association hosts Tokyo Game Show, a massive expo at Makuhari Messe in late September.

October

Pleasantly warm days and cool evenings make this one of the best times to be in Tokyo.

Tokyo International Film Festival

During the last week in October, Tokyo International Film Festival screens works from Japanese and international directors with English subtitles.

Tokyo Designers Week

Tokyo Designers Week attracts the international design world with a large exhibition at Meiji-jingū Gaien, usually around the end of October; shops and galleries around Aoyama and Gaienmae put on special displays.

Chrysanthemum Festivals

Chrysanthemums are the flower of the season (and the royal family), and dazzling displays are put on from late October to mid-November in Hibiya-kōen (p69) and at shrines including Meiji-jingū (p115) and Yasukuni-jinja (p140).

November

Jidai Matsuri

On National Culture Day, 3 November, locals dressed in splendid costumes representing figures from Japanese history parade around Sensō-ji (p166) in Asakusa for the Jidai Matsuri (Festival of the Ages).

Tori-no-ichi

On 'rooster' days in November, 'Otori' shrines such as Hanazono-jinja (p128) hold fairs called Tori-no-ichi (*tori* means rooster); the day is set according to the old calendar, which marks days by the zodiac. Vendors hawk *kumade* – rakes that literally symbolise 'raking in the wealth'.

Shichi-go-san

This adorable festival in mid-November sees parents dress girls aged seven *(shichi)* and three *(san)* and boys aged five *(go)* in wee kimonos and head to Shintō shrines for blessings.

International Robot Exhibition

The world's largest robot expo (www.nikkan.co.jp/eve/irex/english) takes place in odd-numbered years at Tokyo Big Sight.

Tokyo Filmex

Tokyo Filmex, which kicks off in late November, focuses on emerging directors in Asia and screens most films with English subtitles.

Autumn Leaves

The city's trees undergo magnificent seasonal transformations during *kōyō* (autumn foliage season); Rikugi-en (p139) and Koishikawa Kōrakuen (p140) have spectacular displays; even better are Takao-san (p194) and Nikkō (p182), outside the city.

December

Restaurants and bars are filled with Tokyoites hosting *bōnenkai* (end-of-the-year parties).

Gishi-sai

On 14 December, Sengaku-ji (p93) hosts a memorial service honouring the 47 *rōnin* (masterless samurai) who famously avenged their fallen master; locals dressed as the loyal retainers parade through nearby streets.

Winter Illuminations

Couples dressed in their finest head out to admire the seasonal illuminations in places such as Roppongi and Marunouchi.

Toshikoshi Soba

Eating buckwheat noodles on New Year's Eve, a tradition called *toshikoshi soba*, is said to bring luck and longevity – the latter symbolised by the length of the noodles.

Joya-no-kane

Temple bells around Japan ring 108 times at midnight on 31 December, a purifying ritual called *joya-no-kane*. Sensō-ji (p166) draws the biggest crowds in Tokyo.

With Kids

In many ways, Tokyo is a parent's dream: hyperclean, safe and with every mod-con. The downside is that many of the top attractions aren't as appealing to younger ones. Older kids and teens, however, should get a kick out of Tokyo's pop culture and neon streetscapes.

Anime City

Ghibli Museum

See the magical world of famed animator Miyazaki Hayao *(Ponyo, Spirited Away)* at Ghibli Museum (p128). There's a mini-theatre and a life-sized stuffed model of the cat bus from *My Neighbor Totoro.*

Suginami Animation Museum

At this museum (p128) you can learn the history of anime in Japan and practise drawing on light tables.

Odaiba

Local families love Odaiba. At the National Museum of Emerging Science & Innovation (p178) meet humanoid robot ASIMO, see a planetarium show and interact with hands-on exhibits.

At 'onsen theme park', Ōedo Onsen Monogatari (p180), kids wear *yukata* (lightweight kimono) and play old-fashioned carnival games. There's also virtual-reality arcade Tokyo Joypolis (p180), one of the world's tallest Ferris wheels and a giant statue of anime character Gundam. Restaurants are family-friendly.

Ueno

Sprawling Ueno-kōen (p158) has a zoo (with pandas) and the fascinating National Science Museum (p158). See swords and armour at Tokyo National Museum (p155).

Trains

Japanese kids love trains, chances are yours will too. A platform ticket to see the *shinkansen* (bullet train) costs ¥130. Another popular train-spotting location is Shinjuku Station's southern terrace, overlooking the multiple tracks that feed the world's busiest train station.

Play

Tokyo Dome City

There's plenty of activity at Tokyo Dome City (p140): thrill rides, play areas and baseball at Tokyo Dome.

Karaoke

Spend a rainy day at a karaoke parlour such as Shidax Village (p110).

Super Potato Retro-kan

Show the kids your favourite old video games at retro arcade, Super Potato (p152).

Sony Building

At Sony (p76), play Playstation games (for free); try out the latest Sony gadgets.

KiddyLand

Multistorey toy-emporium KiddyLand (p123) has only-in-Japan character goods, action figures and model kits.

Purikura no Mecca

Snap family photos at high-tech photo booths at Purikura no Mecca (p112).

Tokyo Disney Resort

Brave the long lines at Disney (p180), Asia's most visited amusement park.

Like a Local

Tokyo is far more liveable than you may think. Get beyond the skyscrapers, the omnipresent neon and the crowds and you'll find a city that's more like a patchwork of towns, each with its own character and characters.

ROBIN MACDOUGALL / GETTY IMAGES ©

estaurants in Shinjuku (p125)

Hang Out with the Locals

Spend an afternoon in one of these neighbourhoods loved by locals.

Shimo-Kitazawa (p108) A bastion of counterculture for decades, with snaking alleys, secondhand stores, coffee shops, hole-in-the-wall bars and live music halls.

Yanaka (p160) One of the few places in the city with many prewar wooden buildings. It's long been a favourite of artists and there are studios and galleries here, as well as old-time shops and cafes.

Daikanyama & Naka-Meguro (p98) Twin districts that feel light years away from hectic Shibuya, just minutes away. Daikanyama has fashionable boutiques; Naka-Meguro has a leafy canal flanked by restaurants and cafes.

Kichijōji (p128) Oft-voted the best place in Tokyo to live. It has a woodsy park and lanes chock-a-block with clothing shops, funky cafes and casual restaurants. It's popular with students.

Jimbōchō (p152) A favourite destination for local bibliophiles with more than 100 secondhand bookshops. As you'd expect, there are lots of cafes.

Nakano (p128) Tokyo's underground *otaku* (anime and manga fans) haunt, without the flash and bang of Akihabara.

Get to Know the Old City

Literally the 'low city', Shitamachi was where merchants and artisans lived during the Edo period. The city is no longer carved up so neatly; however, many of the old patterns remain. On the east side of the city, former Shitamachi neighbourhoods remain a tangle of alleys and tightly packed quarters, with traditional architecture, artisan workshops and small businesses.

The term 'Shitamachi' is still used to describe neighbourhoods that retain this old-Tokyo vibe, such as Asakusa and Fukagawa. Not everyone in Tokyo is enamoured with the city's forward push; the Shitamachi lifestyle has its staunch defenders. Spend an afternoon strolling through one of these districts and you'll see a whole other side to the city – one that is utterly down-to-earth and unpretentious.

Join the Celebrations

Hanami, the spirited parties that occur every spring under the boughs of the cherry trees, is Tokyo's most famous celebration, but festivals happen year-round. This is especially true during the summer months, when every neighbourhood has its own festival – a custom that goes back centuries. These riotous spectacles usually include a parade of *mikoshi* (portable shrines) by locals in traditional garb (which sometimes means only loincloths and short coats on the men).

Street fairs and *hanabi taikai* (firework displays) draw crowds dressed in colourful *yukata* (lightweight kimonos). And where there are festivals there are stalls selling food and beer. Don't be shy: by all means join in the merry-making. Websites such as **Go Tokyo** (www.gotokyo.org/en/index.html) and **Time Out Tokyo** (www.timeout.jp/en/tokyo) have listings.

Eat Like a Local

Think Seasonally

They may live in concrete boxes but Tokyoites are still attuned to the rhythms of nature – at least when it comes to food. Share their excitement over the first *takenoko* (young bamboo shoots) in spring or *sanma* (mackerel pike) in autumn. Even fast food restaurants and convenience stores offer seasonal treats, luring customers in for the taste of the month.

Look Up

If you're accustomed to scanning the street at ground level, you stand to miss out on a lot in Tokyo. In downtown areas restaurants are stacked on top of each other, creating multiple storeys of competing vertical neon signs. Most department stores, and even some office buildings, have food courts on the top floors with restaurants that are often surprisingly good.

Drink Like a Local

With small apartments and thin walls, most Tokyoites do their entertaining outside the home. A *nomikai* is literally a 'meet up to drink,' and they typically take place in restaurants or *izakaya* (Japanese pub-eatery). A 'party plan' is arranged, consisting of a course of food and a couple of hours of *nomihōdai* (all-you-can-drink booze; a good word to know). Never mind the stereotype about Japanese people being quiet and reserved – *nomikai* are loud and animated. There's no worry about disturbing the neighbours – or cleaning up.

Bathe Like a Local

Public bathhouses *(sentō)* have a centuries' old tradition in Tokyo. Though their numbers are dwindling, most communities still have one. Serious devotees take advantage of extras such as saunas, gossip with neighbours or just to soak longer than would be fair at home (with others clamouring for a turn). Custom calls for a beer afterwards.

Bike Around

Tokyo may not have many bike lanes but that doesn't stop people from taking to the streets on two wheels. Young salarymen commute to the office on racing bikes and housewives shuttle toddlers to preschool on *denki-jitensha,* hybrid electric bicycles. Cycling is an attractive alternative to waiting out the first train or an expensive taxi ride home, and you'll see young people on bikes in the evening, high heels and all.

Connect

With the language barrier it can be hard to connect with locals, though bars with a reputation for attracting a foreign clientele tend to also attract cosmopolitan, English-speaking Japanese. Events such as Pecha Kucha night at SuperDeluxe (p87), and the various art and music mixers held at Pink Cow (p86) all attract an international crowd.

For Free

Tokyo consistently lands near the top of the list of the world's most expensive cities. Yet many of the city's top sights cost nothing. Free festivals and events take place year round too, especially during the warmer months.

Shrines & Temples

Shintō shrines are usually free in Tokyo and most Buddhist temples charge only to enter their *honden* (main hall). So two of the city's most famous sights, Sensō-ji (p166) and Meiji-jingū (p115), won't cost you a thing. Throughout the year festivals take place at shrines and temples, allowing visitors a peek into Tokyo's traditional side.

Museums & Galleries

Tokyo has many free niche museums. Often no bigger than a room, they offer a succinct look at the more plebeian aspects of the city. Learn about Shitamachi artisans at the Traditional Crafts Museum (p168), the history of beer in Japan at Beer Museum Yebisu (p92) or the threat of parasites at Meguro Parasitological Museum (p92). Some museums are free on International Museum Day (18 May), though naturally this attracts crowds. Galleries are free to enter too. You'll find these scattered around the city, especially in Ginza (p69). Don't miss the public art in Nishi-Shinjuku (p127).

Markets

Spend hours wandering the lanes of Tsukiji Market (p67), the world's biggest fish market, or check out old-fashioned open-air market Ameya-yokochō (p158). There's a weekend farmers' market (p119) in Aoyama. In summer, festivals and markets hosted by Tokyo's ethnic communities set up across from Yoyogi-kōen (p116), and often include free performances.

Parks & Gardens

Spend the day people watching in one of Tokyo's excellent public parks, like Yoyogi-kōen (p116) or Inokashira-kōen (p129). Grab a *bentō* (boxed lunch) from a convenience store for a cheap and easy picnic.

Architecture & City Views

Tokyo has some fascinating buildings, such as the designer boutiques lining Omotesandō (p118) in Harajuku and the Nakagin Capsule Tower (p70) near Ginza. Some skyscrapers, including the Tokyo Metropolitan Government Offices (p127), have free observatories on the upper floors.

On the Cheap

Museum Discounts The GRUTT Pass (p248) offers free or discounted admissions to over 70 attractions.

Lunch Restaurants that charge several thousand yen per person for dinner often serve lunch for ¥1000.

¥100 Stores Stock up on sundries (even food and souvenirs) at these cheap emporiums.

After 5pm In the evening, grocery stores, bakeries and department-store food halls slash prices on *bentō*, baked goods and sushi.

Before 6pm Afternoon karaoke costs less than half of what you would pay during peak evening hours.

Alternative Accommodation All-night *manga kissa* (cafes for reading comic books) and spas double as ultra-discount places to sleep (p198).

Tokyo Cheapo This expat-run website (http://tokyocheapo.com) is full of ideas to enjoy Tokyo on the cheap.

Seafood *bentō* (boxed meal)

Eating

As visitors to Tokyo quickly discover, the people here are absolutely obsessed with food. The city has a varied and vibrant dining scene and a strong culture of eating out – popular restaurants are packed most nights of the week. One bowl of steaming noodles is all it takes to find yourself hooked.

Rāmen burger

Tokyo Dining Scene

We're hard pressed to think of something you can't get to eat in Tokyo. There are traditional restaurants that have been serving the same dishes, in the same way, for generations. There are also internationally acclaimed chefs reimaging just what is possible on a plate. It's a truly cosmopolitan dining scene: there are whole neighbourhoods known for just one cuisine, like Kagurazaka (French) and Shin-Okubo (Korean).

You can get superlative meals on any budget, from a simple bowl of noodles to the multicourse procession of edible art that is *kaiseki*, Japan's classic haute cuisine. The biggest restaurant buzzword these days, however, is '*cosupa*' – the Japanese way of saying 'cost performance'. Diners want solid, good meals at a price that will allow them to come back again and again, and we can't blame them. Never mind the record number of Michelin stars – or Unesco naming *washoku* (Japanese food) an 'intangible cultural heritage' – this is the best thing that could happen to the Tokyo dining scene.

Taking the idea of cost-performance to the extreme are Tokyo's standing restaurants, which have sprung up by the dozens in recent years. By doing away with the trappings of formal dining (you know, like chairs), these restaurants can pack in more customers. Rather than just reaping the profits, however, they pass the savings on to diners; as a result, once-a-year special outings, such as going out for fine French food, can be monthly occurrences. One chain of standing restaurants – the names

NEED TO KNOW

Price Range

The following price codes represent the cost of a meal for one person:

¥	less than ¥2000
¥¥	¥2000 to ¥6000
¥¥¥	more than ¥6000

Opening Hours

- Most restaurants open roughly 11.30am to 2.30pm for lunch and 6pm to 10pm for dinner. Chains usually stay open through the afternoon. *Izakaya* open around 5pm and run until 11pm or later.

Reservations

- Reservations are recommended for high-end places or for bigger groups; popular places fill up quickly.

Paying

- If a bill hasn't already been placed on your table, ask for it by catching your server's eye and making a cross in the air with your index fingers.
- Payment is usually settled at the counter.
- Traditional or smaller restaurants may not accept credit cards.

Tipping

- Tipping is not customary, though most high-end restaurants will add a 10% service charge.

Etiquette

- Don't stick your chopsticks upright in your rice or pass food from one pair of chopsticks to another – both are reminiscent of funereal rites.

Websites

- **Tokyo Food Page** (www.bento.com) Run by a *Japan Times*' dining columnist.
- **Tabelog** (http://tabelog.com) Japan's most popular customer-review website (in Japanese).
- **Gurunavi** (www.gnavi.co.jp/en) Restaurant directory (in English, but the Japanese version has more info and coupons).

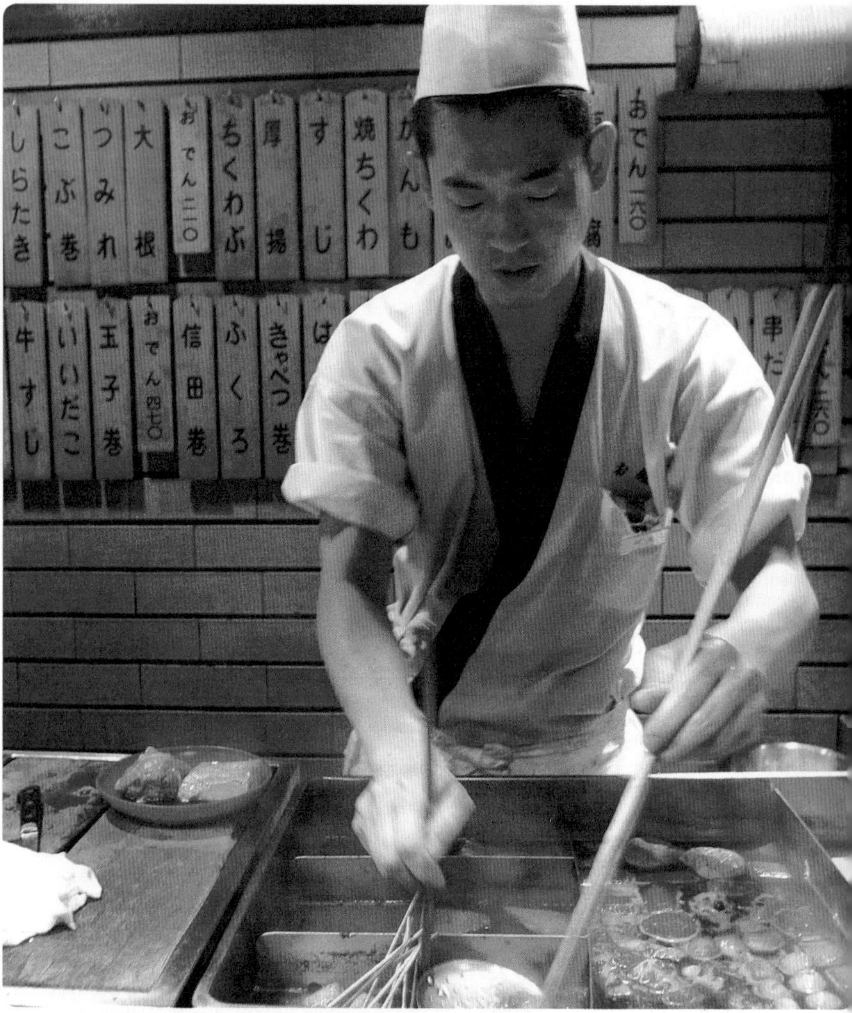

OLIVIER CIRENDINI / GETTY IMAGES ©

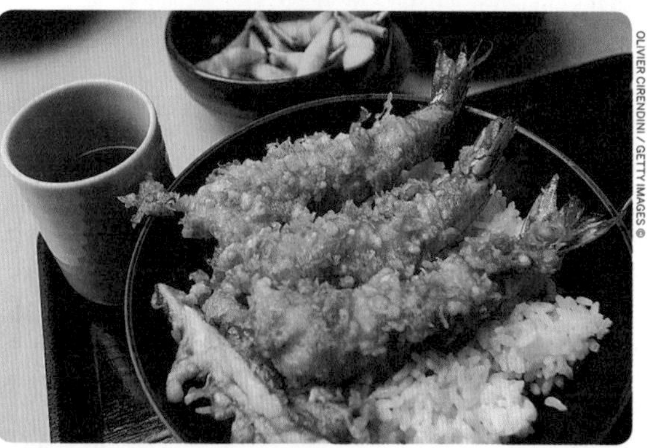

Above: A chef cooking *oden* (p37) restaurant, Shinjuku
Left: Tempura (p37)

all begin with 'Ore no', for example Ore-no-Dashi (p70) – is famous for poaching chefs from top-tier restaurants.

Two other trends you should know about are bistros and burgers, both of which have been taken up by Tokyo chefs with their typical attention to detail. France and America (respectively) should be worried.

Top Tokyo Dining Experiences

➡ Noshing on *yakitori* and knocking back beers with Tokyo's workday warriors under the train tracks in Yurakuchō.

➡ Gazing upon (and sampling) all the glorious delights to be found in a department-store food hall.

➡ Making an early morning trip to Tsukiji Market, followed by sushi breakfast in the market.

➡ Visiting a traditional festival and getting *yaki-soba* (fried noodles) or *okonomiyaki* hot off the grill.

➡ Grabbing late-night noodles after a rousing round of karaoke.

➡ Splurging on an *omakase* (chef's tasting menu) at a top-class sushi restaurant.

Eat Like a Local

When you enter a restaurant in Japan the staff will likely all greet you with a hearty '*Irasshai!*' (Welcome!). In all but the most casual places, where you seat yourself, the waiter or waitress will next ask you '*Nan-mei sama?*' (How many people?). Indicate the answer with your fingers, which is what the Japanese do. You may also be asked if you would like to sit at a *zashiki* (low table on the tatami), at a *tēburu* (table) or the *kauntā* (counter). Once seated you will be given an *o-shibori* (hot towel), a cup of tea or water (this is free) and a menu.

If you're unsure what to order, you can say '*Omakase de onegaishimas[u]*' (I'll leave it up to you). It's probably a good idea to set a price cap, like: '*Hitori de san-zen-en*' (one person for ¥3000).

When your food arrives, it's the custom to say '*Itadakimasu*' (literally 'I will receive' but closer to 'bon appétit' in meaning) before digging in. All but the most extreme type-A chefs will say they'd rather have foreign visitors enjoy their meal than agonise over getting the etiquette right. Still, there's nothing that makes a Japanese chef grimace more than out-of-towners who over-season their food – a little soy sauce and wasabi goes a long way (and heaven forbid, don't pour soy sauce all over your rice; it makes it much harder to eat with chopsticks).

On your way out, it's polite to say '*Gochisō-sama deshita*' (literally 'it was a feast'; a respectful way of saying you enjoyed the meal) to the staff.

What to Eat

SUSHI

Sushi (raw fish and rice seasoned with vinegar) actually comes in many forms, like *maki-zushi* (sushi rolls) and *chirashi-zushi* (assorted toppings arranged over a bowl of rice); however, the most well-known form of sushi, *nigiri-zushi* – the bite-sized slivers of fish draped over pedestals of rice – is

A FOODIE'S DAY IN TOKYO

Get an early start with a latte at Turret Coffee (p75) in Tsukiji, then head to Tsukiji Market (p67) and visit the inner market (open 9am to 11am) followed by a tour through the stalls of the outer market (open 6am to 2pm). There's plenty to snack on here, such as *tamago-yaki* (rolled omelette) and grilled oysters. Save room for sushi lunch at one of the stores in the market, such as Daiwa Sushi (p71) (it's popular so expect a line). Tea shop Cha Ginza (p75) has a stall in the outer market, but it's worth taking a short subway (or taxi) ride to their shop in Ginza, where you can sit and enjoy *matcha* (powdered green tea) and traditional sweets.

Then take the subway to Nihombashi, where you can wander through the great basement food hall at Tokyo's oldest department store, Mitsukoshi (p64). Nearby shopping mall Coredo Muromachi (p64) also has branches of some famous food vendors that date to the days of the original Nihombashi Market (replaced by Tsukiji Market in 1935).

Next head north to Ueno, and walk down the old-fashioned outdoor market, Ameya-yokochō (p158), on your way to Shinsuke (p161), one of Tokyo's best *izakaya* (Japanese pub-eateries). If you still have energy after dinner, head to Shinjuku for a nightcap at Zoetrope (p133), which stocks the world's best selection of Japanese whiskies.

actually a Tokyo speciality. This kind of sushi is also called 'Edo-mae', meaning in the style of Edo, the old name for Tokyo. Sushi was originally designed as a method to make fish last longer; the vinegar in the rice was a preserving agent and older forms of sushi, more common in western Japan, taste much more of vinegar. Edo-mae sushi was developed in the 19th century as a snack for busy merchants to eat on the spot. There was less need for preservation because Tokyo Bay could provide a steady stream of fresh fish.

If you visit one of Tokyo's top sushi counters, most likely you'll be served a belly-busting set course of seasonal *nigiri-zushi.* At sushi restaurants, ordering a set or a course is almost always more economical than ordering a la carte. However, you don't have to pay through the nose for sushi that's leagues better than what you can get back home. For a more casual experience, try a *kaiten-zushi* (回転寿司), where ready-made plates of sushi are sent around the restaurant on a conveyor belt. The best thing about these restaurants is that you don't have to worry about ordering: just grab whatever looks good as it goes by.

Nori soba (buckwheat noodles with seaweed)

NOODLES

Tokyo runs on noodles: you'll see the workforce slurping away at *tachigui* (立ち食い; stand-and-eat) noodle bars in and around train stations. And yes, slurping is key: noodles are to be eaten at whip-speed and the slurping helps cool your mouth while you eat. At most *tachigui* and corner shops you buy a ticket for your meal from a vending machine, and hand it to the chef.

Noodles shops are usually divided into Japanese-style noodles – *soba* (buckwheat noodles) and udon (thick white wheat noodles) – and Chinese-style noodles, otherwise known as *rāmen.* Around the Kantō area of Japan (which includes Tokyo) *soba* is more popular than udon. That said, most counter shops sell both, served in a large bowl of hot broth flavoured with *dashi* (fish stock) and soy sauce.

There are upscale Japanese noodle restaurants, too. These places usually have an option for cooled noodles, served with a concentrated bowl of broth on the side in which to dip them. Noodle connoisseurs prefer this style (since hot soup quickly turns al dente noodles to mush). One common dish is *zaru-soba,* buckwheat noodles served at room temperature on a bamboo mat. The better *soba* restaurants serve *to-wari* (十割; 100% buckwheat) noodles; otherwise they're made of a blend of buckwheat and wheat.

Rāmen originated in China, but its popularity in Japan is epic. Your basic *rāmen* is a big bowl of crinkly egg noodles in broth, served with toppings such as *chāshū* (sliced roast pork), *moyashi* (bean sprouts) and *negi* (leeks). There are four basic categories of soup: rich *tonkotsu* (pork bone), mild *shio* (salt), savoury *shōyu* (soy sauce) and hearty miso. Given the option, most diners get their noodles *katame* (literally 'hard' but more like al dente). If you're really hungry, ask for *kaedama* (another serving of noodles), usually only a couple of hundred yen more.

JAPANESE CLASSICS

Tokyo has a strong artisan tradition and that extends to food too. Instead of serving a variety of dishes, restaurants in Tokyo that cover the classics tend to specialise in just one dish – one they've been perfecting for decades. You know it's going to be good when a place can stay in business serving just one thing. A list of must-tries:

Yakitori (焼き鳥) Charcoal-grilled skewers of chicken seasoned with *tare* (sauce) or *shio* (salt); veggies are available, too.

Tempura (天ぷら) Seafood and vegetables deep-fried in a fluffy, light batter, flavoured with salt or a light sauce mixed with grated *daikon* (radish).

Sukiyaki (すき焼き) Thin slices of beef cooked piece by piece in a broth of soy sauce, sugar and sake at your table, then dipped in raw egg.

Shabu-shabu (しゃぶしゃぶ) Thin slices of beef or pork swished briefly in a light, boiling broth then seasoned with *goma* (sesame-seed) or *ponzu* (citrus-based) sauce.

Tonkatsu (豚カツ) Tender pork cutlets breaded and deep-fried, served with a side of grated cabbage.

Unagi (うなぎ) Freshwater eel grilled over coals and lacquered with a rich, slightly sweet sauce.

Okonomiyaki (お好み焼き) Savoury pancake stuffed with cabbage plus meat or seafood (or cheese or kimchi), which you grill at the table and top with *katsuo bashi* (bonito flakes), *nori* (seaweed), mayonnaise and Worcestershire sauce.

Oden (おでん) A hot wintertime dish of fish cakes, hard-boiled egg and vegetables in *dashi* (fish stock) broth.

Where to Eat

SHOKUDŌ

Dining trends may come and go but *shokudō* (食堂; all-around, inexpensive eateries) remain. The city's workers take a significant number of their meals at these casual joints; you'll find them around every train station and in tourist areas.

Most serve *teishoku* (定食; set-course meal), which includes a main dish of meat or fish, a bowl of rice, miso soup, a small salad and some *tsukemono* (pickles). They also usually serve a small variety of *washoku* (和食; Japanese food) and *yōshoku* (洋食; Western food) staples – things like *kare-raisu* (カレーライス; curry on rice) and *omu-raisu* (オムライス; omelette on rice). Many will have a *kyō-no-ranchi* (今日のランチ; daily lunch special), which is a safe bet if you're at a loss for what to order.

IZAKAYA

Izakaya (居酒屋) translates as 'drinking house' – the Japanese equivalent of a pub. Here food is ordered for the table a few dishes at a time and washed down with plenty of beer, sake or *shōchū* (strong distilled alcohol often made from potatoes).

Dining beneath the railway tracks in Yūrakuchō (p70)

There are traditional *izakaya* that serve classics such as grilled fish (焼き魚; *yaki-zakana*) and those that serve creative, fusion fair; ones with rustic interiors and ones with flashy decor. Either way, you'll find a lively, casual atmosphere. Depending on how much you drink, you can expect to spend about ¥2500 to ¥5000 per person.

FOOD STALLS & TRUCKS

Food stalls are called *yatai* (屋台) and you can find them on market streets, in alleyways of Shitamachi neighbourhoods or under train tracks. Festivals always have rows of *yatai*.

Food trucks gather around the Tokyo International Forum around lunchtime on weekdays for the office crowd. They also make an appearance at the weekend farmers' market (p119) in Aoyama. And keep an eye out for Tokyo's original food trucks: the *yaki-imo* (roasted whole sweet potato) carts that rove the city from October to March crooning '*yaki-imohhhhh…!*'. On a cold day, these stone-roasted treats warm your hands and your insides.

Food to Go

The Japanese frown upon eating in public places (on the subway for example); festivals and parks are two big exceptions.

CONVENIENCE STORES

Konbini (コンビニ; convenience stores) are a way of life for many Tokyoites. Indeed, there seems to be a Lawson, 7-Eleven or Family Mart on just about every corner. In addition to *bentō* (boxed meals) and sandwiches, other *konbini* staples include: *onigiri* (おにぎり), a triangle of rice and *nori* enveloping something savoury (tuna salad or marinated kelp, for example); *niku-man* (肉まん), steamed buns filled with pork, curry and more; and *oden,* which can be found stewing by the register in the winter.

DEPARTMENT STORE FOOD HALLS

The below-ground floors of Tokyo's department stores hold fantastic food halls called *depachika* (literally 'department store basement'). Dozens of vendors offer a staggering array of foodstuffs of the highest order, freshly prepared and often gorgeously packaged for presentation as gifts (excellent if you find yourself dining at a Japanese person's house). Look for museum-quality cakes, flower-shaped *okashi* (sweets) and *bentō* that look too

Top: Diners at an *izakaya* (Japanese pub-eatery)
Middle: Plastic food models in a restaurant window
Bottom: *Rāmen* (noodles in broth)

good to eat. Two *depachika* to try are Isetan (p136) in Shinjuku and Mitsukoshi (p64) in Nihombashi.

SUPERMARKETS & MARKETS

Unfortunately, supermarkets are rare in the big hubs where most hotels and sights are located. However, you can find expat fave Kinokuniya International Supermarket (p119) in Aoyama. Supermarket Natural House, which stocks vegetarian prepared foods, has a branch nearby; there's also one in the basement of Takashimaya in Nihombashi.

On weekends, farmers' markets take place around the city and are a good place to get fresh fruit and bread, plus packaged goods (such as miso and pickles) to take home. Check out the blog **Japan Farmers Markets** (www.japanfarmersmarkets.com) to see what's happening where.

Vegetarian

Vegetarianism, and especially veganism, is not common in Tokyo, though there is more awareness than there used to be. More and more restaurants are able to accommodate the request: '*Bejitarian dekimasu ka*' (Can you do vegetarian?). One thing to be aware of is that often dishes that look vegetarian are not (miso soup, for example) because they were prepared with *dashi* (fish stock); it's best to double check.

Cooking Classes

A Taste of Culture (www.tasteofculture.com) Established by noted Japanese culinary expert Elizabeth Andoh, these courses encompass everything from market tours to culinary classes, all imbued with deep cultural knowledge. Courses are seasonal and fill up fast. Half-day courses (including lunch) start at ¥7000 per person.

Buddha Bellies (http://buddhabelliestokyo.jimdo.com) Professional sushi chef and sake sommelier Ayuko leads small classes in sushi, *bentō* and udon making. Prices start at ¥7000 per person for a 2½-hour course.

Eating by Neighbourhood

- **Marunouchi & Nihombashi** (p62) Midrange options for the local office crowd in Marunouchi; classic Japanese in Nihombashi.
- **Ginza & Tsukiji** (p70) Upscale restaurants and the best sushi in the city.
- **Roppongi & Around** (p84) Both break-the-bank and midrange options, with a good selection of international cuisines.
- **Ebisu, Meguro & Around** (p93) Cosmopolitan and hip, with excellent dining options in all price ranges.
- **Shibuya & Shimo-Kitazawa** (p105) Lively, inexpensive restaurants that cater to a young crowd in Shibuya; good *izakaya* in Shimo-Kitazawa.
- **Harajuku & Aoyama** (p117) Fashionable midrange restaurants and excellent lunch options aimed at shoppers.
- **Shinjuku & West Tokyo** (p129) Gorgeous high-end restaurants, under-the-tracks dives and everything in between.
- **Kōrakuen & Northwest Tokyo** (p141) French restaurants and tiny gems in Kagurazaka; great ethnic food in northwest Tokyo.
- **Akihabara & Around** (p150) Famous for historic eateries in Kanda, comfort food in Akihabara.
- **Ueno & Yanaka** (p161) Classic Japanese restaurants, mostly midrange and budget.
- **Asakusa & Sumida River** (p171) Unpretentious Japanese fare, old-school charm and modest prices.
- **Odaiba & Tokyo Bay** (p179) Restaurants popular with teens and families; lots of big chains.

Bean-filled pastries, a popular Japanese sweet

Lonely Planet's Top Choices

Kyūbey (p71) Rarefied Ginza sushi at its finest.

Afuri (p93) Cult noodle shop with light, citrus-infused broth.

Shinsuke (p161) Century-old *izakaya* adored by sake aficionados.

Kikunoi (p85) Gorgeous *kaiseki* in the classic Kyoto style.

Tonki (p97) *Tonkatsu* raised to an art.

Higashi-Yama (p96) Modern Japanese cuisine in a chic, minimalist setting.

Best by Budget

¥

Tsurutontan (p84) Huge bowls of udon noodles with oodles of toppings.

Harajuku Gyōza Rō (p117) Addictive dumplings served all night.

Maisen (p119) Delectable *tonkatsu* in a former bathhouse.

¥¥

Hōnen Manpuku (p63) Gourmet traditional Japanese.

Tsunahachi (p132) Expertly fried tempura.

Kado (p145) Classic home-cooking in an old house.

¥¥¥

Kozue (p132) Exquisite Japanese cuisine and stunning night views over Shinjuku.

Tofuya-Ukai (p85) Handmade tofu becomes haute cuisine.

Matsukiya (p108) Melt-in-your-mouth sukiyaki.

Best by Cuisine

Tokyo Specialities

Komagata Dojō (p171) Landmark restaurant serving *dojō-nabe* (loach hotpot) for 200 years.

Kappō Miyako (p172) The best place to try *fukagawa-meshi* (rice steamed with clams).

Tomoegata (p173) Steaming pots of *chanko-nabe*, the protein-rich stew that fattens up sumo wrestlers.

Seafood

Yanmo (p119) Extravagant spreads of seafood prepared Japanese-style.

Trattoria Tsukiji Paradiso! (p71) Linguine and clams instead of sushi at Tsukiji Market.

Kaikaya (p108) Fun and funky with seafood served a dozen ways.

Sushi

Daiwa Sushi (p71) Famed sushi counter inside Tsukiji Market.

Sushi-no-Midori (p108) Huge sets of sushi for small prices.

Numazukō (p129) Tokyo's best conveyor-belt sushi restaurant.

Noodles

Nagi (p132) *Rāmen* pilgrimage spot in bohemian Golden Gai.

Kururi (p141) *Miso-rāmen* that draws lines down the street.

Kanda Yabu Soba (p150) Historic *soba* restaurant.

Yakitori

Bird Land (p71) Upscale *yakitori* from free-range, heirloom birds.

Tetchan (p133) Rough-and-tumble joint in an old market.

Regional Japanese

d47 Shokudō (p105) Regional specialities from around Japan.

Warayakiya (p85) Rustic *izakaya* serving food from rural Shikoku.

Best for Old Tokyo Atmosphere

Hantei (p162) Deep-fried skewers in a century-old heritage house.

Otafuku (p172) Charming 100-year-old *oden* restaurant.

Omoide-yokochō (p129) Atmospheric *yakitori* stalls near the train tracks.

Best Izakaya

Shirube (p109) Loud and lively with creative fusion dishes.

Jōmon (p84) Cosy counter joint dishing up grilled meats.

Ippo (p96) Specialises in fish and sake – need we say more?

Best for Vegetarians

Mominoki House (p119) Gourmet macrobiotic fare.

Nagi Shokudō (p105) Hip vegan hang-out.

Eat More Greens (p84) Veggie tapas and decadent salads.

Best for Brunch

Rose Bakery (p62) Quiches, tarts and cakes galore.

Lauderdale (p84) Souffles, salads and sidewalk seating.

Best Bistros

Beard (p97) Inspired French in a stylish setting.

Ahiru Store (p111) Tiny eight-seater local fave.

Best for Sweets

Ouca (p96) Ice cream in only-in-Japan flavours.

Amanoya (p150) Old-time Japanese sweets.

Drinking & Nightlife

Make like Lady Gaga in a karaoke box; sip sake with an increasingly rosy salaryman in a tiny postwar bar; or dance under the rays of the rising sun at an enormous bayside club: that's nightlife, Tokyo-style. The city's drinking culture embraces everything from refined teahouses and indie coffee shops to craft-beer pubs and pet cafes.

Drinking Culture

Drinking in all its forms is a social lubricant in Japan. If alcohol is not your bag, fear not as the city is as packed with cafes and teahouses as it is bars and clubs. Cafes are also where you'll tap into the latest fads and fashions such as *cosplay* (costume play) at maid cafes or rent-by-the-hour pets at cat, dog, bird and bunny cafes.

Where to Drink

Roppongi has the lion's share of foreigner-friendly bars, while Shinjuku offers the retro warren Golden Gai and the gay-bar district Ni-chōme.

Other top party districts include youthful Shibuya and Harajuku; Shimbashi and Yurakuchō which teem with salarymen; and Ebisu and nearby Daikanyama both of which have some excellent bars.

BARS & IZAKAYA

Tokyo's drinking establishments run the gamut from *tachinomi-ya* (standing-only bars) to ritzy cocktail lounges. A staple is the humble *nomiya,* patronised by businessmen and regular customers. Some will demur at serving foreigners who don't speak or read Japanese.

Izakaya can be cheap places for beer and food in a casual atmosphere resembling that of a pub; more upmarket ones are wonderful places to sample premium sake and the distilled spirit *shōchū.*

In summer, beer gardens open up on department-store roofs, hotel grounds and gardens. Many of these places offer all-you-can-eat-and-drink specials for around ¥4000 per person.

KARAOKE & CLUBS

If you've never tried a karaoke box (a small room rented by you and a few of your friends), it's definitely less embarrassing than singing in a bar in front of strangers. With booze and food brought directly to your room, it can easily become a guilty pleasure; rooms generally cost around ¥700 per person per hour.

Tokyo holds its own with London and New York when it comes to top dance venues. Top international DJs and domestic artists do regular sets at venues with body-shaking sound systems. Most clubs kick off after 10pm or so, when the volume increases and the floor fills, and continue until dawn (or later).

CAFES & TEAHOUSES

Chain cafes such as Doutor, Tully's or Starbucks (a nonsmoking oasis with free wi-fi) are common. But don't miss the opportunity to explore Tokyo's vast range of *kissa* (short for *kissaten,* nonchain cafes) and tea rooms – many are gems of retro or contemporary design, sport art galleries or are showcases for a proprietor's beloved collection, such as vintage jazz records or model trains.

NEED TO KNOW

Cheers

Don't forget to say (or yell, depending on the venue) *'Kampai!'* when toasting your drinking buddies.

Prices

To avoid a nasty shock when the bill comes, check prices and cover charges before sitting down. If you are served a small snack *(o-tsumami)* with your first round, you'll usually be paying a cover charge of a few hundred yen or more.

Smoking

Tokyo remains a smoker's paradise, but there's a small but growing number of nonsmoking bars and cafes.

Etiquette & Tipping

It's customary to pour for others and wait for them to refill your glass. At smaller bars, male bartenders are often called 'master' and their female counterparts are 'mama-san'. There's no need to tip in bars.

Opening Hours

Tokyo's night spots stay open from 5pm well into the wee hours.

Beware

Avoid *sunakku* (snack bars), cheap hostess bars that charge hefty sums, and *kyabakura* (cabaret clubs), exorbitant hostess clubs that are often fronts for prostitution. These are concentrated in Shinjuku's Kabukichō and Roppongi.

Websites

- **Beer in Japan** (http://beerinjapan.com/bij) The microbrewery scene.
- **Nonjatta** (http://nonjatta.blogspot.com) Comprehensive source on Japanese whisky.
- **Sake-world.com** (http://sake-world.com) Site of leading non-Japanese sake authority John Gauntner.
- **25Cafes.com** (www.25cafes.com) Reviews smoke-free cafes across Tokyo.
- **Tokyo Cheapo** (http://tokyocheapo.com) Where to drink if you're short on cash.

What to Drink

SAKE & SHŌCHŪ

Japan's national beverage is sake, aka *nihonshū* (酒 or 日本酒). Made from rice it comes in a wide variety of grades, flavours and regions of origin. According to personal preference, sake can be served hot *(atsu-kan)*, but premium ones are normally served well chilled *(reishu)* in a small jug *(tokkuri)* and poured into tiny cups known as *o-choko* or *sakazuki*.

More popular than sake, the clear spirit *shōchū* (焼酎) is made from a variety of raw materials including potato and barley. Because of its potency (alcohol content of around 30%) *shōchū* is usually served diluted with hot water *(oyu-wari)* or in a *chūhai* cocktail with soft drinks or tea.

BEER

Biiru (beer; ビール) is by far Japan's favourite tipple. Lager reigns supreme, although several breweries also offer darker beers. The major breweries – Kirin, Asahi, Sapporo and Suntory – have been joined by a growing number of microbreweries who generally produce a far superior product in terms of taste.

In bars you can order either *nama biiru* (draught beer) or bottled beer in many varieties. Hoppy, a cheap, low-alcohol mix of carbonated malt and hops that debuted in 1948, is also found on the menus of some retro *izakaya* (Japanese pub-eatery) and bars.

WHISKY

Japan produces some of the finest whiskies in the world and Tokyo now has a growing number of dedicated whisky and scotch bars where travellers can sample the best of the major makers Suntory and Nikka, as well as products from several other active single-malt distilleries in Japan and abroad.

COFFEE & TEA

Tokyo has plenty of cafes where passionate baristas coax the best from roasted coffee beans. It's the varieties of local tea that you may not be so familiar with. Green tea is the most commonly served here. *Matcha,* the powdered form of the leaf, features in the traditional tea ceremony and has a high caffeine kick. *Sencha* is medium-grade green tea, while *o-cha* and the brownish *bancha* is the regular stuff. You may also come across *mugicha* (roasted barley tea).

Lonely Planet's Top Choices

Golden Gai (p133) Travel back in time and wander this postwar maze of intimate bars.

Popeye (p173) Get very merry working your way through the most beers on tap in Tokyo.

These (p87) Cuddle up over a cocktail in a nook of this library-like bar in Nishi-Azabu.

Kagaya (p71) Fun and games in an *izakaya* with the incomparable Mark-san.

SuperDeluxe (p87) Tokyo's most interesting club with an eclectic line-up of events.

Bear Pond Espresso (p108) Regularly tipped as serving Tokyo's best espresso.

Best Bars with a View

New York Bar (p135) Make like Bill Murray in the Park Hyatt's starry jazz bar.

Two Rooms (p119) Cool views and a cool crowd, plus an outdoor terrace.

The Bar (p180) Hidden gem offering killer Tokyo Bay vistas.

Best Clubs

Womb (p110) Four levels of lasers and strobes at this Shibuya club fixture.

Air (p97) House and techno rule at this hip Ebisu hangout.

Ageha (p180) One of Asia's largest clubs, set on Tokyo Bay.

Best Tea & Coffee

Cha Ginza (p75) Stylish contemporary version of a teahouse in heart of Ginza.

Lucite Gallery (p173) Views of Tokyo Sky Tree from this former home of a geisha.

Omotesando Koffee (p122) Designer gem; has a branch in Toronomon Hills too.

Cafe de l'Ambre (p75) Decades-old Ginza bolthole, specialising in aged beans from around the world.

Best Craft Beer

Craft Beer Market (p63) With several outlets and a good food menu.

Good Beer Faucets (p108) Fine choice of ales in Shibuya.

Harajuku Taproom (p122) Serves the beers of Baird Brewing.

Best Gay Venues

Advocates Café (p133) Start your Ni-chōme night at this popular corner bar.

Town House Tokyo (p75) Spacious Shimbashi gay bar attracting salarymen and others.

Arty Farty (p135) Rub shoulders (and other body parts) on this bar's packed dance floor.

Best Karaoke

Festa Iikura (p86) Fancy dress + karaoke = fab night out.

'Cuzn Homeground (p173) Offering a wild night of warbling in Asakusa.

Shidax Village (p110) Sing your heart out in a deluxe karaoke box.

Best for Cocktails & Spirits

Zoetrope (p133) Sample premium whiskies at this Shinjuku hole-in-the-wall.

Agave (p86) Try top-brand tequila in this cavern-like Roppongi bar.

Fuglen Tokyo (p111) Aeropress coffee by day and creative cocktails by night.

Best Quirky Places

Fukurou-no-mise (p75) Be mesmerised by the many beautiful breeds at this owl cafe.

N3331 (p151) Ultimate trainspotters' cafe occupying a former train platform.

Samurai (p135) Classic jazz at this *kissa* stacked with 2500 *maneki-neko* (praying cats).

Nakame Takkyū Lounge (p97) Hang with ping-pong-playing hipsters in Naka-meguro.

Entertainment

Tokyo's range of entertainment is impressive. Take your pick from smoky jazz bars, grand theatres, rockin' live houses, comedy shows and major sports events. And don't be afraid of sampling the traditional performing arts: the major venues that stage these shows will offer earphones or subtitles with an English translation of the plots and dramatic dialogue.

Traditional Performing Arts

Little can prepare the uninitiated for the lavish costumes, sets, make up and acting of a classic kabuki play. This highly dramatic, visually arresting form of theatre, with all male performers, is the best known of Japan's traditional performing arts, but there are other forms you can readily view in Tokyo, too, including the stately, slow moving drama of *nō*, and bunraku plays with large puppets expertly manipulated by up to three black-robed puppeteers.

Contemporary Theatre

Language can be a barrier to the contemporary theatre scene, as nearly all productions are in Japanese. Sometimes, though, a show's visual creativity compensates, such as with the camp, colourful musical review shows of Takarazuka. The long-running **Tokyo International Players** (www.tokyoplayers.org) regularly perform English-language theatre, as do the more recently formed **Black Stripe Theater** (http://blackstripetheater.com). You can also catch English and other language shows at **Festival/Tokyo** (http://festival-tokyo.jp/en/), usually held each November.

Dance

While Tokyo has Western dance performances, including shows by **Tokyo Ballet** (http://thetokyoballet.com), it's the home-grown forms of movement that are likely to be of more interest. Keep an eye out for special dance shows in Asakusa and elsewhere by Tokyo's rare communities of geisha.

Top troupes specialising in the avant-garde genre *butō,* in which dancers use their naked or seminaked bodies to express the most elemental human emotions, include **Sankai Juku** (www.sankaijuku.com) and **Dairakudakan Kochūten** (www.dairakudakan.com) based in Kichijoji. Blending elements of Japanese pop culture, folklore and acrobatic dance are **Tokyo Dolores** (www.facebook.com/tokyodolores/info).

Live Music

All kinds of live music, including rock, blues, jazz, classical and electronica, can be seen performed live in Tokyo. Big international acts often appear at major venues such as Tokyo Budōkan or Tokyo Dome. There are also many good small live houses for intimate shows.

Sports

Sports fans are well served with baseball matches held at Tokyo Dome and Jingū Baseball Stadium during the April to October season. Even if you're not in town for one of the year's big sumo tournaments (in January, May and September), it's still possible to watch wrestlers training daily at their stables.

Lonely Planet's Top Choices

National Theatre (p88) Top-notch *nō*, bunraku and other drama in a grand setting.

Kabuki-za (p70) A visual and dramatic feast of traditional theatre awaits inside and out.

Setagaya Public Theatre (p110) Renowned for contemporary drama and dance.

New National Theatre (p135) State-of-the-art venue for opera, ballet, dance and theatre.

Ryōgoku Kokugikan (p175) Clash of sumo titans at the seasonal tournaments.

Best Jazz Clubs

Shinjuku Pit Inn (p135) Tokyo jazz-scene institution for serious devotees.

Blue Note Tokyo (p122) See world-class performers at this sophisticated venue.

Cotton Club (p64) Centrally located venue for high-pedigree performers.

Best for Traditional Arts

National Nō Theatre (p122) Watch dramas unfold slowly on an elegant cypress stage.

Asakusa Engei Hall (p174) Best venue for traditional *rakugo* (comedic monologue).

Oiwake (p174) Listen to indigenous tunes at this rare *minyō izakaya* (pub where traditional folk music is performed).

Best Live Houses

Unit (p99) Offering both live gigs and DJs to a stylish crowd.

Club Quattro (p111) Slick venue with emphasis on rock and roll and world music.

WWW (p110) Great views of the stage for all at this happening Shibuya live house.

Best Contemporary Theatre

Tokyo Takarazuka Theatre (p75) Glitzy, all-female musical revues and plays.

Honda Theatre (p111) Largest of Shimo-Kito's free-wheeling performance spaces.

Best for Spectator Sports

Ryōgoku Kokugikan (p175) Location of the three annual Tokyo sumo *bashō*.

Tokyo Dome (p146) Home to the Yomiuri Giants, Japan's top baseball team.

Jingū Baseball Stadium (p124) The base of Tokyo underdogs Yakult Swallows.

Best Classical Music Venues

Suntory Hall (p88) Gorgeous 2000-seat hall hosting major international performers.

Tokyo International Forum (p58) Location for the La Folle Journee au Japon classical-music festival.

Tokyo Bunka Kaikan (p163) Great acoustics and interiors at this Ueno-kōen venue.

NEED TO KNOW

Tickets

The easiest way to get tickets for many live shows and events is at one of the **Ticket Pia** (チケットぴあ) kiosks scattered across Tokyo. Their online booking site is in Japanese only.

Websites

- **Metropolis** (http://metropolisjapan.com) What's going on across Tokyo's arts and entertainment scene.
- **Kabuki Web** (www.kabuki-bito.jp/eng/top.html) Book tickets online for Shochiku's theatres, including Kabuki-za.
- **Japan Times** (www.japantimes.co.jp/events) Listings from the daily English-language newspaper.
- **Creativeman** (http://creativeman.co.jp) Tickets for some theatre and music shows.
- **Tokyo Stages** (http://tokyostages.wordpress.com) All about the city's theatre scene.
- **Tokyo Dross** (http://tokyodross.blogspot.jp) Listings for live music and other events.
- **Tokyo Jazz** (http://tokyojazzsite.com) Low-down on the jazz scene.

Cinemas

The best time to go to the movies in Tokyo is Cinema Day (generally 1st of the month) when all tickets cost ¥1000 instead of the regular price of ¥1800.

Wooden dolls for sale

Shopping

Since the Edo era, when courtesans set the day's trends in towering geta (traditional wooden sandals), Tokyoites have lusted after both the novel and the outstanding. The city remains the trendsetter for the rest of Japan, and its residents shop – economy be damned – with an infectious enthusiasm. Join them in the hunt for the cutest fashions, the latest gadgets or the perfect teacup.

Fashion

A generation ago, Ginza *depāto* (department stores) were the supreme arbiters of style. Ginza is still the city's most established shopping district, but for the most part, Tokyo's fashion scene has shifted westward to neighbourhoods such as Shibuya, Harajuku, Aoyama and Daikanyama. All these districts are chock-a-block with boutiques; the edgier ones tucked away on side streets. You'll recognise many of the international brand names, but you'll also encounter a lot of Japanese labels, too. Young shoppers in particular prefer cheaper domestic brands that can turn out *kawaii* (cute) renditions of the latest global trends in a way that appeals to Japanese sensibilities.

Secondhand shops also have a following among young Tokyoites; Shimo-Kitazawa and Kōenji are two neighbourhoods that are locally famous for having lots of vintage clothing shops. You'll find merchandise to be expensive but of excellent quality.

While not exactly on the cutting edge of style, Uniqlo is the go-to store for staples such as T-shirts and socks; you'll find branches in most neighbourhoods.

Crafts

Fortunately, trendy Tokyo still has a strong artisan tradition. Older neighbourhoods on the east side of town such as Asakusa and Ningyochō have shops that sell woven bamboo boxes and indigo-dyed *noren* (cloth hung as a sunshade, typically carrying the name of the shop or premises) – much like they did a hundred (or more) years ago. There's also a new generation of craftspeople who are no less devoted to *monozukuri* (the art of making things), but who are channelling more contemporary needs and tastes. Look to the creators who have set up in the newly developed 2k540 Aki-Oka Artisan mall under the elevated tracks between Akihabara and Okachi-machi.

Collector Culture

Akihabara's *otaku* (geeks) are the greatest ambassadors of Japan's collector culture. But they're hardly an isolated example, and anime (Japanese animation) and manga (comic books) aren't the only obsessions. You don't have to go further than famous *otaku* haunts such as Akihabara and Nakano to find stores that specialise in model trains, radio parts, vintage cameras and nostalgic toys. Go further afield and you'll find shops specialising in mid-century Americana, 1980s fashion and obsure music genres. Given the appetite for such collectors' items, a lot of fascinating and obscure things wind up in Tokyo, regardless of where they originated from.

Kimonos

New kimonos are prohibitively expensive – a full set can easily cost a million yen; used kimonos, on the other hand, can be found for as little as ¥1000 – though one in good shape will cost more like ¥10,000. It takes a lot of practice to get down the art of tying an *obi* (sash) properly, so it's a good idea to get shop staff to help you (though there's no reason you can't just wear one like a dressing gown and forgo the sash entirely). Another option is a *yukata,* a lightweight, cotton kimono that's easier to wear. During the summer you can find these at department stores and even Uniqlo new for under ¥10,000. Used kimonos and *yukata* can also be found year-round for bargain prices at flea markets.

NEED TO KNOW

Opening Hours

- Department stores: 10am to 8pm
- Electronic stores: 10am to 10pm
- Boutiques: noon to 8pm

Service

Service is attentive, increasingly so at more expensive stores, where sales staff will carry your purchase to the door and send you off with a bow. If you're feeling a little claustrophobic, you can put both yourself and the clerk at ease with '*Mitteiru dake desu*' ('I'm just looking').

Paying

Traditional and smaller stores may not accept credit cards.

Duty Free

Major department stores and electronics stores offer duty-free shopping; increasingly, so do smaller-scale shops. Look for stickers in the windows that say 'tax-free shop'. To qualify, you must show your passport and spend more than ¥10,000 in any one shop (or ¥5000 on consumables). For more details see http://enjoy.taxfree.jp. Otherwise, sales tax is 8%.

Sizes

All sorts of sizing systems are used and often you'll find only a 'medium' that's meant to fit everyone (but is smaller than a 'medium' in a Western country). To ask if you can try something on say '*Kore o shichaku dekimas ka?*'

Sales

Clothing sales happen, sadly, just twice a year in Japan: at the beginning of January (after the New Year's holiday) and again in the beginning of July.

Websites

- **Tokyo Fashion** (http://tokyofashion.com) Info on the latest trends and boutiques.
- **Spoon & Tamago** (www.spoon-tamago.com) Blog covering Japanese design, with shopping recommendations.

Shopping by Neighbourhood

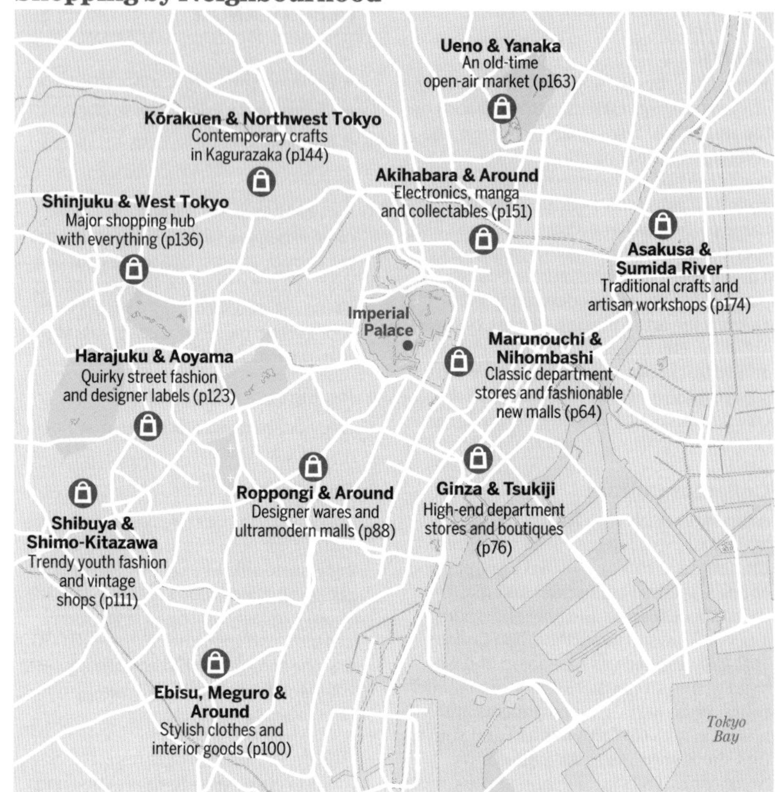

Antique Fairs & Flea Markets

Flea markets and antique fairs pop up regularly around Tokyo; odds are there will be at least one on when you visit. Many take place on the grounds of Shintō shrines, which adds an extra dimension to the experience of trolling for ceramics, costume jewellery, old prints and the like. Though bargaining is permitted, remember that it is considered bad form to drive too hard a bargain. Note that sometimes shrine events (or weather) interfere with markets. For an updated schedule of the city's flea markets, see www.frma.jp (in Japanese).

Electronics

So well known for its electronics shops is Akihabara that it is nicknamed 'Denki-gai' – literally 'Electric Town'. However the big chain shops such as Yodobashi Camera, Bic Camera and Laox can be found in major hubs such as Shinjuku, Shibuya, Ueno and Ikebukuro. Despite the 'camera' in the name, these shops sell all sorts of things, including computers, household appliances and various electronic beauty gadgets (the latter include items you might not find at home). You can shop duty-free, but these days it's unlikely that you'll land much of a bargain.

Variety Stores

Tokyo is full of variety stores that carry an offbeat selection of beauty goods, clever kitchen gadgets and other quirky sundries in attractive packaging. The collective name for such goods is *zakka* – 'miscellaneous things' – and they're intended to add a little colour, ease or joy to daily life. Variety stores are excellent for souvenir hunting. Also keep an eye out for ¥100 stores – variety stores for the budget-minded.

Lonely Planet's Top Choices

Tōkyū Hands (p111) Fascinating emporium of miscellaneous oddities.

2k540 Aki-Oka Artisan (p151) Modern artisan bazaar under the train tracks.

LaForet (p123) Harajuku department store stocked with quirky and cutting-edge brands.

Akomeya (p76) Beautifully packaged, traditional gourmet foodstuffs.

Tokyo Hotarudo (p174) Treasure trove of early 20th century accessories and homewares.

Best for Fashion

Sou-Sou (p124) Traditional Japanese clothing with contemporary panache.

Dover Street Market (p76) Comme des Garcons and other avant-garde labels.

Fake Tokyo (p112) A hotbed of up-and-coming Japanese fashion designers.

Kapital (p100) Denim woven on vintage looms and lush, hand-dyed textiles.

Best for Traditional Crafts

Takumi (p76) One-stop shop for earthy traditional crafts from all over Japan.

Japan Traditional Crafts Aoyama Square (p88) High-end showroom for Japanese artisan work.

Musubi (p123) Versatile patterned cloths in classic and contemporary designs.

Bengara (p174) Beautiful linen *noren* (hanging door curtains).

Best Markets

Ōedo Antique Market (p58) Quality vendors on the first and third Sunday of the month at Tokyo International Forum.

Tsukiji Outer Market (p67) Daily morning market brimming with food and foodstuffs.

Nogi-jinja Antique Flea Market (p80) Bric-a-brac at Nogi-jinja on the fourth Sunday of the month.

Best for Homewares

Do (p100) Artisan-made homewares from around Japan.

Soi (p174) Japanese-modern crockery and vintage pieces.

Muji (p64) Minimalist, utilitarian and utterly indispensable homewares at reasonable prices.

Best for Anime, Manga & Character Goods

Mandarake Complex (p152) Home sweet home for anime and manga fans.

KiddyLand (p123) Toy emporium stocked with character goods.

Nakano Broadway (p128) Retro shopping mall stocked with vintage toys and other collectibles.

Best for Kimonos

Gallery Kawano (p124) Vintage kimonos in good condition.

Tsukikageya (p111) *Yukata* in punk-rock prints.

Chicago Thrift Store (p124) Bargain bins of second-hand kimonos and *yukata*.

Best Shopping Streets

Takeshita-dōri (p116) Tokyo's famous teen fashion bazaar.

Amazake Yokochō (p62) Old-Tokyo strip of craft shops and snack counters.

Meguro-dōri (p100) Tokyo's interior design strip.

Best for Art & Books

Daikanyama T-Site (p98) Designer digs for art and travel tomes.

Tolman Collection (p88) Gallery representing contemporary Japanese print artists.

Best Variety Stores

RanKing RanQueen (p136) The latest must-have consumer products ranked by popularity.

Don Quijote (p136) Oddball assortment of weird loot.

Best Malls

mAAch ecute (p152) Craft and food stores in a former train station.

Coredo Muromachi (p64) Excellent for top-class made-in-Japan fashion and food items.

Best Department Stores

Isetan (p136) Trendy Japanese fashion brands and a great basement food hall.

Mitsukoshi (p64) Classic department store selling kimonos and gourmet food.

Explore Tokyo

TOKYO'S TOP SIGHTS

Neighbourhoods at a Glance

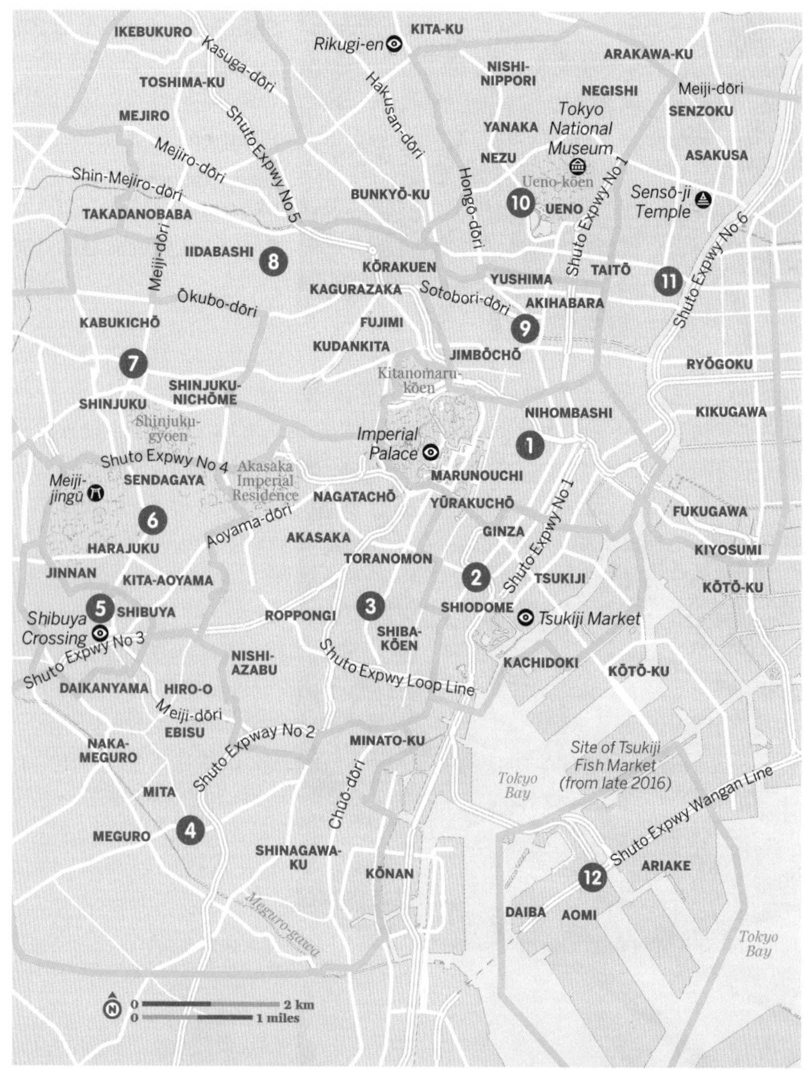

❶ Marunouchi & Nihombashi p54

Marunouchi is a high-powered business district. Its top draw is the Imperial Palace, Tokyo's symbolic centre. Neighbouring Nihombashi is the city's geographic centre, a historic neighbourhood with shops and restaurants that date to the era of the shogun.

❷ Ginza & Tsukiji p65

Ginza is Tokyo's most polished neighbourhood, a fashion centre resplendent with department stores, art galleries and exclusive restaurants; the city's kabuki theatre, Kabuki-za, is here, too. A short walk away is a luxury commercial centre of a different sort: Tsukiji Market.

❸ Roppongi & Around p77

Legendary for its nightlife, Roppongi has reinvented itself in the last decade, with the addition of the forward-looking microcities Roppongi Hills and Tokyo Midtown and several new art museums. It's now downright sophisticated (at least during the day).

❹ Ebisu, Meguro & Around p90

This broad collection of hip neighbourhoods, which includes Daikanyama and Naka-Meguro, has riverside cafes, trendy boutiques, interior-design shops, niche museums and great dining.

❺ Shibuya & Shimo-Kitazawa p101

Shibuya is the heart of Tokyo's youth culture and hits you over the head with its sheer presence: the omnipresent flow of people, glowing video screens and pure exuberance. A short train-ride away, Shimo-Kitazawa is a beloved, bohemian haunt.

❻ Harajuku & Aoyama p113

Harajuku is one of Tokyo's biggest draws, thanks to its stately shrine, Meiji-jingū, outré street fashion and impressive contemporary architecture. Neighbouring Aoyama is a shopping and dining district for the city's fashionable elite.

❼ Shinjuku & West Tokyo p125

Shinjuku – with the world's busiest train station, city views from atop the Tokyo Metropolitan Government Offices and swarming crowds pushing down neon-lit streets – is a fantastic introduction to Tokyo. It's also a major nightlife district. West of Shinjuku is a collection of funky residential neighbourhoods and the magical Ghibli Museum.

❽ Kōrakuen & Northwest Tokyo p137

Kōrakuen is home to Tokyo Dome, where the Yomiuri Giants baseball team plays. Kagurazaka, a former geisha neighbourhood is nearby. Further afield is the city's most attractive traditional garden, Rikugien.

❾ Akihabara & Around p147

Akihabara is synonymous with electronics and *otaku* (geek) culture and is the home of all things anime and manga. Nearby Kanda has shrines, galleries, traditional restaurants and a down-to-earth vibe.

❿ Ueno & Yanaka p153

Ueno is the cultural heart of Tokyo. Its central park, Ueno-kōen, has the city's highest concentration of museums, including the Tokyo National Museum. Neighbouring Yanaka feels like a quaint village where time stopped several decades ago.

⓫ Asakusa & Sumida River p164

Tokyo's eastern neighbourhoods, on the banks of the Sumida-gawa, have an old-Tokyo feel, with traditional restaurants and artisan shops. Asakusa is home to the centuries-old temple, Sensō-ji; Ryōgoku has the sumo stadium Ryōgoku Kokugikan.

⓬ Odaiba & Tokyo Bay p176

This collection of artificial islands on Tokyo Bay was developed as a family-oriented entertainment district, with shopping malls, arcades and the onsen theme-park Ōedo Onsen Monogatari. More grown-up attractions include pleasure-boat cruises.

Marunouchi & Nihombashi

IMPERIAL PALACE AREA | MARUNOUCHI AREA | NIHOMBASHI AREA

Neighbourhood Top Five

❶ Strolling the manicured gardens of the **Imperial Palace** (p56) and watching for VIP visitors in horse-drawn carriages.

❷ Being blown away by the beautiful displays at the fascinating **Intermediateque** (p58).

❸ Comparing the classic and contemporary architecture of **Tokyo Station** (p58) and **Tokyo International Forum** (p58).

❹ Browsing the outstanding collection of impressionist works at the **Bridgestone Museum of Art** (p59).

❺ Eyeballing the sculpted dragons on **Nihombashi** (p59) and sailing under the bridge on a river cruise.

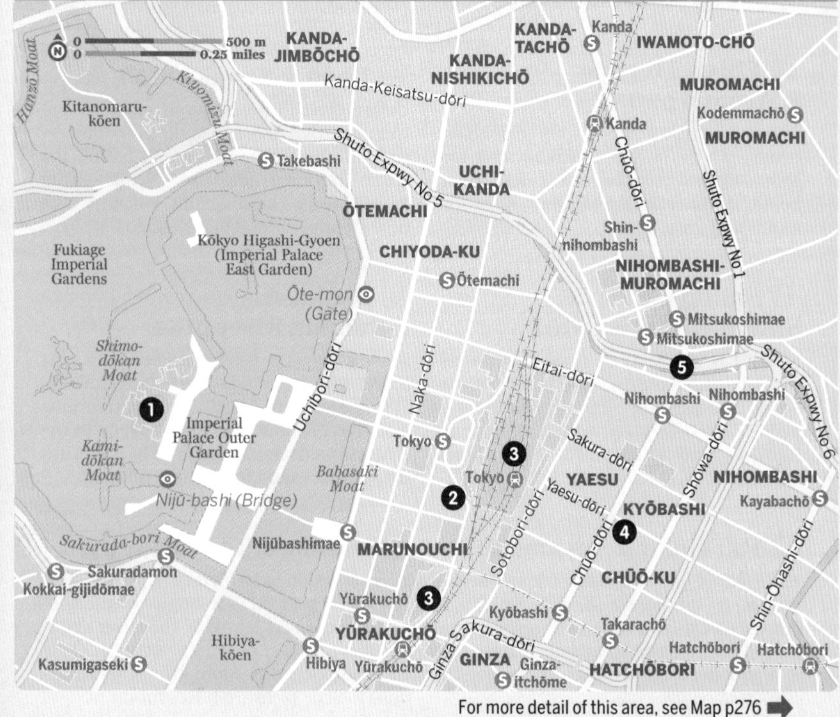

For more detail of this area, see Map p276

Explore Marunouchi & Nihombashi

Tokyo's geographical and spiritual heart is the Imperial Palace. The majority of the compound, encased in a broad moat, remains off-limits to the general public as it's the home of Japan's emperor. However, in the Imperial Palace East Garden you can admire the remains of the mammoth stone walls that once constituted Edo Castle, the largest fortress in the world. Kitanomaru-kōen, north of the main palace area, is renowned for the springtime cherry blossoms by its northern gate, and contains a trio of decent arts and science museums.

Immediately east of the palace, the once drab business stronghold of Marunouchi has blossomed in recent years with a slew of new and revamped buildings including high-end hotels, shops and restaurants. Tree-lined Naka-dōri has morphed into one of Tokyo's most pleasant thoroughfares, the ideal way to saunter from Tokyo Station's handsomely reappointed red-brick entrance to Yūrakuchō, taking in the dramatic architecture of Tokyo International Forum on the way.

Also having undergone a recent architectural facelift is Nihombashi, also spelled Nihonbashi, northeast of Tokyo Station. Joining the elegant department stores Mitsukoshi and Takashimaya here is the new Coredo Muromachi shopping, dining and entertainment complex. In neighbouring Kyōbashi, you'll also find several top-class art museums. In the coming years expect to see Ōtemachi, north of Marunouchi and west of Nihombashi, undergoing a similar makeover.

Local Life

- **Market** At Tokyo International Forum's twice monthly Ōedo Antique Market (p59) you can find unusual and unique souvenirs and gifts.
- **Shopping** Browse high-end boutiques along Marunouchi's Naka-dōri or craft and gourmet-food stores on Ningyōchō's Amazake Yokochō (p62).
- **Exercise** Jog or cycle around the Imperial Palace (p56), or get a gentle workout from the rental pedal boats in the north section of the moat.

Getting There & Away

- **Train** The Yamanote and other JR lines, including the Narita Express and *shinkansen* services, stop at Tokyo Station. Yūrakuchō Station, one stop south, is also convenient for the area.
- **Subway** The Marunouchi line connects with Tokyo Station. The Mita, Chiyoda and Hanzōmon lines also have stops nearby. The Ginza line is handy for Kyōbashi and Nihombashi.

Lonely Planet's Top Tip

At the foot of Nihombashi is a landing from which you can board boats run by **Tokyo Bay Cruise** (Map p276; ☎5679-7311; www.ss3.jp; 45/60min cruises ¥1500/2000; Ⓢ Ginza line to Mitsukoshimae, exit B5 or B6) for a unique perspective of the city. Lasting either 45 minutes or an hour, the cruises proceed along the Nihombashi-gawa, under the historic bridges and the expressway built above the river, out to the Sumida-gawa, or make a loop around Nihombashi-gawa to Kanda-gawa.

Best Places to Eat

- Hōnen Manpuku (p63)
- Taimeike (p63)
- Rose Bakery (p62)

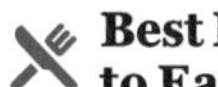
For reviews, see p62

Best Places to Drink

- Cafe Salvador (p63)
- Manpuku Shokudō (p63)
- Peter: the Bar (p63)

For reviews, see p63

Best Places to Shop

- Coredo Muromachi (p64)
- Mitsukoshi (p64)
- KITTE (p64)

For reviews, see p64

FRANK DEIM / GETTY IMAGES ©

TOP SIGHT
IMPERIAL PALACE AREA

Home to Emperor Akihito and Empress Michiko, the palace itself is closed to the public. However, the palace's beautiful east garden is freely open, offers a respite from the city bustle and a chance to view the impressive remains of Edo Castle. The northern park section Kitanomaru-kōen harbours art and science museums and the Olympic venue Nippon Budōkan.

Imperial Palace

The verdant grounds of Japan's Imperial Palace occupy the site of the original Edo-jō, the Tokugawa shōgunate's castle when they ruled the land. In its heyday this was the largest fortress in the world, though little remains of it today apart from the moat and stone walls, parts of which you can view up close in the Imperial Palace East Garden. The present palace, completed in 1968, replaced the one built in 1888, which was largely destroyed during WWII.

As it's the home of Japan's emperor and some of the imperial family, the palace buildings are all off limits. It is possible, however, to take a free tour (lasting around one hour and 15 minutes) of a small part of the surrounding grounds, but you must book ahead through the Imperial Household Agency's website or by phoning. Reservations are taken between a month and four days in advance – you'd be wise to apply as early as possible. Tours run twice daily (10am and 1.30pm, Monday to Friday), but not on public holidays and afternoons from late July through to the end of August. Remember to bring your passport and arrive at least 10 minutes before the start of your tour at the **Kikyō-mon** (桔梗門).

If you're not on the tour, two palace bridges – the iron **Nijū-bashi** and the stone **Megane-bashi** – comprise a famous landmark which can be viewed from the southwest corner of Imperial Palace Plaza. Behind the bridges rises the Edo-era **Fushimi-yagura** watchtower.

DON'T MISS...

- Imperial Palace East Garden
- Nijū-bashi
- Kitanomaru-kōen

PRACTICALITIES

- 皇居; Kōkyo
- Map p276
- ☎3213-1111
- http://sankan.kunaicho.go.jp/english/index.html
- 1 Chiyoda, Chiyoda-ku
- S Chiyoda line to Ōtemachi, exits C13b & C10

Imperial Palace East Garden

Crafted from part of the original castle compound, the **Imperial Palace East Garden** (東御苑; Kōkyo Higashi-gyoen; ⏲9am-4pm Nov-Feb, to 4.30pm Mar–mid-Apr, Sep & Oct, to 5pm mid-Apr–Aug, closed Mon & Fri year-round) FREE has been open to the public since 1968. Here you can get up-close views of the massive stones used to build the castle walls, and even climb the ruins of one of the keeps, off the upper Honmaru lawn.

Entry is free, but the number of visitors at any one time is limited, so it never feels crowded. There are three gates: **Ōte-mon** (大手門; S Chiyoda line to Ōtemachi, exit C13b or C10) on the east side and **Hirakawa-mon** (平川門; S Tōzai line to Takebashi, exit 1a) and **Kitahanebashi-mon** (北桔橋門; S Tōzai line to Takebashi, exit 1a) on the north side. Most people enter through Ōte-mon, the closest gate to Tokyo Station, and once the principal entrance to Edo Castle. Just inside the gate you may want to drop by the **Museum of Imperial Collections** (三の丸尚蔵館; Sannomaru Shozokan; www.kunaicho.go.jp/e-culture/sannomaru/sannomaru.html; ⏲9am-4pm Jan–mid-Apr, Sep & Oct, to 4.30pm mid-Apr–Aug, 3.30pm Nov-Feb) FREE, which mounts small exhibits from the 9500-plus artworks owned by the imperial family.

Kitanomaru-kōen

Split from the Imperial Palace and the East Garden by part of the moat and the Shuto Expressway, leafy **Kitanomaru-kōen** (北の丸公園; www.env.go.jp/garden/kokyogaien/english/index.html; S Hanzōmon line to Kudanshita, exit 2, S Takebashi line, exit 1a) is home to the National Museum of Modern Art (MOMAT; p58), its annex the Crafts Gallery (p58), the Science Museum (p58) and the Nippon Budōkan (p64) events hall.

The park's northern gate **Tayasu-mon** (田安門; S Hanzōmon line to Kudanshita, exit 2), dates from 1636, making it the oldest existing gate to what was once Edo Castle.

The **Chidori-ga-fuchi moat** that surrounds Kitanomaru-kōen explodes with cherry blossoms in spring, making it a prime *hanami* (cherry-blossom-viewing party) spot. You can also rent pedal boats here to view the blossoms from the water.

IMPERIAL PALACE CYCLING COURSE

Every Sunday (bar rainy days), 150 free bicycles are provided for use along the 3.3km **cycling course** (パレスサイクリングコース; ☎3211-5020; www.jbpi.or.jp/english/pc1.html; Babasakimon Police Box; ⏲10am-3pm Sun; S Chiyoda line to Nijūbashimae, exit 2) between Iwaida Bridge and Hirakawa-mon. Bikes are given on a first-come, first-served basis and can be picked up next to the Babasaki-mon police box.

The palace grounds are open on 2 January and 23 December (the Emperor's birthday). All well-wishers can come and greet the imperial family who stand and wave at specified times from a balcony in front of the palace.

Free two-hour guided **walking tours** (https://tfwt.sharepoint.com/Pages/default.aspx) of the Imperial Palace East Garden are available every Saturday; meet at the Marunouchi central exit of Tokyo Station before 1pm.

Imperial Palace Area

IMPERIAL PALACE PALACE

See p56.

NATIONAL MUSEUM OF MODERN ART (MOMAT) MUSEUM

Map p276 (国立近代美術館; Kokuritsu Kindai Bijutsukan; ☎5777-8600; www.momat.go.jp/english; 3-1 Kitanomaru-kōen, Chiyoda-ku; adult/student ¥420/130, extra for special exhibitions; ⏰10am-5pm Tue-Thu, Sat & Sun, to 8pm Fri; Ⓢ Tōzai line to Takebashi, exit 1b) This collection of over 9000 works is one of the country's best. All pieces date from the Meiji period onwards and impart a sense of a more modern Japan through portraits, photography and contemporary sculptures and video works. There's a wonderful view from the museum towards the Imperial Palace East Garden.

CRAFTS GALLERY MUSEUM

Map p276 (東京国立近代美術館 工芸館; www.momat.go.jp/english; 1 Kitanomaru-kōen, Chiyoda-ku; adult/child ¥210/70, 1st Sun of month free; ⏰10am-5pm Tue-Sun; Ⓢ Tōzai line to Takebashi, exit 1b) Housed in a vintage red-brick building this annex of MOMAT stages excellent changing exhibitions of *mingei* (folk crafts): ceramics, lacquerware, bamboo, textiles, dolls and much more. Artists range from living national treasures to contemporary artisans. The building was once the headquarters of the imperial guards, and was rebuilt after its destruction in WWII.

SCIENCE MUSEUM, TOKYO MUSEUM

Map p276 (科学技術館; ☎3212-8544; www.jsf.or.jp; 2-1 Kitanomaru-kōen, Chiyoda-ku; adult/child ¥720/260; ⏰9.30am-4pm Thu-Tue; Ⓢ Tōzai line to Takebashi, exit 1b) Featuring a wide selection of exhibits aimed primarily at children and teenagers, the Science Museum has little in the way of English explanations, but you can ask for a free English pamphlet guide. Even without this or an understanding of Japanese, you can still have fun standing inside a soap bubble or watching a whole variety of scientific experiments.

WADAKURA FOUNTAIN PARK PARK

Map p276 (和田倉噴水公園; www.env.go.jp/garden/kokyogaien/english/point04.html; 1-3 Kōkyo-Gaien, Chiyoda-ku; Ⓢ Chiyoda line to Ōtemachi, exits C13b & C10) FREE At the northeast corner of the broad grassy, moat-surrounded Imperial Palace Plaza is this small, pretty park. The two fountains here celebrate the weddings of the current Emperor Akihito and Empress Michiko in 1961 and Crown Prince Naruhito and Princess Masako in 1995.

Marunouchi Area

★ INTERMEDIATEQUE MUSEUM

Map p276 (☎5777-8600; www.intermediateque.jp; 2nd & 3rd fl, JP Tower, 2-7-2 Marunouchi, Chiyoda-ku; ⏰11am-6pm Tue, Wed, Sat, Sun, to 8pm Thu & Fri; 🚉 JR Yamanote line to Tokyo, Marunouchi exit) FREE Dedicated to interdisciplinary experimentation, Intermediateque cherry picks from the vast collection of the University of Tokyo (Tōdai) to craft a fascinating and wholly contemporary museum experience. Go from viewing the best ornithological taxidermy collection in Japan to a giant pop-art print or the beautifully encased skeleton of a dinosaur.

TOKYO STATION LANDMARK

Map p276 (東京駅; www.tokyostationcity.com/en; 1-9 Marunouchi, Chiyoda-ku; 🚉 JR lines to Tokyo Station) Following a major renovation and expansion completed in time for its centenary in 2014, Tokyo Station is in grand form. Kingo Tatsuno's elegant brick building on the Marunouchi side has been expertly restored to include domes faithful to the original design. Tokyo Station Hotel (p198) occupies the south end of the building; to the north is **Tokyo Station Gallery** (www.ejrcf.or.jp/gallery; Tokyo Station, 1-9-1 Marunouchi, Chiyoda-ku; admission varies; ⏰10am-6pm Tue-Thu, Sat & Sun, to 8pm Fri; 🚉 JR lines to Tokyo, Marunouchi north exit), which hosts interesting exhibitions and the useful JR East Travel Service Center (p253).

Tokyo Station City, the name for the general nontransport complex, includes, on the eastern Yaesu side, **Daimaru** (☎3212-8011; www.daimaru.co.jp/tokyo; 1-9-1 Marunouchi, Chiyoda-ku; ⏰10am-9pm, restaurants 11am-11pm; 🚉 JR lines to Tokyo Station, Yaesu exit) department store, and a vast and bewildering network of underground shopping and dining arcades.

TOKYO INTERNATIONAL FORUM ARCHITECTURE

Map p276 (東京国際フォーラム; ☎5221-9000; www.t-i-forum.co.jp; 3-5-1 Marunouchi, Chiyoda-ku; 🚉 JR Yamanote line to Yūrakuchō, central exit) FREE This architectural marvel designed by Rafael Viñoly houses a convention and

THE GREENING OF MARUNOUCHI

The ongoing rejuvenation of the Marunouchi, Ōtemachi and Yūrakuchō districts by Mitsubishi Estates incorporates a fair amount of greenery in the form of roof-top lawns (at KITTE), vertical gardens (at Marunouchi Brick Square) and trees (along Naka-dōri).

The greenest of the green, though, is local recruitment firm **Pasona** (パソナ; Map p276; 6734-1260; 2-6-4 Ōtemachi, Chiyoda-ku; 9am-5.30pm Mon-Fri; S Tōzai line to Ōtemachi, exit B6) FREE. The exterior of their office is clad in plants, while inside around 200 species of fruits, vegetables, rice and herbs make up their urban farm. Staff take meetings beneath trellises from which tomato plants and grape vines dangle. The company canteen, surrounded by flowers, hosts classical-music miniconcerts each day at noon.

arts centre, with seven auditoriums and a spacious courtyard in which concerts and events are held. The eastern wing looks like a glass ship plying the urban waters; take the lift to the 7th floor and look down on the tiny people below. Visit for the twice-monthly **Ōedo Antique Market** (大江戸骨董市; www.antique-market.jp; 9am-4pm 1st & 3rd Sun of month; JR Yamanote line to Yūrakuchō, Kokusai Forum exit) and the daily food trucks serving bargain meals and drinks to local office workers.

IDEMITSU MUSEUM OF ARTS MUSEUM

Map p276 (出光美術館; www.idemitsu.co.jp/museum; 9th fl, Teigeki Bldg, 3-1-1 Marunouchi, Chiyoda-ku; adult/child/student ¥1000/free/700; 10am-5pm, closed Mon; S Hibiya line to Hibiya, exit B3) You'll find here an excellent collection of Japanese art, sprinkled with Chinese and Korean pottery and a few stray Western pieces. There is no permanent display, with exhibits changing every few months to showcase different aspects of the collection.

MITSUBISHI ICHIGŌKAN MUSEUM MUSEUM

Map p276 (三菱一号館美術館; http://mimt.jp/english; 2-6-2 Marunouchi, Chiyoda-ku; adult/child ¥1600/500; 10am-6pm Tue, Wed & Sun, to 8pm Thu-Sat; S Chiyoda line to Nijūbashimae, exit 1) This museum showcases European art from the late 19th to the mid-20th centuries, with a focus on its holdings of Toulouse-Lautrec works. Also on the premises are Cafe 1894 (p63) and archive rooms (admission free) with period decor and furniture.

Nihombashi Area

NIHOMBASHI (NIHONBASHI) BRIDGE

Map p276 (日本橋; www.nihonbashi-tokyo.jp; S Ginza line to Mitsukoshimae, exits B5 & B6) Guarded by bronze lions and dragons this handsome 1911-vintage granite bridge over Nihombashi-gawa is sadly obscured by the overhead expressway. It's notable as the point from which all distances were measured during the Edo period and as the beginning of the great trunk roads (the Tōkaidō, the Nikkō Kaidō, etc) that took *daimyō* (feudal lords) between Edo and their home provinces.

BRIDGESTONE MUSEUM OF ART MUSEUM

Map p276 (ブリヂストン美術館; www.bridgestone-museum.gr.jp; 1-10-1 Kyōbashi, Chūō-ku; adult/student ¥800/500; 10am-6pm Tue-Thu, Sat & Sun, to 8pm Fri; S Ginza line to Kyōbashi, exit 6) Amassed by Bridgestone founder Ishibashi Shōjiro, this is one of the best French impressionist collections you will find in Asia. Though European painting is undoubtedly the main attraction (think Renoir, Ingres, Monet, Corot, Matisse, Picasso, Kandinsky et al), the museum also exhibits sculpture and some works by Japanese impressionists, as well as European pieces that employ abstract or neoclassical aesthetics.

MITSUI MEMORIAL MUSEUM MUSEUM

Map p276 (三井記念美術館; www.mitsui-museum.jp; 7th fl, Mitsui Main Bldg, 2-1-1 Nihombashi-Muromachi, Chūō-ku; adult/student ¥1000/500; 10am-5pm Tue-Sun; S Ginza line to Mitsukoshimae, exit A7) Stately wood panelling surrounds a small collection of traditional Japanese art and artefacts, including ceramics, paintings, and *nō* (stylised Japanese dance-drama) masks, amassed over three centuries by the families behind today's Mitsui conglomerate.

KITE MUSEUM MUSEUM

Map p276 (凧の博物館; 3271-2465; www.tako.gr.jp/eng/museums_e/tokyo_e.html; 5th fl, 1-12-10 Nihombashi, Chūō-ku; adult/child ¥200/100; 11am-5pm Mon-Sat; S Ginza line to Nihombashi, exit C5) There are 300 or so kites in this small but fascinating museum, located above the restaurant Taimeiken, including brilliantly painted ones based on folk characters, woodblock prints or samurai

1

3

1. Imperial Palace (p56)
One of the palace's most famous landmarks, the Nijū-bashi bridge, with the palace in the background.

2. Tokyo International Forum (p58)
This soaring architectural gem houses an arts and convention centre.

3. Kitanomaru-kōen (p57)
Boats ply the waters of Chidori-ga-fuchi moat, which surrounds Kitanomaru Park, during cherry-blossom season.

WORTH A DETOUR

NINGYŌCHŌ

East of Nihombashi, towards the Sumida-gawa, is **Ningyōchō**, a *shitamachi* (old downtown Tokyo) area well worth exploring for its small temples, shrines, craft shops, food stalls, and atmospheric places to eat and drink. *Ningyō* means doll – these and puppets were once made here when Ningyōchō was a hub for the performing arts. Kabuki is still performed at **Meiji-za** (明治座; Map p292; ☎3666-6666; www.meijiza.co.jp; 2-31-1 Nihonbashi-Hamachō , Chūō-ku; Ⓢ Shinjuku line to Hamachō, exit A2) theatre and you can view the dolls and puppets of Jusaburō Tsujimura at **Jusaburō-kan** (ジュサブロー館; Map p276; ☎3661-0035; http://jusaburo.net/jusaburo.html; 3-6-9 Nihonbashi-Ningyōchō, Chūō-ku; admission ¥1000; ⏲10am-4.30pm Thu-Tue; Ⓢ Hibiya line to Ningyōchō, exit A5).

Zone in on **Amazake Yokochō** (甘酒横丁; Map p276; Ⓢ Hibiya line to Ningyōchō, exit A1) a delightful shopping street lined with age-old businesses and named after the sweet, milky sake drink *amazake;* you can sample it at **Futaba** (双葉; Map p276; www.futaba-tofu.jp; 2-4-9 Nihombashi-Ningyōchō, Chūō-ku; ⏲7am-7pm; Ⓢ Hibiya line to Ningyōchō, exit A1), along with various sweet and savoury eats made from tofu. Also along here is colourful crafts shop **Yūma** (ゆうま; Map p276; www.yuma-oda.com; 2-32-5 Nihombashi-Ningyōchō, Chuo-ku; ⏲10.30am-6.30pm; Ⓢ Hibiya line to Ningyōchō, exit A1).

West across Ningyōchō-dōri from Amazake Yokochō, you'll easily spot **Tamahide** (Map p276; ☎3668-7651; www.tamahide.co.jp; 1-17-1 Nihombashi-Ningyōchō, Chūō-ku; oyakodon from ¥1300; dinner course menu from ¥5800; ⏲11.30am-1pm daily, 5-10pm Mon-Fri, 4-10pm Sat & Sun; Ⓢ Hibiya line to Ningyōchō, exit A1) by the line of customers outside waiting for a space inside the restaurant which has been serving up its signature *oyakodon* (chicken cooked in a sweet soy sauce with egg and served over a bowl of rice) since 1760.

A few blocks northeast from Amazake Yokochō, facing a neighbourhood park, is **Brozers' Hamburger** (Map p276; http://brozers.co.jp; 2-28-5 Nihonbashi Ningyōchō, Chūō-ku; hot dog/burger from ¥600/1000; ⏲11am-9.30pm Mon-Thu, to 10.30pm Fri & Sat, to 7.30pm Sun; 🄴; Ⓢ Hibiya line to Ningyōchō, exit A3), one of Tokyo's best burger joints.

armour. None are particularly old (they're made of paper, after all), but they're amazing to admire nonetheless. Ask for an English booklet at reception.

NATIONAL FILM CENTRE — ARTS CENTRE

Map p276 (東京国立近代美術館フィルムセンター; www.momat.go.jp/english/nfc/index.html; 3-7-6 Kyōbashi, Chūō-ku; screenings adult/student ¥500/300, gallery ¥200/70; ⏲gallery 11am-6.30pm Tue-Sat, check website for screening times; Ⓢ Ginza line to Kyōbashi, exit 1) Here you'll find an archive of Japanese and foreign films, as well as books, periodicals, posters and other materials. There are daily screenings of classic films at bargain prices but few have English subtitles. There are English captions, however, on the worthwhile 7th-floor gallery, which charts the history and evolution of Japanese cinema.

EATING

★ROSE BAKERY MARUNOUCHI — BAKERY ¥

Map p276 (ローズベーカリー 丸の内; ☎3212-1715; http://rosebakery.jp; Meiji-Yasada Bldg, 2-1-1 Marunouchi, Chiyoda-ku; cakes, quiches from ¥410, lunch set ¥1350; ⏲11am-7pm; 🄴; Ⓢ Chiyoda line to Nijūbashimae, exit 3) Tokyo has taken to Paris' Rose Bakery style of dining. Branches of this delicious organic cafe have popped up here in the Comme des Garçons boutique as well as at the same fashion company's Dover Street Market in Ginza and Isetan in Shinjuku. Vegetarians are well served but it is also for those who fancy a full English fry-up for weekend brunch.

TOKYO RĀMEN STREET — RĀMEN ¥

Map p276 (東京ラーメンストリート; www.tokyoeki-1bangai.co.jp/ramenstreet; B1 First Avenue Tokyo Station, 1-9-1 Marunouchi, Chiyoda-ku; rāmen from ¥800; ⏲7.30am-10.30pm; 🅡 JR lines to Tokyo Station, Yaesu south exit) Eight handpicked *rāmen-ya* operate minibranches in this basement arcade on the Yaesu side of Tokyo Station. All the major styles are covered – from *shōyu* (soy-sauce base) to *tsukemen* (cold noodles served on the side).

MEAL MUJI YŪRAKUCHŌ — DELI ¥

Map p276 (MealMUJI有楽町; ☎5208-8241; www.muji.net/cafemeal/; 3-8-3 Marunouchi, Chiyoda-ku; meals from ¥780; ⏲10am-9pm; ⊖📝; 🅡 JR Yamanote line to Yūrakuchō, Kyōbashi exit) Those who subscribe to the Muji lifestyle will be delighted to know that the 'no name brand' experience goes beyond neutral-toned notebooks, containers and linens. Meal MUJI follows the 'simpler is better' mantra with fresh deli fare uncluttered by chemicals and unpronounceable ingredients.

★HŌNEN MANPUKU JAPANESE ¥¥

Map p276 (豊年萬福; ☎3277-3330; www.hounenmanpuku.jp; 1-8-16 Nihombashi-Muromachi, Chūō-ku; mains ¥1280-1850; ⏲11.30am-2.30pm, 5-11pm Mon-Sat, 5-10pm Sun; 🅔; Ⓢ Ginza line to Mitsukoshimae, exit A1) Offering a riverside terrace in warmer months, Hōnen Manpuku's interior is dominated by *washi* (Japanese handmade paper) lanterns beneath which patrons tuck into bargain-priced beef or pork sukiyaki and other traditional dishes. Lunchtime set menus are great value.

TAIMEIKE JAPANESE ¥¥

Map p276 (たいめいけん; ☎3271-2464; www.taimeiken.co.jp; 1-12-10 Nihombashi, Chūō-ku; lunch from ¥800; omelette ¥1950; ⏲11am-8.30pm Mon-Sat, to 8pm Sun; Ⓢ Ginza line to Nihombashi, exit C5) *Yōshoku,* Western dishes adapted to Japanese tastes, has been the draw here since 1931, in particular their borsch and coleslaw. For the food movie *Tampopo* (1985), they created *Tampopo omuraisu* (an omelette atop tomato-flavoured rice) and it's been a signature dish ever since.

NIHONBASHI DASHI BAR JAPANESE ¥¥

Map p276 (日本橋だし場 はなれ; ☎5205-8704; www.ninben.co.jp; 1st fl, Coredo Muromachi 2-3-1 Nihombashi-Muromachi, Chuo-ku; mains from ¥840, lunch/dinner set course from ¥950/1500; ⏲11am-10pm; Ⓢ Ginza line to Mitsukoshimae, exit A4) A key ingredient of the stock *dashi* is flakes of *katsuobushi* (dried bonito) which the Nihombashi-based Ninben have been making and selling since the Edo period. In this restaurant the company showcases its product in myriad ways. If you just want to sample the stock there's a takeaway soup bar in Coredo Muromachi 1 (open 10am to 8pm).

CAFE 1894 INTERNATIONAL ¥¥

Map p276 (カフェ1894; http://mimt.jp/cafe1894; 2-6-2 Marunouchi, Chiyoda-ku; lunch set from ¥1480, coffee ¥525; ⏲11am-11pm Mon-Thu, Sat & Sun, to 2am Fri; Ⓢ Chiyoda line to Nijūbashimae, exit 1) Occupying a faithful replica of the bank that once operated here, Cafe 1894 has vaulted ceilings and handsome woodwork as well as a tempting menu of well-presented dishes including sandwiches, salads, pasta and steak.

DRINKING & NIGHTLIFE

★CAFE SALVADOR CAFE

Map p276 (www.cafecompany.co.jp/brands/salvador/marunouchi; 3-2-3 Marunouchi, Chiyoda-ku; ⏲7am-11pm Mon-Fri, 10am-11pm Sat, 10am-8pm Sun; @📶; 🚉JR Yūrakuchō line to Yūrakuchō, Kokusai Forum exit) Comfy sofas, piles of glossy magazines, quirky art on the walls, free wi-fi and plenty of electricity outlets, make this affordable counter-service cafe one of the most convivial along ritzy Naka-dōri. Plenty of caffeinated drinks are supplemented by salads, sandwiches and fresh bakes.

MANPUKU SHOKUDŌ IZAKAYA

Map p276 (まんぷく食堂; ☎3211-6001; www.manpukushokudo.com; 2-4-1 Yūrakuchō, Chiyoda-ku; cover charge ¥300; ⏲24hr; 🚉JR Yamanote line to Yūrakuchō, central exit) Down your beer or sake as trains rattle overhead on the tracks that span Harumi-dōri at Yūrakuchō.

PETER: THE BAR COCKTAIL BAR

Map p276 (☎6270-2763; http://tokyo.peninsula.com/en/fine-dining/peter-lounge-bar; 1-8-1 Yūrakuchō, Chiyoda-ku; ⏲noon-midnight, to 1am Fri & Sat; Ⓢ Hibiya line to Hibiya, exits A6 & A7) The Peninsula's Peter: The Bar distinguishes itself with dress-circle views across the Imperial Palace, Hibiya Park and Ginza as well as a generous happy hour (5pm to 8pm Sunday to Thursday) when drinks and snacks are all ¥800.

SO TIRED BAR

Map p276 (ソータイアード; ☎5220-1358; www.heads-west.com/shop/so-tired.html; 7th fl, Shin-Marunouchi Bldg, 1-5-1 Marunouchi, Chiyoda-ku; ⏲11am-4am Mon-Sat, to 11pm Sun; 🚉JR lines to Tokyo, Marunouchi north exit) The best thing about this bar on the lively 7th floor of the Shin-Maru Building is that you can buy a drink at the counter and take it out to the terrace.

CRAFT BEER MARKET MITSUKOSHIMAE BEER HALL

Map p276 (Craft Beer Market三越前店; ☎6262-3145; www.craftbeermarket.jp; Coredo Muromachi 3, 1-5-5 Nihombashi-Muromachi, Chūō-ku; cover ¥300; ⏲11am-2pm, 5-11.30pm Mon-Fri, 11am-11.30pm Sat & Sun; Ⓢ Ginza line to Mitsukoshimae, exit A4) If trawling Nihombashi's shops has given you a thirst, this craft-beer pub has some 30 kinds of ales and Japanese snacks. There are other branches in **Awajichō** (Map p290; 2-9-1 Kanda-Awajichō, Chiyoda-ku; ⏲11.30am-2pm, 5-11.30pm Mon-Fri; Ⓢ Marunouchi line to Awajichō, exit A4), **Jimbōchō** (Map p290;

2-11-15 Kanda-Jimbōchō, Chiyoda-ku; ⌚11.30am-2pm, 5-11.30pm Mon-Sat; Ⓢ Hanzomon line to Jimbōchō, exit A7) and **Toranomon** (クラフトビア マーケット; Map p280; 1-23-3 Nishi-Shimbashi, Minato-ku; ⌚11.30am-2pm, 5-11.30pm Mon-Fri; Ⓢ Ginza line to Toranomon, exit 1).

ENTERTAINMENT

COTTON CLUB — JAZZ

Map p276 (コットンクラブ; ☎3215-1555; www.cottonclubjapan.co.jp; 2-7-3 Marunouchi, Chiyoda-ku; ⌚shows begin 7pm, 9.30pm Mon-Sat, 5pm, 8pm Sun; JR lines to Tokyo Station, Marunouchi south exit) You're more likely to hear contemporary international jazz stars here than musicians harking back to the 1920s New York club it honours. Also on the roster is a medley of interesting Japanese artists. Check the website for schedules.

NIPPON BUDŌKAN — LIVE MUSIC, MARTIAL ARTS

Map p276 (日本武道館; ☎3216-5100; http://nipponbudokan.web.fc2.com; 2-3 Kitanomaru-kōen, Chiyoda-ku; Ⓢ Hanzōmon line to Kudanshita, exit 2) The 14,000-plus-seat Budōkan, a legendary concert hall for big acts from the Beatles to Beck, was originally built for the martial-arts championships (judo, karate, kendō, aikidō) of the 1964 Olympics (budō means 'martial arts') and will be pressed into service again for the 2020 event.

SHOPPING

★MITSUKOSHI — DEPARTMENT STORE

Map p276 (三越; ☎3241-3311; www.mitsukoshi.co.jp; 1-4-1 Nihombashi-Muromachi, Chūō-ku; ⌚10am-7pm; Ⓢ Ginza line to Mitsukoshimae, exit A2) Mitsukoshi's venerable Nihombashi branch was Japan's first department store. It's a grand affair with an entrance guarded by bronze lions and a magnificent statue of Magokoro, the Goddess of Sincerity, rising up from the centre of the ground floor.

★COREDO MUROMACHI — MALL

Map p276 (コレド室町; http://mi-mo.jp/pc/lng/eng/muromachi.html; 2-2-1 Nihonbashi-Muromachi, Chūō-ku; ⌚11am-7pm most shops; Ⓢ Ginza line to Mitsukoshimae, exit A4) Spread over three buildings, this stylish new development hits its stride at Coredo Muromachi 3. It houses several well-curated floors of top-class, Japanese-crafted goods including cosmetics, fashion, homewares, eyeglasses and speciality food.

KITTE — MALL

Map p276 (https://jptower-kitte.jp/en; 2-7-2 Marunouchi, Chiyoda-ku; ⌚11am-9pm Mon-Sat, to 8pm Sun; JR lines to Tokyo, Marunouchi south exit) This slick shopping mall at the foot of JP Tower incorporates the restored facade of the former Tokyo Central Post Office. It is notable for its atrium around which are arrayed a quality selection of craft-orientated Japanese brand shops selling homewares, fashion, accessories and lifestyle goods.

MUJI — CLOTHING, HOMEWARES

Map p276 (無印良品; www.muji.com; 3-8-3 Marunouchi, Chiyoda-ku; ⌚10am-9pm; JR Yamanote line to Yūrakuchō, Kyōbashi exit) The flagship store of the famously understated brand sells elegant, simple clothing, accessories and homewares. There are many other outlets across Tokyo, including a good one in Tokyo Midtown, but the Yūrakuchō store also has bicycle rental and a great cafeteria.

BIC CAMERA — ELECTRONICS

Map p276 (ビックカメラ; ☎5221-1111; www.biccamera.co.jp; 1-11-1Yūrakuchō, Chiyoda-ku; ⌚10am-10pm; JR Yamanote line to Yūrakuchō, Kokusai Center exit) Cameras are just the start of the electronic items and much more (toys, sake, medicine and cosmetics) sold in this mammoth discount store occupying a block. Shopping here is like being inside a very noisy computer game but it's worth enduring for the discounts and the tax-free deals available to tourists.

TOKYO CHARACTER STREET — TOYS

Map p276 (東京キャラクターストリート; www.tokyoeki-1bangai.co.jp; B1 First Avenue Tokyo Station, 1-9-1 Marunouchi, Chiyoda-ku; ⌚10am-8.30pm; JR lines to Tokyo Station, Yaesu exit) From Doraemon to Domo-kun, Hello Kitty to Ultraman, Japan knows *kawaii* (cute) and how to merchandise it. Some 15 Japanese TV networks and toy manufacturers operate stalls selling official plush toys, sweets, accessories and the all-important miniature character to dangle from your mobile phone.

TAKASHIMAYA — DEPARTMENT STORE

Map p276 (高島屋; www.takashimaya.co.jp/tokyo/store_information; 2-4-1 Nihombashi, Chūō-ku; ⌚10am-8pm; Ⓢ Ginza line to Nihombashi, Takashimaya exit) The design of Takashimaya's flagship store (1933) tips its pillbox hat to New York's Gilded Age with marble columns, chandeliers and uniformed female elevator operators. Take your passport and you can get a free Shoppers Discount card giving you 5% off purchases over ¥3000.

Ginza & Tsukiji

GINZA | SHIODOME | TSUKIJI

Neighbourhood Top Five

❶ Feasting your eyes and stomach on denizens of the deep at **Tsukiji Market** (p67).

❷ Browsing some of Japan's poshest shops and top department stores in **Ginza** (p76).

❸ Being entertained by the technicolor spectacle of kabuki drama at **Kabuki-za** (p70).

❹ Sipping green tea in the beautiful bayside garden **Hama-rikyū Onshi-teien** (p69).

❺ Snacking on *yakitori* (chicken skewers) with salarymen and women under the tracks at **Yūrakuchō** (p70).

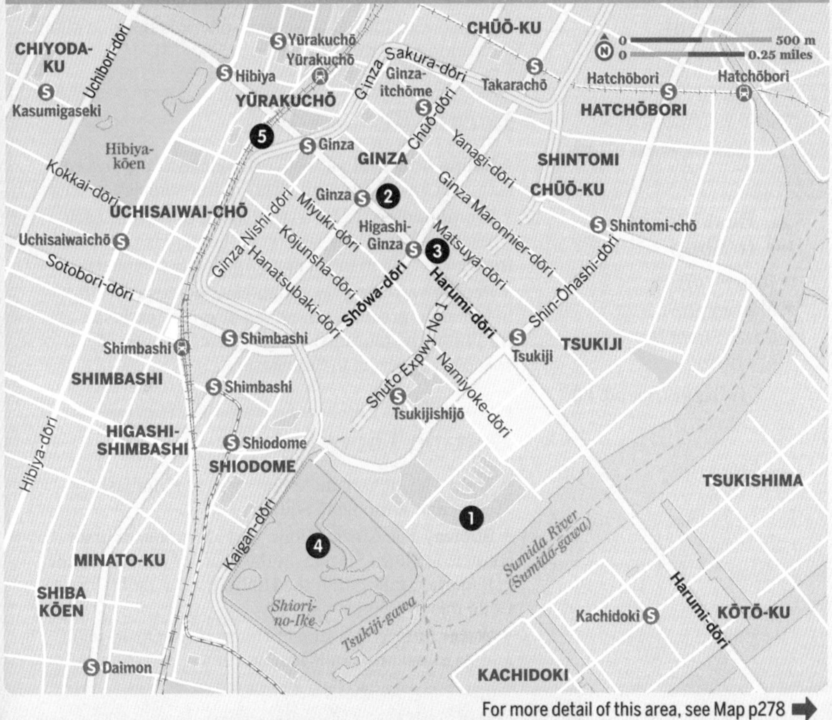

For more detail of this area, see Map p278 ➡

Lonely Planet's Top Tip

Join salarymen and women freshening up at **Komparu-yu** (金春湯; Map p278; www002.upp.so-net.ne.jp/konparu; 8-7-5 Ginza, Chūō-ku; admission ¥460; ⏲2-10pm Mon-Sat; 🚇Ginza line to Shimbashi, exit 1 or 3), a simple bathhouse that's been located on a Ginza side street since 1863. Tile art includes old-school koi (carp) and the traditional Mt Fuji motifs.

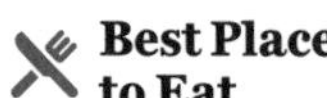

Best Places to Eat

- Ore-no-dashi (p70)
- Kyūbey (p71)
- Trattoria Tsukiji Paradiso! (p71)

For reviews, see p70 ➡

Best Places to Drink

- Kagaya (p71)
- Cha Ginza (p75)
- Cafe de l'Ambre (p75)

For reviews, see p71 ➡

Best Places to Shop

- Takumi (p76)
- Akomeya (p76)
- Dover Street Market Ginza (p76)

For reviews, see p76 ➡

Explore Ginza & Tsukiji

Proudly ranking alongside Fifth Avenue and the Champs-Élysées, Ginza is one of the most famous shopping districts in the world. However, the growing popularity of other parts of Tokyo for high-end shopping have caused Ginza to relax its exclusivity in recent years. Now alongside Mikimoto pearls and Louis Vuitton you'll also find the likes of Uniqlo. Amid the expense-account establishments, there are also plenty of affordable dining and drinking options, including classy *rāmen* (noodle) bars and stand-up joints serving everything from fancy French dishes to sushi.

Speaking of sushi, next to Ginza is Tsukiji, currently home to the world's largest fish market. The wholesale market, where the famous bluefin tuna auctions are held, is set to move across Tokyo Bay to a new home in Toyosu in late 2016. Meanwhile, business is booming for the mouth-watering array of food-related businesses of the outer market which will remain here post 2016. The good news is that you don't need to be up before the crack of dawn to sample the best of Tsukiji or the surrounding area, which includes Hama-rikyū Onshi-teien, a gorgeous bayside garden that's home to a serene traditional teahouse.

Providing a 21st-century backdrop to the manicured greenery of Hama-rikyū are the skyscrapers of Shiodome and the monorail running through it from Shimbashi (also spelled Shinbashi), the birthplace of Japan's railways. The vaulted spaces beneath the train lines here remain one of Tokyo's most atmospheric spots for a night of drinking and dining.

Local Life

- **Eating** Browse Mitsukoshi and Matsuya's *depachika* – basement food floors with plenty of free samples on offer.
- **Promenading** Go for a stroll along Chūō-dōri each weekend, when a long section of the road is traffic free from noon to 5pm (until 6pm, April to September).
- **People-watching** Spot high-class hostesses, clad in kimonos, greeting salarymen at *ryōtei* (exclusive traditional restaurants); you may even see one of Tokyo's rare geisha in Shimbashi.

Getting There & Away

- **Train** The JR Yamanote line stops at Shimbashi Station and Yūrakuchō Station.
- **Subway** The Ginza, Hibiya and Marunouchi lines connect at Ginza Station, in the heart of Ginza. For the fish market, take either the Hibiya line to Tsukiji or the Ōedo line to Tsukijishijō.
- **Water bus** Ferries stop at Hama-rikyū Onshi-teien and go to Asakusa and Odaiba.

TOP SIGHT
TSUKIJI AREA

Until late 2016, this is the location of Tsukiji Market, also known as Tsukiji Fish Market, which is most famous for selling every type of fish and seafood imaginable. The world's biggest seafood market is arguably Tokyo's top sight but the action also spills over into the equally enjoyable outer market *(jōgai-shijō)* which will stay put when the wholesale market moves to Toyosu.

Inner Market

Around 2000 tonnes of seafood, worth around US$15 million, is traded daily in the **inner market** *(jōgai-shijō)* in an atmosphere that is both frenetic and finely orchestrated with handcarts, forklifts and 'turret' electric trucks performing a perfect high-speed choreography across a 23-hectare site. It's an amazing sight, attracting hoards of visitors, particularly on Saturday.

Come November 2016, all wholesale operations will move to a new, state-of-the-art facility on Toyosu, 2.3km southeast across Tokyo Bay. You can see models and plans of the new market, which will include a viewing area able to accommodate some 500 visitors, at the **Tokyo Ichiba Project** (www.tokyoichiba-project.metro.tokyo.jp; 5-2-1 Tsukiji, Chūō-ku; ⏲9am-2pm Mon-Fri, to 3pm Sat). This exhibition is located next to **Uogashi-yokochō** (魚がし横町; sushi set ¥3150; ⏲5am-2pm), a cluster of tiny restaurants, food and souvenir stalls within the *jōnai-shijō,* easily spotted by the long line of people queuing for **sushi** at famous outlets such as Daiwa Sushi (p71).

Don't despair if you miss the tuna auctions. The **Seafood Intermediate Wholesalers' Area** (水産仲卸業者売場; ⏲9-11am) officially opens to visitors at 9am. This is where you can see all kinds of sea creatures laid out in styrofoam crates. It's a photographer's paradise,

DON'T MISS...

- Tuna auction
- Melon auction
- Sushi for breakfast
- Browsing the outer market

PRACTICALITIES

- 東京都中央卸売市場, Tokyo Metropolitan Central Wholesale Produce
- Map p278
- ☎3261-8326
- www.tsukiji-market.or.jp
- 5-2-1 Tsukiji, Chūō-ku
- ⏲5am-1pm; closed Sun, most Wed & all public holidays
- Ⓢ Hibiya line to Tsukiji, exit 1

MELON AUCTION

Attending the **melon auction** (S Ōedo line to Tsukijishijomae, exit A1) in the Vegetable and Fruits Wholesale Market section of the inner market is far less fuss than the tuna auction; just turn up and watch from around 9am.

Dress down when visiting the market and wear waterproof shoes. Wrap up well if you attend the tuna auction as it's very chilly in the auction area.

TOURS

Tsukiji Market Information Centre (☎3541-6521; www.tsukijitour.jp; 4-7-5 Tsukiji, Chūō-ku; tour per person from ¥8800; ⏰8.30am-3pm market days; S Hibiya line to Tsukiji, exit 2) runs the most popular tour (minimum of two people), which starts with a video and finishes with a sushi lunch.

New Tsukiji Tour (http://homepage3.nifty.com/tokyoworks/Tsukiji-Tour/newtsukijitour.html; tour per person ¥7500) is run by ex-Tsukiji-auction-house employee Nakamura Naoto. These walking tours (for one to six people) go behind the scenes of the market.

but you need to avoid getting in the way. The market, which has occupied this location with minimal changes since 1935, was not designed for mass tourism. Please exercise caution and respect when visiting so as not to spoil the opportunity for future visitors.

Tuna Auctions

Tsukiji's star attraction is *maguro* (bluefin tuna), as big as submarine torpedos and weighing up to 300kg: the sight (and sound) of these flash-frozen whoppers being auctioned is a classic Tokyo experience, worth getting up early (or staying up late) for.

Visitors start showing up for one of the 120 places to view the tuna auction from around 3.30am at the **Fish Information Center** (おさかな普及センター; Osakana Fukyū Senta; Kachidoki Gate, 6-20-5 Tsukiji, Chūō-ku) at the northwest corner of the market. It's on a first-come, first-served basis so it pays to get here well before the first batch of 60 visitors go into to see the auctions between 5.25am and 5.50am; the second batch is from 5.50am to 6.15am. Public transport doesn't start until around 5am, so you'll either need to walk or take a taxi to the market.

In the past, the authorities have suspended viewing of the tuna auctions because of inappropriate behaviour by tourists, so please follow the rules. Over the busy new-year period viewings are usually cancelled.

Outer Market

As equally fascinating as the inner market, **Tsukiji Outer Market** (場外市場; Jōgai Shijō; ⏰5am-2pm) is a one-stop shop for anything you need to prepare and serve a great Japanese meal. Here, rows of vendors hawk goods from dried fish and seaweed to rubber boots, crockery and fine-quality kitchen knives; pick up a map from **Information Centre Plat Tsukiji** (☎6264-1925; www.tsukiji.or.jp; 4-16-2 Tsukiji, Chuo-ku; ⏰9.30am-1.30pm Mon-Sat, 10am-2pm Sun) on Namiyōke-dori, where you can also buy souvenirs.

Freshly shucked oysters and fat slices of *tamagoyaki* (sweet and savoury rolled omelettes) are great snacks to sample here while on the go. Alternatively there are many restaurants and cafes, including market-worker's favourite Kimagure-ya (p71).

Also drop by **Namiyoke-jinja** (波除神社; www.namiyoke.or.jp; 6-20-37 Tsukiji, Chūō-ku; S Hibiya line to Tsukiji, exit 1), the Shintō shrine where Tsukiji's workers and residents come to pray. Giant lion masks used in the area's annual festival flank the entrance and there are dragon-shaped taps over the purification basins.

SIGHTS

Ginza

TSUKIJI MARKET MARKET

See p67.

TSUKIJI HONGWAN-JI BUDDHIST TEMPLE

Map p278 (築地本願寺; ☎3541-1131; www.tsukijihongwanji.jp; 3-15-1 Tsukiji, Chūō-ku; ⏲6am-5pm; Ⓢ Hibiya line to Tsukiji, exit 1) FREE When this branch of the mother temple in Kyoto fell victim to the Great Kantō Earthquake of 1923, it was rebuilt in a classical Indian style, making it one of the most distinctive Buddhist places of worship in Tokyo.

Talks in English about Dharma are usually held on the last Saturday of the month from 5.30pm. See the temple website for more information.

HIBIYA-KŌEN PARK

Map p278 (日比谷公園; www.tokyo-park.or.jp/english/park/detail_02.html#hibiya; 1-6 Hibiya-kōen, Chiyoda-ku; Ⓢ Hibiya line to Hibiya, exits A10 & A14) FREE Built around the turn of the 20th century at the height of the Meiji era, this leafy park situated just west of Ginza was Tokyo's first European-style park complete with fountains and ponds.

It's a pleasant spot for a break and you can eat here surrounded by greenery at the long-established Western-style restaurant **Matsumotorō** (松本楼; Map p278; ☎3503-1451; www.matsumotoro.co.jp; 1-2 Hibiya-kōen, Chiyoda-ku; lunch/dinner from ¥1000/2000; ⏲11am-1pm & 5-9pm; Ⓢ Hibiya line to Hibiya, exit A10 or A14).

Shiodome

★HAMA-RIKYŪ ONSHI-TEIEN GARDENS

Map p278 (浜離宮恩賜庭園; Detached Palace Garden; www.tokyo-park.or.jp/park/format/index028.html; 1-1 Hama-rikyū-teien, Chūō-ku; adult/child ¥300/free; ⏲9am-5pm; Ⓢ Ōedo line to Shiodome, exit A1) This beautiful garden, one of Tokyo's finest, is all that remains of a shogunal palace that once extended into the area now occupied by Tsukiji Market. The main features are a large duck pond with an island that's home to a charming tea pavilion, **Nakajima no Ochaya** (中島の御茶屋; tea set ¥500; ⏲9am-4.30pm), as well as some wonderfully manicured trees (black pine, Japanese apricot, hydrangeas etc), some of which are hundreds of years old.

Besides visiting the park as a side trip from Ginza or Tsukiji, consider travelling by boat to or from Asakusa via the Sumida-gawa (Sumida River).

ADVERTISING MUSEUM TOKYO MUSEUM

Map p278 (アド・ミュージアム東京; www.admt.jp; basement fl, Caretta Bldg, 1-8-2 Higashi-Shimbashi, Minato-ku; ⏲11am-6.30pm Tue-Fri, to 4.30pm Sat; Ⓢ Ōedo line to Shiodome, Shimbashi Station exit) FREE This collection is run by Dentsu, Japan's largest advertising agency. It covers everythsing from woodblock-printed handbills from the Edo period to sumptuous art nouveau and art deco Meiji- and Taisho-era works to the best of today. English signage is minimal, but the strong graphics of many of the ads stand alone. If you see advertising as art, it's a spectacle, and there are video consoles to watch award-winning TV commercials from around the world.

GINZA'S GALLERIES

There are plenty of free shows to view at Ginza's commercial galleries. **Shiseido Gallery** (資生堂ギャラリー; Map p278; ☎3572-3901; www.shiseido.co.jp/e/gallery/html; Basement fl, 8-8-3 Ginza, Chūō-ku; ⏲11am-7pm Tue-Sat, to 6pm Sun; Ⓢ Ginza line to Shimbashi, exits 1 & 3) FREE specialises in experimental art; **Gallery Koyanagi** (ギャラリー小柳; Map p278; ☎3561-1896; www.gallerykoyanagi.com; 8th fl, 1-7-5 Ginza, Chūō-ku; ⏲11am-7pm Tue-Sat; Ⓢ Ginza line to Ginza, exit A9) exhibits notable local and international artists; **Ginza Graphic Gallery** (ギンザ・グラフィック・ギャラリー; Map p278; ☎3571-5206; www.dnp.co.jp/gallery/ggg; 7-7-2 Ginza, Chūō-ku; ⏲11am-7pm Tue-Fri, to 6pm Sat; Ⓢ Ginza line to Ginza, exit A2) FREE focuses on advertising and poster art; and **Tokyo Gallery + BTAP** (東京画廊; Map p278; ☎3571-1808; www.tokyo-gallery.com; 7th fl, 8-10-5 Ginza, Chūō-ku; ⏲11am-7pm Tue-Fri, to 5pm Sat; Ⓢ Ginza line to Shimbashi, exit 1 or 3) FREE shows challenging, often political works by Japanese and Chinese artists.

TOP SIGHT KABUKI-ZA THEATRE

The flamboyant facade of this venerable theatre, recently reconstructed to incorporate a tower block, makes a strong impression. It is a good indication of the extravagant dramatic flourishes that are integral to the traditional performing art of kabuki.

A full kabuki performance comprises three or four acts (usually from different plays) over an afternoon or an evening (typically 11am to 3.30pm or 4.30pm to 9pm), with long intervals between the acts. Be sure to rent a headset for blow-by-blow explanations in English, and pick up a *bentō* (boxed meal) to snack on during the intervals.

If four-plus hours sounds too long, 90 sitting and 60 standing tickets are sold on the day for each single act. They are at the back of the auditorium but still provide good views. Some acts tend to be more popular than others, so ask ahead as to which to catch and arrive at least 1½ hours before the start of the performance.

Only die-hard fans will be interested in the small museum on the 5th floor of the tower, but come up here anyway to take a breather in the lovely rooftop garden.

DON'T MISS

- One-act tickets
- Theatre facade
- Rooftop garden

PRACTICALITIES

- 歌舞伎座
- Map p278
- 3545-6800
- www.kabuki-bito.jp/eng
- 4-12-15 Ginza, Chūō-ku
- tickets ¥4000-20,000, single-act tickets ¥800-2000
- Hibiya line to Higashi-Ginza, exit 3

NAKAGIN CAPSULE TOWER ARCHITECTURE
Map p278 (中銀カプセルタワー; www.nakagincapsule.com; 8-16-10 Ginza, Chūō-ku; S Ōedo line to Tsukijishijō, exit A3) A Facebook campaign has been started by some residents and fans to save Kurokawa Kishō's early-1970s building, which is a seminal work of Metabolist architecture. The tower's self-contained pods, which can be removed whole from a central core and replaced elsewhere, are in various states of decay but it's still a very impressive design. It's possible to arrange to stay here via Airbnb.

EATING

Ginza

★ORE-NO-DASHI JAPANESE ¥
Map p278 (俺のだし; 3571-6762; www.oreno.co.jp/en/eaterycat/dashi; 7-6-6 Ginza; dishes from ¥380-1480; 5pm-2am Mon-Fri, 4-11pm Sat & Sun; ; S Ginza line to Ginza, exit A2) The Ore-no chain – where you stand to eat gourmet dishes prepared by skilled chefs at bargain prices – has been a massive success in Ginza. This one specialises in *oden* – delicious morsels simmered in *dashi* (fish stock). There are seats here too and a good wine list.

YŪRAKUCHŌ SANCHOKU INSHOKUGAI JAPANESE ¥¥
Map p278 (有楽町産直飲食街; www.sanchoku-inshokugai.com/yurakucho; International Arcade, 2-1-1 Yūrakuchō, Chiyoda-ku; most 24hr; JR Yamanote line to Yūrakuchō, Yūrakuchō exit) Stalls dishing up *yakitori* have long huddled under the railway tracks here. This red-lantern-lit alleyway is a more modern collective which sticks to the cheap, cheerful and smoky formula, but uses quality ingredients sourced direct from producers around the country. Alongside steak from Hokkaido and seafood from Shizuoka, there's also a beef *rāmen* stall.

NATARAJ INDIAN ¥¥
Map p278 (ナタラジ; 5537-1515; www.nataraj.co.jp; 7th-9th fl, 6-9-4 Ginza, Chūō-ku; mains/set courses from ¥1048/2381; 11.30am-11pm; ; S Ginza line to Ginza, exit A2) Vegetarian and vegans rejoice. Nataraj brings its warm colours and low-key elegance to its three-storey Ginza branch. Sizeable set meals include appealing choices such

as pumpkin curry and chickpea pakora, which go down well with organic wines and beers.

★KYŪBEY SUSHI ¥¥¥

Map p278 (久兵衛; ☎3571-6523; www.kyubey.jp; 8-7-6 Ginza, Chūō-ku; sushi sets lunch ¥5000-8400, dinner from ¥10,500; ⏲11.30am-2pm & 5-10pm Mon-Sat; 📵; Ⓢ Ginza line to Shimbashi, exit 3) Since 1936, Kyūbey's quality and presentation has won it a moneyed and celebrity clientele. Even so, this is a supremely foreigner-friendly and relaxed restaurant. Expect personal greetings in English by the owner Imada-san and his team of talented chefs who will make and serve your sushi, piece by piece. For a real treat, order the *kaiseki* (Japanese haute cuisine) menu served on pottery by famed artisan Kitaoji Rosanjin (¥31,500). There's an exhibition of Rosanjin pieces on the restaurant's 4th floor.

MARU JAPANESE ¥¥¥

Map p278 (銀座圓; ☎5537-7420; www.maru-mayfont.jp/ginza; 2nd fl, Ichigo Ginza 612 Bldg, 6-12-15 Ginza, Chūō-ku; lunch/dinner from ¥1100/6000; ⏲11.30am-2pm & 5.30-9pm Mon-Sat; 📵; Ⓢ Ginza line to Ginza, exit A3) Maru offers a contemporary take on *kaiseki* fine dining. The chefs are young and inventive, and the appealing space is dominated by a long, wooden, open kitchen counter across which you can watch them work. Its good-value lunches offer a choice of mainly fish dishes.

Maru's **Harajuku branch** (圓; Map p288; ☎6418-5572; basement fl, 5-50-8 Jingūmae, Shibuya-ku; dishes ¥450-1800, course from ¥5000; ⏲6pm-1am Mon-Fri, 5pm-1am Sat, 5pm-midnight Sun; 🚭📵; Ⓢ Ginza line to Omote-sandō, exit B2) is only open for dinner.

BIRD LAND YAKITORI ¥¥¥

Map p278 (バードランド; ☎5250-1081; http://ginza-birdland.sakura.ne.jp; 4-2-15 Ginza, Chūō-ku; dishes ¥150-1200, set meals ¥6000-8000; ⏲5-9.30pm Tue-Sat; 📵; Ⓢ Ginza line to Ginza, exit C6) As sauve as it gets for gourmet grilled chicken. Chefs in whites behind a U-shaped counter dispense *yakitori* in all shapes, sizes, colours and organs – don't pass up the dainty serves of liver pâté or the tiny cup of chicken soup. Enter beneath Suit Company. Reservations are recommended.

In the same basement corridor is Sukiyabashi Jiro of *Jiro Dreams of Sushi* fame.

Tsukiji & Shiodome

KIMAGURE-YA SANDWICHES ¥

Map p278 (気まぐれ屋; 6-21-6 Tsukiji, Chūō-ku; sandwiches from ¥140; ⏲5am-10am; Ⓢ Hibiya line to Tsukiji, exit 1) Tsukiji Market workers and locals adore the *ebi-katsu sando* (deep-fried prawn sandwiches) made by genial Matsubara-san out of a stall in his grandfather's old barber shop – and so will you. He also serves one of the cheapest coffees (¥140) you'll find in Tokyo.

★TRATTORIA TSUKIJI PARADISO! ITALIAN ¥¥

Map p278 (☎3545-5550; www.tsukiji-paradiso.com; 6-27-3 Tsukiji, Chūō-ku; mains ¥1500-3600; ⏲11am-2pm & 6-10pm; Ⓢ Hibiya line to Tsukiji, exit 2) Paradise for food lovers, indeed. This charming, aqua-painted trattoria plays on its proximity to Tsukiji with seafood pasta dishes that will make you want to lick the plate clean. Its signature linguine is packed with shellfish in a scrumptious tomato, chilli and garlic sauce. Lunch (from ¥980) is a bargain; book for dinner.

★DAIWA SUSHI SUSHI ¥¥

Map p278 (大和寿司; ☎3547-6807; Bldg 6, 5-2-1 Tsukiji, Chūō-ku; sushi sets ¥3500; ⏲5am-1.30pm Mon-Sat, closed occasional Wed; 🚭; Ⓢ Ōedo line to Tsukijishijomae, exit A1) Waits of over one hour are commonplace at Tsukiji's most famous sushi bar, after which you'll be expected to eat and run. But it's all worth it once your first piece of delectable sushi hits the counter. Unless you're comfortable ordering in Japanese, the standard set (seven *nigiri*, plus *maki* and miso soup) is a good bet; there's a picture menu. Daiwa Sushi is located within the *jōnai-shijō* (inner market) of Tsukiji Market.

DRINKING & NIGHTLIFE

★KAGAYA IZAKAYA

Map p278 (加賀屋; ☎3591-2347; www1.ocn.ne.jp/~kagayayy/index.html; B1 fl, Hanasada Bldg, 2-15-12 Shimbashi, Minato-ku; ⏲7pm-midnight Mon-Sat; 🚉 JR Yamanote line to Shimbashi, Shimbashi exit) It is safe to say that there is no other bar owner in Tokyo who can match Mark Kagaya for brilliant lunacy. His side-splitting antics are this humble *izakaya*'s

1

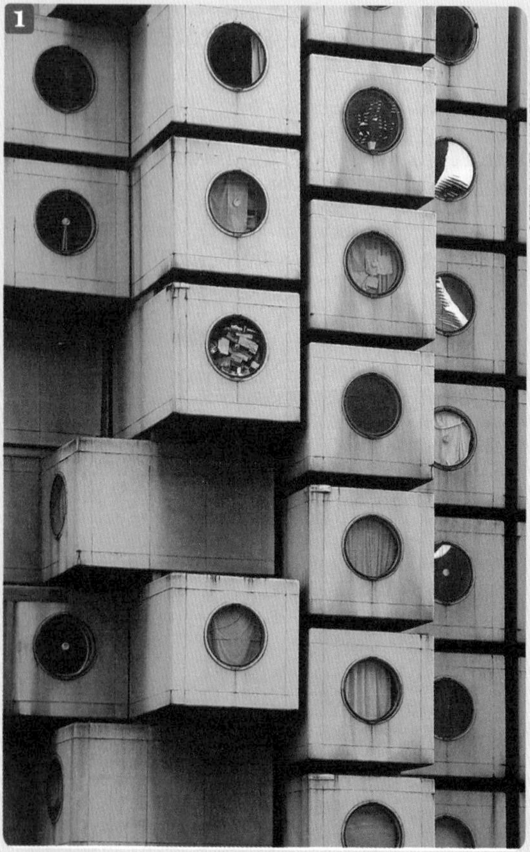

THOMAS VOLSTORF / GETTY IMAGES ©

2

4

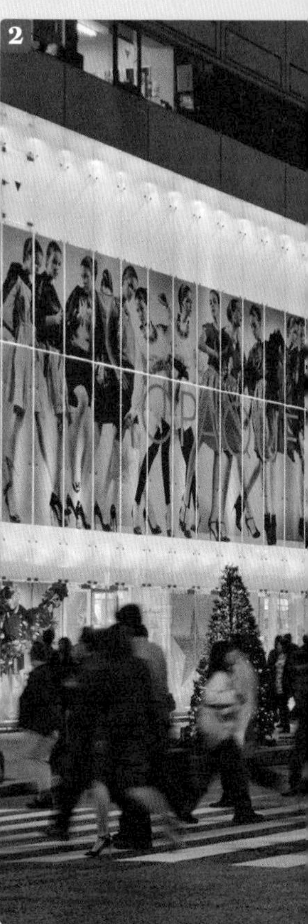

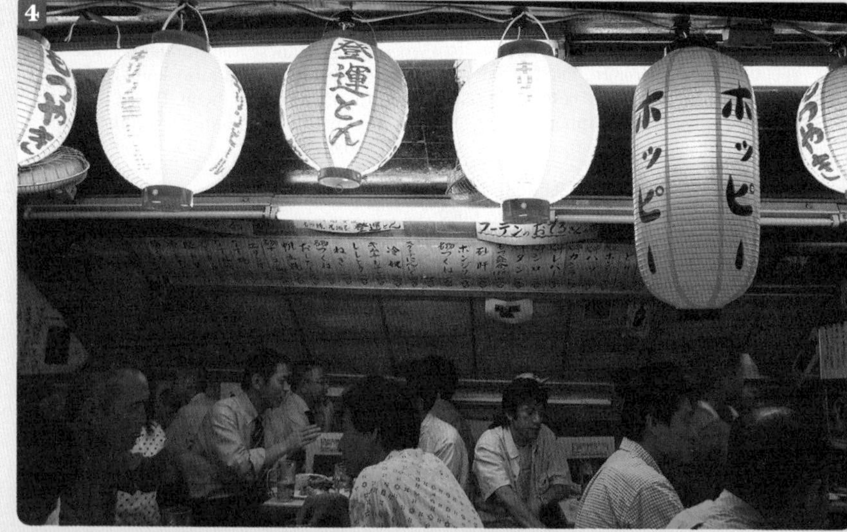

1. Nakagin Capsule Tower (p70)
Kurokawa Kishō's futuristic 1970s apartment building features self-contained, removable pods.

2. Retail therapy in Ginza (p76)
This famous shopping district is home to some of Tokyo's most exclusive boutiques and top department stores.

3. Hama-rikyū Onshi-teien (p69)
Once the site of a shogunal palace, now a vast garden with skyscraper views.

4. Dining in Ginza (p70)
Patrons enjoy a meal at a *yakitori* restaurant.

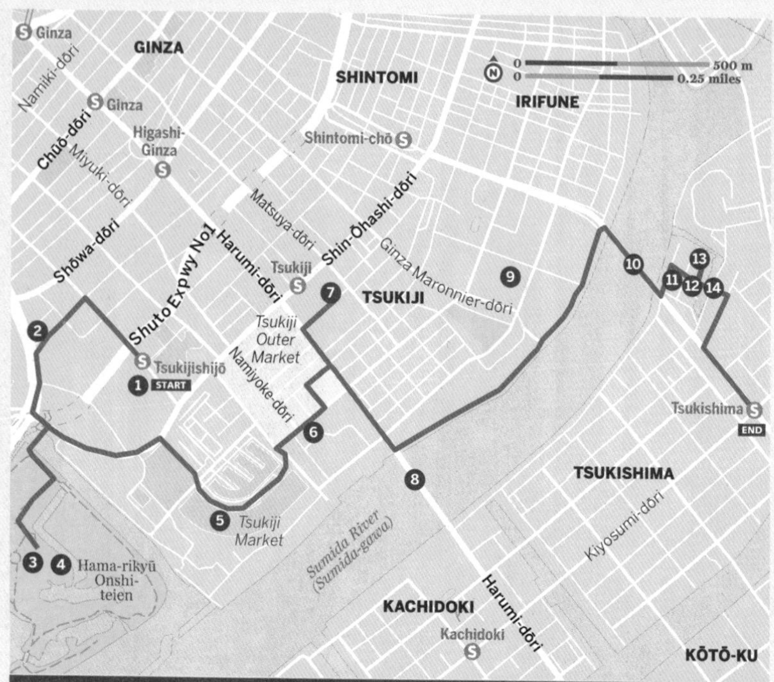

Neighbourhood Walk **Tsukiji**

START TSUKIJISHIJŌ STATION, EXIT A2
END TSUKISHIMA STATION, EXIT 6
LENGTH 3.5KM; THREE HOURS

If you do this walk in the morning you will catch the action around Tsukiji and can have lunch in the area.

Take exit A2 from Tsukijishijō Station and walk north along Hanatsubaki-dōri past **1 Asahi Shimbun**, one of Japan's major daily newspapers. Turn left into the side street just before the major intersection with Shōwa-dōri. Look for the giant pile of stacked cubes that is **2 Nakagin Capsule Tower** (p70).

Follow the raised expressway left until you reach the crossing for **3 Hama-rikyū Onshi-teien** (p69). Stroll around one of Tokyo's loveliest traditional gardens, breaking for a cup of *matcha* (powdered green tea) at **4 Nakajima no Ochaya** (p69).

From the gardens follow Shin-Ōhashi-dōri right to **5 Tsukiji Market** (p67). Explore the inner market, emerging at the area's most popular shrine, **6 Namiyoke-jinja** (p68). You are now in the outer market. Weave your way through the grid of shop-lined alleys to **7 Tsukiji Hongwan-ji** (p69), one of Tokyo's most architecturally distinctive temples.

Return to Harumi-dōri and walk towards the Sumida River. Turn left before the **8 Kachidoki-bashi** on the riverside walkway that runs past **9 St Luke's International Hospital**, then cross **10 Tsukuda Ohashi**. Across the bridge, on the left side, is Tsukuda-jima (Island of Cultivated Rice Fields), a charming neighbourhood with traditional shops such as **11 Tenyasu Honten**, selling *tsukudani* (seafood preserved in a mixture of soy sauce, salt and sugar), and the 11th-generation chopsticks maker and lacquerware artist **12 Nakajima Hideyasu**.

Pay your respects at Shintō shrine **13 Sumiyoshi-jinja**, then cross the attractive red-railed **14 Tsukudako-bashi** over a tidal inlet that is a popular filming location for TV and movies. Nearby is Tsukishima Station.

star attraction, although his mum's nourishing home cooking also hits the spot. Bookings are essential.

★CAFE DE L'AMBRE CAFE

Map p278 (カフェ・ド・ランブル; ☎3571-1551; www.h6.dion.ne.jp/~lambre; 8-10-15 Ginza, Chūō-ku; coffee from ¥650; ⊙noon-10pm Mon-Sat, to 7pm Sun; 🚇Ginza line to Ginza, exit A4) The sign over the door here reads 'Coffee Only' but, oh, what a selection. In business since 1948, l'Ambre specialises in aged beans from all over the world, which the owner still roasts himself.

★CHA GINZA TEAHOUSE

Map p278 (茶・銀座; www.uogashi-meicha.co.jp/shop/ginza; 5-5-6 Ginza, Chūō-ku; tea set ¥500; ⊙11am-6pm, shop until 7pm Tue-Sun; SGinza line to Ginza, exit B3) At this slick contemporary tearoom, it costs ¥600 for either a cup of perfectly prepared *matcha* (green tea), and a small cake or two, or for a choice of *sencha* (premium green tea). Buy your token for tea at the shop on the ground floor which sells top-quality teas from various growing regions in Japan.

FUKUROU-NO-MISE CAFE

Map p278 (フクロウのみせ; http://ameblo.jp/fukurounomise; 1-27-9 Tsukishima, Chuo-ku; entry incl a drink from ¥2000; ⊙2-6pm Wed & Thu, 2-9pm Fri, noon-9pm Sat, noon-6pm Sun; SŌedo line to Tsukishima, exit 10) Make like Harry Potter with many beautiful breeds of owl at this originator of the bird-cafe concept. The owls are well looked after and nonchalant about having their photo taken on your shoulder. One-hour slots are reserved on a first-come, first-served basis; turn up early before the cafe opens to secure a place.

AUX AMIS DES VINS WINE BAR

Map p278 (オザミデヴァン; ☎3567-4120; https://auxamis.com/desvins; 2-5-6 Ginza, Chūō-ku; ⊙11.30am-1.30pm & 6pm-midnight Sat-Thu, to 2am on Fri; SYūrakuchō line to Ginza-itchōme, exits 5 & 8) Even when it rains, the plastic tarp comes down and good wine is drunk alleyside. The enclosed upstairs seating area is warm and informal, and you can order snacks to go with your wine or full *prix fixe* dinners. A solid selection of wine comes by the glass (¥800) or by the bottle.

GINZA SUKI BAR BAR

Map p278 (銀座スキバー; ☎3573-5544; 5th fl, 6-3-5 Ginza, Chūō-ku; ⊙6pm-2am; SGinza line to Ginza, exit C3) Located on the top floor of a stack of bars, this fun place decorated in street art is way more hip than the norm for expense-account Ginza. There is a small outside balcony and no cover charge.

TURRET COFFEE CAFE

Map p278 (http://ja-jp.facebook.com/Turret-COFFEE; 2-12-6 Tsukiji, Chūō-ku; ⊙7am-6pm Mon-Sat, noon-6pm Sun; SHibiya line to Tsukiji, exit 2) Kawasaki Kiyoshi set up his plucky indie coffee shop next to Starbucks. It takes its name from the three-wheeled delivery trucks that beetle around Tsukiji – there's one on the premises. Ideal for an early-morning espresso en route to or from the market.

TOWN HOUSE TOKYO GAY BAR

Map p278 (☎3289-8558; www13.ocn.ne.jp/~t_h_tky/toppage/tht_top.htm; 6th fl, Koruteire Ginza Bldg, 1-11-5 Shimbashi, Minato-ku; cover incl 1 drink from ¥1000; SGinza line to Shimbashi, exit 3) This long-running joint is friendly to *gaijin* (foreigners; literally 'outside people') and has been serving a wide-ranging crowd for years. It provides plenty of space and even a long balcony for a breather. It has karaoke on Fridays and the occasional underwear-only party on Saturday.

☆ ENTERTAINMENT

SHIMBASHI EMBUJŌ THEATRE THEATRE

Map p278 (新橋演舞場; ☎3541-2600; www.kabuki-bito.jp/eng/contents/theatre/shimbashi_enbujo.html; 6-18-2 Ginza, Chūō-ku; tickets ¥3000-17,000; SHibiya line to Higashi-Ginza, exit 6) As well as operating Tokyo's premier kabuki theatre Kabuki-za, Shōchiku stages traditional theatre here. The current venue dates from 1982 and is also used for straight plays, musicals and Super-kabuki (a modern interpretation of the genre).

TOKYO TAKARAZUKA THEATRE THEATRE

Map p278 (宝塚劇場; ☎5251-2001; http://kageki.hankyu.co.jp/english/index.html; 1-1-3 Yūrakuchō, Chiyoda-ku; tickets ¥3500-11,000; SHibiya line to Hibiya, exits A5 & A13) If you love camp, this is for you. The all-female Takarazuka revue, going back to 1914, stages highly stylised musicals in Japanese (English synopses are available) where a mostly female audience swoons over actresses, some of who are in drag.

SHOPPING

★TAKUMI
CRAFTS

Map p278 (たくみ; ☎3571-2017; www.ginza-takumi.co.jp; 8-4-2 Ginza, Chūō-ku; ⊙11am-7pm Mon-Sat; SGinza line to Shimbashi, exit 5) You'll be hard-pressed to find a more elegant selection of traditional folk crafts, including toys, textiles and ceramics from around Japan. Ever thoughtful, the shop also encloses information detailing the origin and background of the pieces if you make a purchase.

★AKOMEYA
FOOD

Map p278 (☎6758-0271; www.akomeya.jp; 2-2-6 Ginza, Chūō-ku; ⊙ shop 11am-9pm, restaurant 11.30am-10pm; SYūrakuchō line to Ginza-itchome, exit 4) Rice is at the core of Japanese cuisine and drink. This stylish store sells not only many types of the grain but also products made from it (such as sake), a vast range of quality cooking ingredients and a choice collection of kitchen, home and bath items. There's also a good, casual restaurant here where rice, unsurprisingly, features heavily on the menu.

★DOVER STREET MARKET GINZA
FASHION

Map p278 (DSM; ☎6228-5080; http://ginza.doverstreetmarket.com; 6-9-5 Ginza, Chūō-ku; ⊙11am-8pm Sun-Thu, to 9pm Fri & Sat; SGinza line to Ginza, exit A2) A department store as envisioned by Kawakubo Rei (of Comme des Garcons), DSM has seven floors of avant-garde brands, including several Japanese labels and everything in the Comme des Garçons line-up. The quirky art installations alone make it worth the visit.

In the same building, which is connected to Uniqlo, is a rooftop shrine, a branch of **Rose Bakery** (Map p278; ☎5537-5038; 7th fl, Ginza Komatsu West, 6-9-5 Ginza, Chūō-ku; baked goods from ¥400, meals from ¥1000; ⊙11am-9pm Mon-Fri, 9am-9pm Sat & Sun; SGinza line to Ginza, exit A2) and **Komatsu Bar** (Map p278; www.komatsubar.jp; 7th fl, Ginza Komatsu West, 6-9-5 Ginza, Chūō-ku; ⊙4pm-midnight Mon-Sat; SGinza line to Ginza, exit A2).

SONY BUILDING
ELECTRONICS

Map p278 (ソニービル; ☎3573-2371; www.sonybuilding.jp; 5-3-1 Ginza, Chūō-ku; ⊙11am-7pm; SGinza, Hibiya or Marunouchi line to Ginza, exit B9) Where Sony shows off and sells its latest digital and electronic gizmos. Kids will love the free Playstation games, while adults tend to lose an hour or so perusing all the latest audio and video accessories.

UNIQLO
FASHION

Map p278 (ユニクロ; www.uniqlo.com; 5-7-7 Ginza, Chūō-ku; ⊙11am-9pm; SGinza line to Ginza, exit A2) This now-global brand has made its name by sticking to the basics and tweaking them with style. Offering inexpensive, quality clothing, this is the Tokyo flagship store with 11 floors and items you won't find elsewhere.

NATSUNO
HOMEWARES

Map p278 (夏野; www.e-ohashi.com; 6-7-4 Ginza, Chūō-ku; ⊙10am-8pm Mon-Sat, to 7pm Sun; SGinza line to Ginza, exit B3) Shelf after shelf of *ohashi* (chopsticks) in wood, lacquer, and even gold leaf line the walls of this intimate shop, alongside plenty of *hashi-oki* (chopstick rests) to match. Prices run from a few hundred yen to ¥10,000. On the 6th floor, its sister shop Konatsu sells adorable tableware for kids.

ITŌYA
ARTS & CRAFTS

Map p278 (伊東屋; www.ito-ya.co.jp; 2-7-15 Ginza, Chūō-ku; ⊙10.30am-8pm Mon-Sat, to 7pm Sun; SGinza line to Ginza, exit A13) Nine floors of stationery-shop love awaits visual-art professionals and seekers of office accessories, with both everyday items and luxury such as fountain pens and Italian leather agendas. You'll also find *washi* (fine Japanese handmade paper), *tenugui* (beautifully hand-dyed thin cotton towels) and *furoshiki* (wrapping cloths).

HAKUHINKAN
CHILDREN

Map p278 (博品館; www.hakuhinkan.co.jp; 8-8-11 Ginza, Chūō-ku; ⊙11am-8pm; Ginza line to Shimbashi, exits 1 & 3) This layer cake of a 'toy park' is crammed with character toys, the hottest squawking video games, seas of colourful plastic, the softest plush toys ever invented and even a model racetrack (¥200 per five minutes) on the 4th floor.

Roppongi & Around

ROPPONGI | SHIBA-KŌEN | TORANOMON | AKASAKA | NISHI-AZABU | AZABU-JŪBAN

Neighbourhood Top Five

1 Enjoying contemporary art and panoramic urban views from **Mori Art Museum** (p79) and **Tokyo City View** (p79).

2 Imbibing, karaoke-ing and living it up in the best **bars and clubs** (p86) of Roppongi and Nishi-Azabu.

3 Pondering cutting-edge art, architecture and design ideas at **21_21 Design Sight** (p79) in Tokyo Midtown.

4 Walking through the massive entrance gate to the venerable temple **Zōjō-ji** (p80) and seeing **Tokyo Tower** (p80) in the background.

5 Digging very curvy architecture and top-notch exhibitions at the **National Art Center, Tokyo** (p79).

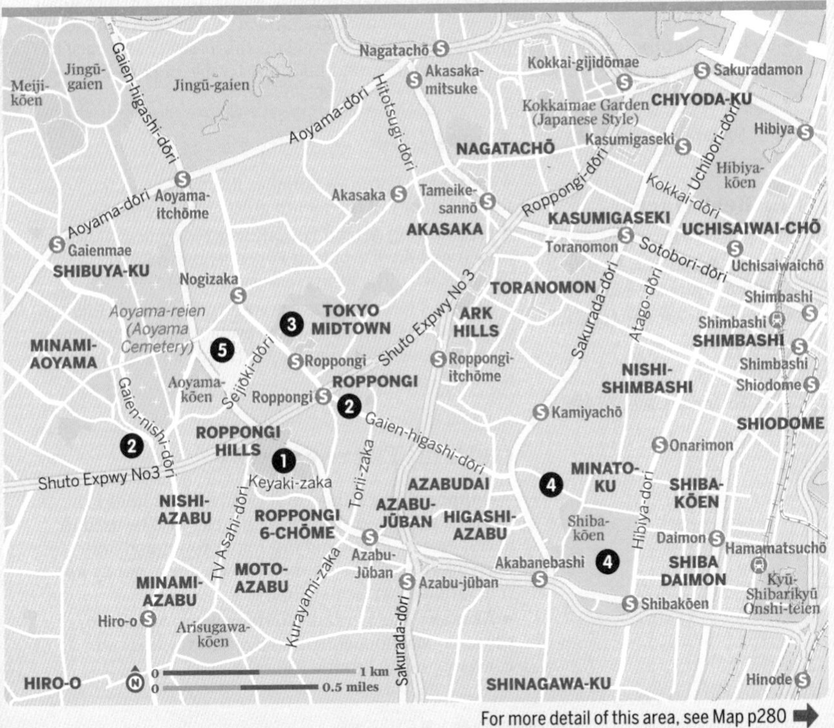

For more detail of this area, see Map p280

Lonely Planet's Top Tip

Keep your ticket stub for Mori Art Museum, Suntory Museum of Art or the National Art Center, Tokyo, and when you visit one of the other two galleries you'll be entitled to a discount on admission. At any of these venues, pick up the *Art Triangle Roppongi* walking map, which lists dozens of smaller galleries in the area.

Best Places to Eat

- Tofuya-Ukai (p85)
- Kikunoi (p85)
- Warayakiya Akasaka (p85)

For reviews, see p84

Best Places to Drink

- Pink Cow (p86)
- Janome (p87)
- These (p87)

For reviews, see p86

Best Places to Shop

- Japan Traditional Crafts Aoyama Square (p88)
- Tolman Collection (p88)
- Souvenir From Tokyo (p89)

For reviews, see p88

Explore Roppongi & Around

Long one of Tokyo's prime nightlife districts, Roppongi has diversified over the last decade, adding arts, culture and high-end shopping to its menu of attractions. The successful mixed-use real-estate developments Roppongi Hills and Tokyo Midtown have transformed the area. Similar projects in neighbouring Akasaka and Toranomon are now putting the spotlight on those districts, too.

You can easily spend a day exploring the Roppongi Art Triangle, its points anchored by the lofty Mori Art Museum in Roppongi Hills, Suntory Museum of Art in Tokyo Midtown and the National Art Center, Tokyo. As night falls, Roppongi Crossing becomes a magnet for an international crowd of hedonistic party-goers and club touts. Head downhill towards either Nishi-Azabu or Azabu-Jūban for more sophisticated dining and drinking options.

Akasaka's proximity to the National Diet, Japan's parliament, defines it as a high-end entertaining district for politicians and bureaucrats. In recent years it has become far less exclusive, particularly in the area around the Akasaka Sakas entertainment development. Nearby you'll find the illustrious Hie-jinja, an important Shintō shrine; a beautiful 400-year-old garden at the Hotel New Ōtani; and the National Theatre, which is the state-sponsored home of traditional performing arts.

Near Toranomon Station is the new Toronomon Hills development and the elegant Musee Tomo. Further south is the Shiba-kōen (Shiba Park) area. Here you can ascend or just admire the retro-glam Tokyo Tower and pace the grounds of the grand Buddhist temple of Zōjō-ji.

Local Life

- **Markets** There's an antiques flea market on the fourth Sunday of the month at Nogi-jinja (p80).
- **Networking** Attend PechaKucha (www.pechakucha.org/cities/tokyo) events at SuperDeluxe (p87) to discover what the local creatives are up to.
- **Events** The covered arena next to Roppongi Hills' Mohri Garden regularly hosts events and performances such as those for Roppongi Art Night (www.roppongiartnight.com) in April.

Getting There & Away

- **Roppongi** The Hibiya and Ōedo subway lines run through Roppongi. The Ōedo line can also be used to access Azabu-Jūban and the Tokyo Tower and Shiba-kōen area. Nogizaka on the Chiyoda line is handy for the National Art Center, Tokyo.
- **Akasaka** The Yūrakuchō, Hanzōmon, Namboku, Chiyoda, Marunouchi and Ginza subway lines all converge in and around Akasaka.

SIGHTS

Roppongi

ROPPONGI HILLS LANDMARK

Map p280 (六本木ヒルズ; www.roppongihills.com/en; 6-chōme Roppongi, Minato-ku; ⏰11am-11pm; Ⓢ Hibiya line to Roppongi, exit 1) It's over a decade old, but Roppongi Hills remains the gold standard for real-estate developments in Tokyo. The centrepiece of the office, shopping, dining and entertainment complex is the 54-storey Mori Tower, home to the Mori Art Museum and Tokyo City View observatory. Scattered around it is public art such as Louise Bourgeois' giant, spiny **Maman spider sculpture** and the benches-cum-sculptures along Keyakizaka-dōri, as well as the re-created Edo-style **Mohri Garden**.

MORI ART MUSEUM MUSEUM

Map p280 (森美術館; www.mori.art.museum; 52nd fl, Mori Tower, Roppongi Hills, 6-10-1 Roppongi, Minato-ku; adult/child/student ¥1500/500/1000; ⏰10am-10pm Wed-Mon, to 5pm Tue, Sky Deck 10am-10pm; Ⓢ Hibiya line to Roppongi, exit 1) Atop Mori Tower this gigantic gallery space sports high ceilings, broad views and thematic programs that continue to live up to all the hype associated with Roppongi Hills. Contemporary exhibits are beautifully presented and include superstars of the art world from both Japan and abroad.

Admission to the museum is shared with **Tokyo City View** (東京シティビュー; Map p280; ☎6406-6652; www.roppongihills.com/tcv/en; 52nd fl, Mori Tower, Roppongi Hills, 6-10-1 Roppongi, Minato-ku; incl with admission to Mori Art Museum, observatory only adult/child/student ¥1500/500/1000; ⏰10am-11pm Mon-Thu & Sun, to 1am Fri & Sat; Ⓢ Hibiya line to Roppongi, exit 1), which wraps itself around the 52nd floor. From this 250m-high vantage point you can see 360-degree views of the seemingly never-ending city. Weather permitting you can also pop out to the rooftop Sky Deck (additional ¥500; 11am to 8pm) for alfresco views.

TOKYO MIDTOWN LANDMARK

Map p280 (東京ミッドタウン; www.tokyo-midtown.com/en; 9-7 Akasaka, Minato-ku; ⏰11am-11pm; Ⓢ Ōedo line to Roppongi, exit 8) With a similar design and urban-planning blueprint to the one that made Roppongi Hills so successful, this sleek complex brims with sophisticated bars, restaurants, shops, art galleries, a hotel and leafy public spaces. Escalators ascend alongside human-made waterfalls of rock and glass, bridges in the air are lined with backlit *washi* (Japanese handmade paper) and planters full of soaring bamboo draw your eyes through skylights to the lofty heights of the towers above.

Behind the complex is **Hinokichō-kōen**. Formerly a private garden attached to an Edo-period villa, Hinokichō was reopened as a public park. The adjacent **Midtown Garden** is a cherry-tree-lined grassy space that makes a perfect spot for a picnic.

SUNTORY MUSEUM OF ART MUSEUM

Map p280 (サントリー美術館; ☎3479-8600; www.suntory.com/sma; 4th fl, Tokyo Midtown, 9-7-4 Akasaka, Minato-ku; admission varies, free for children & junior-high-school students; ⏰10am-6pm Sun-Thu, to 8pm Fri & Sat; 🚇Ōedo line to Roppongi, exit 8) Since its original 1961 opening, the Suntory Museum of Art has subscribed to an underlying philosophy of lifestyle art. Rotating exhibitions focus on the beauty of useful things: Japanese ceramics, lacquerware, glass, dyeing, weaving and such. Its current Midtown digs, designed by architect Kuma Kengō, are both understated and breathtaking.

21_21 DESIGN SIGHT MUSEUM

Map p280 (21_21デザインサイト; ☎3475-2121; www.2121designsight.jp; Tokyo Midtown, 9-7-6 Akasaka, Minato-ku; adult/child ¥1000/free; ⏰11am-8pm Wed-Mon; Ⓢ Ōedo line to Roppongi, exit 8) An exhibition and discussion space dedicated to all forms of design, the 21_21 Design Sight acts as a beacon for local art enthusiasts, whether they be designers themselves or simply onlookers. The striking concrete and glass building, bursting out of the ground at sharp angles, was designed by Pritzker Prize–winning architect Andō Tadao.

NATIONAL ART CENTER, TOKYO MUSEUM

Map p280 (国立新美術館; ☎5777-8600; www.nact.jp; 7-22-1 Roppongi, Minato-ku; admission varies; ⏰10am-6pm Wed, Thu & Sat-Mon, to 8pm Fri; Ⓢ Chiyoda line to Nogizaka, exit 6) Designed by Kurokawa Kishō, this architectural beauty has no permanent collection, but boasts the country's largest exhibition space for visiting shows, which have included Renoir, Modigliani and the Japan

Media Arts Festival. Apart from exhibitions, a visit here is recommended to admire the building's awesome undulating glass facade, its cafes atop giant inverted cones and the great gift shop Souvenir From Tokyo (p89).

FUJIFILM SQUARE MUSEUM

Map p280 (フジフイルム スクエア; http://fujifilmsquare.jp/en; 9-7-3 Akasaka, Tokyo Midtown, Minato-ku; 11am-7pm; Hibiya line to Roppongi, exit 4A) FREE This small gallery on the ground floor of the Tokyo Midtown West Tower is a fascinating look at the history of cameras, from 18th-century camera obscuras to zoetropes to the latest Fujifilm DSLRs. There are two galleries of photography, as well as a computer with a database of vintage Fujifilm TV ads starring Japanese celebs such as electronica group YMO.

NOGI-JINJA SHINTO SHRINE

Map p280 (乃木神社; www.nogijinja.or.jp; 8-11-27 Akasaka, Minato-ku; 9am-5pm; S Chiyoda line to Nogizaka, exit 1) This shrine honours General Nogi Maresuke, a famed commander in the Russo-Japanese War. Hours after Emperor Meiji's funerary procession in 1912, Nogi and his faithful wife committed ritual suicide, following their master into death. An **antiques flea market** is held on the shrine grounds on the fourth Sunday of each month (9am to 4pm).

General Nogi's Residence (旧乃木邸; Map p280; 8-11-32 Akasaka, Minato-ku; 9am-4pm; Chiyoda line to Nogizaka, exit A1) FREE is up the hill from the shrine. This is where Nogi disembowelled himself and his wife slit her throat; it's open to the public only on 12 and 13 September. The rest of the year you can peek through the windows of the barracks-style wooden residence and notice the mash-up of Japanese and Western styles that defined the Meiji period (think a tatami room with a Western fireplace).

AOYAMA REI-EN CEMETERY

Map p280 (青山霊園; 2-32-2 Minami-Aoyama, Minato-ku; Chiyoda line to Nogizaka, exit 5 or Ginza line to Gaienmae, exit 1B) The cherry-tree-lined paths of Japan's first public cemetery are used by locals as shortcuts through the neighbourhood and as a place for picnics during *hanami* (cherry-blossom viewing) season. Accessible either from Roppongi or Aoyama it's a peaceful place for a stroll and the elaborate stone-carved tombs are rather impressive.

Buried here are John Manjiro, the shipwrecked young fisherman who became the first Japanese person to go to America; and Professor Ueno, owner of Hachikō, a dog famous in Japan for returning faithfully to wait for his master at Shibuya Station for nine years after Ueno died suddenly in 1925.

Shiba-kōen

TOKYO TOWER TOWER

Map p280 (東京タワー; www.tokyotower.co.jp/english; 4-2-8 Shiba-kōen, Minato-ku; adult/child main deck ¥900/400, plus special deck ¥1600/800; observation deck 9am-10pm; Ōedo line to Akabanebashi, Akabanebashi exit) Something of a shameless tourist trap, this 1958-vintage tower remains a beloved symbol of the city's post-WWII rebirth. At 333m it's 13m taller than the Eiffel Tower, which was the inspiration for its design. It's also painted bright orange and white in order to comply with international aviation safety regulations. The main observation deck is at 145m (there's another 'special' deck at 250m). There are loftier views at the more expensive Tokyo Sky Tree.

There is an **aquarium** on the 1st floor. The 3rd floor has an exhibit of anime show *One Piece,* which may appeal to fans.

ZŌJŌ-JI BUDDHIST TEMPLE

Map p280 (増上寺; 3432-1431; www.zojoji.or.jp/en/index.html; 4-7-35 Shiba-kōen, Minato-ku; dawn-dusk; S Ōedo line to Daimon, exit A3) FREE One of the most important temples of the Jōdō (Pure Land) sect of Buddhism, Zōjō-ji dates from 1393 and was the funerary temple of the Tokugawa regime. It's an impressive sight, particularly the main gate, **Sangedatsumon** (解脱門), constructed in 1605, with its three sections designed to symbolise the three stages one must pass through to achieve nirvana. The **Daibonsho** (Big Bell; 1673) is a 15-tonne whopper considered one of the great three bells of the Edo period.

Like many sights in Tokyo, Zōjō-ji's original structures have been relocated, and were subject to war, fire and other natural disasters. It has been rebuilt several times in recent history, the last time in 1974.

On the temple grounds there is a large collection of statues of the bodhisattva Jizō, said to be a guide during the transmigration of the soul, as well as a majestic Himalayan cedar planted by US president Ulysses S Grant in 1879.

⊙ Toranomon

MUSÉE TOMO MUSEUM

Map p280 (智美術館; ☎5733-5131; www.musee-tomo.or.jp; 4-1-35 Toranomon, Minato-ku; adult/student ¥1000/500; ⊙11am-6pm Tue-Sun; Ⓢ Hibiya line to Kamiyachō, exit 4B) One of Tokyo's most elegant and tasteful museums is named after Kikuchi Tomo, whose collection of contemporary Japanese ceramics wowed them in Washington and London before finally being exhibited at home. Exhibitions change every few months but can be relied on to be atmospheric and beautiful. The museum's classy French restaurant **Voie Lactée** (lunch/dinner from ¥2300/8000) overlooks a lovely garden and has a star-studded ceiling.

TORANOMON HILLS LANDMARK

Map p280 (http://toranomonhills.com; 1-23 Toranomon, Minato-ku; 📶; Ⓢ Ginza line to Toranomon, exit 1) Opened in mid-2014, the 52-storey, 247m Toranomon Hills complex, topped by the Andaz Hotel, is Mori Buildings' latest modification of Tokyo's cityscape. Apart from the hotel, there are pleasant places to eat and drink and a small public garden.

The complex sits at the head of the new tree-lined boulevard Shin-Tora-dōri (also referred to as General MacArthur Rd), a section of Circular Route 2, a major highway construction project that will link Ariake on Odaiba through to Yotsuya and Kanda in time for the 2020 Olympics.

⊙ Akasaka

HIE-JINJA SHRINE

Map p280 (日枝神社; www.hiejinja.net; 2-10-5 Nagatachō, Chiyoda-ku; ⊙dawn-dusk; Ⓢ Ginza line to Tameike-sannō, exits 5 & 7) FREE Enshrining the deity of sacred Mt Hiei, northeast of Kyoto, this hilltop shrine has been the protector shrine of Edo Castle (now the Imperial Palace) since it was first built in 1478. Host of one of Tokyo's three liveliest *matsuri* (festivals), Sannō-sai, it's an attractive place best approached by the tunnel of red *torii* on the hill's western side. There are also escalators up the hill from Tameike-sannō.

The shrine's present location dates from 1659, though it was destroyed in the 1945 bombings and later rebuilt in 1967.

On the left, inside the main eastern entrance gate, the carved monkey clutching one of her young is emblematic of the shrine's ability to offer protection against the threat of a miscarriage.

NATIONAL DIET LANDMARK

Map p280 (国会議事堂; ☎tours 5521-7445; www.sangiin.go.jp; 1-7-1 Nagatachō, Chiyoda-ku; ⊙8am-5pm Mon-Fri, closed national holidays; Ⓢ Marunouchi line to Kokkai-gijidōmae, exit 1) Built on a site once inhabited by feudal lords, Japan's current parliament building was completed in 1936 and houses two chambers – the Shūgi-in (House of Representatives; the Lower House) and the Sangi-in (House of Councillors; the Upper House). Free one-hour tours of parts of the building and grounds are available when the Diet is not in session (ring the day before to confirm).

The tours take in the public gallery, the emperor's room (from where he addresses the Diet at the start of each session) and central hall, which features a floor mosaic of a million pieces of marble, and murals depicting the four seasons. An English pamphlet is available if there's no English-speaking guide when you arrive. Visit in the afternoon to avoid being tacked onto the larger tour groups.

HOTEL NEW ŌTANI GARDENS, MUSEUM

(ホテルニューオータニ; www.newotani.co.jp/en/tokyo/index.html; 4-1 Kioi-chō, Chiyoda-ku; ⊙6am-10pm; Ⓢ Ginza line to Akasaka-mitsuke, exit D) FREE The New Ōtani was a showplace hotel when it opened in 1964 to coincide with the Tokyo Olympics. Even though this is no longer considered the pinnacle of Tokyo's luxury hotels, it remains worth visiting for its beautiful 400-year-old **garden**, which once belonged to a Tokugawa regent, and for the **New Ōtani Art Museum** (ニューオータニ美術館; ☎3221-4111; www.newotani.co.jp/group/museum/index.html; guests/nonguests free/from ¥500; ⊙10am-6pm Tue-Sun; Ⓢ Ginza line to Akasaka-mitsuke, exit D), which displays a decent collection of modern Japanese and French paintings, as well as woodblock prints.

SŌGETSU KAIKAN BUILDING

Map p280 (草月会館; ☎3408-1151; www.sogetsu.or.jp/e; 7-2-21 Akasaka, Minato-ku; ⊙9.30am-5.30pm Mon-Fri; Ⓢ Ginza line to

1
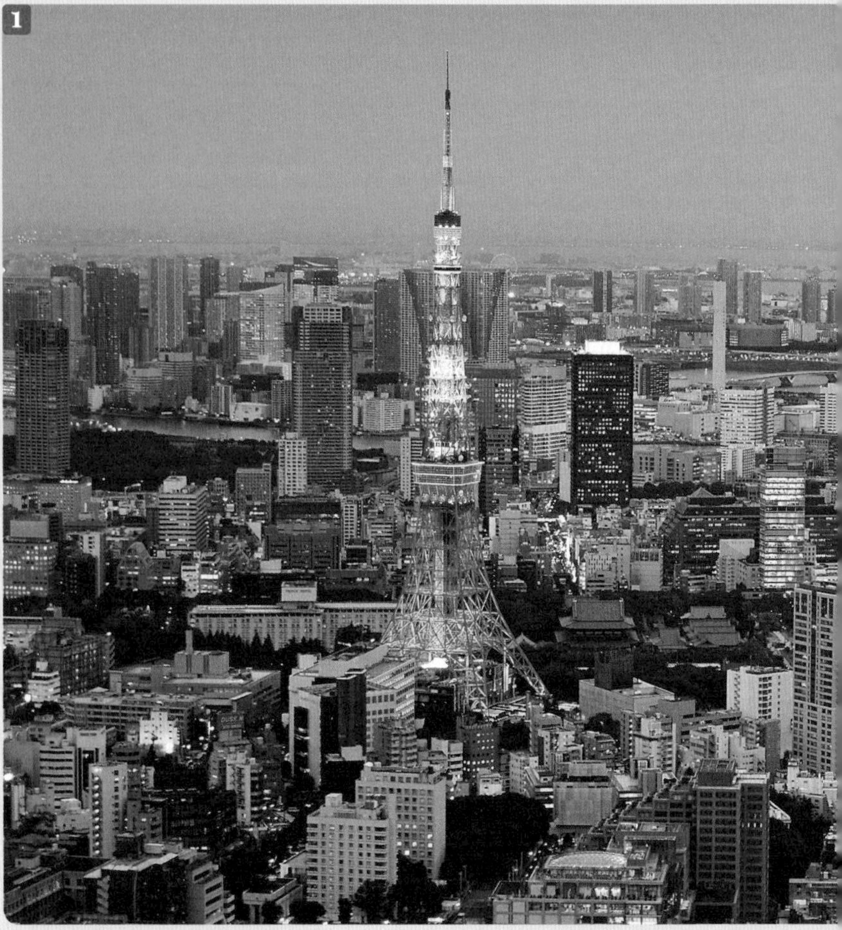

4

TOM BONAVENTURE / GETTY IMAGES ©

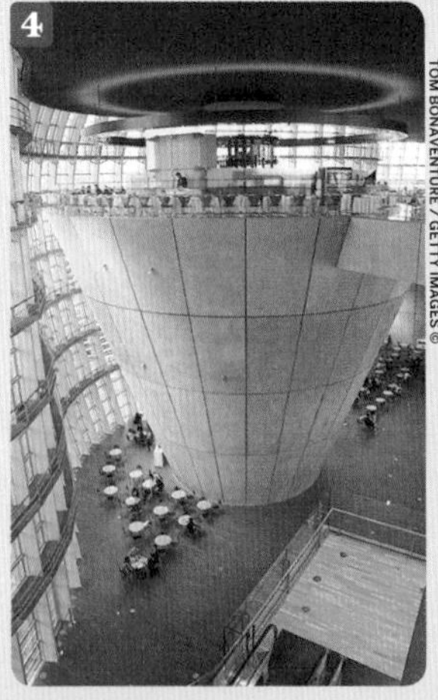

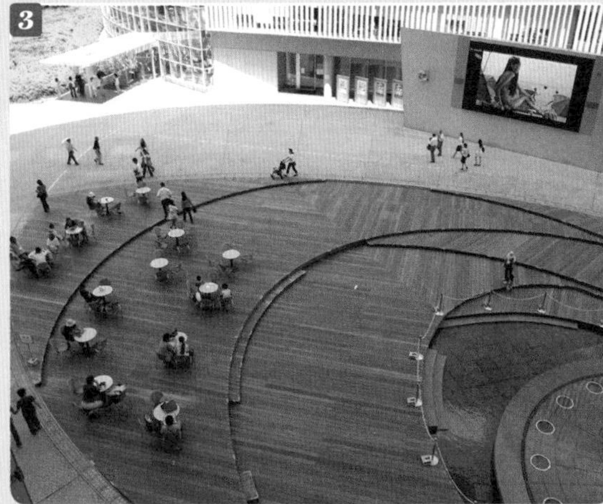

3

FRANK DEIM / GETTY IMAGES ©

1. Tokyo City View (p79)
The view of the city and Tokyo Tower from the Sky Deck.

2. Zōjō-ji (p80)
Wooden votives given as offerings at this Buddhist temple.

3. Roppongi Hills (p79)
Diners enjoy the alfresco setting at this work-live-and-play complex.

4. National Art Center, Tokyo (p79)
Famed for blockbuster exhibitions and its impressive undulating facade.

LAURIE NOBLE / GETTY IMAGES ©

Aoyama-itchōme, exit 4) Sōgetsu is one of Japan's leading schools of avant-garde ikebana (flower arranging), offering classes in English. Even if you have no interest in flower arranging, it's worth taking a peek in for the building (1977) designed by Tange Kenzō, and the giant, climbable piece of installation art by the revered Japanese-American sculptor Isamu Noguchi, which occupies the lobby.

EATING

Roppongi

TSURUTONTAN NOODLES ¥

Map p280 (つるとんたん; www.tsurutontan.co.jp; 3-14-12 Roppongi, Minato-ku; udon ¥680-1800; ⊙11am-8am; 🍴📋; S Hibiya line to Roppongi, exit 5) Huge bowls of udon (thick, wheat noodles) are the speciality here. Go for simple (topped with seaweed or pickled plum), exotic (udon carbonara) or filling (Tsuruton *zanmai*: topped with fried tofu, tempura and beef).

JŌMON IZAKAYA ¥¥

Map p280 (ジョウモン; ☎3405-2585; www.teyandei.com/jomon_rop; 5-9-17 Roppongi, Minato-ku; skewers ¥150-1600; ⊙6pm-5am; 🍴📋; S Hibiya line to Roppongi, exit 3) This wonderfully cosy kitchen has bar seating, rows of ornate *shōchū* (liquor) jugs lining the wall and hundreds of freshly prepared skewers splayed in front of the patrons – don't miss the heavenly *zabuton* beef stick (¥400). It's almost directly across from the Family Mart – look for the name in Japanese on the door.

HONMURA-AN SOBA ¥¥

Map p280 (本むら庵; ☎5772-6657; www.honmuraantokyo.com; 7-14-18 Roppongi, Minato-ku; dishes from ¥1000, set dinner ¥6500; ⊙noon-2.30pm, 5.30-10pm Tue-Sun, closed 1st & 3rd Tue of month; 📋; S Hibiya line to Roppongi, exit 4) This fabled *soba* shop, once located in Manhattan, now serves its handmade buckwheat noodles at this minimalist noodle shop on a Roppongi side street. The delicate flavour of these noodles is best appreciated when served on a bamboo mat, with tempura or with dainty slices of *kamo* (duck).

LAUDERDALE INTERNATIONAL ¥¥

Map p280 (☎3405-5533; www.lauderdale.co.jp; 6-15-1 Roppongi, Minato-ku; mains from ¥1400; ⊙7am-midnight Mon-Fri, from 8am Sat & Sun; 📶📋; S Hibiya line to Roppongi, exit 1) Just off chic Keyaki-zaka and sporting a spacious outdoor terrace, this is an on-trend, all-day dining space that works as well for breakfast as it does for dinner. Weekend brunch is very popular here, particularly the egg dishes.

Nishi-Azabu

CHINESE CAFE 8 CHINESE ¥

Map p280 (中国茶房8; ☎5414-5708; www.chinesecafe8.com; 2nd fl, 3-2-13 Nishi-Azabu, Minato-ku; dishes from ¥550; ⊙24hr; 🍴📋; S Hibiya line to Roppongi, exit 1) Cheap-and-cheerful Chinese known for its cheeky decor, Peking Duck served at any hour and abrupt service (in that order).

GONPACHI IZAKAYA ¥

Map p280 (権八; ☎5771-0170; www.gonpachi.jp/nishiazabu; 1-13-11 Nishi-Azabu, Minato-ku; skewers ¥180-1500, lunch sets weekday/weekend from ¥800/2050; ⊙11.30am-3.30am; 📋; S Hibiya line to Roppongi, exit 2) Over the last decade this cavernous Edo-style space (which inspired a memorable set in Quentin Tarantino's *Kill Bill*) has cemented its rep as a Tokyo dining institution with other less-memorable branches scattered around the city. *Kushiyaki* (charcoal-grilled skewers) are served here alongside noodles, tempura and sushi.

Azabu-Jūban & Shiba-kōen

TOKYO CURRY LAB CURRY ¥

Map p280 (東京カレーラボ; 2nd fl, Tokyo Tower, 4-2-8 Shiba-kōen, Minato-ku; meals ¥1000-1350; ⊙11am-10pm; 📋; S Hibiya line to Kamiyachō, exit 1) Curry rice is like baked beans on toast – a comfort food beloved of nearly all Japanese. This neatly designed outlet, tucked under the soaring spires of Tokyo Tower has a sci-fi feel with personal TVs at each bar stool. The hilariously illustrated place mats (you'll see) make the perfect 'Tokyo is weird' souvenir.

EAT MORE GREENS VEGETARIAN ¥

Map p280 (イートモアグリーンズ; ☎3798-3198; www.eatmoregreens.jp; 2-2-5 Azabu-Jūban, Minato-ku; mains from ¥950; ⊙11am-11pm; @🍴📋;

Namboku line to Azabu-Jūban, exit 4) Inspired by the greengrocers and farmers' markets of NYC, this appealing cafe has an airy interior or outdoor patio to enjoy a delicious assortment of vegetarian and vegan dishes, including cakes and doughnuts – the mushroom rice is divine.

HAINAN JEEFAN SHOKUDŌ SINGAPOREAN ¥

Map p280 (海南鶏飯食堂; www.route9g.com/en; 6-11-16 Roppongi, Minato-ku; mains ¥850-1300; 11.30am-2pm, 6-11pm; closed 3rd Mon of month; ; Namboku line to Azabu-Jūban, exit 5) This cosy, white-walled 'hawker-style Asian canteen' is a small slice of Singapore near Roppongi Hills. Hainan-style chicken rice, Singapore's national dish, is the speciality. Steamed chicken and rice springs to life with the addition of accompanying sauces (detailed eating instructions are offered), alongside other equally tasty Southeast Asian dishes. It's located in the alley behind the main street.

★**TOFUYA-UKAI** KAISEKI ¥¥¥

Map p280 (とうふ屋うかい; 3436-1028; www.ukai.co.jp/english/shiba; 4-4-13 Shibakōen, Minato-ku; lunch/dinner set menu from ¥5500/8400; 11.30am-10pm (last order 8pm); ; Toei Ōedo line to Akabanebashi, exit 8) One of Tokyo's most gracious restaurants is located in a former sake brewery (moved from northern Japan), with an exquisite traditional garden, in the shadow of Tokyo Tower. Seasonal preparations of tofu and accompanying dishes are served in the refined *kaiseki* (Japanese haute cuisine) style. Make reservations well in advance.

Akasaka

★**WARAYAKIYA AKASAKA** IZAKAYA ¥¥

Map p280 (わらやき屋 赤坂; 4540-7647; www.diamond-dining.com/shops/warayakiya; 3-12-3 Akasaka, Minato-ku; cover charge per person ¥380, dishes ¥1300-1800; 5pm-2am Mon-Fri, 5-10pm Sat & Sun; ; Chiyoda line to Akasaka, exits 1 & 2) This chain *izakaya* (Japanese pub-eatery) specialises in *Tosa-ryōri*, the food of Kōchi Prefecture in Shikoku. It is easily spotted by the giant black wave and lanterns decorating its facade, as well as the spectacular flames rising from the straw-fed grill where delicious grilled foods such as seared bonito and chicken are prepared.

There's another branch in **Roppongi** (わらやき屋 六本木; Map p280; 4540-6573; www.diamond-dining.com/shops/warayakiya; 6-8-8 Roppongi, Minato-ku; cover charge per person ¥380, dishes from ¥1000; 5pm-5am Mon-Sat, 5-11pm Sun; Hibiya line to Roppongi, exit 3) as well as the associated **Shimanto-gawa** (四万十川; Map p278; 4540-6297; www.diamond-dining.com/shops/shimantogawa; 2-1-21 Yūrakuchō, Chiyoda-ku; cover charge per person ¥380, dishes from ¥1000; 4-11.30pm; ; Ginza line to Hibiya, exit A4) in Yūrakuchō.

AKASAKA ICHIRYU BEKKAN KOREAN ¥¥

Map p280 (赤坂一龍 別館; 3582-7008; 2-13-17 Akasaka, Minato-ku; seolleongtang ¥1620; 24hr; Chiyoda line to Akasaka, exit 2) While it won't win any awards for its decor, this three-decades old, round-the-clock joint is beloved for its heart-warming rendition of the Korean beef-noodle soup *seolleongtang*. It's served with a full range of traditional Korean side dishes including spicy *kimchee*. Look for a steaming bowl of noodles on the street outside.

HAYASHI IZAKAYA ¥¥

Map p280 (林; 3582-4078; www.sumiyaki-hayashi.jp; 4th fl San-no Kaikan, 2-14-1 Akasaka, Minato-ku; dishes ¥200-1000, course menu from ¥6480; 11.30am-2pm Mon-Fri, 5.30-10pm Mon-Sat; ; Chiyoda line to Akasaka, exit 2) Ensconce yourself in your *hori-kotatsu* (low table with hollowed-out space in the floor for your legs) or on a log bench, and drape a napkin made of kimono fabric over your lap. Kindly staff grill *yakitori* (chicken and other meats or vegetables grilled on skewers) over *irori* (hearths) set into your table.

KOBACHI-YA VEGETARIAN ¥¥

Map p280 (小鉢や; 3584-0002; www.kobachi-ya.com; B1 fl, Shinario Kaikan, 5-4-16 Akasaka, Minato-ku; lunch from ¥1200, dishes from ¥1000; 11.30am-2pm, 5.30-9.30pm Mon-Fri; ; Chiyoda line to Akasaka, exit 7) It has hearty macrobiotic lunch sets of vegetable curry with salad and miso soup, or a variety of veggie and grain dishes perfect for those who don't eat meat. A wider menu is served in the evening, including soy-milk desserts. Vegan dishes are also possible.

★**KIKUNOI** KAISEKI ¥¥¥

Map p280 (菊乃井; 3568-6055; http://kikunoi.jp; 6-13-8 Akasaka, Minato-ku; lunch/dinner course from ¥5670/8960; lunch seating noon-1pm, dinner seating 5-8pm; Chiyoda line to Akasaka, exit 7) Exquisitely prepared seasonal dishes are as beautiful as they are delicious at this two Michelin-starred, Tokyo outpost of a three-generation-old Kyoto-based *kaiseki* restaurant. Kikunoi's Chef Murata has written a book translated into English on *kaiseki* that the staff helpfully use to explain the dishes you are served, if you don't speak Japanese. Reservations are necessary.

DRINKING & NIGHTLIFE

Roppongi

★PINK COW BAR

Map p280 (ピンクカウ; www.thepinkcow.com; B1 fl, Roi Bldg, 5-5-1 Roppongi, Minato-ku; ⌚5pm-late Tue-Sun; Ⓢ Hibiya line to Roppongi, exit 3) With its animal-print decor, rotating display of local artwork and terrific all-you-can-eat buffet (¥2000) every Friday and Saturday, the Pink Cow is a funky, friendly place to hang out. Also host to stitch-and-bitch evenings, writers' salons and indie-film screenings, it's a good bet if you're in the mood to mix with a creative crowd.

DOWNSTAIRS COFFEE COFFEE

Map p280 (www.mercedes-benz-connection.com/tokyo; 7-3-10 Roppongi, Minato-ku; ⌚7am-11pm; 📶; Ⓢ Ōedo line to Roppongi, exit 8) Streamer Coffee Company provides the gourmet joe for this spacious cafe with free wi-fi, big shared tables and a view onto the attached Mercedes Benz showroom. It does good-value breakfast and lunch set menus, as well as doughnuts decorated with the Mercedes Benz logo.

SALSA SUDADA DANCE

Map p280 (サルサスダーダ; www.salsasudada.org; 3rd fl, Fusion Bldg, 7-13-8 Roppongi, Minato-ku; Fri & Sat ¥2000, Sun-Thu free; ⌚6pm-2am; 🚇Hibiya line to Roppongi, exit 4B) Tokyo's salsa fanatics come here to mingle and merengue. If you don't know how to dance, they'll teach you (1½-hour lessons held nightly; ¥1500).

FESTA IIKURA KARAOKE

Map p280 (フェスタ飯倉; ☎5570-1500; www.festa-iikura.com; 3-5-7 Azabudai, Minato-ku; 3hr room & meal plan from ¥5000; ⌚5pm-5am Mon-Sat; Ⓢ Hibiya line to Kamiyachō, exit 2) Kill two *tori* with one stone and savour some sushi while singing your heart out. Excellent service and complimentary costume rentals make this one of the best places to perfect your rendition of 'My Sharona' – we know you've been practising…

★AGAVE BAR

Map p280 (アガヴェ; ☎3497-0229; www.agave.jp; B1 fl, 7-15-10 Roppongi, Minato-ku; ⌚6.30pm-2am Mon-Thu, to 4am Fri & Sat; Ⓢ Hibiya or Ōedo line to Roppongi, exit 2) Rawhide chairs, *cruzas de rosas* (crosses decorated with roses) and tequila shots for the willing make Agave a good place for a long night in search of the sacred worm. Luckily, this gem in the jungle that is Roppongi is more about savouring the subtleties of its 400-plus varieties of tequila than tossing back shots of Cuervo.

MISTRAL BLEU/TRAIN BAR BAR

Map p280 (ミストラルブルー; www.trainbar.com; 5-5-1 Roppongi, Minato-ku; ⌚6pm-5am Mon-Sat; Ⓢ Hibiya line to Roppongi, exit 3) This hole in the wall is about as unpretentious as it gets in Roppongi. The many foreign customers who have drained cheap beers here have left their mark – every surface, even the light bulbs, is covered with signatures.

WARNING ABOUT ROPPONGI NIGHTLIFE

Roppongi is quite innocent, even upmarket, during the day. However, at night the footpaths along Gaien-Higashi-dōri, south of Tokyo Midtown, become populated with hawkers trying to entice patrons into clubs, promising age-old entertainment such as women and liquor. Some of these touts can be aggressive, others just chatty. Use caution if you follow them, as instances of spiked drinks followed by theft, beatings and blackouts have been reported to the point where Western embassies have issued warnings. Exercise common sense and healthy scepticism. If someone offers you illegal drugs, leave.

PASELA KARAOKE

Map p280 (パセラ; www.pasela.co.jp; 5-16-3 Roppongi, Minato-ku; per hour, per person Sun-Thu ¥1100, Fri & Sat ¥1300; 24hr; Hibiya line to Roppongi, exit 3) With decor that is a cut above the other yodelling parlours, Pasela offers six floors of karaoke rooms (including swanky VIP suites), an extensive selection of Western songs, wine, champagne and sweets on the menu, and a Mexican bar-restaurant in the basement.

Azabu-Jūban

★THE GARDEN CAFE

Map p280 (3470-4611; www.i-house.or.jp/eng/facilities/tealounge; International House of Japan, 5-11-16 Roppongi, Minato-ku; 7am-10pm; ; Ōedo line to Azabu-Jūban, exit 7) Stare out from this serene tea lounge across the beautiful late-16th-century garden, hidden behind International House of Japan. There are plenty of tempting pastries and cakes, as well as more substantial meals should you wish to linger – and who could blame you!

Nishi-Azabu

★SUPERDELUXE LOUNGE

Map p280 (スーパー・デラックス; 5412-0515; www.super-deluxe.com; B1 fl, 3-1-25 Nishi-Azabu, Minato-ku; admission varies; Hibiya line to Roppongi, exit 1B) This groovy basement performance space, also a cocktail lounge and club of sorts, stages everything from hula-hoop gatherings to literary evenings and creative presentations in the 20 x 20 PechaKucha (20 slides x 20 seconds) format. Check the website for event details. It's in an unmarked brown-brick building by a shoe-repair shop.

★THESE LOUNGE

Map p280 (テーゼ; 5466-7331; www.these-jp.com; 2-15-12 Nishi-Azabu, Minato-ku; cover charge ¥500; 7pm-4am, to 2am Sun; Hibiya line to Roppongi, exit 3) Pronounced *tay*-zay, this delightfully quirky, nook-ridden space calls itself a library lounge and overflows with armchairs, sofas, and books on the shelves and on the bar. Imbibe champagne by the glass, whiskies or seasonal-fruit cocktails. Bites include escargot garlic toast, which goes down very nicely with a drink in the secret room on the 2nd floor. Look for the flaming torches outside.

MUSE CLUB

Map p280 (ミューズ; 5467-1188; www.muse-web.com; B1 fl, 4-1-1 Nishi-Azabu, Minato-ku; admission women/men incl 2 drinks free/¥3000; 9pm-late Mon-Fri, from 10pm Sat & Sun; Hibiya line to Roppongi, exit 3) This catacomb-like underground club with intimate booths, dance floors and billiards, has an excellent mix of locals and foreigners. There's something for everyone here, whether you want to dance up a storm or just feel like playing darts or table tennis.

BULLET'S CLUB

Map p280 (ブレッツ; www.bul-lets.com; B1 fl, Kasumi Bldg,1-7-11 Nishi-Azabu, Minato-ku; admission ¥2000; 7-11pm, but varies with events; Hibiya line to Roppongi, exit 2) This mellow basement space plays worldwide trance and ambient sounds for barefoot patrons. Mattresses in the middle of the floor provide refuge from the madding crowd, but don't get the wrong idea – it's not always tranquillity.

Toranomon & Around

★JANOME CAFE, BAR

Map p280 (ジャノメ; http://littletyo.com; 1-2-1 Atago, Minato-ku; 8.30am-11pm Mon-Fri, noon-6pm Sat; ; Hibiya line to Kamiyachō, exit 3) Once a sushi shop and some vacant land, Janome is the base for the 'Little Tokyo' project which combines a quirky cool cafe, bar, gallery and design shop with an events space. With free wi-fi it's a great hang-out in an area that, thanks to the adjacent Toronomon Hills development, is on the up and up.

★TORANOMON KOFFEE COFFEE

Map p280 (http://ooo-koffee.com; 2nd fl, Toranomon Hills Mori Tower, 1-23-3 Toranomon, Minato-ku; 7am-7pm; ; Ginza line to Toranomon, exit 1) Coffee making is treated as an exact science at the Toranomon Hill's outpost of cult-coffee stand Omotesando Koffee. Here you'll find gleaming espresso machines, test tubes of coffee beans and baristas in white lab coats practising their craft with precise attention to detail.

SAKE PLAZA SAKE

Map p278 (日本酒造会館; www.japansake.or.jp; 1-1-21 Nishi-Shimbashi, Minato-ku; 10am-5.30pm Mon-Fri; Ginza line to Toranomon, exit 9) Sake Plaza isn't a bar, but who cares when you can get five thimbles of regionally brewed sake for only ¥525. This showroom and tasting space is an ideal place to learn about the national drink as well as start off a night's drinking. It's on the ground floor of the Japan Sake Brewers Association Building (日本酒造会館).

ENTERTAINMENT

NATIONAL THEATRE TRADITIONAL THEATRE

(国立劇場; Kokuritsu Gekijō; ☎3265-7411; www.ntj.jac.go.jp/english; 4-1 Hayabusa-chō, Chiyoda-ku; tickets from ¥1500; S Hanzōmon line to Hanzōmon, exit 1) This is the capital's premier venue for traditional performing arts with a 1600-seat and a 590-seat auditorium. Performances include kabuki, *gagaku* (music of the imperial court) and bunraku (classic puppet theatre). Earphones with English translation are available for hire (¥650 plus ¥1000 deposit). Check the website for performance schedules.

BILLBOARD LIVE LIVE MUSIC

Map p280 (ビルボードライブ東京; ☎3405-1133; www.billboard-live.com; 4th fl, Tokyo Midtown, 9-7-4 Akasaka, Minato-ku; ⏲5.30-9.30pm Mon-Fri, 5-9pm Sat & Sun; @; S Ōedo line to Roppongi, exit 8) This glitzy amphitheatre-like space plays host to major foreign talent as well as Japanese jazz, soul and rock groups who all come in to shake the rafters. The service is excellent and the drinks are reasonably priced.

KINGYO CABARET

Map p280 (金魚; ☎3478-3000; www.kingyo.co.jp; 3-14-17 Roppongi, Minato-ku; admission from ¥3500; ⏲shows 7.30pm & 10pm Tue-Sun; S Hibiya line to Roppongi, exit 3) Next to a cemetery off Roppongi's main drag, cheeky Kingyo puts on a glitzy, colourful and sexually tame cabaret of pretty boys, glammed-up *nyū hāfu* (transsexual) and drag-queen performers. There are a couple of shows each night, and you'll be expected to buy drinks and snacks on top of admission.

STB 139 JAZZ

Map p280 (スイートベイジル; ☎5474-1395; http://stb139.co.jp; 6-7-11 Roppongi, Minato-ku; admission ¥3000-7000; ⏲6-11pm Mon-Sat; S Hibiya line to Roppongi, exit 3) A large, lovely space that draws big-name domestic and international jazz acts running the gamut of the genre; check the website for the current line-up. This classy joint is also a good place to have an Italian dinner before a show; call for reservations between 11am and 8pm Monday to Saturday.

B-FLAT JAZZ

Map p280 (ビーフラット; http://bflat.biz; B1 fl Sakae Bldg, 6-6-4 Akasaka, Minato-ku; admission from ¥2500; ⏲6.30-11pm; S Chiyoda line to Akasaka, exit 5A) This hip jazz club often features local and European talent, as well as healthy doses of Latin jazz. Shows start at 7.30pm and 9.15pm.

SUNTORY HALL CLASSICAL MUSIC

Map p280 (☎3505-1001; www.suntory.com/culture-sports/suntoryhall; Ark Hills, 1-13-1 Akasaka, Minato-ku; S Ginza Line to Tameike-sannō, exit 13) This is one of the best venues at which to attend a classical concert with a busy schedule including accomplished musicians. Its 2000-seat main hall has one of the largest organs in the world.

SHOPPING

★JAPAN TRADITIONAL CRAFTS AOYAMA SQUARE CRAFTS

Map p280 (伝統工芸 青山スクエア; http://kougeihin.jp/home.shtml; 8-1-22 Akasaka, Minato-ku; ⏲11am-7pm; S Ginza line to Aoyama-itchōme, exit 4) Supported by the Japanese Ministry of Economy, Trade and Industry, this is as much a showroom as a shop exhibiting a broad range of traditional crafts, including lacquerwork boxes, woodwork, cut glass, paper, textiles and earthy pottery. The emphasis is on high-end pieces, but you'll find beautiful things in all prices ranges here.

TOLMAN COLLECTION ARTS & CRAFTS

(トールマンコレクション; ☎3434-1300; www.tolmantokyo.com; 2-2-18 Shiba-Daimon, Minato-ku; ⏲11am-7pm Wed-Mon; S Ōedo line to Daimon, exit A3) Based in a traditional wooden building, this reputable gallery represents nearly 50 leading Japanese artists of printing, lithography, etching, woodblock and more. Quality prints start at around ¥10,000 and rise steeply from there. From Daimon Station, walk west towards Zōjo-ji temple. Turn left at the shop Create. You'll soon see the gallery on your left.

Owner Norman Tolman has been collecting modern and contemporary Japanese print art for 50 years and has authored many books on the subject. He has a second **gallery** (Map p280; 3-17-8 Nishi-Shimbashi, Minato-ku; S Hibiya line to Kamiyachō, exit 3) close to Toranomon Hills specialising in antique Imari porcelain.

SOUVENIR FROM TOKYO — SOUVENIRS

Map p280 (スーベニアフロムトーキョー; www.souvenirfromtokyo.jp; basement fl, National Art Center Tokyo, 7-22-2 Roppongi, Minato-ku; ⏲10am-6pm Sat-Mon, Wed, Thu, to 8pm Fri; S Chiyoda line to Nogizaka, exit 6) An expert selection of homegrown design bits and bobs that make for perfect, unique souvenirs: a mobile by Tempo, zigzag tote from Mint Designs or a set of cheeky tea cups from Amabro, for example.

BLUE & WHITE — CRAFTS

Map p280 (ブルー アンド ホワイト; http://blueandwhitetokyo.com; 2-9-2 Azabu-Jūban, Minato-ku; ⏲10am-6pm Mon-Sat, 11am-6pm Sun; S Namboku or Ōedo line to Azabu-Jūban, exit 4) Expat American Amy Katoh sells traditional and contemporary items such as *tenugui* (hand-dyed towels) indigo-dyed *yukata* (light cotton kimono), bolts of nubby cloth and painted chopsticks. Pick through dishes of ceramic beads or collect bundled-up swatches of fabric for your own creations. Katoh's inspiration is the cherubic Japanese good-luck goddess Otafuku, who smiles from every corner of the shop.

JAPAN SWORD — ANTIQUES

Map p280 (日本刀剣; ☎3434-4324; www.japansword.co.jp; 3-8-1 Toranomon, Minato-ku; ⏲9.30am-6pm Mon-Fri, to 5pm Sat; S Ginza line to Toranomon, exit 2) If you're looking for a samurai sword or weaponry, this venerable place sells the genuine article – including antique sword guards and samurai helmets dating from the Edo period – as well as convincing replicas crafted by hand. Be sure to enquire about export and transport restrictions.

DON QUIJOTE — VARIETY

Map p280 (www.donki.com/search/shop_detail_en.php?st_store_id=31; 3-14-10 Roppongi, Minato-ku; ⏲24hr; S Hibiya line to Roppongi, exit 3) The Roppongi branch of this jam-packed bargain castle is where Japanese kids of all ages come to stock up for fun. Donki (as it's known by locals) sells everything from household goods and electronics to French-maid costumes, at cut-rate prices. You'll need to hack your way through cluttered aisles, but it's possible to find some really funky gifts here.

AXIS DESIGN — DESIGN

Map p280 (アクシスビル; www.axisinc.co.jp; 5-17-1 Roppongi, Minato-ku; ⏲11am-7pm; S Hibiya line to Roppongi, exit 3) Salivate over some of Japan's most innovative interior design at this high-end design complex of galleries and shops selling art books, cutting-edge furniture and other objets d'art.

Highlights include **Nuno** (布; ☎3582-7997; www.nuno.com; basement fl, Axis Bldg, 5-17-1 Roppongi, Minato-ku; ⏲11am-7pm Mon-Sat; 🚇Hibiya line to Roppongi, exit 3), whose innovative fabrics incorporating objects from feathers to *washi* appear in New York's Museum of Modern Art, and **Living Motif** (リビング・モティーフ; ☎3587-2784; www.livingmotif.com; Axis, 5-17-1 Roppongi, Minato-ku; ⏲11am-7pm; S Hibiya line to Roppongi, exit 3) with three floors of soothing, contemporary design (both Japanese and international) from cushions to candle holders.

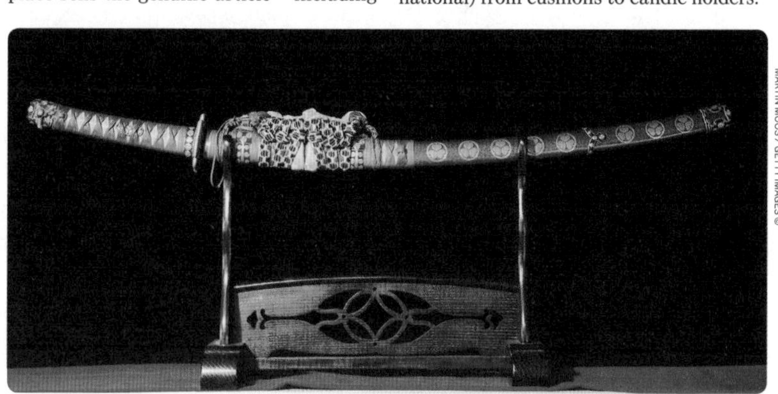

MARTIN MOOS / GETTY IMAGES ©

Display at Japan Sword

Ebisu, Meguro & Around

EBISU | MEGURO | SHIROKANE | TAKANAWA | DAIKANYAMA | NAKA-MEGURO | GOTANDA

Neighbourhood Top Five

❶ Exploring the shops and leafy lanes of fashionable neighbourhoods **Daikanyama** and **Naka-Meguro** (p98), a world away from frenetic central Tokyo.

❷ Learning about the history of beer in Japan at the **Beer Museum Yebisu** (p92).

❸ Discovering an urban oasis in the gardens and teahouses of **Happō-en** (p93).

❹ Catching an exhibition in the newly restored art-deco estate that houses the **Tokyo Metropolitan Teien Art Museum** (p92).

❺ Squeezing into a space at one of Ebisu's popular standing bars, such as **Buri** (p97).

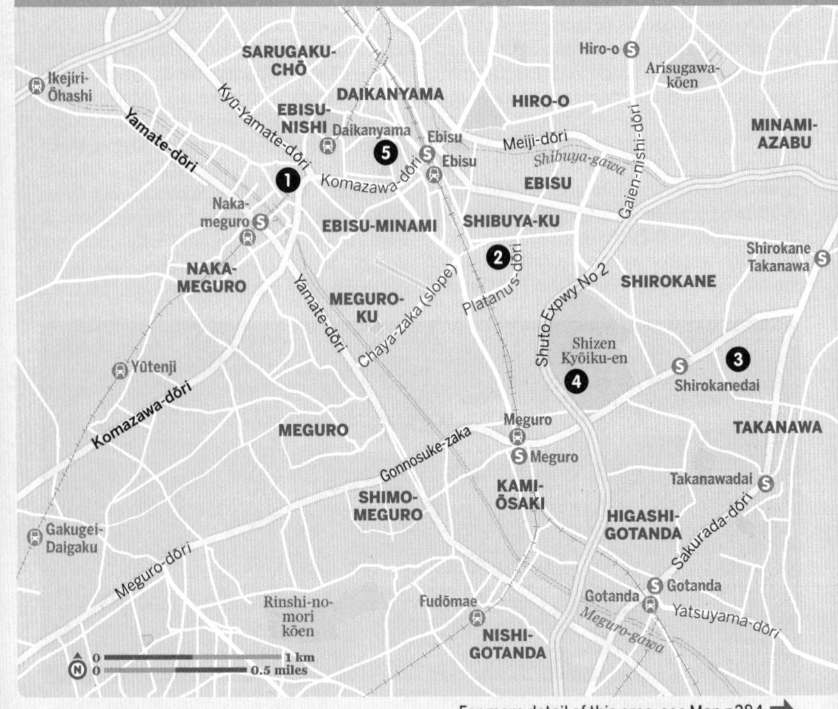

For more detail of this area, see Map p284

Explore Ebisu, Meguro & Around

Named for the prominent beer manufacturer that once provided a lifeline for most of the neighbourhood's residents, Ebisu is now a hip area, with shops, bars and restaurants. It's not the hub that Shinjuku is; rather, Ebisu represents Tokyo on a more human scale. Anchoring the neighbourhood is the Yebisu Garden Place complex, which includes two good museums, Beer Museum Yebisu and Tokyo Metropolitan Museum of Photography (closed until mid-2016 for renovations).

After a morning in Ebisu you could head to Daikanyama and Naka-Meguro – both are within walking distance. These adjacent neighbourhoods are the favourite haunts of fashion, art and media types, whose tastes are reflected in the shops and restaurants here. If you've been craving a slow day, punctuated by cafe stops and book stores, this will do the trick.

One stop south of Ebisu is Meguro, another midsized node on the JR Yamanote line. Nearby Shirokane and Takanawa are posh residential districts. This is an undervisited section of the city, though there are a number of sights. Here you can sip tea in a garden, light incense at a historic temple or examine the centuries-old pottery used in tea ceremonies – and see nary another traveller.

It's well worth sticking around this area for the evening. Foodies will find much to ooh and aah over here, as these neighbourhoods are chock-a-block with small, but highly rated restaurants. Ebisu has several bar strips that are popular with young professionals.

Local Life

- **Eating** Locals pile into retro arcade Ebisu-yokochō (p96) for grilled fish, fried noodles and copious amounts of beer.
- **Events** Yebisu Garden Place (p92), with its wide open plaza, hosts weekend events year-round, including a twice-monthly farmers' market (first and third Sundays).
- **Hang-outs** Ebisu is known for its lively *tachinomi-ya* (standing bars); Naka-Meguro for its riverside cafes and hard-to-find lounges.

Getting There & Away

- **Train** The JR Yamanote line stops at Ebisu, Meguro, Gotanda and Shinagawa stations. The Tōkyū Tōyoko line runs from Shibuya to Daikanyama and Naka-Meguro.
- **Subway** The Hibiya line runs through Ebisu to Naka-Meguro. The Namboku and Mita lines stop at Meguro and Shirokanedai. The Asakusa line runs from Gotanda Station to Takanawadai and Sengaku-ji.
- **Bus** Buses No 1, 2, 6 and 7 run from the west exit of Meguro Station along Meguro-dōri, stopping at Ōtori-jinja-mae.

Lonely Planet's Top Tip

Daikanyama and Naka-Meguro get a late start; don't expect cafes or boutiques to open before 11am (and sometimes not until noon). The exception is Daikanyama T-Site, which opens from 7am.

Best Places to Eat

- Tonki (p97)
- Afuri (p93)
- Higashi-Yama (p96)
- Beard (p97)
- Yakiniku Champion (p96)

For reviews, see p93

Best Places to Drink

- Nakame Takkyū Lounge (p97)
- Buri (p97)
- Kinfolk (p99)
- Enjoy House (p97)

For reviews, see p97

Best Places to Shop

- Okura (p98)
- Kapital (p100)
- Do (p100)
- Vase (p99)

For reviews, see p100

SIGHTS

Ebisu

BEER MUSEUM YEBISU MUSEUM

Map p284 (エビスビール記念館; www.sapporoholdings.jp/english/guide/yebisu; 4-20-1 Ebisu, Shibuya-ku; 11am-7pm Tue-Sun; JR Yamanote line to Ebisu, east exit) FREE Photos, vintage bottles and posters document the rise of Yebisu, and beer in general, in Japan at this small museum located where the actual Yebisu brewery stood until 1988. At the 'tasting salon' you can sample four kinds of Yebisu beer (¥400 each). It's behind the Mitsukoshi department store at Yebisu Garden Place.

TOKYO METROPOLITAN MUSEUM OF PHOTOGRAPHY MUSEUM

Map p284 (東京都写真美術館; www.syabi.com; 1-13-3 Mita, Meguro-ku; admission ¥600-1650; 10am-6pm Tue, Wed, Sat & Sun, to 8pm Thu & Fri; JR Yamanote line to Ebisu, east exit) Tokyo's principal photography museum is closed until August 2016 for renovations. In addition to drawing on its extensive collection, the museum also hosts travelling shows (usually several exhibitions happen simultaneously; ticket prices depend on how many you see). The museum is at the far end of Yebisu Garden Place, on the right side if you're coming from Ebisu Station.

YAMATANE MUSEUM OF ART MUSEUM

Map p284 (山種美術館; www.yamatane-museum.or.jp; 3-12-36 Hiroo, Shibuya-ku; adult/child/student ¥1000/free/800, special exhibits extra; 10am-5pm Tue-Sun; JR Yamanote line to Ebisu, west exit) When Western ideas entered Japan following the Meiji Restoration (1868), many artists set out to master oil and canvas. Others poured new energy into *nihonga* (Japanese style painting, usually done with mineral pigments on silk or paper) and the masters are represented here. From the collection of 1800 works, a small number are displayed in thematic exhibitions.

YEBISU GARDEN PLACE BUILDING

Map p284 (恵比寿ガーデンプレイス; www.gardenplace.jp; 4-20 Ebisu, Shibuya-ku; JR Yamanote line to Ebisu, east exit) This shopping and cultural centre was built on the site of the original Yebisu Beer Brewery (1889) that gave the neighbourhood its name. The large central plaza regularly hosts events and markets on weekends.

LOCAL KNOWLEDGE

MEGURO-GAWA HANAMI

If you're in town during *hanami* (blossom-viewing) season, don't miss one of the city's best parties, along the **Meguro-gawa** (目黒川; Map p284; S Hibiya line to Naka-Meguro) in Naka-Meguro. Here vendors line the canal selling more upmarket treats than you'll find anywhere else. Rather than stake out a space to sit, visitors stroll under the blossoms, hot wine in hand.

Meguro

TOKYO METROPOLITAN TEIEN ART MUSEUM MUSEUM

Map p284 (東京都庭園美術館; www.teien-art-museum.ne.jp; 5-21-9 Shirokanedai, Minato-ku; admission varies; 10am-6pm, closed 2nd & 4th Wed each month; JR Yamanote line to Meguro, east exit) Although the Teien museum hosts regular art exhibitions – usually of decorative arts – its appeal lies principally in the building itself: it's an art-deco structure, a former princely estate built in 1933, designed by French architect Henri Rapin. The museum reopened in late 2014 after a lengthy renovation and now includes a modern annex designed by artist Sugimoto Hiroshi.

INSTITUTE FOR NATURE STUDY PARK

Map p284 (自然教育園; Shizen Kyōiku-en; www.ins.kahaku.go.jp; 5-21-5 Shirokanedai, Meguro-ku; adult/child ¥310/free; 9am-4.30pm Tue-Sun Sep-Apr, to 5pm Tue-Sun May-Aug, last entry 4pm; JR Yamanote line to Meguro, east exit) What would Tokyo look like left to its own natural devices? Since 1949 this park, affiliated with the Tokyo National Museum, has let the local flora go wild. There are wonderful walks through its forests, marshes and ponds. No more than 300 people are allowed in at a time, which makes for an even more peaceful setting.

MEGURO PARASITOLOGICAL MUSEUM MUSEUM

Map p284 (目黒寄生虫館; http://kiseichu.org; 4-1-1 Shimo-Meguro, Meguro-ku; 10am-5pm Tue-Sun; 2 or 7 from Meguro Station to

Ōtori-jinja-mae, 🚉JR Yamanote line to Meguro, west exit) FREE Here's one for fans of the grotesque: this small museum was established in 1953 by a local doctor concerned by the increasing number of parasites he was encountering due to unsanitary postwar conditions. The grisly centrepiece is an 8.8m-long tapeworm found in the body of a 40-year-old Yokohama man.

The museum is about a 1km walk from Meguro Station; the entrance is on the ground floor of a small apartment building, just uphill from the Ōtori-jinja-mae bus stop.

Shirokane & Takanawa

HAPPŌ-EN GARDENS

(八芳園; www.happo-en.com/english; 1-1-1 Shirokanedai, Minato-ku; 10am-8.30pm; S Namboku line to Shirokanedai, exit 2) This gorgeous oasis is actually the grounds of a banquet hall, but anyone is free to enter and walk through the gardens (though some areas are occasionally roped off for weddings). Don't miss the row of bonsai, which includes a 520-year-old pine tree. At the teahouse Muan, you can stop for some *matcha* (powdered green tea) and a sweet (¥800).

SENGAKU-JI BUDDHIST TEMPLE

(泉岳寺; www.sengakuji.or.jp; 2-11-1 Takanawa, Minato-ku; 7am-6pm Apr-Sep, to 5pm Oct-Mar; S Asakusa line to Sengaku-ji, exit A2) The story of the 47 *rōnin* (masterless samurai) who avenged their master, Lord Asano – put to death after being tricked into pulling a sword on a rival – is legend in Japan. They were condemned to commit seppuku (ritual suicide by disembowelment) and their remains were buried at this temple. It's a sombre place, with fresh incense rising from the tombs, placed there by visitors moved by the samurai's loyalty.

There is a small exhibition hall (admission adult/child ¥500/250) with artefacts and a video (available in English) that illustrate the story of the *rōnin*.

HATAKEYAMA COLLECTION MUSEUM

(畠山記念館; www.ebara.co.jp/csr/hatakeyama; 2-20-12 Shirokanedai, Minato-ku; adult/child/student ¥500/free/350; 10am-5pm Tue-Sun Apr-Sep, to 4.30pm Oct-Mar; S Asakusa line to Takanawadai, exit A2) Get a feel for *wabi-sabi* – the aesthetic of perfect imperfections that guides the tea ceremony – at this museum specialising in the earthy pottery and art associated with the traditional ceremony. The museum closes for weeks at a time in between exhibitions.

WORTH A DETOUR

HARA MUSEUM OF CONTEMPORARY ART

Housed in a Bauhaus-style mansion from the 1930s, the **Hara Museum of Contemporary Art** (原美術館; www.haramuseum.or.jp; 4-7-25 Kita-Shinagawa, Shinagawa-ku; adult/student ¥1100/700; 11am-5pm Tue & Thu-Sun, to 8pm Wed; 🚉JR Yamanote line to Shinagawa, Takanawa exit) hosts cutting-edge exhibitions from Japanese and international artists. There are also fascinating permanent installations designed especially for the house's nooks and crannies. The garden-view cafe and excellent gift shop will make you extra glad you made the trip. It's 1.5km from Shinagawa Station; check the website for a map.

EATING

Ebisu

★AFURI RĀMEN ¥

Map p284 (あふり; 1-1-7 Ebisu, Shibuya-ku; noodles from ¥750; 11am-5am; 🚉JR Yamanote line to Ebisu, east exit) Hardly your typical, surly *rāmen-ya*, Afuri has upbeat young cooks and a hip industrial interior. The unorthodox menu might draw eye-rolls from purists, but house specialities such as *yuzu-shio* (a light, salty broth flavoured with yuzu, a type of citrus) draw lines at lunchtime. Order from the vending machine.

UDON YAMACHŌ UDON ¥

Map p284 (うどん山長; 1-1-5 Ebisu, Shibuya-ku; noodles from ¥630; 11.30am-4pm, 5pm-4.30am; 🚉JR Yamanote line to Ebisu, east exit) Go for bowls of udon (thick wheat noodles) in this stylish noodle joint alongside the Shibuya-gawa. In the evening you can tack on sides (such as seasonal veg tempura) and flasks of sake. The shop,

1

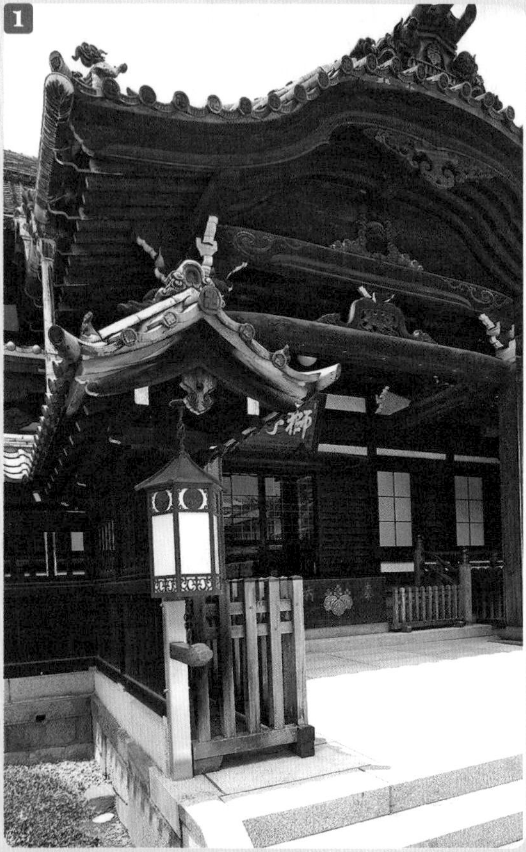

MARTIN HLADIK / GETTY IMAGES ©

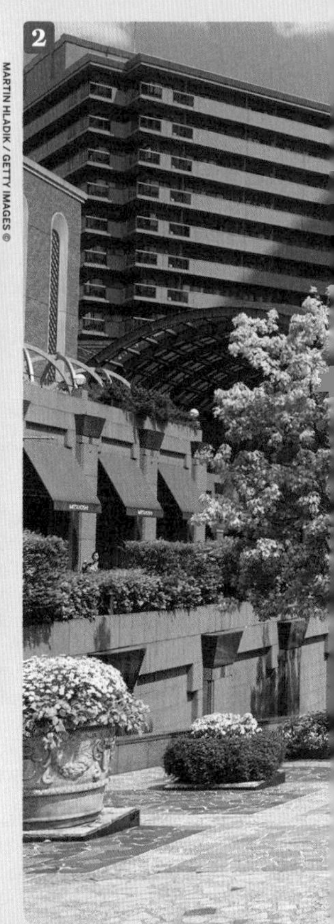

2

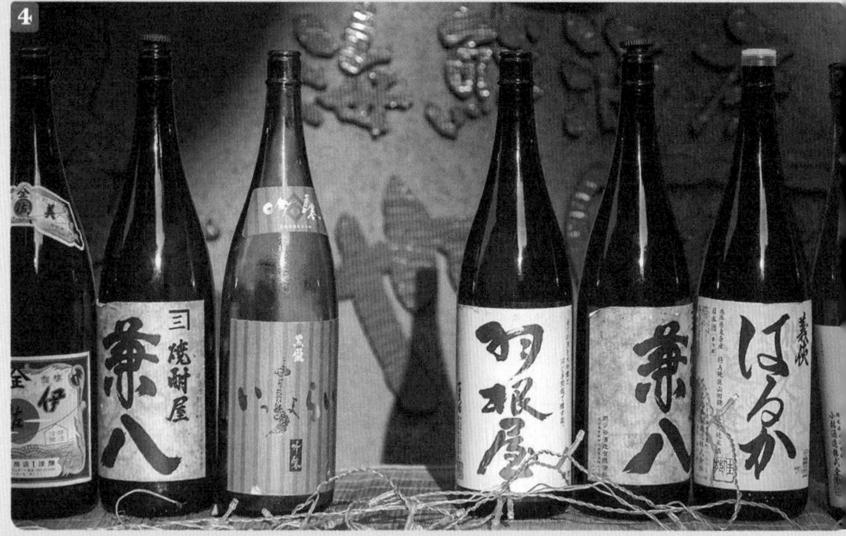

4

1. Sengaku-ji (p93)
The remains of 47 'masterless samurai' are buried at this temple.

2. Yebisu Garden Place (p92)
Home to Tokyo Metropolitan Museum of Photography and Beer Museum Yebisu.

3. Institute for Nature Study (p92)
Stroll through untamed forests at this peaceful park.

4. Dining in Daikanyama (p96)
Empty sake bottles make a colourful display outside a restaurant in this fashionable enclave.

LOCAL KNOWLEDGE

ALLEYWAY EATS

Locals love **Ebisu-yokochō** (恵比寿横町; www.ebisu-yokocho.com; 1-7-4 Ebisu, Shibuya-ku; dishes ¥500-1500; ⌚5pm-late; 🚉JR Yamanote line to Ebisu, east exit), a retro arcade chock-a-block with food stalls dishing up everything from grilled scallops to *yaki soba* (fried buckwheat noodles). Seating is on stools, while tables are fashioned from various items such as repurposed beer crates. It's a loud, lively, (and smoky) place, especially on a Friday night.

You won't find English menus, but the adventurous can get away with pointing at their fellow diners' dishes (you'll be sitting cheek-to-jowl with them). Even if you don't stop to eat it's worth strolling through. The entrance is marked with a rainbow-coloured sign.

with white curtains over the door, is next to a park with a slide shaped like an octopus.

OUCA ICE CREAM ¥

Map p284 (櫻花; www.ice-ouca.com; 1-6-6 Ebisu, Shibuya-ku; ice cream from ¥390; ⌚11am-11.30pm Mar-Oct, noon-11pm Nov-Feb; 🚉JR Yamanote line to Ebisu, east exit) Green tea isn't the only flavour Japan has contributed to the ice-cream playbook; other delicious innovations available at Ouca include *kurogoma* (black sesame) and *beni imo* (purple sweet potato).

TA-IM ISRAELI ¥

Map p284 (タイーム; ☎5424-2990; www.ta-imebisu.com; 1-29-16 Ebisu, Shibuya-ku; lunch from ¥1200, dinner mains from ¥1480; ⌚11.30am-2.30pm, 6-11pm Thu-Tue; 🚭📝🍽; 🚉JR Yamanote line to Ebisu, east exit) Swing by this convivial counter joint for authentic Israeli cooking – felafel, schnitzel, hummus and more – from expat Dan Zuckerman. It's a tiny place; call ahead in the evening.

YAKINIKU CHAMPION BARBECUE ¥¥

Map p284 (焼肉チャンピオン; ☎5768-6922; 1-2-8 Ebisu, Shibuya-ku; dishes ¥780-3300, course from ¥5250; ⌚5pm-12.30am Mon-Fri, to 1am Sat, 4.30pm-midnight Sun; 🍽; 🚉JR Yamanote line to Ebisu, west exit) Ready for an introduction into the Japanese cult of *yakiniku* (Korean barbecue)? Champion's sprawling menu includes everything from sweetbreads to the choicest cuts of grade A5 *wagyū* (Japanese beef). You can't go wrong with popular dishes such as *kalbi* (short ribs, ¥980). It's very popular, best to reserve ahead.

IPPO IZAKAYA ¥¥

Map p284 (一歩; ☎3445-8418; 2nd fl, 1-22-10 Ebisu, Shibuya-ku; dishes ¥500-1500; ⌚6pm-3am; 🚉JR Yamanote line to Ebisu, east exit) This mellow little *izakaya* (Japanese pub-eatery) specialises in simple pleasures: fish and sake (there's an English sign out front that says just that). The friendly chefs speak some English and can help you decide what to have grilled, steamed, simmered or fried. The entrance is up the wooden stairs.

✂ Daikanyama & Naka-Meguro

HANABI JAPANESE ¥

(2-16-11 Aobadai, Meguro-ku; dishes around ¥800; ⌚11.30am-midnight; 🍽; Ⓢ Hibiya line to Naka-Meguro) Hanabi has an enviable location right on the promenade that runs along Naka-Meguro's Meguro-gawa. It's perfect for people-watching (and blossom-spotting in season). The *sakana shio-yaki* (fish grilled with salt, ¥1000) lunch special is excellent. In the evening the menu is more varied, including Japanese staples, pizza, pasta and salads.

BOMBAY BAZAR INTERNATIONAL ¥

Map p284 (ボンベイバザー; www.bombay-bazar.jp; 20-11 Sarugaku-chō; mains from ¥900; ⌚11.30am-7.30pm; 🚭📝🍽; 🚉Tōkyū Tōyoko line to Daikanyama) Mismatched furniture and 'found' objects conspire to make this cafe look like a hippie camp. There's a spin-the-globe menu of pizzas, pastas and curries made with organic veggies.

★HIGASHI-YAMA JAPANESE ¥¥

(ヒガシヤマ; ☎5720-1300; www.higashiyama-tokyo.jp; 1-21-25 Higashiyama, Meguro-ku; lunch/dinner courses from ¥2500/4500; ⌚11.30am-2pm Tue-Sat, 6pm-1am Mon-Sat; 🍽; Ⓢ Hibiya line to Naka-Meguro) Higashi-Yama serves gorgeous modern Japanese cuisine paired with gorgeous crockery. The interior, a rustic take on minimalism, is stunning too. The restaurant is all but hidden, on a side street with little signage; see the website for a map. Tasting courses make ordering easy;

the 'chef's recommendation' course (¥8200) is a worthwhile splurge. Best to book ahead.

Stay for an after-dinner drink in the stark, dimly lit basement lounge.

Meguro

★TONKI TONKATSU ¥

Map p284 (とんき; 1-2-1 Shimo-Meguro, Meguro-ku; meals ¥1900; 4-10.45pm Wed-Mon, closed 3rd Mon of month; JR Yamanote line to Meguro, west exit) One of Tokyo's best *tonkatsu* (crumbed pork cutlet) restaurants, Tonki has a loyal following. The seats at the counter – where you can watch the perfectly choreographed chefs – are the most coveted. From the station, walk down Meguro-dōri, take a left at the first alley and look for a white sign and *noren* (doorway curtains) across the sliding doors.

GANKO DAKO STREET FOOD ¥

Map p284 (頑固蛸; 3-11-6 Meguro, Meguro-ku; 6 for ¥500; 11am-1am; JR Yamanote line to Meguro, west exit) This street stall dishes out steaming hot *tako-yaki* (grilled octopus dumplings). It's located, unfortunately, across from the Meguro Parasitological Museum; nonetheless, Ganko Dako draws them in – check out the celebrity signings on the wall.

★BEARD BISTRO ¥¥

Map p284 (5496-0567; http://b-e-a-r-d.com; 1-17-22 Meguro, Meguro-ku; mains from ¥1700; 5.30-10.30pm Tue-Sat, 10am-1.30pm Sun; JR Yamanote line to Meguro, west exit) One of Tokyo's new hottest restaurants, Beard serves up casual, creative bistro fare inspired by the peripatetic chef's travels. It's a small place, so reservations are recommended. Sunday brunch, featuring dense ricotta hot cakes (¥1200), is popular, too; bookings aren't accepted for brunch, so turn up early or just before closing.

DRINKING & NIGHTLIFE

★NAKAME TAKKYŪ LOUNGE LOUNGE

Map p284 (中目卓球ラウンジ; 2nd fl, Lion House Naka-Meguro, 1-3-13 Kami-Meguro, Meguro-ku; cover before/after 10pm ¥500/800; 7pm-2am Mon-Sat; Hibiya line to Naka-Meguro) *Takkyū* means table tennis and it's a serious sport in Japan. This hilarious bar looks like a university table-tennis clubhouse – right down to the tatty furniture and posters of star players on the wall. It's in an apartment building next to a parking garage (go all the way down the corridor past the bikes); ring the doorbell for entry.

BURI BAR

Map p284 (ぶり; 1-14-1 Ebisu-nishi, Shibuya-ku; 5pm-3am; JR Yamanote line to Ebisu, west exit) Buri – the name means 'super' in Hiroshima dialect – is one of Ebisu's most popular *tachinomi-ya* (standing bars). On almost any night you can find a lively crowd packed in around the horseshoe-shaped counter here. Generous quantities of sake (over 50 varieties; ¥750) are served semi-frozen, like slushies, in colourful jars.

AIR CLUB

Map p284 (エアー; www.air-tokyo.com; basement fl, Hikawa Bldg, 2-11 Sarugaku-chō, Shibuya-ku; cover from ¥2500; from 10pm Thu-Tue; Tōkyū Tōyoko line to Daikanyama) DJs spin mostly house and techno here, and the sound system is top of the line. Expect a good night out on any Friday or Saturday night. Keep an eye out for Frames (フレイムス) – the entrance to the basement club is inside. Bring your ID.

ENJOY HOUSE BAR

Map p284 (http://enjoyhouse.jugem.jp; 2nd fl, 2-9-9 Ebisu-nishi, Shibuya-ku; drinks from ¥600; noon-late; JR Yamanote line to Ebisu, west exit) Decked out with velveteen booths, fairy

LOCAL KNOWLEDGE

TOKYO CLUB SCENE

DJ and *Japan Times* music writer Mike Sunda weighs in on Tokyo's club scene.

Best Clubs

Shibuya wins for quantity, but neighbouring Daikanyama has two of the city's best clubs: Air (p97) and Unit (p99). Air combines a superlative sound system with an equally impeccable booking policy. Unit covers the more eclectic and experimental strands of the electronic spectrum. For after-hours fun head to Oath (p122) in Aoyama: a cult favourite spot among local club-goers, with parties that often carry on as late as noon the following day.

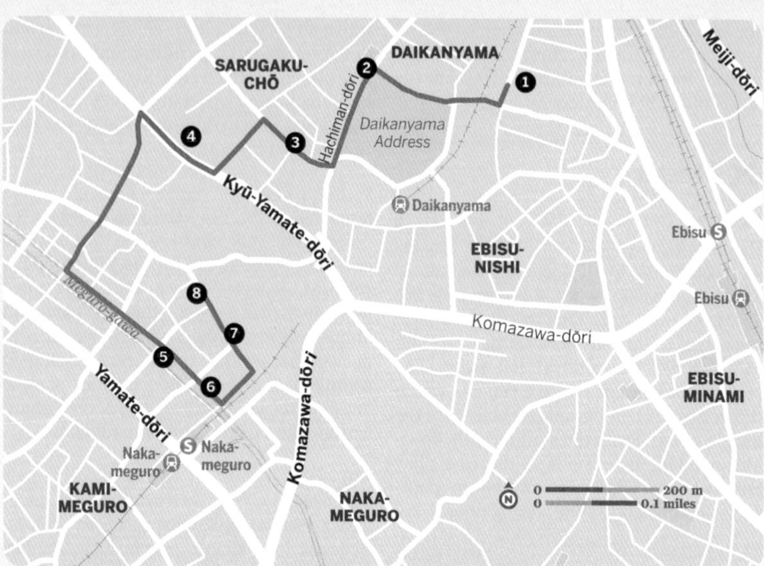

Local Life
Shopping in Daikanyama & Naka-Meguro

Just one stop from Shibuya, but a world away, Daikanyama is an upscale residential enclave with sidewalk cafes, fashionable boutiques and an unhurried pace. Neighbouring Naka-Meguro is Daikanyama's bohemian little sister, home to second-hand shops and secret lounge bars. At the heart of the neighbourhood is the Meguro-gawa, a canal with a leafy promenade.

❶ Kooky Boutiques
While Daikanyama is wealthy, it's not uptight. Some of Tokyo's most out-there boutiques are here: **Harcoza** (ハルコ座; Map p284; www.harcoza.com; 2-15-9 Ebisu-Nishi, Shibuya-ku; ⏱11am-7pm Wed-Mon; Tōkyū Tōyoko line to Daikanyama, north exit) specialises in candy-coloured clothing and accessories with a DIY art-school vibe.

❷ Japanese Designers
Many homegrown designers have flagship stores here, like Tsumori Chisato and Sunao Kuwahara, with shops in the **La Fuente Building** (ラ・フェンテ; Map p284; 11-1 Sarugakuchō, Shibuya-ku; ⏱11am-8pm; Tōkyū Tōyoko line to Daikanyama, main exit). Look for local brands Frapbois and Mercibeaucoup.

❸ Traditional Meets Modern
Surrounded by trendy boutiques, **Okura** (オクラ; Map p284; 20-11 Sarugaku-chō, Shibuya-ku; ⏱11.30am-8pm Mon-Fri, 11am-8.30pm Sat & Sun; Tōkyū Tōyoko line to Daikanyama) has staples such as jeans, T-shirts and work shirts dyed in traditional indigo. The building is unique too – it looks like a farmhouse. If you're hungry, Bombay Bazar (p96) is next door.

❹ Booklovers' Paradise
Locals love **Daikanyama T-Site** (代官山T-SITE; Map p284; http://tsite.jp/daikanyama; 17-5 Sarugaku-chō, Shibuya-ku; ⏱7am-2am; Tōkyū Tōyoko line to Daikanyama). This stylish shrine to the printed word has fantastic books on travel, art, design and food (some in English). You can even sit at the in-house Starbucks and read all afternoon – if you can get a seat.

❺ A Leafy Stroll
Lined with cherry trees and a walking path, the **Meguro-gawa** (more a river than a canal) gives Naka-Meguro its village vibe. On either side are quirky boutiques and cafes, such as Hanabi (p96), overlooking the water.

The Meguro-gawa under the cover of cherry-tree blossoms

6 Treasure Hunting
One of Naka-Meguro's tiny, impeccably curated boutiques, **Vase** (Map p284; 1-7-7 Kami-Meguro, Meguro-ku; ⌚noon-8pm; Ⓢ Hibiya line to Naka-Meguro) stocks cutting-edge designers and vintage pieces (for men and women). It's in a little white house set back from the Meguro-gawa (the name is on the post box).

7 Hidden Art
Possibly the city's tiniest art gallery, **The Container** (Map p284; http://the-container.com; 1-8-30 Kami-Meguro, Meguro-ku; ⌚11am-9pm Wed-Mon, to 8pm Sat & Sun; Ⓢ Hibiya line to Naka-Meguro) is literally a shipping container within a hair salon. It doesn't get much more Tokyo than that.

8 Drinks with Bikes
Call it a day with a cocktail at **Kinfolk** (キンフォーク; Map p284; www.kinfolklife.com/tokyo; 2nd fl, 1-11-1 Kami-Meguro, Meguro-ku; ⌚6pm-midnight; Ⓢ Hibiya line to Naka-Meguro), a dim, moody lounge run by the custom bicycle makers of the same name. It's in an old house with the ceiling cut away to expose the wooden rafters; the entrance is up a rickety metal staircase above a restaurant.

lights and foliage, Enjoy House is a deeply funky place to spend the evening. DJs spin regularly, but there's still no cover charge. By day it's a burger shop. Look for the name painted in red letters in English on the 2nd-floor window.

BAR MARTHA BAR
Map p284 (バー・マーサ; www.martha-records.com/martha/index.html; 1-22-23 Ebisu, Shibuya-ku; cover ¥800, drinks from ¥800; ⌚7pm-5am; 🚉JR Yamanote line to Ebisu, east exit) It's hard to say which is more impressive at this dim, moody bar: the whisky list or the collection of records. The latter are played on spot-lit turntables, amplified by a 1m-tall vintage Tannoy speaker. The somewhat steep cover includes bar snacks.

WHAT THE DICKENS! PUB
Map p284 (ワット・ザ・ディッキンズ; www.whatthedickens.jp; 4th fl, 1-13-3 Ebisu-nishi, Shibuya-ku; ⌚5pm-late Tue-Sat, to midnight Sun; 🚉JR Yamanote line to Ebisu, west exit) This British pub is a long-time favourite of down-to-earth expats and cosmopolitan Japanese alike. The beer and pub grub are well up to scratch, while there are local bands that play for free nightly. It has an unlikely location inside a building that looks like adobe decorated with a mosaic of a hummingbird.

SARUTAHIKO COFFEE CAFE
Map p284 (猿田彦珈琲; http://sarutahiko.co; 1–6–6 Ebisu, Shibuya-ku; coffee from ¥390; ⌚8am-12.30am Mon-Fri, 10am-12.30am Sat & Sun; 🚉JR Yamanote line to Ebisu, east exit) Even though it has only a few seats inside, Sarutahiko Coffee is Ebisu's most popular caffeine pit stop, thanks to its rich, flavourful coffee. Both hand-drip and espresso drinks are served.

☆ ENTERTAINMENT

★UNIT LIVE MUSIC
Map p284 (ユニット; ☎5459-8630; www.unit-tokyo.com; 1-34-17 Ebisu-nishi, Shibuya-ku; ¥2500-5000; 🚉Tōkyū Tōyoko line to Daikanyama) On weekends, this subterranean club has two shows: live music in the evening and a DJ-hosted event after hours. Acts range from Japanese indie bands to overseas artists making their Japanese debut. Unit is less grungy than other Tokyo live

GRAHAM CROUCH / GETTY IMAGES ©

A restaurant in Daikanyama (p98)

houses; it draws a stylish young crowd and, thanks to its high ceilings, it doesn't get too smoky.

LIQUID ROOM LIVE MUSIC

Map p284 (リキッドルーム; ☎5464-0800; www.liquidroom.net; 3-16-6 Higashi, Shibuya-ku; 🚇JR Yamanote line to Ebisu, west exit) When this storied concert hall moved to Ebisu from seedy Kabukichō it cleaned up its act, but Liquid Room is still a great place to catch big-name acts in an intimate setting. Both Japanese and international bands play here, and every once in a while there's an all-night gig. Tickets sell out fast.

SHOPPING

Ebisu

KAPITAL FASHION

Map p284 (キャピタル; http://kapital.jp; 2-20-2 Ebisu, Shibuya-ku; ⏰11am-8pm; 🚇JR Yamanote line to Ebisu, west exit) One of Japan's hottest brands, Kapital is a world away from Tokyo's pop image. The label is known for its premium denim, dyed a dozen times the traditional way, earthy knits and lushly patterned scarves.

Meguro

Meguro-dōri, the broad boulevard that runs southwest from Meguro Station, is known as Tokyo's interior-design district. Some 30 shops punctuate a 3km stretch of the road, starting after the intersection with Yamate-dōri. Even if you're not planning to shop, it's interesting to poke around and imagine what Tokyo's concrete-box apartments might look like on the inside.

When you've had enough, simply hop on any bus heading back up Meguro-dōri; they all stop at Meguro Station. Note that many stores close on Wednesdays.

MEISTER HOMEWARES

Map p284 (マイスター; www.meister-mag.co.jp; 4-11-4 Meguro, Meguro-ku; ⏰11am-8pm Thu-Tue; 🚌No 1, 2, 6 or 7 from Meguro Station to Moto-Keibajō-mae) Highly covetable Japanese modern homewares. Original items include sculptural *chōchin* (paper lanterns) and etched glass tumblers.

DO HOMEWARES

(ドー; www.claska.com/gallery; 2nd fl, Claska Hotel, 1-3-18 Chūō-chō, Meguro-ku; ⏰11am-7pm; 🚇Tokyū-Tōyoko line to Gakugei Daigaku, east exit) Contemporary takes on classic Japanese household goods and artisan wares from around Japan.

OTSU FURNITURE ANTIQUES

(オツファニチュア; www.demode-furniture.net/otsu; 1-4-9 Takaban, Meguro-ku; ⏰11am-8pm; 🚌No 2, 6 or 7 from Meguro Station to Takaban) Early-20th-century Japanese antiques, refinished in-house; especially good for moody, vintage lamps.

Gotanda

GOOD DAY BOOKS BOOKS

(グッド デイ ブックス; www.gooddaybooks.com; 3rd fl, 2-4-2 Nishi-Gotanda, Shinagawa-ku; ⏰11am-8pm Mon-Sat, to 6pm Sun; 🚇JR Yamanote line to Gotanda, west exit) Tokyo's best source for second-hand English-language books has a good selection of titles on Japanese culture and language. From Gotanda Station, head right from the ticket gates, then right again, following the tracks until you see the Big Size Shoes store on the ground floor.

Shibuya & Shimo-Kitazawa

SHIBUYA | SHINSEN

Neighbourhood Top Five

❶ Losing yourself in the crowds at **Shibuya Crossing** (p103), and getting swept along in the beating heart of desire, aspiration and materialism that is Shibuya.

❷ Eating, drinking and shopping your way down the neighbourhood's buzzing main drag, **Shibuya Center-gai** (p104).

❸ Wandering the tiny alleys of **Shimo-Kitazawa** (p108), a bohemian enclave.

❹ Singing your heart out at all-night karaoke parlour **Shidax Village** (p110).

❺ Scoping out the club scene on **Dōgenzaka** (p104), also known as Love Hotel Hill.

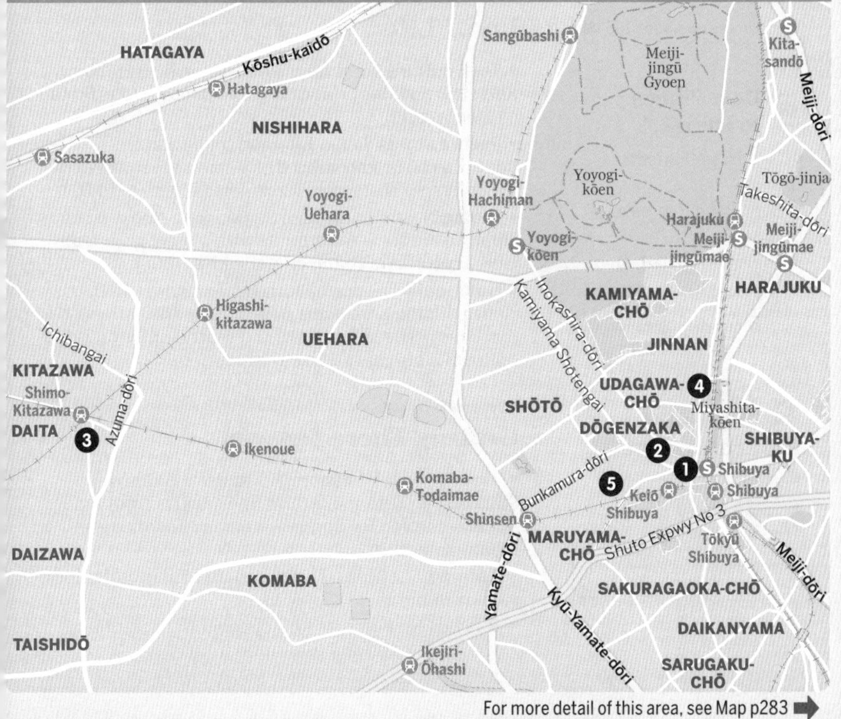

For more detail of this area, see Map p283

Lonely Planet's Top Tip

Missed the last train? You're not alone – or stuck for options. Shibuya has plenty for night crawlers who were lured out late by the neighbourhood's charms but who'd rather not fork over the yen for a taxi ride home. In addition to love hotels and *manga kissa* (cafes where you pay by the hour to read manga, Japanese comic books), consider waiting for the first train at a karaoke parlour; most offer discounted all-night packages from midnight to 5am.

Best Places to Eat

- d47 Shokudō (p105)
- Matsukiya (p108)
- Shirube (p109)
- Kaikaya (p108)

For reviews, see p105

Best Places to Drink

- Good Beer Faucets (p108)
- Bear Pond Espresso (p108)
- Fuglen Tokyo (p111)
- Tight (p110)

For reviews, see p108

Best Places for Entertainment

- WWW (p110)
- Setagaya Public Theatre (p110)
- Club Quattro (p111)

For reviews, see p110

Explore Shibuya & Shimo-Kitazawa

Shibuya has few sights, but makes up for it with sheer presence. As you exit the station you'll first hit Japan's busiest intersection, Shibuya Crossing – a neon-lit scene that has become synonymous with Tokyo. From here, the pedestrian traffic carries onto Shibuya Center-gai, the neighbourhood's main artery, lined with shops, cheap eateries and bars.

The area around Center-gai is primarily a teen hangout. On the east side of Shibuya Station, the new Shibuya Hikarie complex is part of an effort to redevelop the neighbourhood and bring in a more adult (and moneyed) vibe. Inside you'll find a handful of cultural attractions, several floors of restaurants and tonnes of shopping.

Further afield, 3km southwest of central Shibuya, is the cosy neighbourhood of Shimo-Kitazawa, with small, quirky shops, good restaurants and hole-in-the-wall bars around every corner. It's popular with students, but also with an artsy and intellectual grown-up crowd. There's an active underground music and theatre scene here, too.

Shibuya is, above all, an entertainment district and it really comes alive at night. There are dance clubs, live-music venues, theatres and cinemas galore. While weekends are the busiest, you'll find people from all over Tokyo here any night of the week. Bars and karaoke parlours stay open until dawn.

Local Life

- **Teen culture** Local teens love fashion hive Shibuya 109 (p112) and the 'print club' photo booths at Purikura no Mecca (p112).
- **Record stores** Shimo-Kitazawa (p108) and the Udagawa-chō neighbourhood of Shibuya are studded with tiny specialist record shops popular with local DJs.
- **Dining** Nearer to Shinsen Station (one stop west of Shibuya) are some restaurants with a more grown-up vibe. Try Kaikaya (p108) or Matsukiya (p108).
- **Hang-outs** The neighbourhood Tomigaya (p111), along with the Kamiyama *shōtengai* (market street) that runs between Tomigaya and central Shibuya, is the centre of a hip cafe and bistro scene.

Getting There & Away

- **Train** The JR Yamanote line stops at Shibuya Station. The Keiō Inokashira line departs from Keiō Shibuya Station for Shinsen, Komaba-Todaimae and Shimo-Kitazawa.
- **Subway** The Ginza, Hanzōmon and Fukutoshin lines stop in Shibuya.
- **Bus** Bus No 1 departs for Roppongi from platform No 58 of the east exit bus terminal.

TOP SIGHT
SHIBUYA CROSSING

Step out of Shibuya Station after dark and you'll find yourself in the Tokyo of your dreams: an awesome spectacle of giant video screens and neon streets radiating out like a starburst and an omnipresent flow of people. Rumoured to be the busiest intersection in the world (and definitely in Japan), Shibuya Crossing is an epic sight. Perhaps nowhere else says 'Welcome to Tokyo' better than this.

The Scramble

Shibuya Crossing, also known as Shibuya Scramble, is like a giant beating heart, sending people in all directions with every pulsing light change. Hundreds of people – and at peak times said to be over 1000 people – cross at a time, coming from all directions at once yet still managing to dodge each other with a practised, nonchalant agility. Then, in the time that it takes for the light to go from red to green again, all corners have replenished their stock of people – like a video on loop. It's a prime photo opportunity (even better, video). There's a particularly hypnotic view over the crossing from the Starbucks on the 2nd floor of the Q-front building across the street (though it's hard to get a seat).

The intersection is most impressive after dark on a Friday or Saturday night, when the crowds pouring out of the station are dressed in their finest and neon-lit by the signs above. Enter the thick of it and you'll brush by some of Shibuya's infamous characters: the fun-loving *gyaru* (teenage girls who prioritise shopping over studying) in colourful clothes and high-heel boots, her male counterpart (the tousle-haired *gyaru-o*) and the impetuous scouts looking to lure young women into working at dubious clubs. The rhythms here are, however, tied to the train station and after the last train pulls out for the night, the intersection becomes eerily quiet.

DON'T MISS...

- The Scramble at night

PRACTICALITIES

- 渋谷スクランブル交差点; Shibuya Scramble
- Map p283
- 🚉JR Yamanote line to Shibuya, Hachikō exit

SIGHTS

SHIBUYA CROSSING
STREET

See p103.

HACHIKŌ STATUE
STATUE

Map p283 (ハチ公像; Hachikō Plaza; JR Yamanote line to Shibuya, Hachikō exit) Come meet Tokyo's most famous pooch, Hachikō. This Akita dog came to Shibuya Station every day to meet his master, a professor, returning from work. The professor died in 1925, but Hachikō kept coming to the station until his own death 10 years later. The story became legend and a small statue was erected in the dog's memory in front of Shibuya Station.

The surrounding plaza is Tokyo's most popular rendezvous point and is always abuzz with trendy teens.

SHIBUYA CENTER-GAI
STREET

Map p283 (渋谷センター街; Shibuya Sentā-gai; JR Yamanote line to Shibuya, Hachikō exit) Shibuya's main drag is closed to cars and chock-a-block with fast-food joints and high-street fashion shops. At night, lit bright as day, with a dozen competing soundtracks (coming from who knows where), wares spilling onto the streets, shady touts in sunglasses, and strutting teens, it feels like a block party – or Tokyo's version of a classic Asian night market.

MYTH OF TOMORROW
PUBLIC ART

Map p283 (明日の神話; Asu no Shinwa; JR Yamanote line to Shibuya, Hachikō exit) Okamoto Tarō's mural, *Myth of Tomorrow* (1967), was commissioned by a Mexican luxury hotel but went missing two years later. It finally turned up in 2003 and, in 2008, the haunting 30-metre-long work, which depicts the atomic bomb exploding over Hiroshima, was installed inside Shibuya Station. It's on the 2nd floor, on the way to the Inokashira line.

HIKARIE SKY LOBBY

The 11th floor 'Sky Lobby' of Shibuya Hikarie has excellent views, particularly at dusk (and some comfy benches). There's also a scale model of what Shibuya will look like when the massive redevelopment of the neighbourhood finishes in 2027 (hint: more glass towers).

SHIBUYA HIKARIE
BUILDING

Map p283 (渋谷ヒカリエ; www.hikarie.jp; 2-21-1 Shibuya, Shibuya-ku; JR Yamanote line to Shibuya, east exit) This glistening 34-storey tower, which opened in 2012, is just the first step in what promises to be a massive redesign of Shibuya.

Sandwiched between the shops on the lower floors and the offices on the upper floors are a couple of free worthwhile cultural sights on the 8th floor. At the one-room **d47 Museum** (www.hikarie8.com/d47museum; 11am-8pm), lifestyle brand D&D Department combs the country for the platonic ideals of the utterly ordinary: the perfect broom, bottle opener, or salt shaker (to name a few examples). See rotating exhibitions of their latest finds from all 47 prefectures. The excellent d47 Design Travel shop is next door. **Tomio Koyama Gallery** (小山登美夫ギャラリー; www.tomiokoyamagallery.com; 11am-8pm) is a branch of one of Tokyo's more influential contemporary art galleries, which shows both Japanese and international artists.

DŌGENZAKA
NEIGHBOURHOOD

Map p283 (道玄坂; Love Hotel Hill; JR Yamanote line to Shibuya, Hachikō exit) Dōgenzaka, named for a 13th-century highway robber, is a maze of narrow streets. Home to one of Tokyo's largest clusters of love hotels (hotels for amorous encounters), it's also known as Love Hotel Hill. It's more than a little seedy, but some of the older hotels have fantastical (if not a bit chipped and crumbling) facades.

SPAIN-ZAKA
STREET

Map p283 (スペイン坂; JR Yamanote line to Shibuya, Hachikō exit) Shibuya's most atmospheric little alley is typical Tokyo bricolage with a Mediterranean flavour: a mismatch of architecture styles, cutesy clothing stores and a melting pot of restaurants all along a narrow, winding brick lane.

TOGURI MUSEUM OF ART
MUSEUM

Map p283 (戸栗美術館; www.toguri-museum.or.jp; 1-11-3 Shōto, Shibuya-ku; adult/child/student ¥1000/400/700; 9.30am-5.30pm Tue-Sun; JR Yamanote line to Shibuya, Hachikō exit) The Toguri Museum of Art has an excellent collection of Edo-era ceramics, displayed in informative, thematic exhibitions. It's about a 1km walk from Shibuya

WORTH A DETOUR

NIHON MINGEI-KAN

The *mingei* (folk crafts) movement was launched in the early 20th century to promote the works of ordinary craftspeople over cheaper, mass-produced goods. Central to the *mingei* philosophy is *yo no bi* (beauty through use). The excellent **Japan Folk Crafts Museum** (日本民藝館; Mingeikan; http://mingeikan.x0.com; 4-3-33 Komaba, Meguro-ku; adult/student ¥1100/600; 10am-4.30pm Tue-Sun; Keiō Inokashira line to Komaba-Todaimae, west exit), west of Shibuya, houses a collection of some 17,000 pieces in a farmhouse-like building designed by one of the movement's founders. From Komaba-Tōdaimae Station, walk with the train tracks on your left; when the road turns right (after about five minutes), the museum will be on your right.

Station; you'll see blue signs on the utility poles (in Japanese) marking the way when you get close.

EATING

Shibuya

★D47 SHOKUDŌ JAPANESE ¥

Map p283 (d47食堂; www.hikarie8.com/d47shokudo/about.shtml; 8th fl, Shibuya Hikarie, 2-21-1 Shibuya, Shibuya-ku; meals ¥1100-1680; 11am-2.30pm, 6-11pm; JR Yamanote line to Shibuya, east exit) There are 47 prefectures in Japan and d47 serves a changing line-up of *teishoku* (set meals) that evoke the specialities of each, from the fermented tofu of Okinawa to the stuffed squid of Hokkaido. A larger menu of small plates is available in the evening. Picture windows offer birds-eye views over the trains coming and going at Shibuya Station.

SAGATANI SOBA ¥

Map p283 (嵯峨谷; 2-25-7 Dōgenzaka, Shibuya-ku; noodles from ¥280; 24hr; JR Yamanote line to Shibuya, Hachikō exit) Proving that Tokyo is only expensive to those who don't know better, this all-night joint serves up bamboo steamers of delicious noodles for just ¥280 (and beer for ¥150). You won't regret 'splurging' on the ごまだれそば (*goma-dare soba;* buckwheat noodles with sesame dipping sauce) for ¥380. Look for the stone mill in the window and order from the vending machine.

FOOD SHOW SUPERMARKET ¥

Map p283 (フードショー; basement fl, 2-24-1 Shibuya, Shibuya-ku; 10am-9pm; JR Yamanote line to Shibuya, Hachikō exit) This take-away paradise in the basement of Shibuya Station has steamers of dumplings, crisp *karaage* (Japanese-style fried chicken), heaps of salads and cakes almost too pretty to eat. Look for discount stickers on *bentō* (boxed meals) and sushi sets after 5pm. A green sign pointing downstairs marks the entrance at Hachikō Plaza.

NAGI SHOKUDŌ VEGAN ¥

Map p283 (なぎ食堂; http://nagi-shokudo.jugem.jp; 15-10 Uguisudani-chō, Shibuya-ku; lunch/dinner set ¥1000/1500; noon-4pm, 6-11pm Mon-Sat, to 4pm Sun; JR Yamanote line to Shibuya, west exit) A vegan haven in fast-food laced Shibuya, Nagi serves up dishes such as felafel with tofu sauce and stir-fried pumpkin with coriander. It's a low-key, homey place with mismatched furniture. Look for it at the intersection with the post office.

VIRON BAKERY ¥

Map p283 (5458-1770; 33-8 Udagawa-chō, Shibuya-ku; sandwiches ¥600-1200; 9am-10pm; JR Yamanote line to Shibuya, Hachikō exit) A fantastic French bakery (it apparently imports the flour from the motherland), Viron serves up sandwiches and quiches to take away.

TABELA MEDITERRANEAN ¥

Map p283 (タベラ; www.uplink.co.jp/tabela; 37-18 Udagawa-chō, Shibuya-ku; mains ¥900-1400; noon-11pm; JR Yamanote line to Shibuya, Hachikō exit.) Gone too long without a hummus fix? Tabela will sort you out, and serve you tagine on the terrace while you watch the comings and goings on Shibuya's hip Kamiyama *shōtengai* (market street).

1

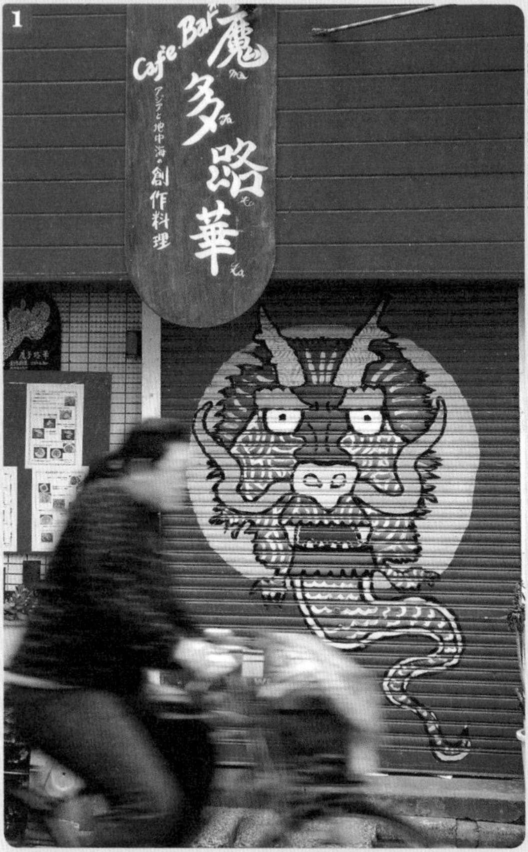
Cafe·Bar
魔多路華
アジアと地中海の創作料理

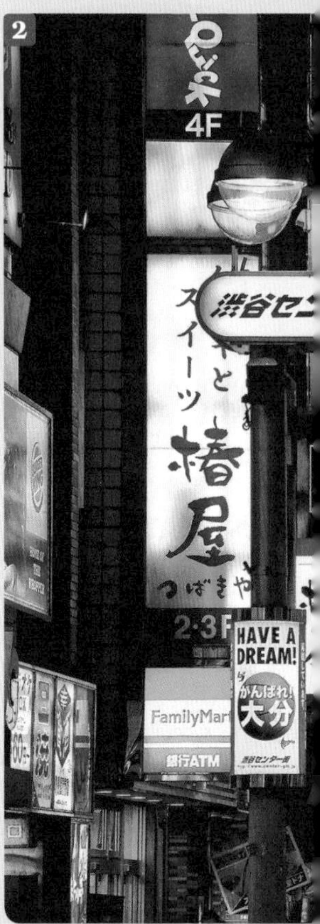

2

4F
スイーツ
椿屋
つばきや
2·3F
HAVE A DREAM!
がんばれ!
大分
FamilyMart
銀行ATM

LONELY PLANET / GETTY IMAGES ©

4

堂書店

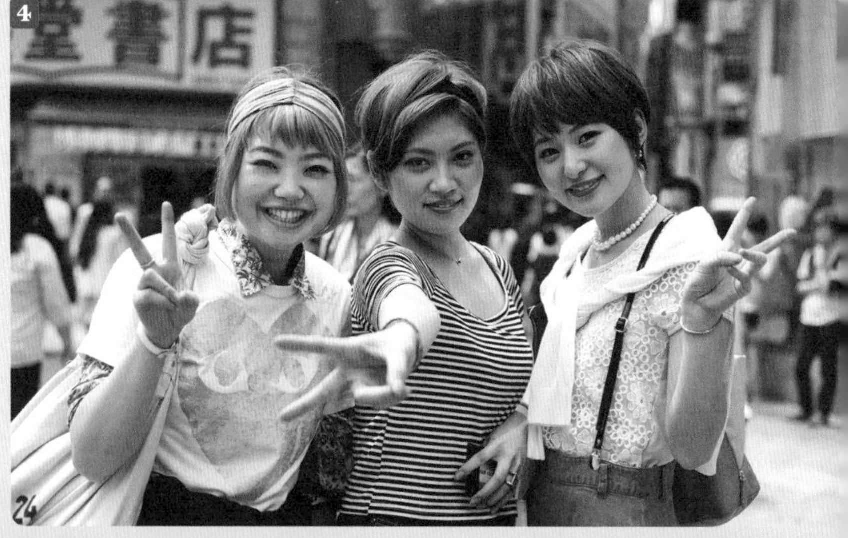

DAVID GEE / GETTY IMAGES ©

1. Shimo-Kitazawa (p108)
A cyclist passes a colourful dragon mural in this artsy neighbourhood.

2. Sibuya Center-gai (p104)
The neighbourhood's neon-lit main artery, lined with shops, eateries and bars, comes alive at night.

3. Hachikō Statue (p104)
Takeshi Ando's bronze statue of the famously faithful dog is a popular meeting place in Shibuya.

4. Youth culture (p102)
Girls pose on a street in Shibuya, a popular haunt for young Tokyoites.

3

LAURIE NOBLE / GETTY IMAGES ©

SUSHI-NO-MIDORI SUSHI ¥¥

Map p283 (寿司の美登利; www.sushinomidori.co.jp; 4th fl, Mark City, 1-12-3 Dōgenzaka, Shibuya-ku; meals ¥800-2800; ⏲11am-10pm; 🚭📄; 🚉JR Yamanote line to Shibuya, Hachikō exit) Locally famous for its generous, exceedingly reasonable sushi sets, Sushi-no-Midori almost always has a line. Take a number from the ticket machine (and, if the line is long, head out for a little shopping). It's least crowded around 3pm on weekdays.

Shinsen

KAIKAYA SEAFOOD ¥¥

Map p283 (開花屋; ☎3770-0878; www.kaikaya.com; 23-7 Maruyama-chō, Shibuya-ku; lunch from ¥780, dishes ¥680-2300; ⏲11.30am-2pm, 5.30-11.30pm Mon-Fri, 5.30-11.30pm Sat & Sun; 🚭📄; 🚉JR Yamanote line to Shibuya, Hachikō exit) Kaikaiya is one chef's attempt to bring the beach to Shibuya. Almost everything on the menu is caught in nearby Sagami Bay and the superfresh seafood is served both Japanese and Western-style. One must try *maguro no kama* (tuna collar). Kaikaya is a boisterous, popular place; reservations are recommended. From Dōgenzaka, turn right after the police box and the restaurant, with a red awning, will be on your right.

★MATSUKIYA SUKIYAKI ¥¥¥

Map p283 (松木家; ☎3461-2651; 6-8 Maruyama-chō, Shibuya-ku; sukiyaki from ¥5250; ⏲11.30am-1.30pm, 5-11pm Mon-Sat; 📄; 🚉JR Yamanote line to Shibuya, Hachikō exit) Matsukiya has been making sukiyaki (thinly sliced beef, simmered and then dipped in raw egg) since 1890 and they really, really know what they're doing. It's worth upgrading to the premium course (¥7350) for even meltier meat, cooked to perfection at your table. There's a white sign out front and the entrance is up some stairs. Reservations are recommended.

DRINKING & NIGHTLIFE

★GOOD BEER FAUCETS BAR

Map p283 (グッドビアフォウセッツ; http://shibuya.goodbeerfaucets.jp; 2nd fl, 1-29-1 Shōtō, Shibuya-ku; beer from ¥800; ⏲5pm-midnight Mon-Thu, Sat, to 3am Fri, 4-11pm Sun; 🚭📶; 🚉JR Yamanote line to Shibuya, Hachikō exit) With 40

Local Life
Hanging out in Shimo-Kitazawa

The narrow streets of 'Shimokita' are barely passable by cars, meaning a streetscape like a dollhouse version of Tokyo. It's been a favourite haunt of generations of students, musicians and artists and there's a lively street scene all afternoon and evening. If hippies – not bureaucrats – ran Tokyo, the city would look a lot more like Shimo-Kitazawa.

❶ An Old Market

Take the north exit from Shimo-Kitazawa Station and head right until you see the entrance to an old, post-WWII **covered market**. On its last legs (and scheduled to be demolished), it's a beloved symbol of the neighbourhood. A few vendors still stubbornly run shops here, and will until the end.

❷ DIY fashion

Next stop: **Shimokita Garage Department** (東洋百貨店; 2-25-8 Kitazawa, Setagaya-ku; ⏲noon-8pm; 🚉Keiō Inokashira line to Shimo-Kitazawa, north exit), a not-quite-so dilapidated covered market, with stalls selling DIY accessories and second-hand clothes. Colourful murals mark the entrance.

❸ Vintage Shopping

The bohemian vibe translates to a love of vintage clothing; **Haight & Ashbury** (2nd fl, 2-37-2 Kitazawa, Setagaya-ku; ⏲noon-10pm; 🚉Keiō Inokashira line to Shimo-Kitazawa, north exit) is the neighbourhood's best second-hand store.

❹ Espresso Break

Need a pick me up? **Bear Pond Espresso** (☎5454-2486; www.bear-pond.com; 2-36-12 Kitazawa, Setagaya-ku; coffee ¥300-700; ⏲10.30am-6pm Wed-Mon; 🚭📄; 🚉Keiō Inokashira line to Shimokitazawa, north exit) makes thick, syrupy espresso that has inspired a militant following.

❺ Record Stores

Shimo-Kitazawa is known for its hole-in-the-wall record stores, such as **Otonomad** (オトノマド; www.otonomad.com; 3-26-4 Kitazawa, Setagaya-ku; ⏲1-8pm Mon-Sat,

An alley in Shimo-Kitazawa

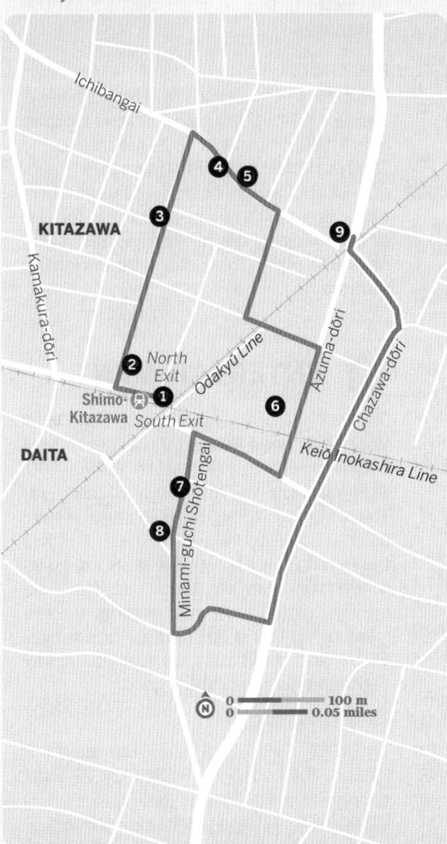

noon-7pm Sun; Keiō Inokashira line to Shimo-Kitazawa, north exit), is particularly good for vintage J-Rock, soul and world music.

6 Fringe Theatre

Along Azuma-dōri – typical Shimokita with low-slung buildings and retro street signs – is Tokyo's underground theatre district. There are half-a-dozen theatres in just a few blocks, including the Honda Theatre (p111).

7 The Southside

Compared to the more laidback northside, Shimokita's southside is an entertainment centre, with bars and live-music houses. Bright, bustling **Minami-guchi Shōtengai** is the main drag.

8 Izakaya Dinner

Duck down a side street and look for the white door curtains at the entrance to **Shirube** (汁べゑ; 3413-3785; 2-18-2 Kitazawa, Setagaya-ku; dishes ¥580-880; 5.30pm-midnight; ; Keiō Inokashira line to Shimo-Kitazawa, south exit). This rowdy, popular *izakaya* (Japanese pub-eatery) mixes classic dishes with fusion ones. Book on weekends and don't miss the *aburi-saba* (blowtorch grilled mackerel).

9 Never Never Land

Twinkling lights mark the entrance of late-night haunt **Never Never Land** (ネヴァーネヴァーランド; 3-19-3 Kitazawa, Setagaya-ku; 6pm-2am; Keiō Inokashira line to Shimo-Kitazawa, north exit), a classic Shimokita bar: smoky, loud and filled with bohemian characters.

GETTING TICKETS

To get theatre and concert tickets, hit up **Ticket Pia** (チケットぴあ; Map p283000) on the 4th floor of Shibuya Hikarie (p104). Note that some venues stop selling advanced tickets one to three days before the show.

shiny taps, Good Beer Faucets has one of the city's best selections of Japanese craft brews and regularly draws a full house of locals and expats. The interior is chrome and concrete (and not at all grungy). Come for happy hour (5pm to 8pm Monday to Thursday, 4pm to 7pm Sunday) and get ¥200 off any beer.

WOMB CLUB

Map p283 (ウーム; www.womb.co.jp; 2-16 Maruyama-chō, Shibuya-ku; cover ¥2000-4000; ⏰11pm-late Fri & Sat, 4-10pm Sun; 🚇JR Yamanote line to Shibuya, Hachikō exit) A longtime (in club years, at least) fixture on the Tokyo scene, Womb gets a lot of big name international DJs playing mostly house and techno. Frenetic lasers and strobes splash across the heaving crowds, which usually jam all four floors. Warning: can get sweaty.

TIGHT BAR

Map p283 (タイト; www.tight-tokyo.com; 2nd fl, 1-25-10 Shibuya, Shibuya-ku; drinks from ¥500; ⏰6pm-2am Mon-Sat, to midnight Sun; 🚇JR Yamanote line to Shibuya, Hachikō exit) This teeny-tiny bar is wedged among the wooden shanties of Nonbei-yokochō, a narrow nightlife strip along the JR tracks. Like the name suggests, it's a tight fit, but the lack of seats doesn't keep regulars away: on a busy night, they line the stairs. Look for the big picture window.

SHIDAX VILLAGE KARAOKE

Map p283 (シダックスビレッジ; 1-12-13 Jinnan, Shibuya-ku; per 30min Mon-Thu ¥580, Fri-Sun ¥610; ⏰11am-5am Sun-Thu, to 6am Fri & Sat; 🚇JR Yamanote line to Shibuya, Hachikō exit) Topped by a massive red neon sign, Shidax outshines all the other karaoke joints in the neighbourhood with spacious rooms and hundreds of English songs. A *nomihōdai* course (all-you-can-drink, two hours for ¥2040) is a sure bet for overcoming any lingering shyness. Nonsmoking rooms are available; rates are cheaper before 6pm.

BEAT CAFE BAR

Map p283 (www.facebook.com/beatcafe; basement fl, 2-13-5 Dōgenzaka, Shibuya-ku; drinks from ¥500; ⏰7pm-5am; 🚇JR Yamanote line to Shibuya, Hachikō exit) Join an eclectic mix of local and international regulars at this comfortably shabby bar among the nightclubs and love hotels of Dōgenzaka. It's a known hang-out for musicians and music fans; check the website for info on parties (and after parties). Look for Gateway Studio on the corner; the bar is in the basement.

SOUND MUSEUM VISION CLUB

Map p283 (www.vision-tokyo.com; basement fl, 2-10-7 Dōgenzaka, Shibuya-ku; cover ¥2000-3500; ⏰10pm-late; 🚇JR Yamanote line to Shibuya, Hachikō exit) With a sleek modern interior and not so much of a cruisy vibe, Vision is downright classy for this side of Shibuya. It's a big space too, with four dance floors. Music varies from hip-hop to electro to techno, with mostly local DJs spinning.

RUBY ROOM CLUB

Map p283 (ルビールーム; www.rubyroomtokyo.com; 2nd fl, 2-25-17 Dōgenzaka, Shibuya-ku; cover from ¥1500; ⏰8pm-late; 🚇JR Yamanote line to Shibuya, Hachikō exit) This tiny, sparkly gem of a cocktail lounge hosts both DJs and live-music events. It's an appealing spot for older kids hanging out in Shibuya. Tuesday is open-mic night (free entry with two-drink minimum).

☆ ENTERTAINMENT

★WWW LIVE MUSIC

Map p283 (www-shibuya.jp/index.html; 13-17 Udagawa-chō, Shibuya-ku; tickets ¥2000-5000; 🚇JR Yamanote line to Shibuya, Hachikō exit) Tokyo's newest, big-hitting music venue used to be an art-house cinema. It still has the tiered floor (though the seats are gone) so everyone can see the stage. The lineup varies from indie pop to punk to electronica, but this is one of those rare venues where you could turn up just about any night and hear something good.

SETAGAYA PUBLIC THEATRE PERFORMING ARTS

(世田谷パブリックシアター; ☎5432-1526; www.setagaya-pt.jp; 4-1-1 Taishidō, Setagaya-ku; tickets ¥3500-7500; 🚇Tōkyū Den-en-toshi line to Sangenjaya, Carrot Tower exit) The best of Tokyo's public theatres, Setagaya Public Theatre puts on contemporary dramas as well as modern *nō* (a stylised dance-drama, performed on a bare stage) and sometimes *butō* (an avant-garde form of dance). The smaller **Theatre Tram** shows more experimental works. Both are located inside the Carrot Tower building connected to Sangenjaya Station, a five-minute train ride from Shibuya.

CLUB QUATTRO — LIVE MUSIC

Map p283 (クラブクアトロ; ☎3477-8750; www.club-quattro.com; 32-13-4 Udagawa-chō, Shibuya-ku; tickets ¥3000-4000; ; JR Yamanote line to Shibuya, Hachikō exit) This small, intimate venue has the feel of a slick nightclub. Though there's no explicit musical focus, emphasis is on rock and roll and world music, generally of high quality. Expect a more grown-up, artsy crowd than the club's location – near Center-gai – might lead you to expect.

SHELTER — LIVE MUSIC

(シェルター; www.loft-prj.co.jp/SHELTER; 2-6-10 Kitazawa, Setagaya-ku; tickets ¥2000-3500; Keiō Inokashira line to Shimo-Kitazawa, south exit) Of all the venues on the Shimo-Kitazawa circuit, this small basement club, going strong for more than 20 years now, has the most consistently solid line-up. It can be an excellent place to catch (and even meet) up-and-coming artists, usually of the rock persuasion.

UPLINK — CINEMA

Map p283 (アップリンク; www.uplink.co.jp; 37-18 Udagawa-chō, Shibuya-ku; tickets ¥1500-1800; JR Yamanote line to Shibuya, Hachikō exit) Uplink screens independent films and documentaries (domestic and foreign) during the day and at night in a tiny art-house cinema with comfy chairs. Before or after enjoy tasty Mediterranean food at ground-floor restaurant Tabela (p105).

HONDA THEATRE — THEATRE

(本多劇場; www.honda-geki.com; 2-10-15 Kitazawa, Shibuya-ku; Keiō Inokashira line to Shimo-Kitazawa, south exit) This is the original, and the biggest, of Shimo-Kitazawa's independent *shōgekijō* (small theatres). If you have a fair helping of Japanese ability, this is a good place to start digging into Tokyo's theatre scene.

SHOPPING

★TŌKYŪ HANDS — VARIETY

Map p283 (東急ハンズ; http://shibuya.tokyu-hands.co.jp; 12-18 Udagawa-chō, Shibuya-ku; 10am-8.30pm; JR Yamanote line to Shibuya, Hachikō exit) This DIY and *zakka* (miscellaneous goods) store has eight fascinating floors of everything you didn't know you needed. Like reflexology slippers, bee-venom face masks and cartoon-character-shaped rice-ball moulds. It's perfect for souvenir hunting, too. There's another branch inside Takashimaya Times Square in Shinjuku.

WORTH A DETOUR

TOMIGAYA

Leave the brash youth culture of Center-gai behind. Just a 15-minute walk away is Tomigaya, a fashionable enclave known for its bistros and cafes. Some spots worth checking out:

Ahiru Store (アヒルストア; ☎5454-2146; 1-19-4 Tomigaya, Shibuya-ku; dishes ¥400-1800; 6pm-midnight Mon-Fri, 3-9pm Sat; ; S Chiyoda line to Yoyogi-kōen, exit 2) This tiny eight-seat bistro, dishing up home-made sausages, fresh-baked bread and bio wines, has a huge local following. Reservations are accepted only for 6pm; otherwise join the queue.

Fuglen Tokyo (www.fuglen.com; 1-16-11 Tomigaya, Shibuya-ku; 8am-10pm Mon & Tue, to 1am Wed-Sun; ; S Chiyoda line to Yoyogi-kōen, exit 2) This Tokyo outpost of a long-running Oslo coffee shop serves Aeropress coffee by day and creative cocktails by night.

Tsukikageya (月影屋; www.tsukikageya.com; 1-9-19 Tomigaya, Shibuya-ku; noon-8pm Thu-Sun; S Chiyoda line to Yoyogi Kōen, exit 2) Forget cute. Natsuki Shigeta designs *yukata* (cotton kimonos) for men, women and babies. The *yukata* have a punk-rock slant that pair with wild accessories.

FAKE TOKYO FASHION

Map p283 (www.faketokyo.com; 18-4 Udagawa-chō, Shibuya-ku; ⌚noon-10pm; 🚇JR Yamanote line to Shibuya, Hachikō exit) This is one of the best places in the city to discover hot new Japanese designers. It's actually two shops in one: downstairs is Candy, full of brash, unisex streetwear; upstairs is Sister, which specialises in more ladylike items, both new and vintage. Look for the 'Fake Tokyo' banners out front.

SHIBUYA 109 FASHION

Map p283 (渋谷109; Ichimarukyū; www.shibuya109.jp/en/top; 2-29-1 Dōgenzaka, Shibuya-ku; ⌚10am-9pm; 🚇JR Yamanote line to Shibuya, Hachikō exit) See all those dolled-up teens walking around Shibuya? This is where they shop. Nicknamed *marukyū,* this cylindrical tower houses dozens of small boutiques, each with their own carefully styled look. Even if you don't intend to buy anything, you can't understand Shibuya without making a stop here.

PARCO DEPARTMENT STORE

Map p283 (パルコ; www.parco-shibuya.com; 15-1 Udagawa-chō, Shibuya-ku; ⌚10am-9pm; 🚇JR Yamanote line to Shibuya, Hachikō exit) Not your typical fussy department store, Parco customers are more likely to be art-school students than ladies who lunch. Lots of Japanese fashion designers have shops here.

TOWER RECORDS MUSIC

Map p283 (タワーレコード; http://tower.jp/store/Shibuya; 1-22-14 Jinnan, Shibuya-ku; ⌚10am-11pm; 🚇JR Yamanote line to Shibuya, Hachikō exit) This eight-storey temple of music has a deep collection of Japanese and world music. Even if you're not into buying, it can be a great place to browse and discover local artists. There's also a good selection of books and magazines in English on the 2nd floor.

LOFT VARIETY

Map p283 (ロフト; www.loft.co.jp; 18-2 Udagawa-chō, Shibuya-ku; ⌚10am-9pm; 🚇JR Yamanote line to Shibuya, Hachikō exit) This emporium of homewares, stationery and accessories specialises in all that is cute and covetable. The 1st floor is particularly ripe for souvenir-hunting.

FRANK DEIM / GETTY IMAGES ©

Shibuya 109

SHIBUYA HIKARIE MALL

Map p283 (渋谷ヒカリエ; www.hikarie.jp; 2-21-1 Shibuya, Shibuya-ku; ⌚10am-9pm; 🚇JR Yamanote line to Shibuya, east exit) The first five floors of this glass skyscraper are filled with the latest trendy boutiques. In the basement levels are dozens of gourmet take-away counters.

SPORTS & ACTIVITIES

PURIKURA NO MECCA ARCADE

Map p283 (プリクラのメッカ; 1-23-10 Jinnan, Shibuya-ku; purikura ¥400; ⌚10am-9pm; 🚇JR Yamanote line to Shibuya, Hachikō exit) It's easy to see why teens get sucked into the cult of *purikura* ('print club', aka photo booths): the digitally enhanced photos automatically airbrush away blemishes and add doe eyes and long lashes for good measure (so you come out looking like an anime version of yourself). After primping and posing, decorate the images on screen with touch pens.

Harajuku & Aoyama

HARAJUKU | AOYAMA | GAIENMAE

Neighbourhood Top Five

❶ Making a wish at **Meiji-jingū** (p115). Leave the city behind as you pass through the towering *torii* (gate) and follow the wooded, gravel path to Tokyo's most famous Shintō shrine.

❷ Scouting new looks on **Takeshita-dōri** (p116) and around the backstreets of Harajuku.

❸ Stretching out on the lawn of **Yoyogi-kōen** (p116), one of Tokyo's largest parks.

❹ Gawking at the architectural wonders (and eyebrow-raising consumerism) along **Omote-sandō** (p116).

❺ Retreating into the calm galleries and gardens of **Nezu Museum** (p116).

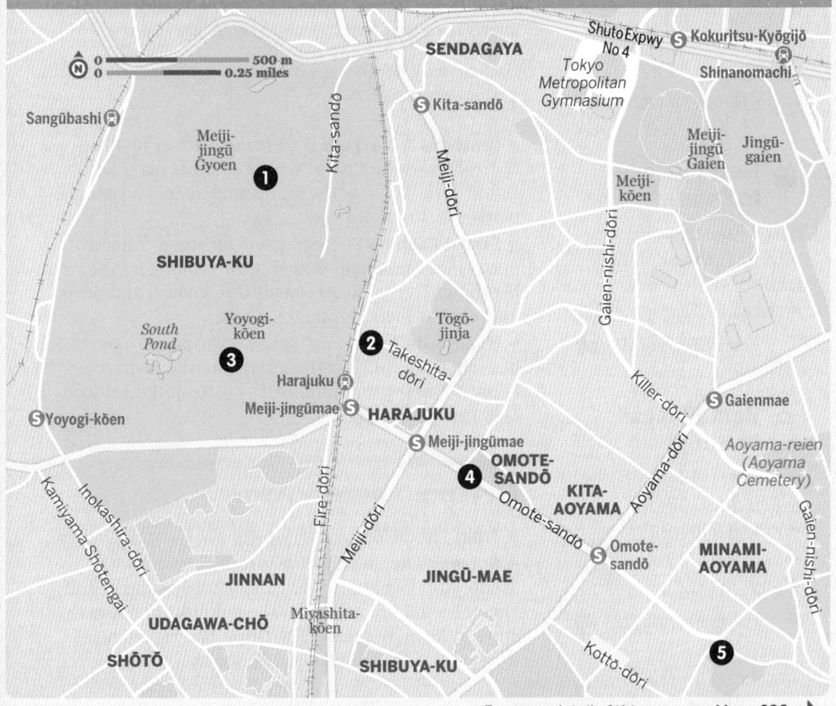

For more detail of this area, see Map p288

Lonely Planet's Top Tip

The recent arrival of fast-fashion megachains (such as H&M) hasn't pushed Harajuku fashion off the map; it's just pushed it further into the backstreets. Ura-Hara (literally 'behind Harajuku') is the nickname for the maze of backstreets behind Omote-sandō. Here you'll find the tiny, eccentric shops and second-hand stores from which Harajuku hipsters cobble together their head-turning looks. Whether your aim is acquisitive or more of the anthropological sort, it's worth spending some time exploring these streets.

Best Places to Eat

- Yanmo (p119)
- Maisen (p119)
- Harajuku Gyōza-Rō (p117)

For reviews, see p117

Best Places to Drink

- Two Rooms (p119)
- Omotesando Koffee (p122)
- Harajuku Taproom (p122)

For reviews, see p119

Best Places to Shop

- Laforet (p123)
- Sou-Sou (p124)
- KiddyLand (p123)
- Musubi (p123)
- RagTag (p123)

For reviews, see p123

Explore Harajuku & Aoyama

The twin neighbourhoods of Harajuku and Aoyama, linked by the boulevard Omote-sandō, are primarily shopping districts. On weekends, Harajuku in particular gets very crowded, with seas of people moving at the pace of a languid shuffle. This is great for people-watching: park yourself at a cafe on Omote-sandō and watch the city's living catwalk unfurl in real time. However, if you're more interested in the sights, or simply covering a lot of ground in one day, it is better to visit on a weekday.

For sightseeing, the best route is to start the morning with a visit to Meiji-jingū. If it's a weekend and the weather's nice, pop over to Yoyogi-kōen after visiting the shrine. Then work your way down Takeshita-dōri and Omote-sandō (p118); the latter known for its contemporary architecture. There are a handful of other small museums and art spaces along the way, too.

Of course, one of the primary reasons to come here is to shop, and you can easily spend a whole day (or three) doing just that. In Harajuku you'll find mostly trendy, youthful duds; in moneyed Aoyama it's sophisticated high fashion. (Somewhere in between is Ura-Hara, Harajuku's backstreets, where Tokyo's street trends are born). As befitting any shopping neighbourhood, both Harajuku and Aoyama have excellent lunch options and cafes.

Once the shops close, Harajuku becomes much quieter. Aoyama too, though there are some swank establishments here that fuel the well-heeled after hours.

Local Life

- **Festivals & Markets** During the warmer months, festivals take place most weekends at the plaza across from Yoyogi-kōen (p116). Year-round, there's a farmers' market (p119) in Aoyama.
- **Street Fashion** Photographers for street-fashion magazines line Omote-sandō (p116) looking for the next big thing. Teens and 20-somethings know it and dress for a shot at their 15 minutes of fame.
- **Hang-outs** Two Rooms (p119) is the place to see and be seen; Oath (p122) is the where after-hours parties happen. During the summer it's all about the outdoor beer gardens (p122).

Getting There & Away

- **Train** The JR Yamanote line stops at Harajuku Station.
- **Subway** The Chiyoda line runs beneath Omote-sandō, stopping at Meiji-jingūmae (for Harajuku) and Omote-sandō (for Aoyama). The Fukutoshin line also stops at Meiji-jingūmae. The Ginza and Hanzōmon lines both stop at Omote-sandō Station.

TOP SIGHT

MEIJI-JINGŪ (MEIJI SHRINE)

Tokyo's grandest Shintō shrine is dedicated to the Emperor Meiji and Empress Shōken. The reign of the Emperor Meiji (1868–1912) coincided with the country's transformation from isolationist, feudal state to modern nation. Constructed in 1920, the shrine was destroyed in WWII air raids and rebuilt in 1958; however, unlike so many of Japan's postwar reconstructions, Meiji-jingū has an authentic feel. The shrine itself occupies only a small fraction of the sprawling forested grounds.

Several wooden *torii* (gates) mark the entrance to Meiji-jingū. The largest, created from a 1500-year-old Taiwanese cypress, stands 12 metres high. It's the custom to bow upon passing through a *torii,* which marks the boundary between the ordinary and the sacred. Another rite: before approaching the main shrine, visitors purify themselves by pouring water over their hands at the *temizuya* (font).

The main shrine is made of cypress from the Kiso region of Nagano. Every day at 8am and 2pm a priest strikes a large drum as part of a ritual offering of food to the deities enshrined here. Should you wish to make an offering too (at any time), toss a five-yen coin in the box, bow twice, clap your hands twice and then bow again. To the right of the main shrine, you'll see kiosks selling *ema* (wooden plaques on which prayers are written) and *omamori* (charms).

The 70 hectares of forested grounds contain some 120,000 trees collected from all over Japan. On the left, along the path towards the main shrine, is the entrance to **Meiji-jingū Gyoen** (明治神宮御苑; Inner Garden; admission ¥500; ⏲9am-4.30pm, to 4pm Nov-Feb), a landscaped garden. It once belonged to a feudal estate; however, when the grounds passed into imperial hands, the emperor himself designed the iris garden to please the empress. The garden is most impressive in June when the irises bloom; the azaleas in April are pretty too.

DON'T MISS

- *Torii*
- Main shrine
- Meiji-jingū Gyoen

PRACTICALITIES

- 明治神宮
- Map p288
- www.meijijingu.or.jp
- 1-1 Yoyogi Kamizono-chō, Shibuya-ku
- ⏲dawn-dusk
- 🚉JR Yamanote line to Harajuku, Omote-sandō exit

SIGHTS

Harajuku

MEIJI-JINGŪ SHINTO SHRINE
See p115.

TAKESHITA-DŌRI STREET
Map p288 (竹下通り; JR Yamanote line to Harajuku, Takeshita exit) This is Tokyo's famous teen-fashion bazaar, where trendy duds sit alongside the trappings of various fashion subcultures (colourful tutus for the *decora;* Victorian dresses for the Gothic Lolitas). Be warned: this pedestrian alley is a pilgrimage site for teens from all over Japan, which means it can get packed.

YOYOGI-KŌEN PARK
Map p288 (代々木公園; JR Yamanote line to Harajuku, Omote-sandō exit) If it's a sunny and warm weekend afternoon you can count on there being a crowd lazing around the large grassy expanse that is Yoyogi-kōen. You can also usually find revellers and noisemakers of all stripes, from hula-hoopers to African drum circles to a group of retro greasers dancing around a boom box. It's an excellent place for a picnic and probably the only place in the city where you can reasonably toss a frisbee without fear of hitting someone. During the warmer months, festivals take place on the plaza across from the park.

OMOTE-SANDŌ STREET
Map p288 (表参道; Ginza line to Omote-sandō, exits A3 & B4, JR Yamanote line to Harajuku, Omote-sandō exit) This regal boulevard was originally designed as the official approach to Meiji-jingū. Now it's a fashionable strip lined with high-end boutiques. Those designer shops come in designer buildings, which means Omote-sandō is also one of the best places in the city to see contemporary architecture (p118).

UKIYO-E ŌTA MEMORIAL MUSEUM OF ART MUSEUM
Map p288 (浮世絵太田記念美術館; 3403-0880; www.ukiyoe-ota-muse.jp; 1-10-10 Jingūmae, Shibuya-ku; adult ¥700-1000, child free; 10.30am-5.30pm Tue-Sun, closed 27th to end of month; JR Yamanote line to Harajuku, Omote-sandō exit) This small, peaceful museum houses the excellent *ukiyo-e* (woodblock prints) collection of Ōta Seizo, the former head of the Toho Life Insurance Company. Seasonal, thematic exhibitions are easily digested in an hour and usually include a few works by masters such as Hokusai and Hiroshige.

The shop in the basement sells beautifully printed *tenugui* (traditional hand-dyed thin cotton towels).

DESIGN FESTA ART GALLERY
Map p288 (デザインフェスタ; 3479-1442; www.designfestagallery.com; 3-20-2 Jingūmae, Shibuya-ku; 11am-7pm; JR Yamanote line to Harajuku, Takeshita exit) FREE Design Festa has been a leader in Tokyo's DIY art scene for over a decade. The madhouse building itself is worth a visit; it's always evolving. Inside there are a dozen small galleries rented by the day. Design Festa also sponsors a twice-yearly exhibition (p25), actually Asia's largest art fair, at Tokyo Big Sight.

CAT STREET STREET
Map p288 (キャットストリート; JR Yamanote line to Harajuku, Omote-sandō exit) Had enough of crowded Harajuku? Exit, stage right, for Cat Street, a windy road lined with a mishmash of boutiques and more room to move. The retail architecture is also quite a spectacle, as this is where smaller brands strike their monuments to consumerism if they can't afford to do so on the main drag.

YOYOGI NATIONAL STADIUM ARCHITECTURE
Map p288 (国立代々木競技場; Kokuritsu Yoyogi Kyōgi-jō; 2-1-1 Jinnan, Shibuya-ku; JR Yamanote line to Harajuku, Omote-sandō exit) This early masterpiece by architect Tange Kenzō was built for the 1964 Olympics. The stadium, which looks vaguely like a samurai helmet, uses suspension bridge technology – rather than beams – to support the roof.

Aoyama

NEZU MUSEUM MUSEUM
Map p288 (根津美術館; 3400-2536; www.nezu-muse.or.jp; 6-5-1 Minami-Aoyama, Minato-ku; adult/child/student ¥1000/free/800, special exhibitions extra ¥200; 10am-5pm Tue-Sun; Ginza line to Omote-sandō, exit A5) Nezu Museum offers a striking blend of old and new: a renowned collection of Japanese, Chinese and Korean antiquities in a gallery space designed by contemporary architect

Kuma Kengo. Select items from the extensive collection are displayed in seasonal exhibitions.

Behind the galleries is a woodsy strolling garden laced with stone paths and studded with teahouses and sculptures. There's a glass-walled cafe (also designed by Kuma), too.

TARO OKAMOTO MEMORIAL MUSEUM MUSEUM

Map p288 (岡本太郎記念館; http://taro-okamoto.or.jp; 6-1-19 Minami-Aoyama, Minato-ku; adult/child ¥620/310; 10am-6pm Wed-Mon; S Ginza line to Omote-sandō exit A5) A painter and sculpture, Okamoto Tarō was Japan's most recognised artist from the post-WWII period, a rare avant-garde figure with mass appeal. His works are both playful and sinister, life-affirming and chaotic. This small museum, which includes a sculpture garden, is inside the artist's home.

Gaienmae

WATARI MUSEUM OF CONTEMPORARY ART MUSEUM

Map p288 (ワタリウム美術館; Watari-Um; 3402-3001; www.watarium.co.jp; 3-7-6 Jingūmae, Shibuya-ku; adult/student ¥1000/800; 11am-7pm Tue & Thu-Sun, to 9pm Wed; S Ginza line to Gaienmae, exit 3) This progressive and often provocative museum was built in 1990 to a design by Swiss architect Mario Botta. Exhibits range from retrospectives of established art-world figures (such as Yayoi Kusama and Nam June Paik) to graffiti and landscape artists – with some exhibitions spilling onto the surrounding streets.

There's an excellent art bookstore, **On Sundays** (Map p288; www.watarium.co.jp; 3-7-6 Jingūmae, Shibuya-ku; 11am-8pm; S Ginza line to Gaienmae, exit 3), in the basement.

EATING

Harajuku

★HARAJUKU GYŌZA-RŌ GYOZA ¥

Map p288 (原宿餃子楼; 6-4-2 Jingūmae, Shibuya-ku; 6 gyōza ¥290; 11.30am-4.30am; JR Yamanote line to Harajuku, Omote-sandō exit) *Gyōza* (dumplings) are the only thing on the menu here, but you won't hear any complaints from the regulars who queue up to get their fix. Have them *sui* (boiled) or *yaki* (pan-fried), with or without *niniku* (garlic) or *nira* (chives) – they're all delicious. Expect to wait on weekends.

LOCAL KNOWLEDGE

GOLDEN GINGKOS

In late fall, the trees along Ichō Namiki (Gingko Avenue) in Gaienmae turn a glorious shade of gold. Locals know to grab a seat at **Royal Garden Café** (ローヤルガーデンカフェ; Map p280; 5414-6170; www.royal-gardencafe.com; 2-1-19 Kita-Aoyama, Minato-ku; 11am-11pm; S Ginza line to Gaienmae, exit 4A) for the best views.

KYŪSYŪ JANGARA RĀMEN ¥

Map p288 (九州じゃんがら; 1-13-21 Jingūmae, Shibuya-ku; rāmen ¥630-1130; 10.45am-midnight Mon-Fri, from 10am Sat & Sun; JR Yamanote line to Harajuku, Omote-sandō exit) Come to this popular shop to sample the elegantly thin noodles, silky *chāshū* (roast pork) and righteous *karashi takana* (hot pickled greens) for which Kyūshū-style *rāmen* (noodles in broth) is famous. You can't go wrong with ordering *zembu-iri* (everything in).

SAKURA-TEI OKONOMIYAKI ¥

Map p288 (さくら亭; 3479-0039; www.sakuratei.co.jp; 3-20-1 Jingūmae, Shibuya-ku; okonomiyaki ¥950-1350; 11am-11pm; JR Yamanote line to Harajuku, Takeshita exit) Grill your own *okonomiyaki* (savoury pancakes) at this funky place inside the gallery Design Festa. During lunch (11am to 3pm) you can get 90 minutes of all-you-can-eat, plus a drink, for just ¥1060.

AGARU SAGARU NISHI IRU HIGASHI IRU KAISEKI ¥¥

Map p288 (上ル下ル西入ル東入ル; 3403-6968; www.agarusagaru.com; basement fl, 3-25-8 Jingūmae, Shibuya-ku; lunch/dinner course ¥1000/3990; noon-2pm, 5.30-11.30pm Mon-Sat; JR Yamanote line to Harajuku, Takeshita exit) In the evening, the young, friendly chefs here serve a procession of artful dishes that are Kyoto-inspired but tweaked for Tokyoites' been-there-done-that tastes. Also, it looks like a cave. Reservations are recommended for dinner.

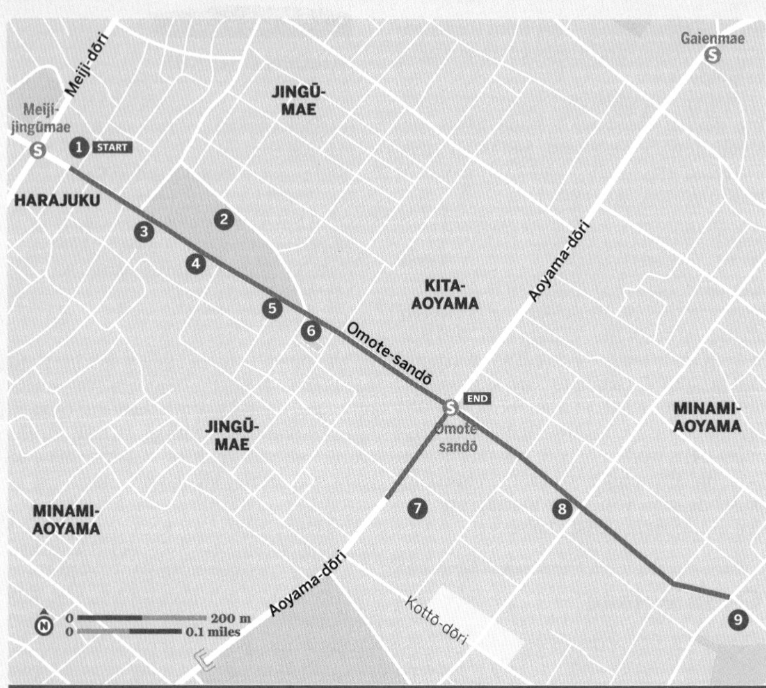

Neighbourhood Walk
Omote-sandō Architecture

START TOKYŪ PLAZA
END NEZU MUSEUM
LENGTH 1.5KM; 1½ HOURS

Omote-sandō is like a walk-through showroom of who's who of contemporary architecture. Here you'll see buildings from four of Japan's six Pritzker Prize winners: Maki Fumihiko, Andō Tadao, SANAA (Sejima Kazuyo and Nishizawa Ryūe) and Itō Toyō.

Start at the intersection of Omote-sandō and Meiji-dōri, with ❶ **Tokyū Plaza** (2012), a castle-like structure by up-and-coming architect Nakamura Hiroshi. The entrance is a dizzying hall of mirrors and there's a spacious roof garden on top.

Next up is something a little more understated: Tadao's deceptively deep ❷ **Omotesandō Hills** (2003). This high-end shopping mall spirals around a sunken central atrium.

Across the street, the ❸ **Dior Building** (2003), designed by SANAA, has a filmy exterior that seems to hang like a dress. Nearby, a glass cone marks the unlikely location of the ❹ **Japan Nursing Association** (2004), designed by Kurokawa Kishō.

Aoki Jun's ❺ **Louis Vuitton Building** (2002) has offset panels of tinted glass behind sheets of metal mesh that are meant to evoke a stack of trunks. There's an art gallery on the 7th floor.

Climb onto the elevated crosswalk to better admire Toyō's construction for ❻ **Tod's** (2004). The criss-crossing strips of concrete take their inspiration from the zelkova trees below; they're also structural.

Fumihiko's 1985 ❼ **Spiral Building** is worth a detour down Aoyama-dōri. The patchwork, uncentred design is a nod to Tokyo's own incongruous landscape. Inside, a spiralling passage doubles as an art gallery.

You can't miss the convex fishbowl that is the ❽ **Prada Aoyama Building** (2003). Created by Herzog and de Meuron, it kicked off the design race down Omote-sandō.

A thicket of bamboo marks the entrance to the traditional-meets-modern Kuma Kengō building that houses the excellent ❾ **Nezu Museum** (p116).

MOMINOKI HOUSE ORGANIC ¥¥

Map p288 (もみの木ハウス; http://omotesando.mominokihouse.net; 2-18-5 Jingūmae, Shibuya-ku; lunch/dinner set from ¥800/3200; ⏰11.30am-10pm; 🚭📝📋; 🚉JR Yamanote line to Harajuku, Takeshita exit) 🌿 Boho Tokyoites have been coming here for tasty macrobiotic fare since 1976. The casual, cosy dining room has seen some famous visitors too, such as Paul McCartney. Chef Yamada's menu is heavily vegetarian, but also includes free-range chicken and *Ezo shika* (Hokkaidō venison, ¥4800).

Aoyama & Gaienmae

★MAISEN TONKATSU ¥

Map p288 (まい泉; http://mai-sen.com; 4-8-5 Jingūmae, Shibuya-ku; lunch/dinner from ¥995/1680; ⏰11am-10pm; 🚭📋; Ⓢ Ginza line to Omote-sandō, exit A2) You could order something else (like fried shrimp), but everyone else will be ordering the famous *tonkatsu* (breaded, deep-fried pork cutlets). There are different grades of pork on the menu, including prized *kurobuta* (black pig), but even the cheapest is melt-in-your-mouth divine. The restaurant is housed in an old public bathhouse. A takeaway window serves delicious *tonkatsu sando* (sandwich).

PARIYA INTERNATIONAL ¥

Map p288 (パリヤ; 3-12-14 Kita-Aoyama, Minato-ku; meals from ¥1030; ⏰11.30am-11pm; 🚭📝📋; Ⓢ Ginza line to Omote-sandō, exit B2) Pariya is the local cafeteria for the fashionable set. Grab a tray and choose one main, one salad and one side dish (or two salads and a side for veggies). It's not cheap slop though; typical dishes include shrimp croquettes and curried potato salad. There are colourful cupcakes and gelato for dessert.

WORLD BREAKFAST ALLDAY INTERNATIONAL ¥

Map p288 (http://world-breakfast-allday.com; 3-1-23 Jingūmae, Shibuya-ku; meals ¥1000-1600; ⏰7.30am-9pm; 📝; Ⓢ Ginza line to Gaienmae, exit 3) Each month this restaurant hones in on a particular country's breakfast tradition, from Indian *idli* (fermented rice and lentil cakes) to Brazilian *pao de queijo* (cheese buns). Classic English breakfasts and muesli are served continuously. With one long table and an open kitchen, it feels like someone's house.

LOCAL KNOWLEDGE

WEEKEND MARKETS

On weekends a **farmers' market** (Map p288; www.farmersmarkets.jp; ⏰10am-4pm Sat & Sun; Ⓢ Ginza line to Omote-sandō, exit B2), with colourful produce and food trucks, sets up on the plaza in front of the United Nations University on Aoyama-dōri. On Saturdays, a small antique market takes place, too.

KINOKUNIYA INTERNATIONAL SUPERMARKET SUPERMARKET ¥

Map p288 (紀ノ国屋 インターナショナル; www.super-kinokuniya.jp/store/international; basement fl, AO bldg, 3-11-7 Kita-Aoyama, Minato-ku; ⏰9.30am-9pm; 📝; Ⓢ Ginza line to Omote-sandō, exit B2) Kinokuniya carries expat lifesavers such as Marmite and peanut butter, crusty, wholegrain bread and cheeses galore (at a price of course).

★YANMO SEAFOOD ¥¥¥

Map p288 (やんも; www.yanmo.co.jp/aoyama/index.html; basement fl, T Place bldg, 5-5-25 Minami-Aoyama, Minato-ku; lunch/dinner course from ¥1100/7560; ⏰11.30am-2pm, 6-10.30pm Mon-Sat; 🚭; Ⓢ Ginza line to Omote-sandō, exit A5) Fresh caught seafood from the nearby Izu Peninsula is the speciality at this upscale, yet unpretentious restaurant. If you're looking to splash out on a seafood dinner this is a great place to do so. The reasonably priced courses include sashimi, steamed and grilled fish. Lunch is a bargain, but you might have to queue. Reservations are essential for dinner.

DRINKING & NIGHTLIFE

★TWO ROOMS BAR

Map p288 (トゥールームス; ☎3498-0002; www.tworooms.jp; 5th fl, AO bldg, 3-11-7 Kita-Aoyama, Minato-ku; ⏰11.30am-2am Mon-Sat, to 10pm Sun; Ⓢ Ginza line to Omote-sandō, exit B2) Expect a crowd dressed like they don't care that wine by the glass starts at ¥1500. You can eat here too, but the real scene is at night by the bar. Call ahead (staff speak English) on Friday or Saturday night to reserve a table on the terrace, which has sweeping views towards the Shinjuku skyline.

1

LAURIE NOBLE / GETTY IMAGES ©

2

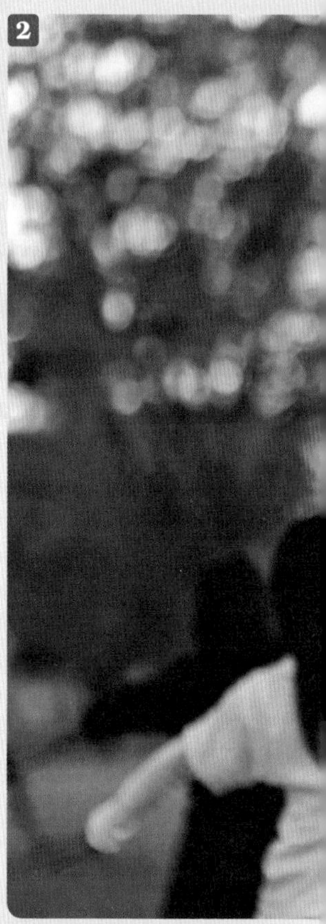

4

ALFIE GOODRICH – JAPANORAMA / GETTY IMAGES ©

1. Yoyogi-kōen (p116)
Rockabilly guys strut their stuff in Harajuku's popular park.

2. Yoyogi-kōen (p116)
Fan dancers practise their graceful moves.

3. Omote-sandō (p118)
This boulevard linking Harajuku and Aoyama is home to designer shops and contemporary architecture.

4. Yoyogi National Stadium (p116)
Built for the 1964 Olympics, the innovative design by Tange Kenzō uses suspension-bridge technology to support the roof.

MAREMAGNUM / GETTY IMAGES ©

LOCAL KNOWLEDGE

SUMMER BEER GARDENS

Summer beer gardens are a Tokyo tradition (typically running late May to early September). Two of the city's best are within Meiji-jingū Gaien (the 'Outer Garden' of Meiji-jingū). **Mori-no Beer Garden** (森のビアガーデン; Map p280; www.rkfs.co.jp/brand/beer_garden_detail.html; 1-7-5 Kita-Aoyama, Minato-ku; men/women ¥4000/3800; ⊙5-10pm Mon-Fri, 3-10pm Sat & Sun; 🅁JR Sōbu line to Shinanomachi) hosts up to 1000 revellers for all-you-can-eat-and-drink spreads of beer and barbecue under a century-old tree.

At the more patrician **Sekirei** (鶺鴒; Map p280; ☎3746-7723; www.meijikinenkan.gr.jp/restaurant/company/sekirei; Meiji-kinenkan, 2-2-23 Moto-Akasaka, Minato-ku; beer from ¥800; ⊙4.30-10.30pm Mon-Sat, 5.30-10.30pm Sun; 🅁JR Sōbu line to Shinanomachi), you can quaff beer on the neatly clipped lawn of the stately Meiji Kinenkan; traditional Japanese dance is performed nightly around 8pm.

HARAJUKU TAPROOM PUB

Map p288 (原宿タップルーム; http://bairdbeer.com/en/taproom; 2nd fl, 1-20-13 Jingūmae, Shibuya-ku; ⊙5pm-midnight Mon-Fri, noon-midnight Sat & Sun; 🚭; 🅁JR Yamanote line to Harajuku, Takeshita exit) Baird's Brewery is one of Japan's most successful and consistently good craft breweries. This is one of their two Tokyo outposts, where you can sample more than a dozen of their beers on tap; try the top-selling Rising Sun Pale Ale. Japanese pub-style food is served as well.

OMOTESANDO KOFFEE CAFE

Map p288 (http://ooo-koffee.com; 4-15-3 Jingūmae, Shibuya-ku; espresso ¥250; ⊙10am-7pm; Ⓢ Ginza line to Omote-sandō, exit A2) Tokyo's most *oshare* (stylish) coffee stand is a minimalist cube set up inside a half-century-old traditional house. Be prepared to circle the block trying to find it, but know that an immaculate macchiato and a seat in the garden await you.

OATH BAR

(http://bar-oath.com; 4-5-9 Shibuya, Shibuya-ku; ⊙9pm-5am Mon-Thu, to 8am Fri & Sat, 5-11pm Sun; Ⓢ Ginza line to Omote-sandō, exit B1) A tiny space along a somewhat forlorn strip of highway, Oath is a favourite after-hours destination for clubbers – helped no doubt by the ¥500 drinks and lack of cover charge. Underground DJs spin here sometimes, too.

A TO Z CAFE CAFE

Map p288 (エートゥーゼットカフェ; 5th fl, 5-8-3 Minami-Aoyama, Minato-ku; ⊙11.30am-11.30pm; Ⓢ Ginza line to Omote-sandō, exit B3) Artist Yoshitomo Nara teamed up with design firm Graf to create this spacious and only slightly off-kilter cafe. Along with wooden schoolhouse chairs, whitewashed walls and a small cottage, you can find a few scattered examples of Nara's work.

MONTOAK CAFE

Map p288 (モントーク; 6-1-9 Jingūmae, Shibuya-ku; ⊙11am-3am; 🚭; 🅁JR Yamanote line to Harajuku, Omote-sandō exit) This smoky glass cube is a calm, dimly lit retreat from the busy streets. It's perfect for holing up with a pot of tea or carafe of wine and watching the crowds go by. Or, if the weather is nice, score a seat on the terrace.

☆ ENTERTAINMENT

NATIONAL NŌ THEATRE TRADITIONAL THEATRE

(国立能楽堂; Kokuritsu Nō-gakudō; ☎3423-1331; www.ntj.jac.go.jp/english; 4-18-1 Sendagaya, Shibuya-ku; tickets from ¥2600; 🅁JR Sōbu line to Sendagaya) The traditional music, poetry and dances that *nō* (stylised Japanese dance-drama) is famous for unfold here on an elegant cypress stage. Each seat has a small screen that can display an English translation of the dialogue. Shows take place only a few times a month.

The theatre is 400m from Sendagaya Station; from the exit, walk right along the main road and turn left at the traffic light.

BLUE NOTE TOKYO JAZZ

Map p288 (ブルーノート東京; www.bluenote.co.jp; 6-3-16 Minami-Aoyama, Minato-ku; tickets from ¥6800; ⊙5.30pm-1am Mon-Sat, 5pm-12.30am Sun; Ⓢ Ginza line to Omote-sandō, exit B3) The serious cognoscenti roll up to this, Tokyo's prime jazz spot, to take in the likes of Maceo Parker, Herbie Hancock and Doctor John. Just like its sister acts in New York and Milan, the digs here are classily decorated with dark wood and deep velvet.

CROCODILE LIVE MUSIC, COMEDY

Map p288 (クロコダイル; www.crocodile-live.jp; basement fl, 6-18-8 Jingūmae, Shibuya-ku; S Chiyoda line to Meiji-jingūmae, exit 1) Decked out in neon, mirrors and chrome, Crocodile is a classic dive. Live music of all sorts plays here nightly, but the most popular event is the English comedy night put on by Tokyo Comedy Store on the last Friday of the month (admission ¥1500). Advanced bookings are recommended; see www.tokyocomedy.com/improvazilla_main_stage_show.

SHOPPING

Harajuku

★LAFORET FASHION

Map p288 (ラフォーレ; www.laforet.ne.jp; 1-11-6 Jingūmae, Shibuya-ku; 11am-8pm; JR Yamanote line to Harajuku, Omote-sandō exit) Laforet has been a beacon of cutting-edge Harajuku style for decades. Don't let the Topshop on the ground floor fool you; lots of quirky, cult favourite brands still cut their teeth here.

★MUSUBI SPECIALITY SHOP

Map p288 (むす美; http://kyoto-musubi.com; 2-31-8 Jingūmae, Shibuya-ku; 11am-7pm Thu-Tue; JR Yamanote line to Harajuku, Takeshita exit) *Furoshiki* are versatile squares of cloth that can be folded and knotted to make shopping bags and gift wrap. This shop sells pretty ones in both traditional and contemporary patterns. There is usually an English-speaking clerk who can show you how to tie them, or pick up one of the English-language books sold here.

KIDDYLAND TOYS

Map p288 (キデイランド; www.kiddyland.co.jp/en/index.html; 6-1-9 Jingūmae, Shibuya-ku; 10am-9pm; JR Yamanote line to Harajuku, Omote-sandō exit) This multistorey toy emporium is packed to the rafters with character goods. It's not just for kids either; you'll spot plenty of adults on a nostalgia trip down the Hello Kitty aisle.

TOKYO'S TOKYO SOUVENIRS

Map p288 (トーキョーズトーキョー; 5th fl, Tōkyū Plaza, 4-30-3 Jingūmae, Shibuya-ku; 11am-9pm; JR Yamanote line to Harajuku, Omote-sandō exit) Tokyo's Tokyo is betting that you'd love to find something slightly wacky, pop-culture-inflected and 'only in Tokyo' to bring home with you. It's stocked with accessories from local fashion designers, surprisingly useful gadgets and other fun trinkets.

6% DOKI DOKI FASHION, ACCESSORIES

Map p288 (ロクパーセントドキドキ; www.dokidoki6.com; 2nd fl, 4-28-16 Jingūmae, Shibuya-ku; noon-8pm; JR Yamanote line to Harajuku, Omote-sandō exit) Tucked away on an Ura-Hara backstreet, this bubblegum-pink store sells acid-bright accessories that are part raver, part schoolgirl (and 100% Harajuku).

DAISO VARIETY

Map p288 (ダイソー; 1-19-24 Jingūmae, Shibuya-ku; 10am-9pm; JR Yamanote line to Harajuku, Takeshita exit) One of the city's best ¥100 shops, right on Takeshita-dōri, Daiso carries everything you need for a *kawaii* (cute) makeover: fake lashes, feathers and bows (plus useful things such as towels and spoons). It's also great for souvenir hunting.

DOG FASHION, VINTAGE

Map p288 (ドッグ; www.dog-hjk.com/index.html; basement fl, 3-23-3 Jingūmae, Shibuya-ku; noon-8pm; JR Yamanote line to Harajuku, Takeshita exit) Club kids and stylists love the showpiece items at Dog, which is decorated to look like a derelict carnival funhouse. Look for graffiti over the entrance.

ORIENTAL BAZAAR SOUVENIRS

Map p288 (オリエンタルバザー; www.orientalbazaar.co.jp; 5-9-13 Jingūmae, Shibuya-ku; 10am-6pm Mon-Wed & Fri, to 7pm Sat & Sun;

RECYCLE SHOPS

Take Tokyoites love of fashion, pair it with impossibly small closets and what do you get? Possibly the world's best consignment shops, called *risaikuru shoppu* (recycle shop) in Japanese. One to check out is **RagTag** (ラグタグ; Map p288; 6-14-2 Jingūmae, Shibuya-ku; 11am-8pm; JR Yamanote line to Harajuku, Omote-Sandō exit), stocked with labels locals love, such as Comme des Garcons and Vivienne Westwood.

JR Yamanote line to Harajuku, Omote-sandō exit) Oriental Bazaar stocks a wide selection of souvenirs at very reasonable prices. Items to be found here include fans, pottery, *yukata* (light cotton kimonos) and T-shirts, some made in Japan, but others not (read the labels).

CONDOMANIA SPECIALITY SHOP

Map p288 (コンドマニア; 6-30-1 Jingūmae, Shibuya-ku; 11am-9.30pm; JR Yamanote line to Harajuku, Omote-sandō exit) This irreverent outpost must be Tokyo's cheekiest rendezvous point. Popular items include *omamori* (traditional good-luck charms) with condoms tucked inside.

CHICAGO THRIFT STORE VINTAGE

Map p288 (シカゴ; 6-31-21 Jingūmae, Shibuya-ku; 10am-8pm; JR Yamanote line to Harajuku, Omote-sandō exit) Chicago is crammed with all sorts of vintage clothing, but best of all is the extensive collection of used kimonos and *yukata*, priced very low, in the back.

Aoyama

★**SOU-SOU** FASHION

Map p288 (そうそう; 3407-7877; http://sousounetshop.jp; 5-3-10 Minami-Aoyama, Minato-ku; 11am-8pm; S Ginza line to Omote-sandō, exit A5) Sou-Sou gives traditional Japanese clothing items – such as *tabi* (split-toed socks) and *haori* (coats with kimono-like sleeves) – a contemporary spin. It is best known for producing the steel-toed, rubber-soled *jika-tabi* shoes worn by Japanese construction workers in fun, playful designs.

BEDROCK FASHION

Map p288 (ベッドロック; 4-12-10 Jingūmae, Shibuya-ku; 11am-9pm, to 8pm Sun; S Ginza line to Omote-sandō, exit A2) Walking into Bedrock is like stepping into Keith Richards' boudoir, or the costume closet for Pirates of the Caribbean. Enter through a secret staircase in the back of the Forbidden Fruit juice bar.

PASS THE BATON VINTAGE

Map p288 (パスザバトン; www.pass-the-baton.com; 4-12-10 Jingūmae, Shibuya-ku; 11am-9pm Mon-Sat, to 8pm Sun; S Ginza line to Omote-sandō, exit A3) There are all sorts of treasures to be found at this consignment shop, from 1970s designer duds to delicate teacups, personal castaways to dead stock from long defunct retailers. It's in the basement of Omotesandō Hills, but you'll need to enter from a separate street entrance on Omote-sandō.

COMME DES GARÇONS FASHION

Map p288 (コム・デ・ギャルソン; www.comme-des-garcons.com; 5-2-1 Minami-Aoyama, Minato-ku; 11am-8pm; S Ginza line to Omote-sandō, exit A5) Designer Kawakubo Rei threw a wrench in the fashion machine in the early '80s with her dark, asymmetrical designs. That her work doesn't appear as shocking today as it once did speaks volumes for her far-reaching success. This eccentric, vaguely disorienting architectural creation is her brand's flagship store.

GALLERY KAWANO KIMONO

Map p288 (ギャラリー川野; www.gallery-kawano.com; 4-4-9 Jingūmae, Shibuya-ku; 11am-6pm; Ginza line to Omote-sandō, exit A2) Gallery Kawano has a good selection of vintage kimonos in decent shape, priced reasonably (about ¥5000 to ¥15,000). The staff will help you try one on and pick out a matching *obi* (sash); they're less excited about helping customers who try things on but don't intend to buy.

SPORTS & ACTIVITIES

JINGŪ BASEBALL STADIUM BASEBALL

Map p288 (神宮球場; Jingū Kyūjo; 3404-8999; www.jingu-stadium.com; 3-1 Kasumigaoka-machi, Shinjuku-ku; tickets ¥1600-4600; S Ginza line to Gaienmae, exit 3) Jingū Baseball Stadium, built in 1926, is home to the Yakult Swallows, Tokyo's number-two team (but number one when it comes to fan loyalty). Pick up tickets from the booth in front of the stadium; same-day outfield tickets cost just ¥1600 (¥500 for children) and are usually available. Night games start at 6pm; weekend games start around 2pm.

OHARA SCHOOL OF IKEBANA IKEBANA

Map p288 (小原流いけばな; 5774-5097; www.ohararyu.or.jp; 5-7-17 Minami-Aoyama, Minato-ku; per class ¥4000; S Ginza line to Omote-sandō, exit B1) Every Thursday, from 10.30am to 12.30pm, this well-regarded ikebana school teaches introductory flower-arrangement classes in English. Sign up via email by 3pm the day before.

Shinjuku & West Tokyo

NISHI-SHINJUKU | SHINJUKU | OGIKUBŌ | KICHIJŌJI | MITAKA

Neighbourhood Top Five

❶ Exploring the crackling neon canyons of **Shinjuku** (p134). From the narrow lanes of seedy Kabukichō to the main boulevards, the light show here and the sheer volume of dining, drinking and entertainment options are something to behold.

❷ Looking out over the city from the observatory atop the **Tokyo Metropolitan Government Offices** (p127).

❸ Laying on the lawn at **Shinjuku-gyoen** (p127) and gazing up at the skyscrapers.

❹ Immersing yourself in the imagination of animator Hayao Miyazaki at the **Ghibli Museum** (p128) in Mitaka.

❺ Getting cosy in the bars of **Golden Gai** (p133), Shinjuku's literary and artistic hang-out.

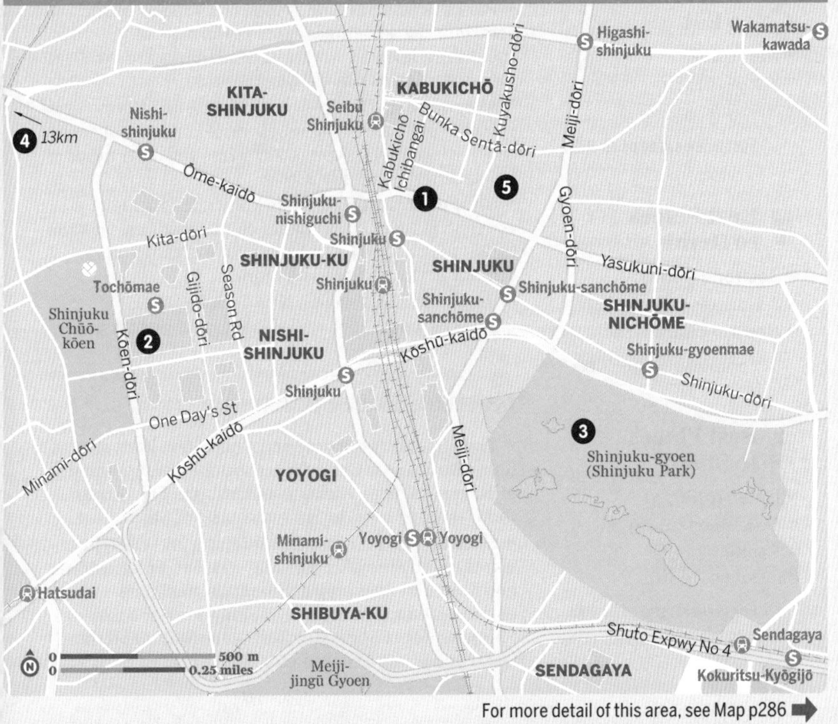

For more detail of this area, see Map p286

Lonely Planet's Top Tip

Shinjuku is nothing if not intimidating. Should you want to grab a quick bite to eat – without having to brave the crowded streets – head to one of the food courts on the top floors of the shopping centres inside Shinjuku Station, such as **Lumine** (ルミネ; Map p286; www.lumine.ne.jp/shinjuku; Shinjuku Station, Shinjuku-ku; ⌚11am-11pm; 🚇JR Yamanote line to Shinjuku, south exit) or **Mylord** (ミロード; Map p286; www.shinjuku-mylord.com; Shinjuku Station, Shinjuku-ku; ⌚11am-11pm; 🚇JR Yamanote line to Shinjuku, south exit). Both have more than a dozen reasonably priced options with plastic food models out the front.

Best Places to Eat

- Nagi (p132)
- Kozue (p132)
- Nakajima (p132)

For reviews, see p129

Best Places to Drink

- Zoetrope (p133)
- Advocates Café (p133)
- New York Bar (p135)

For reviews, see p133 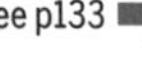

Best Places to Shop

- Isetan (p136)
- Disk Union (p136)
- RanKing RanQueen (p136)

For reviews, see p136

Explore Shinjuku & West Tokyo

Shinjuku is a whole city within the city. Its breadth and scale are simply awesome – over three million people a day pass through the station alone. To the west of the station is Nishi-Shinjuku (West Shinjuku), a planned district of soaring skyscrapers. The Tokyo Metropolitan Government offices are here, along with many company headquarters; it's full of black-suited office workers.

East of the train station is one huge entertainment district. Commuters who pass through Shinjuku on their way home stop off for something to eat and drink, and sometimes stay out until the trains start running the next morning. Tipplers are spoiled for choice here: Shinjuku is that rare Tokyo neighbourhood that truly has something for everyone. It's also home to the nation's largest gay district, Shinjuku-nichōme.

The JR Chūō line runs west of Shinjuku, to commuter towns that gradually grow more suburban the further out you go. Mitaka, a 20-minute train ride from Shinjuku, is home to the magical Ghibli Museum. Neighbouring Kichijoji has been voted the best place to live in Tokyo for 10 years running; with a fantastic park, Inokashira-kōen, plenty of shops and a laid-back vibe, it's easy to see why.

Local Life

- **Parks** Grassy Shinjuku-gyoen is a popular picnic spot; you can sometimes catch performers in Inokashira-kōen on weekends. Both parks are excellent for *hanami* (blossom viewing).
- **Alleyway eats** Omoide-yokochō (p129) and Harmonica-yokochō (p129) are two atmospheric old markets where you can down *yakitori* (skewers of chicken, and other meats or vegetables) and beer like a local.
- **Shopping** Kōenji (p128) is known for its high concentration of secondhand clothing stores; Nakano (p128) is paradise for collectors of old cameras, vintage action figures and more.
- **Romance** The sky-high New York Bar (p135) is famous as a date spot, and also for marriage proposals.

Getting There & Away

- **Train** The JR Yamanote and Chūō-Sōbu lines stop at Shinjuku Station; Chūō-Sōbu continues west, stopping at Nakano, Kōenji, Kichijōji and Mitaka. The private Keio New line stops at Hatsudai, west of Shinjuku.
- **Subway** The Marunouchi, Shinjuku and Ōedo lines run through Shinjuku. The Marunouchi, Fukutoshin and Shinjuku lines stop at Shinjuku-sanchōme, convenient for the east side of Shinjuku. For Nishi-Shinjuku (West Shinjuku), Tochōmae Station on the Ōedo line is more convenient.

SIGHTS

Nishi-Shinjuku

TOKYO METROPOLITAN GOVERNMENT OFFICES — BUILDING

Map p286 (東京都庁; Tokyo Tochō; www.metro.tokyo.jp/ENGLISH/TMG/observat.htm; 2-8-1 Nishi-Shinjuku, Shinjuku-ku; observatories 9.30am-11pm; S Ōedo line to Tochōmae, exit A4) FREE Tokyo's seat of power, designed by Tange Kenzō, looms large and looks somewhat like a pixelated cathedral. Take an elevator from the ground floor of Building 1 to one of the twin 202m-high observatories for panoramic views over the never-ending cityscape (the views are virtually the same from either tower). On a clear day, look west for a glimpse of Mt Fuji.

JAPANESE SWORD MUSEUM — MUSEUM

(刀剣博物館; www.touken.or.jp; 4-25-10 Yoyogi, Shibuya-ku; adult/child/student ¥600/free/300; 9am-4.30pm Tue-Sun; Keiō New line to Hatsudai, east exit) In 1948, after American forces returned the *katana* (Japanese swords) they'd confiscated during the postwar occupation, the national Ministry of Education established a society, and this museum, to preserve the feudal art of Japanese swordmaking. There are dozens of swords on display here, with English explanations throughout.

The museum's location, in a residential neighbourhood, is not obvious. Head down Kōshū-kaidō to the Park Hyatt and make a left, then the second right under the highway, followed by another quick right and left in succession. There's a map on the website.

NTT INTERCOMMUNICATION CENTRE — MUSEUM

(ICC; www.ntticc.or.jp; 4th fl, Tokyo Opera City, 3-20-2 Nishi-Shinjuku, Shinjuku-ku; special exhibitions extra; 11am-6pm Tue-Sun; Keiō New line to Hatsudai) FREE The ICC shows challenging, conceptual works that explore the intersection between art and technology. Make sure to check out the installation in the museum's eerie, echo-free chamber (reservation ticket necessary). Every summer the museum does a program for kids with lots of hands-on, sensory stuff.

There is also a superlative video library, Hive, which you can access from computer terminals in the museum.

LOCAL KNOWLEDGE

SHINJUKU I-LAND ART

An otherwise ordinary office complex, **Shinjuku I-Land** (新宿アイランド; Map p286; 6-5-1 Nishi-Shinjuku, Shinjuku-ku; S Marunouchi line to Nishi-Shinjuku) is home to more than a dozen public artworks, including one of Robert Indiana's *Love* sculptures and two *Tokyo Brushstroke* sculptures by Roy Liechtenstein. The courtyard, with stonework by Giulio Paolini and a dozen restaurants, makes for an attractive lunch or coffee stop.

TOKYO OPERA CITY ART GALLERY — ARTS CENTRE

(www.operacity.jp/ag; 3rd fl, Tokyo Opera City, 3-20-2 Nishi-Shinjuku, Shinjuku-ku; adult/student ¥1000/800; 11am-7pm Tue-Thu & Sun, to 8pm Fri & Sat; Keiō New line to Hatsudai) This contemporary arts centre puts on a variety of exhibitions, including solo shows of current Japanese artists and retrospectives of major modern architects.

Shinjuku

SHINJUKU-GYOEN — PARK

Map p286 (新宿御苑; 3350-0151; www.env.go.jp/garden/shinjukugyoen; 11 Naito-chō, Shinjuku-ku; adult/child ¥200/50; 9am-4.30pm Tue-Sun; S Marunouchi line to Shinjuku-gyoenmae, exit 1) Though Shinjuku-gyoen was designed as an imperial retreat (completed 1906), it's now definitively a park for everyone. The wide lawns make it a favourite for urbanites in need of a quick escape from the hurly-burly of city life. Don't miss the recently renovated greenhouse, with its giant lily pads and perfectly formed orchids, and the cherry blossoms in spring.

KABUKICHŌ — NEIGHBOURHOOD

Map p286 (歌舞伎町; JR Yamanote line to Shinjuku, east exit) Tokyo's most notorious red-light district, which covers several blocks north of Yasukuni-dōri, was famously named for a kabuki theatre that was never built. Instead you'll find an urban theatre of a different sort playing out in the neighbourhood's soaplands (bathhouses just shy of antiprostitution

WORTH A DETOUR

NAKANO & KŌENJI

Nakano (中野) and Kōenji (高円寺) are two neighbourhoods on the Chūō line (just one and two stops, respectively, from Shinjuku) with heaps of character.

Nakano is a big draw for *otaku* (anime and manga fans), who prefer the neighbourhood's underground vibe to Akihabara's brash, commercial one. The scene is centred around **Nakano Broadway** (中野ブロードウェイ; www.nbw.jp; 5-25-15 Nakano, Nakano-ku; JR Chūō line to Nakano, north exit), a vintage 1960s shopping centre (at the end of the equally retro Nakano Sun Mall covered arcade). The original Mandarake is here, but so are dozens of other shops aimed at collectors of all sorts, from vintage toys to antique watches to darts.

Nakano Broadway is also the unlikely location of a string of galleries – called **Hidari Zingaro**, **Pixiv Zingaro** and **Oz Zingaro** – from hugely successful contemporary artist Murakami Takashi. There's a cafe too, **Bar Zingaro** (http://bar-zingaro.jp; 2nd fl, Nakano Broadway, Nakano-ku; coffee ¥520; 11am-9pm Sun-Thu, to 11pm Fri & Sat), decorated with some of the artist's signature smiling flowers.

Kōenji is known for its irreverent, creative spirit, which shows up in the neighbourhood's many quirky clothing shops and grungy live-music halls. One must-see is the **Kita-Kore Building** (キタコレビル; 3-4-11 Kōenji-kita, Suginami-ku; varies; JR Chūō line to Kōenji, north exit), a dilapidated shack of a building housing a handful of outré shops. It's not hard to imagine that Lady Gaga shops there. Look for it on Naka-dōri, the narrow street to the left of the train station's north exit. Down the 'Pal' covered shopping arcade is vintage shop **Spank** (http://spankworld.jp; 4-24-7 Kita-Kōenji, Suginami-ku; 1-8pm; JR Chūō line to Kōenji, south exit), responsible for a sparkly '80s throwback look called 'Fairy-kei' that's popular now.

Finish the day with a meal or drink under the Chūō-line tracks in Kōenji, where polished wine bars sit next to *yakitori* (skewers of chicken, and other meats or vegetables) dives. Stick around for a show at **Ni Man Den Atsu** (二万電圧; www.den-atsu.com; Basement, 1-7-23 Kōenji-Minami, Suginami-ku; S Marunouchi line to Higashi-Kōenji, exit 3), Kōenji's notorious punk venue.

laws), peep shows, cabarets, love hotels and fetish bars. It's generally safe to walk through, though men and women both may attract unwanted attention – best not to go alone.

HANAZONO-JINJA SHINTO SHRINE

Map p286 (花園神社; 5-17 Shinjuku, Shinjuku-ku; 24hr; S Marunouchi line to Shinjuku-sanchōme, exits B10 & E2) During the day merchants from nearby Kabukichō come to this Shintō shrine to pray for the solvency of their business ventures. At night, despite signs asking revellers to refrain, drinking and merrymaking carries over from the nearby bars onto the stairs here.

Ogikubō

SUGINAMI ANIMATION MUSEUM MUSEUM

(杉並アニメーションミュージアム; http://sam.or.jp; 3-29-5 Kami-Ogi, Suginami-ku; 10am-6pm Tue-Sun; JR Chūō line to Ogikubō, north exit) FREE This small museum, designed mostly for kids, covers the history of animation in Japan and its digital future. Temporary exhibits sometimes show cell art from major animators; there are also light tables (where you can practise drawing) and a manga and anime library.

Take any bus from stand number 0 or 1 outside the north exit of Ogikubō Station to Ogikubō Keisastsusho-mae (five minutes, ¥210). Double back to the traffic light and turn right.

Kichijōji & Mitaka

★**GHIBLI MUSEUM** MUSEUM

(ジブリ美術館; www.ghibli-museum.jp; 1-1-83 Shimo-Renjaku, Mitaka-shi; adult ¥1000, child ¥100-700; 10am-6pm Wed-Mon; JR Chūō line to Mitaka, south exit) Master animator Hayao Miyazaki, whose Studio Ghibli produced *Princess Mononoke* and *Spirited Away,* designed this museum. Fans will enjoy the original sketches; kids, even if they're not familiar with the movies, will fall in love with the fairy-tale atmosphere (and the big cat bus). Don't miss the original 20-minute animated short playing on the 1st floor.

Tickets must be purchased in advance, and you must choose the exact time and date you plan to visit.

Purchase tickets online through a travel agent before you arrive in Japan or from a kiosk at any Lawson convenience store in Tokyo (the trickier option, as it will require some Japanese-language ability to navigate the ticket machine). Both options are explained in detail on the website, where you will also find a useful map.

Getting to Ghibli (which is pronounced 'jiburi') is all part of the adventure. A minibus (round trip/one way ¥320/210) leaves for the museum approximately every 20 minutes from Mitaka Station (bus stop number 9). Alternatively, you can walk there by following the canal and turning right when you reach Inokashira-kōen (which will take about 15 minutes). The museum is on the western edge of Inokashira-kōen, so you can also walk there through the park from Kichijōji Station in about 30 minutes.

INOKASHIRA-KŌEN PARK

(井の頭公園; www.kensetsu.metro.tokyo.jp/seibuk/inokashira/index.html; 1-18-31 Goten-yama, Musashino-shi; JR Chūō line to Kichijōji, Kōen exit) One of Tokyo's best parks, Inokashira-kōen has a big pond in the middle with rowboats and swan-shaped pedal boats for rent. There's also an island with an ancient shrine to the sea goddess Benzaiten. Walk straight from the Kōen exit of Kichijōji Station, cross at the light and veer right at Marui ('0101') department store; the park is at the end of the lane. Along the way, you'll pass shops selling takeaway items such as *yakitori* and hot dogs.

HARMONICA-YOKOCHŌ MARKET

(ハーモニカ横丁; http://hamoyoko.com; 1-2 Kichijōji-Honchō, Musashino-shi; JR Chūō line to Kichijōji, north exit) With low ceilings and red paper *chōchin* (lanterns), this old covered market has a definite vintage feel. Some of the vendors – the fishmongers, for example – are equally old school, but there are some trendy boutiques and bars here too. There's a morning market every third Sunday (7am to 10am). Look for the entrance across the street from Kichijōji Station's north exit.

EATING

Nishi-Shinjuku

OMOIDE-YOKOCHŌ YAKITORI $

Map p286 (思い出横丁; Nishi-Shinjuku 1-chōme, Shinjuku-ku; skewers from ¥100; noon-midnight, hours vary by shop; JR Yamanote line to Shinjuku, west exit) Since the postwar days, smoke has been billowing night and day from the *yakitori* stalls that line this alley by the train tracks, literally translated as 'Memory Lane' (and less politely known as Shonben-yokochō, or 'Piss Alley'). Several stalls have English menus.

NUMAZUKŌ SUSHI $

Map p286 (沼津港; Basement, My Bldg, 1-10-1 Nishi-Shinjuku, Shinjuku-ku; plates ¥90-550; 11am-10.30pm; JR Yamanote line to Shinjuku, west exit) Shinjuku's best *kaiten-sushi* (conveyor-belt sushi) restaurant has a long, snaking counter and a huge menu; it's pricier than most but the quality is worth it. It's below the Shinjuku Highway Bus Terminal, two basement floors down. You can also get there via an underground passage from Shinjuku Station; look for the fish-shaped sign over the door.

WORTH A DETOUR

EDO-TOKYO OPEN AIR ARCHITECTURE MUSEUM

The fantastic, yet little-known **Edo-Tokyo Open Air Architecture Museum** (江戸東京たてもの園; www.tatemonoen.jp/english; 3-7-1 Sakura-chō, Koganei-shi; adult/child ¥400/free; 9.30am-5.30pm Tue-Sun Apr-Sep, to 4.30pm Oct-Mar; JR Chūō line to Musashi-Koganei) has a collection of historic buildings rescued from Tokyo's modernising zeal. Among them are an Edo-era farmhouse, a modernist villa and a whole strip of early-20th-century shops, all of which you can enter. From the north exit of Musashi-Koganei Station, take a number 2 or 3 bus for Koganei-koen Nishi-guchi; from the bus stop it's a short walk through Koganei park to the museum.

LONELY PLANET / GETTY IMAGES ©

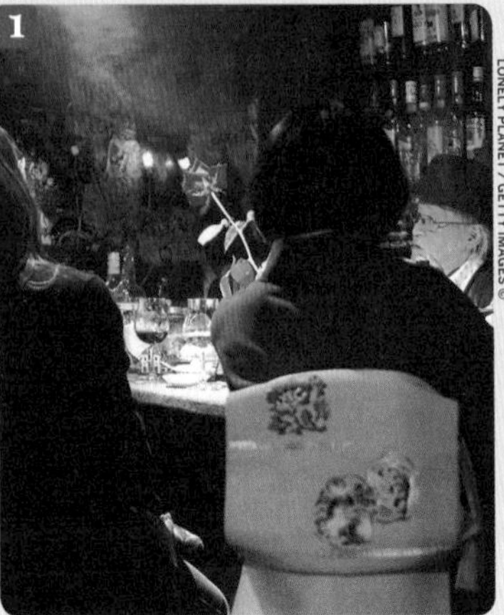

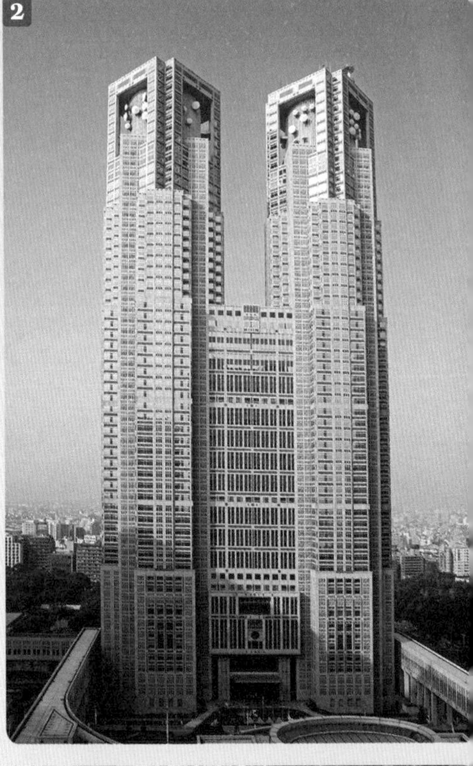

1. Golden Gai (p133)
Customers enjoy a drink in this unique quarter of Tokyo.

2. Tokyo Metropolitan Government offices (p127)
The city's seat of power looms large over the skyline.

3. Omoide-yokochō (p129)
Dine on *yakitori* with the locals in this atmospheric alley.

4. Shinjuku-gyoen (p127)
Autumn foliage lights up this former imperial retreat.

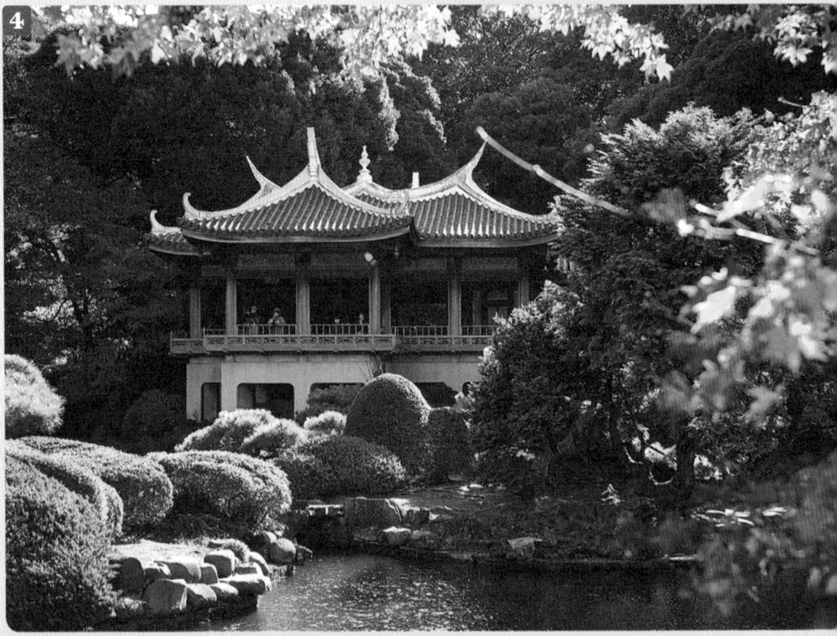

LAURIE NOBLE / GETTY IMAGES ©

LOCAL KNOWLEDGE

THE WAY OF RĀMEN

Chef Ivan Orkin, owner of **Ivan's Rāmen** (www.ivanramen.com; 3-24-7 Minami-Karasuyama, Setagaya-ku; ⏲11.30am-2pm & 6-11pm Mon, Tue, Thu & Fri, 11.30am-9.30pm Sat & Sun, closed Wed & 4th Tue; 📋; 🚉Keio line to Rokakōen), filled us in on the art of noodle slurping and some of his favourite *rāmen* (noodle) shops.

How to Eat It

Rāmen is like a brick-oven pizza – if you let it sit for a few minutes it becomes something different. So you need to start slurping right away, even if it burns a little. Keep slurping, make noise and don't chew.

Where to Eat It

Nagi is one of my favourites. The one in Golden Gai is a great place to go after drinking. I also like Kikanbō (p150) in Kanda. It's sort of new wave. It serves very serious, delicious spicy miso *rāmen*.

TSUKI NO SHIZUKA IZAKAYA $$

Map p286 (月ノ雫; www.tsukino-shizuku.com; 2nd & 3rd fl, 1-12-1 Nishi-Shinjuku, Shinjuku-ku; dishes ¥480-980; ⏲11.30am-2pm & 5pm-midnight Mon-Fri, to 5am Fri, 4pm-5am Sat, 4pm-midnight Sun; 📋; 🚉JR Yamanote line to Shinjuku, west exit) This lively, popular *izakaya* (Japanese pub-eatery) makes ordering easy and fun, with tableside touch-screen devices (in English). Look for staples, such as *kara-age* (fried chicken), sashimi, and *goma-dōfu* (sesame tofu). There's a glowing sign over the stairs.

★KOZUE JAPANESE $$$

Map p286 (梢; ☎5323-3460; http://tokyo.park.hyatt.jp/en/hotel/dining/Kozue.html; 40th fl, Park Hyatt, 3-7-1-2 Nishi-Shinjuku, Shinjuku-ku; lunch/dinner course from ¥2700/15,000; ⏲11.30am-2.30pm & 5.30-9.30pm; 🚭📋; Ⓢ Ōedo line to Tochōmae, exit A4) It's hard to beat Kozue's combination of exquisite, seasonal Japanese cuisine, artisan crockery and soaring views over Shinjuku from the floor-to-ceiling windows. Reservations are essential.

Shinjuku

★NAGI RĀMEN $

Map p286 (凪; www.n-nagi.com; 2nd fl, Golden Gai G2, 1-1-10 Kabukichō, Shinjuku-ku; rāmen from ¥820; ⏲24hr; 📋; 🚉JR Yamanote line to Shinjuku, east exit) The house speciality at this atmospheric noodle joint, up a treacherous stairway in Golden Gai, is *niboshi rāmen* (egg noodles in a broth flavoured with dried sardines). There is almost always a wait; first purchase your order from the vending machine inside, then claim your spot at the end of the line. Look for the sign with a red circle.

★NAKAJIMA KAISEKI $

Map p286 (中嶋; ☎3356-4534; www.shinjyuku-nakajima.com; Basement, 3-32-5 Shinjuku, Shinjuku-ku; lunch/dinner from ¥800/8640; ⏲11.30am-2pm & 5.30-10pm Mon-Sat; 🚭📋; Ⓢ Marunouchi line to Shinjuku-sanchōme, exit A1) In the evening, this Michelin-starred restaurant serves exquisite *kaiseki* (Japanese haute cuisine) dinners. On weekdays, it also serves a set lunch of humble *iwashi* (sardines) for one-tenth the price; in the hands of Nakajima's chefs they're divine. The line for lunch starts to form shortly before the restaurant opens at 11.30am. Look for the white sign at the top of the stairs.

SHINJUKU ASIA-YOKOCHŌ ASIAN $

Map p286 (新宿アジア横丁; Rooftop, 2nd Toa Hall Bldg, 1-21-1 Kabukichō, Shinjuku-ku; dishes from ¥650; ⏲5pm-5am; 📋; 🚉JR Yamanote line to Shinjuku, east exit) A rooftop night market that spans the Asian continent, Asia-yokochō has vendors dishing out everything from Korean *bibimbap* to Vietnamese *pho*. It's noisy, a bit chaotic and particularly fun in a group.

TSUNAHACHI TEMPURA $$

Map p286 (つな八; ☎3352-1012; www.tunahachi.co.jp; 3-31-8 Shinjuku, Shinjuku-ku; lunch/dinner from ¥1296/2268; ⏲11am-10.30pm; 🚭📋; 🚉JR Yamanote line to Shinjuku, east exit) Tsunahachi has been expertly frying prawns and seasonal vegetables for nearly 90 years. The sets are served in courses so each dish comes piping hot. Sit at the counter for the added pleasure of watching the chefs at work. Indigo *noren* (curtains) mark the entrance.

Kichijōji & Mitaka

TETCHAN YAKITORI $

(てっちゃん; 1-1-2 Kichijōji-Honchō, Musashino-shi; ⌚4-11pm; 🚉JR Chūō line to Kichijōji, north exit) Inside the labyrinth warren that is the old covered market Harmonica-yokochō, this no-frills *yakitori* joint fits right in. It's the kind of place that appeals to both college kids and their retired grandparents. There's no English menu, but safe bets include *tsukune* (chicken meatballs), *rebā* (liver) and *tori-momo* (chicken thigh).

PEPA CAFE FOREST THAI $

(ペパカフェフォレスト; www.peppermintcafe.com/forest; 4-1-5 Inokashira, Mitaka-shi; dishes from ¥780; ⌚noon-10pm; 🚭📋; 🚉JR Chūō line to Kichijōji, Kōen exit) This funky terrace cafe inside Inokashira-kōen serves tasty Thai classics, ice cream, coffee and beer. It's across the pond, if you're coming through the park from Kichijōji Station.

DRINKING & NIGHTLIFE

★ZOETROPE BAR

Map p286 (ゾートロープ; http://homepage2.nifty.com/zoetrope; 3rd fl, 7-10-14 Nishi-Shinjuku, Shinjuku-ku; ⌚7pm-4am Mon-Sat; 🚉JR Yamanote line to Shinjuku, west exit) A must-visit for whisky fans, Zoetrope has no less than 300 varieties of Japanese whisky (from ¥700) behind its small counter – including some no longer commercially available. The owner speaks some English and can help you pick from the daunting menu. He'll also let you choose the soundtrack to play alongside the silent films he screens on the wall.

★ADVOCATES CAFÉ GAY & LESBIAN

Map p286 (アドボケイツカフェ; http://advocates-cafe.com; 2-18-1 Shinjuku, Shinjuku-ku; ⌚6pm-4am, to 1am Sun; Ⓢ Marunouchi line to Shinjuku-sanchōme, exit C8) The scene at this tiny, teeny corner bar overflows onto the street and becomes more like a block party, especially in the summer. Advocates has a popular happy hour – 'beer blast' (all you can drink for ¥1000; 6pm to 9pm) – and is a great place to start the evening, meet new people and find out where the next party is. It's open to all; staff speak English.

GOLDEN GAI

Golden Gai (ゴールデン街; Map p286; 🚉JR Yamanote line to Shinjuku, east exit), a warren of tiny alleys and narrow, two-storey wooden buildings, began as a black market following WWII. It later functioned as a licensed quarter, until prostitution was outlawed in 1958. Now those same buildings are filled with more than a hundred closet-sized bars. Each is as unique and eccentric as the 'master' or 'mama' who runs it. That Golden Gai – prime real estate – has so far resisted the kind of development seen elsewhere in Shinjuku is a credit to these stubbornly bohemian characters.

Bars here usually have a theme – from punk rock to photography – and draw customers with matching expertise and obsessions (many of whom work in the media and entertainment industries). Since regular customers are their bread and butter, many establishments are likely to give tourists a cool reception. Don't take it personally. Japanese visitors unaccompanied by a regular get the same treatment; this is Golden Gai's peculiar, invisible velvet rope. However, there are bars that expressly welcome tourists (with English signs posted on their doors). Note that most bars have a cover charge (usually ¥500 to ¥1500).

The best way to experience Golden Gai is to stroll the lanes and pick a place that suits your mood. If you're stumped, **Albatross G** (アルバトロスG; Map p286; www.alba-s.com/index.html; 1-1-7 Kabukichō, Shinjuku-ku; cover charge ¥500, drinks from ¥500; ⌚7pm-5am; 🚉JR Yamanote line to Shinjuku, east exit) and **Araku** (亜楽; Map p286; www.facebook.com/bar.araku; 2nd fl, G2-dōri, 1-1-9 Kabukichō, Shinjuku-ku; ⌚8pm-5am Mon-Sat; 🚉JR Yamanote line to Shinjuku, east exit) are two good bets. Noodle shop Nagi is here, too.

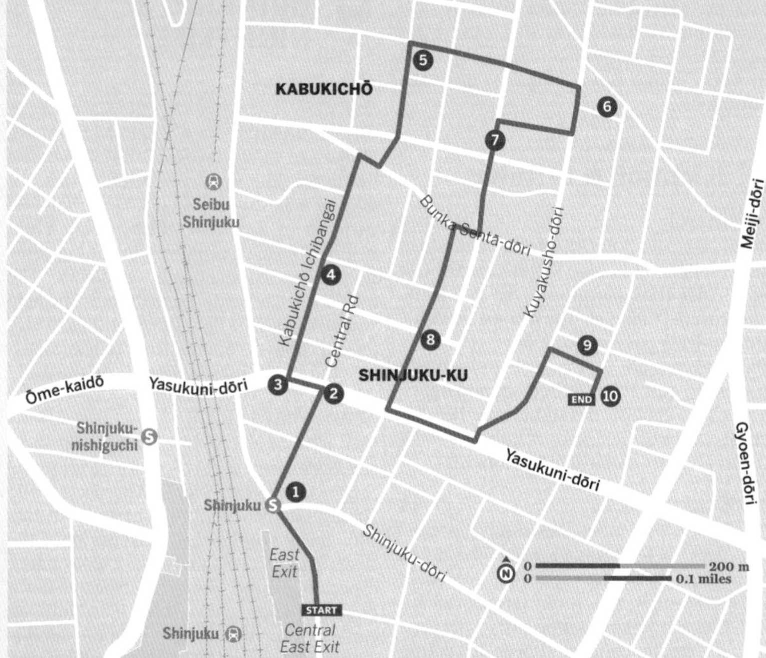

Neighbourhood Walk
Shinjuku at Night

START SHINJUKU STATION (EAST EXIT)
END HANAZONO-JINJA
LENGTH 2KM; TWO HOURS

Shinjuku's east side is lively any night of the week, though Fridays are the most crowded. Take the east exit and follow the signs out of the station for Kabukichō. Above ground, you should see the big screen of **1 Studio Alta** (スタジオアルタ), a popular Shinjuku meeting spot.

Take the pedestrian street on your left to Yasukuni-dōri, Shinjuku's main drag, where *izakaya* (Japanese pub-eateries) are stacked several stories high, along with karaoke parlours and all-night noodle joints. At all-night emporium **2 Don Quijote** (p136) you can pick up everything from a bottle of wine to a nurse's costume.

One block west is the flashing red **3 torii** (gate) that marks the entrance to Kabukichō, Tokyo's biggest red-light district. **4 Kabukichō Ichibangai**, the lane that leads into the heart of the neighbourhood, is a strange mix of 'hostess bars' (staffed by sexily clad, flirtatious young women), 'information centres' (which match customers with establishments that suit their particular, uh, needs) and otherwise ordinary restaurants.

There are more innocent ways to blow off steam in Kabukichō, too. Look for **5 Oslo Batting Centre** (オスローバッティングセンター) on the corner. It's ¥300 for 20 pitches if you feel like taking a swing.

To the right is a row of **6 love hotels** (hotels for amorous encounters). Kabukichō is also known for **7 host bars**, where bleach-blond pretty boys wait to do for the gals what hostess bars do for the guys. You'll see plenty of signs for these.

On your left you'll pass the eye-searing entrance to the **8 Robot Restaurant** (p135), home to one of Kabukichō's most bizarre spectacles (which is saying something). Back on Yasukuni-dōri, turn left. Look for the stone-paved, tree-lined path on your left that leads to atmospheric **9 Golden Gai** (p133) and get yourself a drink. Before calling it a night, pay your respects at **10 Hanazono-jinja** (p128).

★NEW YORK BAR BAR

Map p286 (ニューヨークバー; ☎5323-3458; http://tokyo.park.hyatt.com; 52nd fl, Park Hyatt, 3-7-1-2 Nishi-Shinjuku, Shinjuku-ku; ⏲5pm-midnight Sun-Wed, to 1am Thu-Sat; Ōedo line to Tochōmae, exit A4) You may not be lodging at the Park Hyatt, but you can still ascend to the 52nd floor to swoon over the sweeping nightscape from the floor-to-ceiling windows at this bar (of *Lost in Translation* fame). There's a cover charge of ¥2200 after 8pm (7pm Sunday) and live music nightly; cocktails start at ¥1800. Note: dress code enforced.

On the 41st floor, the **Peak Bar** offers views that are arguably just as good, in a quieter setting. There's no cover here and you can take advantage of the generous 'Twilight Time' all-you-can-drink deal (5pm to 9pm; ¥4200, unlimited canapes included).

SAMURAI BAR

Map p286 (サムライ; http://jazz-samurai.seesaa.net; 5th fl, 3-35-5 Shinjuku, Shinjuku-ku; ⏲6pm-1am; JR Yamanote line to Shinjuku, southeast exit) Never mind the impeccable record collection, this eccentric jazz *kissa* (cafe where jazz records are played) is worth a visit just for the owner's impressive collection of 2500 *maneki-neko* (beckoning cats). Look for the sign next door to Disc Union and take the elevator. There's a ¥300 cover charge (¥500 after 9pm); drinks from ¥650.

ARTY FARTY GAY & LESBIAN

Map p286 (アーティファーティ; www.arty-farty.net; 2nd fl, 2-11-7 Shinjuku, Shinjuku-ku; ⏲6pm-1am; Ⓢ Marunouchi line to Shinjuku-sanchōme, exit C8) A fixture on Tokyo's gay scene for many a moon, Arty Farty welcomes all in the community to come shake a tail feather on the dance floor here. It usually gets going later in the evening. Weekend DJ events sometimes have a cover charge (¥1000 to ¥2000), which includes entrance to sister club the Annex, around the corner.

BAR GOLDFINGER LESBIAN

Map p286 (http://goldfingerparty.com/bar/top; 2-12-11 Shinjuku, Shinjuku-ku; ⏲from 6pm Thu-Mon, closing time varies; Ⓢ Marunouchi line to Shinjuku-sanchōme, exit C8) This mostly ladies-only bar in Shinjuku-nichōme has a lowbrow-chic decor – it's designed to look like a '70s motel – and a friendly vibe; drinks for ¥700. Men are allowed on Mondays and Fridays. On the third Saturday of every month, the bar hosts Tokyo's most popular lesbian party, **Goldfinger** (www.goldfingerparty.com), held at a larger venue; check the website for details.

BERG CAFE

Map p286 (ベルグ; www.berg.jp; Basement, Lumine Est, 3-38-1 Shinjuku, Shinjuku-ku; ⏲7am-11pm; ; JR Yamanote line to Shinjuku, east exit) This long-running coffee shop inside Shinjuku Station has more personality than the average chain, and is cheaper too (just ¥216 for a cup). The *mōningu setto* (morning set; ¥399) includes coffee, hard-boiled egg and toast. Look for the 'Food Pocket' sign to the left of the east-exit ticket gates.

☆ ENTERTAINMENT

ROBOT RESTAURANT CABARET

Map p286 (ロボットレストラン; ☎3200-5500; www.robot-restaurant.com; 1-7-1 Kabukichō, Shinjuku-ku; tickets ¥7000; ⏲shows at 4pm, 5.55pm, 7.50pm & 9.45pm; JR Yamanote line to Shinjuku, east exit) This Kabukichō spectacle is wacky Japan at its finest, with giant robots manned by bikini-clad women and enough neon to light all of Shinjuku. Reservations aren't necessary but they're highly recommended. If you've booked ahead, be sure to arrive at least 30 minutes before the show. Look for discount tickets in English-language free mags around town.

SHINJUKU PIT INN JAZZ

Map p286 (新宿ピットイン; ☎3354-2024; www.pit-inn.com; Basement, 2-12-4 Shinjuku, Shinjuku-ku; admission from ¥3000; ⏲matinee 2.30pm, evening show 7.30pm; Ⓢ Marunouchi line to Shinjuku-sanchōme, exit C5) This is not the kind of place you come to talk over the music. Aficionados have been coming here for more than 40 years to listen to Japan's best jazz performers. Weekday matinees feature new artists and cost only ¥1300.

NEW NATIONAL THEATRE PERFORMING ARTS

(新国立劇場; Shin Kokuritsu Gekijō; ☎5351-3011; www.nntt.jac.go.jp/english/index.html; 1-1-1 Hon-machi, Shibuya-ku; Keio New line to Hatsudai, theatre exit) Tokyo's premier public performing-arts centre includes state-of-the-art venues for opera, dance and theatre. Many of the plays and dance productions are Japanese; the opera stage is usually given over to visiting international productions.

LOFT LIVE MUSIC

Map p286 (ロフト; www.loft-prj.co.jp; B2 fl, 1-12-9 Kabukichō, Shinjuku-ku; JR Yamanote line to Shinjuku, east exit) The chequerboard stage here has hosted the feedback and reverb of many a Tokyo punk over the last 35 years. The music is loud and usually good.

SHOPPING

★ISETAN DEPARTMENT STORE

Map p286 (伊勢丹; www.isetan.co.jp; 3-14-1 Shinjuku, Shinjuku-ku; 10am-8pm; S Marunouchi line to Shinjuku-sanchōme, exits B3, B4 & B5) Most department stores play to conservative tastes, but this one doesn't. Women should head to the Re-Style section on the 2nd floor for an always changing line-up of up-and-coming Japanese designers. Men get a whole building of their own (connected by a passageway). Don't miss the basement food hall, featuring some of the country's top purveyors of sweet and savoury goodies.

★DISK UNION MUSIC

Map p286 (ディスクユニオン; 3-31-4 Shinjuku, Shinjuku-ku; 11am-9pm; JR Yamanote line to Shinjuku, east exit) Scruffy Disk Union is known by local audiophiles as Tokyo's best used CD and vinyl store. Eight storeys carry a variety of musical styles; if you still can't find what you're looking for there are several other branches in Shinjuku that stock more obscure genres (pick up a map here).

★RANKING RANQUEEN VARIETY

Map p286 (ランキンランキン; Basement, Shinjuku Station, Shinjuku-ku; 10am-11pm; JR Yamanote line to Shinjuku, east exit) If it's trendy, it's here. This clever shop stocks only the top-selling products in any given category, from eyeliner and soft drinks to leg-slimming massage rollers. Look for it just outside the east-exit ticket gates of JR Shinjuku Station.

BINGOYA CRAFTS

Map p286 (備後屋; www.quasar.nu/bingoya; 10-6 Wakamatsu-chō, Shinjuku-ku; 10am-7pm Tue-Sun, closed 3rd Sat & Sun; S Toei Ōedo line to Wakamatsu-Kawada) Bingoya has five floors of quality, unpretentious crafts sourced from all over Japan. There's a particularly good selection of folksy pottery and textiles. Since it's a little out of the way, it's better for buyers than browsers; the store can help arrange shipping overseas. It's just in front of Wakamatsu-Kawada Station; look across the main street, to the right.

DON QUIJOTE VARIETY

Map p286 (ドン・キホーテ; 5291-9211; www.donki.com; 1-16-5 Kabukichō, Shinjuku-ku; 24hr; JR Yamanote line to Shinjuku, east exit) This fluorescent-lit bargain castle is filled to the brink with weird loot. Chaotic piles of knock-off electronics and designer goods sit alongside sex toys, fetish costumes and packaged foods. Though it's now a national chain, it started as a rare (at the time) 24-hour store for the city's night workers.

BICQLO CLOTHING, ELECTRONICS

Map p286 (ビックロ; 3-29-1 Shinjuku, Shinjuku-ku; 10am-10pm; S Marunouchi line to Shinjuku-sanchōme, exit A5) This mash-up store brings two of Japan's favourite retailers – electronics outfitter Bic Camera and budget clothing chain Uniqlo – under one roof. So you can match your new camera to your new hoodie. It's bright white: you can't miss it.

KINOKUNIYA BOOKS

Map p286 (紀伊國屋書店; www.kinokuniya.co.jp; Takashimaya Times Sq, 5-24-2 Sendagaya, Shibuya-ku; 10am-8pm; JR Yamanote line to Shinjuku, south exit) The 6th floor has a broad selection of foreign-language books and magazines, including English-teaching texts.

Kōrakuen & Northwest Tokyo

KŌRAKUEN | KUNDANSHITA | ICHIGAYA | HANZŌMON | MEJIRO | IKEBUKURO

Neighbourhood Top Five

❶ Soaking up the peaceful, contemplative atmosphere of a classic Japanese garden. **Rikugi-en** (p139) is considered the city's most beautiful. **Koishikawa Kōrakuen** (p140) is a close second.

❷ Wandering the old-world alleys of **Kagurazaka** (p144), an old geisha quarter with enticing shops and cafes.

❸ Cheering on Japan's number-one baseball team, the Yomiuri Giants, at **Tokyo Dome** (p146).

❹ Bath-hopping at the over-the-top onsen complex **Spa La Qua** (p146).

❺ Passing through the proud, bronze *torii* (gates) at **Yasukuni-jinja** (p140), a shrine with deep political resonance.

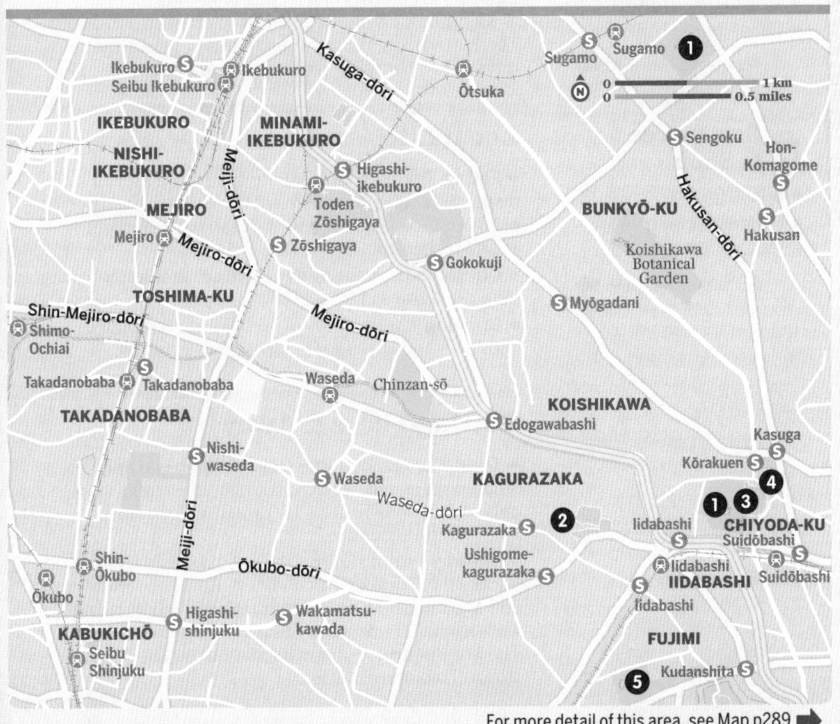

For more detail of this area, see Map p289 ➡

Lonely Planet's Top Tip

If you plan to explore several sights in Tokyo's northwest districts, try to work in a ride on Tokyo's last streetcar. The Toden Arakawa line (p141) passes near Chinzan-sō and Zōshigaya-reien through sleepy residential districts you wouldn't otherwise see.

Best Places to Eat

- Kururi (p141)
- Kado (p145)
- Le Bretagne (p145)

For reviews, see p141

Best Places to Drink

- Beer Bar Bitter (p145)
- Mugimaru 2 (p144)
- Canal Cafe (p145)

For reviews, see p145

Best Places to Shop

- Kukuli (p144)
- Puppet House (p146)
- Baikatei (p144)

For reviews, see p146

Explore Kōrakuen & Northwest Tokyo

The neighbourhoods northwest of the Imperial Palace are off the tourist trail, yet have some fascinating sights. If you're keen to see a traditional Japanese garden, there are some fantastic examples here. Rikugi-en is the city's most famous and well worth the detour. Koishikawa Kōrakuen, with a more convenient location, is beautiful as well. Next door to Koishikawa Kōrakuen is the entertainment complex Tokyo Dome City, which includes a baseball stadium, amusement park, spa complex and dozens of shops and restaurants. Nearby, the neighbourhood Kagurazaka, with its narrow cobblestone lanes, presents an alternative picture of Tokyo – that of a hundred years ago.

South of Kōrakuen, in Kudanshita, are two controversial attractions: Yasukuni-jinja and its adjacent museum Yūshū-kan, which covers Japan's warring past. Anyone with an interest in Japanese history (or Asian geopolitics) should make a stop here. On a lighter note, there are also some pleasant strolls nearby, along the Imperial Palace moats, Hanzo-bōri and Soto-bōri.

In the northwest corner of Tokyo, Ikebukuro is a big, brash transport hub, not dissimilar to Shinjuku, with department stores, and bar and restaurant strips. Nearby, however, are some wealthy residential districts that hide a handful of overlooked sights, such as the garden Chinzan-sō and the cemetery Zōshigaya-reien.

Kagurazaka is one of Tokyo's top dining destinations. There are many exclusive restaurants priced quite extravagantly, but there are some affordable options, too.

Local Life

- **Eating** Kagurazaka is said to have more French restaurants than anywhere outside France; the diverse neighbourhoods of northwest Tokyo have excellent ethnic restaurants.
- **Outdoors** On a sunny day there are few better places than the terrace at Canal Cafe (p145).
- **Drinking** The east side of Ikebukuro is crammed with bars and *izakaya* (Japanese pub-eateries).

Getting There & Away

- **Train** The JR Sōbu line stops at Iidabashi and Suidōbashi (rapid-service JR Chūō–line trains stop only at Suidōbashi). The JR Yamanote line stops at Mejiro and Ikebukuro.
- **Subway** Useful stations include Iidabashi (Nanboku, Yūrakuchō, Tōzai and Ōedo lines), Kōrakuen (Nanboku and Marunouchi lines), Kagurazaka (Tōzai line) and Kudanshita (Hanzōmon, Tōzai and Shinjuku lines). The Marunouchi, Yūrakuchō and Fukutoshin lines stop at Ikebukuro Station.

WORTH A DETOUR

TOP SIGHT RIKUGI-EN

Tokyo's most beautiful garden is hidden in the city's north. Built by a feudal lord in 1702, with a large central pond, it was designed to reflect the aesthetic of traditional Waka poetry. Walkways pass over hills, stone bridges, trickling streams and scenes inspired by famous poems.

Teahouses

Rikugi-en has two vintage teahouses, where you can sit and rest, taking in the scenery. The **Tsutsuji-chaya** dates to the Meiji period and is perfectly primed for viewing the maples in autumn. The Takimi-chaya is perched on the edge of the stream. At **Fukiage-chaya**, a more modern construction, you can drink *matcha* (¥500) alfresco while overlooking the pond.

Poetic Views

The bridge, **Togetsukyō**, created from two huge stone slabs, references a poem about a crane flying over a moonlit field. Stone markers around the garden make note of other scenic views, many of which reference famous works of Japanese or Chinese literature. Climb to the top of the **Fujishiro-tōge**, a hill named after a real one in Wakayama Prefecture, for views over the whole garden.

Seasonal Blooms

Something is almost always in bloom at Rikugi-en, though the garden is most famous for its maple leaves, which turn bright red in late autumn, usually around late November or early December. During this time, the park stays open later and the trees are illuminated after sunset. In early spring you can catch plum blossoms, followed by the flowering of the magnificent weeping cherry tree near the entrance.

DON'T MISS...

- Teahouses
- Togetsukyō
- View from Fujishiro-tōge
- Maples in late autumn

PRACTICALITIES

- 六義園
- 6-16-3 Hon-Komagome, Bunkyō-ku
- adult/child ¥300/free
- 9am-5pm
- JR Yamanote line to Komagome, south exit

SIGHTS

Kōrakuen

KOISHIKAWA KŌRAKUEN GARDENS

Map p289 (小石川後楽園; 1-6-6 Kōraku, Bunkyō-ku; adult/child ¥300/free; ⊙9am-5pm; 🚉JR Sōbu line to Iidabashi, exit C3) Established in the mid-17th century as the property of the Tokugawa clan, this formal strolling garden incorporates elements of Chinese and Japanese landscaping. It's among Tokyo's most attractive gardens, although nowadays the *shakkei* (borrowed scenery) also includes the other-worldly Tokyo Dome. Don't miss the Engetsu-kyō (Full-Moon Bridge), which dates from the early Edo period.

TOKYO DOME CITY ATTRACTIONS AMUSEMENT PARK

Map p289 (東京ドームシティアトラクションズ; ☎3817-6001; www.tokyo-dome.co.jp/e; 1-3-61 Kōraku, Bunkyō-ku; attractions ¥420-1030; ⊙10am-9pm; 🚉JR Chūō line to Suidōbashi, west exit) The top attraction at this amusement park next to Tokyo Dome is the 'Thunder Dolphin' (¥1030), a roller coaster that cuts a heart-in-your-throat course in and around the tightly packed buildings of downtown. There are plenty of low-key, child-friendly rides as well. You can buy tickets for individual rides or a day pass (adult/child ¥3900/2100; after 5pm adult ¥2900).

BASEBALL HALL OF FAME & MUSEUM MUSEUM

Map p289 (野球体育博物館; www.baseball-museum.or.jp; 1-3-61 Kōraku, Bunkyō-ku; adult/child ¥600/200; ⊙10am-6pm Tue-Sun Mar-Sep, to 5pm Oct-Feb; 🚉JR Chūō line to Suidōbashi, west exit) How did baseball come to be a Japanese obsession? This museum chronicles baseball's rise from a hobby imported by an American teacher in 1872 to the Japanese team winning the bronze medal at the 2004 Olympics. Be sure to pick up the comprehensive English-language pamphlet. The entrance to the museum is adjacent to Gate 21 of Tokyo Dome.

LOCAL KNOWLEDGE

GIRL GEEKS

Ikebukuro's **Otome Road** (乙女ロード; 🚉JR Yamanote line to Ikebukuro, east exit), literally 'Maiden Road', has many of the same anime and manga stores that you see in Akihabara – but they're full of goods that girl geeks love. Look for it across the street from the west edge of the Sunshine City shopping complex, just beyond the highway overpass.

TOKYO DAI-JINGŪ SHINTO SHRINE

Map p289 (東京大神宮; ☎3262-3566; www.tokyodaijingu.or.jp/english; 2-4-1 Fujimi, Chiyoda-ku; ⊙6am-9pm; 🚉JR Sōbu line to Iidabashi, west exit) This is the Tokyo branch of Ise-jingū, Japan's mother shrine in Mie Prefecture. Credited with establishing the Shintō wedding ritual, Tokyo Dai-jingū is a popular pilgrimage site for young Tokyoites hoping to get hitched.

Kundanshita, Ichigaya & Hanzōmon

YASUKUNI-JINJA SHINTO SHRINE

Map p289 (靖国神社; www.yasukuni.or.jp; 3-1-1 Kudan-kita, Chiyoda-ku; ⊙6am-5pm; Ⓢ Hanzōmon line to Kudanshita, exit 1) Literally 'For the Peace of the Country Shrine', Yasukuni is the memorial shrine to Japan's war dead, around 2.5 million souls. Completed in 1869, it has *torii* made of steel and bronze. It is also incredibly controversial: in 1979 14 class-A war criminals, including WWII general Hideki Tōjō, were enshrined here.

YŪSHŪ-KAN MUSEUM

Map p289 (遊就館; www.yasukuni.or.jp; 3-1-1 Kudankita, Chiyoda-ku; adult/student ¥800/500; ⊙9am-4pm; Ⓢ Hanzōmon line to Kudanshita, exit 1) Most history museums in Japan skirt the issue of war or focus on the burden of the common people. Not so here: it begins with Japan's samurai tradition and ends with its defeat in WWII. It is also unapologetic and has been known to boil the blood of some visitors with its particular view of history.

NATIONAL SHŌWA MEMORIAL MUSEUM MUSEUM

Map p289 (昭和館; Shōwa-kan; www.showakan.go.jp; 1-6-1 Kudan-minami, Chiyoda-ku; adult/child/student ¥300/80/150; ⊙10am-5.30pm; 🚉Hanzōmon line to Kudanshita, exit 4) This museum of WWII-era Tokyo gives a sense of everyday life for the common people: how they ate, slept, dressed, studied, prepared for war and endured martial law, famine and loss of loved ones. Audio guide is free.

MIZUMA ART GALLERY GALLERY

Map p289 (www.mizuma-art.co.jp; 2nd fl, 3-13 Ichigaya-tamachi, Shinjuku-ku; ⊙11am-7pm Tue-Sat;

JR Sōbu line to Ichigaya, exit 1) Run by Tokyo art-world figure Sueo Mizuma, Mizuma Art Gallery represents some of Japan's more successful contemporary artists, such as Aida Makoto and Konoike Tomoko. Shows often feature *neo-nihonga* (Japanese-style paintings with contemporary panache). It's in a metal building above a small parking lot.

JCII CAMERA MUSEUM MUSEUM

Map p289 (日本カメラ博物館; www.jcii-cameramuseum.jp; 25 Ichiban-chō, Chiyoda-ku; adult/child ¥300/free; 10am-5pm Tue-Sun; S Hanzōmon line to Hanzōmon, exit 4) Among the hundreds of vintage cameras on display here is a 1839 Giroux daguerreotype, the world's first camera. Japan wasn't far behind: the ornate Tsui-kin, Japan's first camera, came out 1854; it's also on display here.

Behind the museum, in a separate building, is the JCII Photo Salon, which hosts free photography exhibits.

Mejiro & Ikebukuro

CHINZAN-SŌ GARDENS

(椿山荘; www.hotel-chinzanso-tokyo.jp; 2-10-8 Sekiguchi, Bunkyō-ku; 10am-9.30pm; S Yūrakuchō line to Edogawa-bashi, exit 1A) FREE This woodsy strolling garden was once the estate of a Meiji-era statesman. The pathways are lined with a number of antiquities transported from all over Japan. Most notable is a 16.7m three-storey pagoda, estimated at nearly a millennium old, which was transported from the Hiroshima area. From exit 1A, walk west for 10 minutes along the Kanda-gawa canal until the gate to Chinzan-sō appears on your right.

ST MARY'S CATHEDRAL TOKYO CHURCH

(東京カテドラル聖マリア大聖堂; Sekiguchi Cathedral; www.tokyo.catholic.jp; 3-16-15 Sekiguchi, Bunkyō-ku; 9am-5pm; S Yurakuchō line to Edogawabashi, exit 1A) Rising nearly 40m tall and glistening in the sun, this stainless-steel contemporary cathedral was completed in 1955. It's the work of Japan's foremost modern architect, Tange Kenzō, and structural and acoustic engineers from the University of Tokyo.

IKEBUKURO EARTHQUAKE HALL MUSEUM

(池袋防災館; Ikebukuro Bōsai-kan; www.tfd.metro.tokyo.jp/hp-ikbskan; 2-37-8 Nishi-Ikebukuro, Tōshima-ku; 9am-5pm Wed-Mon, closed 3rd Wed of month; JR Yamanote line to Ikebukuro, Metropolitan exit) FREE This public-safety centre has a room that simulates a real earthquake. It's obviously intended for school children, but travellers are welcome here, too. You may want to skip the whole two-hour safety course and just go for the shake down, which is no joke – on our last visit we experienced a reenactment of the 1923 Kantō quake that was thoroughly rattling.

WORTH A DETOUR

TOKYO'S LAST STREETCAR

Given Tokyo's tangled streets, it's hard to imagine that streetcars were common here until the 1960s. The **Toden Arakawa line** (都電荒川線; one way ¥165) is the only one left within central Tokyo. The route arcs across the north of the city from Minowabashi in the east to Waseda in the west, from where it's a 10-minute walk to the gardens of Chinzan-sō. Along the way, you'll pass homes with hanging laundry, pocket parks and plenty of the sort of everyday street life that most visitors miss. The cemetery Zōshigaya-reien also falls on the route.

MYONICHIKAN ARCHITECTURE

(明日館; Jiyu Gakuen Girls' School; www.jiyu.jp; 2-31-3 Nishi-Ikebukuro, Toshima-ku; tour with/without coffee ¥600/400; 10am-4pm Tue-Sun; JR Yamanote line to Ikebukuro, Metropolitan exit) Lucky the girls who went to the Frank Lloyd Wright–designed 'School of the Free Spirit' (Jiyu Gakuen). Built in 1921, it functioned as a school until the 1970s and was then reopened as a public space in 2001. Visitors can tour the facilities and have coffee in the common room.

ZŌSHIGAYA-REIEN CEMETERY

(雑司ヶ谷霊園; 4-25-1 Minami-Ikebukuro, Toshima-ku; 8.30am-5.15pm; Toden Arakawa line to Toden Zōshigaya) FREE On the outskirts of Ikebukuro, this cemetery has the city's largest collection of literary greats. Pick up an English-language map from the office and hunt down the graves of Natsume Sōseki, Nagai Kafu and Lafcadio Hearn, among others.

EATING

★KURURI RAMEN ¥

Map p289 (麺処くるり; 3-2 Ichigaya-Tamachi, Shinjuku-ku; noodles ¥700-950; 11am-9pm; JR Sōbu line to Iidabashi, west exit) The line-up of *rāmen* (noodle) fanatics outside this

LONELY PLANET / GETTY IMAGES ©

TOM BONAVENTURE / GETTY IMAGES ©

GREG ELMS / GETTY IMAGES ©

1. Koishikawa Kōrakuen (p140)
This formal strolling garden was established in the mid-17th century.

2. Tokyo Dome (p146)
Fans cheer on the Yomiuri Giants baseball team.

3. Tokyo festivals (p24)
Take in the sounds of traditional drumming at one of the city's festivals.

4. Kagurazaka (p144)
Enjoy a glimpse of colourful kimonos in this charming neighbourhood.

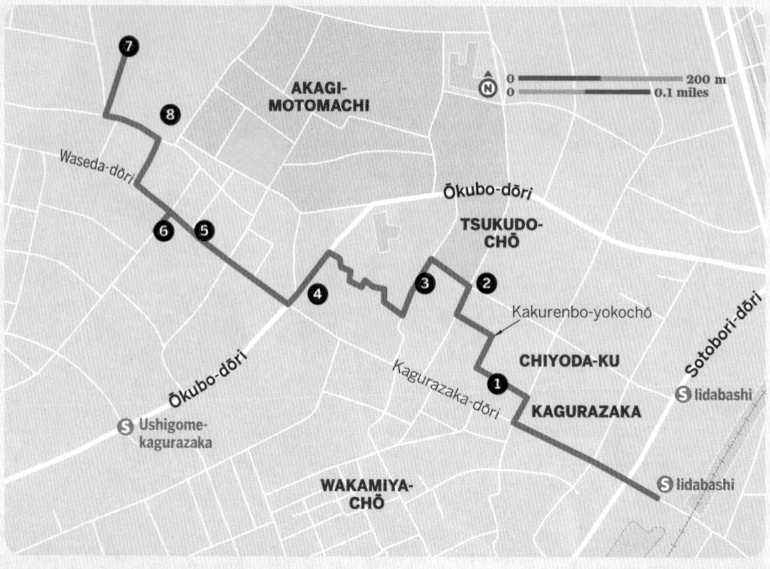

Local Life
Exploring Kagurazaka

At the start of the 20th century, Kagurazaka was a fashionable *hanamachi* – a pleasure quarter where geisha entertained. Though the geisha have disappeared, the neighbourhood retains the glamour and charm. These days it is a popular destination for Tokyoites, who enjoy wandering the narrow cobblestone lanes or whiling away the day in one of the many cafes.

❶ In the Footsteps of Geisha
Walk up Kagurazaka-dōri, turn right at Royal Host restaurant and then take the first left onto **Geisha Shinmichi**. This narrow lane was once where geisha lived and worked. Though it's now home to residences and restaurants, the paving stones remain.

❷ Traditional Crafts
At the end of attractive side-street Honta-yokochō is **Kukuli** (Map p289; www.kukuli.co.jp; 1-10 Tsukudo-chō, Shinjuku-ku; ⌚11am-7pm; 🚇JR Yamanote line to Iidabashi, west exit), one of several shops specialising in traditional craftwork. It has hand-dyed textiles (like scarves and tea towels) with a modern touch.

❸ Cobblestone Alleyways
Winding cobblestone alley **Hyogo-yokochō** is the neighbourhood's oldest and most atmospheric lane. Here you'll see *ryōtei*: exclusive, traditional Japanese restaurants (for which Kagurazaka is famous).

❹ Tea Break in an Old House
Follow the twisting stone-paved road. The old house almost covered in ivy is **Mugimaru 2** (ムギマル2; Map p289; ☎5228-6393; www.mugimaru2.com; 5-20 Kagurazaka, Shinjuku-ku; coffee ¥550; ⌚noon-9pm Thu-Tue; Ⓢ Tozai line to Kagurazaka, exit 1), a favourite local hang-out. Climb the narrow staircase and grab a spot on the floor beside a low table. The speciality is *manjū* (steamed buns).

❺ Pastry Chefs in Action
Award-winning, 80-year-old confectioner **Baikatei** (梅花亭; Map p289; 6-15 Kagurazaka, Shinjuku-ku; ⌚10am-8pm; Ⓢ Tōzai line to Kagurazaka, exit 1) turns out gorgeous *wagashi* (Japanese-style sweets). Watch the chefs at work, whipping humble beans and rice into pastel flowers, from the window in the back.

❻ Handmade Accessories
The ever-changing selection at **Sada** (貞; Map p289; www.sadakagura.com; 6-58 Kagu-

SOSHIRO / GETTY IMAGES ©

Woman in traditional geisha dress, Kagurazaka

razaka, Shinjuku-ku; ⌚noon-7pm; Ⓢ Tōzai line to Kagurazaka, exit 1) includes clothes and pretty accessories handmade in Japan. Some items are contemporary; others have a traditional Japanese feel, made with kimono material.

7 A Contemporary Shrine

Akagi-jinja (赤城神社; Map p289; http://akagi-jinja.jp; 1-10 Akagi-Motomachi, Shinjuku-ku; Ⓢ Tōzai line to Kagurazaka, exit 1), Kagurazaka's signature shrine, looks nothing like the traditional ones around the city. In 2010 the shrine, which can trace its history back centuries, was remodelled by Kengo Kuma, one of Japan's most prominent architects. The result is a sleek glass box.

8 Dinner at Kado

Set in a gorgeous home, half-hidden by a wooden facade, **Kado** (カド; Map p289; ☎3268-2410; http://kagurazaka-kado.com; 1-32 Akagi-Motomachi, Shinjuku-ku; lunch/dinner sets from ¥800/3150; ⌚11.30am-2.30pm & 5-11pm; 🚭📵; 🚉Tōzai line to Kagurazaka, exit 1) serves delicious seasonal courses (like firefly squid in vinegar miso dressing); reservations recommended. For something light, the bar in the foyer serves dishes à la carte.

cramped, anonymous noodle shop proves its street cred among connoisseurs. The *miso-rāmen* (みそらぁめん) broth is swamp-thick, incredibly rich and absolutely delicious. There's no sign, but it's next to a liquor shop with a striped awning; buy a ticket inside from the machine.

★ LE BRETAGNE FRENCH ¥

Map p289 (ル ブルターニュ; ☎3235-3001; www.le-bretagne.com/e/top.html; 4-2 Kagurazaka, Shinjuku-ku; crêpes ¥750-1850; ⌚11.30am-10.30pm Tue-Sat, to 10pm Sun; 🚭📝📵; 🚉JR Sōbu line to Iidabashi, west exit) This French-owned cafe is credited with starting the Japanese rage for crêpes. Savoury buckwheat galettes are made with ham and cheese imported from France; the sweet ones – served with the likes of apple compote and ice cream – are divine.

MUCHA-AN SOBA ¥

(無茶庵; ☎3943-5489; 2-10-8 Sekiguchi, Bunkyō-ku; noodles from ¥1050; ⌚11.30am-3pm & 5-8pm; 🚭📵; Ⓢ Yūrakuchō line to Edogawabashi, exit 1A) Perched on a hill inside Chinzan-sō gardens (p141), this shop in a wood-built former ryokan makes its own soba (buckwheat) noodles. Get them served simply, as *seiro* (noodles on bamboo mat with dipping sauce on the side) or as part of an elaborate lunch set with tempura. It's best to reserve on the weekend and holidays.

CANAL CAFE ITALIAN ¥¥

Map p289 (カナルカフェ; ☎3260-8068; www.canalcafe.jp; 1-9 Kagurazaka, Shinjuku-ku; lunch from ¥1600, dinner mains ¥1500-2800; ⌚11.30am-11pm Tue-Sat, to 9.30pm Sun; 🚭📝📵; 🚉JR Sōbu line to Iidabashi, west exit) Along the languid moat that forms the edge of Kitanomaru-kōen, this is one of Tokyo's best alfresco dining spots. The restaurant serves tasty wood-fired pizzas, seafood pastas and grilled meats, while over on the 'deck side' you can settle in with a sandwich, muffin or just a cup of coffee.

DRINKING & NIGHTLIFE

★ BEER BAR BITTER BAR

Map p289 (ビアバービター; www.beerbar-bitter.com; 2nd fl, 1-14 Tsukudochō, Shinjuku-ku; ⌚5pm-2am Sun-Fri; 🚉JR Sōbu line to Iidabashi, west exit) This Kagurazaka hideaway has Belgian beer on tap and a moody, industrial interior. Look for it above a bistro called Viande and take the stairs on the right.

LOCAL KNOWLEDGE

ETHNIC EATS

Northwest Tokyo is home to several foreign communities: Shin-Ōkubo is known as Koreatown, Takadanobaba has a small community of people from Myanmar and Ikebukuro's Chinatown is second only to the one in Yokohama. If you need a break from Japanese food, you'll find some tempting options in these 'hoods. Here are a few local favourites:

Shin-chan (辛ちゃん; Map p286; 1-2-9 Hyakunin-chō, Shinjuku-ku; dishes from ¥980; noon-5am; JR Yamanote line to Shin-Ōkubo) In Shin-Ōkubo's Koreatown, Shin-chan specialises in spicy Korean-style fried chicken and is popular with homesick Korean exchange students. There's a picture menu and dishes are big enough to share. Look for the twinkling blue lights out front.

Ruby (ルビー; 3-8-5 Takadanobaba, Toshima-ku; mains ¥780; 11.30am-2.30pm & 5pm-midnight Mon-Fri, 5pm-5am Sat & Sun; JR Yamanote line to Takadanobaba, Waseda exit) Takadanobaba's Myanmar community gathers here for *mohinga* (rice-noodle soup) and *laphete thote* (salad of pickled tea leaves) made with ingredients sent over by the owner's mother back in Myanmar. There's a picture menu.

Yong Xiang Sheng Jian Guan (永祥生煎館; 1st fl, City Hotel, 1-29-2 Nishi-Ikebukuro, Toshima-ku; 6 dumplings for ¥570; 11.30am-10pm; JR Yamanote line to Ikebukuro, west exit) This takeaway counter deals in Shanghai street food, namely *sheng jian bao* (pan-fried pork buns; called *yaki-shōronpo* in Japan). Warning: they're as hot as they are delicious.

ENTERTAINMENT

JAZZ SPOT INTRO — JAZZ

(イントロ; www.intro.co.jp; Basement, NT Bldg, 2-14-8 Takadanobaba, Shinjuku-ku; 6.30pm-midnight Mon-Thu, to 1am Fri, to 5am Sat, 5pm-midnight Sun; JR Yamanote line to Takadanobaba, Waseda exit) This little club – which gives away a quarter of its floor space to a grand piano – holds jam sessions almost nightly (Monday and Fridays are for drinking and talking shop). It's most well known for its 12-hour Saturday sessions that run until 5am. Bonus: no cover charge.

SHOPPING

★PUPPET HOUSE — CRAFTS

Map p289 (パペットハウス; www.puppet-house.co.jp; 1-8 Shimomiyabi-chō, Shinjuku-ku; 11am-7pm Tue-Sat; JR Sōbu line to Iidabashi, east exit) Japan's only dedicated puppet shop is a showcase for one-of-a-kind handmade marionettes from around the world. It's obviously a labour of love and the English-speaking owner is happy to show you how to make the puppets walk, skip and dance. Look for the sign of Punch at the entrance to an alley.

LA RONDE D'ARGILE — HOMEWARES

Map p289 (ラ・ロンダジル; http://la-ronde.com; 11 Wakamiya-chō, Shinjuku-ku; 11.30am-6pm Tue-Sat; S Ōedo line to Ushigome-Kagurazaka, exit A2) A changing selection of homewares made by local artisans fill two floors of this old house turned shop.

SPORTS & ACTIVITIES

★TOKYO DOME — BASEBALL

Map p289 (東京ドーム; www.tokyo-dome.co.jp/e; 1-3 Kōraku, Bunkyō-ku; tickets ¥2200-6100; JR Chūō line to Suidōbashi, west exit) Tokyo Dome (aka 'Big Egg') is home to the Yomiuri Giants. Love 'em or hate 'em, they're the most consistently successful team in Japanese baseball. If you're looking to see the Giants in action, the baseball season runs from the end of March to the end of October. Tickets sell out in advance; get them early at www.giants.jp/en.

SPA LAQUA — ONSEN

Map p289 (スパ ラクーア; www.laqua.jp; 5th-9th fl, Tokyo Dome City, 1-3-61 Kōraku, Bunkyō-ku; admission weekday/weekend ¥2634/2958; 11am-9am; S Marunouchi line to Kōrakuen, exit 2) One of Tokyo's few true onsen (hot springs), this chic spa complex relies on natural hot-spring water from 1700m below ground. There are indoor and outdoor baths, saunas and a bunch of add-on options, such as *akasuri* (Korean-style whole-body exfoliation). It's a fascinating introduction to Japanese health and beauty rituals.

Akihabara & Around

AKIHABARA | KANDA

Neighbourhood Top Five

❶ Experiencing blazing neon, the maid cafes, the latest electronic gadgets and *otaku* (geek) vibe of **Akihabara Electric Town** (p149).

❷ Encountering dinosaurs made from old plastic toys amid the contemporary art galleries at **3331 Arts Chiyoda** (p149).

❸ Browsing the cream of Japanese crafts and cuisine at the beneath-train-tracks-malls **2k540 Aki-Oka Artisan** (p151), **Chabara** (p152) and **mAAch ecute** (p152).

❹ Learning the art of paper folding at the **Origami Kaikan** (p149).

❺ Enjoying a moment of quiet contemplation at **Kanda Myōjin** (p149) and the nearby cafes **Imasa** (p151) and **Amanoya** (p150).

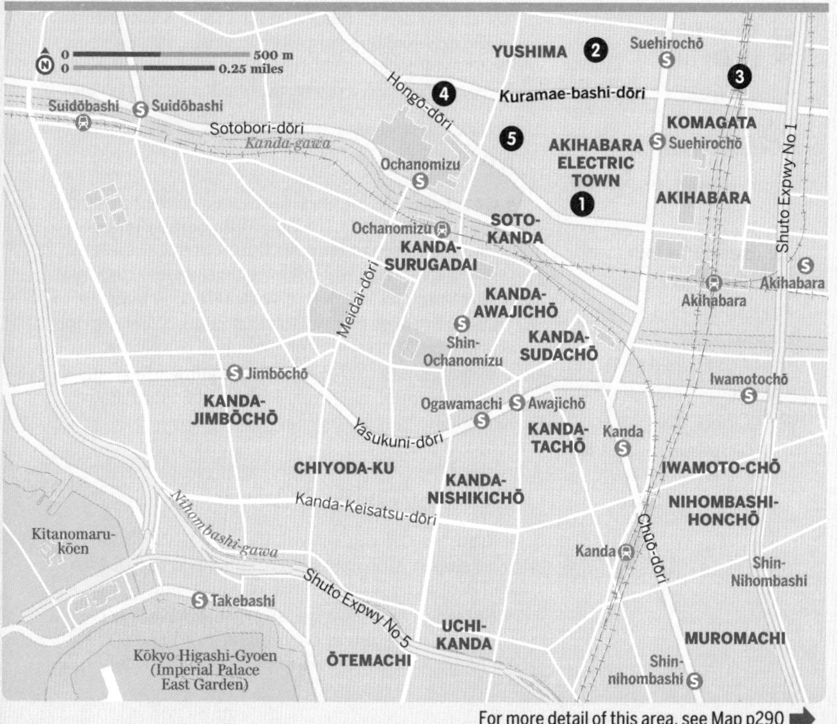

For more detail of this area, see Map p290 ➡

Lonely Planet's Top Tip

Check electronics prices in your home country online before buying big-ticket items in Akihabara; they may or may not be a good deal. If you do buy, have your passport handy since travellers spending more than ¥10,001 in a single day at selected shops can get a refund of the consumption tax (8%). For a list of duty-free shops offering this service, see www.akiba.or.jp.

Best Places to Eat

- Isegen (p150)
- Kanda Yabu Soba (p150)
- Botan (p150)

For reviews, see p150

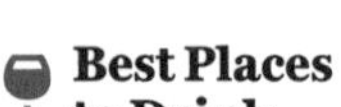

Best Places to Drink

- Imasa (p151)
- N3331 (p151)
- Cafe Asan (p151)

For reviews, see p151

Best Places to Shop

- 2k540 Aki-Oka Artisan (p151)
- mAAch ecute (p152)
- Mandarake Complex (p152)

For reviews, see p151

Explore Akihabara & Around

Long a hub of Tokyo's electronics trade, Akihabara is today more synonymous with *otaku* (geeks) and their love of anime, manga and J-pop culture. Even if you haven't the faintest idea of who or what AKB48 or Gundam is, Akiba, as it's popularly known, is still well worth visiting for its buzzing, quirky atmosphere, shopping malls and the contemporary arts of 3331 Arts Chiyoda.

Along neon-lined Chūō-dōri, you're sure to encounter *cosplay* (costume play) maids enticing customers into maid cafes. Electric Town is across the street, and holds a dense concentration of electronics shops, comic and DVD retailers and figurine sellers. Respite is available in the 2k540 Aki-Oka Artisan arcade, with its serene atmosphere and eclectic, craft-oriented shops.

Head south across the Mansei-bashi to discover mAAch ecute, another sophisticated under-the-tracks shopping and dining complex. A short walk south is Kanda, a major transport hub that is undergoing an infrastructure upgrade. Here you'll find some of Tokyo's most traditional restaurants as well as come-as-you-are noodle bars and convivial *izakaya* (Japanese pub-eateries) packed with carousing salarymen.

West of Akihabara, in the vicinity of Ochanomizu, are an interesting trio of religious buildings: the Shintō shrine Kanda Myōjin, the Confucian shrine Yushima Seidō, and the Russian Orthodox Nicholai Cathedral. If you want to stretch your legs further, Origami Kaikan has fine displays on the art of folding paper into exquisite shapes. Paper in the form of books, magazines and poster art is the raison d'etre of Jimbōchō, a dream destination for bibliophiles.

Local Life

- **Cosplay** Catch anime fans dressed as their favourite characters, particularly along Akihabara's Chūō-dōri on Sundays (1pm to 6pm April to September, to 5pm October to March) when it becomes a pedestrian zone.
- **Festivals** The area bursts with extra creativity during Trans Arts Tokyo (www.kanda-tat.com), a contemporary arts fest held between September and November.
- **Video games** Go old-school and join enthusiasts playing Pacman and Street Fighter at Super Potato Retro-kan.

Getting There & Away

- **Train** The JR Yamanote, Sōbu, and Keihin-Tōhoku lines stop at Akihabara. Ochanomizu on the JR Chūō and Sōbu lines is convenient for other sights.
- **Subway** The Hibiya line stops near Akihabara, while the Ginza line stops at Suehirochō and Kanda. The Shinjuku and Hanzōmon lines stop at Jimbōchō.

SIGHTS

Akihabara

AKIHABARA ELECTRIC TOWN
NEIGHBOURHOOD

Map p290 (秋葉原電気街; Akihabara Denki-Gai; JR Yamanote line to Akihabara, Electric Town exit) Post WWII, Akihabara Station became synonymous with a black market for radio parts and other electronics. After the 1960s and '70s when the district was *the* place to hunt for bargains on new and used electronics, Akihabara saw its top shopping mantle increasingly usurped by discount stores elsewhere in the city. It has long since bounced back by reinventing itself as the centre of the *otaku* universe, catching J-pop culture fans in its gravitational pull.

Now you are as likely to find intricately designed plastic models of anime characters, self-penned pornographic comics and *cosplay* outfits as you are electric circuits, fuses and wires in the place locals call Akiba. To make some sense of it all pick up an English map at **Tokyo Anime Center Akiba Info** (東京アニメセンターAkiba Info; Map p290; www.animecenter.jp; 2nd fl, Akihabara UDX Bldg, 4-14-1 Soto-Kanda, Chiyoda-ku; 11am-7pm Tue-Sun; JR Yamanote line to Akihabara, Electric Town exit); the helpful staff here also speak English.

3331 ARTS CHIYODA
ART GALLERY

Map p290 (6803 2441; www.3331.jp/en; 6-11-14 Soto-Kanda, Chiyoda-ku; noon-7pm Wed-Mon; ; Ginza line to Suehirochō, exit 4) FREE Interesting galleries and creative studios now occupy this former high school which has morphed into a forward-thinking arts hub for Akiba. It's a fascinating place to explore. There's a good cafe and shop selling cute design items, as well as a play area for kids stocked with recycled toys and colourful giant dinosaurs made of old plastic toys.

AKIHABARA RADIO CENTER
BUILDING

Map p290 (秋葉原ラジオセンター; 1-14-2 Soto-Kanda, Chiyoda-ku; hours vary; JR Yamanote line to Akihabara, Electric Town exit) Strictly for old-school electronics *otaku*, this two-storey warren of several dozen electronics stalls under the elevated railway is the original, still-beating heart of Akihabara. By old-school, we mean connectors, jacks, LEDs, switches, semiconductors and other components. It's worth a peek as a cultural study; the easiest access is the narrow entrances under the tracks on Chūō-dōri.

Kanda & Around

ORIGAMI KAIKAN
CRAFTS

Map p290 (おりがみ会館; 3811-4025; www.origamikaikan.co.jp; 1-7-14 Yushima, Bunkyō-ku; shop 9am-6pm, gallery 10am-5.30pm Mon-Sat; JR Chūō or Sōbu lines to Ochanomizu, Hijiri-bashi exit) FREE This exhibition centre and workshop is dedicated to the quintessential Japanese art of origami which you can learn to do yourself in classes here. There's a shop/gallery on the 1st floor, a gallery on the 2nd, and a workshop on 4th where you can watch the process of making, dyeing and decorating origami paper.

Admission is free, but origami lessons (offered most days in Japanese) cost ¥1000 to ¥2500 for one to two hours, depending on the complexity of that day's design. First-timers would do well to try for a class with the centre's director, Kobayashi Kazuo.

KANDA MYŌJIN (KANDA SHRINE)
SHINTO SHRINE

Map p290 (神田明神; www.kandamyoujin.or.jp; 2-16-2 Soto-kanda, Chiyoda-ku; JR Chūō or Sōbu lines to Ochanomizu, Hijiri-bashi exit) FREE Tracing its history back to AD 730, this splendid Shintō shrine boasts vermillion-lacquered halls surrounding a stately courtyard, where you'll also find the pet pony Akari. Its present location dates from 1616 and the *kami* (gods) enshrined here are said to bring luck in business and in finding a spouse. In mid-May on odd-numbered years, this is the home shrine of the Kanda Matsuri, one of Tokyo's top three festivals.

NIKOLAI CATHEDRAL
CHURCH

Map p290 (ニコライ堂; 3295-6879; www.orthodoxjapan.jp; 4-1-3 Kanda-Surugadai, Chiyoda-ku; admission ¥300; 1-4pm Apr-Sep, 1-3.30pm Oct-Mar, 1-6pm every Mon; S Chiyoda line to Shin-Ochanomizu, exit 2) This Russian Orthodox cathedral, complete with a distinctive Byzantine-style architecture, was first built in 1891 under the supervision of English architect Josiah Conder. The original copper dome was damaged in the 1923 earthquake, forcing the church to downsize to the (still enormous) dome that's now in place.

The church is named for St Nikolai of Japan (1836–1912), who first arrived as chaplain of the Russian consulate in the port city of Hakodate (Hokkaidō) and through missionary work soon amassed about 30,000 faithful.

YUSHIMA SEIDŌ (YUSHIMA SHRINE) SHRINE

Map p290 (湯島聖堂; www.seido.or.jp; 1-4-25 Yushima, Bunkyō-ku; ⏱9.30am-5pm Apr-Sep, to 4pm Oct-Mar; 🚉JR Chūō or Sōbu lines to Ochanomizu, Hijiribashi exit) FREE Established in 1691 and later used as a school for the sons of the powerful during the Tokugawa regime, this is one of Tokyo's handful of Confucian shrines. There's a Ming-dynasty bronze statue of Confucius in its black-lacquered main hall. The sculpture is visible only from 1 to 4 January and the fourth Sunday in April, but you can turn up at weekends and holidays to see the building's interior.

TOKYO WONDER SITE HONGO ART GALLERY

Map p290 (トーキョーワンダーサイト本郷; www.tokyo-ws.org; 2-4-16 Hongo, Bunkyō-ku; ⏱hours vary; 🚉JR Chūō or Sōbu line to Ochanomizu, Ochanomizu-bashi exit) FREE Tokyo Wonder Site comprises three floors of galleries with the aim of promoting new and emerging artists. There is a regularly changing program of exhibitions, competitions and lectures in a range of media. Check the website before setting out.

GALLERY KURA GALLERY

Map p290 (Gallery蔵; http://ocha-navi.solacity.jp; Sola City, 4-6 Kanda Surugandai, Chiyoda-ku; ⏱11am-7pm Mon, Wed-Fri, 10.30am-6pm Sat & Sun; S Chiyoda line to Shin-Ochanomizu, exit B2) FREE Tucked away amid the new Sola City development is this exhibition space occupying a relocated 1917 storehouse once used by the area's book distributors. Various art shows and events are held here.

EATING

Kanda

KANDA YABU SOBA SOBA $

Map p290 (神田やぶそば; ☎3251-0287; www.yabusoba.net; 2-10 Kanda-Awajichō, Chiyoda-ku; noodles ¥700-2000; ⏱11.30am-8.30pm; 📵; S Marunouchi line to Awajichō, exit A3) This venerable buckwheat noodle shop has had a total rebuild following a fire in 2013. When you walk in, staff singing out the orders is one of the first signs that you've arrived in a singular, ageless place. Come here for classic handmade noodles and accompaniments such as shrimp tempura (*ten-seiro soba*) or slices of duck (*kamo-nanban soba*).

KIKANBŌ RĀMEN $

Map p290 (鬼金棒; http://karashibi.com; 2-10-8 Kaji-chō, Chiyoda-ku; rāmen from ¥780; ⏱11am-9.30pm Mon-Sat, to 4pm Sun; 🚉JR Yamanote line to Kanda, north exit) The *karashibi* (カラシビ) spicy miso rāmen here has a cult following. Choose your level of *kara* (spice) and *shibi* (strange mouth-numbing sensation created by Japanese sanshō pepper). We recommend *futsu-futsu* (regular for both) for first-timers; *oni* (devil) level costs an extra ¥100. Look for the red door curtains and buy an order ticket from the vending machine.

KOMAKI SHOKUDŌ VEGAN $

Map p290 (こまきしょくどう; http://konnichiha.net/fushikian; Chabara, 8-2 Kanda Neribei-chō, Chiyoda-ku; set meals from ¥980; ⏱11am-7.30pm; 🚉JR Yamanote line to Akihabara, Electric Town exit) A Kamakura cooking school specialising in *shōjin-ryōri* (Buddhist-style vegan cuisine) runs this cafe within the Chabara food market. Their nonmeat meals and dishes are tasty and they sell some of the ingredients they use.

AMANOYA DESSERTS $

Map p290 (天野屋; www.amanoya.jp; 2-8-15 Soto-Kanda, Chiyoda-ku; desserts from ¥500; ⏱10am-6pm Mon-Sat, to 5pm Sun; 🚉JR Chūō or Sōbu lines to Ochanomizu, Hijiribashi exit) The owner of this charming dessert cafe is a bit of a collector, as you'll discover from the eclectic bits and bobs on display ranging from model trains to carved masks. Motherly women doll out sweet treats, such as *mochi* rice cakes, as well *amazake*, a mildly alcoholic milky sake beverage that's long been a house speciality.

ISEGEN JAPANESE $$

Map p290 (いせ源; ☎3251-1229; www.isegen.com; 1-11-1 Kanda-Sudachō, Chiyoda-ku; dishes from ¥1000; ⏱11.30am-2pm & 5-9pm Mon-Sat, closed Sat Jun-Aug; 📵; S Marunouchi line to Awajichō, exit A3) This illustrious fish restaurant, in business since the 1830s, operates out of a handsomely crafted 1930 wooden building. The speciality is *ankō-nabe* (monkfish stew; ¥3400 per person, minimum order for two) served in a splendid communal tatami room.

BOTAN SUKIYAKI $$$

Map p290 (ぼたん; ☎3251-0577; http://r.gnavi.co.jp/g198900; 1-15 Kanda-Sudachō, Chiyoda-ku; set meals from ¥7300; ⏱11.30am-9pm Mon-Sat; 📵; S Marunouchi line to Awajichō, exit A3) Botan has been making a single, perfect dish in the same traditional wooden house since the 1890s. Sit cross-legged on rattan mats as chicken *nabe* (meat cooked in broth with vegetables) simmers over a charcoal brazier next to you, allowing you to take in the scent of prewar Tokyo. Try to get a seat in the handsome upstairs dining room.

DRINKING

★IMASA — CAFE

Map p290 (井政; ☎3258-0059; www.kanda-imasa.co.jp; 2-16 Soto-Kanda, Chiyoda-ku; drinks ¥600; ⊙11am-4pm Mon-Fri; 🚉JR Chūō or Sōbu lines to Ochanomizu, Hijiribashi exit) It's not every day that you get to sip your coffee or tea in a cultural property. Imasa is the real deal, an old timber merchant's shophouse dating from 1927 but with Edo-era design and detail, and a few pieces of contemporary furniture. Very few houses like this exist in Tokyo or are open to the public.

N3331 — CAFE

Map p290 (☎5295-2788; http://n3331.com; 2nd fl, mAAch ecute 1-25-4 Kanda-Sudachō, Chiyoda-ku; ⊙11am-10.30pm Mon-Sat, to 8.30pm Sun; 🚉JR Yamamote line to Akihabara, Electric Town exit) Climb the original white-tile-clad stairs to the former platform of Mansei-bashi Station to find this ultimate trainspotters' cafe. Through floor to ceiling windows, watch commuter trains stream by while you sip on coffee, craft beer or sake and enjoy snacks.

CAFE ASAN — CAFE

Map p290 (☎6803-0502; www.cafeasan.jp; 2k540 Aki-oka Artisan, 5-9-9 Ueno, Taitō-ku; ⊙11.30am-7pm Thu-Tue; 📶; Ⓢ Ginza line to Suehirochō, exit 2) With hammock-style chairs, free wi-fi and plugs for computers and smartphones, this is a popular cafe with the digital generation. Manga and anime are a subtle design theme here, all fitting for Akiba, but the real draw are the made-to-order souffle hotcakes that are well worth waiting the 20 minutes or so they take to make.

MILONGA NUEVA — CAFE

Map p290 (ミロンガヌオーバ; ☎3295-1716; 1-3 Kanda-Jimbōchō, Chiyoda-ku; ⊙10.30am-10.30pm Mon-Fri, 11.30am-7pm Sat & Sun; Ⓢ Shinjuku line to Jimbōchō, exit A7) Off an alley parallel to Yasukuni-dōri, this wonderfully retro cafe plays old tango tunes on the sound system and serves up blends such as Kilimanjaro coffee for ¥650.

@HOME CAFE — CAFE

Map p290 (@ほぉ〜むカフェ; www.cafe-athome.com; 4th-7th fl, 1-11-4 Soto-Kanda, Chiyoda-ku; drinks from ¥500; ⊙11.30am-10pm Mon-Fri, 10.30am-10pm Sat & Sun; 🚉JR Yamanote line to Akihabara, Electric Town exit) *Kawaii* (cute) waitresses, dressed as French maids, play children's games with customers at this quintessential 'maid cafe'. You'll be welcomed as *go-shujinsama* (master) the minute you enter. It's a little titillating, perhaps, but this is no sex joint – just (more or less) innocent fun for Akiba's *otaku*. Dishes, such as curried rice, are topped with smiley faces.

ENTERTAINMENT

AKB48 THEATRE — POP CULTURE

Map p290 (www.akb48.co.jp/english/overseas/index.html; 8th fl, Don Quijote, 4-3-3 Soto-Kanda, Chiyoda-ku; 🚉JR Yamanote line to Akihabara, Electric Town exit) This J-pop phenomenon is a girl group of 60 rotating members who perform in shifts at their very own workhouse…er… theatre in the heart of Akihabara. Tickets for sell-out shows are awarded by lottery; overseas visitors can try their luck by sending an email to sfar@akb48.co.jp one month in advance of coming to Japan – see the website for further details. If you're curious to see what the big deal is, pop into **AKB48 Cafe** (Map p290; http://akb48cafeshops.com; 1-1 Kanda Hanagaoka-chō, Chiyoda-ku; ⊙11am-11pm; 🚉JR Yamanote line to Akihabara, Electric Town exit) where videos of the group play on loop and look-a-like waitresses serve cutesy concoctions to slack-jawed fans.

CLUB GOODMAN — LIVE MUSIC

(☎3862-9010; http://clubgoodman.com; B1 fl, AS Bldg, 55 Kanda-Sakumagashi, Chiyoda-ku; cover from ¥1500; 🚉JR Yamanote line to Akihabara, Electric Town exit) In the basement of a building with a guitar shop and recording studios, it's no surprise that this live house is a favourite with Tokyo's indie-scene bands and their fans.

SHOPPING

★2K540 AKI-OKA ARTISAN — CRAFTS

Map p290 (アキオカアルチザン; www.jrtk.jp/2k540; 5-9-23 Ueno, Taitō-ku; ⊙11am-7pm Thu-Tue; 🚉Ginza line to Suehirochō, exit 2) This ace arcade under the JR tracks (its name refers to the distance from Tokyo Station) offers an eclectic range of stores selling Japanese-made goods – everything from pottery to cute aliens, a nod to Akihabara from a mall that is more akin to

Kyoto than Electric Town. The best for colourful crafts is **Nippon Hyakkuten** (日本百貨店; http://nippon-dept.jp). Also look for customisable wood cases for your digital life at **Hacoa** (ハコア), dainty kaleidoscopes at **Sōshin Kaleidoscopes** (創心万華鏡) or figurines at **Studio Uamou** (ｽﾀｼﾞｵ ｳｱﾓｳ), showcasing the cartoonish creations of designer Takagi Ayako. The latter shares space with **Boo** (遊食家; Map p290; 2k540 Aki-Oka Artisan, 5-9-9 Ueno, Taitō-ku; ⏲11.30am-2pm, 5pm-midnight Mon, Tue, Thu-Sat, 11am-8pm Sun) 🌿, one of a handful of quirky cafes here.

MAACH ECUTE
MALL

Map p290 (www.maach-ecute.jp; 1-25-4 Kanda-Sudachō, Chiyoda-ku; ⏲11am-9pm Mon-Sat, to 8pm Sun; 🚉Chūō or Sōbu lines to Akihabara, Electric Town exit) JR has another shopping and dining hit on its hands with this complex crafted from the old station and railway arches at Mansei-bashi. Crafts, homegoods, fashions and food from across Japan are sold here; look out for **Tatazumai** which stocks more than 50 types of craft beer, cider and sakes, and **Obscura Coffee Roasters**.

★MANDARAKE COMPLEX
MANGA, ANIME

Map p290 (まんだらけコンプレックス; www.mandarake.co.jp; 3-11-2 Soto-Kanda, Chiyoda-ku; ⏲noon-8pm; 🚉JR Yamanote line to Akihabara, Electric Town exit) When *otaku* dream of heaven, it probably looks a lot like this giant go-to store for manga and anime. Eight storeys are piled high with comic books and DVDs, action figures and cell art just for starters. The 5th floor is devoted to women's comics, while the 4th floor is for men.

CHABARA
FOOD

Map p290 (ちゃばら; www.jrtk.jp/chabara; 8-2 Kanda Neribei-chō, Chiyoda-ku; ⏲11am-8pm; 🚉JR Yamanote line to Akihabara, Electric Town exit) This under-the-train-tracks shopping mall focuses on artisan food and drinks from across Japan, including premium sake, soy sauce, sweets, teas and crackers – all great souvenirs and presents.

AKIHABARA RADIO KAIKAN
MANGA, ANIME

Map p290 (秋葉原ラジオ会館; http://akihabara-radiokaikan.co.jp; 1-15-6 Soto-kanda, Chiyoda-ku; ⏲11am-8pm; 🚉JR Yamanote line to Akihabara, Electronic Town exit) Despite its name, Radio Kaikan has nothing to do with radios and everything to do with Japanese pop culture. It was completely rebuilt in 2014 to include nine floors of shops selling manga, anime, collectables such as models and figurines, fanzines, costumes and gear. Shops include Volks for dolls, **K-Books** (Kブックス; Map p290; www.k-books.co.jp; 3rd fl, Akihabara Radio Kaikan, Chiyoda-ku) and **Kayōdō Hobby Lobby** (海洋堂ホビーロビー; Map p290; ☎3253-1951; www.kaiyodo.co.jp; 5th fl, Akihabara Radio Kaikan, 1-15-6 Soto-kanda, Chiyoda-ku; ⏲11am-8pm Thu-Tue).

TECHNOLOGIA
ELECTRONICS

Map p290 (テクノロジア; www.technologia.co.jp; 4-12-9 Soto-Kanda, Chiyoda-ku; ⏲11am-7pm Fri-Wed; 🚉Ginza line to Suehirochō, exit 2) Are you on the lookout for a bipedal humanoid robot? Or would a talking Hello Kitty do the trick? Technologia specialises in DIY robot kits (from ¥50,000) with numerous motors and dance routines. It also carries a range of electronic components, robot combat DVDs, magazines and other robot goods.

YODOBASHI AKIBA
ELECTRONICS

Map p290 (ヨドバシカメラAkiba; www.yodobashi-akiba.com; 1-1 Kanda Hanaoka-chō, Chiyoda-ku; ⏲9.30am-10pm; 🚉JR Yamanote line to Akihabara, Shōwa-tōriguchi exit) This is the monster branch of Shinjuku's Yodobashi Camera where many locals shop. It has eight floors of electronics, cameras, toys, appliances, CDs and DVDs at an in-store branch of Tower Records, and even restaurants. Ask about export models and VAT-free purchases.

JIMBŌCHŌ BOOKSTORES
BOOKS

Map p290 (Ⓢ Hanzōmon line to Jimbōchō, exits A1, A6 or A7) This fascinating neighbourhood of more than 170 new and second-hand booksellers is proof that the printed word is alive and well in Tokyo. Amid tottering stacks of volumes you'll find everything from antique guidebooks of the Yoshiwara pleasure district to obscure sheet music from your favourite symphony.

ACTIVITIES

SUPER POTATO RETRO-KAN
ARCADE

Map p290 (スーパーポテトレトロ館; www.superpotato.com; 1-11-2 Soto-kanda, Chiyoda-ku; ⏲11am-8pm Mon-Fri, from 10am Sat & Sun; 🚉JR Yamanote line to Akihabara, Electric Town exit) Are you a gamer keen to sample retro computer games? On the 5th floor of this store specialising in used video games, there's a retro video arcade where you can get your hands on some old-fashioned consoles.

Ueno & Yanaka

UENO | YUSHIMA | YANAKA

Neighbourhood Top Five

❶ Getting schooled in Japanese art history at the **Tokyo National Museum** (p155), the finest collection of Japanese art in the world and home to samurai swords, *ukiyo-e* (woodblock prints) and gilded screens.

❷ Strolling through expansive **Ueno-kōen** (p158), chock-a-block with museums, temples and even a zoo.

❸ Exploring the winding lanes, temples and art galleries of **Yanaka** (p160), where time stands still.

❹ Absorbing the sights, sounds and smells of the old-fashioned outdoor market, **Ameya-yokochō** (p158).

❺ Dining in one of the neighbourhood's historic restaurants, such as the *izakaya* (Japanese pub-eatery) **Shinsuke** (p161).

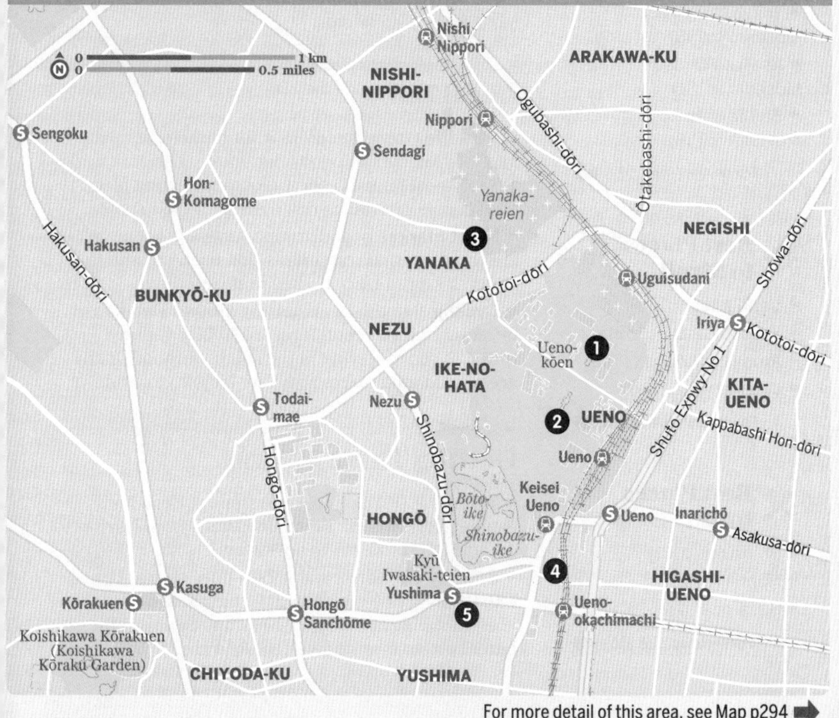

For more detail of this area, see Map p294 ➡

Lonely Planet's Top Tip

While it's possible to get around these neighbourhoods on foot, the 'tōzai' (東西; east-west) route of the **Megurin** (めぐりん; www.city.taito.lg.jp/index/kurashi/kotsu/megurin; single-ride/day pass ¥100/300) community bus does a helpful loop around the area. Useful stops include No 2, across from the Ueno Park exit at Ueno Station, No 9 in front of Yanaka Cemetery (Yanaka Rei-en Iriguchi) and No 12 for Yanaka Ginza (Yanaka Ginza Yomise-dōri). Stops are announced on the bus, which runs approximately every 15 minutes from 7am to 7pm.

Best Museums

- Tokyo National Museum (p155)
- Asakura Chōso Museum (p161)
- Shitamachi Museum (p158)

For reviews, see p155

Best Places to Stroll

- Ueno-kōen (p158)
- Yanaka Ginza (p159)
- Ameya-yokochō (p158)
- Yanaka-reien (p161)

For reviews, see p158

Best Places to Eat

- Shinsuke (p161)
- Hantei (p162)
- Sasa-no-Yuki (p161)

For reviews, see p161

Explore Ueno & Yanaka

Ueno, revolving around its sprawling park, Ueno-kōen, has been one of Tokyo's top draws since the Edo period. You could easily spend a whole day just exploring the park. Start in the morning at the Tokyo National Museum and wend your way southward, hitting a few other museums, the zoo and the centuries-old shrines and temples that dot the park. Temporary exhibitions can draw huge crowds, but you'll find the permanent collections of most museums blissfully quiet. Wrap up the day with a stroll through the retro street market Ameya-yokochō.

Within walking distance of Ueno is Yanaka, famous locally as the neighbourhood that time forgot. Having survived, miraculously, the Great Kantō Earthquake and the allied fire-bombing of WWII (not to mention the slash and burn modernising of the postwar years), Yanaka has a high concentration of vintage wooden structures. But that's not all that makes Yanaka unique: it has more than a hundred temples, relocated from around Tokyo during an Edo-era episode of urban restructuring. Many artists also live and work in the neighbourhood. Simply put, it's a fantastic place to wander. It's popular with Tokyoites though too, and can get crowded on weekends. There are also a handful of charming museums here and in neighbouring Yushima that see few tourists.

With the exception of the area around Ueno Station, these districts get pretty quiet at night, though Yanaka has a few hip hang-outs.

Local Life

- **Park life** On weekends, look for buskers, acrobats and food vendors in Ueno-kōen (p158). The park is also Tokyo's most famous cherry-blossom viewing place, with people arriving at dawn to claim their spots.
- **Night market** In and around Ameya-yokochō (p158) are several casual restaurants that open up onto the street. It's a fun place to dine in the evening.
- **Cycling** Join the locals getting around Yanaka by bicycle with a rental from Tokyo Bike Gallery (p162). If you're staying in the neighbourhood, many accommodation places also have bicycles to lend.

Getting There & Away

- **Train** The JR Yamanote line stops at Ueno and Nippori (for Yanaka). Keisei line trains from Narita Airport stop at Keisei Ueno Station.
- **Subway** The Ginza and Hibiya lines stop at Ueno. The Chiyoda line runs along the west side of Ueno-kōen, stopping at Yushima, Nezu and Sendagi; the latter two stops are convenient for Yanaka.

TOP SIGHT
TOKYO NATIONAL MUSEUM

If you visit only one museum in Tokyo, make it this one. Established in 1872, the world's largest collection of Japanese art covers ancient pottery, Buddhist sculpture, samurai swords, colourful *ukiyo*-e, gorgeous kimonos and much, much more.

The Tokyo National Museum is divided into several buildings, the most of important of which is the **Honkan** (Main Gallery), which houses the collection of Japanese art. Visitors with only an hour or two should hone in on the galleries here. The building itself is in the Imperial Style of the 1930s, with art deco flourishes throughout.

Next on the priority list is the enchanting **Gallery of Hōryū-ji Treasures**, which displays masks, scrolls and gilt Buddhas from Hōryū-ji (in Nara Prefecture, dating from 607) in a spare, elegant, box-shaped contemporary building (1999) by Taniguchi Yoshio. Nearby, to the west of the main gate, is the Kuro-mon (Black Gate), transported from the Edo-era mansion of a feudal lord. On weekends it opens for visitors to pass through.

Visitors with more time can explore the recently renovated, three-storied **Tōyōkan** (Gallery of Eastern Antiquities), with its collection of Buddhist sculptures from around Asia and delicate Chinese ceramics. The **Heiseikan**, accessed via a passage on the 1st floor of the Honkan, houses the Japanese Archaeological Gallery, full of pottery, talismans and articles of daily life from Japan's palaeolithic and neolithic periods.

The museum also regularly hosts temporary exhibitions (which cost extra), within the halls of the Heiseikan; these can be fantastic, but often lack the English signage found throughout the rest of the museum.

DON'T MISS...

- Honkan
- Gallery of Hōryū-ji Treasures

PRACTICALITIES

- 東京国立博物館; Tokyo Kokuritsu Hakubutsukan
- Map p294
- www.tnm.jp
- 13-9 Ueno-kōen, Taitō-ku
- adult/student/child & senior ¥620/¥410/free
- 9.30am-5pm Tue-Thu year round, to 8pm Fri, to 6pm Sat & Sun (Mar-Dec)
- JR Yamanote line to Ueno, Ueno-kōen exit

Tokyo National Museum

HISTORIC HIGHLIGHTS

It would be a challenge to take in everything the sprawling Tokyo National Museum has to offer in a day. Fortunately, the Honkan (Main Gallery) is designed to give visitors a crash course in Japanese art history from the Jōmon era (13,000–300 BC) to the Edo era (AD 1603–1868). The works on display here are rotated regularly, to protect fragile ones and to create seasonal exhibitions – you're always guaranteed to see something new.

Buy your ticket from outside the main gate then head straight to the Honkan with its sloping tile roof. Stow your coat in a locker and take the central staircase up to the 2nd floor, where the exhibitions are arranged chronologically. Allow two hours for this tour of the highlights.

The first room on your right starts from the beginning with **ancient Japanese art** ❶. Be sure to pick up a copy of the brochure Highlights of Japanese Art at the entrance.

Continue to the **National Treasure Gallery** ❷. 'National Treasure' is the highest distinction awarded to a work of art in Japan. Keep an eye out for more National Treasures, labelled in red, on display in other rooms throughout the museum.

Moving on, stop to admire the **art of the Imperial court** ❸, the **samurai armour and swords** ❹ and the **ukiyo-e and kimono** ❺.

Next, take the stairs down to the 1st floor, where each room is dedicated to a different craft, such as lacquerware or ceramics. Don't miss the excellent examples of **religious sculpture** ❻ and **folk art** ❼.

Finish your visit with a look inside the enchanting **Gallery of Hōryū-ji Treasures** ❽.

Ukiyo-e & Kimono (Room 10)
Chic silken kimono and lushly coloured *ukiyo-e* (woodblock prints) are two icons of the Edo era (AD 1603–1868) *ukiyo* – the 'floating world', or world of fleeting beauty and pleasure.

Japanese Sculpture (Room 11)
Many of Japan's most famous sculptures, religious in nature, are locked away in temple reliquaries. This is a rare chance to see them up close.

MUSEUM GARDEN

Don't miss the garden if you visit during the few weeks it's open to the public in spring and autumn.

Heiseikan & Japanese Archaeology Gallery

Research & Information Centre

❽

Hyōkeikan

Kuro-mon

Main Gate

Gallery of Hōryū-ji Treasures
Surround yourself with miniature gilt Buddhas from Hōryū-ji, said to be one of Japan's oldest Buddhist temples, founded in 607. Don't miss the graceful Pitcher with Dragon Head, a National Treasure.

REBECCA MILNER ©

REBECCA MILNER ©

Samurai Armour & Swords (Rooms 5 & 6)

Glistening swords, finely stitched armour and imposing helmets bring to life the samurai, those iconic warriors of Japan's medieval age.

Art of the Imperial Court (Room 3-2)

Literature works, calligraphy and narrative picture scrolls are displayed alongside decorative art objects, which allude to the life of elegance led by courtesans a thousand years ago.

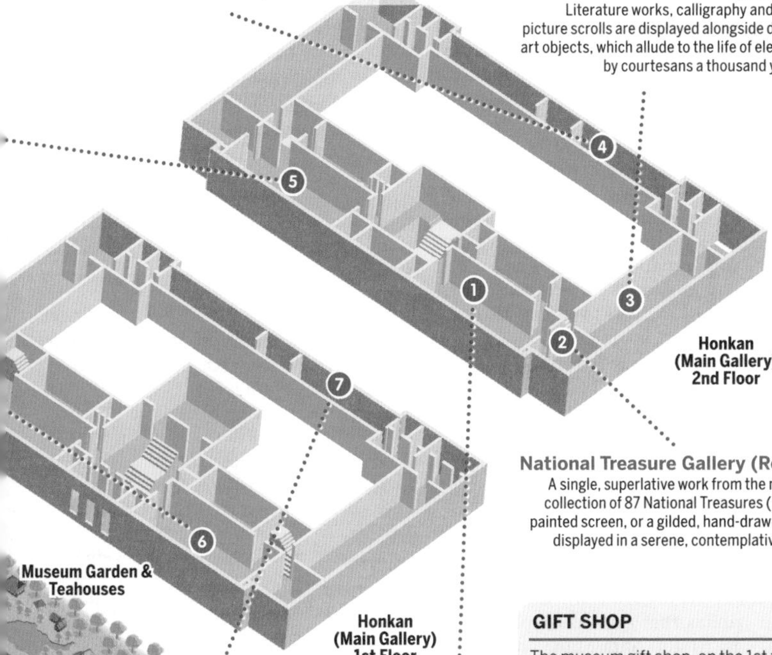

Honkan (Main Gallery) 2nd Floor

Honkan (Main Gallery) 1st Floor

Museum Garden & Teahouses

Honkan (Main Gallery)

Tōyōkan (Gallery of Eastern Antiquities)

National Treasure Gallery (Room 2)

A single, superlative work from the museum's collection of 87 National Treasures (perhaps a painted screen, or a gilded, hand-drawn sutra) is displayed in a serene, contemplative setting.

GIFT SHOP

The museum gift shop, on the 1st floor of the Honkan, has an excellent collection of Japanese art books in English.

Dawn of Japanese Art (Room 1)

The rise of the Imperial court and the introduction of Buddhism changed the Japanese aesthetic forever. These clay works from previous eras show what came before.

Folk Culture (Room 15)

See artefacts from Japan's historical minorities – the indigenous Ainu of Hokkaidō, the Kirishitan (persecuted Christians of the middle ages) and the former Ryūkyū Empire, now Okinawa.

REBECCA MILNER ©

REBECCA MILNER ©

SIGHTS

Ueno

TOKYO NATIONAL MUSEUM MUSEUM

See p155.

UENO-KŌEN PARK

Map p294 (上野公園; ⌚5am-11pm; 🚊JR Yamanote line to Ueno, Ueno-kōen & Shinobazu exits) Sprawling Ueno-kōen has wooded pathways that wind past centuries-old temples and shrines – even a zoo. At the southern tip is a large pond, Shinobazu-ike, choked with lily pads. Stroll down the causeway to **Benten-dō** (弁天堂; Map p294; ☎3821-4638; 2-1 Ueno-kōen, Taitō-ku; ⌚9am-5pm; 🚊JR Yamanote line to Ueno, Shinobazu exit) FREE, a temple dedicated to Benzaiten (the water goddess). From here you can get a good look at the birds and botany that thrive in the park; you can also rent row boats (per hour ¥600). Navigating the park is easy, thanks to large maps in English.

UENO ZOO ZOO

Map p294 (上野動物園; Ueno Dōbutsu-en; www.tokyo-zoo.net; 9-83 Ueno-kōen, Taitō-ku; adult/child ¥600/free; ⌚9.30am-5pm Tue-Sun; 🚊JR Yamanote line to Ueno, Ueno-kōen exit) Located in Ueno-kōen, Japan's oldest zoo is home to animals from around the globe, but the biggest attractions are two giant pandas that arrived from China in 2011 – Rī Rī and Shin Shin. There's also a whole area devoted to lemurs, which makes sense given Tokyoites' love of all things cute.

UENO TŌSHŌ-GŪ SHINTO SHRINE

Map p294 (上野東照宮; www.uenotoshogu.com; 9-88 Ueno-kōen, Taitō-ku; admission ¥500; ⌚9.30am-4.30pm; 🚊JR Yamanote line to Ueno, Shinobazu exit) Like its counterpart in Nikkō (p182), this shrine inside Ueno-kōen was built in honour of Tokugawa Ieyasu, the warlord who unified Japan. Resplendent in gold leaf and ornate details, it dates from 1651 (though it recently underwent a touch-up). You can get a pretty good look from outside the gate, if you want to skip the admission fee.

In January and February there is a spectacular peony garden (joint admission ¥1000).

KIYŌMIZU KANNON-DŌ BUDDHIST TEMPLE

Map p294 (清水観音堂; 1-29 Ueno-kōen, Taitō-ku; ⌚9am-4pm; 🚊JR Yamanote line to Ueno, Shinobazu exit) Ueno-kōen's Kiyōmizu Kannon-dō is one of Tokyo's oldest structures: established in 1631 and in its present position since 1698, it has survived every disaster come its way. It's a miniature of the famous Kiyomizu-dera in Kyoto and is a pilgrimage site for women hoping to conceive.

AMEYA-YOKOCHŌ MARKET

Map p294 (アメヤ横町; 4 Ueno, Taitō-ku; 🚊JR Yamanote line to Ueno, Ueno-kōen exit) Step into this alley paralleling the JR Yamanote line tracks, and ritzy, glitzy Tokyo feels like a distant memory. This open-air market got its start as a black market, post WWII, when American goods were sold here. Today, it's filled with vendors selling everything from fresh seafood and exotic cooking spices to jeans and sneakers.

SHITAMACHI MUSEUM MUSEUM

Map p294 (下町風俗資料館; ☎3823-7451; www.taitocity.net/taito/shitamachi; 2-1 Ueno-kōen, Taitō-ku; adult/child ¥300/100; ⌚9.30am-4.30pm Tue-Sun; 🚊JR Yamanote line to Ueno, Shinobazu exit) This museum re-creates life in the plebeian quarters of Tokyo during the Meiji and Taishō periods (1868–1926), before the city was twice destroyed by the Great Kanto Earthquake and WWII. There are old tenement houses and shops that you can enter.

NATIONAL SCIENCE MUSEUM MUSEUM

Map p294 (国立科学博物館; Kokuritsu Kagaku Hakubutsukan; www.kahaku.go.jp; 7-20 Ueno-kōen, Taitō-ku; adult/child ¥600/free; ⌚9am-5pm Tue-Thu, Sat & Sun, to 8pm Fri; 🚊JR Yamanote line to Ueno, Ueno-kōen exit) The Japan Gallery here showcases the rich and varied wildlife of the Japanese archipelago, from the bears of Hokkaido to the giant beetles of Okinawa. Elsewhere in the museum: a rocket launcher, a giant squid, an Edo-era mummy, and a digital seismograph that charts earthquakes in real time. There's English signage throughout, plus an English-language audio guide (¥300).

NATIONAL MUSEUM OF WESTERN ART MUSEUM

Map p294 (国立西洋美術館; Kokuritsu Seiyō Bijutsukan; www.nmwa.go.jp; 7-7 Ueno-kōen, Taitō-ku; adult/student ¥420/130, 2nd & 4th Sat of the month free; ⌚9.30am-5.30pm Tue-Thu, Sat & Sun, to 8pm Fri; 🚊JR Yamanote line to Ueno, Ueno-kōen exit) The permanent collection here runs from medieval Madonna and child images to 20th-century abstract expressionism, but is strongest in French impressionism, including a whole gallery of Monet. The main building was designed by Le Corbusier in the late 1950s and is now on Unesco's World Heritage List.

TOKYO METROPOLITAN MUSEUM OF ART MUSEUM

Map p294 (東京都美術館; www.tobikan.jp; 8-36 Ueno-kōen, Taitō-ku; admission varies; ⌚9.30am-5.30pm Tue-Thu, Sat & Sun, to 8pm Fri; 🚉JR Yamanote line to Ueno, Ueno-kōen exit) This museum hosts blockbuster shows on loan from international museums (such as New York's Metropolitan Museum of Art). Other exhibition halls are given over to local artistic associations, whose shows include works (ceramics, calligraphy etc) from living artists.

⊙ Yushima

KYŪ IWASAKI-TEIEN HISTORIC BUILDING

Map p294 (旧岩崎邸庭園; ☎3823-8340; http://teien.tokyo-park.or.jp/en/kyu-iwasaki/index.html; 1-3-45 Ike-no-hata, Taitō-ku; adult/child ¥400/free; ⌚9am-5pm; Ⓢ Chiyoda line to Yushima, exit 1) This grand residence was once the villa of Hisaya Iwasaki, son of the founder of Mitsubishi, and is now a fascinating example of how the cultural elite of the early Meiji period tried to straddle east and west. Built in 1896, it has been open to the public since 2001.

YOKOYAMA TAIKAN MEMORIAL HALL MUSEUM

Map p294 (横山大観記念館; http://members2.jcom.home.ne.jp/taikan/index.htm; 1-4-24 Ike-no-hata, Taitō-ku; adult/child ¥550/200; ⌚10am-4pm Thu-Sun; Ⓢ Chiyoda line to Yushima, exit 1) Early-20th-century artist Yokoyama Taikan was one of the masters of modern *nihonga* (Japanese-style painting). Inside his former residence, a traditional Japanese structure with a garden, are changing displays of his works and those of his contemporaries. The museum closes for several weeks in June, August and December.

YUSHIMA TENJIN SHINTO SHRINE

Map p294 (湯島天神, Yushima Tenmangu; 3-30-1 Yushima, Bunkyō-ku; ⌚6am-8pm; Ⓢ Chiyoda line to Yushima, exit 1) In the 14th century, the spirit of a renowned scholar was enshrined here, leading to the shrine's current popularity: it receives countless students who come to pray for academic success, especially during school-entrance-exam season.

⊙ Yanaka

YANAKA GINZA STREET

Map p294 (谷中銀座; 🚉JR Yamanote line to Nippori, north exit) Yanaka Ginza is pure, vintage mid-20th-century Tokyo, a pedestrian street lined with butcher shops, vegetable vendors and the like. Most Tokyo neighbourhoods once had stretches like these (until supermarkets took over). It's popular with Tokyoites from all over the city, who

LOCAL KNOWLEDGE

ARTISTS' TOWN YANAKA

Yanaka and its surrounds have been an artists' haven for centuries – thanks to all the temples that once provided a steady stream of commissions, explains Allan West, an artist himself and a resident of Yanaka for more than 20 years. Tokyo University of the Arts (also known as Geidai, Japan's top art school), is in nearby Ueno, another reason artists often settle around here.

West (a Geidai graduate) makes his paints the old-fashioned way, by grinding precious stones, such as lapis lazuli and malachite. Only a handful of stores remain in all of Japan that sell such materials – nearly half of which are in Yanaka. You can stop by his studio, **Edokoro** (繪処アランウエスト; Map p294; ☎3827-1907; www.allanwest.jp; 1-6-17 Yanaka, Taitō-ku; ⌚1-5pm, from 3pm Sun, closed irregularly; Ⓢ Chiyoda line to Nezu, exit 1) FREE, and sometimes even catch him at work, making gilded screens and scrolls.

To get a feel for the artist's life in Yanaka, West recommends a visit to the Yokoyama Taikan Memorial Hall and the Asakura Chōso Museum (p161); the latter, he says, is 'really spectacular – the kind of space only a sculptor could think of.'

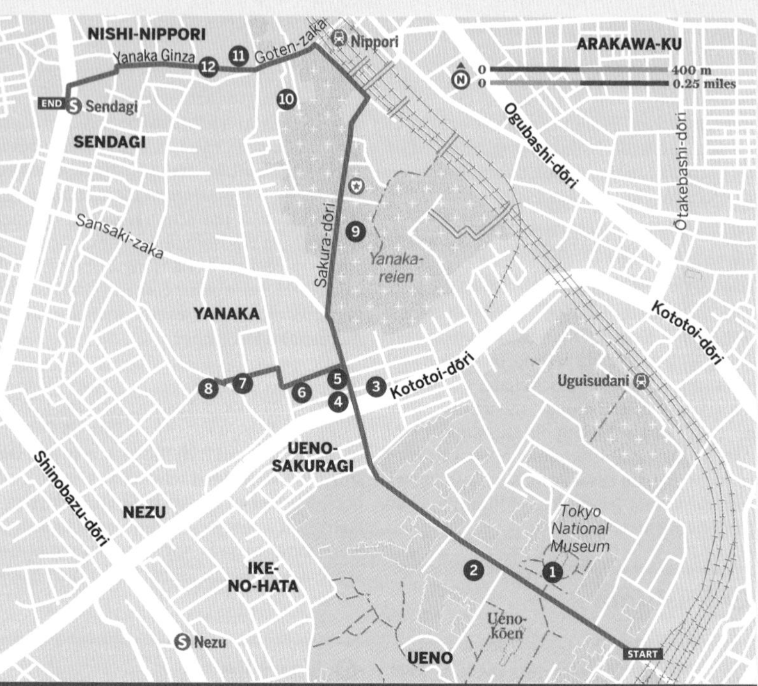

Neighbourhood Walk Yanaka

START TOKYO NATIONAL MUSEUM
FINISH SENDAGI STATION
LENGTH 3KM; TWO HOURS

If you have time, visit the **1 Tokyo National Museum** (p155) before you start exploring Yanaka, with its temples, galleries and old wooden buildings. If not, simply follow the road northwest out of **2 Ueno-kōen** (p158) until you hit Kototoi-dōri. At the corner is the **3 Shitamachi Museum Annex** (p161), actually a preserved, century-old liquor store. Across the street is **4 Kayaba Coffee** (p162), if you need a pick-me-up.

From here, it's a short walk to **5 SCAI the Bathhouse** (p161), a classic old public bathhouse turned contemporary art gallery. It's a worthwhile detour to continue down to **6 Edokoro** (p159), the studio of painter Allan West, and to see the ancient, thick-trunked **7 Himalayan cedar tree** on the corner. In and around here, you'll pass many temples, including **8 Enju-ji**, where Nichikasama, the 'god of strong legs' is enshrined; it's popular with runners. Feel free to stop in any of the temples, just be respectful and keep your voice low.

Now double back towards the entrance of **9 Yanaka-reien** (p161), one of Tokyo's most atmospheric and prestigious cemeteries (also a favourite sunning spot of the neighborhood's many stray cats). When you exit the cemetery, continue with the train tracks on your right, climbing until you reach the bridge, which overlooks the tracks (a favorite destination for trainspotters).

Head left and look for the sign pointing towards the **10 Asakura Chōso Museum** (p161), the home studio of an early-20th-century sculptor and now an attractive museum. Back on the main drag, continue down the **11 Yūyake Dandan** – literally the 'Sunset Stairs' – to the classic mid-20th-century shopping street, **12 Yanaka Ginza** (p159). Pick up some snacks from the vendors here, then hunker down on a milk crate on the side of the road with the locals and wash it all down with a beer.

Walk west and you can pick up the subway at Sendagi Station.

come to soak up the nostalgic atmosphere, plus the locals who shop here.

ASAKURA CHŌSO MUSEUM MUSEUM

Map p294 (朝倉彫塑館; www.taitocity.net/taito/asakura; 7-16-10 Yanaka, Taitō-ku; adult/student ¥400/150; ⏲9.30am-4.30pm Tue-Thu, Sat & Sun; JR Yamanote line to Nippori, north exit) Sculptor Asakura Fumio (artist name Chōso; 1883–1964) designed this atmospheric house himself, which includes a central water garden, a studio with vaulted ceilings and a 'sunrise room'. It's now a museum with a number of the artist's signature realist works, mostly of people and cats, on display.

YANAKA-REIEN CEMETERY

Map p294 (谷中霊園; 7-5-24 Yanaka, Taitō-ku; JR Yamanote line to Nippori, west exit) One of Tokyo's largest graveyards, Yanaka-reien is the final resting place of more than 7000 souls, many of whom were quite well known in their day. It's also where you'll find the tomb of Yoshinobu Tokugawa (徳川慶喜の墓), the last shōgun.

SCAI THE BATHHOUSE ART GALLERY

Map p294 (スカイザバスハウス; 3821-1144; www.scaithebathhouse.com; 6-1-23 Yanaka, Taitō-ku; ⏲noon-6pm Tue-Sat; S Chiyoda line to Nezu, exit 1) FREE Once a 200-year-old bathhouse, now a cutting-edge gallery space, SCAI showcases Japanese and international artists in its austere vaulted space.

DAIMYO CLOCK MUSEUM MUSEUM

Map p294 (大名時計博物館; Daimyō Tokei Hakubutsukan; 2-1-27 Yanaka, Taito-ku; adult/child ¥300/100; ⏲10am-4pm Tue-Sun, closed Jul-Sep & 25 Dec-14 Jan; S Chiyoda line to Nezu, exit 1) Before the 1860s, only samurai lords could see these fascinating clocks, called *wadokei*, that tell time according to variable hours named after animals of the Chinese zodiac. The museum itself is a ramshackle old building.

SHITAMACHI MUSEUM ANNEX HISTORIC BUILDING

Map p294 (下町風俗資料館; 2-10-6 Uenosakuragi, Taitō-ku; ⏲9.30am-4.30pm Tue-Sun; S Chiyoda line to Nezu, exit 1) FREE This century-old liquor shop (which operated until 1986) was returned to its original state, with old sake barrels, weights, measures and posters.

EATING

Ueno & Yushima

YABU SOBA SOBA $

Map p294 (上野やぶそば; 3831-4728; 6-9-16 Ueno, Taitō-ku; ⏲11.30am-8.30pm Thu-Tue; JR Yamanote line to Ueno, Hirokōji exit) This busy, famous place rustles up top-class *soba* (buckwheat noodles). There's a picture menu to help you choose. Look for the black-granite sign in front that says in English 'Since 1892'.

★SHINSUKE IZAKAYA $$

Map p294 (シンスケ; 3832-0469; 3-31-5 Yushima, Bunkyō-ku; ⏲5-9.30pm Mon-Fri, to 9pm Sat; S Chiyoda line to Yushima, exit 3) In business since 1925, Shinsuke is pretty much the platonic ideal of an *izakaya*: long cedar counter, 'master' in *happi* (traditional short coat) and *hachimaki* (traditional headband) and smooth-as-silk *dai-ginjo* (premium grade sake). The only part that seems out of place is the friendly staff who go out of their way to explain the dishes in English.

Really, this is the kind of place that should be intimidating for travellers, but isn't at all, and the food – contemporary updates of classics – is fantastic. Don't miss the *kitsune raclette* – deep-fried tofu stuffed with raclette cheese.

SASA-NO-YUKI TOFU $$

Map p294 (笹乃雪; 3873-1145; 2-15-10 Negishi, Taitō-ku; dishes ¥400-700, lunch/dinner course from ¥2200/5000; ⏲11.30am-8pm Tue-Sun; JR Yamanote line to Uguisudani, north exit) Sasa-no-Yuki opened its doors in the Edo period, and continues to serve its signature dishes, with tofu made fresh every morning with water from the shop's own well. Some treats to expect: *ankake-dofu* (tofu in a thick, sweet sauce) and *goma-dofu* (sesame tofu). The best seats overlook a tiny garden with a koi pond.

Vegetarians should not assume everything is purely veggie – ask before ordering. There is bamboo out front.

IZU-EI HONTEN UNAGI $$

Map p294 (伊豆栄本店; www.izuei.co.jp; 2-12-22 Ueno, Taitō-ku; set meals ¥2160-4860; ⏲11am-9.30pm; JR Yamanote line to Ueno, Hirokōji exit) Izu-ei's twin delights are its delicious *unagi* (eel) and its elegant, traditional

BICYCLE RENTAL

Ueno-kōen and Yanaka are great places to stroll; they're also great places to cycle. Hipster bicycle manufacturer **Tokyo Bike** (Map p294; www.tokyobike.com; 4-2-39 Yanaka, Taitō-ku; ¥1000 per day; 11.30am-5.30pm Fri-Tue; JR Yamanote line to Nippori, west exit) in Yanaka rents seven-speed city bikes for the afternoon. Reserve one in advance by sending an email with your name, desired day, and height.

atmosphere, with waitresses in kimonos and tatami seating (there are chairs, too).

There's another branch inside Ueno-kōen, **Izu-ei Umekawa-tei** (梅川亭; Map p294; 4-34 Ueno-kōen, Taitō-ku; 11am-3pm, 5-10pm Mon-Fri, 11am-10pm Sat & Sun; ; JR Yamanote line to Ueno, Ueno-kōen exit).

Yanaka

NEZU NO TAIYAKI SWEETS $

Map p294 (根津のたいやき; 1-23-9-104 Nezu, Bunkyō-ku; taiyaki ¥170; 10.30am until sold out, closed irregularly; ; Chiyoda line to Nezu, exit 1) This street stall, beloved of locals for half a century, sells just one thing: *taiyaki*, hot, sweet, bean-jam buns shaped like *tai* (sea bream) – a fish considered to be lucky. Come early before they sell out (always by 2pm, and sometimes by noon).

★**HANTEI** TRADITIONAL JAPANESE $$

Map p294 (はん亭; 3828-1440; www.hantei.co.jp/nedu.html; 2-12-15 Nezu, Bunkyō-ku; lunch/dinner course from ¥3150/2835; noon-3pm & 5-10pm Tue-Sun; ; Chiyoda line to Nezu, exit 2) Housed in a beautifully maintained, century-old traditional wooden building, Hantei is a local landmark. Delectable skewers of seasonal *kushiage* (fried meat, fish and vegetables) are served with small, refreshing side dishes. Lunch courses include eight sticks and dinner courses start with six, after which you'll continue to receive additional rounds (¥210 per skewer) until you say stop.

KAMACHIKU UDON $$

Map p294 (釜竹; 5815-4675; http://kamachiku.com/top_en; 2-14-18 Nezu, Bunkyō-ku; noodles from ¥850, small dishes ¥350-850; 11.30am-2pm Tue-Sun, 5-9pm Tue-Sat; ; Chiyoda line to Nezu, exit 1) Udon (thick, wheat noodles) made fresh daily is the speciality at this popular restaurant, in a beautifully restored brick warehouse from 1910. In addition to noodles, the menu includes lots of *izakaya*-style small dishes (such as grilled fish and veggies). Expect to queue on weekends.

NAGOMI YAKITORI $$

Map p294 (和味; 3821-5972; 3-11-11 Yanaka, Taitō-ku; skewers from ¥180; 5pm-midnight; ; JR Yamanote line to Nippori, north exit) On Yanaka Ginza, Nagomi deals in juicy skewers of *ji-dori* (free-range chicken). There are plenty of grilled veggie options, too. Wash it all down with a bowl of chicken soup *rāmen*. Look for the sake bottles in the window.

DRINKING & NIGHTLIFE

TORINDŌ TEAHOUSE

Map p294 (桃林堂; 1-5-7 Ueno-Sakuragi, Taitō-ku; tea set ¥810; 9am-5pm; Chiyoda line to Nezu, exit 1) Sample a cup of paint-thick *matcha* (powdered green tea) at this tiny teahouse on the edge of Ueno-kōen. Tradition dictates that the bitter tea be paired with something sweet, so choose from the artful desserts in the glass counter, then pull up a stool at the communal table. It's a white building with persimmon-coloured door curtains.

KAYABA COFFEE CAFE

Map p294 (カヤバ珈琲; http://kayaba-coffee.com; 6-1-29 Yanaka, Taitō-ku; drinks from ¥400; 8am-11pm Mon-Sat, to 6pm Sun; Chiyoda line to Nezu, exit 1) This vintage 1930s coffee shop (the building is actually from the '20s) in Yanaka is a hang-out for local students and artists. Come early for the 'morning set' (coffee and a sandwich for ¥700). In the evenings, Kayaba morphs into a bar.

BOUSINGOT BAR

Map p294 (ブーザンゴ; 3823-5501; www.bousingot.com; 2-33-2 Sendagi, Bunkyō-ku; drinks from ¥450; 6-11pm Wed-Mon; Chiyoda line to Sendagi, exit 1) It's fitting that Yanaka, which refuses to trash the past, would have a bar that doubles as a used bookstore. Sure, the books are in Japanese but you can still enjoy soaking up the atmosphere with some resident book lovers.

WARRIOR CELT PUB

Map p294 (www.warriorcelt.jp; 3rd fl, 6-9-22 Ueno, Taitō-ku; pints ¥900; ⏲5pm-midnight; JR Yamanote line to Ueno, Hirokōji exit) A long-running, authentic pub, the Warrior Celt is the rare expat hang-out on the east side of town. There's live music most weekends, ranging from rock to celtic folk. Pints go for ¥600 during happy hour (5pm to 7pm) and all night on Thursdays for ladies.

ENTERTAINMENT

TOKYO BUNKA KAIKAN CLASSICAL MUSIC

Map p294 (東京文化会館; 5-45 Ueno-kōen, Taitō-ku; JR Yamanote line to Ueno, Ueno-kōen exit) The Tokyo Metropolitan Symphony Orchestra and the Tokyo Ballet all make regular appearances at this large hall inside Ueno-kōen. Prices vary wildly; look out for monthly morning classical-music performances that cost only ¥500.

Tokyo Bunka Kaikan is also the main venue for **Tokyo Haru-sai** (東京春祭; www.tokyo-harusai.com/index_e.html), the classical-music festival that takes place every spring.

SHOPPING

ISETATSU CRAFTS

Map p294 (いせ辰; ☎3823-1453; 2-18-9 Yanaka, Taitō-ku; ⏲10am-6pm; S Chiyoda line to Sendagi, exit 1) Dating back to 1864, this venerable stationery shop specialises in *chiyogami:* gorgeous, colourful paper made using woodblocks.

YANAKA MATSUNOYA HOMEWARES

Map p294 (谷中松野屋; www.matsunoya.jp; 3-14-14 Nishi-Nippori, Arakawa-ku; ⏲11am-7pm Wed-Mon, from 10am Sat & Sun; JR Yamanote line to Nippori, west exit) On Yanaka Ginza, Matsunoya sells household goods – baskets, brooms and canvas totes, for example – simple in beauty and form, handmade by local artisans.

NIPPORI FABRIC TOWN FABRICS

Map p294 (日暮里繊維街; Nippori Sen-i-gai; http://nippori-senigai.com; Nippori Chūō-dōri, Arakawa-ku; ⏲hours vary; JR Yamanote line to Nippori, east exit) If you have a notion to sew, this stretch of shops east of Nippori Station – selling buttons, brocade, kimono fabric scraps and more – will hit you like a proverbial bolt. Take the north gate to the east exit; once you're out of the station, a map on your right will point you in the right direction.

SPORTS & ACTIVITIES

ROKURYU KŌSEN BATHHOUSE

Map p294 (六龍鉱泉; 3-4-20 Ikenohata, Taitō-ku; admission ¥460; ⏲3.30-11pm Tue-Sun; S Chiyoda line to Nezu, exit 2) Ancient leaves that work their way up the pipes here give the water an amber hue, and the minerals are reputed to be excellent for your skin. The bath is located down a small lane next to a shop with a green awning.

Fabrics on display in Yanaka

Asakusa & Sumida River

ASAKUSA | OSHIAGE | RYŌGOKU | KIYOSUMI | FUKAGAWA

For more detail of this area, see Map p291 and p292

Neighbourhood Top Five

❶ Soaking up the atmosphere (and the incense) at Asakusa's centuries-old temple complex, **Sensō-ji** (p166).

❷ Catching the salt-slinging, belly-slapping ritual of sumo at **Ryōgoku Kokugikan** (p175).

❸ Learning about life in old Edo at the city's excellent history museum, the **Edo-Tokyo Museum** (p170).

❹ Scaling the world's tallest tower, **Tokyo Sky Tree** (p168), and seeing the capital at your feet.

❺ Shopping for handmade goods in Asakusa's many traditional craft stores, such as **Bengara** (p174).

Explore Asakusa & Sumida River

Welcome to Tokyo's east side, the area long known as Shitamachi (the 'Low City'), where the city's merchants and artisans lived during the Edo period (1603–1868). Asakusa (ah-*saku*-sah), with its grand temple complex, is one of Tokyo's principal tourist destinations. During the day, Sensō-ji is pretty much always jam-packed. Step off the main drags though and you'll find far fewer tourists, and the craft shops and mum-and-dad restaurants that have long defined these quarters.

The neighbourhoods east of the Sumida-gawa – Oshiage, Ryōgoku, Fukagawa and Kiyosumi – look much like they have for decades, having experienced little of the development seen elsewhere in the city. Tokyo Sky Tree, just across the river from Asakusa in Oshiage, is the exception. This is the city's newest tourist attraction, with a shopping and entertainment complex at its base. Make it your last stop of the day, to see the city all lit up at night.

Ryōgoku has two key sights, the sumo stadium and the Edo-Tokyo Museum. Further south, Fukagawa and Kiyosumi have a handful of worthy sights (a temple, a shrine, a garden and some museums) yet remain fairly off the radar. Walking around these neighbourhoods can give you a feel for the old-Tokyo culture of the city's east side.

Local Life

➡ **Street food** Asakusa brims with street-food vendors (p173), especially along Nakamise-dōri.

➡ **Festivals** The 15th and 28th of each month are festival days at Fukagawa Fudō-dō (p171) and Tomioka Hachiman-gū (p171), with food stalls and a flea market.

➡ **Hang-outs** Escape the all-inclusive Tokyo Sky Tree complex and hang with the Oshiage locals at Shishimaru Shokudō (p172).

Getting There & Away

➡ **Train** The Tsukuba Express stops at Tsukuba Express Asakusa Station, west of Sensō-ji. The Tōbu Sky Tree line leaves from Tōbu Asakusa Station for Tokyo Sky Tree Station. The JR Sōbu line goes to Ryōgoku.

➡ **Subway** The Ginza line stops at Asakusa. The Asakusa line stops at a separate Asakusa Station and at Oshiage. The Ōedo line connects the Ryōgoku, Kiyosumi and Fukagawa areas via Ryōgoku, Kiyosumi-Shirakawa and Monzen-Nakachō Stations. The Hanzōmon line also stops at Oshiage and Kiyosumi-Shirakawa.

➡ **Water bus** Tokyo Cruise and Tokyo Mizube Cruising Line ferries stop at separate piers in Asakusa; Tokyo Mizube Cruising Line also stops in Ryōgoku.

Lonely Planet's Top Tip

Tokyo Mizube Cruising Line (東京水辺ライン; Map p291; www.tokyo-park.or.jp/waterbus) water buses depart from Niten-mon Pier in Asakusa for Odaiba, via Ryōgoku. It's actually the most convenient way to get between Asakusa and Ryōgoku (one way 10 minutes, ¥310) and is the perfect way for travellers short on time to sample a river cruise.

Best Places to Eat

➡ Otafuku (p172)

➡ Irokawa (p172)

➡ Asakusa Imahan (p172)

➡ Rokurinsha (p172)

For reviews, see p171 ➡

Best Places to Drink

➡ Popeye (p173)

➡ Lucite Gallery (p173)

➡ Kamiya Bar (p173)

➡ 'Cuzn Homeground (p173)

For reviews, see p173 ➡

Best Places to Shop

➡ Tokyo Hotarudo (p174)

➡ Bengara (p174)

➡ Soi (p174)

For reviews, see p174 

TOM BONAVENTURE / GETTY IMAGES ©

TOP SIGHT
SENSŌ-JI

Sensō-ji is the capital's oldest temple, older than Tokyo itself. According to legend, in AD 628, two fishermen brothers pulled out a golden image of Kannon (the bodhisattva of compassion) from the nearby Sumida-gawa. Sensō-ji was built to enshrine it. Today the temple stands out for its old-world atmosphere – a glimpse of a bygone Japan that is rarely visible in Tokyo today.

Kaminari-mon

The temple precinct begins at the majestic Kaminari-mon, which means Thunder Gate. An enormous *chōchin* (lantern), which weighs 670kg, hangs from the centre. On either side are a pair of ferocious protective deities: Fūjin, the god of wind, on the right; and Raijin, the god of thunder, on the left. Kaminari-mon has burnt down countless times over the centuries; the current gate dates to 1970.

Nakamise-dōri Shopping Street

Beyond Kaminari-mon is the bustling shopping street, Nakamise-dōri. With its souvenir stands it feels rather touristy, though that's nothing new: Sensō-ji has been Tokyo's top tourist sight for centuries, since travel was restricted to religious pilgrimages during the feudal era. In addition to the usual T-shirts, you can also find Edo-style crafts and oddities (such as wigs done up in traditional hairstyles). There are also numerous snack vendors serving up crunchy *sembei* (rice crackers) and *age-manju* (deep-fried *anko* – bean-paste – buns).

At the end of Nakamise-dōri is **Hōzō-mon**, another gate with fierce guardians. On the gate's back side are a pair of 2500kg, 4.5m-tall *waraji* (straw sandals) crafted for Sensō-ji by some 800 villagers in northern Yamagata Prefecture. These are meant to symbolise

DON'T MISS

- Kaminari-mon
- Nakamise snack vendors
- Incense cauldron at the Main Hall
- Temple Lights at Sunset
- Getting an *omikuji*

PRACTICALITIES

- 浅草寺
- Map p291
- www.senso-ji.jp
- 2-3-1 Asakusa, Taitō-ku
- 24hr
- S Ginza line to Asakusa, exit 1

the Buddha's power, and it's believed that evil spirits will be scared off by the giant footwear.

Main Hall

In front of the grand **Hondō** (Main Hall), with its dramatic sloping roof, is a large cauldron with smoking incense. The smoke is said to bestow health and you'll see people wafting it over their bodies. The current Hondō was constructed in 1958, replacing the one destroyed in the WWII air raids. The style is similar to the previous one, though the roof tiles are made of titanium.

The Kannon image (a tiny 6cm) is cloistered away from view deep inside the main hall (and admittedly may not exist at all). Nonetheless, a steady stream of worshippers visit the temple to cast coins, pray and bow in a gesture of respect. Do feel free to join in.

Off the courtyard stands a 53m-high **five-storey pagoda**, a 1973 reconstruction of a pagoda built by Tokugawa Iemitsu. The current structure is the second-highest pagoda in Japan.

Asakusa-jinja

Located on the east side of the temple complex is **Asakusa-jinja** (浅草神社; www.asakusajinja.jp/english; ⌚9am-4.30pm), built in honour of the brothers who discovered the Kannon statue that inspired the construction of Sensō-ji. (Historically, Japan's two religions, Buddhism and Shintō were intertwined and it was not uncommon for temples to include shrines and vice versa). This section of Sensō-ji survived WWII, and Asakusa-jinja's current structure dates to 1649. Painted a deep shade of red, it is a rare example of early-Edo architecture.

Next to the shrine is the temple complex's eastern gate, **Niten-mon**, standing since 1618. Though it appears minor today, this gate was the point of entry for visitors arriving in Asakusa via boat – the main form of transport during the Edo period.

Awashima-dō

Sensō-ji includes many other smaller temples. One to visit is Awashima-dō, on the western edge of the temple grounds, which dates to the late 17th century. The deity enshrined here is a guardian of women, and the temple is the site of a curious ancient ritual: *hari-kuyō* (the needle funeral). Annually on 8 February, monks perform last rites for broken or old sewing needles. Kimono makers and seamstresses express their thanks to the needles by sticking them in a block of soft tofu.

FORTUNE-TELLING

Part of the fun of visiting a temple is getting your fortune told by an *omikuji* (paper fortune). Drop ¥100 into the slots by the wooden drawers at either side of the approach to the main hall, then grab a silver canister and shake it. Extract a stick and note its number (in kanji). Replace the stick, find the matching drawer and withdraw a paper fortune (there's English on the back). If you pull out 大凶 (*dai-kyō*, Great Curse), never fear. Just tie the paper on the nearby rack, ask the gods for better luck, and try again!

The main hall and its gates are illuminated every day from sunset until 11pm. The minutes just before the sun sinks make for some of the best pictures of this photogenic sanctuary.

FESTIVALS

During the first three days of the New Year more than 2.5 million people visit Sensō-ji to pray for the year to come. Asakusa-jinja is the epicentre of one of Tokyo's most important festivals, May's Sanja Matsuri (p25), which draws another 1.5 million visitors.

SIGHTS

Asakusa

SENSŌ-JI BUDDHIST TEMPLE
See p166.

SUPER DRY HALL ARCHITECTURE
Map p291 (フラムドール; Flamme d'Or; 1-23-1 Azuma-bashi, Sumida-ku; S Ginza line to Asakusa, exit 4) Designed by Philippe Starck and completed in 1989, the Asahi Beer headquarters, with its telltale golden plume, is a Tokyo landmark. The golden bit – which weighs more than 300 tonnes – is open to interpretation: Asahi likes to think it is the foam to the building's beer mug. Locals call it the 'golden turd'.

AMUSE MUSEUM MUSEUM
Map p291 (アミューズミュージアム; www.amusemuseum.com; 2-34-3 Asakusa, Taitō-ku; adult/student ¥1080/864; 10am-6pm; S Ginza line to Asakusa, exit) Here you'll find a fascinating collection of Japanese folk articles, mainly clothing, gathered by famed ethnologist Tanaka Chūzaburō. On another floor there's a video tutorial (with English subtitles) on how to find secret meaning in *ukiyo-e* (woodblock prints). Don't miss the roof terrace, which looks over the Sensō-ji temple complex.

CHINGO-DŌ BUDDHIST TEMPLE
Map p291 (鎮護堂; 2-3-1 Asakusa, Taitō-ku; 6am-5pm; S Ginza line to Asakusa, exit 1) This small, peaceful temple is actually part of Sensō-ji but has a separate entrance on Dembō-in-dōri. It pays tribute to the *tanuki* (racoon-like folkloric characters), who figure in Japanese myth as mystical shapeshifters and merry pranksters. They are also said to protect agains fire and theft, which is why you'll often see *tanuki* figurines in front of restaurants.

RICKSHAW RIDES

Hang around the entrance to Sensō-ji long enough and you're bound to get approached by a scantily clad, strapping young man offering you...a ride in his *jinrikisha* (rickshaw). Rides start at ¥3000 per 10 minutes for two people (¥2000 for one person).

TAIKO DRUM MUSEUM MUSEUM
Map p291 (太鼓館; Taiko-kan; www.miyamoto-unosuke.co.jp/taikokan; 4th fl, 2-1-1 Nishi-Asakusa, Taitō-ku; adult/child ¥500/150; 10am-5pm Wed-Sun; S Ginza line to Tawaramachi, exit 3) There are hundreds of drums from around the world here, including several traditional Japanese *taiko*. The best part is that you can actually play most of them (those marked with a music note).

TRADITIONAL CRAFTS MUSEUM MUSEUM
Map p291 (江戸下町伝統工芸館; Edo Shitamachi Dentō Kōgeikan; www.city.taito.lg.jp/index/kurashi/shigoto/jibasangyo/kogeikan; 2-22-13 Asakusa, Taitō-ku; 10am-8pm; S Ginza line to Asakusa, exit 1) FREE Asakusa has a long artisan tradition and changing exhibitions of local crafts – such as Edo-kiriko (cut glass) – are on display here. Demonstrations are held on Saturdays and Sundays (between 11am and 5pm).

HANAYASHIKI AMUSEMENT PARK
Map p291 (花やしき; www.hanayashiki.net/index.html; 2-28-1 Asakusa, Taitō-ku; adult/child ¥1000/500; 10am-6pm; S Ginza line to Asakusa, exit 1) Japan's oldest amusement park has creaky old carnival rides and heaps of vintage charm. Once you're inside, you can buy tickets for rides (which cost a few hundred yen each). A haunted-house attraction here allegedly housed a real ghost that is said to still appear on the grounds.

Oshiage

TOKYO SKY TREE TOWER
Map p291 (東京スカイツリー; www.tokyo-skytree.jp; 1-1-2 Oshiage, Sumida-ku; admission 350m/450m observation decks ¥2060/3090; 8am-10pm; S Hanzōmon line to Oshiage, Sky Tree exit) Tokyo Sky Tree opened in May 2012 as the world's tallest 'free-standing tower' at 634m. Its silvery exterior of steel mesh morphs from a triangle at the base to a circle at 300m. There are two observation decks, at 350m and 450m. You can see more stuff during daylight hours – at peak visibility you can see up to 100km away, all the way to Mt Fuji – but it is at night that Tokyo appears truly beautiful.

The panorama from the lower observatory, the Tembō Deck, is spectacular. Don't miss the small section of glass floor panels, where you can see – dizzyingly – all the way to the ground. The upper observatory,

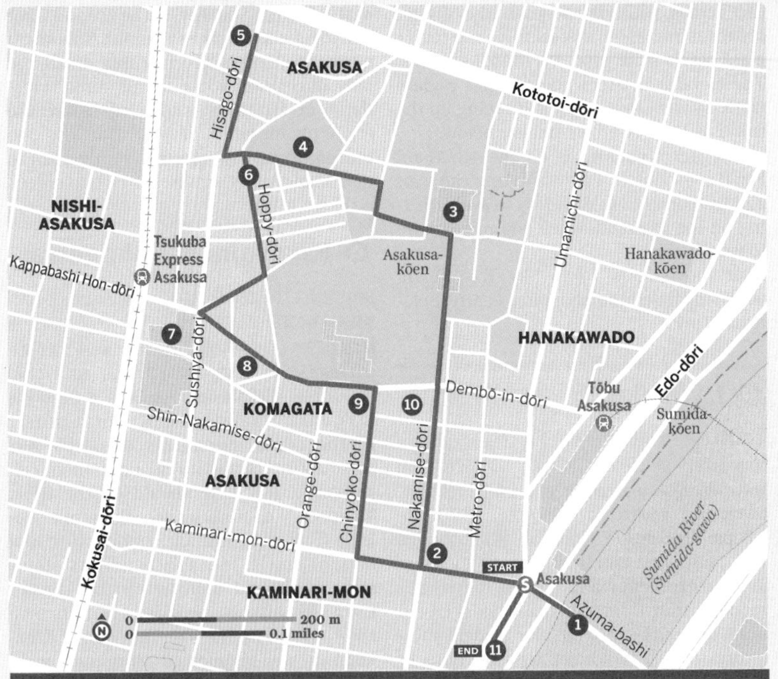

Neighbourhood Walk Shitamachi

START ASAKUSA STATION, EXIT 4
END EF
LENGTH 2.5KM; 2½ HOURS, PLUS LUNCH

This walk takes in the major sights in Asakusa, while giving you a feel for the flavour of Shitamachi (the old Edo-era 'Low City'). First head over to **1 Azuma-bashi**. Originally built in 1774, it was once the point of departure for boat trips to the Yoshiwara pleasure district, north of Asakusa. From here you can get a good look at the golden flame of Super Dry Hall and the even more incongruent Tokyo Sky Tree, both across the river.

Retrace your steps to **2 Kaminari-mon**, the entrance to the grand temple complex, **3 Sensō-ji** (p166). Spend some time exploring the temple's highlights. Afterwards, walk past the nostalgic amusement park, **4 Hanayashiki** (p168), an Asakusa fixture since 1853.

Next take a detour up the covered arcade to the **5 Traditional Crafts Museum** (p168), where you can see the work of local artisans. Then head down the lane called **6 Hoppy-dōri** (p173), lined with *yakitori* stalls. Go on, have a few skewers and a beer.

Pop over to look at lantern-lit **7 Asakusa Engei Hall** (p174), reminiscent of the vaudeville halls that were once common here. The theatre is part of the Rokku district of Asakusa, a famous (and famously bawdy) entertainment district during the century before WWII. Pay a visit to vintage store **8 Tokyo Hotarudo** (p174), where the goods pay homage to this era, when Asakusa was thought of as the Montmartre of Tokyo.

If you resisted the charms of Hoppy-dōri you can have a meal at **9 Daikokuya** (p171), an old-school tempura restaurant, along Dembō-in-dōri, a strip with crafty stores. Don't miss the centuries-old comb store **10 Yonoya Kushiho** (p174).

Take one of the roads parallel to Nakamise – a world away from the tourist hordes – and finish up at **11 Ef** (p174), a cafe in a 19th-century wooden warehouse.

the Tembō Galleria, beneath the digital broadcasting antennas, features a circular glass corridor for more vertiginous thrills. The elevator between the two has a glass front, so you can see yourself racing up the tower as the city grows smaller below.

The ticket counter is on the 4th floor. You'll see signs in English noting the wait and the current visibility. Try to avoid visiting on the weekend, when you might have to wait in line.

At the base is Tokyo Sky Tree Town, which includes the shopping centre Solamachi (p175).

⊙ Ryōgoku

EDO-TOKYO MUSEUM MUSEUM

Map p292 (江戸東京博物館; ☎3626-9974; www.edo-tokyo-museum.or.jp; 1-4-1 Yokoami, Sumida-ku; adult/child ¥600/free; ⏰9.30am-5.30pm Tue-Sun, to 7.30pm Sat; 🚉JR Sōbu line to Ryōgoku, west exit) This history museum does an excellent job laying out Tokyo's miraculous transformation from feudal city to modern capital, through city models, miniatures of real buildings, reproductions of old maps and *ukiyo-e* (woodblock prints). Don't miss the life-sized replica of the original Nihombashi. There is English signage throughout and there's also a free audio guide available (¥1000 deposit).

SUMO MUSEUM MUSEUM

Map p292 (相撲博物館; www.sumo.or.jp/sumo_museum; 1-3-28 Yokoami, Sumida-ku; ⏰10am-4.30pm Mon-Fri; 🚉JR Sōbu line to Ryōgoku, west exit) FREE Located on the ground floor of Ryōgoku Kokugikan Stadium, this small museum displays the pictures of all the past *yokozuna* (top-ranking sumo wrestlers), or for those who lived before the era of photography, *ukiyo-e*. During sumo tournaments, the museum is only open to ticket holders; otherwise it's free to enter.

⊙ Kiyosumi & Fukagawa

MUSEUM OF CONTEMPORARY ART, TOKYO (MOT) MUSEUM

Map p292 (東京都現代美術館; www.mot-art-museum.jp; 4-1-1 Miyoshi, Kōtō-ku; adult/child ¥500/free; ⏰10am-6pm Tue-Sun; Ⓢ Ōedo line to Kiyosumi-Shirakawa, exit B2) For a primer in the major movements of post-WWII Japanese art, a visit to the permanent collection gallery here should do the trick. Temporary exhibitions, on changing subjects (including fashion, architecture and design) cost extra. The building's stone, steel and wood architecture by Yanagisawa Takahiko is a work of art in its own right. The museum is on the edge of Kiba-kōen, a well-signposted 10-minute walk from the subway station.

KIYOSUMI-TEIEN GARDENS

Map p292 (清澄庭園; http://teien.tokyo-park.or.jp/en/kiyosumi/index.html; 3-3-9 Kiyosumi, Kōtō-ku; adult/child ¥150/free; ⏰9am-5pm; Ⓢ Ōedo line to Kiyosumi-Shirakawa, exit A3) One of Tokyo's most picturesque retreats, Kiyosumi-teien started out in 1721 as the villa of a *daimyō* (domain lord; regional

WORTH A DETOUR

SHIBAMATA

At the eastern edge of Tokyo, the neighbourhood of Shibamata is known for its atmospheric streets and workaday feel that make it a comfy-cosy throwback to the post-WWII period. It's also famous for being the setting of the long-running film franchise *Otoko wa Tsurai Yo* (It's Tough Being a Man; 1968–95), about a fedora-sporting, plaid-blazer-wearing, working-class everyman in a suburb just outside the big city.

Shibamata's main street, **Taishakuten-sandō** (帝釈天参道), does indeed feel like a film set, lined with dozens of wood-built shops specialising in *unagi* (eel), *sembei* (flavoured rice crackers) and *kusa-dango* (sweet bean-paste dumplings wrapped in leaves). The street ends at the small temple **Taishakuten** (帝釈天), which boasts exquisite wood carvings. Nearby is Tokyo's only remaining human-powered ferry **Yagiri no Watashi** (矢切の渡し; 1-way adult/child ¥200/100; ⏰9.30am-4.30pm daily Apr-Nov, Sat & Sun only Dec-Mar), which has plied the Edo-gawa since the Edo period.

To reach Shibamata, take the Keisei line from Oshiage and transfer at Keisei-Takasago to the Keisei Kanamachi line (¥185, about 20 minutes). Taishakuten-sandō begins about 100m from the station.

lord under the shōguns). After the villa was destroyed in the 1923 earthquake, Iwasaki Yatarō, founder of the Mitsubishi Corporation, purchased the property. He used company ships to transport prize stones here from all over Japan, which are set around a pond ringed with Japanese black pine, hydrangeas and Taiwanese cherry trees.

FUKAGAWA EDO MUSEUM MUSEUM
Map p292 (深川江戸資料館; 1-3-28 Shirakawa, Kōtō-ku; adult/child ¥400/50; ⌚9.30am-5pm, closed 2nd & 4th Mon of month; S Ōedo line to Kiyosumi-Shirakawa, exit A3) During the Edo period (1603–1868), Fukagawa was a typical working-class neighbourhood, with narrow alleys and tenement homes. You can see what it likely looked like at this indoor museum, complete with a fire-lookout tower, life-sized facades and buildings you can enter.

FUKAGAWA FUDŌ-DŌ BUDDHIST TEMPLE
Map p292 (深川不動尊; 1-17-13 Tomioka, Kōtō-ku; ⌚8am-6pm, to 8pm on festival days; S Ōedo line to Monzen-Nakachō, exit 1) Fukagawa Fudō-dō, which belongs to the esoteric Shingon sect, is very much an active temple. Fire rituals (called *'goma'*) take place daily in an auditorium in the Hondō (Main Hall) at 9am, 11am, 1pm, 3pm and 5pm, plus 7pm on festival days (1st, 15th, 28th of each month). Sutras are read, drums are pounded and various amulets and objects are passed over the flames in blessing.

There's also a trippy prayer corridor with 9500 miniature Fudōmyō (a fierce-looking representation of Buddha's determination) crystal statues. Upstairs is a gallery depicting all 88 temples of the 1400km pilgrimage route on the island of Shikoku; it is said that offering a prayer at each alcove has the same effect as visiting each temple.

TOMIOKA HACHIMAN-GŪ SHINTO SHRINE
Map p292 (富岡八幡宮; 1-20-3 Tomioka, Kōtō-ku; S Ōedo line to Monzen-Nakachō, exit 1) Founded in 1627, this shrine is famous as the birthplace of the sumo tournament. Around the back of the main building is the *yokozuna* stone, carved with the names of each of these champion wrestlers. Near the entrance are the two gilded, jewel-studded *mikoshi,* used in the Fukagawa Hachiman (p26) festival in mid-August; the larger one weighs 4.5 tonnes. A **flea market** takes place here on the 15th and 28th of most months, from around 8am to sunset.

> **ASAKUSA TOURIST INFORMATION CENTER**
>
> The roof terrace of the Asakusa Culture Tourist Information Center (p253) has fantastic views of Tokyo Sky Tree. Free guided tours of Asakusa depart from here on Saturdays and Sundays at 11am and 1.15pm.

EATING

Asakusa

DAIKOKUYA TEMPURA ¥
Map p291 (大黒家; www.tempura.co.jp/english/index.html; 1-38-10 Asakusa, Taitō-ku; meals ¥1550-2100; ⌚11am-8.30pm Mon-Fri, to 9pm Sat; 📖; S Ginza line to Asakusa, exit 1) Near Nakamise-dōri, this is the place to get old-fashioned tempura fried in pure sesame oil, an Asakusa speciality. It's in a white building with a tile roof. If there's a queue (and there often is), you can try your luck at the annexe one block over.

KOMAGATA DOJŌ TRADITIONAL JAPANESE ¥
Map p291 (駒形どぜう; ☎3842-4001; 1-7-12 Komagata, Taitō-ku; mains from ¥1550; ⌚11am-9pm; 🚭📖; S Ginza line to Asakusa, exits A2 & A4) Since 1801, Komagata Dojō has been simmering and stewing *dojō* (Japanese loach, which looks something like a miniature eel). *Dojō-nabe* (loach hotpot), served here on individual *hibachi* (charcoal stove), was a common dish in the days of Edo, but few restaurants serve it today. The open seating around wide, wooden planks heightens the traditional flavour. There are lanterns out front.

SOMETARŌ OKONOMIYAKI ¥
Map p291 (染太郎; 2-2-2 Nishi-Asakusa, Taitō-ku; mains ¥390-880; ⌚noon-10pm; 📖; S Ginza line to Tawaramachi, exit 3) Sometarō is a fun and funky place to try *okonomiyaki* (savoury Japanese-style pancakes filled with meat, seafood and vegetables that you cook yourself). This historic, vine-covered house is

a friendly spot where the menu includes a how-to guide for even the most culinarily challenged.

★**OTAFUKU** TRADITIONAL JAPANESE ¥¥

Map p291 (大多福; ☎3871-2521; www.otafuku.ne.jp; 1-6-2 Senzoku, Taitō-ku; oden ¥110-550, course ¥5400; ⊙5-11pm Tue-Sat, to 10pm Sun; 📖; 🚊Tsukuba Express line to Asakusa, exit 1) Celebrating its centenary in 2015, Otafuku specialises in *oden,* classic Japanese stew. It's simmered at the counter and diners pick what they want from the pot, one or two items at a time. You can dine cheaply on radishes and kelp, or splash out on scallops and tuna – either way you get to soak up Otafuku's convivial, old-time atmosphere.

Look for a shack-like entrance and lantern on the northern side of Kototoi-dōri.

★**IROKAWA** UNAGI ¥¥

Map p291 (色川; ☎3844-1187; 2-6-11 Kaminarimon, Taitō-ku; sets from ¥2500; ⊙11.30am-1.30pm & 5-8.30pm Mon-Sat; 🚭📖; SGinza line to Asakusa, exit 2) This tiny restaurant has a real old Edo flavour and is one of the best, unpretentious *unagi* (eel) restaurants in town. The menu is simple: a 'small' gets you two slices of charcoal-grilled eel over rice, a 'large' gets you three. The chef grills everything right behind the counter. Look for the light-green building with plants out front.

★**ASAKUSA IMAHAN** SUKIYAKI ¥¥¥

Map p291 (浅草今半; ☎3841-1114; www.asakusaimahan.co.jp/index.html; 3-1-12 Nishi-Asakusa, Taitō-ku; lunch/dinner course from ¥3780/7130; ⊙11.30am-9.30pm; 🚭📖; SGinza line to Tawaramachi, exit 3) For a meal to remember, swing by this famous beef restaurant, in business since 1895. Choose between courses of *sukiyaki* (sautéed beef dipped in raw egg) and *shabu-shabu* (beef blanched in broth); prices rise according to the grade of meat. For diners on a budget, Imahan sells a limited number of cheaper lunch sets (from ¥1500).

KAPPABASHI KITCHENWARE TOWN

Kappabashi-dōri (合羽橋通り; Map p291; SGinza line to Tawaramachi, exit 3) is the country's largest wholesale restaurant-supply and kitchenware district. Gourmet accessories include bamboo steamer baskets, lacquer trays, neon signs and *chōchin* (paper lanterns). It's also where restaurants get their freakishly realistic plastic food models. **Ganso Shokuhin Sample-ya** (元祖食品サンプル屋; Map p291; www.ganso-sample.com; 3-7-6 Nishi-Asakusa, Taitō-ku; ⊙10am-5.30pm; SGinza line to Tawaramachi, exit 3) has a showroom of tongue-in-cheek ones plus keychains and kits to make your own.

Oshiage

★**ROKURINSHA** RĀMEN ¥

Map p291 (六厘舎; www.rokurinsha.com; 6th fl, Solamachi, 1-1-2 Oshiage, Sumida-ku; rāmen from ¥850; ⊙10.30am-11pm; 🚭📖; SHanzōmon line to Oshiage, exit B3) Rokurinsha's specialty is *tsukemen* – *rāmen* noodles served on the side with a bowl of concentrated soup for dipping. The noodles here are thick and perfectly al dente and the soup is a rich *tonkotsu* (pork bone) base. It's an addictive combination that draws lines to this outpost in Tokyo Sky Tree Town.

SHISHIMARU SHOKUDŌ IZAKAYA ¥

Map p291 (ししまる食堂; 1-16-7 Oshiage, Sumida-ku; dishes ¥330-800; ⊙6-11pm Mon, 11.30am-2pm & 6-11pm Tue-Fri, 11.30am-3pm Sat; 🖊; SHanzōmon line to Oshiage, exit A1) The house speciality at this eccentric little joint in the shadow of Tokyo Sky Tree is *te-uchi udon* (handmade wheat noodles); other dishes to sample include *tori-ten* (chicken tempura) and *kurokke* (deep-fried potato croquettes). There's homemade *karin* (quince) brandy, too. There is a ¥200 cover charge in the evening. Look for the orange awning out front.

Ryōgoku, Kiyosumi & Fukagawa

KAPPŌ MIYAKO TRADITIONAL JAPANESE ¥

Map p292 (割烹みや古; ☎3633-0385; 2-7-1 Tokiwa, Kōtō-ku; ⊙11.30am-2pm & 4.30-8pm Tue-Sun; 🚭; SToei Ōedo line to Morishita, exit A7) Centuries ago, when Fukagawa was basically a tidal flat, hungry locals would gather clams at the shore, resulting in the neighbourhood's signature dish: *fukagawa-meshi* (rice steamed with clams). At lunchtime, this 90-year-old restaurant serves a piping hot '*fukagawa meshi* set'

LOCAL KNOWLEDGE

STREET FOOD

Asakusa is great for street food. Here are some local favourites:

Hoppy-dōri (ホッピー通り; Map p291; 2-5 Asakusa, Taito-ku; skewers from ¥120; Tsukuba Express to Asakusa, exit 4) Along the street popularly known as Hoppy-dōri – 'Hoppy' is a cheap malt beverage – food vendors set out stools and tables for customers to nosh on cheap *yakitori* from noon until late.

Iriyama Sembei (入山煎餅; Map p291; 1-13-4 Asakusa, Taitō-ku; sembei from ¥120; 10am-6pm Fri-Wed; Tsukuba Express to Asakusa, exit 4) At this century-old shop you can watch *sembei* (rice crackers) being hand-toasted on charcoal grills. Get them hot as takeaway or packaged as souvenirs.

Chōchin Monaka (ちょうちんもなか; Map p291; 2-3-1 Asakusa, Taitō-ku; ice cream ¥280; 10am-5.30pm; ; S Ginza line to Asakusa, exit 1) Traditionally, *monaka* are wafers filled with sweet bean jam. At this little stand on Nakamise-dōri, they're filled with ice cream instead – in flavours such as *matcha* (powdered green tea) and *kuro-goma* (black sesame).

(¥1500) that includes miso soup and pickles. Seating is on tatami; look for the bamboo and ivy out front.

TOMOEGATA NABE ¥

Map p292 (巴潟; www.tomoegata.com; 2-17-6 Ryōgoku, Sumida-ku; lunch/dinner from ¥860/3130; 11.30am-2pm & 5-11pm; ; JR Sōbu line to Ryōgoku, east exit) If you're keen to try *chanko-nabe* – the protein-rich stew that fattens up sumo wrestlers – Tomoegata is a great place to do it. The daily lunch special includes a reasonably sized individual serving of *chanko-nabe*. In the evening, groups can splash out on huge steaming pots filled with beef, scallops, mushrooms and tofu.

DRINKING & NIGHTLIFE

★POPEYE PUB

Map p292 (ポパイ; www.40beersontap.com; 2-18-7 Ryōgoku, Sumida-ku; 5-11pm Mon-Sat; ; JR Sōbu line to Ryōgoku, west exit) Popeye boasts an astounding 70 beers on tap, including the world's largest selection of Japanese beers – from Echigo Weizen to Hitachino Nest Espresso Stout. The happy-hour deal (5pm to 8pm) offers select brews with free plates of pizza, sausages and other munchables. It's extremely popular and fills up fast; get here early to grab a seat.

From the station's west exit, take a left on the main road and pass under the tracks; take the second left and look for Popeye on the right.

★LUCITE GALLERY CAFE

Map p292 (ルーサイトギャラリー; http://lucite-gallery.com; 1-28-8 Yanagibashi, Taitō-ku; coffee ¥500; varies; JR Sōbu line to Asakusa-bashi, east exit) In the former Yanagibashi entertainment district, this cafe and gallery was once the home of geisha and popular singer Ichimaru. Rotating exhibits by potters and other artists are shown in the downstairs tatami rooms, while the 2nd-floor cafe opens to a verandah overlooking the Sumida River. It's a five-minute walk east of Asakusa-bashi Station.

KAMIYA BAR BAR

Map p291 (神谷バー; 3841-5400; www.kamiya-bar.com; 1-1-1 Asakusa, Taitō-ku; 11.30am-10pm Wed-Mon; S Ginza line to Asakusa, exit 3) One of Tokyo's oldest Western-style bars, Kamiya opened in 1880 and is still hugely popular – though probably more so today for its enormous, cheap draft beer (¥1020 for a litre). Its real speciality, however, is Denki Bran, a herbal liquor that's been produced in-house for over a century. Order at the counter, then give your tickets to the server.

'CUZN HOMEGROUND BAR

Map p291 (http://homeground.jpn.com; 2-17-9 Asakusa, Taitō-ku; beer ¥800; 11am-6am; ; S Ginza line to Tawaramachi, exit 3) Run by a wild gang of local hippies, 'Cuzn is the kind of bar where anything can happen: a barbecue, a jam session or all-night karaoke, for example.

KAPPABASHI COFFEE CAFE

Map p291 (合羽橋珈琲; www.kappabashi-coffee.com; 3-25-11 Nishi-Asakusa, Taitō-ku; coffee ¥450; ⏲8am-8pm; 🚭; 🚉Tsukuba Express to Asakusa, exit 2) This stylish coffee shop has a Japanese modern interior with an *irori* (traditional hearth) in the middle and picture windows looking out onto the street. In addition to hand-drip coffee, light meals are served.

EF CAFE

Map p291 (エフ; ☎3841-0442; www.gallery-ef.com; 2-19-18 Kaminari-mon, Taitō-ku; coffee ¥550; ⏲11am-midnight Mon, Wed, Thu, Sat, to 2am Fri, to 10pm Sun; Ⓢ Ginza line to Asakusa, exit 2) Set in a 19th-century wooden warehouse that beat the 1923 earthquake and WWII, this wonderfully cosy space serves coffee, tea and, after 6pm, cocktails and beer. Be sure to check out the gallery in the back.

ASAHI SKY ROOM BAR

Map p291 (アサヒスカイルーム; ☎5608-5277; 22F, Asahi Super Dry Bldg, 1-23-1 Azuma-bashi, Sumida-ku; beer ¥720; ⏲10am-9pm; Ⓢ Ginza line to Asakusa, exit 4) Spend the day at the religious sites and end at the Asahi altar, on the 22nd floor of the golden-tinged Asahi Super Dry Building. The venue itself isn't noteworthy, but the views over the Sumida-gawa are spectacular, especially at sunset.

ENTERTAINMENT

OIWAKE TRADITIONAL MUSIC

Map p291 (追分; ☎3844-6283; www.oiwake.info; 3-28-11 Nishi-Asakusa, Taitō-ku; admission plus 1 food & 1 drink ¥2000; ⏲5.30pm-midnight; 🚉Tsukuba Express to Asakusa, exit 1) Oiwake is one of Tokyo's few *minyō izakaya,* pubs where traditional folk music is performed. It's a homey place, where the waitstaff and the musicians – who play *tsugaru-jamisen* (a banjo-like instrument), hand drums, and bamboo flute – are one and the same. Sets start at 7pm and 9pm; children are welcome for the early show. Seating is on tatami.

ASAKUSA ENGEI HALL COMEDY

Map p291 (浅草演芸ホール; ☎3841-6545; www.asakusaengei.com; 1-43-12 Asakusa, Taitō-ku; adult/student ¥2800/2300; ⏲shows 11.40am-4.30pm & 4.40-9pm; Ⓢ Ginza line to Tawaramachi, exit 3) Asakusa was once full of theatres like this one, where traditional *rakugo* (comedic monologue) and other forms of comedy are performed along with juggling, magic and the like. It's all in Japanese, but the linguistic confusion is mitigated by lively facial expressions and props, which help translate comic takes on universal human experiences.

SHOPPING

★TOKYO HOTARUDO VINTAGE

Map p291 (東京蛍堂; http://tokyohotarudo.com; 1-41-8 Asakusa, Taitō-ku; ⏲11am-8pm Wed-Sun; 🚉Tsukuba Express to Asakusa, exit 5) This curio shop is run by an eccentric young man who prefers to dress as if the 20th century hasn't come and gone already. If you think that sounds marvellous, then you'll want to check out his collection of vintage dresses and bags, antique lamps, watches, and decorative objets d'art.

The entrance is tricky: look for a vertical black sign with a pointing finger.

★BENGARA CRAFTS

Map p291 (べんがら; www.bengara.com; 1-35-6 Asakusa, Taitō-ku; ⏲10am-6pm Mon-Fri, to 7pm Sat & Sun, closed 3rd Thu of month; Ⓢ Ginza line to Asakusa, exit 1) By now you're familiar with *noren,* the curtains that hang in front of shop doors. This store sells beautiful ones, made of linen and coloured with natural dyes (like indigo or persimmon) or decorated with ink-brush paintings. There are smaller items too, such as pouches and book covers, made of traditional textiles.

★SOI HOMEWARES

Map p291 (2nd fl, 3-25-11 Nishi-Asakusa, Taitō-ku; ⏲noon-6pm Tue-Sun; 🚉Tsukuba Express to Asakusa, exit 2) If you visit just one homewares store in Kappabashi, make it this one. There's a well-edited selection of ceramics and glassware, new and vintage, plus some really cute *tenugui* (printed clothes) to wrap them in.

YONOYA KUSHIHO ACCESSORIES

Map p291 (よのや櫛舗; 1-37-10 Asakusa, Taitō-ku; ⏲10.30am-6pm Thu-Tue; Ⓢ Ginza line to Asakusa, exit 1) Even in a neighbourhood where old is not out of place, Yonoya Kushiho stands out: this little shop has been selling handmade boxwood combs since 1717. Yonoya also sells old-fashioned hair ornaments (worn with the elaborate up-dos of courtesans in the past) and modern trinkets.

FUJIYA CRAFTS

Map p291 (ふじ屋; 2-2-15 Asakusa, Taitō-ku; ⌚10.30am-6.30pm Fri-Wed; Ⓢ Ginza line to Asakusa, exit 1) Fujiya specialises in *tenugui:* dyed cloths of thin cotton that can be used as tea towels, kerchiefs, gift wrap (the list goes on; they're surprisingly versatile). Here they come in traditional designs and humorous modern ones.

SOLAMACHI MALL

Map p291 (ソラマチ; 1-1-2 Oshiage, Sumida-ku; ⌚10am-9pm; Ⓢ Hanzōmon line to Oshiage, exit B3) It's not all cheesy Sky Tree swag here at this mall under the tower (though you can get 634m-long rolls of Sky Tree toilet paper). Shops on the 4th floor offer a better-than-usual selection of Japanese-y souvenirs, including pretty trinkets made from kimono fabric and quirky fashion items.

SPORTS & ACTIVITIES

★RYŌGOKU KOKUGIKAN SUMO

Map p292 (両国国技館, Ryōgoku Sumo Stadium; ☎3623-5111; www.sumo.or.jp; 1-3-28 Yokoami, Sumida-ku; admission ¥2200-14,800; 🚉JR Sōbu line to Ryōgoku, west exit) If you're in town when a tournament is on – for 15 days each January, May and September – catch the big boys in action at Japan's largest sumo stadium. Doors open at 8am, but the action doesn't heat up until the senior wrestlers hit the ring around 2pm. Tickets can be bought online one month before the start of the tournament.

A limited number of general-admission tickets are sold only on the day of the match from the box office in front of the stadium. You'll have to line up very early (say 6am) on the last couple of days of the tournament to snag one.

If you get there in the morning when the stadium is still pretty empty, you can usually sneak down to the box seats. You can rent a radio (¥100 fee, plus ¥2000 deposit) to listen to commentary in English. Stop by the basement restaurant to sample *chanko-nabe* for just ¥250 a bowl.

ℹ WATCHING SUMO PRACTICE

Not in town for a sumo tournament? You can still catch an early-morning practice session at a 'stable' – where the wrestlers live and practise. Overseas visitors are welcome at **Arashio Stable** (荒汐部屋; Arashio-beya; Map p292; ☎3666-7646; www.arashio.net/tour_e.html; 2-47-2 Hama-chō, Nihombashi, Chūō-ku; Ⓢ Toei Shinjuku line to Hamachō, exit A2) FREE, so long as they mind the rules (check the website). Visit between 7.30am and 10am – you can watch through the window or on a bench outside the door. There is no practise during tournament weeks.

JAKOTSU-YU BATHHOUSE

Map p291 (蛇骨湯; ☎3841-8645; www.jakotsuyu.co.jp; 1-11-11 Asakusa, Taitō-ku; admission ¥460; ⌚1pm-midnight Wed-Mon; Ⓢ Ginza line to Tawaramachi, exit 3) Unlike most *sentō* (public baths), the tubs here are filled with pure hot-spring water, naturally the colour of weak tea. Another treat is the lovely, lantern-lit, rock-framed *rotemburo* (outdoor bath). Jakotsu-yu is a welcoming place; it has English signage and doesn't have a policy against tattoos. It's an extra ¥200 for the sauna; ¥140 for a small towel.

MOKUHANKAN PRINTMAKING

Map p291 (木版館; ☎070-5011-1418; http://mokuhankan.com/parties; 2nd fl, 1-41-8 Asakusa, Taitō-ku; per person ¥2000; ⌚10am-5.30pm; 🚉Tsukuba Express to Asakusa, exit 5) Try your hand at making *ukiyo-e* at this studio run by expat David Bull. Hour-long 'print parties' take place daily; sign up online. There's a shop here too, where you can see Bull and Jed Henry's humorous Ukiyo-e Heroes series – prints featuring videogame characters in traditional settings.

Odaiba & Tokyo Bay

Neighbourhood Top Five

❶ Seeing the city's night lights twinkling in Tokyo Bay from the promenades of **Odaiba Kaihin-kōen** (p178) or the terrace of a waterfront restaurant.

❷ Soaking in the hot-spring baths at **Ōedo Onsen Monogatari** (p180) and enjoying the old-Edo theme-park atmosphere.

❸ Being amazed by life-like robots and other cutting-edge technology at the **National Museum of Emerging Science & Innovation** (p178).

❹ Cruising across Tokyo Bay on a pleasure boat (p178) while you enjoy a meal or drinks.

❺ Enjoying family days out at **Tokyo Disney Resort** (p180) and **Tokyo Sea Life Park** (p178).

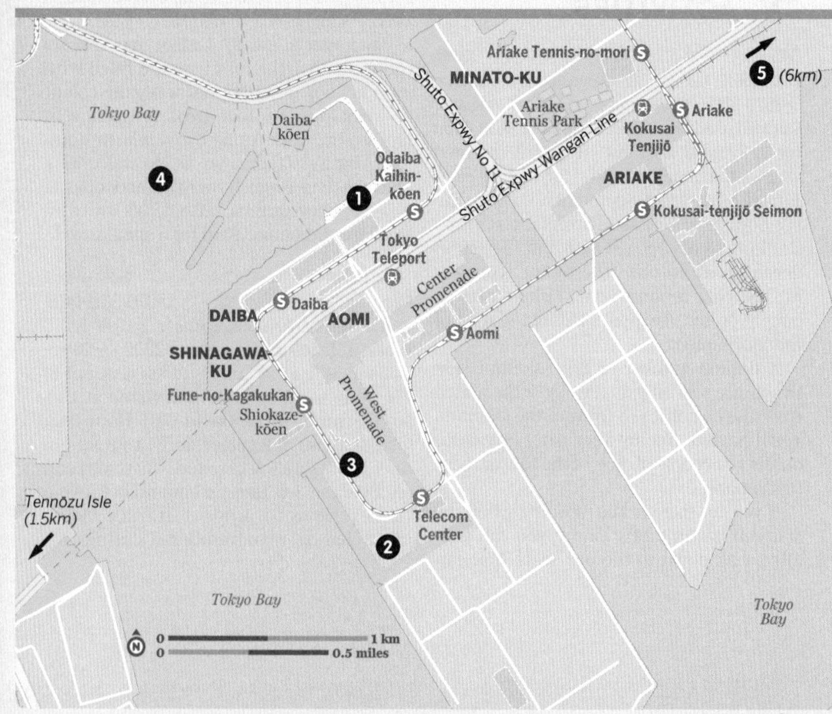

For more detail of this area, see Map p293

Explore Odaiba & Tokyo Bay

In central Tokyo, it's easy to forget that the city started as a seaside town. Not so on Odaiba, a human-made island tethered to the mainland by the 798m Rainbow Bridge.

Although gun emplacements were set up on islets here back in the mid-19th century to protect Tokyo against foreign attack, Odaiba was developed mostly in the 1990s and offers buildings on a grand scale, with broad streets, spacious parks and waterfront views. There's even an artificial beach overlooked by a kitschy replica of the *Statue of Liberty*; you'll definitely feel as though you're in an alternative Tokyo. Should you visit in the evening there's the bonus of romantic twinkling views of bay and city skyline.

Ōedo Onsen Monogatari and the National Museum of Emerging Science and Innovation are Odaiba's prime attractions; both can easily take up a half-day or more. There's also striking contemporary architecture, notably the Fuji Television Japan Broadcast Centre and the convention centre Tokyo Big Sight.

Tokyo's youngsters and families can't get enough of Odaiba's several malls, with masses of chain stores, restaurants and amusements under one roof. They're less interesting for foreign tourists; however, if you're travelling with kids, these all-in-one complexes can be excellent on rainy days.

Tokyo Bay can also be appreciated from the water on pleasure cruises, several of which stop off in Odaiba or across on the eastern edge of the city.

Local Life

➡ **Boat cruises** Groups of friends and colleagues organise private parties on the bay, particularly during the summer and winter holidays.

➡ **Photo spot** Waterfront-park Odaiba Kaihin-kōen is popular with amateur photographers working to perfect their city-by-night shot.

➡ **Conventions** Crowds descend on Tokyo Big Site for major conventions such as the comic market Comiket (www.comiket.co.jp) and Tokyo Game Show.

Getting There & Away

➡ **Monorail** The Yurikamome line runs from Shimbashi through Odaiba to Toyos; stops include Shijo-mae, the location for the new central Tokyo fish and fresh-produce market.

➡ **Train** The Rinkai line runs from Osaki through Odaiba to Shin-Kiba, stopping at Tennōzu Isle, Tokyo Teleport and Kokusai Tenjijō Stations.

➡ **Boat** Tokyo Cruise boats stop at Odaiba Kaihin-kōen (Odaiba Seaside Park), Palette Town and Tokyo Big Sight.

Lonely Planet's Top Tip

It's a long walk from one end of Odaiba to the other. If you intend to spend the day here, invest in a day pass (adult/child ¥820/410) for the Yurikamome line. The monorail is an attraction itself, with the best seats right up front. From Shimbashi Station, the monorail snakes through the Shiodome skyscrapers before arching up to cross the Rainbow Bridge to Odaiba where it connects all the main attractions.

Best Places to Eat

➡ Bills (p179)

➡ Hibiki (p179)

➡ TY Harbor Brewery (p179)

For reviews, see p179 ➡

Best Places to Drink

➡ The Bar (p180)

➡ Jicoo the Floating Bar (p180)

➡ Waterline (p179)

For reviews, see p180 ➡

Best Places to Play

➡ National Museum of Emerging Science & Innovation (p178)

➡ Tokyo Joypolis (p180)

➡ RiSūPia (p178)

For reviews, see p178 

SIGHTS

NATIONAL MUSEUM OF EMERGING SCIENCE & INNOVATION (MIRAIKAN) MUSEUM

Map p293 (未来館; www.miraikan.jst.go.jp; 2-3-6 Aomi, Kōtō-ku; adult/child ¥620/210; ⏲10am-5pm Wed-Mon; 🚉Yurikamome line to Telecom Centre) *Miraikan* means 'hall of the future', and the fascinating exhibits here present the science and technology that will shape the years to come. Lots of hands-on displays make this a great place for kids and curious adults. There are several demonstrations, too, including the humanoid robot Asimo and the lifelike android Otonaroid. The Gaia dome theatre/planetarium has an English audio option and is popular; reserve your seats as soon as you arrive.

ODAIBA KAIHIN-KŌEN PARK

Map p293 (お台場海浜公園; Odaiba Marine Park; www.tptc.co.jp/en/park/tabid/846/Default.aspx; 1-4-1 Daiba, Minato-ku; ⏲24hr; 🚉Yurikamome line to Odaiba Kaihin-kōen) One of the best views of Tokyo is from this park's promenades and elevated walkways – especially at night when old-fashioned *yakatabune* (low-slung wooden boats), bedecked with lanterns, traverse the bay. Also here you'll find an 800m-long human-made **beach** and an 11m replica of the **Statue of Liberty** (Map p293) – a very popular photo op with the Rainbow Bridge in the background.

TOKYO SEA LIFE PARK AQUARIUM

(葛西臨海水族館; www.tokyo-zoo.net/english/kasai/main.html; 6-2-3 Rinkai-chō, Edogawa-ku; adult/child ¥700/350; ⏲9.30am-4pm Thu-Tue; 🚉JR Keiyō line to Kasai Rinkai-kōen) The focal point of Kasai Rinkai-kōen, the largest park of Tokyo's central 23 wards, is this mammoth aquarium where the highlight is a doughnut-shaped tank filled with sleek, silvery bluefin tuna. As well as sealife from many different oceanic habitats you can also see cute penguins, auks and puffins here.

RISŪPIA MUSEUM

Map p293 (リスーピア; www.risupia.panasonic.co.jp; Panasonic Centre Tokyo, 3-5-1 Ariake, Kōtō-ku; adult/child ¥500/free; ⏲10am-6pm Tue-Sun; 🚉Yurikamome line to Ariake) At the Panasonic showroom, this museum has hands-on exhibits illustrating maths and science principles. The 1st-floor Quest Gallery is free but the 3rd-floor Discovery Field, which charges admission, is more fun. Look out for the 'prime number' air-hockey game that uses numbers instead of pucks. There are explanations throughout in English.

FERRIS WHEEL TOWER

Map p293 (大観覧車; Dai-kanransha; www.dai-kanransha.com/g_date.html; 1-3-10 Aomi, Kōtō-ku; rides ¥920; ⏲10am-10pm; 🚉Yurikamome line to Aomi) Even if you don't take a spin in one of the world's tallest Ferris wheels, it's great eye candy when illuminated at night in a rainbow of colours.

TOKYO BAY PLEASURE CRUISES

Those low-slung wooden boats out on the bay, bedecked with lanterns, are *yakatabune* and they've been a Tokyo tradition since the days of Edo. They're used for private parties, which usually include all-you-can-eat-and-drink banquets and karaoke. Pull together 20 people and you can arrange a 2½-hour feast aboard a *yakatabune* through **Funasei** (船清; ☎5479-2731; www.funasei.com; 1-16-8 Kita-shinagawa, Shinagawa-ku; per person ¥10,800; 🚉Keikyu line to Kita-shinagawa). Once a month they run a general cruise for ¥10,000 that anyone can join (minimum two people, advance reservation necessary; see website for details).

Also offering reservations for as few as two people, and one of the cheapest *yakatabune* deals around with prices starting at ¥4900 per person, is **Tsukishima Monja Yakatabune** (月島もんじゃ屋形船; ☎3533-6699; www.4900yen.com; 2-6-3 Shin-Kiba, Kōtō-ku; per person from ¥4900; Ⓜ Yūrakuchō line to Shin-Kiba, main exit). Food and drink is very basic though – beers, soft drinks and *monja-yaki*, a savoury, scrambled batter-style dish. Also the departure point is far flung Shin-Kiba pier, a short shuttle-bus ride from Shin-Kiba Station.

Wine-and-dine cruises around Tokyo Bay on multilevel Western-style ships are offered on the **Symphony** (www.symphony-cruise.co.jp; lunch/dinner cruises from ¥6200/8200; 🚉JR Yamanote line to Hamamatsuchō) and **Vingt-et-un** (☎3436-2121; www.vantean.co.jp; lunch/dinner cruises from ¥9000/16,000; 🚉Yurikamome line to Takeshiba).

WORTH A DETOUR

TENNŌZU ISLE

Odaiba is not the only location in Tokyo where you can enjoy waterfront views while dining or drinking. In the old Terada Warehouses on Tennōzu Isle (www.e-tennoz.com/en), **TY Harbor Brewery** (5479-4555; www.tyharborbrewing.co.jp; 2-1-3 Higashi-Shinagawa, Shinagawa-ku; lunch sets ¥1200-1700, dinner mains from ¥1700; 11.30am-2pm & 5.30-10pm; ; Rinkai line to Tennōzu Isle, exit B) has set up a number of operations. As well brewing its own beer on the premises, the restaurant serves excellent burgers, steaks and crab cakes. Next to the brewery is its floating lounge **Waterline** (ウォーターラインラウンジ; www.tyharborbrewing.co.jp; 2-1-3 Higashi-Shinagawa, Minato-ku; Rinkai line to Tennōzu Isle, exit B), where you can nestle into a comfy sofa and sip one of TY's signature brews. And brewers yeast is used for the extensive menu of breads baked at its neighbouring cafe, **Breadworks** (5479-3666; www.tyharborbrewing.co.jp; 2-1-6 Higashi-shinagawa, Shinagawa-ku; breads & pastries from ¥200; 8am-8pm).

Tennōzu Isle, which is on the west side of Tokyo Bay in Shinagawa ward, can be reached in nine minutes from Odaiba via the Rinkai line from Tokyo Teleport Station.

DIVER CITY TOKYO PLAZA — PLAZA

Map p293 (6380-7800; www.divercity-tokyo.com; 1-1-10 Aomi, Kōtō-ku; Yurikamome line to Daiba) This Odaiba mall distinguishes itself more with its nonshopping attractions, including the mixed amusement and sports park **Round1 Stadium**, a rooftop **skate park** and **Gundam Front Tokyo** (http://gundamfront-tokyo.com/en), an exhibition based on the popular robot anime. An 18m-tall model of one of the **Gundam** (ガンダム) robots stands in front of the mall and is a great photo op.

FUJI TV — ARCHITECTURE

Map p293 (フジテレビ; 5500-8888; 2-4-8 Daiba, Minato-ku; observation deck adult/child ¥500/¥300; 10am-6pm Tue-Sun; Yurikamome line to Daiba) Designed by the late, great Kenzō Tange, the Fuji TV headquarters building is recognisable by the 90-degree angles of its scaffolding-like structure. It is topped by a 1200-tonne ball, which includes an observation deck. Pick up an English guide at the desk out front for information on a self-guided tour.

TOKYO BIG SIGHT — LANDMARK

Map p293 (東京ビッグサイト; Tokyo International Exhibition Hall; www.bigsight.jp/english/index.html; 3-11-1 Ariake, Kōtō-ku; Yurikamome line to Kokusai-tenjijō) Officially known as Tokyo International Exhibition Hall, Tokyo Big Sight's striking architecture includes four giant upside-down pyramids.

Also look outside for the giant red-handled **Saw sculpture** (Map p293) by Claes Oldenburg and Coosje Van Bruggen.

EATING

Odaiba's malls are packed with food courts and chain restaurants.

★BILLS — INTERNATIONAL ¥

Map p293 (ビルズ; www.bills-jp.net; 3rd fl, Seaside Mall, DECKS Tokyo Beach, 1-6-1 Daiba, Minato-ku; mains from ¥1300; 9am-10pm Mon-Fri, 8am-10pm Sat & Sun; ; Yurikamome line to Odaiba Kaihin-kōen) Australian chef Bill Granger has had a big hit with his restaurant chain in Japan – unsurprising given how inviting and spacious a place this is. The menu includes his classics such as ricotta hotcakes, and lunch and dinner mains such as *wagyū* burgers.

★HIBIKI — JAPANESE ¥

Map p293 (響; www.dynac-japan.com/hibiki; 6th fl, Aqua City Odaiba, 1-7-1 Daiba, Minato-ku; lunch sets ¥1000, dishes ¥750-1700; 11am-3pm & 5-10pm Mon-Fri, 11am-11pm Sat & Sun; ; Yurikamome line to Daiba, south exit) The menu here features seasonal dishes, hearty grilled meats and fresh tofu, along with sake, *shōchū* (strong distilled alcohol often made from potatoes) and glittering views across the bay. The lunch set is a good deal and includes a small salad bar; choose your main dish from the samples out the front.

ODAIBA TAKOYAKI MUSEUM — JAPANESE ¥

Map p293 (お台場たこ焼きミュージアム; 4th fl, Seaside Mall, DECKS Tokyo Beach, 1-6-1 Daiba, Minato-ku; takoyaki from ¥400; 11am-9pm; Yurikamome line to Odaiba Kaihin-kōen) Seven different stalls dish up variations on the classic fried batter and octopus balls usually served at street stalls at festivals and events.

DRINKING & NIGHTLIFE

★THE BAR COCKTAIL BAR

Map p293 (☎5530-8309; 13th fl, the SOHO, 2-7-4 Aomi, Kōtō-ku; cover charge ¥300; ⏱3pm-midnight Mon-Fri; 🚇Yurikamome line to Telecom Centre) Atop the SOHO building, this sleek bar offers to-die-for views of Tokyo Bay from its floor-to-ceiling windows. Go up a level for access to the roof for even better views with your drink. Find directions on how to access the bar in the convenience store on the ground floor of the building.

★JICOO THE FLOATING BAR COCKTAIL BAR

Map p293 (ジークザフローティングバー; ☎0120-049-490; www.jicoofloatingbar.com; admission ¥2600; ⏱8-10.30pm Thu-Sat; 🚇Yurikamome line to Hinode or Odaiba Kaihin-kōen) For a few nights a week, the futuristic cruise-boat *Himiko*, designed by manga and anime artist Leiji Matsumoto, morphs into this floating bar. Board on the hour at Hinode pier and the half-hour at Odaiba Kaihin-kōen. Space is limited; make a reservation online.

CANTEEN CAFE

Map p293 (ザキャンティーン; the SOHO, 2-7-4 Aomi, Kōtō-ku; ⏱9am-10pm Mon-Fri, 10am-6pm Sat, bar Mon-Fri; 🚭📶; 🚇Yurikamome line to Telecom Centre) On the ground floor of an office building, this contemporary design cafe serves up coffee and lunch specials in a colourful, relaxed setting.

AGEHA CLUB

(アゲハ; www.ageha.com; 2-2-10 Shin-Kiba, Kōtō-ku; admission ¥2500-4000; ⏱11pm-5am Fri & Sat; 🚇Yūrakuchō line to Shin-Kiba, main exit) This gigantic waterside club, the largest in Tokyo, rivals any you'd find in LA or Ibiza. Top international and Japanese DJs appear here. Free buses run to the club from the east side of Shibuya Station on Roppongi-dōri; check the website for details and bring photo ID.

SHOPPING

VENUS FORT MALL

Map p293 (ヴィーナスフォート; ☎3599-0700; www.venusfort.co.jp; 1-3-15 Aomi, Kōtō-ku; ⏱10am-9pm; 🚇Yurikamome line to Aomi) Some effort has been made at Venus Fort to avoid the cookie-cutter style of other Odaiba malls. The interior of the 2nd floor mimics Italian streetscapes with fountains and ceilings that simulate the sky shifting from day to night. It's a fun, kitschy shopping experience, but takes a turn for the very weird at **Strange Love** (Map p293; www.strangelove.co.jp; 2nd fl, Venus Fort, 1-3-15 Aomi, Kōtō-ku; 🚇Yurikamome line to Aomi), an antiques and curio store for those with adult tastes.

SPORTS & ACTIVITIES

★ŌEDO ONSEN MONOGATARI ONSEN

Map p293 (大江戸温泉物語; www.ooedoonsen.jp; 2-6-3 Aomi, Kōtō-ku; adult/child from ¥1980/900, after 6pm from ¥1480/900; ⏱11am-9am, last entry 7am; 🚇Yurikamome line to Telecom Centre, Rinkai line to Tokyo Teleport with free shuttle bus) Just to experience the truly Japanese phenomenon that is an amusement park centred on bathing is reason enough to visit. The baths, which include gender-divided indoor tubs and *rotemburo* (outdoor baths), are filled with real onsen (hot-spring) water, pumped from 1400m below Tokyo Bay. The *iwashioyoku* (hot-stone bath) and *tsunaburo* (hot-sand bath) cost extra, as do massages, and require reservations. Visitors with tattoos will be denied admission.

★TOKYO DISNEY RESORT AMUSEMENT PARK

(東京ディズニーリゾート; www.tokyodisneyresort.co.jp; 1-1 Maihama, Urayasu-shi; 1-day ticket for 1 park adult/child ¥6400/4200, after 6pm ¥3400; ⏱varies by season; 🚇JR Keiyō line to Maihama) At this very popular resort, you'll find not only Tokyo Disneyland, modelled after the California original, but also Tokyo DisneySea, a clever add-on that caters more to adults. Tickets can be booked online and it's worth packing a *bentō* (boxed meal), as on-site restaurants are almost always overrun with diners.

TOKYO JOYPOLIS AMUSEMENT PARK

Map p293 (東京ジョイポリス; http://tokyo-joypolis.com; 3rd-5th fl Decks Tokyo Beach, 1-6-1 Daiba, Minato-ku; adult/child ¥800/300, all-rides passport ¥3900/2900, passport after 5pm ¥2900/1900; ⏱10am-10pm; 🚇Yurikamome line to Odaiba Kaihin-kōen) This indoor amusement park is stacked with virtual-reality attractions and adult thrill rides; there are rides for little ones, too. Separate admission and individual ride tickets (most ¥500) are available, as well as an unlimited 'passport'.

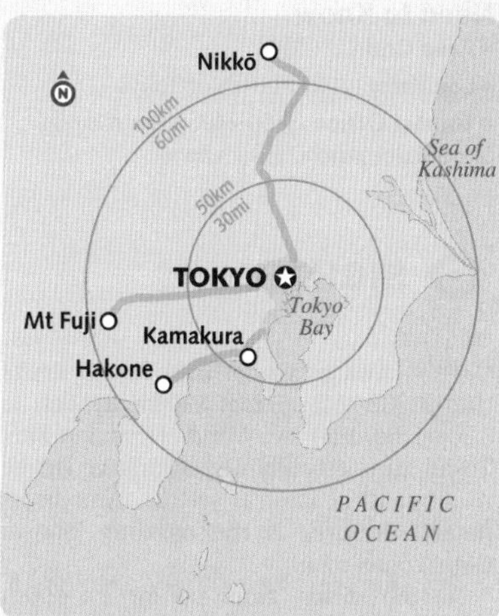

Day Trips from Tokyo

Nikkō p182

Take in the grandeur of old Edo at the spectacular shrines and temples of Nikkō, in the wooded mountains north of Tokyo.

Hakone p186

A centuries-old onsen (hot-spring) resort, Hakone offers beautiful landscape, a serene lake, traditional inns and even the smoking remains of a volcano.

Kamakura p189

An ancient feudal capital, seaside Kamakura is packed with temples and shrines, plus the famous Daibutsu (Big Buddha) statue.

Mt Fuji p192

Follow the pilgrim trail up Japan's most famous peak for a sunrise to beat all others, or admire views of the perfect snowcapped cone from below.

Nikkō 日光

Explore

Nikkō's premier attraction is its cluster of World Heritage shrines and temples, set amongst towering cedars. Among these is Tōshō-gū, an elaborate shrine rebuilt in 1634 as a memorial to the first Tokugawa shogun. The major sights, a 30-minute walk (or a five-minute bus ride) from the train station, can be visited on foot in an afternoon; however, it's well worth budgeting more time to explore. In the hills beyond are a smattering of smaller sights, often overlooked by the crowds.

On weekends and holidays, Nikkō can become extremely packed. It's best to visit early on a weekday; alternatively, stay the night to get an early start and use the extra day to explore the mountains, marshlands and onsen (p239) of the sprawling Nikkō National Park.

The Best...

- **Sight** Tōshō-gū
- **Place to Eat** Gyōshintei (p185)
- **Place to Sleep** Nikkō Kanaya Hotel (p185)

Top Tip

Nikkō is most attractive – and thus most crowded – in October when the hills blaze red. During this time expect serious traffic delays on the way to Chūzen-ji Onsen.

Getting There & Around

- **Train** From Tokyo, Tōbu-Nikkō line trains leave from Tōbu Asakusa Station (it's well signposted from the subway). You can usually get last-minute seats on the hourly reserved *tokkyū* (limited-express) trains (¥2700, 110 minutes). *Kaisoku* (rapid) trains (¥1360, 2½ hours, hourly from 5.39am to 4.50pm) require no reservation; be sure to ride in the last two cars (some cars may separate at an intermediate stop). Note that with either train, you may need to change at Shimo-Imaichi.
- **Bus** In front of Nikkō Station, buses leave regularly for the short trip to Shinkyō, the bus stop for the World Heritage sites (¥200, five minutes).

Need to Know

- **Area Code** ☎0288
- **Location** 120km north of Tokyo
- **Tourist Office** (☎54-2496; www.nikko-jp.org; 591 Gokomachi; ⏲9am-5pm)

SIGHTS

★TŌSHŌ-GŪ — SHINTO SHRINE

(東照宮; www.toshogu.jp; 2301 Sannai; adult/child ¥1300/450; ⏲8am-4.30pm Apr-Oct, to 3.30pm Nov-Mar) A World Heritage Site, Tōshō-gū is a brilliantly decorative shrine in a beautiful natural setting. Among its notable features is the dazzling 'Sunset Gate' Yōmei-mon.

As the shrine gears up for its 400th anniversary a major restoration program is underway. Until at least 2018, the Yōmei-mon and Shimojinko (one of the Three Sacred Storehouses) will be obscured by scaffolding. Don't be put off visiting, as Tōshō-gū remains an impressive sight. A new museum building is also set to open during 2015.

The stone steps of **Omotesandō** lead past the towering stone *torii* (entrance gate) **Ishidorii** (石鳥居), and the **Gōjūnotō** (五重塔; Five Storey Pagoda), an 1819 reconstruction of the mid-17th-century original, to **Omotemon** (表門), Tōshō-gū's main gateway, protected on either side by Deva kings.

In Tōshō-gū's initial courtyard are the **Sanjinko** (三神庫; Three Sacred Storehouses); on the upper storey of the Kamijinko (upper storehouse) are relief carvings of 'imaginary elephants' by an artist who had never seen the real thing. Nearby is the **Shinkyūsha** (神厩舎; Sacred Stable), adorned with relief carvings of monkeys. The allegorical 'hear no evil, see no evil, speak no evil' simians demonstrate three principles of Tendai Buddhism.

Further into Tōshō-gū's precincts, to the left of the drum tower, is **Honji-dō** (本地堂), a hall known for the painting on its ceiling of the Nakiryū (Crying Dragon). Monks demonstrate the hall's acoustical properties by clapping two sticks together. The dragon 'roars' (a bit of a stretch) when the sticks are clapped beneath its mouth, but not elsewhere.

Once the scaffolding comes off in 2018, the **Yōmei-mon** (陽明門; Sunset Gate) will be grander than ever, its gold leaf and intricate, coloured carvings and paintings of flowers, dancing girls, mythical beasts and Chinese sages, all shiny and renewed. Worrying that the gate's perfection might arouse envy in the gods, those responsible for its construction had the final supporting pillar placed upside down as a deliberate error.

Gōhonsha (御本社), the main inner courtyard, includes the **Honden** (本殿; Main Hall) and **Haiden** (拝殿; Hall of Worship). Inside these halls are paintings of the 36 immortal poets of Kyoto, and a ceiling-painting pattern from the Momoyama period; note the 100 dragons, each different. *Fusuma* (sliding door) paintings depict a *kirin* (a mythical beast that's part giraffe and part dragon).

To the right of the Gōhonsha is **Sakashita-mon** (坂下門), into which is carved a tiny wooden sculpture of the **Nemuri-neko** (眠り猫; Sleeping Cat) that's famous for its lifelike appearance (though admittedly the attraction is lost on some visitors). From here it's an uphill path through towering cedars to the appropriately solemn **Oku-miya** (奥宮), Ieyasu's tomb.

Bypassed by nearly everyone at Tōshō-gū is the marvellous **Nikkō Tōshō-gū Museum of Art** (日光東照宮美術館; ☎54-0560; http://www.toshogu.jp/shisetsu/bijutsu.html; 2301 Yamanouchi; adult/child ¥800/400; ⏲9am-4.30pm Apr-Oct, to 3.30pm Nov-Mar) in the old shrine offices, showcasing fine paintings on its doors, sliding screens, frames and decorative scrolls, some by masters including Yokoyama Taikan and Nakamura Gakuryo. Follow the path to the right of Omote-mon to find it.

RINNŌ-JI — BUDDHIST TEMPLE

(輪王寺; ☎54-0531; http://rinnoji.or.jp; 2300 Yamanouchi; adult/child ¥400/200; ⏲8am-4.30pm Apr-Oct, to 3.30pm Nov-Mar) This Tendai-sect temple was founded 1200 years ago by Shōdō Shōnin. The exterior of the **Sambutsu-dō** (三仏堂; Three-Buddha Hall) is under wraps for restoration until 2020. Inside sit a trio of 8m gilded wooden Buddha statues: Amida Nyorai (a primal deity in the Mahayana Buddhist canon), flanked by Senjū (deity of mercy and compassion) and Batō (a horse-headed Kannon).

TAIYŪIN-BYŌ — SHINTO SHRINE

(大猷院廟; adult/child ¥550/250; ⏲8am-4.30pm Apr-Oct, to 3.30pm Nov-Mar) Ieyasu's grandson Iemitsu (1604–51) is buried here and although it houses many of the same elements as Tōshō-gū (storehouses, drum tower, Chinese-style gates etc), the more intimate scale and setting in a cryptomeria forest make it very appealing.

Look for dozens of lanterns donated by *daimyō* (domain lords), and the gate Niō-mon, the guardian deities of which have a hand up (to welcome those with pure hearts) and a hand down (to suppress those with impure hearts).

FUTARASAN-JINJA — SHINTO SHRINE

(二荒山神社; www.futarasan.jp; adult/child ¥200/100) Set among cypress trees, this very atmospheric shrine was also founded by Shōdō Shōnin; the current building dates from 1619, making it Nikkō's oldest. It's the protector shrine of Nikkō

DISCOUNT PASSES

Passes are available at the **Tōbu Sightseeing Service Center** (Map p291; ☎3841-2871; www.tobu.co.jp/foreign; ⏲7.45am-5pm) in Asakusa Station and at Tōbu Nikkō Station. Note there's a surcharge (weekday/weekend & holiday ¥1080/1160, one way) if you ride the limited-express Spacia trains.

➡ **Two-Day Nikkō Pass** (adult/child ¥2670/1340) Valid for two days, this includes round-trip *kaisoku* (rapid) train travel between Asakusa, Nikkō and Kinugawa Onsen, buses within Nikkō, and admission to the sites covered in the combination ticket.

➡ **All Nikkō Pass** (adult/child ¥4520/2280) Includes the same deal on trains and buses as the World Heritage Pass, plus transportation to and from Chūzen-ji and Yumoto Onsen, but not admission to the sights. Valid for four days.

➡ **Tōbu Nikkō Buss Free Pass** If you've already got your rail ticket, two-day bus-only passes allow unlimited rides between Nikkō and Chūzen-ji Onsen (adult/child ¥2000/1000) or Yumoto Onsen (adult/child ¥3000/1500), including the World Heritage Site area.

➡ **Sekai-isan-meguri** (World Heritage Bus Pass; adult/child ¥500/250) Covers the area between Nikkō's train stations and the shrine precincts.

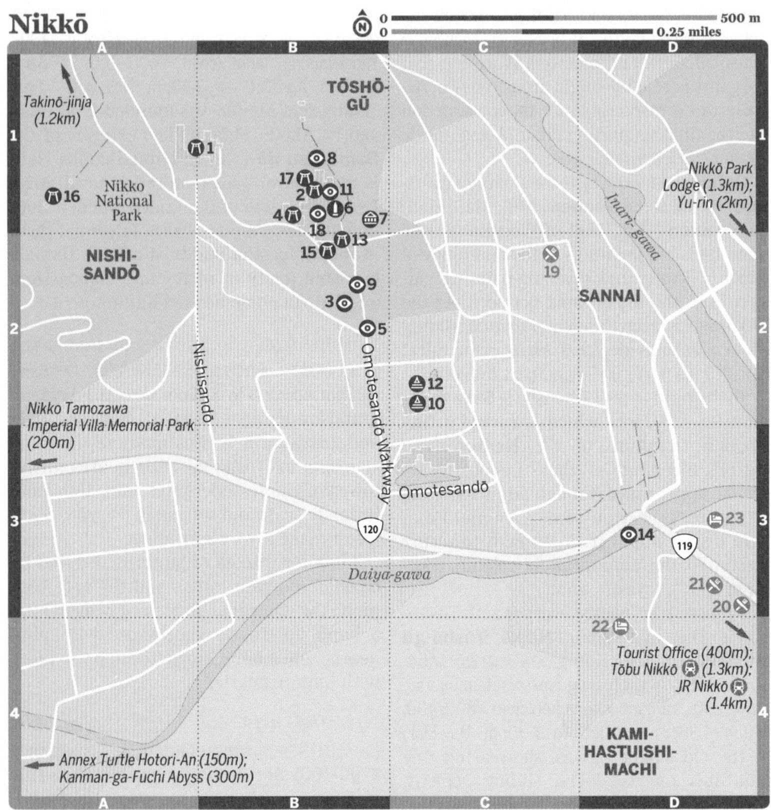

Nikkō

Sights

1 Futarasan-jinja A1
2 Gōhonsha B1
3 Gōjūnotō B2
4 Honji-dō B1
5 Ishi-dorii B2
6 Nemuri-neko B1
7 Nikkō Tōshō-gū Museum of Art B1
8 Okumiya B1
9 Omote-mon B2
10 Rinnō-ji C2
11 Sakashita-mon B1
12 Sambutsu-dō C2
13 Sanjinko B2
14 Shin-kyō D3
15 Shinkyūsha B2
16 Taiyūin-byō A1
17 Tōshō-gū B1
18 Yōmei-mon B1

Eating

19 Gyōshintei C2
20 Hippari Dako D3
21 Nagomi-chaya D3

Sleeping

22 Nikkō Kanaya Hotel D4
23 Nikkorisou Backpackers D3

itself, dedicated to Nantai-san (2484m); the mountain's consort, Nyotai-san; and their mountainous progeny, Tarō. There are other branches of the shrine on Nantai-san and by Chūzenji-ko.

SHIN-KYŌ HISTORIC SITE

(神橋; crossing fee ¥300) This highly photographed red footbridge is located at the sacred spot where Shōdō Shōnin was said to have been carried across the Daiya River on the backs of two giant serpents. It's a reconstruction of the 17th-century original.

NIKKŌ TAMOZAWA IMPERIAL VILLA MEMORIAL PARK HISTORIC SITE
(日光田母沢御用邸記念公園; ☎53-6767; www.park-tochigi.com/tamozawa; 8-27 Hon-chō; adult/child ¥510/260; ⏲9am-4pm Wed-Mon) About 1km west of Shin-kyō bridge, this splendidly restored imperial palace of more than 100 rooms showcases superb craftsmanship, with parts of the complex dating from the Edo, Meiji and Taishō eras. Apart from the construction skills involved, there are brilliantly detailed screen paintings and serene garden views framed from nearly every window.

TAKINŌ-JINJA SHINTO SHRINE
(滝尾神社) FREE About 1km north of Futarasan-jinja, close by the Shiraito Falls, is this serene, delightfully less crowded, shrine that has a history stretching back to 820. The stone gate, called **Undameshi-no-torii**, dates back to Iemitsu's time. Before entering, it's customary to try your luck tossing three stones through the small hole near the top.

KANMAN-GA-FUCHI ABYSS PARK
(憾満ガ淵) Escape the crowds along this wooded path lined with a collection of *jizō* statues (the small stone effigies of the Buddhist protector of travellers and children). After passing the Shin-kyō bridge follow the Daiya-gawa west for about 1km, crossing another bridge near Jyoko-ji temple en route.

EATING

The speciality in Nikkō is *yuba*, the skin that forms when making tofu (really, it's a delicacy!). Note that many restaurants close early or irregularly in Nikkō, especially outside of the peak season.

HIPPARI DAKO YAKITORI ¥
(ひっぱり凧; 1011 Kamihatsu-ishimachi; meals ¥550-900; ⏲11am-8pm; 🍴📄) An institution for over a quarter of a century among foreign travellers, as layers of business cards tacked to the walls testify, this no-frills restaurant serves comfort-food meals, including curry udon, *yuba* sashimi and *yaki-udon* (fried noodles).

NAGOMI-CHAYA JAPANESE ¥¥
(和み茶屋; ☎54-3770; 1016 Kamihatsu-ishi; dishes/set-course meals from ¥450/1620; ⏲11.30am-4pm Thu-Tue) A faithful picture menu makes ordering simple at this sophisticated arts-and-crafts-style cafe near the top of Nikkō's main drag. The beautifully prepared *kaiseki* style lunches are a great deal.

★**GYŌSHINTEI** KAISEKI ¥¥¥
(尭心亭; ☎53-3751; www.meiji-yakata.com/gyoushin; 2339-1 Sannai; set-course lunch/dinner from ¥2138/4514; ⏲11am-7pm; 🍴📄) Splash out on deluxe spreads of vegetarian *shōjin-ryōri,* featuring local bean curd and vegetables served half a dozen delectable ways, or the *kaiseki* courses which include fish. The elegant tatami dining room overlooks a carefully tended garden which is part of the Meji-no-Yakata compound of chic restaurants close by the World Heritage Sites.

SLEEPING

The nicer places to stay are in the residential or wooded fringes of town. English is spoken at all of the following.

NIKKORISOU BACKPACKERS HOSTEL ¥
(☎080-9449-1545; http://nikkorisou.com/eng.html; 1107 Kamihatsu-ishi-machi; dm/s/d with shared bathroom from ¥2600/3600/6200; 📶) The closest hostel to the World Heritage Site offers a riverside location, relaxed, friendly vibe and a good-sized kitchen for self-catering. The rental bicycles at ¥500 a day are a deal.

ANNEX TURTLE HOTORI-AN INN ¥¥
(☎53-3663; www.turtle-nikko.com; 8-28 Takumi-chō; s/tw ¥6500/12,600; 🚭❄@📶) More modern than the original Turtle Inn, with Japanese- and Western-style rooms plus river views from the onsen bath.

★**NIKKŌ KANAYA HOTEL** HOTEL ¥¥¥
(日光金谷ホテル; ☎54-0001; www.kanaya-hotel.co.jp; 1300 Kamihatsu-ishimachi; tw from ¥17,820; ❄@📶) This grand lady from 1893 wears her history like a well-loved, if not slightly worn, dress. The newer wing has Japanese-style rooms with excellent vistas, spacious quarters and private bathrooms; the cheaper rooms in the main building are Western style and have an appealing old-fashioned ambience.

Hakone 箱根

Explore

Hakone is a natural wonder, with hot springs and a shimmering lake set among forested peaks. Add to that a dizzying variety of transport options: the standard route takes visitors from the Hakone-Yumoto in a narrow-gauge switchback train to Gōra; on the way it's worth stopping off at the excellent Hakone Open Air Museum and/or the Okada Museum of Art. You continue by funicular and ropeway to steaming Ōwakudani before ending with a cruise across **Ashino-ko** (芦ノ湖), the lake featured in the iconic image of Mt Fuji with the *torii* of the Hakone-jinja rising from the water.

During holidays, Hakone is busy. To beat the crowds, visit during the week. You'll need the whole day, especially if you plan to soak in one of its excellent onsen baths.

The Best...

➡**Sight** Hakone Open Air Museum

➡**Onsen** Tenzan Tōji-Kyō

➡**Tea Break** Amazake-chaya

Top Tip

The Hakone Freepass (adult/child from Shinjuku ¥5140/1500, valid for two days), available at Odakyū stations, is a great investment as it covers the return express train fare from Shinjuku to Hakone-Yumoto, unlimited use of most transport around Hakone and discounts at many attractions. If you choose tos ride the Romance Car limited express train to or from Hakone you'll have to pay an extra ¥890 each way.

Getting There & Away

➡ **Train** The Odakyū line runs from Shinjuku Station to Hakone-Yumoto. You can take either the convenient Romance Car (¥2080, 85 minutes) or the *kyūkō* (express) service (¥1190, two hours), although the latter may require a transfer in Odawara. From Hakone-Yumoto, the Hakone-Tōzan line (¥400, 40 minutes) continues on to Gōra.

➡ **Bus** Hakone Tōzan (which is included in the Hakone Freepass) and Izu Hakone buses run between Hakone-Yumoto, Gōra, Hakone-machi and Moto-Hakone, stopping at all the major attractions in between.

Need to Know

➡**Area Code** ☎ 0460

➡**Location** 92km southwest of Tokyo

➡**Tourist Office** (☎85-8911; www.hakone.or.jp; ⏰9am-5.45pm)

SIGHTS

★HAKONE OPEN-AIR MUSEUM — MUSEUM

(彫刻の森美術館; www.hakone-oam.or.jp; 1121 Ninotaira; adult/child ¥1600/800; ⏰9am-4.30pm) On a rolling, leafy hillside setting, this safari for art lovers includes an impressive selection of 19th- and 20th-century Japanese and Western sculptures (including works by Henry Moore, Rodin and Miró) as well as an excellent Picasso Pavilion with more than 300 works ranging from paintings and glass art to tapestry.

★OKADA MUSEUM OF ART — MUSEUM

(岡田美術館; ☎87-3931; www.okada-museum.com; 483-1 Kowakidani; adult/student ¥2800/1800; ⏰9am-4.30pm) Showcasing the dazzling Japanese, Chinese and Korean art treasures of industrialist Okada Kazuo, this mammoth museum should not be missed. You could spend hours marvelling at the beauty of so many pieces, including detailed screen paintings and exquisite pottery. The museum is opposite the Kowakien stop.

ŌWAKUDANI — VOLCANO

(大桶谷; www.kanagawa-park.or.jp/owakudani) FREE The 'Great Boiling Valley' was created 3000 years ago when Kami-yama erupted and collapsed, also forming Ashino-ko. Hydrogen sulfide steams from the ground here and the hot water is used to boil onsen *tamago*, eggs blackened in the sulphurous waters, which you can buy to eat (they're fine inside).

HAKONE MUSEUM OF ART — MUSEUM

(箱根美術館; www.moaart.or.jp; 1300 Gōra; adult/child ¥900/free; ⏰9.30am-4.30pm, closed Thu) Sharing grounds with a lovey velvety moss garden and teahouse (¥700 *matcha* green tea and sweet), this museum has a collection of Japanese pottery dating from as far back as the Jōmon period (some 5000 years ago). The gardens are spectacular in autumn.

HAKONE SEKISHO — MUSEUM

(箱根関所, Hakone Checkpoint Museum; www.hakonesekisyo.jp; 1 Hakone-machi; adult/child ¥500/250; ⏰9am-4.30pm Mar-Nov, to 4pm Dec-Feb)

WORTH A DETOUR

OLD HAKONE HIGHWAY

Up the hill from the Moto-Hakone bus stop is the entrance to the stone-paved **Old Hakone Highway** (箱根旧街道), part of the Edo-era Tokkaidō, which leads back to Hakone-Yumoto (about 3½ hours) via the village of **Hatajuku** (畑宿), where you can visit the **Hatajuku Yosegi Kaikan** (畑宿寄木会館; ☎0460-85-8170; 103 Hakone-machi) to find out more about the craft of marquetry practiced in the area.

About 30 minutes' walk from Moto-Hakone you'll also pass the wonderful **Amazake-chaya** (甘酒茶屋; 395-1 Futoko-yama; drinks & snacks from ¥400; ⏲7am-5.30pm), a traditional teahouse where you can enjoy a cup of *amazake* (a thick sweet drink made from rice used to make sake; ¥400) with a traditional sweet, *mochi* (sticky rice cake, from ¥400).

You're free to walk through this 2007 reconstruction of the feudal-era checkpoint on the Old Tōkaidō Hwy, but if you want to enter any of the buildings you'll need to buy a ticket. One displays Darth Vader-like armour and grisly implements used on lawbreakers. There's basic English explanations on only some displays.

HAKONE-JINJA SHINTO SHRINE

(箱根神社; ⏲9am-4pm) A pleasant stroll around Ashino-ko follows a cedar-lined path to this shrine set in a wooded grove, in Moto-Hakone. Its signature red *torii* rises from the lake; get your camera ready.

ONSEN

Hakone offers bathing options galore. Apart from the following facilities open to the general public, ask at the Tourist Information Centre for a list of onsen hotels and ryokan that allow day visitors (typical admission fee is ¥1000).

★HAKONE YURYŌ ONSEN

(箱根湯寮; ☎85-8411; www.hakoneyuryo.jp; 4 Tonosawa; adult/child ¥1400/700, private baths from ¥3900; ⏲10am-8pm Mon-Fri, to 9pm Sat & Sun) A free shuttle bus will whisk you in three minutes from Hakone-Yumoto station to this idyllic onsen complex ensconsed in the forest. The *rotemburo* (outdoor baths) are spacious, and leaf shaded. There's also private ones you can book in advance. No tattoos allowed. It's also around a five-minute walk from Tonosawa Station on the Hakone-Tōzan line.

TENZAN TŌJI-KYŌ ONSEN

(天山湯治郷; www.tenzan.jp; 208 Yumoto-chaya; adult/child ¥1300/650; ⏲9am-10pm) Soak in *rotemburo* of varying temperatures and designs (one is constructed to resemble a natural cave) at this large, popular bath 2km southwest of town. To get here, take the 'B' Course shuttle bus from the bridge outside the Hakone-Yumoto Station (¥100). Tattoos are allowed.

YUNESSUN ONSEN

(箱根小涌園ユネッサン; www.yunessun.com; 1297 Ninotaira; Yunessun adult/child ¥2900/1600, Mori-no-Yu adult/child ¥1900/1200, both ¥4100/2100; ⏲9am-7pm Mar-Oct, to 6pm Nov-Feb) Best described as an onsen amusement park with a whole variety of baths and outdoor water slides, Yunessun is mixed bathing so you'll need to bring a swimsuit; the connected Mori-no-Yu complex (11am to 9pm) is traditional single-sex bathing. Take a bus from Hakone-machi, Gōra or Hakone-Yumoto to the Kowakien stop.

EATING & DRINKING

GYŌZA CENTER JAPANESE ¥

(餃子センター; ☎82-3457; www.gyozacenter.com; 1300 Gōra; mains from ¥800; ⏲11.30am-3pm & 5-8pm, closed Sat; 📄) The humble *gyōza* (dumpling) stars at this cosy, long-running restaurant, in a dozen different varieties. No vegetarian options though, unfortunately. It's between Gōra and Chōkoku-no-mori Stations on a corner, with an English sign.

MIYAFUJI SUSHI ¥¥

(鮨みやふじ; www.miyanoshita.com/miyafuji/index.html; 310 Miyanoshita; meals from ¥1680; ⏲11.30am-3pm & 5.30-8pm Fri-Wed; 📄) A short walk uphill from Fujiya Hotel, this friendly sushi shop is known for its *aji-don* (brook trout over rice). Look for the English sign.

Hakone Region

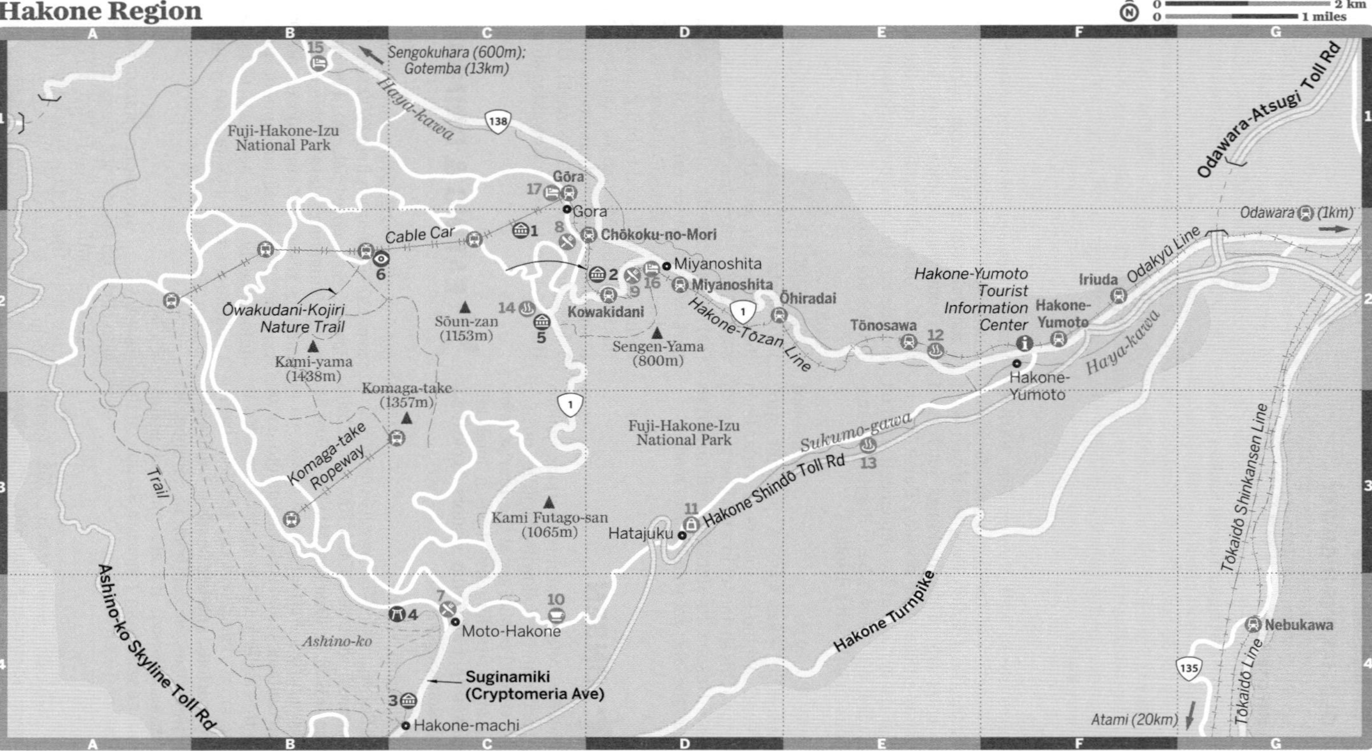

BAKERY & TABLE INTERNATIONAL ¥¥

(☎85-1530; www.bthjapan.com; 9-1 Moto-Hakone; mains ¥1000-2500) There are options that appeal to everyone at this lakeside venue with a footbath terrace outside. The take-away bakery is on the ground floor, a cafe is one floor up and the restaurant serving fancy open sandwiches and crêpes above that.

SLEEPING

Staying at one of Hakone's (often pricey) lodgings is one of the main reasons for visiting. Here are our top choices in different price ranges, all with onsen baths.

★HAKONE TENT HOSTEL ¥

(☎050-5874-1900; http://hakonetent.com; 1320-257 Gora; dm/s/d/tr with shared bathroom ¥3500/4000/9000/13,500;) Best hostel by far in Hakone, with an ace contemporary design blending punk and trad elements in a stylish makeover of a run-down ryokan to include a sleek, wooden lobby bar and lounge. Shin, Candy and their mates, the friendly young Japanese who run the place, got the place started through crowdfunding.

Hakone Region

Sights

1 Hakone Museum of Art C2
2 Hakone Open-Air Museum D2
3 Hakone Sekisho C4
4 Hakone-jinja C4
5 Okada Museum of Art C2
6 Ōwakudani B2

Eating

7 Bakery & Table C4
8 Gyōza Center C2
9 Miyafuji D2

Drinking & Nightlife

10 Amazake-chaya C4

Shopping

11 Hatajuku Yosegi Kaikan D3

Sports & Activities

12 Hakone Yuryō E2
13 Tenzan Tōji-kyō E3
14 Yunessun C2

Sleeping

15 Fuji Hakone Guest House B1
16 Fujiya Hotel D2
17 Hakone Tent C1

FUJI HAKONE GUEST HOUSE GUESTHOUSE ¥¥

(富士箱根ゲストハウス; ☎84-6577; www.fujihakone.com; 912 Sengokuhara; s/d from ¥6500/11,100;) Run by a welcoming English-speaking family, this guesthouse has handsome tatami rooms, cosy indoor and outdoor onsen with divine volcanic waters, and a wealth of information on sights and hiking in the area. Take the T-course bus to Senkyōrō-mae from Odawara Station (stop four; ¥1050, 50 minutes) or Tōgendai (¥380, 10 minutes). There's an English sign close by.

FUJIYA HOTEL HOTEL ¥¥¥

(富士屋ホテル; ☎82-2211; www.fujiyahotel.jp; 359 Miyanoshita; d from ¥21,670;) One of Japan's finest Western-heritage hotels, the beautifully detailed Fujiya opened in 1878 and played host to Charlie Chaplin back in the day (room 45). Now sprawled across several wings, it remains dreamily elegant. It's worth a visit to soak up the retro atmosphere, stroll through the hillside gardens and greenhouse and to have tea in the lounge.

Kamakura 鎌倉

Explore

Kamakura has dozens of temples and shrines – a legacy of its glory days as the country's first feudal capital (1192–1333). Fortunately for visitors, several of the more important ones form a neat path from Kita-Kamakura Station to Kamakura Station and are easily visited on foot. The Daibutsu (Big Buddha) and Hase-dera, Kamakura's most famous attractions, lie to the west in Hase, reachable by a short ride on the old-fashioned Enoden Line or a hike through the hills along the Daibutsu Hiking Course. Get an early start if you plan to do the hike.

For souvenir shopping, head to narrow Komachi-dōri, to the left of Kamakura Station's east exit. Kamakura's beach, Yuigahama, is a sandy stretch with a smattering of eateries and bars frequented by the hippies and surfers who call Kamakura home.

The Best...

➡ **Sight** Daibutsu

➡ **Hike** Daibutsu Hiking Course (p192)

➡ **Place to Eat** Matsubara-an (p192)

Top Tip

Bikes are perfect for touring Kamakura's temples and shrines; get wheels at **Kamakura Rent-a-Cycle** (レンタサイクル; per hour/day ¥800/1800; ⌚8.30am-5pm), outside the station's east exit.

Getting There & Away

➡ **Train** JR Yokosuka–line trains run to Kamakura from Tokyo (¥920, 56 minutes), via Shinagawa (¥720, 46 minutes). The Shōnan Shinjuku line runs from the west side of Tokyo (Shibuya, Shinjuku and Ikebukuro, all ¥920) in about an hour, though some trains require a transfer at Ōfuna. The Enoden (Enoshima Dentetsu) line runs past Hase, where the Daibutsu is, along the coast to Enoshima.

➡ **JR Kamakura-Enoshima Free Pass** (adult/child ¥700/350) Valid for one day from Ōfuna or Fujisawa Stations; unlimited use of JR trains around Kamakura, the Shōnan monorail between Ōfuna and Enoshima, and the Enoden Enoshima line.

➡ **Odakyū Enoshima/Kamakura Free Pass** (from Shinjuku/Fujisawa ¥1470/610) Valid for one day; includes transport to Fujisawa Station (where it meets the Enoden Enoshima line), plus use of the Enoden.

Need to Know

➡ **Area Code** ☎0467

➡ **Location** 65km south of Tokyo

➡ **Tourist Office** (鎌倉市観光協会観光総合案内所; ☎22-3350; ⌚9am-5pm)

SIGHTS & ACTIVITIES

DAIBUTSU — MONUMENT

(大仏; www.kotoku-in.jp; Kōtoku-in, 4-2-28 Hase; adult/child ¥200/150; ⌚8am-5.30pm Apr-Sep, to 5pm Oct-Nov) Kamakura's most iconic sight, an 11.4m bronze statue of Amida Buddha (*amitābha* in Sanskrit), is in Kōtoku-in, a Jōdo-sect temple. Completed in 1252, it's said to have been inspired by Yoritomo's visit to Nara (where Japan's biggest Daibutsu holds court) after the Minamoto clan's victory over the Taira clan. Once housed in a huge hall, today the statue sits in the open, the hall having been washed away by a tsunami in 1495.

HASE-DERA — BUDDHIST TEMPLE

(長谷寺, Hase Kannon; www.hasedera.jp; 3-11-2 Hase; adult/child ¥300/100; ⌚8am-4.30pm) The focal point of this Jōdo-sect temple, one of the most popular in the Kantō region, is a 9m-high carved wooden *jūichimen* (11-faced) Kannon statue. Kannon (*avalokiteshvara* in Sanskrit) is the bodhisattva of infinite compassion and, along with Jizō, is one of Japan's most popular Buddhist deities. The temple is about 10 minutes' walk from the Daibutsu and dates back to AD 736, when the statue is said to have washed up on the shore near Kamakura.

TSURUGAOKA HACHIMAN-GŪ — SHINTO SHRINE

(鶴岡八幡宮; http://hachimangu.or.jp; 2-1-31 Yukinoshita; ⌚9am-4pm) FREE Kamakura's most important shrine is, naturally, dedicated to Hachiman, the god of war. Minamoto Yoritomo himself ordered its construction in 1191 and designed the pine-flanked central promenade that leads to the coast. The sprawling grounds are ripe with historical symbolism: the Gempei Pond, bisected by bridges, is said to depict the rift between the Minamoto (Genji) and Taira (Heike) clans.

ENGAKU-JI — BUDDHIST TEMPLE

(円覚寺; www.engakuji.or.jp; 409 Yamanouchi; adult/child ¥300/100; ⌚8am-4.30pm Mar-Nov, to 4pm Dec-Feb) One of Kamakura's five major Rinzai Zen temples, Engaku-ji was founded in 1282 as a place where Zen monks might pray for soldiers who lost their lives defending Japan against Kublai Khan. All of the temple structures have been rebuilt over the centuries; the Shariden, a Song-style reliquary, is the oldest, last rebuilt in the 16th century. At the top of the long flight of stairs is the Engaku-ji bell, the largest bell in Kamakura, cast in 1301.

★KENCHŌ-JI — BUDDHIST TEMPLE

(建長寺; www.kenchoji.com; 8 Yamanouchi; adult/child ¥300/100; ⌚8.30am-4.30pm) Established in 1253, Japan's oldest Zen monastery is still active today. The central Butsuden (Buddha Hall) was brought piece

Kamakura

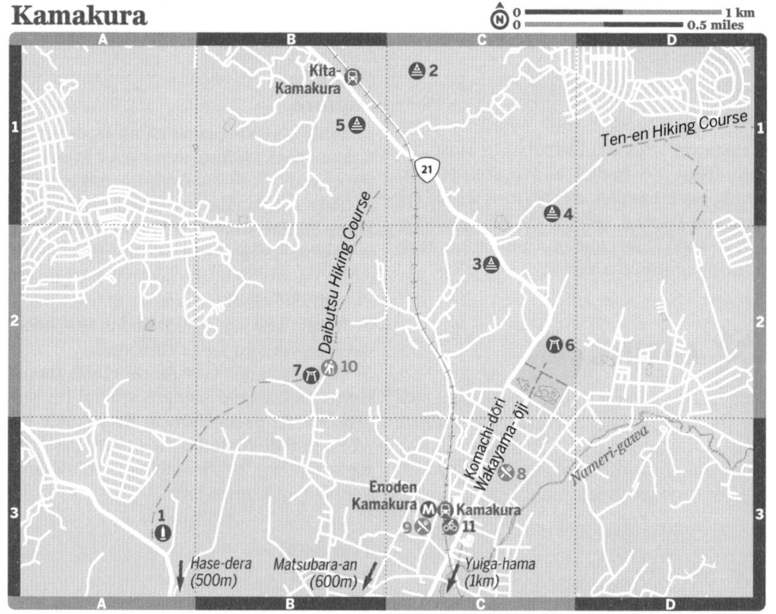

Kamakura

Sights

1 Daibutsu A3
2 Engaku-ji C1
3 Ennō-ji C2
4 Kenchō-ji C1
5 Tōkei-ji B1
6 Tsurugaoka Hachiman-gū C2
7 Zeniarai-benten B2

Eating

8 Bowls Donburi Café C3
9 Wander Kitchen C3

Sports & Activities

10 Daibutsu Hiking Course B2
Engaku-ji .... (see 2)
Kenchō-ji .... (see 4)

Transport

11 Kamakura Rent-a-Cycle C3

by piece from Tokyo in 1647. Its Jizō Bosatsu statue, unusual for a Zen temple, reflects the valley's ancient function as an execution ground – Jizō consoles lost souls. Other highlights include a bell cast in 1253 and the juniper grove, believed to have sprouted from seeds brought from China by Kenchō-ji's founder some seven centuries ago.

TŌKEI-JI BUDDHIST TEMPLE
(東慶寺; www.tokeiji.com; 1367 Yamanouchi; adult/child ¥200/100; ⏲8.30am-5pm Mar-Oct, to 4pm Nov-Feb) Across the railway tracks from Engaku-ji, Tōkei-ji is famed as having served as a women's refuge. A woman could be officially recognised as divorced after three years as a nun in the temple precincts. Today, there are no nuns; the grave of the last abbess can be found in the cemetery, shrouded by cypress trees.

ENNŌ-JI BUDDHIST TEMPLE
(円応寺; 1543 Yamanouchi; admission ¥200; ⏲9am-4pm Mar-Nov, to 3pm Dec-Feb) Ennō-ji is distinguished by its statues depicting the judges of hell. According to the Juo concept of Taoism, which was introduced to Japan from China during the Heian period (794–1185), these 10 judges decide the fate of souls, who, being neither truly good nor truly evil, must be assigned to spend eternity in either heaven or hell. Presiding

over them is Emma (Yama), a Hindu deity known as the gruesome king of the infernal regions.

DAIBUTSU HIKING COURSE HIKING

This 3km wooded trail connects Kita-Kamakura with the Daibutsu in Hase (allow about 1½ hours) and passes several small, quiet temples and shrines, including **Zeniarai-benten** (銭洗弁天; 2-25-16 Sasuke; ⌚8am-4pm) FREE, one of Kamakura's most alluring Shintō shrines.

EATING

Vegetarians can eat well in Kamakura: pick up the free, bilingual *Vegetarian Culture Map* at the tourist office. Snackers will love Komachi-dōri, with its *sembei* (rice cracker) vendors and ice-cream stands.

BOWLS DONBURI CAFÉ JAPANESE ¥

(鎌倉どんぶりカフェbowls; http://bowls-cafe.jp; 2-14-7 Komachi; meals ¥880-1680; ⌚11am-3pm & 5-10pm;) The humble *donburi* (rice bowl) gets a hip, healthy remake here at this modern, bright cafe, with toppings such as roasted tuna, soy sauce and sesame oil. You get a discount if you discover the word *atari* at the bottom of the bowl. Also serves excellent coffee and has free wi-fi and computer terminals with internet.

WANDER KITCHEN INTERNATIONAL ¥

(☎61-4751; http://wanderkitchen.net; 15 Onarimachi; sweets/lunch from ¥400/1000; ⌚noon-8pm;) It's worth searching out this charmingly decorated, retro-chic wooden house with a small garden out front for its cool vibe and tasty meals, cakes and drinks. It's tucked away just off the main street about five minutes' walk south of the west exit of Kamakura Station.

★**MATSUBARA-AN** NOODLES ¥¥

(松原庵; ☎61-2299; http://matsubara-an.com/kamakura/shop.php; 4-10-3 Yuiga-hama; mains ¥860-1720; ⌚11am-9pm;) Dinner reservations are recommended for this upscale *soba* restaurant in a lovely old house. Try the tempura *goma seiro soba* (al dente noodles served cold with sesame dipping sauce). Dine alfresco or indoors where you can watch noodles being handmade. From Yuiga-hama Station (Enoden line) head towards the beach and then take the first right. Look for the blue sign.

Mt Fuji 富士山

Explore

Roughly 300,000 people climb Japan's most famous peak (3776m) every year. Even with the crowds, the view from the top at dawn is truly spectacular (weather permitting). Many climbers opt to hike the whole thing at night (*dangan-tozan*; literally 'bullet climb') to arrive at the summit for sunrise. The official climbing season is from 1 July to 31 August when mountain huts are open; weekdays see far fewer climbers.

Even if you don't opt for the climb, there's gorgeous lakeland scenery around the volcano's base, particularly at **Kawaguchi-ko**, while in **Fuji-Yoshida**, the original pilgrim town for Fuji, is the ancient, atmospheric temple Fuji Sengen-jinja.

The Best...

➡**Sight** Mt Fuji

➡**Temple** Fuji Sengen-jinja

➡**Place to Eat** Hōtō Fudō (p194)

Top Tip

Weather can make or break your climb; check the conditions (www.snow-forecast.com/resorts/Mount-Fuji/6day/top) before setting out. And make sure you're fully prepared for wet and freezing conditions even if the forecast is for fine weather.

Getting There & Away

➡ **Bus** From 1 July to 31 August, **Keiō Dentetsu Bus** (☎03-5376-2222; www.highwaybus.com) runs direct buses (¥2700, 2½ hours; reservations necessary) from the Shinjuku Highway Bus Terminal to Mt Fuji Fifth Station. The same company runs buses year-round to Kawaguchi-ko (¥1750, 1¾ hours; reservations necessary), also leaving from the Shinjuku Highway Bus Terminal. From roughly mid-April to early December, buses run between Kawaguchi-ko and Mt Fuji Fifth Station (one way/return ¥1540/2100, 50 minutes). The schedule is highly seasonal; check with **Fujikyū Yamanashi bus** (☎0555-72-6877; http://transportation.fujikyu.co.jp) for current details. At the height of the climbing season there are buses until 9.15pm – ideal for climbers intending to make an overnight ascent.

Need to Know

- **Area Code** ☎0555
- **Location** 110km west of Tokyo
- **Tourist Office** (☎22-7000; ⊙9am-5pm) Next to Fujisan (Mt Fuji) train station.

SIGHTS & ACTIVITIES

MT FUJI HIKING

(富士山) Fuji is divided into 10 'stations' from base (first station) to summit (10th), but most climbers start from one of the four fifth stations, reachable by road. The most popular is **Kawaguchi-ko Trail**, accessed from the **Fuji Subaru Line Fifth Station**, because of its direct access by bus from Shinjuku Station. From the fifth stations, allow five to six hours to reach the top and about three hours to descend, plus 1½ hours for circling the crater at the top.

Trails below the fifth stations are now used mainly as short hiking routes, but you might consider the challenging but rewarding 19km hike from base to summit on the historic **Old Yoshidaguchi Trail**, which starts at Fuji Sengen-jinja in the town of Fuji-Yoshida. You can start from the station or take a bus part of the way to Umagaeshi (¥500). The *Climbing Mt Fuji* brochure, available at the tourist centres at both Fujisan and Kawaguchi-ko Stations, is useful.

FUJI SENGEN-JINJA SHINTO SHRINE

(冨士浅間神社; ☎22-0221; http://sengenjinja.jp/index.html; 5558 Kami-Yoshida, Fuji-Yoshida; ⊙grounds 24hr; staffed 9am-5pm) FREE A necessary preliminary to the Mt Fuji ascent was a visit to this deeply wooded, atmospheric temple, which has been located here since the 8th century. Notable points include a 1000-year-old cedar; its main gate, which is rebuilt every 60 years (slightly larger each time); and its two one-tonne *mikoshi* (portable shrines) used in the annual Yoshida no Himatsuri (Yoshida Fire Festival). From Fujisan Station it's a 20-minute uphill walk, or take a bus to Sengen-jinja-mae (¥150, five minutes).

MT FUJI: KNOW BEFORE YOU GO

Climbing Fuji-san is a serious challenge. It's high enough for altitude sickness, and as on any mountain, the weather can be volatile. You can count on it being close to freezing in the morning, even in summer.

At a minimum, bring clothing appropriate for cold and wet weather, including a hat and gloves. If you're climbing at night, bring a torch (flashlight) or headlamp and spare batteries. Descending the mountain is much harder on the knees than ascending; hiking poles can really help.

From the fifth stations and up, dozens of mountain huts offer hikers simple hot meals and a place to sleep. Although most offer little more than a blanket on the floor sandwiched between other climbers, they fill up fast – reservations are recommended (and are essential on weekends). Most huts allow you to rest inside as long as you order something. Camping is not permitted on the mountain.

Authorities strongly caution against climbing outside the regular season, when the weather is highly unpredictable and first-aid stations on the mountain are closed. Many mountain huts on the Yoshida Trail do stay open through mid-September, when conditions may still be good for climbing; none open before late June, when snow still blankets the upper stations.

Outside of the climbing season, check weather conditions carefully before setting out, bring appropriate equipment, do not climb alone, and be prepared to retreat at any time. Once snow or ice is on the mountain, Fuji becomes a very serious and dangerous undertaking and should only be attempted by those with winter mountaineering equipment and plenty of experience. Off-season climbers must register with the local police department; download the form from the Fuji-Yoshida City website and fax it in (http://www.city.fujiyoshida.yamanashi.jp; fax 0555-224-1180). The website also has an up-to-date list of mountain huts and contact information.

The *Shobunsha Yama-to-kōgen Mt Fuji Map* (山と高原地図・富士山; in Japanese), available at major bookshops, is the most comprehensive map of the area.

WORTH A DETOUR

HIKING TAKAO-SAN & OKU-TAMA

Less than an hour by train from Shinjuku, Takao-san (高尾山; 599m) is the mountain right on Tokyo's doorstep. The most popular trail (No 1) takes about 3¼ hours round-trip and passes a temple, **Yaku-ō-in** (薬王院; 042-661-1115; www.takaosan.or.jp/english/about.html; 2177 Takao-machi, Hachioji-shi; 24hr) FREE. Alternatively, a cable car and a chairlift can take you part of the way up (adult/child one way ¥480/240, return ¥930/460). Keiō-line offices have free trail maps in English, or check www.takaotozan.co.jp.

From Shinjuku Station, take the Keiō line (*jun-tokkyū*; ¥370, 47 minutes) to Takaosanguchi. The tourist village, trail entrances, cable car and chairlift are a few minutes away to the right. JR Pass holders can travel to Takao Station on the JR Chūō line (48 minutes) and transfer to the Keiō line to Takaosanguchi (¥120, two minutes).

You can continue for another hour to Oku-Tama. Here you'll find lofty cedars and more trail options. The **tourist information centre** (御岳ビジターセンター; 0428-78-9363; 38-5 Mitake-san; 9am-4.30pm Tue-Sun), near Oku-Tama Station, has English maps as well as information on trail conditions (note that many can get dangerously icy during the winter months). One moderate five-hour climb follows the Nokogiri Ridge to **Nokogiri-yama** (鋸山; 1109m) and continues to **Ōdake-san** (大岳山; 1267m), which has superb vistas, and **Mitake-san** (御岳山; 929m), a charming old-world hamlet with an ancient shrine. This is one trail that will get icy during winter.

A **cable car** (www.mitaketozan.co.jp; one way/return ¥590/1110; 7.30am-6.30pm) leads down from Mitake-san to Takimoto, where buses (¥280, 10 minutes) run to Mitake Station on the Ōme line; otherwise it's a 30-minute walk. JR Ōme–line trains run from Shinjuku to Oku-Tama (¥1080, one hour 50 minutes) and Mitake (¥890, 90 minutes); you may need to transfer at both Tachikawa and Ōme Stations.

KACHI KACHI YAMA ROPEWAY ROPEWAY

(カチカチ山ロープウェイ; www.kachikachiyama-ropeway.com; 1163-1 Azagawa; 1 way/return adult ¥410/720, child ¥210/360; 9am-5pm) On the lower eastern edge of the lake, this ropeway runs to the **Fuji Viewing Platform** (1104m). If you have time, there is a 3½-hour hike from here to **Mitsutōge-yama** (三つ峠山; 1785m); it's an old trail with excellent Fuji views. Ask at Kawaguchi-ko Tourist Information Center for a map.

EATING

SAKURADA UDON JAPANESE ¥

(桜井うどん; 5-1-33 Shimo-Yoshida; noodles ¥350; 10am-2pm Mon-Sat) Fuji-Yoshida is famous for its *te-uchi udon* (chunky white flour noodles), with some 60 places serving them for lunch. Just off the main drag, this is a good spot to sample the dish sitting cross-legged on tatami. Look for the blue *noren* (curtains) next to the Status Pub.

HŌTŌ FUDŌ NOODLES ¥¥

(ほうとう不動; 72-8511; www.houtou-fudou.jp; 707 Kawaguchi; hōtō ¥1080; 11am-7pm) *Hōtō* are Kawaguchi-ko's local noodles, hand-cut and served in a thick miso stew with vegetables. It's a hearty meal best sampled at this chain with five branches around town. This is the most architecturally interesting one, an igloo-like building in which you can also sample *basashi* – horsemeat sashimi (¥1080).

SLEEPING

★**K'S HOUSE MT FUJI** HOSTEL ¥

(83-5556; http://kshouse.jp/fuji-e/index.html; 6713-108 Funatsu; dm from ¥2500, d with/without bathroom ¥7800/6800;) K's is expert at providing a welcoming atmosphere, spacious Japanese-style rooms and English-speaking staff. There's a fully loaded kitchen, mountain bikes for hire and comfy common areas to meet fellow travellers/climbers and free pick-up from Kawaguchi-ko Station. Its bar, **Zero Station** (6pm-midnight), is stumbling distance away. Rooms fill up fast during the climbing season.

FUJISAN HOTEL MOUNTAIN HUT ¥

(富士山ホテル; 22-0237; www.fujisanhotel.com; per person with/without 2 meals from ¥8350/5950) One of the largest and most popular rest huts open on Mt Fuji during the climbing season. There are English-speaking staff here.

Sleeping

Tokyo is known for being an expensive place to sleep; however, more and more attractive budget and midrange options are popping up every year. The best deals are on the east side of town, in neighbourhoods such as Ueno and Asakusa. As with pretty much anywhere in Tokyo, you can expect high levels of cleanliness and service.

Boutique Hotels

Boutique hotels haven't really caught on in Tokyo; there are only a few. This is perhaps because the concept – intimate and with memorable decor – is too similar to that of a hotel with a more sleazy repute: the love hotel.

Business Hotels

Functional and economical, 'business hotels' are geared to the lone traveller on business. The compact rooms usually have semidouble beds (140cm across; roomy for one, a bit of a squeeze for two) and tiny en suite baths. They're famous for being deeply unfashionable, though many chains have updated their rooms in recent years. Expect to pay from ¥9000 to ¥12,000 (or ¥12,000 to ¥18,000 for double occupancy). Most accept credit cards.

Capsule Hotels

Capsule hotels offer rooms the size of a single bed, with just enough headroom for you to sit up. Think of it like a bunk bed with more privacy (and a reading light, TV and alarm clock). Most are men-only, though some have floors for women, too. Prices range from ¥3500 to ¥5000, which usually includes access to a large shared bath and sauna. Most only accept cash and do not permit guests with visible tattoos.

Hostels

In the last five years, Tokyo hostels have gone from ordinary to outstanding. Always known for being clean and well managed, they now outdo themselves to provide cultural activities and social events for guests. Most have a mixture of dorms and private rooms, and cooking and laundry facilities. Expect to pay about ¥2800 for a dorm and ¥7500 for a private room (double occupancy).

Luxury Hotels

In the top-end bracket, you can expect to find the amenities of deluxe hotels anywhere in the world: satellite TV, concierge service in fluent English and enough space to properly unwind. Many of Tokyo's luxury hotels are in high-rise buildings and offer fantastic city views. They also offer direct airport access, via the Limousine Bus.

Ryokan

For a really traditional Japanese experience, with tatami (woven-mat floor) rooms and futon (traditional quilt-like mattress) instead of beds, a ryokan is the way to go. Exclusive establishments can charge upwards of ¥25,000; however, there are a number of relatively inexpensive ryokan in Tokyo, starting around ¥8000 a night (for double occupancy).

Most ryokan have 'family rooms' that can sleep four or five – an economical choice if you're travelling as a group or with kids. Some offer rooms with private baths, but one of the pleasures of staying in a traditional inn is the communal bath. These are segregated by sex, spacious, and sometimes made of cedar or stone. Most inns provide cotton robes called *yukata,* which you can wear to and from the baths. Many ryokan accept cash only.

NEED TO KNOW

Price Ranges
Prices reflect the cost of one night's accommodation for double-occupancy:

¥ under ¥8000

¥¥ ¥8000 to ¥20,000

¥¥¥ over ¥20,000

Tax
Sales tax (8%) applies to hotel rates. There is also a citywide 'accommodation tax' of ¥100 on rooms over ¥10,000 and ¥200 for rooms over ¥15,000.

Rates
Rack rates (including taxes) are quoted here, but prices can vary dramatically and can often be significantly less. Check online for deals.

Reservations
Advance booking is highly recommended. Busy periods include the first week of January, 'Golden Week' (29 April to 5 May) and August.

Websites
- **Lonely Planet** (lonelyplanet.com/Japan/Tokyo/hotels) Reviews, recommendations and booking.
- **Jalan** (www.jalan.net) Popular discount accommodation site.
- **Rakuten Travel** (http://travel.rakuten.com) Local booking site with good deals.
- **Japanican** (www.japanican.com) Accommodation site for foreign travellers run by Japan's largest travel agency.
- **Japanese Inn Group** (www.japaneseinngroup.com) Bookings for ryokan and other small inns.

Lonely Planet's Top Choices

Sawanoya Ryokan (p206) A gem in quiet Yanaka with wonderful hospitality and traditional baths.

Claska (p201) Very cool designer digs in a residential neighbourhood south of Meguro.

Nui (p207) Hipster hostel in a former warehouse near Asakusa.

Park Hyatt Tokyo (p204) Palatial high-rise with otherworldly views in Shinjuku.

Hotel S (p200) Stylish boutique hotel down the road from Roppongi's legendary nightlife.

Khaosan World (p207) Trippy hostel in a former love hotel with superfriendly staff, in Asakusa.

Best by Budget

¥

Toco (p206) Hostel in a charming old wooden house near Ueno.

Kimi Ryokan (p204) Welcoming budget ryokan in northwest Tokyo.

K's House Tokyo (p207) Homey backpacker fave near Asakusa.

¥¥

Shibuya Granbell Hotel (p202) Funky boutique hotel on the quieter side of Shibuya.

Mitsui Garden Hotel Ginza Premier (p199) A great deal in centrally located and upmarket Ginza.

Dormy Inn Premium Shibuya Jingūmae (p203) Lots of amenities and an enviable location in Harajuku.

¥¥¥

Ritz-Carlton Tokyo (p201) Ultraluxe perch in Roppongi, overlooking the whole city.

Palace Hotel Tokyo (p198) Elegant rooms alongside the Imperial Palace in Marunouchi.

The Peninsula Tokyo (p198) Huge rooms, breathtaking views, and every mod-con imaginable.

Best Ryokan

Hōmeikan (p206) Atmospheric, 100-year-old ryokan near Ueno.

Sukeroku No Yado Sadachiyo (p208) Traditional inn with big tatami rooms and fantastic baths, in Asakusa.

Andon Ryokan (p207) Minamalist modern ryokan with rooftop jacuzzi near Asakusa.

Best Views

Tokyo Central Youth Hostel (p205) Youth hostel with city views worthy of a luxury hotel.

Hotel Chinzanso (p205) Rooms overlooking the manicured grounds of a former estate.

Cerulean Tower Tōkyū Hotel (p202) Glittering views over Shibuya and beyond for less than the average luxury hotel.

Best Capsule Hotels

9 Hours (p202) Futuristic pods in Narita Airport.

Capsule & Sauna Century (p202) Capsules and a huge bath in the thick of Shibuya.

Where to Stay

Neighbourhood	For	Against
Marunouchi & Nihombashi	Convenient for all sights and for travel out of the city	Area is mostly businesspeople; sky-high prices and quiet on weekends
Ginza & Tsukiji	Ginza's shops and restaurants at your doorstep; handy for early-morning visits to the fish market	Congested and few inexpensive options compared to other districts
Roppongi & Around	A wealth of good eating and drinking options, as well as sights	Roppongi can be noisy at night; if you're not into the nightlife there's little reason to stay here
Ebisu, Meguro & Around	On the useful JR Yamanote line; near major hubs but with fewer crowds; great bars and restaurants	No major sights in the neighbourhood, and can feel removed from the action
Shibuya & Shimo-Kitazawa	Convenient transport links; plenty of nightlife and a buzzing streetscape	Youth-centric area has no real adult vibe; extremely crowded; possible sensory overload
Harajuku & Aoyama	On the JR Yamanote line; great shopping and some key sights nearby	Few options and big crowds
Shinjuku & West Tokyo	Superb transport links for all of Tokyo's big sights, a wealth of food and nightlife options	Very crowded around station area; cheap options are clustered around the red-light district
Kōrakuen & Northwest Tokyo	Very central; attractive upscale options in Kagurazaka; good budget options in Ikebukuro	Central locations quiet at night and on weekends; Ikebukuro is crowded and remote
Akihabara & Around	Kanda options are central to big sights and surrounded by easy transport links	Area is mostly for businesspeople and has little charm
Ueno & Yanaka	Ryokan (traditional Japanese inns) abound; lots of greenery and museums; easy airport access	The good ryokan here tend to be isolated in residential neighborhoods
Asakusa & Sumida River	Atmospheric old-city feel, convenient for east Tokyo sights; great budget options	Asakusa is quiet at night, and a good 20-minute subway ride from more central areas

Marunouchi & Nihombashi

YAESU TERMINAL HOTEL BUSINESS HOTEL ¥¥

Map p276 (八重洲ターミナルホテル; ☎3281-3771; www.yth.jp; 1-5-14 Yaesu, Chūō-ku; s/d ¥11,500/16,500; ; JR lines to Tokyo, Yaesu north exit) This sleek little business hotel on cherry-tree-lined Sakura-dōri has contemporary lines and a minimalist look. Though room sizes are generally tiny, they're decently priced for this neighbourhood and showcase modern, sporting, contemporary art by radiographic artist Steven Meyers.

PALACE HOTEL TOKYO LUXURY HOTEL ¥¥¥

Map p276 (パレスホテル東京; ☎3211-5211; www.palacehoteltokyo.com; 1-1-1 Marunouchi, Chiyoda-ku; r/ste from ¥50,000/124,000; ; Chiyoda line to Ōtemachi, exit C13B) With its prestigious address, the gorgeously renovated Palace Hotel offers the refinement and elegance that its name suggests. Sniff the botanically perfumed air as you stride its plush corridors. Request a room with a balcony – they're a bit more expensive but worth it for the chance to soak up private alfresco views of the city.

THE PENINSULA TOKYO LUXURY HOTEL ¥¥¥

Map p276 (ザ・ペニンシュラ東京; ☎6270-2288; www.peninsula.com/tokyo; 1-8-1 Yūrakuchō, Chiyoda-ku; r from ¥67,000; ; JR lines to Yūrakuchō, Hibiya exit) One almost gets a feeling of guilty extravagance when sprawling out in the Peninsula's vast rooms (starting at 51 sq metres), which overlook the Imperial Palace and Hibiya Moat, and have floor-to-ceiling windows. Latticed caramel woodwork, sumptuous marble bathrooms and a dark central atrium unite in a delicious symphony of design.

TOKYO STATION HOTEL LUXURY HOTEL ¥¥¥

Map p276 (東京ステーションホテル; ☎5220-1112; www.tokyostationhotel.jp; 1-9-1 Marunouchi, Chiyoda-ku; r from ¥41,000; ; JR lines to Tokyo, Marunouchi south exit) Representing a return to the classics, the Tokyo Station Hotel has brushed up handsomely as part of the heritage building's restoration. Rooms are spacious and decorated in an opulent European fashion, with tall ceilings, marble

ONLY-IN-TOKYO SLEEPING ALTERNATIVES

Add a cultural experience, and save a little money, by staying the night in one of these only-in-Tokyo sleeping alternatives.

Love Hotels

At these hotels for amorous encounters – known in Japanese as *rabu hoteru* (or *rabuho*, for short) – you can stop for a short afternoon 'rest' (from ¥2500) or an overnight 'stay' (from ¥6500); you can't stay consecutive nights, though. Some love hotels have over-the-top interiors (and amenities that range from costumes to video-game consoles). Pictures of the rooms are usually displayed out front. Take your pick from the dozens of hotels on Dōgenzaka in Shibuya.

Manga-kissa

Manga-kissa are cafes for reading manga (Japanese comics) and surfing the internet. Around the time they started adding private cubicles for DVD-viewing, they became places to sleep too. A 'night pack' (for nine to 12 hours) starts at around ¥1500. **Gran Cyber Cafe Bagus** is one of the nicer chains, with a women's-only area, showers and blanket rentals; there are branches in **Shinjuku** (グランサイバーカフェバグース; Map p286; www.bagus-99.com/shops/gcc_shinjuku; 3rd fl, 3-15-11 Shinjuku, Shinjuku-ku; JR Yamanote line to Shinjuku, east exit) and **Shibuya** (グランサイバーカフェバグース; Map p283; www.bagus-99.com/shops/gcc_shibuya; 6th fl, 28-6 Udagawa-chō, Shibuya-ku; JR Yamanote line to Shibuya, Hachikō exit).

Spas & Saunas

Many spas and saunas – Spa LaQua (p146) and Ōedo Onsen Monogatari (p180) included – have 'relaxation rooms' with mats on the floor or reclining chairs where you can overnight for an extra fee (about ¥1500 to ¥2000).

counters and dripping chandeliers. Some rooms have views of the Imperial Palace.

MANDARIN ORIENTAL TOKYO LUXURY HOTEL ¥¥¥

Map p276 (マンダリン オリエンタル 東京; ☎3270-8800; www.mandarinoriental.com/tokyo; 2-1-1 Nihonbashi-Muromachi, Chūō-ku; r/ste from ¥71,000/171,000; Ⓢ Ginza line to Mitsukoshimae, exit A7) The Mandarin's atrium lobby and all rooms offer breathtaking views. Kimono-weaving designs are part of the exquisite design of the spacious rooms. There are two Michelin-starred restaurants to dine at and, although there is no swimming pool, there are hot tubs in the lofty spa.

MARUNOUCHI HOTEL LUXURY HOTEL ¥¥¥

Map p276 (丸の内ホテル; ☎3215-2151; www.marunouchi-hotel.co.jp; Oazo Bldg, 1-6-3 Marunouchi, Chiyoda-ku; s/d from ¥23,960/32,500; JR lines to Tokyo, Marunouchi north exit) Handy for Tokyo Station (and with great views of the building from many of its rooms), the Marunouchi deftly synthesises modern conveniences with Japanese style. Rooms are a decent size with spacious bathrooms.

HOTEL RYUMEIKAN TOKYO HOTEL ¥¥¥

Map p276 (ホテル龍名館東京; ☎3271-0971; www.ryumeikan-tokyo.jp; 1-3-22 Yaesu, Chūō-ku; s/d ¥18,000/33,000; JR lines to Tokyo, Yaesu north exit) Mixing subtle Japanese details with contemporary design, Ryumeikan strikes the right balance between comfortable amenities, polite service and a winning location close to Tokyo Station. It's a fantastic alternative to the cookie-cutter business digs – several rooms here could even be considered spacious.

Ginza & Tsukiji

★MITSUI GARDEN HOTEL GINZA PREMIER HOTEL ¥¥

Map p278 (三井ガーデンホテル銀座プレミア; ☎3543-1131; www.gardenhotels.co.jp; 8-13-1 Ginza, Chūō-ku; r from ¥16,000; Ⓢ Ginza line to Shimbashi, exit 1) If you book ahead and online, this upmarket business hotel is a steal. It is reasonably priced and has a great location, pleasantly decorated rooms, and a high-rise lobby with killer Shiodome and Tokyo Tower views.

By now the new **Millennium Mitsui Garden Hotel Tokyo** (ミレニアム 三井ガーデンホテル 東京; Map p278; ☎3549-3331; www.gardenhotels.co.jp/eng/millennium-tokyo; 5-11-1 Ginza, Chūō-ku; r from ¥20,300; Ⓢ Hibiya line to Higashi-Ginza, exit A1), nearby in Ginza, should be open. It has slightly larger entry-level rooms.

TŌKYŪ STAY HIGASHI-GINZA BUSINESS HOTEL ¥¥

Map p278 (東急ステイ東銀座; ☎5551-0109; www.tokyustay.co.jp; 4-11-5 Tsukiji, Chūō-ku; s/d from ¥14,000/19,900; Ⓢ Hibiya line to Tskuji, exits 1 & 2) With a giant red snapper painted on the side of the building, you can't miss this place in Tsukiji's outer-market area. It's a combination of business hotel and longer-stay apartments, and all of the comfortable, compact rooms are fitted with washing machine/dryers and kitchenettes.

GINZA GRAND HOTEL BUSINESS HOTEL ¥¥

Map p278 (銀座グランドホテル; ☎3572-4131; www.ginzagrand.com; 8-6-15 Ginza, Chūō-ku; s/d from ¥16,000/23,500; JR Yamanote line to Shimbashi, Ginza exit) This well-located upmarket business hotel has a bright, fresh design with rooms decorated in pleasant mahogany and caramel tones. The 'Audrey' rooms feature special amenities for women.

HOTEL VILLA FONTAINE SHIODOME BUSINESS HOTEL ¥¥

Map p278 (ホテルヴィラフォンテーヌ汐留; ☎3569-2220; www.hvf.jp/eng; 1-9-2 Higashi-Shimbashi, Minato-ku; s/d incl breakfast from ¥13,000/15,000; Ⓢ Ōedo line to Shiodome, exit 10) Cone-shaped lanterns light the high-ceilinged black-marble lobby. Sculptural red blobs and flame-themed art on the walls lead to upmarket rooms with internet, TV and partial views of Hama Rikyū Onshi-teien. With breakfast thrown in, this is an excellent deal.

IMPERIAL HOTEL LUXURY HOTEL ¥¥¥

Map p278 (帝国ホテル; ☎3504-1111; www.imperialhotel.co.jp; 1-1-1 Uchisaiwai-chō, Chiyoda-ku; s/d from ¥42,770/48,710; Ⓢ Hibiya line to Hibiya, exit A13) The present building is the successor to Frank Lloyd Wright's 1923 masterpiece, and small tributes to the architect's style can be found in the lobby and elsewhere. The rooms are not the most stylish in Tokyo but are large, comfortable and

LONGER-TERM RENTALS

If you're a budget traveller planning to settle in Tokyo, you might consider landing first at a *gaijin* (foreigner) house. These are private dwellings that have been partitioned into rooms or apartments, furnished simply and rented out to *gaijin*. (Renting an apartment in Tokyo through ordinary channels can be challenging – with big deposits, a two-year minimum contract and an unfortunate unwillingness to rent to foreign tenants). **Sakura House** (www.sakura-house.com) has a variety of properties all over the city and has long been a right of passage for expats getting started in Tokyo.

Kimi Information Center (www.kimiwillbe.com) also has information on *gaijin* houses, furnished short- and long-term apartment rentals and English teaching jobs.

generally have impressive views; the ones on the Imperial floor are the most up to date. Service here is virtually peerless.

CONRAD TOKYO LUXURY HOTEL ¥¥¥

Map p278 (コンラッド東京; ☎6388-8000; www.conradtokyo.co.jp; 1-9-1 Higashi-Shimbashi, Minato-ku; s/d from ¥40,600/89,500; Ōedo line to Shiodome, exit 10) One of the gigantic, glittery gems of the Shiodome development adjacent to Hama Rikyū Onshi-teien, the Conrad is a strong contender for the attention of upmarket travellers looking for that central, super-sophisticated base. The garden or city views are equally spectacular, as are the varnished hardwood interiors and floor-to-ceiling glassed bathrooms.

Roppongi & Around

★HOTEL S BOUTIQUE HOTEL ¥¥

Map p280 (ホテル S; ☎5771-2469; http://hr-roppongi.jp; 1-11-6 Nishi-Azabu, Minato-ku; r from ¥18,200; Hibiya line to Roppongi, exit 2) The eight styles of room at this boutique property capture the arty design spirit of Roppongi. Some of the more expensive duplex-type rooms have Japanese design elements such as tatami (in charcoal) and circular *hinoki* (cypress-wood) bathtubs. The entry-level rooms are also a cut above the usual. There are serviced apartments here, too, if you're planning a longer stay.

HOTEL VILLA FONTAINE ROPPONGI BUSINESS HOTEL ¥¥

Map p280 (ホテルヴィラフォンテーヌ六本木; ☎3560-1110; www.hvf.jp/eng/roppongi.php; 1-6-2 Roppongi, Minato-ku; s/d from ¥18,500/20,500; Namboku line to Roppongi-itchōme, exit 1, Hibiya line to Roppongi, exit 5) Stylish, modern and reasonably priced, this stylish business-hotel chain offers 140cm-wide beds, a complimentary buffet breakfast and free LAN access if you're lugging a laptop (wi-fi in the lobby only). It's close enough to Roppongi's centre to experience its madness, but far enough away for a quiet sleep. Rates on Sunday are practically half-price.

B ROPPONGI BUSINESS HOTEL ¥¥

Map p280 (ザ・ビー六本木; ☎5412-0451; www.theb-hotels.com/the-b-roppongi/en/index.html; 3-9-8 Roppongi, Minato-ku; s/d incl breakfast from ¥13,600/14,100; Hibiya line to Roppongi, exit 5) The slick, white-brown rooms here range in size from 10 to 31 sq metres, albeit with small, prefab bathrooms. Atmosphere is business-casual and the location is perfect for Roppongi's nocturnal attractions. If it's full there a couple of other B hotels nearby in Akasaka.

HOTEL AVANSHELL AKASAKA BUSINESS HOTEL ¥¥

Map p280 (ホテル アバンシェル赤坂; ☎3568-3456; www.solarehotels.com/hotel/tokyo/hotel-avanshell-akasaka; 2-14-14 Akasaka, Minato-ku; s/d from ¥12,500/15,500; Chiyoda line to Akasaka, exit 2) This hotel is visually appealing and a cut above most business hotels. The rooms are laid out under themes such as 'primo', and have zippy decor ranging from black leather couches and puffy white bedspreads to cool, green tatami spaces.

ASIA CENTER OF JAPAN BUSINESS HOTEL ¥¥

Map p280 (ホテル アジア会館; ☎3402-6111; www.asiacenter.or.jp; 8-10-32 Akasaka, Minato-ku; s/d from ¥8850/10,580; Ginza line to Aoyama-itchōme, exit 4) The decor is generic and forgettable but the rooms are decently sized and staff are old hands at helping foreign visitors. A quiet location but within walking distance of Roppongi.

★RITZ-CARLTON TOKYO LUXURY HOTEL ¥¥¥

Map p280 (ザ・リッツ・カールトン東京; ☎3423-8000; www.ritzcarlton.com; Tokyo Midtown, 9-7-1 Akasaka, Minato-ku; s/ste from ¥73,500/126,500; ; Hibiya line to Roppongi, exit 8) The Ritz-Carlton's lobby – with giant paintings by Sam Francis and views clear to the Imperial Palace – is on the 45th floor, and capacious rooms go up from there. Concierges can do just about anything, and if you send your shoes for a complimentary shine they return in a lovely wooden box.

HOTEL ŌKURA LUXURY HOTEL ¥¥¥

Map p280 (ホテルオークラ東京; ☎3582-0111; www.okura.com; 2-10-4 Toranomon, Minato-ku; s/d from ¥41,580/47,520; ; Hibiya line to Kamiyachō, exit 4B) While the beloved original 1962 hotel, a design classic, has been demolished to make way for a new building (set to open in 2019), the Okura's 1973 vintage South Wing is still in business. It remains very elegant, too, with many identical fixtures, including the famous lobby lanterns. Rooms are bright, large and have tasteful Japanese design touches.

GRAND HYATT TOKYO LUXURY HOTEL ¥¥¥

Map p280 (グランド ハイアット 東京; ☎4333-1234; http://tokyo.grand.hyatt.jp/en/hotel/home.html; 6-10-3 Roppongi, Minato-ku; r from ¥48,000; ; Hibiya line to Roppongi, exits 1C & 3) Architecturally open and bright despite its somewhat labyrinthine layout, the Grand Hyatt is warm and gorgeously chic. Smooth mahogany and natural fabrics give an organic flavour to the rooms, while its Roppongi Hills location imbues it with vibrant energy. Even the bathrooms feature rain-shower fixtures and rough-cut stone, continuing a nature-in-architecture motif.

THE CAPITOL HOTEL TŌKYŪ LUXURY HOTEL ¥¥¥

Map p280 (ザ・キャピトルホテル 東急; ☎3503-0109; www.capitolhoteltokyu.com; 2-10-3 Nagatachō, Chiyoda-ku; r from ¥70,300; ; Ginza or Nanboku lines to Tameike-sannō, exit 6) Neighbours with Japan's Diet as well as the prime minister's residence and office, this tastefully luxurious hotel exudes power and prestige. Fully renovated in recent years, it sports sleek contemporary Japanese design with ripple-effect carpets, soothing monotones in the rooms and *washi* paper lamps.

Ebisu, Meguro & Around

★CLASKA BOUTIQUE HOTEL ¥¥

(クラスカ; ☎3719-8121; www.claska.com/en/hotel; 1-3-18 Chūō-chō, Meguro-ku; s/d from ¥13,200/20,900, weekly per night s ¥8200; ; 1, 2, or 7 from Meguro Station to Shimizu, Tōkyū Tōyoko line to Gakugei Daigaku, east exit) The Claska is hands down Tokyo's most stylish hotel, though you might not know it from the retro business-hotel facade. No two rooms are alike: some have tatami and floor cushions; others have spacious terraces and glass-walled bathrooms. Its 20 rooms fill up fast. The only drawback is the out-of-the-way location, about 2km west of Meguro Station.

The easiest way to get here is by taxi from Meguro Station (about ¥1000, 10 minutes); there's also a bus stop very near the hotel. Free bicycle rentals are available for up to three hours for guests to explore the surrounding neighbourhood, a residential enclave known for its interior-design shops.

WEEKLY DORMY INN MEGURO AOBADAI BUSINESS HOTEL ¥¥

(ウイークリードーミーイン目黒青葉台; ☎6894-5489; www.hotespa.net/weekly/meguro/en; 3-21-8 Aobadai, Meguro-ku; s/d from ¥7400/12,400; ; Hibiya line to Naka-Meguro) If you prefer to base yourself somewhere less hectic – but no less fun – try this business hotel in hip Naka-Meguro. Rooms include a hotplate and fridge. There are laundry machines and free bicycle rentals, too. Wi-fi is weak in some rooms, but fine in the lobby. Breakfast (rice balls) and even dinner (noodles) is included.

HOTEL EXCELLENT EBISU BUSINESS HOTEL ¥¥

Map p284 (ホテルエクセレント恵比寿; ☎5458-0087; www.soeikikaku.co.jp/english/index.html; 1-9-5 Ebisu-nishi, Shibuya-ku; s/d from ¥9400/11,900; ; JR Yamanote line to Ebisu, west exit) This reasonably priced hotel is located a minute's walk from Ebisu Station. Rooms here are small and basic; their proximity to the neighbourhood's excellent restaurants and bars is the real draw. The beds in the double rooms are on the small side for two; the beds in the single and twin rooms are roomy for one.

AIRPORT ACCOMMODATION

For late-night arrivals and early-morning departures, when there's no public transportation, sleeping at the airport is an economical option.

9 Hours (0476-33-5109; http://ninehours.co.jp/en/narita; Narita International Airport Terminal 2; capsule ¥3900;) This slick capsule hotel inside Narita Airport has roomy, space-age pods and separate rooms for men and women. It's possible to stay for only a few hours, too (¥1500, plus ¥500 per hour). One downside: small luggage lockers.

Royal Park Hotel The Haneda (ロイヤルパークホテル ザ 羽田; 6830-1111; www.rph-the.co.jp/haneda/en; Haneda Airport International Terminal; s/d from ¥12,500/16,000;) Haneda Airport's brand-new transit hotel is good value if you factor in the cost of *not* having to take a taxi for late-night arrivals. Rooms have modern decor and are stocked with amenities.

RYOKAN SANSUISŌ RYOKAN ¥¥

(旅館山水荘; 3441-7475; www.sansuiso.net; 2-9-5 Higashi-Gotanda, Shinagawa-ku; s/d from ¥5000/8600; ; JR Yamanote line to Gotanda, east exit) This 10-room inn is run by a friendly older couple. The tatami rooms are cosy and well kept, though the building itself is old; if you're staying two to a room it's worth 'splurging' for a room with a private bathroom (an extra ¥400). Larger rooms can sleep up to five. It's a 500m walk from Gotanda Station, one stop past Meguro on the JR Yamanote line; note that it gets a bit of rail noise from the tracks nearby. From the east exit, follow the tracks south until you reach the river and a towering apartment complex – the inn is behind it.

Shibuya & Shimo-Kitazawa

CAPSULE & SAUNA CENTURY CAPSULE HOTEL ¥

Map p283 (カプセル&サウナセンチュリー; 3464-1777; www.century-grp.com; 1-19-14 Dōgenzaka, Shibuya-ku; capsules from ¥3990; ; JR Yamanote line to Shibuya, Hachikō exit) This men-only capsule hotel perched atop Dōgenzaka hill includes large shared bathrooms, massage chairs and coin laundry machines; the 'deluxe' capsules are slightly bigger. It's a clean, well-run place, and major credit cards are accepted. It's also pretty popular, so it's a good idea to reserve a spot before you head out for the night.

HOTEL FUKUDAYA RYOKAN ¥¥

Map p283 (ホテル福田屋; 3467-5833; www2.gol.com/users/ryokan-fukudaya/index.html; 4-5-9 Aobadai, Meguro-ku; s/d from ¥6600/11,500; ; Keiō line to Shinsen) Hotel Fukudaya offers futons in crisp, white linens on fresh tatami; the Western-style rooms are cheaper, but not as nice. Some rooms have private bathrooms, but there is also a communal *o-furo* (Japanese-style bath). It's in a residential neighbourhood, a seven-minute walk from Shinsen Station or a 20-minute walk from Shibuya.

★SHIBUYA GRANBELL HOTEL BOUTIQUE HOTEL ¥¥¥

Map p283 (渋谷グランベルホテル; 5457-2681; www.granbellhotel.jp; 15-17 Sakuragaoka-chō, Shibuya-ku; s/d from ¥13,000/22,000; ; JR Yamanote line to Shibuya, south exit) Though priced about the same as a business hotel, the Granbell is far more stylish. Some rooms have glass-enclosed bathrooms, Simmons beds and pop-art curtains. The hotel is on the quieter side of Shibuya, towards Daikanyama; still, it's just a few minutes' walk to the station.

The Granbell is also available during the day for a 'rest' (from ¥10,500 for five hours), meaning it doubles as an upscale love hotel.

CERULEAN TOWER TŌKYŪ HOTEL LUXURY HOTEL ¥¥¥

Map p283 (セルリアンタワー東急ホテル; 3476-3000; www.ceruleantower-hotel.com/en; 26-1 Sakuragaoka-chō, Shibuya-ku; s/d from ¥36,828/48,708; ; JR Yamanote line to Shibuya, south exit) If you're going to splurge in Shibuya, this is the place to do it. The Cerulean has big rooms with big beds and stylish, modern decor. Huge picture windows offer views across Shibuya to the Shinjuku skyline and beyond (or towards Tokyo Bay; your pick).

HOTEL METS SHIBUYA BUSINESS HOTEL ¥¥¥

Map p283 (ホテルメッツ渋谷; ☎3409-0011; www.hotelmets.jp/shibuya; 3-29-17 Shibuya, Shibuya-ku; s/d incl breakfast from ¥15,500/25,000; ; JR Yamanote line to Shibuya, new south exit) Super convenient and comfortable, the Hotel Mets is inside Shibuya Station's quiet south exit. For a business hotel it's fairly stylish and the double beds clock in at a roomy 160cm. Bonus: breakfast is included, either a buffet spread or toast and eggs at the in-house cafe. Reception is on the 4th floor.

EXCEL HOTEL TŌKYŪ HOTEL ¥¥¥

Map p283 (エクセルホテル東急; ☎5457-0109; www.tokyuhotelsjapan.com/en/TE/TE_SHIBU/index.html; 1-12-2 Dōgenzaka, Shibuya-ku; s/d from ¥24,948/34,452; ; JR Yamanote line to Shibuya, Hachikō exit) This hotel is right on top of Shibuya Station, a location you'll be grateful for after a long day. Rooms are spacious though ordinary. Prices rise along with the floor numbers, but you can get a pretty good view with a simple upgrade for ¥2000 per night to a 'city view' room. The hotel is part of the Mark City complex.

HOTEL UNIZO BUSINESS HOTEL ¥¥¥

Map p283 (ホテルユニゾ; ☎5457-7557; www.hotelunizo.com/eng/shibuya; 4-3 Udagawa-chō, Shibuya-ku; s/tw from ¥17,490/23,660; ; JR Yamanote line to Shibuya, Hachikō exit) The location, right in the thick of Shibuya, is the draw here. Rooms are compact, though attractively decorated; double beds are 160cm wide. There's a popular cafe on the 2nd floor.

Harajuku & Aoyama

DORMY INN PREMIUM SHIBUYA JINGŪMAE BUSINESS HOTEL ¥¥

Map p288 (ドーミーインプレミアム渋谷神宮前; ☎5774-5489; www.hotespa.net/hotels/shibuya; 6-24-4 Jingūmae, Shibuya-ku; s/d from ¥11,490/15,990; ; JR Yamanote line to Harajuku, Omote-sandō exit) This flashy new property from the Dormy Inn chain of business hotels has typically small rooms with double beds (140cm) but a host of perks: free breakfast and noodles in the evening, laundry facilities, a communal bath and shuttle service to Shibuya Station (7am to noon).

TŌKYŪ STAY AOYAMA PREMIER BUSINESS HOTEL ¥¥¥

Map p288 (東急ステイ青山プレミア; ☎3497-0109; 2-27-18 Minami-Aoyama, Minato-ku; s/d from ¥18,300/31,300; ; S Ginza line to Gaienmae, exit 1A) This is the nicest of the Tōkyū Stay chain of apartment hotels. The rooms are on the small side, but the picture windows (and city views) make up for it; some rooms include a basic kitchenette (with microwave and hotplate) and a washer and dryer. Rates drop slightly (¥1000 to ¥2000 per night) if you book for seven days or more.

Shinjuku & West Tokyo

While proximity to transport-hub Shinjuku Station is a plus, properties around Higashi-Shinjuku and Nishi-Shinjuku subway stations have better rates and are within walking distance of Shinjuku attractions. Note that many budget hotels in Shinjuku that target foreign travellers are in the red-light district, Kabukichō; while it's highly unlikely you'd encounter any real danger, some might find it unpleasant to walk past shady characters night after night.

LADIES 510 CAPSULE HOTEL ¥

Map p286 (レディース510; ☎3200-1945; www.capsule510.jp/ladies510; 2-40-1 Kabukichō, Shinjuku-ku; capsule ¥4300; ; JR Yamanote line to Shinjuku, east exit) This is a clean, well-run capsule hotel just for women in Kabukichō. Park your stuff in the narrow locker on arrival and switch to the pyjamas provided; towels, hairbrushes and skin creams are also included. There's a shared bath, sauna, cafe and free iPad rentals. It's a small place and fills up early on weekends.

GREEN PLAZA SHINJUKU CAPSULE HOTEL ¥

Map p286 (グリーンプラザ新宿; ☎3207-4923; www.hgpshinjuku.jp/hotel; 1-29-2 Kabukichō, Shinjuku-ku; capsules from ¥4500; ; JR Yamanote line to Shinjuku, east exit) Smack in the middle of Kabukichō, Green Plaza Shinjuku offers 630 standard and 'upgrade' capsules (with wi-fi and outlets) for men only. There's also a ladies' sauna on the 9th floor that allows women to check in for the night and rest in a communal lounge area (¥3500) or in their own tiny room (¥5300).

E HOTEL HIGASHI-SHINJUKU BUSINESS HOTEL ¥¥

Map p286 (イーホテル東新宿; www.shinjuku-hotel.co.jp/eng; 2-3-15 Kabukichō, Shinjuku-ku; s/d from ¥9000/11,000; ; Ōedo line to Higashi-Shinjuku, exit A1) This traveller favourite has an excellent location (just in front of the Higashi-Shinjuku subway station), friendly staff and lots of city info. Rooms are typically small but have a clean, modern feel and comfortable double beds. Those on the main street might get some noise, but some have nice night views. There's a coffee shop on the ground floor.

SEKITEI RYOKAN ¥¥

(石亭; 3365-5931; http://license-kanren.com/sekitei?lang=en; 2-15-10 Hyakunin-chō, Shinjuku-ku; s/d ¥7800/11,400; ; JR Yamanote line to Shin-Ōkubo) A 15-minute walk north of Shinjuku, Sekitei is a quiet, personable inn with clean and comfortable tatami rooms. Try to book the one with the rock garden running through the centre. Staff speak some English. There's a small lounge and laundry room.

NISHITETSU INN SHINJUKU BUSINESS HOTEL ¥¥

Map p286 (西鉄イン新宿; 3367-5454; www.n-inn.jp/english/hotels/shinjuku; 7-23-2 Nishi-Shinjuku, Shinjuku-ku; s/tw from ¥10,100/16,300; ; Marunouchi line to Nishi-Shinjuku, exit 1) A 10-minute walk west of Shinjuku Station, and next door to the Nishi-Shinjuku subway station, Nishitetsu offers a winning combination of price and location. Rates go down if you book consecutive nights. Rooms are simple and clean – small, but not laughably so. There's a cafe in the lobby and English-speaking staff at the front desk.

KADOYA HOTEL HOTEL ¥¥

Map p286 (かどやホテル; 3346-2561; www.kadoya-hotel.co.jp; 1-23-1 Nishi-Shinjuku, Shinjuku-ku; s/d from ¥9000/14,000; ; JR Yamanote line to Shinjuku, west exit) Kadoya has been welcoming foreign tourists for decades and is above all friendly and accommodating. The standard rooms show their age, but are clean and comfortable, and a steal for Nishi-Shinjuku. The newer 'comfort' rooms (from ¥19,500) have more space, Simmons beds, Japanese-style bathtubs and the best decor. There's also a coin laundry.

CITADINES APARTMENT ¥¥

Map p286 (シタディーン; 5379-7208; www.citadines.com; 1-28-13 Shinjuku, Shinjuku-ku; r from ¥14,256; ; Marunouchi line to Shinjuku-gyoenmae, exit 2) Bright and modern, Citadines has compact studios with queen-sized beds, kitchenettes and a sitting area. Rooms sleep up to three. It's a bit far from the Shinjuku action, though travellers staying for more than a few days will likely come to appreciate the relative quiet. There's a fitness room and laundrette too. English is spoken.

IBIS TOKYO SHINJUKU BUSINESS HOTEL ¥¥

Map p286 (イビス東京新宿; 3361-1111; www.accorhotels.com; 7-10-5 Shinjuku, Shinjuku-ku; s/d ¥13,725/17,250; ; JR Yamanote line to Shinjuku, west exit) The rooms here are tiny, but what you're really paying for is convenience: the hotel is just a couple of minutes' walk from Shinjuku Station. This Ibis is only a couple of years old so the interior still feels fresh. Front desk staff speak English. Note that prices rise (by about ¥3000) on Friday and Saturday nights.

★PARK HYATT TOKYO LUXURY HOTEL ¥¥¥

Map p286 (パークハイアット東京; 5322-1234; http://tokyo.park.hyatt.com; 3-7-1-2 Nishi-Shinjuku, Shinjuku-ku; d from ¥43,000; ; Ōedo line to Tochōmae, exit A4) The Park Hyatt still looks as tasteful and elegant as it did when it opened 20 years ago. The hotel starts on the 41st floor of a Tange Kenzō–designed skyscraper in west Shinjuku, meaning even the entry-level rooms have otherworldly views. Perks for guests include complimentary mobile-phone rentals (you pay for outgoing calls only) and morning yoga classes.

HOTEL CENTURY SOUTHERN TOWER HOTEL ¥¥¥

Map p286 (ホテルセンチュリーサザンタワー; 5354-0111; www.southerntower.co.jp/english; 2-2-1 Yoyogi, Shibuya-ku; s/d ¥23,760/26,136; ; JR Yamanote line to Shinjuku, south exit) This is one of the better deals for accommodation in Shinjuku, with a central location, just a couple of minutes' walk from Shinjuku Station's south exit. There are spacious rooms and big beds. Book a west-facing room for views of Mt Fuji.

Kōrakuen & Northwest Tokyo

KIMI RYOKAN RYOKAN ¥

(貴美旅館; 3971-3766; www.kimi-ryokan.jp; 2-36-8 Ikebukuro, Toshima-ku; s/d from ¥4860/6590; ; JR Yamanote line to Ikebukuro, west exit) Easily one of the best budget ryokan in Tokyo, this convivial inn has tatami rooms of various sizes and a Japanese-style lounge area that's conducive to meeting other travellers. Clean showers and toilets are shared, and there's a lovely Japanese cypress bath. Book well in advance.

TOKYO CENTRAL YOUTH HOSTEL HOSTEL ¥

Map p289 (東京セントラルユースホステル; ☎3235-1107; www.jyh.gr.jp/tcyh; 18th fl, 1-1 Kagurakashi, Shinjuku-ku; ¥4050, with YHA discount ¥3450; ; JR Sōbu line to Iidabashi, west exit) Sitting right on top of Iidabashi Station, which handles five train lines, this clean, well-managed hostel has fantastic transport access. It also has luxury-hotel-worthy night views. The drawbacks: a utilitarian atmosphere, wi-fi in the lobby only and an 11pm curfew. Sleeping is in on basic wooden bunks in gender-segregated dorm rooms. There's a breakfast buffet (¥600) and laundry machines.

There's little signage out front, but it's in the big office building in front of Iidabashi Station; take the elevator to the 18th floor.

WAKANA RYOKAN ¥¥

Map p289 (和可菜; ☎3260-3769; 4-7 Kagurazaka, Shinjuku-ku; r per person ¥10,000; ; JR Sōbu line to Iidabashi, west exit) Nestled among the exclusive restaurants of Kagurazaka's famous cobblestone lane, Hyogo-yokochō, this 60-year-old ryokan was once known as a writer's retreat. In comparison to the atmospheric location, the rooms are ordinary and some get street noise. Little English is spoken, so you might want to enlist the help of a tourist office or Japanese-speaker when booking.

THE AGNES HOTEL BOUTIQUE HOTEL ¥¥¥

Map p289 (アグネスホテル; ☎3267-5505; www.agneshotel.com/foreign/english.html; 2-20-1 Kagurazaka, Shinjuku-ku; s/d ¥22,000/27,000; ; JR Sōbu line to Iidabashi, west exit) Tucked away on a side street in atmospheric Kagurazaka, Agnes feels like a secluded retreat (even though it's only a few minutes' walk to the train station). The 56 rooms, big enough to move around in, are done up in soft colours and come with cushy armchairs.

HOTEL CHINZANSO LUXURY HOTEL ¥¥¥

(椿山荘; ☎3943-0996; www.hotel-chinzanso-tokyo.com; 2-10-8 Sekiguchi, Bunkyō-ku; r from ¥25,200; ; S Yurakuchō line to Edogawabashi, exit 1A) On the grounds of a former estate, Hotel Chinzanso has a manicured strolling garden for a backyard. The rooms are huge, and some look out over the garden. The interior is lavish, strewn with antiques. The downside is the far-flung location and 15-minute walk to the nearest subway station.

TOKYO DOME HOTEL HOTEL ¥¥¥

Map p289 (東京ドームホテル; ☎5805-2111; www.tokyodome-hotels.co.jp/e; 1-3-61 Kōraku, Bunkyō-ku; s/d from ¥22,772/28,712; ; JR Sōbu line to Suidōbashi, west exit) Part of the Tokyo Dome City complex that includes the baseball stadium, this massive hotel (with more than 1000 rooms) is smack in the middle of the city with direct access to Narita Airport, via the Limousine Bus. Rooms are spacious, though ordinary. Some packages include baseball tickets. Fluent English is spoken.

Akihabara & Around

SAKURA HOTEL JIMBŌCHŌ HOSTEL ¥

Map p290 (サクラホテル池袋; ☎3261-3939; www.sakura-hotel.co.jp; 2-21-4 Kanda-Jimbōchō, Chiyoda-ku; dm/s/d from ¥3300/6300/8450; ; Marunouchi line to Jimbōchō, exit A6) A long-standing, great budget option with a sociable atmosphere. Staff are bilingual and helpful, and the rooms, though basic and tiny, are comfortable and clean. There's a 24-hour cafe, a laundry and internet access.

★HILLTOP HOTEL HISTORIC HOTEL ¥¥

Map p290 (山の上ホテル; ☎3293-2311; www.yamanoue-hotel.co.jp; 1-1 Kanda-Surugadai, Chiyoda-ku; s/d from ¥20,396/21,584; ; JR Chūō or Sōbu lines to Ochanomizu, Ochanomizu exit) This art-deco gem from the 1930s exudes personality and charm, with antique wooden furniture and a wood-panelled lounge. Mishima Yukio wrote his last few novels here. The older rooms in the main building come with antique writing desks and leather upholstered chairs.

HOTEL MY STAYS OCHANOMIZU BUSINESS HOTEL ¥¥

Map p290 (ホテルマイステイズ御茶ノ水; ☎5289-3939; www.mystays.jp; 2-10-6 Kanda Awajichō, Chiyoda-ku; s/d from ¥6000/10,000; ; JR Chūō line to Ochanomizu, Hijiribashi exit) This stylish business hotel stands out for its bold brown-and-white colour scheme, great-value prices and extras such as large Simmons beds. It's also handy for Akihabara.

GAKUSHIKAIKAN HOTEL ¥¥

Map p290 (学士会館; ☎3292-5938; www.gakushikaikan.co.jp; 3-28 Kandanishiki-cho, Chiyoda-ku; s/tw incl breakfast from ¥9936/14,363; ; S Hanzamon line to Jimbocho, exit A9) An academic air hangs over this retro hotel that's owned by seven major Japanese universities. It's a quirky place but the rooms are great value given the location and the complimentary breakfast. It has way more style and atmosphere than a comparable business hotel.

NEW CENTRAL HOTEL BUSINESS HOTEL ¥¥

Map p290 (ニューセントラルホテル; ☎3256-2171; www.pelican.co.jp/newcentralhotel; 2-7-2 Kanda-Tachō, Chiyoda-ku; s/d ¥8500/10,300; @; JR Yamanote line to Kanda, west exit) The New Central may be as generic as its white-collar-worker clientele, but the pleasant *sentō* (public bath) facilities (separate for men and women) make it stand out. The location, on a quiet side street, makes this a worthwhile base.

Ueno & Yanaka

★TOCO HOSTEL ¥

(トコ; ☎6458-1686; http://backpackersjapan.co.jp; 2-13-21 Shitaya, Taitō-ku; dm/r from ¥2700/6500; @; S Hibiya line to Iriya, exit 4) A group of friends renovated this old wooden building (which dates to 1920 and was once frequented by geisha) and turned it into one of Tokyo's most attractive hostels. Private tatami rooms and dorms with wooden bunks surround a small garden, and there's a funky bar-lounge out front.

★SAWANOYA RYOKAN RYOKAN ¥¥

Map p294 (旅館澤の屋; ☎3822-2251; www.sawanoya.com; 2-3-11 Yanaka, Taitō-ku; s/d from ¥5184/9720; @; S Chiyoda line to Nezu, exit 1) Sawanoya is a gem in quiet Yanaka, with very friendly staff and all the traditional hospitality you would expect of a ryokan. The shared cypress and earthenware baths are the perfect balm after a long day (some rooms have their own bath, too). The lobby overflows with information about travel options in Japan, and bicycles are available for rent.

★HŌMEIKAN RYOKAN ¥¥

(鳳明館; ☎3811-1181; www.homeikan.com; 5-10-5 Hongō, Bunkyō-ku; s/d from ¥8100/14,040; ; S Ōedo line to Kasuga, exit A6) Atop a slope in a quiet residential neighbourhood, this beautifully crafted wooden ryokan is an old-world oasis in the middle of Tokyo. The main Honkan wing dates from the Meiji era and is registered as an important cultural property, though we prefer the Daimachi Bekkan, with its winding corridors and garden. Rates include breakfast.

The only drawback is that it's a little out of the way.

ANNEX KATSUTARŌ RYOKAN RYOKAN ¥¥

Map p294 (アネックス勝太郎旅館; ☎3828-2500; www.katsutaro.com; 3-8-4 Yanaka, Taitō-ku; s/d from ¥6500/10,800; @; S Chiyoda line to Sendagi, exit 2) More like a modern hotel than a traditional ryokan, the family-run Annex Katsutarō has spotless, thoughtfully arranged tatami rooms with attached bathrooms. Though a bit of a walk from the sights in Ueno, it's ideal for exploring the old Yanaka district. Breakfast and bicycles are available for a small fee.

TOKHOUSE RENTAL HOUSE ¥¥

Map p294 (☎090-9674-4198; www.tokhouse.com; 3-52-9 Sendagi, Bunkyō-ku; s/d/q from ¥8000/10,000/13,000; ; JR Yamanote line to Nishi-Nippori, west exit) For the price of a room in a business hotel you can get your own apartment, with a fully equipped kitchen, in the heart of Yanaka. There's a two-night minimum and a ¥5000 to ¥6000 cleaning fee; ask about discounts for families with children. Richard, the American owner and a long-time Tokyo resident, has lots of tips for exploring the area.

HOTEL GRAPHY BOUTIQUE HOTEL ¥¥

Map p294 (☎3828-7377; www.hotel-graphy.com; 4-5-10 Ikenohata, Taitō-ku; s/d from ¥6600/8200; @; S Chiyoda line to Nezu, exit 2) Hotel Graphy falls somewhere between a boutique hotel and a hostel. It has a hip, modern vibe with a spacious lounge, kitchen, roof terrace – even a yoga room. Rooms are minimalist (read: fairly spartan) and singles have shared bathrooms. Rates drop significantly for weekly and monthly stays.

RYOKAN KATSUTARŌ RYOKAN ¥¥

Map p294 (旅館勝太郎; ☎3821-9808; www.katsutaro.com; 4-16-8 Ike-no-hata, Taitō-ku; s/d from ¥5500/9000; @; S Chiyoda line to

Nezu, exit 2) The original Ryokan Katsutarō has a quiet and family-like atmosphere, with very affable managers. Though the building may be aged, the eight tatami rooms have been renovated without ruining the inn's character; some have en suite bathrooms, others don't. Bicycle rental is available.

TOUGENYA HOTEL BUSINESS HOTEL ¥¥

Map p294 (東金屋ホテル; ☎3834-1601; www.tougane-h.com/e; 3-17-5 Ueno, Taitō-ku; s/d from ¥7000/9000; ; JR Yamanote line to Ueno, Asakusa exit) Connected to Ueno Station by pedestrian passageways, Tougenya is a convenient base for getting around (and getting to and from the airport with luggage). It's also very near the Ueno sights. Rooms are basic and fairly charmless, though the common areas are done up with attractive Japanese touches.

HOTEL COCO GRAND HOTEL ¥¥

Map p294 (ホテルココグラン; ☎5812-1155; www.cocogrand.co.jp; 2-12-14 Ueno, Taitō-ku; s/d from ¥9800/16,800; ; JR Yamanote line to Ueno, Shinobazu exit) The decor of this new hotel, next to Ueno-kōen, is brassy, bordering on love-hotel territory. But there's no arguing with the queen-sized beds, spacious communal bathing facilities (including a sauna) and free breakfast buffet.

Asakusa & Sumida River

Asakusa has emerged as Tokyo's budget-traveller central and has a real backpacker vibe. If you're looking to meet up with other travellers, this is the best place to stay.

★NUI HOSTEL ¥

(ヌイ; ☎6240-9854; http://backpackersjapan.co.jp/nui_en; 2-14-13 Kuramae, Taitō-ku; dm/d from ¥2700/6800; ; S Ōedo line to Kuramae, exit A7) In a former warehouse, this hostel has raised the bar for stylish budget digs in Tokyo. High ceilings mean bunks you can comfortably sit up in and there is an enormous shared kitchen and workspace. Best of all is the ground-floor bar and lounge, with furniture made from salvaged timber; it's a popular local hang-out.

★KHAOSAN WORLD HOSTEL ¥

Map p291 (www.khaosan-tokyo.com/en/world/index.html; 3-15-1 Nishi-Asakusa, Taitō-ku; dm/d from ¥2200/8400, f ¥12,000; ; Tsukuba Express to Asakusa, exit A2) Hands down Tokyo's most oddball hostel, Khaosan World has taken over an ageing love hotel and left much of the design elements intact – things like mirrored ceilings and glittering brocade wallpaper (don't worry: it's clean). There's a wide variety of rooms to choose from, including ones with tatami floors and capsule-style bunks. There are cooking and laundry facilities, too.

★ANDON RYOKAN RYOKAN ¥

(行燈旅館; ☎3873-8611; www.andon.co.jp; 2-34-10 Nihonzutsumi, Taitō-ku; s/d from ¥6020/7140; ; S Hibiya line to Minowa, exit 3) About 2km north of Asakusa, the minimalist and modern Andon Ryokan is fabulously designed in form and function. It has tiny but immaculate tatami rooms and a spectacular upper-floor spa, which can be used privately. The owner collects antiques and will serve you breakfast on dishes worth more than your stay.

Andon also has a full program of cultural events, bike rentals and laundry facilities. It's a five-minute walk from the subway.

K'S HOUSE TOKYO HOSTEL ¥

(ケイズハウス東京; ☎5833-0555; http://kshouse.jp; 3-20-10 Kuramae, Taitō-ku; dm/s/d ¥2900/4500/7200; ; S Ōedo line to Kuramae, exit A6) This homey, modern hostel, with comfy sofas in the living room, cooking facilities and a roof terrace, is a backpacker fave. From exit A6, walk northwest along Asakusa-dōri and turn left at the first corner. K's House is the yellow building at the end of the block.

TOKYO RYOKAN RYOKAN ¥

Map p291 (東京旅館; ☎090-8879-3599; www.tokyoryokan.com; 2-4-8 Nishi-Asakusa, Taitō-ku; r from ¥7000; ; S Ginza line to Tawaramachi, exit 3) This tidy little inn has only three tatami rooms and no en suite bathrooms but tonnes of charm. There are touches of calligraphy, attractive woodwork and sliding screens. The owner, an avid traveller himself, speaks fluent English and is very knowledgable about Asakusa.

KHAOSAN TOKYO KABUKI HOSTEL ¥

Map p291 (☎5830-3673; www.khaosan-tokyo.com/en/kabuki; 1-17-2 Asakusa, Taitō-ku; dm/d from ¥3400/7800; ; S Ginza line to Asakusa, exit 3) A short walk from the sights in Asakusa, this is the most popular of Khaosan's miniempire of quirky hostels.

All rooms have en suite bathrooms. There's a lounge done up like a traditional Japanese living room that makes for a convivial hang-out spot. The staff speak English.

ANNE HOSTEL HOSTEL ¥

Map p292 (浅草橋旅荘庵; ☎5829-9090; http://j-hostel.com; 2-21-14 Yanagibashi, Taitō-ku; dm/tw from ¥2600/6800; ; JR Sōbu line to Asakusabashi, east exit) Located in a former office building, laid-back Anne has standard wooden bunk beds, modern toilets and showers. There's a cosy lounge too, where a simple breakfast (coffee, toast and eggs) is served free of charge. Staff speak English and sometimes put on cultural events. Rates go up ¥300 per person on Saturdays.

RETRO METRO HOSTEL ¥

Map p291 (レトロメトロ; ☎6322-7447; http://retrometrobackpackers.com/index-en.html; 2-19-1 Nishi-Asakusa, Taitō-ku; dm from ¥2600; ; S Ginza line to Tawaramachi, exit 3) The opposite of the big, social hostel, Retro Metro, with just two small dorm rooms, should appeal to more grown-up travellers. It's in an old house with artsy touches and a small kitchen.

SAKURA HOSTEL HOSTEL ¥

Map p291 (サクラホステル; ☎3847-8111; www.sakura-hostel.co.jp; 2-24-2 Asakusa, Taitō-ku; dm/tw ¥3000/8500; ; Tsukuba Express to Asakusa, exit A1) Billed as the largest in Tokyo, this rather utilitarian hostel does have a few perks: superfriendly English-speaking staff and a simple breakfast served in the large common space for just ¥325. Cultural events and tours are held regularly. There are discounts for stays of more than a week.

SUKEROKU NO YADO SADACHIYO RYOKAN ¥¥

Map p291 (助六の宿貞千代; ☎3842-6431; www.sadachiyo.co.jp; 2-20-1 Asakusa, Taitō-ku; d with/without 2 meals from ¥33,600/19,600; ; S Ginza line to Asakusa, exit 1) This stunning ryokan virtually transports its guests to old Edo. Gorgeously maintained tatami rooms are spacious for two people, and all come with modern, Western-style bathrooms. Splurge on an exquisite meal here, and make time for the *o-furo,* one made of fragrant Japanese cypress and the other of black granite. Look for the rickshaw parked outside.

RYOKAN SHIGETSU RYOKAN ¥¥

Map p291 (旅館指月; ☎3843-2345; www.shigetsu.com; 1-31-11 Asakusa, Taitō-ku; s/d ¥8700/15,750; ; S Ginza line to Asakusa, exit 1) South of Sensō-ji, this spotless and atmospheric ryokan has Japanese-style rooms with *shōji* (sliding rice-paper screen) doors and windows. There's a shared *o-furo* made of cedar, with views of Tokyo Sky Tree.

HATAGO BUSINESS HOTEL ¥¥

Map p291 (旅籠; ☎6802-7277; http://asakusahotel.org; 2-6-8 Komagata, Taitō-ku; s/tw from ¥7500/12,000; ; S Ginza line to Asakusa, exit 4) If you're looking for a hotel in this part of town, the new Hatago is a good bet: rooms are typically small but come with tatami floors (even though you sleep on beds) and other Japanese touches. Breakfast is included and the staff speak English. Rates go up on weekends.

Understand Tokyo

Tokyo Today

Tokyo has reinvented itself countless times in the four centuries since its founding. With the 2020 Summer Olympic Games on the horizon, it hopes to do so again, with plans for a greener, friendlier city. Following decades of economic stagnation and a soon-to-be-shrinking workforce, the stakes are high. Does Tokyo still have what it takes to pull off another reincarnation?

Best on Film

Stray Dog (Kurosawa Akira; 1949) Noir thriller set in sweltering, occupied Tokyo.

Tokyo Story (Ozu Yasujirō; 1953) Portrait of a family in rapidly changing, post-WWII Japan.

Lost in Translation (Sofia Coppola; 2003) Disorienting, captivating Tokyo through the eyes of two Americans.

Adrift in Tokyo (2008) Two luckless antiheroes on a long walk through the city.

When a Woman Ascends the Stairs (Naruse Mikio; 1960) Inside the world of a Ginza hostess bar.

Best in Print

Scarlet Gang of Asakusa (Kawabata Yasunari; 1930) Lively chronicle of a gang of street urchins in Asakusa.

Coin Locker Babies (Murakami Ryu; 1980) Coming-of-age story set in a future, literally toxic, Tokyo.

Snakes and Earrings (Kanehara Hitomi; 2003) The fall of a Shibuya 'Barbie girl'.

After Dark (Murakami Haruki; 2004) Colourful characters come together during a night in the life of Tokyo.

A Strange Tale from East of the River (Nagai Kafu; 1937) An unlicensed prostitute in atmospheric, prewar Tokyo.

Tokyo Vision 2020

Since it was announced in 2013 that Tokyo would hold the 2020 Summer Olympics, the city has gone into full preparation mode, enacting its 'Tokyo Vision 2020'. To understand just how much hosting the Olympics means to the city (or at least to the city's image-makers), you have to look back to the 1964 Summer Olympics. The first games to be held in Asia, the 1964 Olympics marked Tokyo's big comeback after the city was all but destroyed in WWII. The powers that be are hoping that the 2020 games will again be symbolic, reaffirming Tokyo's position in the pantheon of world's great cities, following more than two decades of economic malaise and the faltering of its export giants (such as Sony).

Much of the city's current infrastructure dates to the manic preparations leading up to the 1964 games. And while Tokyo sold the International Olympic Commission on a compact games that would use many existing structures, new developments are in store. The most dramatic redevelopment will take place along Tokyo Bay, where many of the events will be held. Already in the works is the Umi-no-Mori (Sea Forest), a vast green space on one of the bay's artificial landfill islands. So far a quarter of the planned 88 hectares of trees has been planted, in compost soil created from park and roadside prunings and heat-treated sewage. When it's completed, around 2016, the park will be five times the size of Hibiya-kōen. Other positive changes to look forward to: a more accessible Tokyo for people with disabilities, expanded wi-fi networks and increased flight capacity for Tokyo's more convenient airport, Haneda.

As a whole, Tokyoites look to the 2020 games as a source of pride, though there has been some hand-wringing in the media that the city and its citizens aren't 'international' enough. That has translated into a renewed interest in English study, and even talk of banning smoking in bars and restaurants. There has been some controversy as well: the New National Stadium, designed by Iraqi-British architect Zaha Hadid and scheduled to be completed in 2019, has been derided by some as an oversized eyesore. The most vocal critic (perhaps unsurprisingly) is Maki Fumihiko, the architect who designed the original National Stadium (which will be replaced by the new one).

Private developers will no doubt seek to ride the Olympic wave as well, meaning even more construction projects. One controversial idea that has been bandied around: allowing casinos.

City of the Future

By now a whole generation has come of age that has known nothing but Japan's lingering economic malaise. They've embraced a sort of 'recession chic', flocking to fast-fashion brands like H&M the way their peers two decades ago took to Burberry scarves. They'll happily queue for hours to land a table (but not a chair) at one of the city's hot, wallet-friendly 'standing restaurants'. When it comes to the future though, they're not so sure: fewer and fewer companies are offering the kind of stable, lifetime employment that had been the bedrock of society for decades. Instead, recent grads are shunted into part-time contract positions with limited mobility and benefits, creating an urban underclass that threatens to become permanent.

Something else noteworthy is slated to happen in 2020: while the population of Japan has been dropping off since 2004, it's predicted that Tokyo's population will peak at 13.35 million in 2020 and then also begin to decline. The birth rate for the capital hovers around 1.1 (even lower than the national average of 1.4). The workforce is shrinking but the country as a whole remains wary of immigration, though there have been programs to bring in nurses and caretakers from Indonesia and the Philippines.

Tokyo is seen as a forerunner – facing the kinds of problems that major modern cities around the world will face as their populations begin a similar tapering off. The city's Tokyo Vision 2020 also includes provisions for making Tokyo a more attractive city in which to live and work – such as more childcare facilities, job centres for senior citizens and special economic zones for foreign companies. If it works, Tokyo could become a model for cities of the future.

if Tokyo were 100 people

12 would be 0-14
68 would be 15-64
20 would be 65 years and over

ethnicity

(% of population)

population per sq km

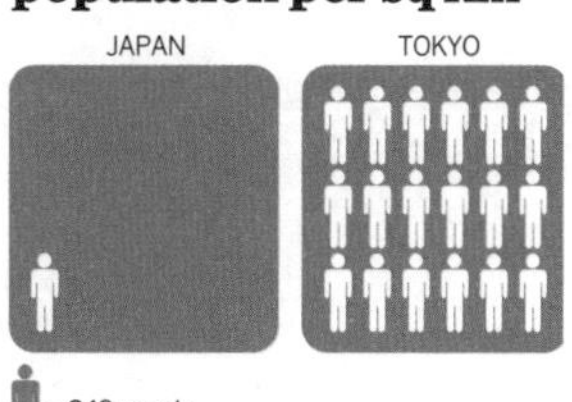

History

Tokyo is one of the world's great cities. It's perhaps surprising then to learn that until 450 years ago it was hardly a blip on the map. Still, while its history might be short, the city has played many roles: samurai stronghold, imperial capital and modern metropolis. Its latest identity as a city of the future – reflected in portrayals in manga (Japanese comics) and anime (Japanese animation) – is just another example of Tokyo's protean nature.

Humble Beginnings

The monstrous metropolis that is Tokyo, population 13 million, has come a long way from its origins as a collection of tidal flats at the mouth of the Sumida-gawa (Sumida River). Its first permanent inhabitants were part of a pottery-producing culture who settled here around 10,000 BC. These early Tokyoites lived as fishers, hunters and food gatherers. Some 4000 years later, wet-rice farming techniques were introduced from Korea, and the Shintō religion also began to develop.

Around AD 300, the proto-Japanese nation began to form in the Kansai area, around what is today Nara Prefecture, under the control of the Yamato clan. These forerunners of the current imperial family claimed descent from the sun goddess Amaterasu. In the 6th century, Buddhism arrived in Japan from China, which had a dramatic effect on the course of events to come. Buddhism introduced a highly evolved system of metaphysics, codes of law and the Chinese writing system, a conduit for the principles of Confucian statecraft. By the end of the 8th century, the Buddhist clerical bureaucracy had become vast, threatening the authority of the nascent imperial administration. The emperor responded by relocating the capital to Heian-kyō (modern day Kyoto). From that point on, Kyoto generally served as the capital until the Meiji Restoration in 1868, when Tokyo became the new chief city.

All of this was happening in the west: Edo (the old name for Tokyo) was still just a sleepy fishing village, and would continue to be so for the next several hundred years.

TIMELINE

10,000 BC

Tokyo area inhabited by pottery-making people during late Neolithic Jōmon period. The Kantō region around Tokyo is among the most densely settled in this era.

AD 710

Japan's first permanent capital established at Nara, ending the practice of moving the capital after an emperor's death. The city is modelled on Chang'an, capital of Tang-dynasty China.

794

Imperial capital moved to Heian-kyō, renamed Kyoto in the 11th century. It is laid out in a grid in accordance with Chinese geomancy principles.

Rise of the Warrior Class

Throughout the Heian period (794–1185), courtly life in the capital developed into a golden age of culture and refinement. Meanwhile, lesser nobles, with little chance of improving their rank and standing, led military excursions to reign in the outer lying provinces. They were accompanied by their loyal retainers, skilled warriors called samurai.

By the 12th century, some of the clans established by these lesser nobles had gained significant power and influence. A feud broke out between two, the Minamoto (also known as Genji) and the Taira (also known as Heike), who were backing different claimants to the imperial throne. The Minamoto were eventually the victors, in 1192, and their leader, Minamoto Yoritomo, created a new position for himself – shogun (generalissimo).

The emperor in Kyoto remained the nation's figurehead, granting authority to the shogun, though in reality it was the shogun who wielded power. Minamoto set up his *bakufu* (military government) in his eastern stronghold, a seaside cove named Kamakura – bringing the seat of power closer to Tokyo for the first time. The Kamakura *bakufu* lasted until 1333, when it was trounced by imperial forces led by the general Ashikaga Takauji. The emperor resumed power; the position of shogun was retained – awarded to Ashikaga – but removed to Kyoto, making the government once again centralised.

Over the next two centuries, the Ashikaga shoguns were increasingly unable to reign in the provincial warlords, called *daimyō,* who had set about consolidating considerable power. Castles and fortresses were erected around the country. One such castle was constructed in the mid-15th century by a warrior poet named Ōta Dōkan in a place called Edo.

Besides loyal samurai, Tokugawa Ieyasu stocked his capital with ninja. Their commander was Hattori Hanzō, renowned for his cunning, deadly tactics that helped Ieyasu at key moments in his career. The ninja master's legacy was enshrined in Hanzōmon, a gate that still exists today at the Imperial Palace.

Battle for Supremacy

By the time Portuguese traders and missionaries arrived in 1543, feudal warlords had carved Japan into a patchwork of fiefdoms. One of the most powerful *daimyō,* Oda Nobunaga of the Chūbu region, near present-day Nagoya, was quick to see how the Portuguese could support his ambitious plans. He viewed their Christianity as a potential weapon against the power of the Buddhist clergy and made ample use of the firearms they introduced. By the time he was assassinated in 1581, Oda had united much of central Japan. Toyotomi Hideyoshi took over the job of consolidating power, but looked less favourably on the growing Christian movement, subjecting it to systematic persecution.

Toyotomi's power was briefly contested by Tokugawa Ieyasu, son of a minor lord allied to Oda. After a brief struggle for power, Tokugawa agreed to a truce with Toyotomi; in return, Toyotomi granted

1457

Ōta Dōkan orders construction of first Edo Castle. Later developed by shōgun Tokugawa Ieyasu in the 17th century, it becomes the largest fortress the world has seen.

1600

Tokugawa Ieyasu, victor in the Battle of Sekigahara, establishes his capital in Edo, beginning 250 years of peace under Tokugawa rule, known as the Edo period.

1638

Sakoku national isolation policy; Japan cuts off all contact with the outside world, except for limited trade with the Dutch and Chinese off Nagasaki. The policy remains until the 1850s.

1657

Great Meireki Fire devastates Edo, killing over 100,000 and destroying two-thirds of the city. Reconstruction plans include the widening of streets to prevent further conflagrations.

SAMURAI: THOSE WHO SERVE

The culture of Kyoto originated in the imperial court. Osaka is still associated with its mercantile roots. Tokyo, meanwhile, is the city of the samurai.

The prime duty of a samurai, a member of the warrior class, was to give faithful service to his *daimyō* (feudal lord). In fact, the origin of the term 'samurai' is closely linked to a word meaning 'to serve'. Over the centuries, the samurai established a code of conduct that came to be known as *bushidō* (the way of the warrior), drawn from Confucianism, Shintō and Buddhism.

Confucianism required a samurai to show absolute loyalty to his lord. Towards the oppressed, a samurai was expected to show benevolence and exercise justice. Subterfuge was to be despised, as were all commercial and financial transactions. A real samurai had endless endurance and total self-control, spoke only the truth and displayed no emotion. Since his honour was his life, disgrace and shame were to be avoided above all else, and all insults were to be avenged.

From Buddhism, the samurai learnt the lesson that life is impermanent – a handy reason to face death with serenity. Shintō provided the samurai with patriotic beliefs in the divine status both of the emperor and of Japan – the abode of the gods.

Seppuku (ritual suicide), also known as hara-kiri, was an accepted means of avoiding dishonour. Seppuku required the samurai to ritually disembowel himself, watched by an aide, who then drew his own sword and lopped off the samurai's head. One reason for this ritual was the requirement that a samurai should never surrender but always go down fighting.

Not all samurai were capable of adhering to their code of conduct – samurai indulging in double-crossing or subterfuge, or displaying outright cowardice, were popular themes in Japanese theatre.

Though the samurai are long gone, there are echoes of *bushidō* in the salaryman corporate warriors of today's Japan. Under the once-prevalent lifetime employment system, employees were expected to show complete obedience to their company, and could not question its decisions if, for example, they were transferred to distant Akita-ken.

him eight provinces in eastern Japan – which included Edo. While Toyotomi intended this to weaken Tokugawa by separating him from his ancestral homeland Chūbu, the upstart looked upon the gift as an opportunity to strengthen his power. He set about turning Edo into a real city.

When Toyotomi Hideyoshi died in 1598, power passed to his son, Toyotomi Hideyori. However, Tokugawa Ieyasu had been busily scheming to secure the shōgunate for himself and soon went to war against those loyal to Hideyori. Tokugawa's forces finally defeated

1707

Mt Fuji erupts, spewing ash over the streets of Edo 100km to the northeast. The stratovolcano is still active today but with a low risk of eruption.

1721

Edo's population grows to 1.1 million as people move in from rural areas, making it the world's largest city. Meanwhile, London's population is roughly 650,000.

1853

Black ships of the US navy arrive in Japan under the command of Commodore Matthew Perry, who succeeds in forcing Japan open to US trade; international port established in Yokohama in 1859.

1868

Meiji Restoration; Tokugawa shogunate loyalists are defeated in civil war. The imperial residence moves to Edo, which is renamed Tokyo.

Hideyori and his supporters at the legendary Battle of Sekigahara in 1600, moving him into a position of supreme power. He chose Edo as his permanent base and began 2½ centuries of Tokugawa rule.

Boomtown Edo

In securing a lasting peace nationwide and ruling from Edo, Tokugawa Ieyasu laid the foundation for Tokyo's ascendancy as one of the world's great cities. In 1603 the emperor appointed him shogun, and the Tokugawa family ruled from Edo Castle (Edo-jō), on the grounds of the current Imperial Palace. The castle became the largest fortress the world had ever seen, with elaborate rituals shaping the lives of its many courtiers, courtesans, samurai and attendants. Edo would also grow to become the world's largest city, topping one million in the early 1700s and dwarfing much older London and Paris, as people from all over Japan flocked here to serve the growing military class.

This was the result of a canny move by the Tokugawa that ensured their hegemony. They implemented the *sankin kōtai* system that demanded that all *daimyō* in Japan spend alternate years in Edo. Their wives and children remained in Edo while the *daimyō* returned to their home provinces. This dislocating policy made it hard for ambitious *daimyō* to usurp the Tokugawas. The high costs of travelling back and forth with a large retinue also eroded their financial power.

Society was made rigidly hierarchical, comprising (in descending order of importance) the nobility, who had nominal power; the *daimyō* and their samurai; the farmers; and finally the artisans and merchants. Class dress, living quarters and even manner of speech were all strictly codified, and interclass movement was prohibited.

The caste-like society imposed by Tokugawa rule divided Edo into a high city (Yamanote) and a low city (Shitamachi). The higher Yamanote (literally 'hand of the mountains') was home to the *daimyō* and their samurai, while the merchants, artisans and lower orders of Edo society were forced into the low-lying Shitamachi (literally 'downtown').

The typical residential neighbourhood of the Shitamachi featured squalid conditions, usually comprising flimsy wooden structures with earthen floors. These shanty towns were often swept by great conflagrations, which locals referred to as *Edo-no-hana,* or flowers of Edo; the expression's bravura sums up the spirit of Shitamachi. Under great privation, Shitamachi subsequently produced a flourishing culture that thumbed its nose at social hardships and the strictures of the shogunate. Increasingly wealthy merchants patronised the kabuki theatre, sumo tournaments and the pleasure quarters of the Yoshiwara

Edo was divided into *machi* (towns) according to profession. It's still possible to stumble across small enclaves that specialise in particular wares. Most famous are Jimbōchō, the bookshop area; Kappabashi, with its plastic food and kitchen supplies; and Akihabara, which now specialises in electronics and manga (comics).

1871

Samurai domain system abolished, and Tokyo Prefecture (Tokyo-fu) established out of the former Musashi Province. Tokyo is initially divided into 15 wards.

1872

Japan's first train line connects Shimbashi in Tokyo with Yokohama to the southwest; Osaka–Kōbe services are launched in 1874 and Osaka–Kyoto services in 1877.

1889

Constitution of the Empire of Japan declared. Based on a Prussian model of constitutional monarchy, the emperor shares power with an elected parliament.

1914

Tokyo Station opens. Designed by Tatsuno Kingo, it begins operations with four platforms. Greatly expanded over the past 100 years, it now serves over 3000 trains per day.

district – generally enjoying a joie de vivre that the dour lords of Edo castle frowned upon. Today, the best glimpses we have into that time come from *ukiyo-e* (woodblock prints).

The 'Eastern Capital' is Born

Edo's transformation from a grand medieval city into a world-class capital required an outside nudge, or *gaiatsu* (external pressure). This came in the form of a fleet of black ships, under the command of US Navy Commodore Matthew Perry, that sailed into Edo-wan (now Tokyo Bay) in 1853. Perry's expedition demanded that Japan open itself to foreign trade after centuries of isolation.

The coming of Westerners heralded a far-reaching social revolution against which the antiquated Tokugawa regime was powerless. In 1867–68, civil war broke out between Tokugawa loyalists and a band of upstart *daimyō* from southern Kyūshū. The latter were victorious, and faced with widespread antigovernment feeling and accusations that the regime had failed to prepare Japan for this threat, the last Tokugawa shogun resigned. Power reverted to Emperor Meiji, in what became known as the Meiji Restoration; though in reality, the southern lords were the real decision makers. In 1868 the seat of imperial power was moved from Kyoto to Edo, and the city renamed Tokyo (Eastern Capital).

The word Meiji means 'enlightenment' and Japan's new rulers pushed the nation into a crash course in industrialisation and militarisation. A great exchange began between Japan and the West: Japanese scholars were dispatched to Europe to study everything from literature and engineering to nation building and modern warfare. Western scholars were invited to teach in Japan's nascent universities.

The new Japanese establishment learned quickly: in 1872 the first railroad opened, connecting Tokyo with the new port of Yokohama, south along Tokyo Bay, and by 1889 the country had a Western-style constitution. In a remarkably short time, Japan achieved military victories over China (1894–95) and Russia (1904–05) and embarked on modern, Western-style empire building, with the annexation of Taiwan (1895), then Korea (1910) and Micronesia (1914).

Nationalists were also busy transforming Shintō into a jingoistic state religion. Seen as a corrupting foreign influence, Buddhism suffered badly – many artefacts and temples were destroyed, and the common people were urged to place their faith in the pure religion of State Shintō.

During the Meiji period, and the following Taishō period, changes that were taking place all over Japan could be seen most prominently in the country's new capital city. Tokyo's rapid industrialisation, uniting around the nascent *zaibatsu* (huge industrial and trading conglomerates), drew

Tokyo Tomes

- *Edo, the City that Became Tokyo* (Naito Akira; 2003)
- *Low City, High City* (Edward Seidensticker; 1970)
- *Tokyo: Exploring the City of the Shogun* (Enbutsu Sumiko; 2007)
- *Tokyo: A Spatial Anthropology* (Jinnai Hidenobu; 1995)
- *Tokyo Now & Then* (Paul Waley; 1984)

1923

Great Kantō Earthquake kills over 140,000. An estimated 300,000 houses are destroyed; a reconstruction plan is only partly realised due to money shortages.

1923

Yamanote line completed. One of Japan's busiest lines, today the 34.5km loop around the heart of Tokyo has 29 stations. It takes trains about an hour to circle the city.

1926

Hirohito ascends the throne to become the Shōwa emperor. Presiding over Japan's military expansion across East Asia and atrocities, he is spared trial by Allied forces after WWII.

1936

In the February 26 Incident, over 1000 Imperial Japanese Army troops stage a coup d'etat, killing political leaders and occupying the centre of Tokyo before surrendering to government loyalists.

job seekers from around Japan, causing the population to grow rapidly. In the 1880s electric lighting was introduced. Western-style brick buildings began to spring up in fashionable areas such as Ginza.

The Great Kantō Earthquake

If the Meiji Restoration sounded the death knell for old Edo, there were two more events to come that were to erase most traces of the old city: the Great Kantō Earthquake and the firebombings of WWII.

According to Japanese folklore, a giant catfish living underground causes earthquakes when it stirs. At noon on 1 September 1923 the catfish really jumped: the Great Kantō Earthquake, a magnitude 7.9 quake that struck south of Tokyo in Sagami Bay, caused unimaginable devastation in Tokyo. More than the quake itself, it was the subsequent fires, lasting some 40 hours, that laid waste to the city, including some 300,000 houses. A quarter of the quake's 142,000 fatalities occurred in one savage firestorm in a clothing depot.

In true Edo style, reconstruction began almost immediately. The spirit of this rebuilding is perhaps best summed up by author Edward Seidensticker in *Tokyo Rising* (1990): popular wisdom had it that any business which did not resume trading within three days of being burnt out did not have a future. Opportunities were lost in reconstructing the city – streets might have been widened and the capital transformed into something more of a showcase.

In 1904 the kimono shop Echigoya, founded in 1673, decided to reinvent itself as Japan's first Western-style department store, Mitsukoshi. The shop in Nihombashi (1914) was called the grandest building east of the Suez Canal. The retailer remains one of the most prestigious shops in Tokyo.

Modern Boys, Modern Girls

Despite the devastating effects of the Great Kantō Earthquake, the first few decades of the 20th century were a time of optimism in Tokyo. Old feudal-era loyalties finally buckled and party politics flourished for the first time, giving rise to the term Taishō Democracy – after the era of the short-lived Taishō emperor (1912–26). In 1925 suffrage was extended to all males, not just property owners (women wouldn't be given the vote until the American occupation after WWII).

Western fashions and ideas, initially the domain of only the most elite, began to trickle down to the middle class. More and more Tokyoites began adopting Western dress (which they most likely traded for kimono as soon as they got home). Cafes and dance halls flourished. Women began to work outside the home, in offices, department stores and factories, enjoying a new freedom and disposable income. Like women around the world in the 1920s, they cut their hair short and wore pants. These were the 'modern girls' – or *moga* for short – who walked arm and arm with their male counterparts, the *moba,* along Ginza, then the most fashionable district in the city.

1944–45

Allied air raids during WWII destroy large swaths of the city, including the Imperial Palace; casualties of more than 100,000 are reported.

1947

New constitution adopted, including Article 9 in which Japan renounces war and the possession of armed forces. Japan's Self-Defense Forces are built into a formidable military arsenal.

1948

Tokyo War Crimes Tribunal concludes, resulting in the execution of six wartime Japanese leaders. In 1978 they are secretly enshrined at Yasukuni-jinja.

1951

Japan signs San Francisco Peace Treaty, officially ending WWII, renouncing Japan's claims to overseas colonies and outlining compensation to Allied territories.

The Beginning of Shōwa & WWII

Following the accession of Emperor Hirohito (*Shōwa tennō* to the Japanese) and the initiation of the Shōwa period in 1926, the democratic spirit of the last two decades was replaced by a quickening tide of nationalist fervour. In 1931 the Japanese invaded Manchuria, and in 1937 embarked on full-scale hostilities with China. By 1940, a tripartite pact with Germany and Italy had been signed and a new order for all of Asia formulated: the Greater East Asia Co-Prosperity Sphere. On 7 December 1941, the Japanese attacked Pearl Harbor, bringing the US, Japan's principal rival in the Asia-Pacific region, into the war.

Despite initial successes, the war was disastrous for Japan. On 18 April 1942, B-25 bombers carried out the first bombing and strafing raid on Tokyo, with 364 casualties. Much worse was to come. Incendiary bombing commenced in 1944, the most devastating of which took place over the nights of 9 and 10 March 1945, when some two-fifths of the city, mainly in the Shitamachi area, went up in smoke and tens of thousands of lives were lost. The same raids destroyed Asakusa's Sensō-ji, and later raids destroyed Meiji-jingū. By the time Emperor Hirohito made his famous capitulation address to the Japanese people on 15 August 1945, much of Tokyo had been decimated – sections of it were almost completely depopulated, like the charred remains of Hiroshima and Nagasaki after they were devastated by atomic bombs. Food and daily necessities were scarce, the population was exhausted by the war effort and fears of marauding US military overlords were high.

BLACK MARKETS

Black markets thrived in the years that followed WWII, when goods by other channels were scarce. The remains of Ueno's black market can be seen in Ameya-yokochō, which is still a lively market. Shinjuku, too, has two former black markets that are now popular places to eat and drink: Omoide-yokochō and Golden Gai.

The Postwar Miracle

Tokyo's phoenix-like rise from the ashes of WWII and its emergence as a major global city is something of a miracle. Once again, Tokyoites did not take the devastation as an opportunity to redesign their city (as did Nagoya, for example), but rebuilt where the old had once stood.

During the US occupation in the early postwar years, Tokyo was something of a honky-tonk town. Now-respectable areas such as Yūrakuchō were the haunt of the so-called *pan-pan* girls (prostitutes).

In 1947, Japan adopted its postwar constitution, with the now-famous Article 9, which barred the use of military force in settling international disputes and maintaining a military for warfare (although the nation does maintain a self-defence force).

By 1951, with a boom in Japanese profits arising from the Korean War, Tokyo rebuilt rapidly, especially the central business district, and the subway began to take on its present form. The once-bombed-out city has never looked back from this miraculous economic growth.

1952

US occupation ends; Japan enters a period of high economic growth. The Korean War provides an incentive for Japanese manufacturers, who supply US forces.

1955

Liberal Democratic Party (LDP) founded; it has a virtually uninterrupted hold on power into the 21st century despite recurring corruption scandals and deep-seated factionalism.

1958

Tokyo Tower (333m) completed, designed for broadcasts and inspired by the Eiffel Tower. By the 1960s it is a tourist magnet and symbol of Japan's high growth.

1964

Tokyo Olympic Games held, marking Japan's postwar reintegration into the international community and the first time the games are hosted by a non-Western country.

RISE OF THE MEGAMALLS

When Roppongi Hills opened in 2003, it was more than just another shopping mall: it was an ambitious prototype for the future of Tokyo. It took developer Mori Minoru (1934–2012) no fewer than 17 years to acquire the land and to construct this labyrinthine kingdom. He envisioned improving the quality of urban life by centralising home, work and leisure into a utopian microcity.

Foreign investment banks and leading IT companies quickly signed up for office space, and Roppongi was positioned as the centre of the new economy – an alternative to Marunouchi, a bastion of traditional (read: old-fashioned) business culture. The nouveau riche who lived, worked and played at Roppongi Hills were christened *Hills-zoku* ('Hills tribe') by the media and their lavish lifestyles were splashed across the tabloids.

Similar projects appeared in succession: Shiodome Shio-site (2004), Tokyo Midtown (2005) and Akasaka Sakas (2008). The newest is Toranomon Hills (2014), another project from Mori Building. While they open to much fanfare, such developments have proved polarising: conceived during the economic bubble of the late '80s and early '90s and unveiled in harder times, the luxury and exclusivity that they project seem out of step with today's lingering economic malaise. Still, Roppongi Hills at least is credited with transforming the neighbourhood of Roppongi, once synonymous with sleazy nightlife, into a cultural attraction.

During the 1960s and '70s, Tokyo reemerged as one of the centres of growing Asian nationalism (the first phase was in the 1910s and '20s). Increasing numbers of Asian students came to Tokyo, taking home with them new ideas about Asia's role in the postwar world.

One of Tokyo's proudest moments came when it hosted the 1964 Summer Olympics. In preparation, the city embarked on a frenzy of construction unequalled in its history. Many Japanese see this time as a turning point in the nation's history, the moment when Japan finally recovered from the devastation of WWII to emerge as a fully fledged member of the modern world economy.

Construction and modernisation continued at a breakneck pace through the '70s, with the interruption of two Middle East oil crises, to reach a peak in the late '80s, when wildly inflated real-estate prices and stock speculation fuelled what is now known as the 'bubble economy'. When the bubble burst in 1991, the economy went into a protracted slump that was to continue, more or less, into the present.

There were other, more disturbing, troubles in Japanese society. In March 1995, members of the Aum Shinrikyō doomsday cult released sarin nerve gas on crowded Tokyo subways, killing 12 and injuring more than 5000. This, together with the devastating Kōbe earthquake

1968–69

Tokyo University students take over administrative buildings to protest the Vietnam War. No one is allowed to graduate in 1969 and entrance exams are cancelled.

1972

Okinawa, captured and held by US forces in WWII, is returned to Japan. High concentration of lingering US military bases on the islands angers locals even today.

1989

Death of Emperor Hirohito; Heisei era begins as Hirohito's son Akihito ascends the throne; stock-market decline begins, initiating a decade-long economic slump in Japan.

1995

Doomsday cult Aum Shinrikyō releases sarin gas on the Tokyo subway, killing 12 and injuring more than 5000. Guru Shōkō Asahara is sentenced to death for Aum-related crimes in 2004.

of the same year, which killed more than 6000 people, signalled the end of Japan's feeling of omnipotence, born of the unlimited successes of the '80s.

21st Century

Based on the price paid for the most expensive real estate in the late 1980s, the land value of Tokyo exceeded that of the entire US. During the late '80s, Japanese companies also bought international icons including Pebble Beach Golf Course, the Rockefeller Center and Columbia Pictures movie studio.

Tokyo has weathered a long hangover since the heady days of the bubble economy. Despite periods of small, but hopeful growth and declarations that 'Japan is back', the economy is still sputtering. In 2014 the administration of Prime Minister Abe Shinzō launched an ambitious stimulus plan – nicknamed 'Abenomics' – that seemed promising but ultimately couldn't pull Japan out of its slump. The raising of the consumption tax the same year, from 5% to 8%, put a squeeze on spending.

Japan is also struggling with its international role, particularly the leeway allowed by its 'Peace Constitution'. In 2004 then Prime Minister Koizumi Junichirō sent Self-Defense Force (SDF) troops to join allied forces in Iraq. Though it was a humanitarian – not combat – mission, this marked the first deployment of Japanese troops overseas since WWII; the move was received with apprehension and even protest. The Defense Agency was promoted to a fully fledged ministry and Japanese military cooperation with the US escalated. In 2014 the Abe administration passed a resolution to reinterpret Article 9 (the peace clause) of the constitution to allow the SDF to come to the aid of an ally under attack. It was a decision that was not supported by the majority of citizens; demonstrations were held in the capital.

On 11 March 2011, a magnitude-9.0 earthquake rocked northeastern Japan resulting in a record-high tsunami that killed nearly 20,000 people and sparked a meltdown at the Daiichi nuclear plant in Fukushima-ken. Tokyo experienced little actual damage, but was shaken nonetheless. The capital itself is long overdue for a major earthquake and for a time the idea of decentralisation was bandied about – to mitigate the effects of a potential disaster. Of greater concern to ordinary citizens was the risk of radioactive contamination of foodstuffs, prompting many to form organisations to petition the government for greater transparency of safety monitoring, and in more extreme cases, the abolition of nuclear power.

With the announcement in 2013 that Tokyo would hold the 2020 Summer Olympics, all talk of decentralisation evaporated. With a renewed focus on turning the city into a showpiece, Tokyo is now focusing on what it does best: building.

2009

LDP loses control of the House of Representatives to the opposition Democratic Party of Japan (DPJ), for only the second time since 1955; by 2012 the LDP are back in power.

2011

Magnitude 9.0 earthquake strikes off Sendai in Tōhoku, unleashing tsunami waves, killing nearly 20,000, and crippling the Fukushima Daiichi nuclear plant.

2012

Tokyo Sky Tree opens as a digital broadcasting tower. At 634m, it is the tallest tower in the world, nearly twice as high as Tokyo Tower.

2013

Tokyo is awarded the 2020 Summer Olympics; plans are set in motion to revitalise the bayfront and make the city a more international destination.

Pop Culture & Technology

A Studio Ghibli movie; a manga (comic) by Tezuka Osamu; platform shoes from Shibuya 109; the latest Sony Playstation: Tokyo is a master at crafting pop-cultural products that catch the attention of the world. Here more people read manga than newspapers, street fashion is more dynamic than that on the catwalk, robots are the stars of anime (Japanese animation) as well as real-life marvels of technology, and everyone, including the police, has a *kawaii* (cute) cartoon mascot.

Manga

Walk into any Tokyo convenience store and you can pick up several phone-directory-sized weekly manga anthologies. Inside you'll find about 25 comic narratives spanning everything from gangster sagas

Above: Pop-culture character Hatsune Miku with a fan, Akihabara (p225)

Top Manga

- *Astro Boy*
- *Barefoot Gen*
- *Black Jack*
- *Doraemon*
- *Lone Wolf and Cub*
- *Nausicaä of the Valley of the Wind*
- *Rose of Versailles*

and teen romance to bicycle racing to *shōgi* (Japanese chess), often with generous helpings of sex and violence. The more successful series are collected in *tankōbon* (volumes) which occupy major sections of bookshops.

No surprise then that manga accounts for about a third of the sales of Japan's US$30-billion book and magazine publishing industry. Major publishers, including Kodansha and Kadokawa, are based in Tokyo and this is where many *mangaka* (manga artists) get their start in the industry. Recently, faced with declining print-magazine sales, publishers have expanded into the booming market for *keitai* manga – comics read on smartphones.

Comiket (www.comiket.co.jp; short for 'Comic Market') is a massive twice-yearly convention for fan-produced amateur manga known as *dōjinshi*. To the untrained eye, *dōjinshi* looks like 'official' manga, but most are parodies (sometimes of a sexual nature) of famous manga titles.

Anime

Top Anime

- *Akira (1988)*
- *My Neighbor Totoro (1988)*
- *Ghost in the Shell (1995)*
- *Tokyo Godfathers (2003)*
- *Mind Game (2004)*

Many manga have inspired anime for TV and cinema. For example, *Nausicaä of the Valley of the Wind*, a 1982 manga by Miyazaki Hayao, Japan's most revered animator and recipient of a lifetime achievement Oscar in 2015, was made into a movie in 1984. Beloved TV anime *Astro Boy* and *Kimba the White Lion* were the first successful manga for Tezuka Osamu (1928–89), an artist frequently referred to as *manga no kamisama* – the 'god of manga'.

In 2014, Studio Ghibli, Japan's most critically successful producer of animated movies, announced it would be halting production to regroup in the light of the retirement of one of its creative lights, Oscar-winner (for *Spirited Away*; 2001) Miyazaki Hayao, and the advanced age of another, Takahata Isao. Takahata Isao was Miyazaki's mentor from

J-POP WHO'S WHO

Japanese pop music, commonly shortened to J-pop, is a major driver of the country's fashion industry. If you can't tell Morning Musume (eight-girl idol group, big in the early 2000s) from Arashi (five-member one-time boy band), then read on for a brief who's who of current J-pop royalty.

➡ **AKB48** Consisting of 60-plus fresh-faced young girls from all over Japan, including one who is entirely computer generated, AKB48 has taken the manufactured idol group to its limit. Divided into three teams, the AKB48 girls have their own TV show, and their own concert hall, coffee shop and theatre in Akihabara. Fans, mostly grown men, line up daily to see these young idols on stage.

➡ **Hamasaki Ayumi** Noted for her chameleon style and high-concept videos, the empress of J-pop, known as Ayu to her adoring fans, is one of the brightest stars in the Avex universe: Avex is one of Japan's biggest recording labels. She has shifted more than 50 million records since her debut in 1998.

➡ **B'z** Matsumoto Tak and Inaba Koshi have been rocking the Japanese charts since 1988. Pronouced 'beez', the duo is one the nation's biggest-selling J-pop acts.

➡ **Kyary Pamyu Pamyu** This pop princess (whose real name is Takemura Kiriko) has been a runaway success since her musical debut in 2011 with PonPonPon. She's been compared to Lady Gaga for her outrageous fashions and self-promotion, which includes being the Harajuku ambassador of *kawaii* (cuteness).

➡ **Mr Children** Nicknamed Misu-Chiru, this four-member band formed in 1988 and have gone on to sell in excess of 50 million records. Lead singer Sakurai Kazutoshi composes most of their songs.

Tokyo fashions

their time working together in the 1960s for animation studio Tōei, and the director of anime classics including *Grave of the Fireflies* (1988) and *Only Yesterday* (1991).

Such news is a concern for fans as Studio Ghilbli's premium product is far superior to the vast majority of low-budget anime, which tends to feature saucer-eyed schoolgirls, cute fluorescent monsters and mechatronic superheroes in recycled and tweaked plots. Nevertheless, the international success of series such as *Mobile Suit Gundam* and *Pokémon* continues to tempt many fans to make the trip to anime's creative source in Tokyo.

Hyperfashion

Visitors are often in awe of Tokyo's incredible sense of style and its broad range of subcultures. It's not uncommon to see Japanese wearing kimonos for special occasions, and *yukata* (light summer kimonos) for fireworks shows and festivals in summer. Everyday wear ranges from the standard-issue salaryman suit (overwhelmingly dark blue or black) to the split-toed shoes and baggy trousers of construction workers.

Tokyo's fashion designers who have become international superstars include Issey Miyake, Yohji Yamamoto and, more recently, Rei Kawakubo of Comme des Garçons. Other designers include Koshino Hiroko and Utsugi Eri. Fujiwara Hiroshi, a renowned streetwear fashion arbiter, also has a huge impact on what Japanese youth wear.

Fashion trends come and go in the blink of a heavily made-up eye in Tokyo. The streets of Harajuku and Shibuya remain the best places in which to view what's currently hot; at the time of research it was the looks

Fashion Websites

Tokyo Fashion (http://tokyo fashion.com)

Tokyo Adorned/ Thomas C Card (www.tokyo adorned.com)

TONY BURNS / GETTY IMAGES ©

Above: Gundam robot, Odaiba (p226)
Left: Manga graphics on lockers, Akihabara

TOKYO'S LOVE AFFAIR WITH THE ROBOT

The success of Shinjuku's Robot Restaurant should have come as no surprise. Long before fantasy *mecha* (a manga/anime term for robot technology) caught on with the likes of Go Nagai's *Mazinger Z* (an anime featuring a flying robot) and the video series (and soon to be a live-action film) *Patlabor*, the Japanese had an affinity for robotic devices. During the Edo period (1603–1868), small mechanical dolls known as *karakuri ningyō* were used by feudal lords to serve tea and entertain guests.

Fast forward to 21st-century Tokyo and human-scale robots are still entertaining people. At Honda Welcome Plaza Aoyama and the National Museum of Emerging Science & Innovation (Miraikan) in Odaiba, Asimo, the world's most advanced humanoid robot, does brief daily demonstrations, including bowing, jogging and posing for photos. Also at Miraikan, marvel as the female android (a human-like robot), Otonaroid, answers questions from the audience and moves in an uncannily human way.

Only in Tokyo would millions cross town to have their photo taken in front of an 18m replica of a robot from the animated Gundam sci-fi series erected in Odaiba. Soon, thanks to SoftBank and Aldebaran Robotics (www.aldebaran.com/en/a-robots/who-is-pepper), many may have a robot at home: in 2014 they launched Pepper, an affordable 1.2m-tall robot designed to read your emotions and act accordingly to cheer you up or join in and enhance your happiness.

proffered by vintage store Bubbles. Less radical and more affordable are Muji and Uniqlo, whose inspired, practical fashions are simple without being bland; the former also offers an amazing selection of household and lifestyle goods, including furniture, stationery and food staples.

Future Tech & Design

It may be a fully automated toilet that sings while you use it, or a smartphone that can also check for bad breath – Japanese are inimitable in their flair for tricking out ordinary gadgets with primo engineering and lots of fun, hot looks. It's all driven by an insatiable desire for novelty.

The humble photo booth, for instance, has evolved beyond recognition in the *purikura* (print club), a minigraphics studio that can spit out extensively user-designed photo stickers and has enough room for you to change into your favourite superhero costume. In addition to ranking your vocalist skills, karaoke music players can count the number of calories burned per song. Inescapable vending machines dispense a cornucopia of consumer goods from underwear to steaming *rāmen* (noodles in broth).

Tokyo brims with such innovative Japanese designs; to see classics head to the display by the Japan Design Council on the 7th floor of Ginza department store, Matsuya. Trade shows such as Tokyo Designers Week (www.tdwa.com/en_index.html) draw the brightest designers and manufacturers from around Japan, as well as massive public attendance.

Pop-Culture Districts

Akihabara & Central Tokyo

Akihabara should be the first stop on any pop-culture Tokyo tour. With its multitude of stores selling anime and manga-related goods, not to mention maid cafes, and all the electronic gizmos imaginable, no other area of the city has such prime geek appeal.

Also check out the Tokyo Character Street arcade of shops beneath Tokyo Station and Pokémon Center near Hamamatsuchō Station.

Tokyo Pop Books

Cruising the Anime City: An Otaku Guide to Neo Tokyo (Patrick Macias, Machiyama Tomohiro; 2004)

A Geek in Japan (Hector Garcia; 2011)

Wrong About Japan (Peter Carey; 2006)

Websites

Culture Japan (www.dannychoo.com)

Tezuka in English (http://tezukainenglish.com/wp)

GhibliWiki (www.nausicaa.net/wiki/Main_Page)

Cosplay fashion, Harajuku

Odaiba

This human-made island with its outlandish architecture and zippy monorail feels like it was designed to resemble an anime version of the city. An enormous Gundam robot statue stands tall outside the shopping-mall Diver City, where there's a Gundam-themed exhibition and cafe. For robots and androids that actually work, don't miss Odaiba's National Museum of Emerging Science & Innovation (Miraikan).

Conventions & Events

Tokyo Games Show (http://expo.nikkeibp.co.jp/tgs) September

Comiket (www.comiket.co.jp) August and December

AnimeJapan (www.animejapan.jp/en) March

Design Festa (http://designfesta.com/en) May

Harajuku & Shibuya

The streets of Harajuku – Takeshita-dōri, Cat St and Omotesandō – remain the best places to survey Tokyo's multiple style tribes. Among the most striking are the *gosurori* (gothic Lolita) kids posing like vampires at noon. Think Halloween meets neo-Victorian with the odd glam-rock accent and you'll get the idea. More wannabe street fashionistas strut their stuff a little further south in Tokyo's trend-Mecca, Shibuya.

Northern Tokyo

Fans of Tezuka Osamu should hop off the JR Yamanote line at Takadanobaba to view a fabulous mural homage to his characters under the railway tracks there. Further north, Ikebukuro is home to a cluster of anime- and manga-related shops and businesses including butler cafes (cosplay theme cafes aimed at geek gals).

Western Tokyo

You'll need to book ahead to visit the massively popular Ghibli Museum at Mitaka, a brilliantly creative mini theme park based around the company's movies. Die-hard anime fans will also want to schedule time in Nakano to cruise the aisles of pop-culture emporium Mandarake.

Arts & Architecture

Tokyo is rivalled only by Kyoto as Japan's centre of arts and culture. The city offers a beguiling blend of the traditional and the contemporary: you could spend the morning gawking at some fantastic examples of modern architecture, the afternoon soaking up the old-world atmosphere of a kabuki play and the evening taking in a contemporary-art exhibition (and the skyline) from a museum atop a skyscraper.

Performing Arts

Traditional Drama & Storytelling

Kabuki

Tokyo had a rich theatre culture when it was Edo (1603–1868). Above all, there was kabuki: captivating, occasionally outrageous and beloved of the townspeople.

Kabuki reached its golden age in Edo, but got its start in Kyoto. Around the year 1600, a charismatic shrine priestess led a troupe of female performers in a new type of dance people dubbed 'kabuki' – a slang expression that meant 'cool' or 'in vogue' at the time. The dancing – rather ribald and performed on a dry riverbed for gathering crowds – was also a gateway to prostitution, which eventually led the Tokugawa establishment to ban the female performers. Adolescent men took their place, though they too attracted amorous admirers (who engaged in the occasional brawl with competing suitors). Finally, in 1653, the authorities mandated that only adult men with shorn forelocks could perform kabuki, which gave rise to one of kabuki's most fascinating elements, the *onnagata* (actors who specialise in portraying women).

When kabuki arrived in Edo, it developed hand in hand with the increasingly affluent merchant class, whose decadent tastes translated into the breathtaking costumes, dramatic music and elaborate stagecraft that have come to characterise the art form. It is this intensely visual nature that makes kabuki accessible to foreign audiences – you don't really have to know the story to enjoy the spectacle. (Tip: if you opt for the cheap seats, bring binoculars).

The plays draw from a repertoire of popular themes, such as famous historical accounts and stories of love-suicide. But more than by plot, kabuki

ARTS EVENTS

February

The year's top animation, manga and digital installations go on display at the **Japan Media Arts Festival**, held at the National Art Center Tokyo.

March

Classical-music festival **Haru-sai** takes place in venues around Ueno. Also: **Art Fair Tokyo**.

April

Performances and larger-than-life installations take over the streets of Roppongi for **Roppongi Art Night**.

May

Weekend-long **Design Festa** is the largest art event in Asia.

July

The **International Gay & Lesbian Film Festival** screens dozens of films from Japan and around the world.

September

The **Tokyo Jazz Festival** has three days of shows by international and local stars.

October

Tokyo International Film Festival screens works by Japanese directors with English subtitles.

November

Tokyo's theatre festival **Festival/Tokyo**, the celebration of interior design that is **Tokyo Designer's Week**, and the film festival **FilmEx** are all on this month. Also: round two for **Design Festa**.

is driven by its actors, who train for the profession from childhood. The leading families of modern kabuki go back many generations, as sons follow their fathers into the *yago* (kabuki acting house) in order to perpetuate an ancestor's name on stage. Thus the generations of certain families (eg Bando and Ichikawa) run into the double digits. The Japanese audience takes great interest in watching how different generations of one family perform the same part. A few actors today enjoy great social prestige, with their activities on and off the stage chronicled in the tabloids.

Kabuki isn't as popular as it once was, though it still has its devout followers. You might be surprised to hear audience members shouting during the play. This is called *kakegoe;* it usually occurs during pivotal moments such as well-known lines of dialogue or *mie* (dramatic poses held for a pause) and expresses encouragement and delight. Actors note they miss this reinforcement when performing overseas.

Ginza's Kabuki-za, in business since 1889, is the last of Tokyo's dedicated kabuki theatres.

Arts Websites

Tokyo Art Beat (www.tokyoart beat.com)

Real Tokyo (www.realtokyo.co.jp)

Tokyo Stages (http://tokyostages.wordpress.com)

Art Info Japan (http://enjp.blouinartinfo.com)

Tokyo Architect (www.tokyo-architect.com)

Nō

Kabuki was seen as too unrefined for the military classes (though they may have secretly enjoyed it). *Nō,* a dramatisation of the aesthetic quality *yūgen* (subtle, elusive beauty), was considered a better match.

Nō has its roots in indigenous Shintō rituals and developed in Kyoto between 1350 and 1450. Rather than a drama in the usual sense, *nō* seeks to express a poetic moment by symbolic and almost abstract means: glorious movements, grand and exaggerated costumes and hairstyles, sonorous chorus and music, and subtle expression. Actors frequently wear masks while they perform before a spare, unchanging set, which features a painting of a large pine tree. Most plays centre around two principal characters: the *shi-te,* who is sometimes a living person but more often a demon or a ghost whose soul cannot rest; and the *waki,* who leads the main character towards the play's climactic moment. The elegant language used is that of the court of the 14th century.

Some visitors find *nō* rapturous and captivating; others (including most Japanese today) find its subtlety all too subtle. The intermissions of *nō* performances are punctuated by *kyōgen* (short, lively, comic farces) – these have a more universal appeal.

Tokyo has its own public theatre dedicated to *nō,* the National Nō Theater, near Harajuku. Masks and costumes are also on display at the Tokyo National Museum.

Rakugo

Rakugo, a form of comedic monologue, was another popular diversion of the working class in Edo. While kabuki tickets fetch a handsome price and carry an air of sophistication, *rakugo* has a down-to-earth vibe. The performer, usually in a kimono, sits on a square cushion on a stage. Props are limited to a fan and hand towel. Some comedians specialise in classic monologues, which date to the Edo and Meiji periods; others pen new ones that address issues relevant to contemporary life. A number of famous comedians, including movie director Kitano Takeshi, have studied *rakugo* as part of their development.

Rakugo is still performed regularly in Tokyo's few remaining *yose* (vaudeville theatres), such as Asakusa Engei Hall. It is sometimes possible, both in Japan and abroad, to catch one of the few comedians who can perform *rakugo* in English, such as Katsuri Kaishi.

Contemporary Movements

Theatre in Tokyo doesn't play the same influential role that it did in the days of Edo or as it does in major Western cities – much to the lament of those involved. Commercially successful theatre tends to fall into two categories: mainstream Western imports (especially musicals) and performances starring celebrities. Still, in wealthy and intellectual residential pockets of the city, public and underground theatres play to full houses.

Every November, Tokyo's month-long theatre festival, Festival/Tokyo (http://festival-tokyo.jp/en), takes place in venues around the city. In addition to new works from Japanese theatre troupes, works from around the world (and particularly Asia) are performed, sometimes with English subtitles.

Underground & Fringe

Theatre around the world spent the 1960s redefining itself, and it was certainly no different in Tokyo. The *angura* (underground) movement of the 1960s saw productions take place in any space available: tents, basements, open spaces and street corners. Some of the figures who emerged during this period, such as Sato Makoto, now creative director at Za Kōenji public theatre, have continued to play a big part in shaping Tokyo's current theatre landscape.

Another important movement, still relevant today, emerged in the 1980s – *shōgeki* (literally 'small theatre', but more like 'fringe theatre'). The most famous of the *shōgeki* theatres, such as Honda Theatre, are clustered in Shimo-Kitazawa. These remain the place to see the works of up-and-coming playwrights and directors.

Some current names to look for include Okada Toshiki and his troupe Chelfitsch, which earned critical acclaim for *Sangatsu no Itsukukan* (Five Days in March; 2004), a hyper-real portrayal of two *furītā* (part-time workers), holed up in a Shibuya love hotel at the start of the second Iraq War. Chelfitsch rely heavily on disjointed, hyper-colloquial language. More accessible to visitors with little or no Japanese ability are the physical, and often risqué, works of Miura Daisuke and his troupe potudo-ru. He recently adapted his award-winning *Ai no Uzu* (Love's Whirlpool; 2005), set at a Roppongi swingers' party, into a film of the same name (2014).

Recommended Reading

From Postwar to Postmodern, Art in Japan 1945–1989 (Dorun Chung; 2013)

Art Space Tokyo (Ashley Rawlings; 2008)

A Hundred Years of Japanese Film (Donald Richie; 2012)

21st Century Tokyo: A Guide to Contemporary Architecture (Julian Worrall & Erez Golani Solomon; 2010)

Butō

Butō is Japan's unique and fascinating contribution to contemporary dance. It was born out of a rejection of the excessive formalisation that characterises traditional forms of Japanese dance, and of an intention to return to more ancient roots. Hijikata Tatsumi (1928–86) is credited with giving the first *butō* performance in 1959; Ōno Kazuo (1906–2010) was also a key figure.

During a performance, one or more dancers use their naked or semi-naked bodies to express the most elemental and intense human emotions. Nothing is forbidden in *butō* and performances often deal with taboo topics such as sexuality and death. For this reason, critics often describe *butō* as scandalous, and *butō* dancers delight in pushing the boundaries of what can be considered beautiful in artistic performance. It's also entirely visual, meaning both Japanese and non-Japanese spectators are on level footing.

Dairakudakan (www.dairakudakan.com), which operates out of a small theatre in Kichijōji, west of Shinjuku, is one of the more active troupes today. You can also sometimes catch *butō* at the Setagaya Public Theatre.

Takarazuka

Takarazuka, musical revues performed by an all-female cast, is one form of commercial theatre that is likely to amuse overseas visitors. Founded in 1913, partly as an inversion of the all-male kabuki theatre and partly as a form of entertainment for a growing male middle class with money to burn, *takarazuka* combines traditional Japanese elements with Western musical styles. Interestingly, in light of its history, its most devoted admirers nowadays are women who swoon with romantic abandon over the troupe's beautiful drag kings. The place to see it is Tokyo Takurazuka Theatre, near Ginza.

Visual Arts

Nihonga

Japan has a rich history of painting, though it owes its origins to China. Traditionally, paintings consisted of black ink or mineral pigments on *washi* (Japanese handmade paper) and were sometimes decorated with gold leaf. These works adorned folding screens, sliding doors and hanging scrolls; never behind glass, they were a part of daily life. Throughout the Edo period, the nobility patronised artists such as those by the Kanō school, who depicted Confucianism subjects, mythical Chinese creatures or scenes from nature.

With the Meiji Restoration (1868) – when artists and ideas were sent back and forth between Europe and Japan – painting necessarily became either a rejection or an embracement of Western influence. Two terms were coined: *yōga* for Western-style works and *nihonga* for works in the traditional Japanese style, though in reality, many *nihonga* artists incorporate shading and perspective into their works, while using techniques from all the major traditional Japanese painting schools.

The best place in Tokyo to see *nihonga* is the Yamatane Museum of Art in Ebisu. The National Museum of Modern Art has some important works as well.

Ukiyo-e

Far from the nature scenes of classical paintings, *ukiyo-e* (woodblock prints, but literally 'pictures of the floating world') were for the common people, used in advertising or in much the same way posters are used today. The subjects of these woodblock prints were images of

JAPANESE TRADITIONAL ARTS

Tea Ceremony

Sadō (the way of tea) is a celebration of the aesthetic principle of *wabi-sabi*, reached when naturalness, spontaneity and humility come together. Many Japanese art forms, including pottery, ikebana (art of flower arranging), calligraphy and garden design, developed in tandem with the tea ceremony. A few of Tokyo's most prestigious hotels have tearooms where ceremonies are performed in English, including the Imperial Hotel; reservations are necessary. You can also see pottery associated with the tea ceremony at the Tokyo National Museum and at the Hatakeyama Collection.

Ikebana

What sets Japanese ikebana (literally 'living flowers') apart from Western forms of flower arranging is the suggestion of space and the symbolism inherent in the choice and placement of the flowers and, in some cases, bare branches. It's not as esoteric as it sounds. Tokyo's classic Ohara School of Ikebana (p124) and the more avant-garde Sōgetsu Kaikan (p81) offer classes in English.

everyday life, characters in kabuki plays and scenes from the 'floating world', a term derived from a Buddhist metaphor for life's fleeting joys.

Edo's particular 'floating world' revolved around pleasure districts such as the Yoshiwara. In this topsy-turvy kingdom, an inversion of the usual social hierarchies imposed by the Tokugawa shogunate, money meant more than rank, actors and artists were the arbiters of style, and prostitutes elevated their art to such a level that their accomplishments matched those of the women of noble families.

The vivid colours, novel composition and flowing lines of *ukiyo-e* caused great excitement when they finally arrived in the West; the French came to dub it 'Japonisme'. *Ukiyo-e* was a key influence on Impressionists and post-Impressionists (eg Toulouse-Lautrec, Manet and Degas). Yet among the Japanese, the prints were hardly given more than passing consideration – millions were produced annually in Edo, often thrown away or used as wrapping paper for pottery. For years, the Japanese were perplexed by the keen interest foreigners took in this art form.

The Ota Memorial Ukiyo-e Museum in Harajuku has fantastic collections from masters such as Hokusai, Hiroshige and Utamaro. You can also see their works at the Tokyo National Museum.

Photography

It's no surprise that the country famous for producing cameras would also produce noteworthy photographers. The most well known are the two bad boys of Japanese photography, Moriyama Daido (b 1938) and Araki Nobuyoshi (b 1940). Moriyama is a tireless chronicler of Tokyo's underbelly. His grainy, monochrome shots of Shinjuku – usually the Kabukichō red-light district – reveal a whole other side of the city. Meanwhile, Araki is known for risqué, erotic images that walk that fine line between art and pornography (though his subject was often his own wife). He takes evocative (and sometimes absurdist) photos of other things too, including the streets of his home town, Tokyo.

Moriyama once worked as an assistant to Hosoe Eikoh (b 1933), another important Japanese photographer. Hosoe's work focuses mostly on the human form (and sometimes with an erotic gleam); a few of his famous subjects include the writer Mishima Yukio and the *butō* dancer Hijikata Tatsumi.

Among the younger generation, Kawauchi Rinko (b 1972) has an impeccable eye for finding the poetic in the ordinary – and making it just offbeat enough to avoid being cliché. Ninagawa Mika (b 1972) is well known for her brightly coloured, sensual and wickedly girly compositions that have appeared on many album and magazine covers.

The Tokyo Metropolitan Museum of Photography is obviously the best place for photo exhibits, though it's closed for renovations through summer 2016. The JCII Photo Salon and Fuji Film Square hold free exhibitions.

Public Art

Robert Indiana's *Love* and Roy Lichtenstein's *Tokyo Brushstrokes* at Shinjuku I-Land, Nishi-Shinjuku

Miyajima Tatsuo's *Counter Void* and Louise Bourgeois' *Maman* at Roppongi Hills

Okamoto Tarō's *Myth of Tomorrow* inside Shibuya Station

Superflat & Beyond

The '90s was a big decade for Japanese contemporary art: love him or hate him, Murakami Takashi brought Japan back into an international spotlight it hadn't enjoyed since 19th-century collectors went wild for *ukiyo-e*. His work makes fantastic use of the flat planes, clear lines and decorative techniques associated with *nihonga,* while lifting motifs from the lowbrow subculture of manga (Japanese comics). As much an artist as a clever theorist, Murakami proclaimed in his 'Superflat' manifesto that his work picked up where Japanese artists left off after the Meiji Restoration – and might just be the future of painting, given that most of us now view the world through the portals of our two-dimensional computer screens. Murakami inspired a whole generation of artists who worked in his 'factory', Kaikai Kiki, and presented their works at his Geisai art fairs.

Another big name concurrent with Murakami is Nara Yoshitomo, known for his paintings and sculptures of punkish tots with unsettling depth. You can see some of his works at A to Z Cafe in Aoyama.

Naturally, younger artists have had trouble defining themselves in the wake of 'Tokyo Pop' – as the highly exportable art of the '90s came to be known. There are a handful of artists gaining recognition for works that could be described as 'neo-*nihonga*'; among them are Tenmyouya Hisashi, Yamaguchi Akira and Konoike Tomoko, all represented by Mizuma Art Gallery. Other names to look out for are those of sculptors Nawa Kohei and Motohiko Odani, who create works of ethereal and frightening beauty, and the collection of irreverent pranksters known as ChimPom.

Roppongi's Mori Art Museum holds a show every three years called Roppongi Crossing, featuring up-and-coming artists. The next one is in autumn 2016.

Cinema

Japan's golden age of cinema in the 1950s – the era of international acclaimed auteurs Ozu Yasujirō, Mizoguchi Kenji and Kurosawa Akira – is responsible for a whole generation of Japanophiles. Ozu (1903–63) was the first great Japanese director, known for his piercing, at times heartbreaking, family dramas. Mizoguchi (1898–1956) began by shooting social-realist works in the 1930s but found critical acclaim with his reimagining of stories from Japanese history and folklore. Kurosawa (1910–98) is the most famous Japanese director to date, and an oft-cited influence for film-makers around the world. His films are intense and psychological; the director favoured strong leading men and worked often with the actor Mifune Toshirō. Kurosawa won the Golden Lion at the Venice International Film Festival and an honoury Oscar for the haunting *Rashomon* (1950), based on the short story of the same name by Ryūnosuke Akutagawa and staring Mifune as a bandit.

Check out the annual anthology of new Japanese writing, Monkey Business (http://monkeybusinessmag.tumblr.com). Literary magazine Granta (www.granta.com) also regularly publishes translations of new works by Japanese writers; in 2014 it did a whole issue on Japan.

In the 1980s, another wave of Japanese film-makers achieved cult status abroad – Itami Jūzō (1933–97) in particular. A child prodigy and former actor, Itami hit it big with his first film *Osōshiki* (The Funeral; 1984), a satirical look at family relations. His second film, *Tampopo* (1985), starring a young Watanabe Ken, is likely responsible for introducing the world to the cult of *rāmen*. Another actor turned director is Kitano Takeshi (b 1947), known also by his comedian name, Beat Takeshi. He is best known for his gangster movies, but his biggest success, *Hanabi* (Fireworks; 1997), is a surprisingly tender tale of an unhinged ex-cop, for which he won the Venice Golden Lion.

One newer director to watch is Sono Sion (b 1961), known for being somewhat of a provocateur. His latest film, *Tokyo Tribe* (2014), is a hip-hop musical set in an alternative Tokyo ruled by warring street gangs.

Literature

Most of Japan's national literature since the Edo period has been penned by authors writing in Tokyo. Consequently, no other city in Japan has a greater hold on the national imagination and, as more and more Japanese works are translated, the global imagination.

Haiku

Japan has a rich poetic tradition, and one that was historically social in nature. Poetry groups would come together to collaborate on long *renga* (linked verse), with each new verse playing off some word or association in the one that came before. *Renga* were composed in a gamelike atmosphere and were more about witty repartee than about creating works to be preserved and read. Sometime in the 17th century, however, the opening stanza of a *renga* became accepted as a standalone poem - and the haiku was born. Today, the haiku is Japan's most widely known form of poetry; at just 17 sparse syllables, it is also the shortest.

Matsuo Bashō (1644–94) is considered the master of the form, and is Japan's most famous poet. He's also the origin of the popular image of the haiku artist as a Zen-like ascetic figure. Yet before Bashō left for the wilds of northeast Japan to pen his opus, *Oku no Hosomichi* (Narrow Roads to the Interior; 1702), he lived in a little hut with a banana tree on the edge of Edo, in the neighbourhood of Fukagawa.

Twentieth-Century Modernism

The most important writer of the modern era, Sōseki Natsume (1867–1916) was born in Tokyo in the last year that it was called Edo. One of the first generation of scholars to be sent abroad, Sōseki studied English literature in London. His ability to convey Japanese subtlety and wit through the lines of the then newly imported Western-style novel, while taking a critical look at modernising Japan and its morals, has endeared him to generations of Japanese readers.

Nobel Prize–winner Kawabata Yasunari (1899–1972) may not have been born in the capital, but he made up for it during his 20s, which he spent living in Asakusa - then Tokyo's equivalent of Paris' Montmartre. His novel *Asakusa Kurenaidan* (The Scarlet Gang of Asakusa; 1930), about the neighbourhood's demimonde, was inspired by his time there.

Japan's other Nobel Laureate, Ōe Kenzaburo (b 1935), confronts modern Japan head-on, using the individual as a stand-in for society in disturbing works such as *Kojinteki na taiken* (A Personal Matter; 1964). Ōe grew up in rural Shikoku but has made Tokyo his home, where, as a vocal pacifist and antinuclear activist, he can still be found speaking at rallies and symposiums. His latest work to be published in English, *The Changeling* (2000), is the first in a series inspired by the suicide of Japanese film director Itami Jūzō, Ōe's brother-in-law.

Japan's most controversial literary figure, Mishima Yukio (1925–70) grew up in central Tokyo, attending the elite Gakushūin (the school attended by the aristocracy). A prolific writer, Mishima wrote essays and *nō* plays in addition to dense, psychological novels. His growing obsession with *bushidō* (the samurai code)

JAPANESE CINEMA

1930s

Directors hone their styles. Watch Ozu Yasujirō's *Umarete wa mita keredo* (I Was Born, But...; 1929); Mizoguchi Kenji's *Naniwa Ereji* (Osaka Elegy; 1936).

1940s

Censors demand nationalist themes. Watch Mizoguchi's classic vendetta story *Chūshingura* (The 47 Rōnin; 1941).

1950s

The golden age of Japanese film. Watch Kurosawa Akira's *Rashōmon* (1950); Mizoguchi's *Ugetsu Monogatari* (1953).

1960s

Colour and prosperity arrive. Watch Ozu's *Sanma no Aji* (An Autumn Afternoon; 1962).

1970s

Ōshima Nagisa brings new-wave visual techniques and raw sex. Watch *Ai no Korīda* (In the Realm of the Senses; 1976).

1980s

Imamura Shōhei and Itami Jūzō earn critical success. Watch Imamura's *Naruyama Bushiko* (The Ballad of Naruyama; 1983); Itami's *Tampopo* (1986).

1990s

Actor Takeshi Kitano emerges as a successful director. Watch *Hana-bi* (Fireworks; 1997).

2000s

Anime and horror flicks boom. Watch Miyazaki Hayao's *Sen to Chihiro no Kamikakushi* (Spirited Away; 2001).

eventually led to a bizarre, failed takeover of the Tokyo headquarters of the Japanese Self-Defense Forces that ended with Mishima committing seppuku (ritual suicide).

Contemporary Writers

Among contemporary novelists, Murakami Haruki (b 1949) is the biggest star, both at home and internationally. His latest work, *Colorless Tsukuru Tazaki and His Years of Pilgrimage* (2013), moved a million copies in a week – and this at a time when bestseller lists in Japan are largely filled with how-to manuals and self-help books. The English translation topped the US bestsellers list when it was released the following year. Of all his books, the one most Japanese people are likely to mention as their favourite is the one that established his reputation, *Norwegian Wood* (1987). It's a wistful story of students in 1960s Tokyo trying to find themselves and each other. Like the main character, Murakami once worked at a record store; the university in the novel is modelled after his alma mater, Waseda University.

The other literary Murakami, Murakami Ryū, is known for darker, edgier works that look at Japan's urban underbelly. His signature work is *Coin Locker Babies* (1980), a coming-of-age tale of two boys left to die in coin lockers. Both survive, though the Tokyo they live to face is literally toxic. His most recent novel, a likewise dystopian work titled *From the Fatherland, with Love* (2005), was translated into English in 2013.

Literature in Japan is not, entirely, a boys' club. Banana Yoshimoto (b 1964) – who picked her pen name because it sounded androgynous – had an international hit with *Kitchen* (1988). More recently, in 2011, her novel *The Lake* (2005) was shortlisted for the Man Asian Literary Prize. In 2003 the prestigious Akutagawa Prize for emerging writers was awarded to two young women: Wataya Risa (b 1984) for the novel *The Back You Want to Kick* and Kanehara Hitomi (b 1983) for the novel *Snakes and Earrings*. Wataya has gone on to have further success, winning the Kenzoburo Oe prize in 2012 for her latest work *Isn't it a pity?*

Edo- & Meiji-Era Buildings

- *Kiyomizu Kannon-do (1631)*
- *Asakusa-jinja (1649)*
- *Tōshō-gu (1651)*
- *Bank of Japan (1896)*
- *Kyū Iwasaki-teien (1896)*
- *Akasaka Palace (1909)*

Architecture

Traditional Architecture

Until the end of the Edo period, the city's houses and shops were almost entirely constructed of wood, paper and tile, and early photos show a remarkable visual harmony in the old skyline. Unfortunately, such structures were also highly flammable and few survived the twin conflagrations of the first half of the 20th century – the Great Kantō Earthquake and WWII. However, traditional elements are still worked into contemporary structures. These include tatami (reed mat) floors

TEMPLE OR SHRINE?

Buddhist temples and Shintō shrines were historically intertwined, until they were forcibly separated by government decree in 1868. But centuries of coexistence means the two resemble each other architecturally; you'll also often find small temples within shrines and vice versa. The easiest way to tell the two apart though is to check the gate. The main entrance of a shrine is a *torii* (gate), usually composed of two upright pillars, joined at the top by two horizontal crossbars, the upper of which is normally slightly curved. *Torii* are often painted a bright vermilion. In contrast, the *mon* (main entrance gate) of a temple is often a much more substantial affair, constructed of several pillars or casements, joined at the top by a multitiered roof. Temple gates often contain guardian figures, usually *Niō* (deva kings).

CONTEMPORARY BUILDINGS

Nakagin Capsule Tower (1972) Apartment building in Ginza with removable pods and a fascinating retro vision of the future, by Kurokawa Kishō.

Super Dry Hall (1989) Instantly recognisable Philippe Starck work topped with an eccentric golden plume, across the bridge from Asakusa.

St Mary's Cathedral (1964) Transcendent stainless-steel church in Mejiro; an early work by Tange Kenzō.

Prada Aoyama Building (2003) Jacques Herzog and Pierre de Meuron's creation in Aoyama is a mosaic of bubbled glass.

Tokyo International Forum (1996) A soaring glass vessel in the heart of Marunouchi, designed by Rafael Vinoly.

National Art Center Tokyo (2006) In Roppongi, an undulating meshwork unsupported by columns; Kurokawa Kishō's last great work.

21_21 Design Sight (2007) Concrete clamshell rising out of the ground, by Andō Tadao, near Roppongi Station.

Tokyo Metropolitan Government Offices (1991) Tange Kenzō's design for city hall in Shinjuku has both heft and airiness, inspired by the cathedrals of Europe.

Myonichikan (1921) Frank Lloyd Wright's charmingly vintage 'School of the Free Spirit', in Nishi-Ikebukuro.

Mode Cocoon Tower (2008) Elliptical webbed tower and a new landmark for Nishi-Shinjuku; designed by Tange Associates.

and *shōji* (sliding rice-paper screen doors), which you'll encounter if you stay in a ryokan (traditional inn) or eat at a traditional restaurant. Temples and shrines, though reconstructions, usually mimic their earlier incarnations.

Foreign Influences

When Japan opened its doors to Western influence following the Meiji Restoration (1868), the city's urban planners sought to remake downtown Tokyo in the image of a European city. A century-long push and pull ensued, between enthusiasts and detractors, architects who embraced the new styles and materials, and those who rejected them. Tokyo Station, with its brick facade and domes looking very much like a European terminus, went up in 1914. Meanwhile, the Tokyo National Museum (1938) was done in what was called the Imperial Style, a sturdy rendering of traditional forms. There was also some meeting in the middle: around the turn of the 20th century it became fashionable among the elite to build houses with both Japanese- and Western-style wings; the Kyū Iwasaki-teien is one example.

A few decades later, the International Style, characterised by sleek lines, cubic forms, and materials such as glass, steel and brick, arrived in Japan. Many structures in this style were put up around Marunouchi and Nihombashi; though many have since been rebuilt to add more floors, the street-floor facades of some buildings still pay homage to the original structures.

Early Style Icons

Modern Japanese architecture really came into its own in the 1960s. The best known of Japan's 20th-century builders was Tange Kenzō (1913–2005), who was influenced by traditional Japanese forms as well as the aggressively sculptural works of French architect Le Corbusier. Some of Tange's noteworthy works include St Mary's Cathedral (1964), the National Gymnasium (1964), the Tokyo Metropolitan Government Offices (1991) and the Fuji Television Japan Broadcast Centre (1996).

Standing 634m tall, Tokyo Sky Tree (2012) is the world's tallest, free-standing tower. It employs an ancient construction technique used in pagodas: a *shimbashira* column (made of contemporary, reinforced concrete), structurally separate from the exterior truss. It acts as a counterweight when the tower sways, cutting vibrations by 50%.

Concurrent with Tange were the 'metabolists', Shinohara Kazuo, Kurokawa Kishō, Maki Fumihiko and Kikutake Kiyonori. The Metabolism movement promoted flexible spaces and functions at the expense of fixed forms in building. Kurokawa's Nakagin Capsule Tower (1972) is a seminal work, designed as pods that could be removed whole from a central core and replaced elsewhere. His last great work, the National Art Center in Roppongi (2006), weaves undulating vertical forms into a strikingly latticed, organic structure.

Kikutake went on to design the Edo-Tokyo Museum (1992). This enormous structure encompasses almost 50,000 sq metres of built space and reaches 62.2m (the height of Edo Castle) at its peak. Meanwhile, Maki's Spiral Building (1985) is a favourite with Tokyo residents for its user-friendly design, gallery space, cafe and shops.

Next-Generation Builders

Since the 1980s a second generation of Japanese architects have emerged who continue to explore both modernism and postmodernism, while incorporating a renewed interest in Japan's architectural heritage. Among them are Itō Toyō and Andō Tadao, both winners of the prestigious Pritzker Architecture Prize. Ando's works are earthy and monumental; Ito's are lighter and more conceptual. Both architects have structures along Omote-sandō (p118).

Across the street from Andō's Omotesandō Hills is the work of one of Ito's protégées, Sejima Kazuyo, who designed the flagship boutique for Dior with her partner Nishizawa Ryūe in the firm SANAA. Sejima and Nishizawa picked up Pritzker awards in 2010. Judges praised their design simplicity, saying that their architecture is 'in direct contrast with the bombastic'.

Meanwhile, Tange protégé Taniguchi Yoshio landed the commission to redesign the Museum of Modern Art (1999) in New York City. He also designed the Gallery of Horyū-ji Treasures at the Tokyo National Museum and Tokyo Sea Life Park. His works are minimal and elegant. Another name to know is Kengo Kuma, known for his use of wood and light. His works in recent years include reboots of the Nezu Museum and the Suntory Museum of Art, Akagi-jinja and the Asakusa Culture Tourist Information Center.

Onsen

Communal bathing, known as *hadaka no tsukiai* (meaning 'naked friendship'), is seen in Japan as a great social leveller. With thousands of onsen (hot springs) scattered across the archipelago, the Japanese have been taking the plunge for centuries. The blissful relaxation that follows a good long soak can turn a sceptic into a convert, and is likely to make you an onsen fanatic. Even in Tokyo there are opportunities for a dip, in either onsen or *sentō* (public bath).

Healing Waters

What sets an onsen apart from an ordinary *sentō* is the nature of the water. Onsen water comes naturally heated from a hot spring and often contains a number of minerals and gases; *sentō* water comes from the tap and is mechanically heated. Onsen are reputed to makes one's skin *sube-sube* (smooth), while the chemical composition of particular

Above: Onsen in Hakone (p186)

waters are also believed to help cure such ailments as high blood pressure, poor circulation and even infertility.

Konyoku (mixed bathing) was the norm in Japan until the Meiji Restoration (1868), when the country sought to align itself with more 'civilised' Western ideas and outlawed the practice. Within Tokyo's central 23 wards you won't encounter it, but in the countryside and on the Izu Islands (where baths may be no more than a pool in a riverbed blocked off with stones, or a tidal basin beside crashing waves) *konyoku* is more common.

Outdoor onsen pools are called *rotemburo* (or *notemburo*). Facilities can be publicly run or attached to a ryokan (traditional Japanese inn) or *minshuku* (Japanese guesthouse).

Onsen Locations

You don't have to travel far outside Tokyo (or leave the city limits at all) to discover onsen. The best have a rustic charm that adds multiple layers to the experience: picture yourself sitting in a *rotemburo* on a snow-flecked riverside or watching the autumn leaves fall. With express train and bus services, it's possible to get there and back in a day, though staying in an *onsen ryokan* (traditional inn with its own baths) is certainly a treat. In addition to having longer use of the baths, a stay typically includes a multicourse dinner of seasonal delicacies and a traditional breakfast.

Many *onsen ryokan* open their baths to day trippers in the afternoon; ask the tourist-information centre where there are places offering *higaeri-onsen* (bathing without accommodation).

In Print

The Japanese Spa: A Guide to Japan's Finest Ryokan and Onsen (Akihiko Seki and Elizabeth Heilman Brooke; 2005)

A Guide to Japanese Hot Springs (Anne Hotta with Yoko Ishiguro; 1986)

Tokyo

Deep beneath the concrete tangle that is Tokyo, there is pure hot-spring water. In the city centre, Spa LaQua (p146) has several floors of upmarket baths. Ōedo Onsen Monogatari (p180), in Odaiba, bills itself as an onsen 'theme park' and includes a re-creation of an old-Edo downtown, along with multiple indoor and outdoor tubs.

Onsen water is also pumped into Jakotsu-yu (p175) in Asakusa, Rokuryu Kōsen (p163) in Ueno, and the century-old **Take-no-Yu** (竹の湯; ☎03-3453-1446; http://homepage3.nifty.com/takenoyu; 1-15-12 Minami-Azabu, Minato-ku; adult/student ¥480/180; ⏰3.30-11.30pm Tue-Thu, Sat & Sun; Ⓢ Namboku line to Azabu-Jūban, exit 1) in Azabu-Jūban, where the bathwater is a mineral-rich, dark-tea colour.

Further afield **Niwa-no-Yu** (庭の湯; ☎03-3990-4126; www.niwanoyu.jp; 3-25-1 Koyama, Nerima-ku; ¥2250, after 6pm ¥1260; ⏰10am-11pm; Ⓢ Seibu Toshima or Ōedo lines to Toshimaen) is a large onsen complex next to the Toshimaen amusement park, 14 minutes west of Ikebukero by direct train. As well as separate male and female bathing areas, there's a swimsuit zone with a big central pool and saunas, where friends and families can hang out together. Hot tubs in landscaped gardens also add to the appeal.

For a truly rustic onsen experience, take a train to the western edge of Tokyo to find **Moegi-no-Yu** (もえぎの湯; www.okutamas.co.jp; 119-1 Hikawa, Okutama, Nishitama-gun; adult/child ¥780/410; ⏰9.30am-8pm Tue-Sun Apr-Jun, Oct & Nov, to 9.30pm Jul-Sep, to 7pm Dec-Mar; 🚆 JR Ome line to Okutama); this is a good spot to relax after a day hiking in the Okutama region and includes *rotemburo* and foot baths. It's a 10-minute walk from Okutama Station.

Hakone

Just under two hours southwest of the city is Tokyo's favorite onsen getaway, Hakone (p186), a centuries-old resort town with several distinct hot springs set among forested peaks. Top public facilities include Hakone Yuryō, Tenzan Tōji-kyō and Yunessun.

Chūzen-ji Onsen & Yumoto Onsen

Onsen are a feature of this beautiful lakeland area 11.5km west of the old pilgrim town of Nikkō, itself around two hours northeast of Tokyo. At the **Nikkō Lakeside Hotel** (日光レークサイドホテル; ☎0288-55-0321; www.tobuhotel.co.jp/nikkolake; 2482 Chūgūshi; s/d from ¥16,500/25,000; ❄📶), in Chūzen-ji Onsen, the wooden bathhouse with milky sulphuric water is open to day trippers (¥1000, 12.30pm to 5pm).

From Chūzen-ji, you can continue on to the quieter hot-springs resort of Yumoto Onsen by bus (¥890, 30 minutes) or by a three-hour hike across picturesque marshland on the **Senjōgahara Shizen-kenkyū-rō** (戦場ヶ原自然研究路; Senjō Plain Nature Trail). For the latter option, take a Yumoto-bound bus and get off at Ryūzu-no-taki (竜頭ノ滝), a waterfall that marks the start of the trail.

In Yumoto Onsen, towards the back of the town, the hot-spring temple **Onsen-ji** (温泉時; adult/child ¥500/300; ⏰9am-4pm) has a humble bathhouse and a tatami lounge for resting weary muscles.

Buses leave twice an hour from both JR Nikkō Station and Tōbu Nikkō Station for Chūzen-ji Onsen (¥1150, 45 minutes) and Yumoto Onsen (¥1700, 1½ hours).

Onsen and *sentō* often refuse entry to people with tattoos because of their association with the *yakuza* (Japanese mafia). If your tattoo is small, you might get away with covering it with medical tape. Otherwise, ask to book a private onsen bath – *onsen ryokan* and *minshuku* often have these.

Sentō

As little as 50 years ago, many private homes in Japan did not have baths, so every evening people headed off to the local neighbourhood *sentō*. More than just a place to wash oneself, the *sentō* served as a kind of community meeting hall, where news and gossip were traded and social ties strengthened.

In 1968, at the peak of their popularity, Tokyo had 2687 *sentō;* now there are around 1000. Some look as though they haven't changed in decades. Others have evolved with the times, adding saunas, jet baths, *denki-buro* (literally an 'electric bath' that's spiked with an electric current; it feels as unsettling as it sounds) and coin laundries.

A soak in a *sentō* is not just a cultural experience, but also an ideal way to recover from a day of sightseeing. Bathhouses can be identified by their distinctive *noren* (half-length curtains over the doorway), which usually bear the hiragana (ゆ; yu) for hot water (occasionally, it may be written in kanji: 湯).

Admission to a *sentō* rarely costs more than ¥500. If you've forgotten any of your toiletries or a towel, you can buy them here for a small price; most open from around 3pm to midnight. Asakusa is particularly good for ambient old-fashioned soaks.

Sentō you can check out are Jakotsu-yu (p175) in Asakusa, Rokuryu Kōsen (p163) near Nezu, and Komparu-yu (p66) in Ginza.

Bathing Etiquette

Bathing isn't just a pastime, it's a ritual – one so embedded in Japanese culture that everyone knows exactly what to do. This can be intimidating to the novice, but really all you need to know to avoid causing alarm is to wash yourself before getting into the bath. It's also a good

Interior of a *sentō* (p239)

idea to memorise the characters for men (男) and women (女), which will be marked on the *noren* hanging in front of the respective baths.

Upon entering an onsen or *sentō,* the first thing you'll encounter is a row of lockers for your shoes. After you pay your admission and head to the correct changing room, you'll find either more lockers or baskets for your clothes. Take everything off here, entering the bathing room with only the small towel.

That little towel performs a variety of functions: you can use it to wash (but make sure to give it a good rinse afterwards) or to cover yourself as you walk around. It is not supposed to touch the water though, so leave it on the side of the bath or – as the locals do – folded on top of your head.

Park yourself on a stool in front of one of the taps and give yourself a thorough wash. Make sure you rinse off all the suds. When you're done, it's polite to rinse off the stool for the next person. At more humble bathhouses you might have little more than a ladle to work with; in that case, crouch low and use it to scoop out water from the bath and pour over your body – taking care not to splash water into the tub – and scrub a bit with the towel.

In the baths, keep splashing to a minimum and your head above the water. Before heading back to the changing room, wipe yourself down with the towel to avoid dripping on the floor.

Online

Sento Guide (www.sentoguide.info) Best English-language resource about bathhouses across Japan.

1010 (www.1010.or.jp/index.php) A searchable database of sentō in Tokyo.

Survival Guide

Transport

ARRIVING IN TOKYO

Most travellers arrive in Tokyo by air. Narita International Airport has long been the primary gateway, but Haneda Airport, with its new international terminal, now sees more and more long-haul flights. Both airports require train or bus rides to get to the capital's downtown area.

Trans-Pacific flights take at least nine hours from North America's west coast, or 12 to 13 hours from the east coast. From Australia, it's a nine- to 10-hour journey. Flights from western Europe can take 12 hours to Tokyo.

Note that non-Japanese visitors are fingerprinted and photographed on arrival. A neat appearance will speed your passage through passport control and customs.

From elsewhere in Japan, Tokyo can be reached by *shinkansen* (bullet train) and by air (often cheaper and faster than the train); all domestic flights go to Haneda Airport.

Flights, tours and rail tickets can be booked online at lonelyplanet.com/bookings.

Narita Airport

The excellent, modern **Narita Airport** (NRT; 成田空港; ☎0476-34-8000; www.narita-airport.jp) is inconveniently located 66km east of Tokyo, in neighbouring Chiba Prefecture. It's divided into two terminals, which are connected by a free shuttle-bus service. The airport website lists which airlines use which terminal. There are **Tourist Information Centres** (1st fl, terminals 1 & 2; ⏲8am-10pm) in both terminals.

Rail

Both Japan Railways (JR) and the independent Keisei line connect Narita Airport and central Tokyo.

Keisei Skyliner (京成スカイライナー; www.keisei.co.jp/keisei/tetudou/skyliner/us) The quickest service into Tokyo runs nonstop to Nippori (¥2470, 36 minutes) and Ueno (¥2470, 41 minutes) Stations, where you can connect to the JR Yamanote line or the subway (Ueno Station only). Trains run twice an hour, 8am to 10pm. Foreign nationals can purchase tickets in advance online for slightly less (¥2200). The Skyliner & Tokyo Subway Ticket, which combines a one-way ticket on the Skyliner and a one-, two- or three-day subway pass, is a good deal.

Keisei Main Line (京成本線) *Kaisoku kyūkō* (limited express; ¥1030, 71 minutes to Ueno) trains follow the same route as the Skyliner but make stops. This is a good budget option. Trains run every 20 minutes during peak hours.

Narita Express (N'EX; 成田エクスプレス; www.jreast.co.jp/e/nex) A swift and smooth option, especially if you're staying on the west side of the city, N'EX trains depart Narita approximately every half-hour between 7am and 10pm for Tokyo Station (¥3020, 53 minutes). They also run less frequently into Shinagawa (¥3110, 65 minutes), Shibuya (¥3110, 73 minutes), Shinjuku (¥3190, 80 minutes) and Ikebukuro (¥3190, 86 minutes). Foreign tourists can purchase return N'EX tickets for ¥4000 (valid for 14 days), a

BAGGAGE SHIPMENT

Baggage couriers provide next-day delivery of your large luggage from Narita and Haneda Airports to any address in Tokyo (around ¥2000 per large bag) or beyond, so you don't have to haul it on the trains. Look for kiosks in the arrival terminals. If you plan on taking advantage of this service, make sure to put the essentials you'll need for the next 24 hours in a small bag.

CLIMATE CHANGE & TRAVEL

Every form of transport that relies on carbon-based fuel generates CO_2, the main cause of human-induced climate change. Modern travel is dependent on aeroplanes, which might use less fuel per kilometre per person than most cars but travel much greater distances. The altitude at which aircraft emit gases (including CO_2) and particles also contributes to their climate change impact. Many websites offer 'carbon calculators' that allow people to estimate the carbon emissions generated by their journey and, for those who wish to do so, to offset the impact of the greenhouse gases emitted with contributions to portfolios of climate-friendly initiatives throughout the world. Lonely Planet offsets the carbon footprint of all staff and author travel.

discount of more than 30% off the standard return fare. Check online or enquire at the JR East Travel Service centres at Narita Airport for the latest deals. Long-haul JR passes are valid on N'EX trains, but you must obtain a seat reservation (no extra charge) from a JR ticket office (see p245).

Bus

Friendly Airport Limousine (☎3665-7220; www.limousinebus.co.jp/en; 1-way fare ¥3150) Operates scheduled, direct, all-reserved buses between Narita Airport and major hotels and train stations in Tokyo. The journey takes 1½ to two hours depending on traffic. At the time of research, discount round-trip 'Welcome to Tokyo Limousine Bus Return Voucher' tickets (¥4500) were available for foreign tourists; ask at the ticket counter at the airport.

Access Narita (アクセス成田; Map p276; ☎0120-600-366; www.accessnarita.jp) Discount buses connect Narita Airport to Tokyo Station and Ginza (¥1000, one to 1¼ hours). There's no ticket counter at the airport, just go directly to bus stop 31 at Terminal 1 or stops 2 or 19 at Terminal 2. You can reserve tickets online (a safer bet for trips to the airport), but unfortunately only in Japanese.

Taxi

This will set you back approximately ¥30,000 and, battling traffic all the way, will usually take longer than the train.

Haneda Airport

Closer to central Tokyo, **Haneda Airport** (HND; 羽田空港; ☎ international terminal 6428-0888; www.tokyo-airport-bldg.co.jp/en) has two domestic terminals and one international terminal, which opened in 2010. Originally, international flights into Haneda only arrived at awkward night-time hours; however, in March 2014, daytime arrivals were added. Still, there's a chance that you might arrive between midnight and 5am, during which time trains, buses and the monorail to central Tokyo will not be running.

Keep in mind the price of a taxi (or the hours spent camped at the airport) when you book your ticket.

There's a **Tourist Information Centre** (2nd fl Arrival Lobby; ⏲5.30am-1am) inside the international terminal.

Monorail

Tokyo Monorail (東京モノレール; www.tokyo-monorail.co.jp/english) Leaving approximately every 10 minutes (5am to midnight) for Hamamatsuchō Station (¥490, 15 minutes), which is a stop on the JR Yamanote line.

Rail

Keikyū (☎5789-8686; www.haneda-tokyo-access.com/en) Airport *kyūkō* trains depart several times an hour (5.30am to midnight) for Shinagawa (¥410, 12 minutes) on the JR Yamanote line. From Shinagawa, some trains continue along the Asakusa subway line, which serves Higashi-Ginza, Nihombashi and Asakusa Stations.

Bus

Friendly Airport Limousine (www.limousinebus.co.jp/en) Coaches connect Haneda with major hubs such as Shibuya (¥1030), Shinjuku (¥1230), Roppongi (¥1130) and Ginza (¥930); fares double after midnight. Travel times vary wildly, taking anywhere from 30 to 90 minutes depending on traffic.

Haneda Airport Express (http://hnd-bus.com) Though more useful for suburban destinations than downtown ones, coaches do travel to handy places such as Shibuya Station (¥1030) and Tokyo Station (¥930) in about an hour, depending on traffic.

Taxi

Taxis cost between ¥4000 and ¥10,000, depending on the destination. To central Tokyo will set you back around ¥7000.

GETTING AROUND TOKYO

Hyperefficient, sparkling clean and virtually crime free, Tokyo's public transport system is the envy of the world. Of most use to travellers is the train and subway system, which is easy to navigate thanks to English signage. Make sure to get a Suica or Pasmo card, which makes transferring between the two a breeze. The only downside is that the whole system shuts down between midnight and 5am, when the city's fleet of taxis picks up the slack.

Train & Subway

Tokyo's rail network includes JR lines, an extensive subway system and private commuter lines that depart in every direction for the suburbs, like spokes on a wheel. Trains arrive and depart precisely on time, and even a minute's delay elicits apologies from conductors. Major transit hubs include Tokyo, Shinagawa, Shibuya, Shinjuku, Ikebukuro and Ueno.

Japan Railways (JR)

The JR network covers the whole country and includes the *shinkansen*. In Tokyo, the above-ground Yamanote and the Chūō and Sōbu lines are the most useful. Tickets start at ¥133 and go up depending on how far you travel.

Yamanote line The most important train line in Tokyo, both in usefulness and cultural significance, the Yamanote line makes a 35km loop around central Tokyo. Stops include many sightseeing destinations, such as Shibuya, Harajuku, Shinjuku, Tokyo and Ueno. JR Yamanote–line trains are silver with a green stripe.

Chūō & Sōbu lines The JR Chūō line cuts through the city centre, from Tokyo Station through Shinjuku to points west as far as Takao; trains on this line are coloured orange. The Sōbu line is contiguous with the Chūō line between Mitaka in the west and Ochanomizu in the city centre, though it makes more stops; after Ochanomizu it heads towards the eastern suburbs passing through Ryōgoku and Akihabara on the way. Sōbu-line cars have a yellow stripe.

Subway

Tokyo has 13 subway lines, nine of which are operated by **Tokyo Metro** (www.tokyometro.jp/en) and four by **Toei** (www.kotsu.metro.tokyo.jp/eng). The lines are colour-coded, making navigation fairly simple.

Unfortunately a transfer ticket is required to change between the two; a Pasmo or Suica card makes this process seamless, but either way a journey involving multiple lines (including JR) comes out costing more. Rides on Tokyo Metro cost ¥165 to ¥237 and on Toei ¥174 to ¥267, depending on how far you travel.

Private Commuter Lines

Private commuter lines service some of the hipper residential neighbourhoods. Trains you may find yourself riding include the Odakyū line (from Shinjuku for Shimo-Kitazawa) and the Tōkyū-Tōyoko line (from Shibuya for Daikanyama and Naka-Meguro). Note that the commuter lines run *tokkyū* (特急; limited-express services), *kyūkō* (急行; ordinary express) and *futsū* (普通; local) trains – make sure you get the right one.

Tickets

➡ If you stubbornly refuse to buy a train pass, you can still purchase paper tickets from vending machines near the ticket gates. If the machine has a touch screen, there will be an option to switch the language to English.

➡ Fare charts are listed above the machines. If you can't work out how much to pay, one easy trick is to buy the lowest price possible and then use one of the 'fare adjustment' machines near

SUICA & PASMO

Getting a prepaid train pass – the interchangeable Suica and Pasmo – is highly recommended, even for a short trip. With this card, fitted with an electromagnetic chip, you'll be able to breeze through the ticket gates of any train or subway station in the city without having to work out fares or transfer tickets. Fares for pass users are slightly less (a couple of yen per journey) than for paper-ticket holders.

Suica and Pasmo also work on buses and can be used to pay for things in some convenience stores, station kiosks and vending machines. To use it, simply wave it over the card reader; you will need to do this to enter and exit the station.

Both Suica and Pasmo cards can be purchased from ticket vending machines in most train and subway stations (Suica from JR line machines and Pasmo from subway and commuter-line machines). There is a minimum charge of ¥1000 plus a deposit of ¥500, refundable if you return your card at a train-station window. You can charge the cards, in increments of ¥1000, at the same vending machines.

DISCOUNT PASSES

City Passes

The following are really only worth it if you plan to hit many neighbourhoods in one day. If you're coming through Narita, a better deal is the **Skyliner & Tokyo Subway Ticket** (¥2800 to ¥3500; see www.keisei.co.jp/keisei/tetudou/skyliner/us/value_ticket/subway.html).

Tokyo Metro One-Day Open Ticket Unlimited rides on Tokyo Metro subway lines only. Purchase at Tokyo Metro stations. It costs ¥710/360 per adult/child.

Common One-Day Ticket for Tokyo Metro & Toei Subway Lines Valid on all 13 lines operating underground in Tokyo. Purchase at Tokyo Metro or Toei stations. It costs ¥1000/500 per adult/child.

Tokyo Combination Ticket Unlimited same-day rides on Tokyo Metro, Toei and JR lines operating in Tokyo. Purchase at stations serviced by any of these lines. It costs ¥1590/800 per adult/child.

Long-Haul Passes

The following passes are fantastic if you plan to travel outside Tokyo; however, they are only available for foreign-passport holders on a tourist visa. The latter two options can be purchased at JR East Travel Service Centers in either airport or at Tokyo Station.

Japan Rail Pass (www.japanrailpass.net) Covers travel on JR trains throughout the nation. A seven-day pass costs ¥29,110 and must be purchased *before* arriving in Japan; 14-day and 21-day passes are also available.

JR East Pass (www.jreast.co.jp/e/eastpass) For unlimited travel on JR trains in eastern Honshū and into the Japan Alps. Costs start at ¥22,000 for either five consecutive days or four days of your choosing within a 30-day period.

JR Kantō Area Pass (www.jreast.co.jp/e/kantoareapass) Three consecutive days of unlimited rides on all Kanto-area JR East lines, including limited-express trains and *shinkansen* (bullet trains; but not the Tōkaidō *shinkansen*) for ¥8300. This is good for travellers wanting to visit the Nikkō and Mt Fuji areas.

the exit gates to settle the difference at the end of your journey.

➡ You'll need a valid ticket to exit the station, so make sure to pick it up when it pops out of the entry gates.

JR TICKET COUNTERS

Larger JR stations have service counters called *midori-no-madoguchi* (緑の窓口; green window, aka JR Ticket Counters). Here you can buy *shinkansen* tickets, make reservations and buy special passes. Credit cards are usually accepted.

Female Carriages

Tokyo's train system is remarkably crime free, but groping male hands have long been a problem for women when trains are packed. Tokyo train lines now reserve women-only carriages at peak times. The carriages are marked with signs (usually pink) in Japanese and English.

Priority Seats

Seats at the end of every train car are set aside as 'priority seats' for elderly, handicapped or pregnant passengers, though Tokyoites largely ignore this. If you think you have greater claims to a priority seat, a gentle *sumimasen* (excuse me) should do the trick.

Stations

Navigating your way around train stations in Tokyo can be confusing, particularly at complex stations such as Shinjuku. Most stations have adequate English signposting, with large yellow signs on the platforms posting exit numbers. Street maps of the area are usually posted near each exit.

EXITS

Since each station will usually have several different exits, you should get your bearings and decide where to exit while still on the platform. When possible, find out which exit to use when you get directions to a destination. If you have your destination written down, you can go to an attended gate and ask the station attendant to direct you to the correct exit.

LOCKERS & TOILETS

Most stations have luggage lockers, which can hold medium-sized bags. These lockers often come in several sizes and cost from ¥200 to ¥600. Storage is good for 24 hours, after which your bags will be removed and taken to the station office.

TRAIN TIPS

➡ Figure out the best route to your destination with the app **Navitime for Japan Travel** (www.navitime.co.jp); you can download routes to be used offline, too.

➡ Avoid rush hour (around 8am to 9.30am and 5pm to 8pm), when 'packed in like sardines' is an understatement. The last train of the night is also usually packed – with drunk people.

➡ When the platform is crowded, Tokyoites will form neat lines on either side of where the doors will be when the train pulls up. Once you're on the train though, all's fair when it comes to grabbing a seat.

➡ It's considered bad form to eat or drink on the train (long-distance trains are an exception). Talking on the phone or having a loud conversation is also frowned upon.

➡ Stand to the left on the escalators.

All train stations have toilets, almost all of which are free of charge. Bring pocket tissues, though, as toilet paper is not always provided. It's also a good idea to pick up a handkerchief at a ¥100 shop.

LOST & FOUND

Larger stations have dedicated lost-and-found windows (labelled in English); otherwise, lost items are left with the station attendant.

JR East Infoline (☎ in English 050-2016-1603; ⏲10am-6pm)

Tokyo Metro Lost & Found (☎3834-5577; www.tokyometro.jp/en/support/lost/index.html; ⏲9am-8pm)

Toei Transportation Lost & Found (☎3816-5700; ⏲9am-8pm)

Bus

Tokyo has an extensive bus network, operated by **Toei** (www.kotsu.metro.tokyo.jp/eng/services/bus.html), though in most cases it's easier to get around by subway.

➡ Fares are ¥210/110 per adult/child; there are no transfer tickets. Deposit your fare into the box as you enter the bus; there's a change machine at the front of the bus that accepts ¥1000 notes.

➡ Most buses have digital signage that switches between Japanese and English. A recording announces the name of each stop as it is reached, so listen carefully and press the button next to your seat when your stop is announced.

Boat

Tokyo Cruise (水上バス; Suijō Bus; ☎0120-977-311; http://suijobus.co.jp) Tokyo Cruise water buses run up and down the Sumida-gawa (Sumida River), roughly twice an hour between 10am and 6pm, connecting Asakusa with Hama-rikyū Onshi-teien (¥740, 35 minutes) and Odaiba (¥1560, 50 minutes). Tickets can be purchased before departure at any pier.

Tokyo Mizube Cruising Line (東京水辺ライン; ☎5608-8869; www.tokyo-park.or.jp/waterbus) Water buses head down the Sumida-gawa from Asakusa to Ryōgoku (¥310), Hama-rikyū Onshi-teien (¥620) and Odaiba (¥1130), and then back up again. Schedules are seasonal, and infrequent in winter. Tickets don't have to be reserved in advance but can be purchased just before departure.

Taxi

Taxis in Tokyo feature white-gloved drivers, seats covered with lace doilies and doors that magically open and close – an experience in itself. They rarely make economic sense though, unless you have a group of four.

➡ Fares start at ¥730 for the first 2km, then rise by ¥90 for every 280m. You also click up about ¥90 every two minutes while you relax in traffic jams.

➡ Between 10pm and 5am fares can rise by as much as 20%.

➡ Train stations and hotels usually have taxi stands where you are expected to queue. In the absence of a stand, you can hail a cab from the street.

➡ A red light means the taxi is free and a green light means it's taken.

➡ Drivers rarely speak any English, though fortunately most taxis now have navigation systems. It's a good idea to have your destination written down in Japanese, or better yet, a business card with an address.

Bicycle

Tokyo is by no means a bicycle-friendly city. Bike lanes are almost nonexistent and you'll see no-parking signs for bicycles everywhere (ignore these at your peril: your bike could get impounded, requiring a half-day excursion to the pound and a ¥3000 fee). Still, you'll see people cycling everywhere and it can be a really fun way to get around the city.

Some hostels and ryokan have bikes to lend. The Rentabike website (http://rentabike.jp) lists places around town that rent bicycles.

Cogi Cogi (☎5459-7330; http://cogicogi.jp/index_en.asp; per day ¥1500; ⏰10am-7pm) This bike-sharing system has ports around the city. There are instructions in English, but it's a little complicated to use and requires you to sign up in advance online.

Car & Motorcycle

Considering the traffic, the confusing roads and the ridiculous cost of parking, the only reason you'd want a car in Tokyo is to get out of the city.

You will need an International Driving Permit, which must be arranged in your own country before you go. It's also wise to get a copy of *Rules of the Road* (¥1000), available from the **Japan Automobile Federation** (☎0570-00-8139; www.jaf.or.jp/e/index.htm; 2-2-17 Shiba, Minato-ku; ⏰9am-5.30pm Mon-Fri; Ⓢ Mita line to Shibakōen, exit A1).

Expect to pay ¥8000 per day for a smallish rental car.

Nippon Rent-a-Car (Map p276; ☎English service desk 3485-7196; www.nipponrentacar.co.jp/english; ⏰9am-5pm Mon-Fri)

Toyota Rent-a-Car (Map p276; ☎5954-8020, toll-free in Japan 0800-7000-815; https://rent.toyota.co.jp/en)

TOURS

Bus

Gray Line (☎3595-5948; www.jgl.co.jp/inbound/index.htm; per person ¥4000-9700) Offers half-day and full-day tours with stops, covering key downtown sights, as well as tours to Hakone. Pick-up service from major hotels is available, otherwise most tours leave from in front of the Dai-Ichi Hotel in Shimbashi.

Hato Bus Tours (☎3435-6081; www.hatobus.com; per person ¥1500-12,000; Ⓡ JR Yamanote line to Hamamatsuchō, south exit) Tokyo's most well-known bus-tour company offers hour-long, half-day and full-day bus tours of the city. Shorter tours cruise by the sights in an open-air double-decker bus; longer ones make stops. Tours leave from the Hato Bus Terminal in Hamamatsuchō.

SkyBus (Map p276; ☎3215-0008; www.skybus.jp; 2-5-2 Marunouchi, Chiyoda-ku; tours adult/child from ¥1600/700, Sky Hop Bus adult/child ¥2500/1200; ⏰ticket office 9am-6pm; Ⓡ JR Yamanote line to Tokyo, Marunouchi south exit) Open-top double-decker buses cruise through different neighbourhoods of the city (for roughly 50 to 80 minutes); most have English-language audio guidance aboard.

Walking

Haunted Tokyo Tours (www.hauntedtokyotours.com; per person from ¥3000) Fun and friendly English-speaking guides take amblers to the scenes of some of the city's most notorious ghost haunts and urban legends. You'll never look at Tokyo the same way again.

Tokyo Metropolitan Government Tours (www.gotokyo.org/en/tourists/guideservice/guideservice/index.html) The Tokyo government tourism bureau can arrange free or fairly cheap walking tours in one of seven different languages with volunteer guides. There are several routes to choose from, each lasting about three hours.

Tokyo SGG Club (www2.ocn.ne.jp/~sgg) Free guided tours of Asakusa (11am to 1.15pm Saturday and Sunday) and Ueno (10.30am to 1.30pm Wednesday and Friday) on a first-come, first-served basis.

True Japan Tours (http://truejapantours.com; per person from ¥4000) Walking tours and cultural experiences (such as learning to wear kimono) with certified, bilingual tour guides.

NAVIGATING TOKYO STREETS

Tokyo is difficult to navigate even for locals. Only the biggest streets have names, and they don't figure into addresses; instead, addresses are derived from districts, blocks and building numbers.

Like most Japanese cities, Tokyo is divided first into *ku* (wards; Tokyo has 23 of them), which in turn are divided into *chō* or *machi* (towns) and then into numbered *chōme* (pronounced cho-may), areas of just a few blocks. Subsequent numbers in an address refer to blocks within the *chōme* and buildings within each block.

It's near impossible to find your destination using the address alone. Smartphones with navigation apps have been a real boon – reason enough to rent a mobile internet device. Many restaurants and venues have useful maps on their websites.

If you truly do get lost, police officers at *kōban* (police boxes) have maps and are always happy to help with directions (though few speak English). At the very least, you should be able to get back to the nearest train station and try again.

Directory A–Z

Discount Cards

Grutt Pass (www.rekibun.or.jp/grutto; pass ¥2000) gives you free or discounted admission to some 70 attractions around town. If you plan on visiting more than a few museums, it's excellent value. All major museums sell them.

Electricity

The Japanese electricity supply is an unusual 100V AC. Appliances with a two-pin plug made for use in North America will work without an adaptor, but may be a bit sluggish.

Emergency

Although most emergency operators don't speak English, they'll immediately refer you to someone who does.

Ambulance (救急車; Kyūkyūsha; ☎119)

Emergency Interpretation (☎emergency translation 5285-8185, medical info 5285-8181; www.himawari.metro.tokyo.jp/qq/qq13enmnlt.asp; ⏲medical info 9am-8pm, emergency translation 5-8pm Mon-Fri, 9am-8pm Sat & Sun) In English, Chinese, Korean, Thai and Spanish.

Fire (消防署; Shōbōsho; ☎119)

Police (警視庁; Keishichō; ☎emergency 110, general 3501-0110; www.keishicho.metro.tokyo.jp) Twenty-four-hour staffed *kōban* (police boxes) are located near most major train stations.

Gay & Lesbian Travellers

Gay and lesbian travellers are unlikely to encounter problems in Tokyo. There are no legal restraints on same-sex sexual activities in Japan apart from the usual age restrictions. Some travellers have reported being turned away or grossly overcharged when checking into love hotels with a partner of the same sex. Otherwise, discrimination is unusual. One note: Japanese of any orientation do not typically engage in public displays of affection.

Tokyo has a small but very lively gay quarter, Shinjuku-nichōme. However, outside this and a handful of other places, the gay scene is all but invisible. Tokyo is tolerant, but it is no Sydney. For more advice on travelling in Tokyo, have a look at **Utopia Asia** (www.utopia-asia.com).

Health

Tokyo enjoys an excellent standard of public hygiene and health (stress-related ailments notwithstanding).

Insurance

The only insurance accepted at Japanese hospitals is Japanese insurance; however, hospitals are legally required to treat you even without this insurance; if you run into trouble, call Japan Helpline. You'll have to pay for the treatment in full and apply for a reimbursement when you get home. Note that smaller clinics often don't accept credit cards. Expect to pay about ¥3000 for a simple visit to an outpatient clinic and from around ¥20,000 and upwards for emergency care.

Medications

Pharmacies in Japan do not carry foreign medications, so it's a good idea to bring your own. In a pinch, reasonable substitutes can be found, but the dosage may be less than what you're used to.

Many commonly prescribed drugs, such as codeine and the ADHD medication Adderall, are actually controlled substances in Japan. Technically you need to prepare a '*yakkan shōmei*' – an import certificate for pharmaceuticals – to bring these in with you, even just for personal use. See the Ministry of Health, Labour and Welfare's website (www.mhlw.go.jp/english/policy/health-medical/pharmaceuticals/01.html) for more details about which medications are classified and how to prepare the form.

NEED HELP?

Japan Helpline (☎0570-000-911; www.jhelp.com/en/jhlp.html; ⏰24hr) English-speaking operators can help you negotiate tricky situations – such as dealing with a police station – or simpler ones, like recovering a bag you left on the subway. If you don't have access to mobile service, use the contact form on its webpage; staff will get back to you right away.

Tokyo Foreign Residents Advisory Center (☎5320-7744; www.metro.tokyo.jp/english/resident/livingin/cont7-01.htm; ⏰9.30am-noon & 1-5pm Mon-Fri) This municipal-run helpline has English-speaking operators who can answer questions on daily life, social customs and other concerns.

Internet Access

Most accommodation in Tokyo has, at the very least, complimentary wi-fi in the lobby.

Having internet in your pocket can be a great help for navigating the city. SIM cards for internet devices and unlocked smartphones are increasingly available. **B-Mobile** (www.bmobile.ne.jp/english) sells prepaid data-only SIM cards online and will ship them to your accommodation or the airport post office.

It is also possible to rent pocket wi-fi devices from **Rentafone Japan** (☎from overseas 81-75-212-0842, toll free within Japan 0120-746-487; www.rentafonejapan.com).

Computers

Ubiquitous *manga kissa* (cafes for reading manga) double as internet cafes.

FedEx Kinko's (フェデックスキンコーズ; per 20min ¥250) Outposts all over central Tokyo (including branches in Shinjuku and Shibuya) have a few computer terminals each, as well as printing and photocopying services.

Terminal (Map p288; http://theterminal.jp/index.html; 3rd fl, 3-22-12 Jingūmae, Shibuya-ku; per 30min ¥325; ⏰24hr; 🚉JR Yamanote line to Harajuku, Takeshita exit) Tokyo's nicest internet cafe has big-screen Macs kitted out with Adobe software and good coffee.

Wi-Fi

Tokyo is not as rich in free wi-fi as you might expect, since most locals rely on their mobile-phone providers for access. A few useful services:

Japan Connected (www.ntt-bp.net/jcfw/en.html) Download this app and register ahead of time for free wi-fi service, courtesy of the national telecom provider NTT, and connect at any 7-Eleven convenience store, subway stations, Narita and Haneda Airports, Roppongi Hills and other locations.

Freespot Access Map (www.freespot.com/users/map_e.html) Map of wi-fi hotspots and instructions in English for tapping into them.

Starbucks (http://starbucks.wi2.co.jp) Sign up in advance for a Starbucks wireless account and connect at any of the 272 (yes, 272) Starbucks in Tokyo for free.

Legal Matters

Japanese police have extraordinary powers compared with their Western counterparts: they have the right to detain a suspect without charging them for up to three days, after which a prosecutor can decide to extend this period for another 20 days. Police also have the authority to choose whether to allow a suspect to phone their embassy or lawyer or not, although, if you do find yourself in police custody, you should insist that you will not cooperate in any way until allowed to make such a call. Your embassy is the first place you should call if given the chance.

Police will speak almost no English; insist that a *tsuyakusha* (interpreter) be summoned; police are legally bound to provide one before proceeding with any questioning. Even if you are able to speak Japanese, it is best to deny it and stay with your native language.

Medical Services

Tokyo enjoys a high level of medical services, though unfortunately, most hospitals

DENGUE FEVER

In summer 2014, Tokyo experienced its first outbreak of dengue fever in 70 years. Dengue fever is a mosquito-borne illness that, while rarely fatal, has no vaccine or cure; the only prevention is to wear mosquito repellant and avoid places where others have been infected. Symptoms include high fever, headaches and body aches (Dengue is also known as 'breakbone fever'); if you experience any of the above, seek medical treatment immediately.

The locus of the outbreak was Harajuku's Yoyogi-kōen, though pathogen-carrying mosquitoes were detected in other city parks too. These parks were closed for several months while pesticides were administered, but have since reopened. It's unclear yet whether dengue will become a regular presence. In the meantime, if you see barriers blocking the entrance to a park or signs with a picture of a mosquito, it's best to stay away.

and clinics do not have doctors and nurses who speak English. Even for those that do, getting through reception can still be challenging. Larger hospitals are your best bet. Most hospitals will accept walk-in patients in the mornings (usually 8am to 11am); be prepared to wait.

Clinics

Primary Care Tokyo (プライマリーケア東京; http://pctclinic.com; 3rd fl, 2-1-16 Kitazawa, Setagaya-ku; ⏲9am-12.30pm Mon-Sat, 2.30-6pm Mon-Fri; 🅁Keiō Inokashira line to Shimo-Kitazawa, south exit) Fluent-English-speaking, American-trained doctor who can address common concerns.

Tokyo Medical & Surgical Clinic (東京メディカルアンドサージカルクリニック; Map p280; ☎3436-3028; www.tmsc.jp; 3-4-30 Shiba-kōen, 2nd fl, Mori Bldg, 32, Minato-ku; ⏲8.30am-5pm Mon-Fri, to noon Sat; ⓈHibiya line to Kamiyachō, exit 1) Well-equipped clinic staffed with English-speaking Japanese and foreign physicians. Twenty-four-hour emergency consultation is also available.

Emergency Rooms

Seibo International Catholic Hospital (聖母病院; ☎3951-1111; www.seibokai.or.jp; 2-5-1 Nakaochiai, Shinjuku-ku; 🅁JR Yamanote line to Mejiro, main exit) Has English-speaking doctors.

St Luke's International Hospital (聖路加国際病院; Seiroka Kokusai Byōin; Map p278; ☎3541-5151; www.luke.or.jp; 9-1 Akashi-chō, Chūō-ku; ⓈHibiya line to Tsukiji, exits 3 & 4) Has English-speaking doctors.

Money

ATMs

Most Japanese bank ATMs do not accept foreign-issued cards. Even if they display Visa and MasterCard logos, most accept only Japan-issued versions of these cards. The following places have ATMs that routinely work with most cards (including Visa, MasterCard, American Express, Plus, Cirrus and Maestro; some MasterCard and Maestro with IC chips may not work). Be aware that many banks place a limit on the amount of cash you can withdraw in one day (often around US$300).

7-Eleven (セブン・イレブン; www.sevenbank.co.jp/english) The Seven Bank ATMs at 7-Eleven convenience stores have English instructions and are available 24 hours a day. Considering that 7-Eleven convenience stores are ubiquitous, this is the easiest option for getting quick cash.

Citibank (シティバンク; www.citibank.co.jp/en) The only bank with ATMs that accept cards from every country; its ATMs are 24-hour. Locations include Shinjuku, Shibuya, Aoyama, Roppongi and Ginza.

Japan Post Bank (ゆうちょ銀行; www.jp-bank.japanpost.jp/en/ias/en_ias_index.html) Post offices have Japan Post Bank ATMs with English instructions; opening hours vary depending on the size of the post office, but are usually longer than regular post-office hours.

Cash

More and more places in Tokyo accept credit cards but it's still a good idea to always keep at least several thousand yen on hand for local transport, inexpensive restaurants and shops (and even some moderately priced restaurants and shops).

The currency in Japan is the yen (¥), and banknotes and coins are easily distinguishable. There are ¥1, ¥5, ¥10, ¥50, ¥100 and ¥500 coins; and ¥1000, ¥2000, ¥5000 and ¥10,000 banknotes (the ¥2000 note is very rarely seen). The ¥1 coin is a lightweight aluminium coin; the bronze-coloured ¥5 and silver-coloured ¥50 coins both have a hole punched in the middle. Prices may be listed using the kanji for yen (円). Prices are usually in Arabic numerals, but occasionally they are in traditional kanji.

Changing Money

With a passport, you can change cash or travellers cheques at any Authorised Foreign Exchange Bank (signs are displayed in English), major post offices, some large hotels and most big department stores.

For currency other than US dollars, larger banks such as Sumitomo Mitsui (SMBC) and Tokyo-Mitsubishi UFJ (MUFG), are a better bet. They can usually change at least US, Canadian and Australian dollars, pounds sterling, euros and Swiss francs. Branches of these banks can be found near all major train stations.

MUFG also operates **World Currency Shop** (www.tokyo-card.co.jp/wcs/wcs-shop-e.php) foreign-exchange counters near major shopping centres. They will exchange a broader range of currencies, including Chinese yuan, Korean won and Taiwan, Hong Kong, Singapore and New Zealand dollars.

Note that you receive a better exchange rate when withdrawing cash from ATMs than when exchanging cash or travellers cheques in Tokyo.

Credit Cards

Businesses that do take credit cards will often display the logo for the cards they accept. Visa is the most widely accepted, followed by MasterCard, American Express and Diners Club. Foreign-issued cards should work fine. Citibank and Japan Post ATMs allow you to take out a cash advance on a foreign-issued credit card.

Tipping & Bargaining

It is not customary to tip, even in the most expensive restaurants and bars. Bargaining is not customary either, with the exception of outdoor markets. In high-end restaurants and hotels, a 10% service fee is added to the bill.

Opening Hours

Standard opening hours:

Banks 9am to 3pm (some to 5pm) Monday to Friday.

Bars Open around 5pm until the wee hours.

Museums Open at 9am or 10am and close at 5pm, with the last entry between 4pm and 4.30pm; often closed on Monday.

Post offices Local post offices generally open 9am to 5pm Monday to Friday.

Restaurants Lunch 11.30am to 2.30pm; dinner 6pm to 10pm; last orders taken about half an hour before closing.

Shops and supermarkets From 10am to 8pm daily.

Public Holidays

If a national holiday falls on a Monday, most museums and restaurants that normally close on Mondays will remain open and close the next day instead.

New Year's Day (Ganjitsu) 1 January

Coming-of-Age Day (Seijin-no-hi) Second Monday in January

National Foundation Day (Kenkoku Kinen-bi) 11 February

Spring Equinox (Shumbun-no-hi) 20 or 21 March

Shōwa Day (Shōwa-no-hi) 29 April

Constitution Day (Kempō Kinem-bi) 3 May

Green Day (Midori-no-hi) 4 May

Children's Day (Kodomo-no-hi) 5 May

Marine Day (Umi-no-hi) Third Monday in July

Mountain Day (Yama-no-hi) 11 August, starting in 2016

Respect-for-the-Aged Day (Keirō-no-hi) Third Monday in September

Autumn Equinox (Shūbun-no-hi) 23 or 24 September

Health & Sports Day (Taiiku-no-hi) Second Monday in October

Culture Day (Bunka-no-hi) 3 November

Labour Thanksgiving Day (Kinrō Kansha-no-hi) 23 November

Emperor's Birthday (Tennō-no-Tanjōbi) 23 December

Safe Travel

The biggest threat to travellers in Tokyo is the city's general aura of safety. It's wise to keep up the same level of caution and common sense that you would back home. Of special note are reports that drink-spiking continues to be a problem in Roppongi (resulting in robbery, extortion and, in extreme cases, physical assault). Be wary of following touts into bars there

UNOFFICIAL HOLIDAYS

During the New Year period, technically only New Year's Day is a holiday in Japan, but the traditional holiday period – called *Shōgatsu* – extends until at least 3 January (and often until 6 January). Expect most businesses to be closed and Tokyo to be very quiet.

Be aware that during the New Year period (29 December to 3 January), the string of national holidays called Golden Week (29 April to 5 May) and the O-Bon festival in mid-August, accommodation may be fully booked or pricier than usual as these are all major travel periods for Japanese.

and in Kabukichō. Women walking through Kabukichō and Dōgenzaka (both are red-light districts) risk being harrassed.

Taxes & Refunds

Japan's consumption tax is 8% and is set to rise to 10% by March 2017. However, the number of shops where you can purchase items tax free is also increasing; these are noted with a 'tax-free' sticker in English on the window. In order to qualify for tax-free shopping, you need to have your passport with you and spend a minimum of ¥10,000 in the store (¥5000 for consumables such as food and cosmetics; these must remain unopened until you leave the country). Since the tax is not charged at point of sale, there is no need to collect a refund when leaving the country; however, you will need to hand in a form affixed to your passport to customs officials when you depart.

Telephone

The country code for Japan is ☎81; Tokyo's area code is ☎03, although some outer suburbs have different area codes. Following the area code, 03 numbers consist of eight digits. The area code is not used if dialling within the same area code from a landline.

Mobile phones start with 090 or 080, plus an eight-digit number. Calls to mobile phones are significantly more expensive than local calls. When dialling Tokyo from abroad, to either a landline or a mobile, drop the first 0; rather, dial ☎81-3 or ☎81-90.

Toll-free numbers begin with 0120, 0070, 0077, 0088 and 0800. For local directory assistance, dial ☎104 (cost ¥105). For international directory assistance in English, dial ☎0057.

Mobile Phones

Japan operates on the 3-G network, so overseas phones with 3-G technology should work in Tokyo. The question of SIM cards is a tricky one in Tokyo. They are not generally available around the city, though kiosks at airports rent micro and nano SIMs that will work in unlocked iPhones or Android phones. Charges for the air time and data you use will be charged to your credit card.

If you want a phone primarily for data, a prepaid card, such as the one from **B-Mobile** (www.bmobile.ne.jp/english/index.html), is the safest choice.

If you want a phone mostly to make calls, it is more economical to rent a basic mobile phone. **Rentafone Japan** (☎from overseas 81-75-212-0842, toll free within Japan 0120-746-487; www.rentafonejapan.com) offers rentals for ¥3900 a week (plus ¥300 for each additional day) and domestic calls cost a reasonable ¥35 per minute.

Public Phones

Public phones do still exist and they work almost 100% of the time; look for them around train stations. Ordinary public phones are green; those that allow you to call abroad are grey and are usually marked 'International & Domestic Card/Coin Phone'.

Local calls cost ¥10 per minute; note that you won't get change on a ¥100 coin. The minimum charge for international calls is ¥100, which buys you a fraction of a minute – good for a quick check-in but not economical for much more. Dial ☎001 010 (KDDI), ☎0041 010 (SoftBank Telecom) or ☎0033 010 (NTT), followed by the country code, area code and local number.

There's very little difference in the rates from the different providers; all offer better rates at night. Reverse-charge (collect) international calls can be made from any pay phone by dialling ☎106.

If you are going to make a significant number of calls, it's worth purchasing a *terehon kādo* (telephone card). These stored-value cards are available from station kiosks and convenience stores in ¥1000 denominations and can be used in grey or green pay phones; phones display the remaining value of your card when it is inserted.

PRACTICALITIES

Newspapers & Magazines

- *Asahi Shimbun* (http://ajw.asahi.com)
- *Japan Times* (www.japantimes.co.jp/events)
- *Metropolis* (http://metropolisjapan.com)

Smoking

- Tokyo has a curious policy: smoking is banned in public spaces but allowed inside bars and restaurants (though nonsmoking bars and restaurants exist, too). Designated smoking areas are set up around train stations.

Weights & Measures

- The metric system is used.
- Some traditional Japanese measurements, especially for area (eg *jō* is the size of a tatami mat).

Phone cards with English instructions are readily available.

Time

Tokyo local time is nine hours ahead of Greenwich Mean Time (GMT). Japan does not observe daylight-saving time, so remember to subtract one hour when working out the time difference with a country using daylight-saving time.

JAPANESE YEARS

In addition to the typical Western calendar, Japan also counts years in terms of the reigns of its emperors – Meiji, Shōwa, et al. The current era is called Heisei (pronounced hay-say) after the ceremonial name bestowed on the current emperor, Akihito, by the Imperial Household Agency. He ascended to the throne in 1989 (Heisei 1); thus 2015 is Heisei 27, 2016 is Heisei 28, and so on.

Toilets

Toilets in Tokyo run the gamut from heated-seat thrones that wash and dry your most intimate areas at the touch of a button (these are called 'washlets') to humble, porcelain squat toilets in the floor.

When using squat toilets, the correct position is facing the hood, away from the door. If you just can't bear a squat toilet, look for the characters 洋式 (*yō-shiki*, Western style) on the stall door. Washrooms for people with a disability are always Western-style. The most common words for toilet in Japanese are トイレ (pronounced 'toire') and お手洗い ('o-tearai'); 女 (female) and 男 (male) will also come in handy.

Public toilets, typically clean, can be found in most train stations; convenience stores usually have toilets you can use too. Toilet paper is usually present, but it's still a good idea to accept those small packets of tissue handed out on the street, a common form of advertising, just in case. Paper towels and hand dryers are often lacking, so Japanese carry a handkerchief for use after washing their hands.

Separate toilet slippers are usually provided in homes and restaurants where you take off your shoes at the entrance; they are typically just inside the toilet door. These are for use in the toilet only, so remember to shuffle out of them when you leave.

Tourist Information

Tokyo has many excellent tourist-information centres (観光案内所; *kankō annaisho;* TICs) with English-speaking staff as well as pamphlets and maps in English. However, with the exception of the JR East Travel Service Center, they cannot make bookings. In addition to the TICs listed below, there are outposts in **Narita** (1st fl, terminals 1 & 2; ⌚8am-10pm) and **Haneda** (2nd fl Arrival Lobby; ⌚5.30am-1am) Airports.

Asakusa Culture Tourist Information Center (浅草文化観光センター; Map p291; ☎3842-5566; http://taitonavi.jp; 2-18-9 Kaminarimon, Taitō-ku; ⌚9am-8pm; Ⓢ Ginza line to Asakusa, exit 2) Run by Taitō-ku, this TIC has lots of info on Asakusa and Ueno, and a Pia ticket counter (for purchasing tickets to concerts and shows), near the entrance to Sensō-ji.

Japan Guide Association (☎3213-2706; www.jga21c.or.jp) Can put you in contact with licensed, professional tour guides.

JNTO Tourist Information Center (Map p276; ☎3201-3331; www.jnto.go.jp; 1st fl, Shin-Tokyo Bldg, 3-3-1 Marunouchi, Chiyoda-ku; ⌚9am-5pm; 🚆JR Yamanote line to Yūrakuchō, Tokyo International Forum exit) Run by the Japan National Tourism Organisation (JNTO), this TIC has information on Tokyo and beyond.

JR East Travel Service Center (JR東日本訪日旅行センター; Map p276; www.jreast.co.jp/e/customer_support/service_center_tokyo.html; Tokyo Station, 1-9-1 Marunouchi, Chiyoda-ku; ⌚7.30am-8.30pm; 🚆JR Yamanote line to Tokyo, Marunouchi north exit) Tourist information, luggage storage, money exchange, and bookings for ski and onsen (hot springs) getaways. There are branches in the two airports, too.

Moshi Moshi Information Space (もしもしインフォメーションスペース; Map p288; 3-23-5 Jingūmae, Shibuya-ku; 🚆JR Yamanote line to Harajuku, Omote-sandō exit) Ship your shopping home, get your nails done and pick up loads of local info at this somewhat unorthodox tourist-information centre run by a private organisation.

Tokyo Tourist Information Center (東京観光情報センター; Map p286; ☎5321-3077; www.gotokyo.org; 1st fl, Tokyo Metropolitan Government bldg 1, 2-8-1 Nishi-Shinjuku, Shinjuku-ku; ⌚9.30am-6.30pm; Ⓢ Ōedo line to Tochōmae, exit A4) Combine a trip to the observatories at the Tokyo Metropolitan Government Offices with a stop at the city's official TIC. There's another branch located right outside the ticket gates of the Keisei Ueno line (which services Narita Airport).

Travellers with Disabilities

Tokyo is making steps to improve universal access (called 'barrier free' here), though it is a slow process. Many new buildings in Tokyo have access ramps, and more and more subway stations have elevators.

For the blind, traffic lights have speakers playing melodies when it is safe to cross, train platforms have raised dots and lines to provide guidance and some ticket machines have Braille. Some attractions also offer free entry to travellers with disabilities and their companion. A fair number of hotels, from the higher end of midrange and above, offer a 'barrier-free' room or two. Still, Tokyo can be rather difficult for travellers with disabilities to negotiate, especially visitors in wheelchairs, who are often forced to make a choice between negotiating stairs or rerouting.

Accessible Japan (www.tesco-premium.co.jp/aj) Details the accessibility of hundreds of sites in Tokyo, including hotels, sights and department stores, as well as general information about getting around Japan. It's not updated regularly.

Japanese Red Cross Language Service Volunteers (www.tok-lanserv.jp/eng) Resources for travellers with disabilities. Click the *Accessible Tokyo* link on the site for good bilingual information on accommodation, activities, sights, shops etc.

Visas

Citizens of 66 countries, including Australia, Canada, Hong Kong, Korea, New Zealand, Singapore, USA, UK and almost all European nations will be automatically issued a *tanki-taizai* (temporary visitor visa) on arrival. Typically this visa is good for 90 days. For a complete list of visa-exempt countries, consult www.mofa.go.jp/j_info/visit/visa/short/novisa.html#list.

Citizens of Austria, Germany, Ireland, Lichtenstein, Mexico, Switzerland and the UK are able to extend this visa once, for another 90 days. To do so, you need to apply at the **Tokyo Regional Immigration Bureau** (東京入国管理局; Tokyo Nyūkoku Kanrikyoku; ☎5796-7111; www.immi-moj.go.jp/english/index.html; 5-5-30 Kōnan, Minato-ku; ⏲9am-noon & 1-4pm Mon-Fri; 🚌99 from Shinagawa Station, east exit to Tokyo Nyūkoku Kanrikyoku-mae, 🚆Rinkai line to Tennōzu Isle) before the initial visa expires.

Resident Cards

Anyone entering Japan on a visa for longer than the standard 90 days for tourists will be issued a resident card. It must be carried at all times as the police can stop you and ask to see the card. If you don't have it, you could be hauled off to the police station to wait until someone fetches it for you – providing you have one.

Work Visas

Arriving in Japan and looking for a job is quite a tough proposition these days, though people still do it and occasionally succeed in finding visa sponsorship. With that said, there are legal employment categories for foreigners that specify standards of experience and qualifications.

Once you find an employer in Japan who is willing to sponsor you, it is necessary to obtain a Certificate of Eligibility from your nearest Japanese immigration office. The same office can then issue your work visa, which is valid for either one or three years. This procedure can take two to three months.

Working-Holiday Visas

Citizens of Australia, Canada, Denmark, France, Germany, Ireland, Korea, New Zealand, Norway, the UK and residents of Hong Kong can apply for a working-holiday visa if they're between 18 and 30. The visa is designed to enable young people to travel extensively during their stay; thus, employment is supposed to be part-time or temporary. In practice, many people work full time. The working-holiday visa must be obtained from a Japanese embassy or consulate abroad. Visit www.mofa.go.jp/j_info/visit/w_holiday/programme.html#2.

Language

Japanese is spoken by more than 125 million people. While it bears some resemblance to Altaic languages such as Mongolian and Turkish and has grammatical similarities to Korean, its origins are unclear. Chinese is responsible for the existence of many Sino-Japanese words in Japanese, and for the originally Chinese kanji characters which the Japanese use in combination with the homegrown hiragana and katakana scripts.

Japanese pronunciation is easy to master for English speakers, as most of its sounds are also found in English. If you read our coloured pronunciation guides as if they were English, you'll be understood. In Japanese, it's important to make the distinction between short and long vowels, as vowel length can change the meaning of a word. The long vowels, shown in our pronunciation guides with a horizontal line on top of them (ā, ē, ī, ō, ū), should be held twice as long as the short ones. It's also important to make the distinction between single and double consonants, as this can produce a difference in meaning. Pronounce the double consonants with a slight pause between them, eg sak·ka (writer).

Note also that the vowel sound ai is pronounced as in 'aisle', air as in 'pair' and ow as in 'how'. As for the consonants, ts is pronounced as in 'hats', f sounds almost like 'fw' (with rounded lips), and r is halfway between 'r' and 'l'. All syllables in a word are pronounced fairly evenly in Japanese.

WANT MORE?

For in-depth language information and handy phrases, check out Lonely Planet's *Japanese Phrasebook*. You'll find it at **shop.lonelyplanet.com**, or you can buy Lonely Planet's iPhone phrasebooks at the Apple App Store.

BASICS

Japanese uses an array of registers of speech to reflect social and contextual hierarchy, but these can be simplified to the form most appropriate for the situation, which is what we've done in this language guide too.

Hello.	こんにちは。	kon·ni·chi·wa
Goodbye.	さようなら。	sa·yō·na·ra
Yes.	はい。	hai
No.	いいえ。	ī·e
Please. (when asking)	ください。	ku·da·sai
Please. (when offering)	どうぞ。	dō·zo
Thank you.	ありがとう。	a·ri·ga·tō
Excuse me. (to get attention)	すみません。	su·mi·ma·sen
Sorry.	ごめんなさい。	go·men·na·sai

You're welcome.
どういたしまして。 dō i·ta·shi·mash·te

How are you?
お元気ですか? o·gen·ki des ka

Fine. And you?
はい、元気です。 hai, gen·ki des
あなたは? a·na·ta wa

What's your name?
お名前は何ですか? o·na·ma·e wa nan des ka

My name is ...
私の名前は wa·ta·shi no na·ma·e wa
…です。 ... des

Do you speak English?
英語が話せますか? ē·go ga ha·na·se·mas ka

I don't understand.
わかりません。 wa·ka·ri·ma·sen

Does anyone speak English?
どなたか英語を do·na·ta ka ē·go o
話せますか? ha·na·se·mas ka

ACCOMMODATION

Where's a ...?	…はどこですか?	... wa do·ko des ka
campsite	キャンプ場	kyam·pu·jō
guesthouse	民宿	min·shu·ku
hotel	ホテル	ho·te·ru
inn	旅館	ryo·kan
youth hostel	ユースホステル	yū·su·ho·su·te·ru

Do you have a ... room?	…ルームはありますか?	...rū·mu wa a·ri·mas ka
single	シングル	shin·gu·ru
double	ダブル	da·bu·ru

How much is it per ...?	…いくらですか?	... i·ku·ra des ka
night	1泊	ip·pa·ku
person	1人	hi·to·ri

air-con	エアコン	air·kon
bathroom	風呂場	fu·ro·ba
window	窓	ma·do

DIRECTIONS

Where's the ...?
…はどこですか? ... wa do·ko des ka

Can you show me (on the map)?
(地図で)教えてくれませんか? (chi·zu de) o·shi·e·te ku·re·ma·sen ka

What's the address?
住所は何ですか? jū·sho wa nan des ka

Could you please write it down?
書いてくれませんか? kai·te ku·re·ma·sen ka

behind ...	…の後ろ	... no u·shi·ro
in front of ...	…の前	... no ma·e
near ...	…の近く	... no chi·ka·ku
next to ...	…のとなり	... no to·na·ri
opposite ...	…の向かい側	... no mu·kai·ga·wa
straight ahead	この先	ko·no sa·ki

Turn ...	…まがってください。	... ma·gat·te ku·da·sai
at the corner	その角を	so·no ka·do o
at the traffic lights	その信号を	so·no shin·gō o
left	左へ	hi·da·ri e
right	右へ	mi·gi e

KEY PATTERNS

To get by in Japanese, mix and match these simple patterns with words of your choice:

When's (the next bus)?
(次のバスは)何時ですか? (tsu·gi no bas wa) nan·ji des ka

Where's (the station)?
(駅は)どこですか? (e·ki wa) do·ko des ka

Do you have (a map)?
(地図)がありますか? (chi·zu) ga a·ri·mas ka

Is there (a toilet)?
(トイレ)がありますか? (toy·re) ga a·ri·mas ka

I'd like (the menu).
(メニュー)をお願いします。 (me·nyū) o o·ne·gai shi·mas

Can I (sit here)?
(ここに座って)もいいですか? (ko·ko ni su·wat·te) mo ī des ka

I need (a can opener).
(缶切り)が必要です。 (kan·ki·ri) ga hi·tsu·yō des

Do I need (a visa)?
(ビザ)が必要ですか? (bi·za) ga hi·tsu·yō des ka

I have (a reservation).
(予約)があります。 (yo·ya·ku) ga a·ri·mas

I'm (a teacher).
私は(教師)です。 wa·ta·shi wa (kyō·shi) des

EATING & DRINKING

I'd like to reserve a table for (two people).
(2人)の予約をお願いします。 (fu·ta·ri) no yo·ya·ku o o·ne·gai shi·mas

What would you recommend?
なにがおすすめですか? na·ni ga o·su·su·me des ka

What's in that dish?
あの料理に何が入っていますか? a·no ryō·ri ni na·ni ga hait·te i·mas ka

Do you have any vegetarian dishes?
ベジタリアン料理がありますか? be·ji·ta·ri·an ryō·ri ga a·ri·mas ka

I'm a vegetarian.
私はベジタリアンです。 wa·ta·shi wa be·ji·ta·ri·an des

I'm a vegan.
私は厳格な菜食主義者です。 wa·ta·shi wa gen·ka·ku na sai·sho·ku·shu·gi·sha des

I don't eat ...	…は 食べません。	... wa ta·be·ma·sen
dairy products	乳製品	nyū·sē·hin
(red) meat	(赤身の) 肉	(a·ka·mi no) ni·ku
meat or dairy products	肉や 乳製品は	ni·ku ya nyū·sē·hin
pork	豚肉	bu·ta·ni·ku
seafood	シーフード 海産物	shī·fū·do/ kai·sam·bu·tsu

Is it cooked with pork lard or chicken stock?
これはラードか鶏の だしを使って いますか? — ko·re wa rā·do ka to·ri no da·shi o tsu·kat·te i·mas ka

I'm allergic to (peanuts).
私は (ピーナッツ)に アレルギーが あります。 — wa·ta·shi wa (pī·nat·tsu) ni a·re·ru·gī ga a·ri·mas

That was delicious!
おいしかった。 — oy·shi·kat·ta

Cheers!
乾杯! — kam·pai

Please bring the bill.
お勘定をください。 — o·kan·jō o ku·da·sai

Key Words

appetisers	前菜	zen·sai
bottle	ビン	bin
bowl	ボール	bō·ru
breakfast	朝食	chō·sho·ku
cold	冷たい	tsu·me·ta·i
dinner	夕食	yū·sho·ku
fork	フォーク	fō·ku
glass	グラス	gu·ra·su
grocery	食料品	sho·ku·ryō·hin
hot (warm)	熱い	a·tsu·i
knife	ナイフ	nai·fu
lunch	昼食	chū·sho·ku
market	市場	i·chi·ba
menu	メニュー	me·nyū
plate	皿	sa·ra
spicy	スパイシー	spai·shī
spoon	スプーン	spūn
vegetarian	ベジタリアン	be·ji·ta·ri·an
with	いっしょに	is·sho ni
without	なしで	na·shi de

SIGNS

入口	**Entrance**
出口	**Exit**
営業中/開館	**Open**
閉店/閉館	**Closed**
インフォメーション	**Information**
危険	**Danger**
トイレ	**Toilets**
男	**Men**
女	**Women**

Meat & Fish

beef	牛肉	gyū·ni·ku
chicken	鶏肉	to·ri·ni·ku
duck	アヒル	a·hi·ru
eel	うなぎ	u·na·gi
fish	魚	sa·ka·na
lamb	子羊	ko·hi·tsu·ji
lobster	ロブスター	ro·bus·tā
meat	肉	ni·ku
pork	豚肉	bu·ta·ni·ku
prawn	エビ	e·bi
salmon	サケ	sa·ke
seafood	シーフード 海産物	shī·fū·do/ kai·sam·bu·tsu
shrimp	小エビ	ko·e·bi
tuna	マグロ	ma·gu·ro
turkey	七面鳥	shi·chi·men·chō
veal	子牛	ko·u·shi

Fruit & Vegetables

apple	りんご	rin·go
banana	バナナ	ba·na·na
beans	豆	ma·me
capsicum	ピーマン	pī·man
carrot	ニンジン	nin·jin
cherry	さくらんぼ	sa·ku·ram·bo
cucumber	キュウリ	kyū·ri
fruit	果物	ku·da·mo·no
grapes	ブドウ	bu·dō
lettuce	レタス	re·tas
nut	ナッツ	nat·tsu
orange	オレンジ	o·ren·ji
peach	桃	mo·mo

peas	豆	ma·me
pineapple	パイナップル	pai·nap·pu·ru
potato	ジャガイモ	ja·ga·i·mo
pumpkin	カボチャ	ka·bo·cha
spinach	ホウレンソウ	hō·ren·sō
strawberry	イチゴ	i·chi·go
tomato	トマト	to·ma·to
vegetables	野菜	ya·sai
watermelon	スイカ	su·i·ka

Other

bread	パン	pan
butter	バター	ba·tā
cheese	チーズ	chī·zu
chilli	唐辛子	tō·ga·ra·shi
egg	卵	ta·ma·go
honey	蜂蜜	ha·chi·mi·tsu
horseradish	わさび	wa·sa·bi
jam	ジャム	ja·mu
noodles	麺	men
pepper	コショウ	koshō
rice (cooked)	ごはん	go·han
salt	塩	shi·o
seaweed	のり	no·ri
soy sauce	しょう油	shō·yu
sugar	砂糖	sa·tō

Drinks

beer	ビール	bī·ru
coffee	コーヒー	kō·hī
(orange) juice	(オレンジ) ジュース	(o·ren·ji·) jū·su
lemonade	レモネード	re·mo·nē·do
milk	ミルク	mi·ru·ku
mineral water	ミネラル ウォーター	mi·ne·ra·ru· wō·tā
red wine	赤ワイン	a·ka wain
sake	酒	sa·ke
tea	紅茶	kō·cha
water	水	mi·zu
white wine	白ワイン	shi·ro wain
yogurt	ヨーグルト	yō·gu·ru·to

QUESTION WORDS

How?	どのように?	do·no yō ni
What?	なに?	na·ni
When?	いつ?	i·tsu
Where?	どこ?	do·ko
Which?	どちら?	do·chi·ra
Who?	だれ?	da·re
Why?	なぜ?	na·ze

EMERGENCIES

Help!
たすけて! tas·ke·te

Go away!
離れろ! ha·na·re·ro

I'm lost.
迷いました。 ma·yoy·mash·ta

Call the police.
警察を呼んで。 kē·sa·tsu o yon·de

Call a doctor.
医者を呼んで。 i·sha o yon·de

Where are the toilets?
トイレはどこですか? toy·re wa do·ko des ka

I'm ill.
私は病気です。 wa·ta·shi wa byō·ki des

It hurts here.
ここが痛いです。 ko·ko ga i·tai des

I'm allergic to ...
私は… アレルギーです。 wa·ta·shi wa ... a·re·ru·gī des

SHOPPING & SERVICES

I'd like to buy ...
…をください。 ... o ku·da·sai

I'm just looking.
見ているだけです。 mi·te i·ru da·ke des

Can I look at it?
それを見ても いいですか? so·re o mi·te mo ī des ka

How much is it?
いくらですか? i·ku·ra des ka

That's too expensive.
高すぎます。 ta·ka·su·gi·mas

Can you give me a discount?
ディスカウント できますか? dis·kown·to de·ki·mas ka

There's a mistake in the bill.
請求書に間違いが あります。 sē·kyū·sho ni ma·chi·gai ga a·ri·mas

ATM	ATM	ē·tī·e·mu
credit card	クレジット カード	ku·re·jit·to· kā·do
post office	郵便局	yū·bin·kyo·ku
public phone	公衆電話	kō·shū·den·wa
tourist office	観光案内所	kan·kō·an·nai·jo

TIME & DATES

What time is it?
何時ですか？ nan·ji des ka

It's (10) o'clock.
(10)時です。 (jū)·ji des

Half past (10).
(10)時半です。 (jū)·ji han des

am	午前	go·zen
pm	午後	go·go

Monday	月曜日	ge·tsu·yō·bi
Tuesday	火曜日	ka·yō·bi
Wednesday	水曜日	su·i·yō·bi
Thursday	木曜日	mo·ku·yō·bi
Friday	金曜日	kin·yō·bi
Saturday	土曜日	do·yō·bi
Sunday	日曜日	ni·chi·yō·bi

January	1月	i·chi·ga·tsu
February	2月	ni·ga·tsu
March	3月	san·ga·tsu
April	4月	shi·ga·tsu
May	5月	go·ga·tsu
June	6月	ro·ku·ga·tsu
July	7月	shi·chi·ga·tsu
August	8月	ha·chi·ga·tsu
September	9月	ku·ga·tsu
October	10月	jū·ga·tsu
November	11月	jū·i·chi·ga·tsu
December	12月	jū·ni·ga·tsu

TRANSPORT

boat	船	fu·ne
bus	バス	bas
metro	地下鉄	chi·ka·te·tsu
plane	飛行機	hi·kō·ki
train	電車	den·sha
tram	市電	shi·den

What time does it leave?
これは何時に出ますか？ ko·re wa nan·ji ni de·mas ka

Does it stop at (...)?
(…)に停まりますか？ (...) ni to·ma·ri·mas ka

Please tell me when we get to (...).
(…)に着いたら教えてください。 (...) ni tsu·i·ta·ra o·shi·e·te ku·da·sai

NUMBERS

1	一	i·chi
2	二	ni
3	三	san
4	四	shi/yon
5	五	go
6	六	ro·ku
7	七	shi·chi/na·na
8	八	ha·chi
9	九	ku/kyū
10	十	jū
20	二十	ni·jū
30	三十	san·jū
40	四十	yon·jū
50	五十	go·jū
60	六十	ro·ku·jū
70	七十	na·na·jū
80	八十	ha·chi·jū
90	九十	kyū·jū
100	百	hya·ku
1000	千	sen

A one-way/return ticket (to ...).
(. . . 行きの)片道/往復切符。 (...·yu·ki no) ka·ta·mi·chi/ō·fu·ku kip·pu

first	始発の	shi·ha·tsu no
last	最終の	sai·shū no
next	次の	tsu·gi no

aisle	通路側	tsū·ro·ga·wa
bus stop	バス停	bas·tē
cancelled	キャンセル	kyan·se·ru
delayed	遅れ	o·ku·re
ticket window	窓口	ma·do·gu·chi
timetable	時刻表	ji·ko·ku·hyō
train station	駅	e·ki
window	窓側	ma·do·ga·wa

I'd like to hire a ...	…を借りたいのですが。	... o ka·ri·tai no des ga
bicycle	自転車	ji·ten·sha
car	自動車	ji·dō·sha
motorbike	オートバイ	ō·to·bai

GLOSSARY

Amida Nyorai – Buddha of the Western Paradise
ANA – All Nippon Airways
-bashi – bridge (also *hashi*)
bashō – sumo tournament
bentō – boxed lunch or dinner, usually containing rice, vegetables and fish or meat
bosatsu – a bodhisattva, or Buddha attendant, who assists others to attain enlightenment
bugaku – dance pieces played by court orchestras in ancient Japan
bunraku – classical puppet theatre that uses life-size puppets to enact dramas similar to those of *kabuki*
chō – city area (for large cities) sized between a *ku* and *chōme*
chōme – city area of a few blocks
Daibutsu – Great Buddha
daimyō – domain lords under the *shōgun*
dōri – street
fugu – poisonous pufferfish, elevated to haute cuisine
futon – cushion-like mattress that is rolled up and stored away during the day
futsū – local train; literally 'ordinary'
gagaku – music of the imperial court
gaijin – foreigner; the contracted form of *gaikokujin* (literally, 'outside country person')
-gawa – river (also *kawa*)
geisha – a woman versed in the arts and other cultivated pursuits who entertains guests
-gū – shrine (also *-jingū* or *-jinja*)
haiden – hall of worship in a shrine
haiku – seventeen-syllable poem
hakubutsukan – museum
hanami – cherry-blossom viewing
hashi – bridge (also *-bashi*); chopsticks
higashi – east
hiragana – phonetic syllabary used to write Japanese words
honden – main building of a shrine
hondō – main building of a temple
ikebana – art of flower arrangement
irori – open hearth found in traditional Japanese homes
izakaya – Japanese pub/eatery
-ji – temple (also *tera* or *dera*)
-jingū – shrine (also *-jinja* or *-gū*)
-jinja – shrine (also *-gū* or *-jingū*)
jizō – bodhisattva who watches over children
JNTO – Japan National Tourist Organization
-jō – castle (also *shiro*)
JR – Japan Railways
kabuki – form of Japanese theatre that draws on popular tales and is characterised by elaborate costumes, stylised acting and the use of male actors for all roles
kaiseki – Buddhist-inspired, Japanese haute cuisine; called *cha-kaiseki* when served as part of a tea ceremony
kaisoku – rapid train
kaiten-sushi – conveyor-belt sushi
kamikaze – literally, 'wind of the gods'; originally the typhoon that sank Kublai Khan's 13th-century invasion fleet and the name adopted by Japanese suicide bombers in the waning days of WWII
kampai – cheers, as in a drinking toast
kanji – literally, 'Chinese writing'; Chinese ideographic script used for writing Japanese
Kannon – Buddhist goddess of mercy
karaoke – a now-famous export where revellers sing along to recorded music, minus the vocals
kawa – river
-ken – prefecture, eg Shiga-ken
kimono – traditional outer garment that is similar to a robe
kita – north
-ko – lake
kōban – local police box
kōen – park
ku – ward
kyōgen – drama performed as comic relief between *nō* plays, or as separate events
kyūkō – ordinary express train (faster than a *futsū*, only stopping at certain stations)
live house – a small concert hall where live music is performed
machi – city area (for large cities) sized between a *ku* and *chōme*
mama-san – older women who run drinking, dining and entertainment venues
maneki-neko – beckoning or welcoming cat figure frequently seen in restaurants and bars; it's supposed to attract customers and trade
matcha – powdered green tea served in tea ceremonies
matsuri – festival
midori-no-madoguchi – ticket counter in large Japan Rail stations, where you can make more complicated bookings (look for the green band across the glass)
mikoshi – portable shrine carried during festivals
minami – south
minshuku – Japanese equivalent of a B&B

mon – temple gate

mura – village

N'EX – Narita Express

Nihon – Japanese word for Japan; literally, 'source of the sun' (also known as *Nippon*)

Nippon – see *Nihon*

nishi – west

nō – classical Japanese drama performed on a bare stage

noren – door curtain for restaurants, usually labelled with the name of the establishment

NTT – Nippon Telegraph & Telephone Corporation

o- prefix used as a sign of respect (usually applied to objects)

obi – sash or belt worn with *kimono*

O-bon – mid-August festivals and ceremonies for deceased ancestors

o-furo – traditional Japanese bath

onsen – mineral hot spring with bathing areas and accommodation

o-shibori – hot towels given in restaurants

pachinko – vertical pinball game that is a Japanese craze

Raijin – god of thunder

ryokan – traditional Japanese inn

ryōri – cooking; cuisine

ryōtei – traditional-style, high-class restaurant; *kaiseki* is typical fare

sabi – a poetic ideal of finding beauty and pleasure in imperfection; often used in conjunction with *wabi*

sakura – cherry trees

salaryman – male employee of a large firm

-sama – a suffix even more respectful than *san*

samurai – Japan's traditional warrior class

-san – a respectful suffix applied to personal names, similar to Mr, Mrs or Ms but more widely used

sentō – public bath

setto – set meal; see also *teishoku*

Shaka Nyorai – Historical Buddha

shakkei – borrowed scenery; technique where features outside a garden are incorporated into its design

shamisen – three-stringed, banjo-like instrument

-shi – city (to distinguish cities with prefectures of the same name)

shinkansen – bullet train (literally, 'new trunk line')

Shintō – indigenous Japanese religion

Shitamachi – traditionally the low-lying, less-affluent parts of Tokyo

shōgun – military ruler of pre-Meiji Japan

shōjin ryōri – Buddhist vegetarian cuisine

shokudō – Japanese-style cafeteria/cheap restaurant

soba – thin brown buckwheat noodles

tatami – tightly woven floor matting on which shoes should not be worn

teishoku – set meal in a restaurant

tokkyū – limited express train

torii – entrance gate to a *Shintō* shrine

tsukemono – Japanese pickles

udon – thick, white, wheat noodles

ukiyo-e – woodblock prints; literally, 'pictures of the floating world'

wabi – a Zen-inspired aesthetic of rustic simplicity

wasabi – spicy Japanese horseradish

washi – Japanese paper

yakuza – Japanese mafia

Zen – a form of Buddhism

FOOD GLOSSARY

Rice Dishes

katsu-don (かつ丼) – rice topped with a fried pork cutlet

niku-don (牛丼) – rice topped with thin slices of cooked beef

oyako-don (親子丼) – rice topped with egg and chicken

ten-don (天丼) – rice topped with tempura shrimp and vegetables

Izakaya Fare

agedashi-dōfu (揚げだし豆腐) – deep-fried tofu in a dashi broth

jaga-batā (ジャガバター) – baked potatoes with butter

niku-jaga (肉ジャガ) – beef and potato stew

shio-yaki-zakana (塩焼魚) – a whole fish grilled with salt

poteto furai (ポテトフライ) – French fries

chiizu-age (チーズ揚げ) – deep-fried cheese

hiya-yakko (冷奴) – cold tofu with soy sauce and spring onions

tsuna sarada (ツナサラダ) – tuna salad over cabbage

Sushi & Sashimi

ama-ebi (甘海老) – shrimp

awabi (あわび) – abalone

hamachi (はまち) – yellowtail

ika (いか) – squid

ikura (イクラ) – salmon roe

kai-bashira (貝柱) – scallop

kani (かに) – crab

katsuo (かつお) – bonito

sashimi mori-awase (刺身盛り合わせ) – a selection of sliced sashimi

tai (鯛) – sea bream

toro (とろ) – the choicest cut of fatty tuna belly

uni (うに) – sea-urchin roe

Yakitori

yakitori (焼き鳥) – plain, grilled white meat

hasami/negima (はさみ/ねぎま) – pieces of white meat alternating with leek

sasami (ささみ) – skinless chicken-breast pieces

kawa (皮) – chicken skin

tsukune (つくね) – chicken meatballs

gyū-niku (牛肉) – pieces of beef

tebasaki (手羽先) – chicken wings

shiitake (しいたけ) – Japanese mushrooms

piiman (ピーマン) – small green peppers

tama-negi (玉ねぎ) – round white onions

yaki-onigiri (焼きおにぎり) – a triangle of rice grilled with *yakitori* sauce

Rāmen

rāmen (ラーメン) – soup and noodles with a sprinkling of meat and vegetables

chāshū-men (チャーシュー麺) – *rāmen* topped with slices of roasted pork

wantan-men (ワンタン麺) – *rāmen* with meat dumplings

miso-rāmen (みそラーメン) – *rāmen* with miso-flavoured broth

chānpon-men (ちゃんぽん麺) – Nagasaki-style *rāmen*

Soba & Udon

soba (そば) – thin brown buckwheat noodles

udon (うどん) – thick white wheat noodles

kake soba/udon (かけそば/うどん) – *soba/udon* noodles in broth

kata yaki-soba (固焼きそば) – crispy noodles with meat and vegetables

kitsune soba/udon (きつねそば/うどん) – *soba/udon* noodles with fried tofu

tempura soba/udon (天ぷらそば/うどん) – *soba/udon* noodles with tempura shrimp

tsukimi soba/udon (月見そば/うどん) – *soba/udon* noodles with raw egg on top

yaki-soba (焼きそば) – fried noodles with meat and vegetables

zaru soba (ざるそば) – cold noodles with seaweed strips served on a bamboo tray

Tempura

tempura moriawase (天ぷら盛り合わせ) – a selection of tempura

shōjin age (精進揚げ) – vegetarian tempura

kaki age (かき揚げ) – tempura with shredded vegetables or fish

Kushiage & Kushikatsu

ika (いか) – squid

renkon (れんこん) – lotus root

tama-negi (玉ねぎ) – white onion

gyū-niku (牛肉) – beef pieces

shiitake (しいたけ) – Japanese mushrooms

ginnan (銀杏) – ginkgo nuts

imo (いも) – potato

Okonomiyaki

mikkusu (ミックスお好み焼き) – mixed fillings of seafood, meat and vegetables

modan-yaki (モダン焼き) – *okonomiyaki* with *yaki-soba* and a fried egg

ika okonomiyaki (いかお好み焼き) – squid *okonomiyaki*

gyū okonomiyaki (牛お好み焼き) – beef *okonomiyaki*

negi okonomiyaki (ネギお好み焼き) – thin *okonomiyaki* with spring onions

Kaiseki

bentō (弁当) – boxed lunch

ume (梅) – regular course

take (竹) – special course

matsu (松) – extra-special course

Unagi

kabayaki (蒲焼き) – skewers of grilled eel without rice

unagi teishoku (うなぎ定食) – full-set *unagi* meal with rice, grilled eel, eel-liver soup and pickles

una-don (うな丼) – grilled eel over a bowl of rice

unajū (うな重) – grilled eel over a flat tray of rice

Alcoholic Drinks

nama biiru (生ビール) – draught beer

shōchū (焼酎) – distilled grain liquor

oyu-wari (お湯割り) – *shōchū* with hot water

chūhai (チューハイ) – *shōchū* with soda and lemon

whisky (ウィスキー) – whisky

mizu-wari (水割り) – whisky, ice and water

Coffee & Tea

kōhii (コーヒー) – regular coffee

burendo kōhii (ブレンドコーヒー) – blended coffee, fairly strong

american kōhii (アメリカンコーヒー) – weak coffee

kōcha (紅茶) – black, British-style tea

kafe ōre (カフェオレ) – cafe au lait, hot or cold

Japanese Tea

o-cha (お茶) – green tea

sencha (煎茶) – medium-grade green tea

matcha (抹茶) – powdered green tea used in the tea ceremony

bancha (番茶) – ordinary-grade green tea, brownish in colour

mugicha (麦茶) – roasted barley tea

Behind the Scenes

SEND US YOUR FEEDBACK

We love to hear from travellers – your comments keep us on our toes and help make our books better. Our well-travelled team reads every word on what you loved or loathed about this book. Although we cannot reply individually to your submissions, we always guarantee that your feedback goes straight to the appropriate authors, in time for the next edition. Each person who sends us information is thanked in the next edition – and the most useful submissions are rewarded with a selection of digital PDF chapters.

Visit **lonelyplanet.com/contact** to submit your updates and suggestions or to ask for help. Our award-winning website also features inspirational travel stories, news and discussions.

Note: We may edit, reproduce and incorporate your comments in Lonely Planet products such as guidebooks, websites and digital products, so let us know if you don't want your comments reproduced or your name acknowledged. For a copy of our privacy policy visit lonelyplanet.com/privacy.

OUR READERS

Many thanks to the travellers who used the last edition and wrote to us with helpful hints, useful advice and interesting anecdotes:

Badong Abesamis, Parham Fazelzadeh, Robert Glass, Shinobu Honjo, Steve Hoy, Laura Huddleston, Adam Keyworth, Neels de Leeuw, HangYu Li, Cristina Miret, Antonio Mogort, Rob Nelson, Torben Retboll, Gregory Schmauch, Roch Stefaniak, Veronica Tam, Jennifer Ward, Mathias Wendt

AUTHOR THANKS

Rebecca Milner

A big thanks to my mom for her company, and to my husband for his tireless patience. To Emi and Steph for their willingness to visit 'just one more bar' and to Jon and Kanna for their cooking. Kyary, Mike, Allan and Ivan: thank you for your 'local knowledge'. Will, Tabata-san, Sayuri, Miyawaki-san, Tristan, Toshiko and Kenichi: I'm grateful for your help and recommendations. And finally to Simon and Laura: thank you for all of your help, guidance and patience.

Simon Richmond

Domo arigato gozaimasu to Kylie Clark and colleagues at JNTO London; Tabata Naoko and colleagues at TCVB; Osawa Kei at Intermediateque; Tokyo friends Toshiko, Kenichi, Giles and William; Masami Takahashi in Hakone; Brent Potter for expert advice on Fuji and for getting me safely up to the summit and back; *Tokyo* coauthor Rebecca, and Laura and Diana for keeping it all running smoothly at Lonely Planet headquarters.

ACKNOWLEDGMENTS

Tokyo Subway Route Map, Bureau of Transportation, Tokyo Metropolitan Government, Tokyo Metro Co Ltd © 2014.6.

Illustrations pp156–7 by Michael Weldon.

Cover photograph: Restaurant in Omoide-Yokochō, Shinjuku; Jon Arnold/AWL.

THIS BOOK

This 10th edition of *Tokyo* was researched and written by Rebecca Milner and Simon Richmond. The 9th edition was written by Timothy N Hornyak and Rebecca Milner, and the 8th edition by Andrew Bender and Timothy N Hornyak. This guidebook was produced by the following:

Destination Editor Laura Crawford
Product Editors Carolyn Boicos, Alison Ridgway
Senior Cartographer Diana Von Holdt
Book Designer Jessica Rose
Assisting Editors Katie Connolly, Kellie Langdon, Charlotte Orr, Sally Schafer
Assisting Cartographers Julie Dodkins, Anthony Phelan, Julie Sheridan
Cover Researcher Naomi Parker
Thanks to Naoko Akamatsu, Kate James, Claire Naylor, Karyn Noble, Martine Power, Ellie Simpson, Luna Soo, Lauren Wellicome, Tony Wheeler

See also separate subindexes for:

EATING P269
DRINKING & NIGHTLIFE P270
ENTERTAINMENT P270
SHOPPING P271
SPORTS & ACTIVITIES P271
SLEEPING P271

Index

Sights 000
Map Pages **000**
Photo Pages **000**

Sights 000
Map Pages **000**
Photo Pages **000**

Sights 000
Map Pages **000**
Photo Pages **000**

EATING

DRINKING & NIGHTLIFE

Sights 000
Map Pages **000**
Photo Pages **000**

ENTERTAINMENT

SHOPPING

SPORTS & ACTIVITIES

SLEEPING

Sights 000
Map Pages **000**
Photo Pages **000**

Tokyo Maps

Sights

- Beach
- Bird Sanctuary
- Buddhist
- Castle/Palace
- Christian
- Confucian
- Hindu
- Islamic
- Jain
- Jewish
- Monument
- Museum/Gallery/Historic Building
- Ruin
- Shinto
- Sikh
- Taoist
- Winery/Vineyard
- Zoo/Wildlife Sanctuary
- Other Sight

Activities, Courses & Tours

- Bodysurfing
- Diving
- Canoeing/Kayaking
- Course/Tour
- Sento Hot Baths/Onsen
- Skiing
- Snorkelling
- Surfing
- Swimming/Pool
- Walking
- Windsurfing
- Other Activity

Sleeping

- Sleeping
- Camping

Eating

- Eating

Drinking & Nightlife

- Drinking & Nightlife
- Cafe

Entertainment

- Entertainment

Shopping

- Shopping

Information

- Bank
- Embassy/Consulate
- Hospital/Medical
- Internet
- Police
- Post Office
- Telephone
- Toilet
- Tourist Information
- Other Information

Geographic

- Beach
- Hut/Shelter
- Lighthouse
- Lookout
- Mountain/Volcano
- Oasis
- Park
- Pass
- Picnic Area
- Waterfall

Population

- Capital (National)
- Capital (State/Province)
- City/Large Town
- Town/Village

Transport

- Airport
- Border crossing
- Bus
- Cable car/Funicular
- Cycling
- Ferry
- Metro/MTR/MRT station
- Monorail
- Parking
- Petrol station
- Skytrain/Subway station
- Taxi
- Train station/Railway
- Tram
- Underground station
- Other Transport

Note: Not all symbols displayed above appear on the maps in this book

Routes

- Tollway
- Freeway
- Primary
- Secondary
- Tertiary
- Lane
- Unsealed road
- Road under construction
- Plaza/Mall
- Steps
- Tunnel
- Pedestrian overpass
- Walking Tour
- Walking Tour detour
- Path/Walking Trail

Boundaries

- International
- State/Province
- Disputed
- Regional/Suburb
- Marine Park
- Cliff
- Wall

Hydrography

- River, Creek
- Intermittent River
- Canal
- Water
- Dry/Salt/Intermittent Lake
- Reef

Areas

- Airport/Runway
- Beach/Desert
- Cemetery (Christian)
- Cemetery (Other)
- Glacier
- Mudflat
- Park/Forest
- Sight (Building)
- Sportsground
- Swamp/Mangrove

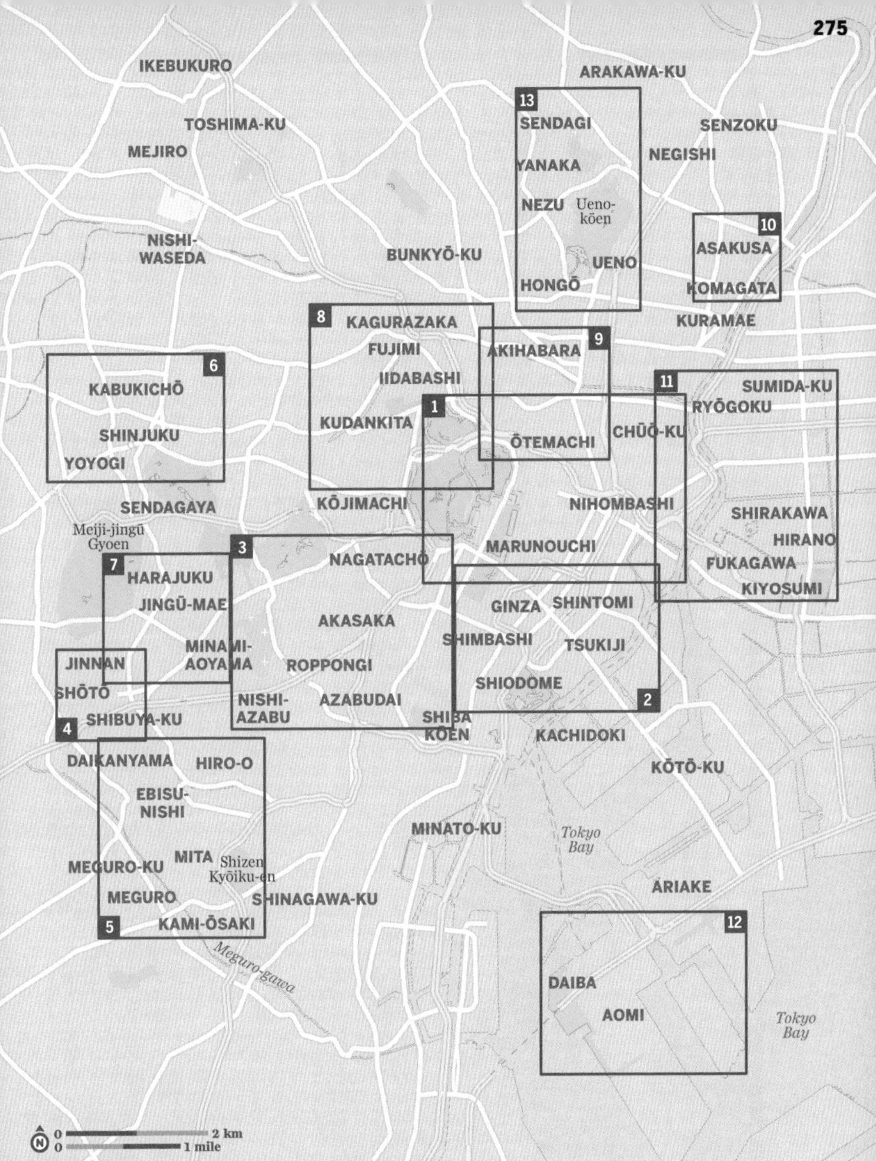
IKEBUKURO
TOSHIMA-KU
MEJIRO
NISHI-WASEDA
BUNKYŌ-KU
ARAKAWA-KU
13
SENDAGI
YANAKA
NEZU
Ueno-kōen
UENO
HONGŌ
SENZOKU
NEGISHI
10
ASAKUSA
KOMAGATA
KURAMAE
8
KAGURAZAKA
FUJIMI
IIDABASHI
KUDANKITA
9
AKIHABARA
1
ŌTEMACHI
CHŪŌ-KU
11
SUMIDA-KU
RYŌGOKU
6
KABUKICHŌ
SHINJUKU
YOYOGI
SENDAGAYA
Meiji-jingū Gyoen
KŌJIMACHI
NIHOMBASHI
MARUNOUCHI
SHIRAKAWA
HIRANO
FUKAGAWA
KIYOSUMI
3
NAGATACHŌ
7
HARAJUKU
JINGŪ-MAE
MINAMI-AOYAMA
AKASAKA
ROPPONGI
GINZA
SHINTOMI
SHIMBASHI
TSUKIJI
SHIODOME
2
JINNAN
SHŌTO
SHIBUYA-KU
4
NISHI-AZABU
AZABUDAI
SHIBA KŌEN
KACHIDOKI
KŌTŌ-KU
DAIKANYAMA
HIRO-O
EBISU-NISHI
MINATO-KU
Tokyo Bay
MEGURO-KU
MITA
Shizen Kyōiku-en
MEGURO
SHINAGAWA-KU
ARIAKE
5
KAMI-ŌSAKI
Meguro-gawa
12
DAIBA
AOMI
Tokyo Bay
0 2 km
0 1 mile

MAP INDEX

MARUNOUCHI & NIHOMBASHI

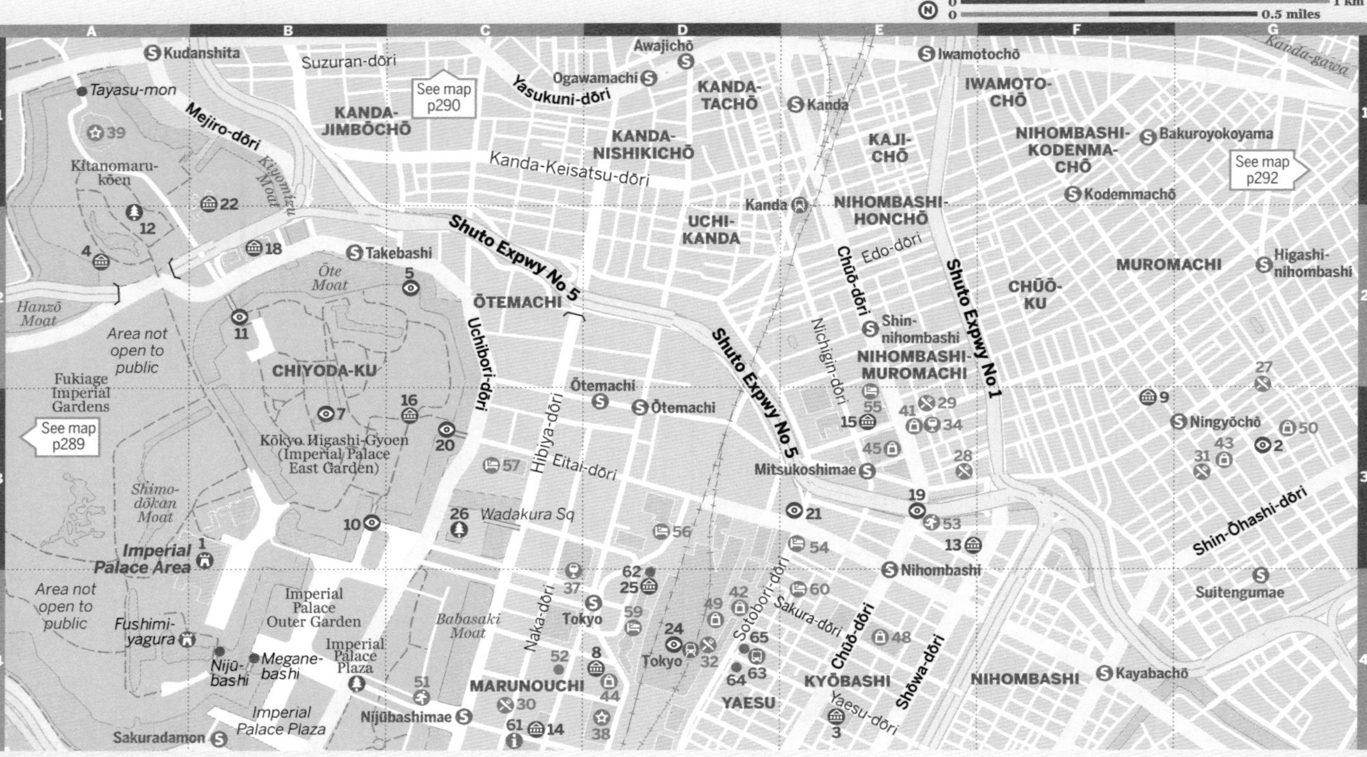

Top Sights (p56)
1 Imperial Palace Area B3

Sights (p58)
2 Amazake Yokochō G3
3 Bridgestone Museum of Art E4
4 Crafts Gallery A2
5 Hirakawa-mon C2
6 Idemitsu Museum of Arts C5
7 Imperial Palace East Garden B3
8 Intermediateque D4
9 Jusaburō-kan F3
10 Kikyō-mon B3
11 Kitahanebashi-mon B2
12 Kitanomaru-kōen (Kitanomaru Park) A2
13 Kite Museum E3
14 Mitsubishi Ichigōkan Museum C4
15 Mitsui Memorial Museum E3
16 Museum of Imperial Collections C3
17 National Film Centre D5
18 National Museum of Modern Art (MOMAT) B2
19 Nihombashi (Nihonbashi) E3
20 Ōte-mon C3
21 Pasona E3
22 Science Museum, Tokyo B1
23 Tokyo International Forum C5
24 Tokyo Station D4
25 Tokyo Station Gallery D4
26 Wadakura Fountain Park C3

Eating (p62)
27 Brozers' Hamburger G2
Cafe 1894 .... (see 14)
28 Hōnen Manpuku E3
Meal MUJI Yūrakuchō .... (see 46)
29 Nihonbashi Dashi Bar E3
30 Rose Bakery Marunouchi C4
Taimeike .... (see 13)
31 Tamahide G3
32 Tokyo Rāmen Street D4

Drinking & Nightlife (p63)
33 Cafe Salvador C5
34 Craft Beer Market Mitsukoshimae E3
35 Manpuku Shokudō C5
36 Peter: The Bar C5
37 So Tired C4

Entertainment (p64)
38 Cotton Club D4
39 Nippon Budōkan A1

Shopping (p64)
40 Bic Camera C5
41 Coredo Muromachi E3
42 Daimaru D4
43 Futaba G3
44 KITTE D4
45 Mitsukoshi E3
46 Muji C5
47 Ōedo Antique Market C5
48 Takashimaya E4
49 Tokyo Character Street D4
50 Yūma G3

Sports & Activities (p55 & p57)
51 Imperial Palace Cycling Course C4
52 SkyBus C4
53 Tokyo Bay Cruise E3

Sleeping (p198)
54 Hotel Ryumeikan Tokyo E3
55 Mandarin Oriental Tokyo E3
56 Marunouchi Hotel D3
57 Palace Hotel Tokyo C3
58 The Peninsula Tokyo C5
59 Tokyo Station Hotel D4
60 Yaesu Terminal Hotel E4

Information (p253)
61 JNTO Tourist Information Center C4
62 JR East Travel Service Center D4

Transport (p243 & p247)
63 Access Narita D4
64 Nippon Rent-a-Car D4
65 Toyota Rent-a-Car D4

GINZA & TSUKIJI

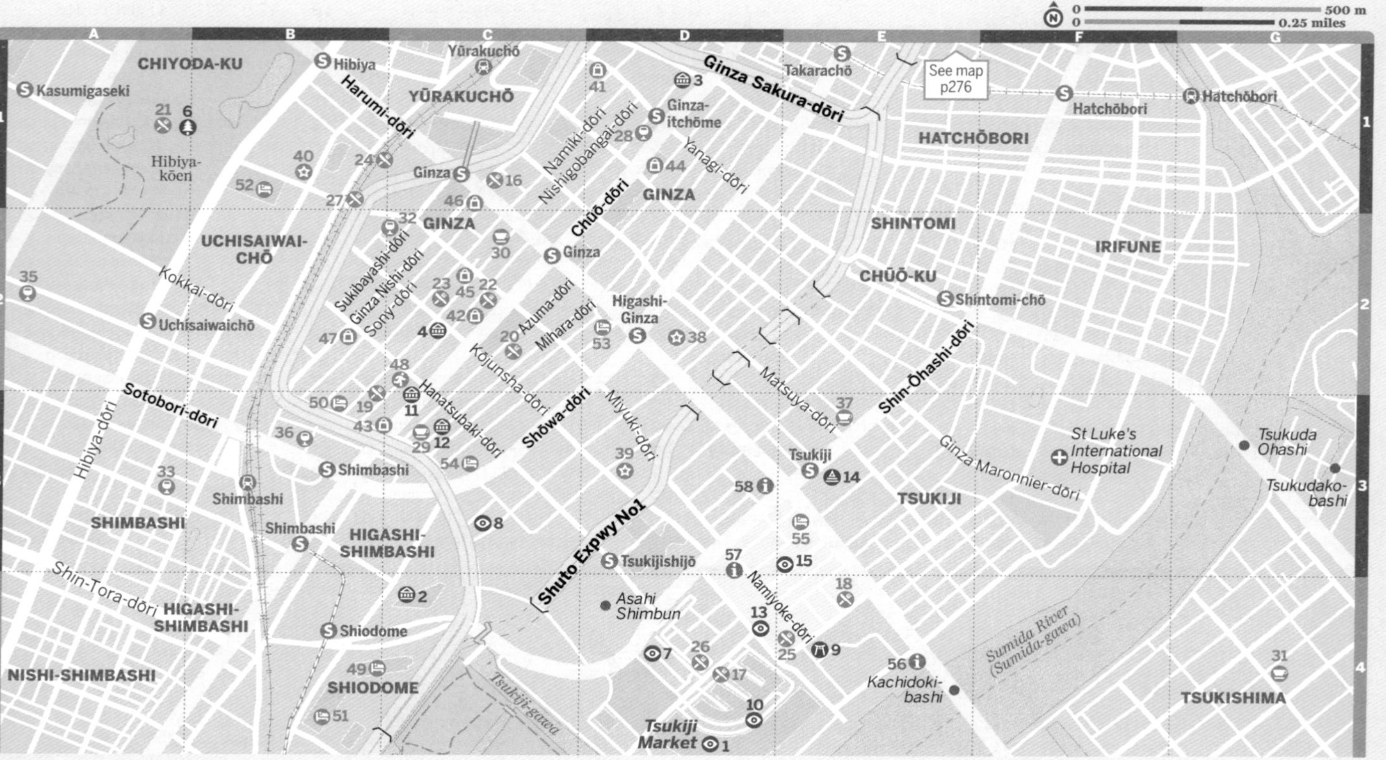

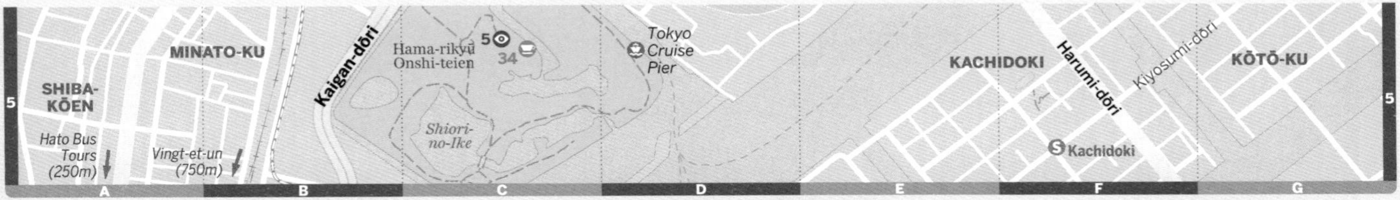

Top Sights (p67)
1 Tsukiji Market ... D4

Sights (p69)
2 Advertising Museum Tokyo ... C4
3 Gallery Koyanagi ... D1
4 Ginza Graphic Gallery ... C2
5 Hama-rikyū Onshi-teien ... C5
6 Hibiya-kōen ... A1
7 Melon Auction ... D4
8 Nakagin Capsule Tower ... C3
9 Namiyoke-jinja ... E4
10 Seafood Intermediate Wholesalers' Area ... D4
11 Shiseido Gallery ... C3
12 Tokyo Gallery + BTAP ... C3
13 Tokyo Ichiba Project ... D4
14 Tsukiji Hongwan-ji ... E3
15 Tsukiji Outer Market ... E3

Eating (p70)
16 Bird Land ... C1
17 Daiwa Sushi ... D4
18 Kimagure-ya ... E4
19 Kyūbey ... B3
20 Maru ... C2
21 Matsumotorō ... A1
22 Nataraj ... C2
23 Ore-no-dashi ... C2
Rose Bakery ... (see 42)
24 Shimanto-gawa ... B1
25 Trattoria Tsukiji Paradiso! ... E4
26 Uogashi-yokochō ... D4
27 Yūrakuchō Sanchoku Inshokugai ... B1

Drinking & Nightlife (p71)
28 Aux Amis Des Vins ... D1
29 Cafe de l'Ambre ... C3
30 Cha Ginza ... C2
31 Fukurou-no-mise ... G4
32 Ginza Suki Bar ... C2
33 Kagaya ... A3
Komatsu Bar ... (see 42)
34 Nakajima no Ochaya ... C5
35 Sake Plaza ... A2
36 Town House Tokyo ... B3
37 Turret Coffee ... E3

Entertainment (p75)
38 Kabuki-za ... D2
39 Shimbashi Embujō Theatre ... D3
40 Tokyo Takarazuka Theatre ... B1

Shopping (p76)
41 Akomeya ... D1
42 Dover Street Market Ginza ... C2
43 Hakuhinkan ... B3
44 Itōya ... D1
45 Natsuno ... C2
46 Sony Building ... C1
47 Takumi ... B2
Uniqlo ... (see 42)

Sports & Activities (p66)
48 Komparu-yu ... C2

Sleeping (p199)
49 Conrad Tokyo ... B4
50 Ginza Grand Hotel ... B3
51 Hotel Villa Fontaine Shiodome ... B4
52 Imperial Hotel ... B1
53 Millennium Mitsui Garden Hotel Tokyo ... D2
54 Mitsui Garden Hotel Ginza Premier ... C3
55 Tōkyū Stay Higashi-Ginza ... E3

Information (p68)
56 Fish Information Center ... E4
57 Information Centre Plat Tsukiji ... D3
58 Tsukiji Market Information Centre ... D3

Key on p282

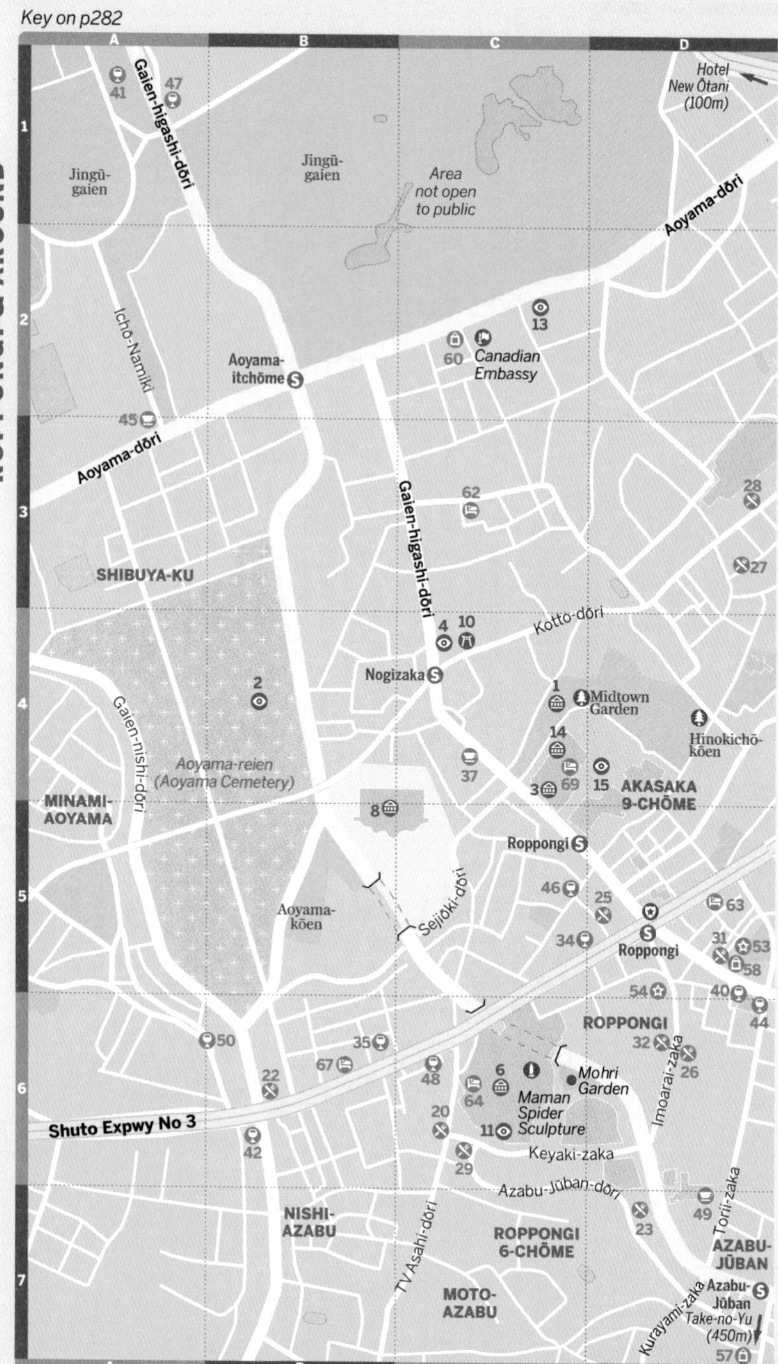

Hotel New Ōtani (100m)
Gaien-higashi-dōri
Jingū-gaien
Area not open to public
Aoyama-dōri
Ichō-Namiki
Aoyama-itchōme
Canadian Embassy
SHIBUYA-KU
Kotto-dōri
Nogizaka
Midtown Garden
Hinokichō-kōen
Gaien-nishi-dōri
Aoyama-reien (Aoyama Cemetery)
AKASAKA 9-CHŌME
MINAMI-AOYAMA
Roppongi
Sejiōki-dōri
Aoyama-kōen
ROPPONGI
Imoarai-zaka
Mohri Garden
Maman Spider Sculpture
Shuto Expwy No 3
Keyaki-zaka
Azabu-Jūban-dōri
Torii-zaka
NISHI-AZABU
ROPPONGI 6-CHŌME
TV Asahi-dōri
AZABU-JŪBAN
MOTO-AZABU
Azabu-Jūban
Kurayami-zaka
Take-no-Yu (450m)

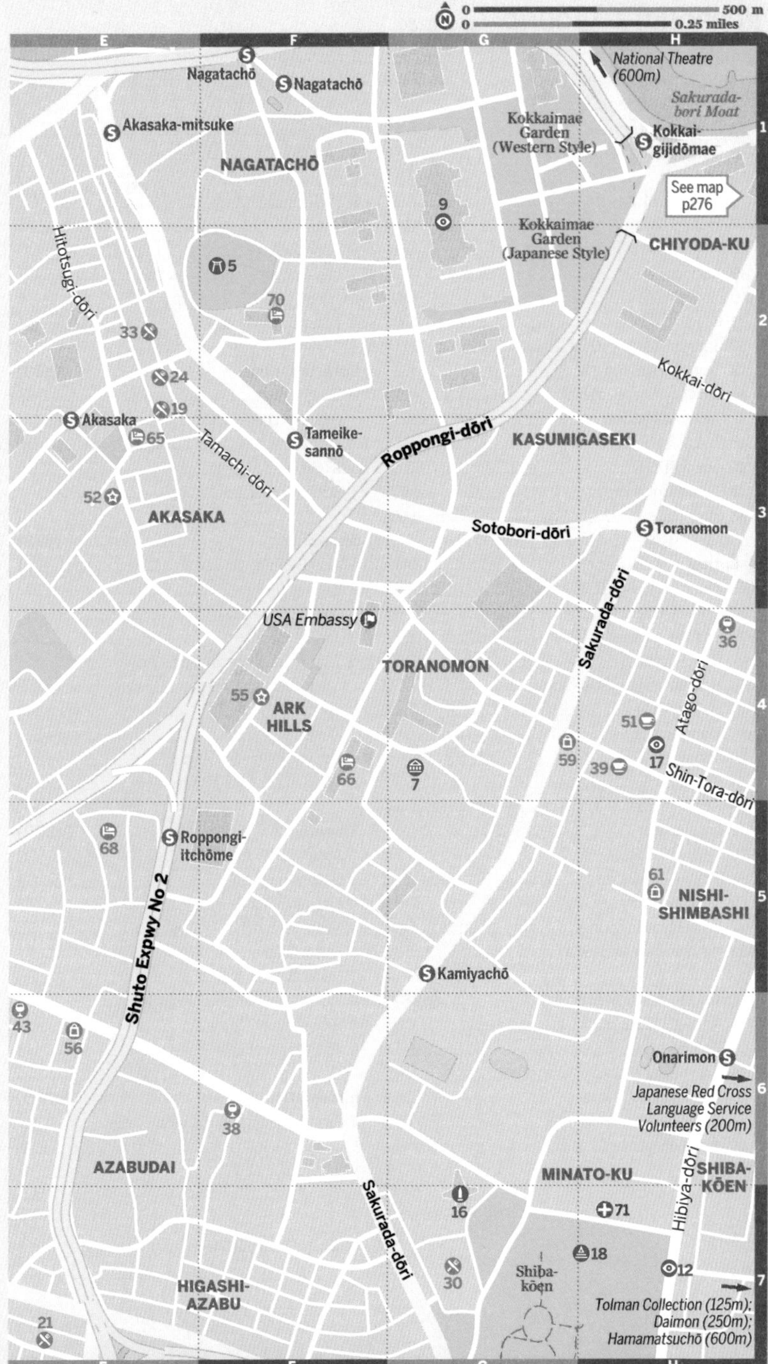

ROPPONGI & AROUND
0 500 m
0 0.25 miles
Nagatachō
Nagatachō
Akasaka-mitsuke
NAGATACHŌ
National Theatre (600m)
Sakurada-bori Moat
Kokkaimae Garden (Western Style)
Kokkai-gijidōmae
See map p276
Kokkaimae Garden (Japanese Style)
CHIYODA-KU
Hitotsugi-dōri
Kokkai-dōri
Akasaka
Tameike-sannō
Roppongi-dōri
KASUMIGASEKI
Tamachi-dōri
AKASAKA
Sotobori-dōri
Toranomon
Sakurada-dōri
USA Embassy
TORANOMON
ARK HILLS
Atago-dōri
Shin-Tora-dōri
Roppongi-itchōme
NISHI-SHIMBASHI
Shuto Expwy No 2
Kamiyachō
Onarimon
Japanese Red Cross Language Service Volunteers (200m)
AZABUDAI
MINATO-KU
SHIBA-KŌEN
Hibiya-dōri
Sakurada-dōri
Shiba-kōen
HIGASHI-AZABU
Tolman Collection (125m); Daimon (250m); Hamamatsuchō (600m)

ROPPONGI & AROUND *Map on p280*

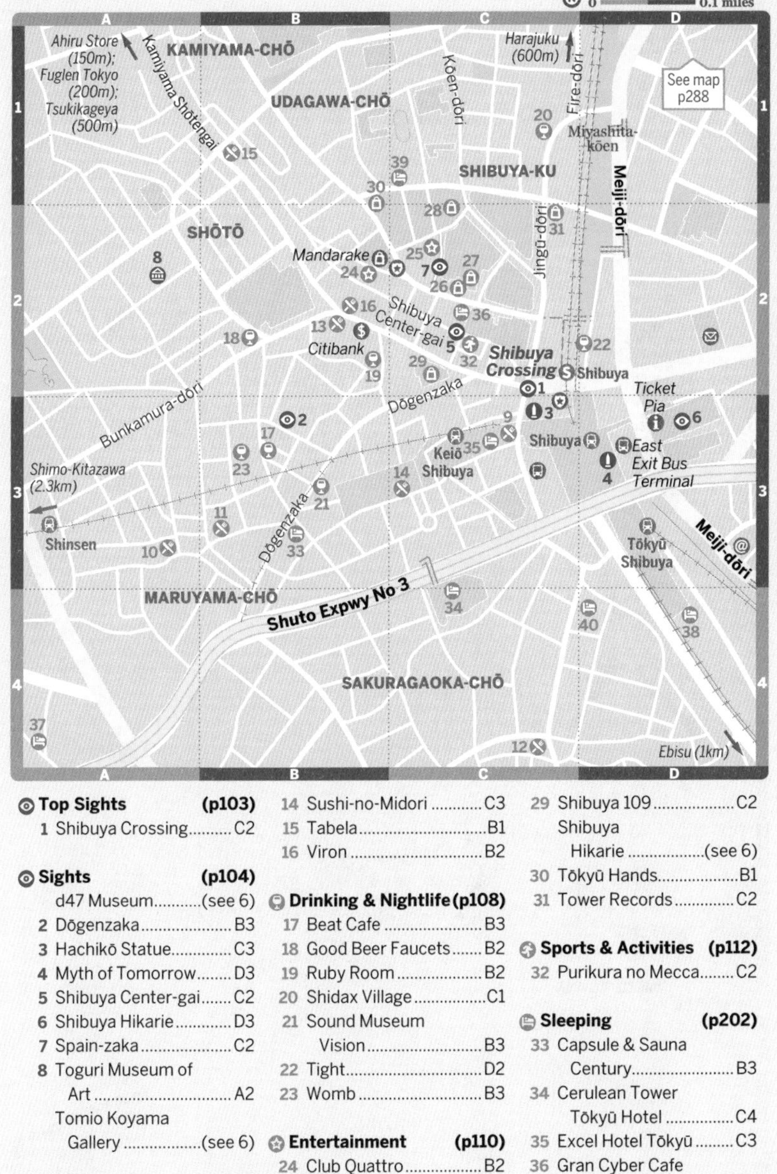

Top Sights (p103)
1 Shibuya Crossing C2

Sights (p104)
d47 Museum .... (see 6)
2 Dōgenzaka B3
3 Hachikō Statue C3
4 Myth of Tomorrow D3
5 Shibuya Center-gai C2
6 Shibuya Hikarie D3
7 Spain-zaka C2
8 Toguri Museum of Art A2
Tomio Koyama Gallery .... (see 6)

Eating (p105)
d47 Shokudō .... (see 6)
9 Food Show C3
10 Kaikaya A3
11 Matsukiya B3
12 Nagi Shokudō C4
13 Sagatani B2
14 Sushi-no-Midori C3
15 Tabela B1
16 Viron B2

Drinking & Nightlife (p108)
17 Beat Cafe B3
18 Good Beer Faucets B2
19 Ruby Room B2
20 Shidax Village C1
21 Sound Museum Vision B3
22 Tight D2
23 Womb B3

Entertainment (p110)
24 Club Quattro B2
Uplink .... (see 15)
25 WWW C2

Shopping (p111)
26 Fake Tokyo C2
27 Loft C2
28 Parco C2
29 Shibuya 109 .... C2
Shibuya Hikarie .... (see 6)
30 Tōkyū Hands B1
31 Tower Records C2

Sports & Activities (p112)
32 Purikura no Mecca C2

Sleeping (p202)
33 Capsule & Sauna Century B3
34 Cerulean Tower Tōkyū Hotel C4
35 Excel Hotel Tōkyū C3
36 Gran Cyber Cafe Bagus C2
37 Hotel Fukudaya A4
38 Hotel Mets Shibuya D4
39 Hotel Unizo C1
40 Shibuya Granbell Hotel D4

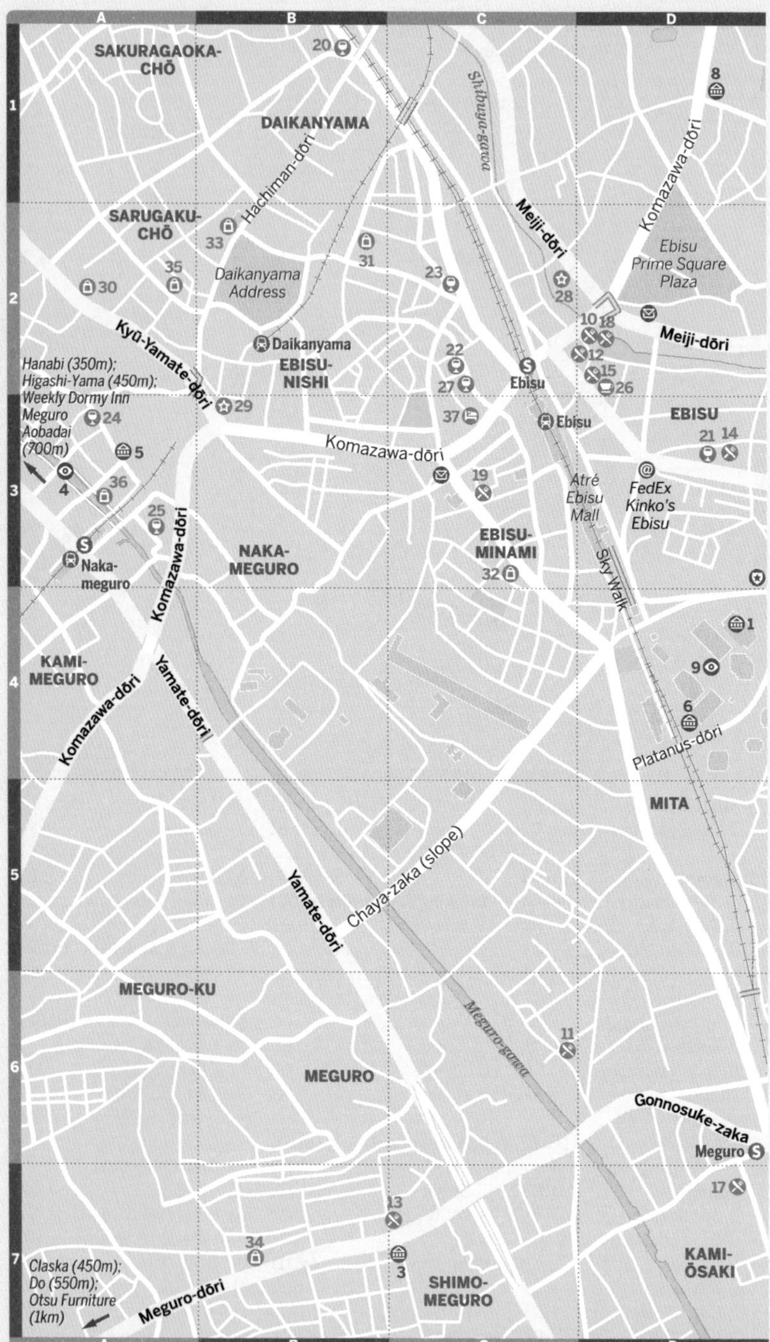
A
B
C
D
1
2
3
4
5
6
7
SAKURAGAOKA-CHŌ
DAIKANYAMA
SARUGAKU-CHŌ
Hachiman-dōri
Shibuya-gawa
Meiji-dōri
Komazawa-dōri
Ebisu Prime Square Plaza
Daikanyama Address
Daikanyama
EBISU-NISHI
Kyū-Yamate-dōri
Hanabi (350m); Higashi-Yama (450m); Weekly Dormy Inn Meguro Aobadai (700m)
Ebisu
EBISU
FedEx Kinko's Ebisu
Atré Ebisu Mall
NAKA-MEGURO
Naka-meguro
EBISU-MINAMI
Sky Walk
KAMI-MEGURO
Yamate-dōri
Platanus-dōri
MITA
Chaya-zaka (slope)
MEGURO-KU
Meguro-gawa
MEGURO
Gonnosuke-zaka
Meguro
KAMI-ŌSAKI
SHIMO-MEGURO
Meguro-dōri
Claska (450m); Do (550m); Otsu Furniture (1km)
1
3
4
5
6
8
9
10
11
12
13
14
15
17
18
19
20
21
22
23
24
25
26
27
28
29
30
31
32
33
34
35
36
37

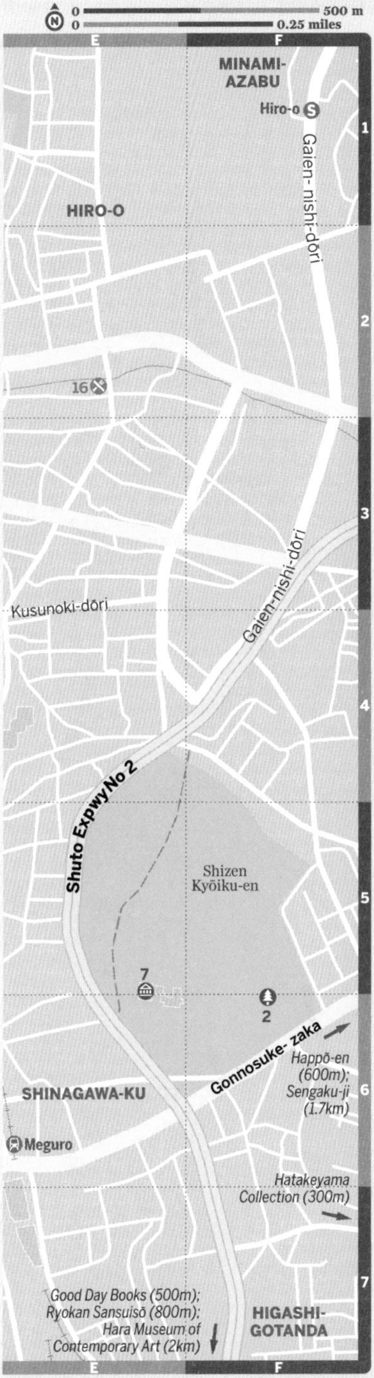
0
500 m
0
0.25 miles
E
F
MINAMI-AZABU
Hiro-o
Gaien-nishi-dōri
HIRO-O
16
Kusunoki-dōri
Gaien-nishi-dōri
Shuto Expwy No 2
Shizen Kyōiku-en
7
2
Gonnosuke- zaka
Happō-en (600m); Sengaku-ji (1.7km)
SHINAGAWA-KU
Meguro
Hatakeyama Collection (300m)
Good Day Books (500m); Ryokan Sansuisō (800m); Hara Museum of Contemporary Art (2km)
HIGASHI-GOTANDA
1
2
3
4
5
6
7
E
F

Sights **(p92)**

1 Beer Museum Yebisu D4
2 Institute for Nature Study F6
3 Meguro Parasitological Museum C7
4 Meguro-gawa A3
5 The Container A3
6 Tokyo Metropolitan Museum of Photography D4
7 Tokyo Metropolitan Teien Art Museum E5
8 Yamatane Museum of Art D1
9 Yebisu Garden Place D4

Eating **(p93)**

10 Afuri D2
11 Beard C6
Bombay Bazar .... (see 35)
12 Ebisu-yokochō D2
13 Ganko Dako C7
14 Ippo D3
15 Ouca D2
16 Ta-im E2
17 Tonki D7
18 Udon Yamachō D2
19 Yakiniku Champion C3

Drinking & Nightlife **(p97)**

20 Air B1
21 Bar Martha D3
22 Buri C2
23 Enjoy House C2
24 Kinfolk Lounge A3
25 Nakame Takkyū Lounge A3
26 Sarutahiko Coffee D2
27 What the Dickens! C2

Entertainment **(p99)**

28 Liquid Room C2
29 Unit B3

Shopping **(p100)**

30 Daikanyama T-Site A2
31 Harcoza B2
32 Kapital C3
33 La Fuente Building B2
34 Meister B7
35 Okura A2
36 Vase A3

Sleeping **(p201)**

37 Hotel Excellent Ebisu C3

SHINJUKU

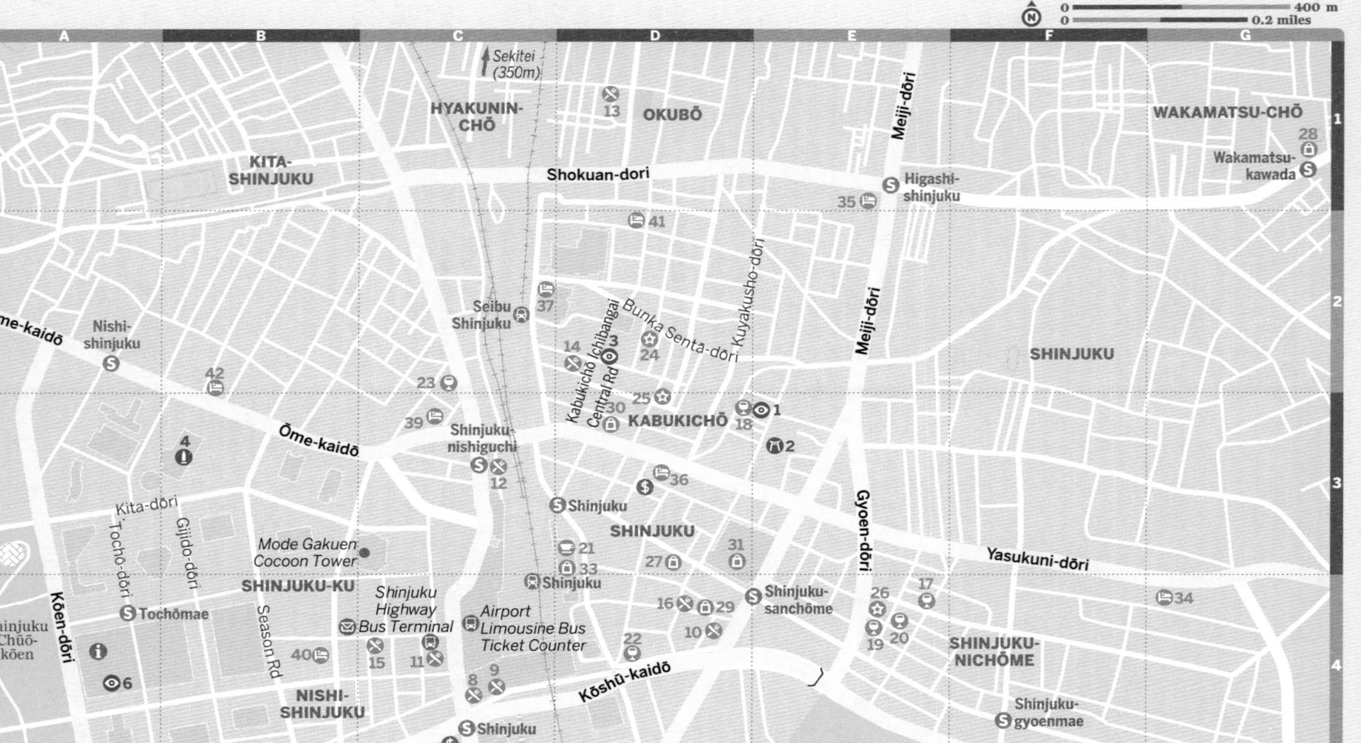

0
400 m
0
0.2 miles
Sekitei (350m)
HYAKUNIN-CHŌ
13
OKUBŌ
Meiji-dōri
WAKAMATSU-CHŌ
28
Wakamatsu-kawada
KITA-SHINJUKU
Shokuan-dori
Higashi-shinjuku
35
41
Kuyakusho-dōri
37
Seibu Shinjuku
Bunka Senta-dōri
Kabukichō Ichibangai
Central Rd
Meiji-dōri
Ōme-kaidō
Nishi-shinjuku
14
3
24
SHINJUKU
42
23
25
1
30
KABUKICHŌ
18
39
Shinjuku-nishiguchi
Ōme-kaidō
4
2
12
36
Shinjuku
Gyoen-dōri
Kita-dōri
SHINJUKU
Tochō-dōri
Gijido-dōri
Mode Gakuen Cocoon Tower
21
31
27
Yasukuni-dōri
33
SHINJUKU-KU
Shinjuku
17
34
Shinjuku Highway Bus Terminal
16
29
Shinjuku-sanchōme
26
Tochōmae
Season Rd
Airport Limousine Bus Ticket Counter
20
Shinjuku Chūō-kōen
Kōen-dōri
10
19
22
SHINJUKU-NICHŌME
40
15
11
9
Kōshū-kaidō
6
8
NISHI-SHINJUKU
Shinjuku-gyoenmae
Shinjuku

Sights (p127)

1 Golden Gai ... E3
2 Hanazono-jinja ... E3
3 Kabukichō ... D2
4 Shinjuku I-Land ... B3
5 Shinjuku-gyoen ... E5
6 Tokyo Metropolitan Government Offices ... A4

Eating (p129)

7 Kozue ... A5
8 Lumine ... C4
9 Mylord ... C4
Nagi ... (see 1)
10 Nakajima ... D4
11 Numazukō ... C4
12 Omoide-yokochō ... C3
13 Shin-chan ... D1
14 Shinjuku Asia-yokochō ... D2
15 Tsuki no Shizuka ... C4
16 Tsunahachi ... D4

Drinking & Nightlife (p133)

17 Advocates Café ... E4
18 Albatross G ... D3
Araku ... (see 1)
19 Arty Farty ... E4
20 Bar Goldfinger ... E4
21 Berg ... D3
Golden Gai ... (see 1)
New York Bar ... (see 43)
22 Samurai ... D4
23 Zoetrope ... C2

Entertainment (p135)

24 Loft ... D2
25 Robot Restaurant ... D3
26 Shinjuku Pit Inn ... E4

Shopping (p136)

27 Bicqlo ... D3
28 Bingoya ... G1
29 Disk Union ... D4
30 Don Quijote ... D3
31 Isetan ... D3
32 Kinokuniya ... D5
33 RanKing RanQueen ... D3

Sleeping (p203)

34 Citadines ... G4
35 E Hotel Higashi-Shinjuku ... E1
36 Gran Cyber Cafe Bagus ... D3
37 Green Plaza Shinjuku ... C2
38 Hotel Century Southern Tower ... C5
39 Ibis Tokyo Shinjuku ... C3
40 Kadoya Hotel ... B4
41 Ladies 510 ... D2
42 Nishitetsu Inn Shinjuku ... B2
43 Park Hyatt Tokyo ... A5

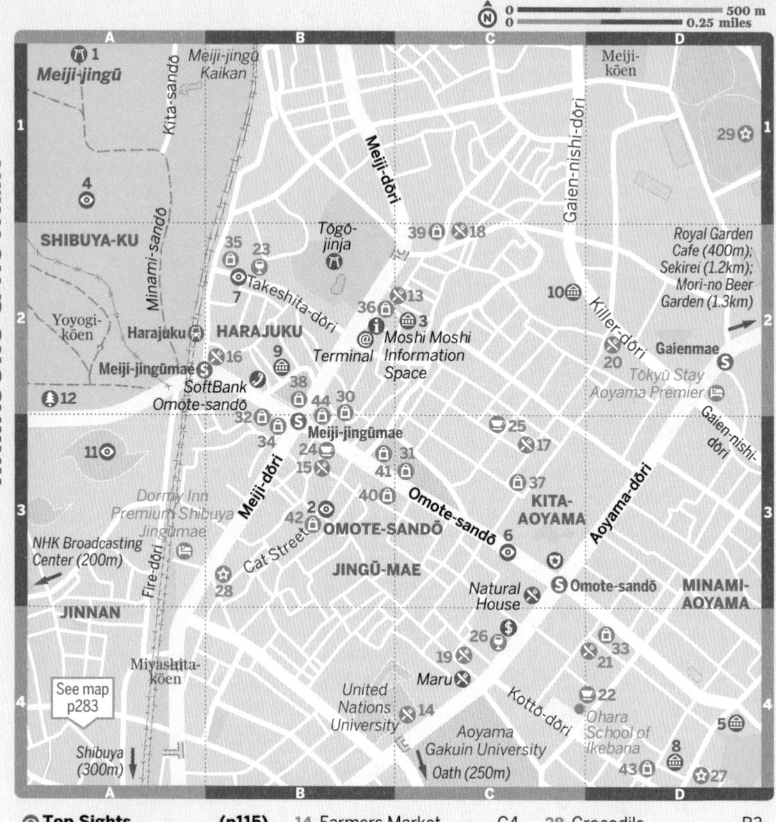

Top Sights (p115)

1 Meiji-jingū......A1

Sights (p116)

2 Cat Street......B3
3 Design Festa......C2
4 Meiji-jingū Gyoen......A1
5 Nezu Museum......D4
6 Omote-sandō......C3
7 Takeshita-dōri......B2
8 Taro Okamoto Memorial Museum......D4
9 Ukiyo-e Ōta Memorial Museum of Art......B2
10 Watari Museum of Contemporary Art......C2
11 Yoyogi National Stadium......A3
12 Yoyogi-kōen......A2

Eating (p117)

13 Agaru Sagaru Nishi Iru Higashi Iru......C2
14 Farmers Market......C4
15 Harajuku Gyōza-rō......B3
Kinokuniya International Supermarket......(see 26)
16 Kyūsyū Jangara......B2
17 Maisen......C3
18 Mominoki House......C2
19 Pariya......C4
Sakura-tei......(see 3)
20 World Breakfast Allday......D2
21 Yanmo......D4

Drinking & Nightlife (p119)

22 A to Z Cafe......D4
23 Harajuku Taproom......B2
24 Montoak......B3
25 Omotesando Koffee......C3
26 Two Rooms......C4

Entertainment (p122)

27 Blue Note Tokyo......D4
28 Crocodile......B3
29 Jingū Baseball Stadium......D1

Shopping (p123)

30 6% Doki Doki......B2
31 Bedrock......C3
32 Chicago Thrift Store......B3
33 Comme des Garçons......D4
34 Condomania......B3
35 Daiso......B2
36 Dog......B2
37 Gallery Kawano......C3
KiddyLand......(see 24)
38 Laforet......B2
39 Musubi......C2
On Sundays......(see 10)
40 Oriental Bazaar......B3
41 Pass the Baton......B3
42 RagTag......B3
43 Sou-Sou......D4
44 Tokyo's Tokyo......B3

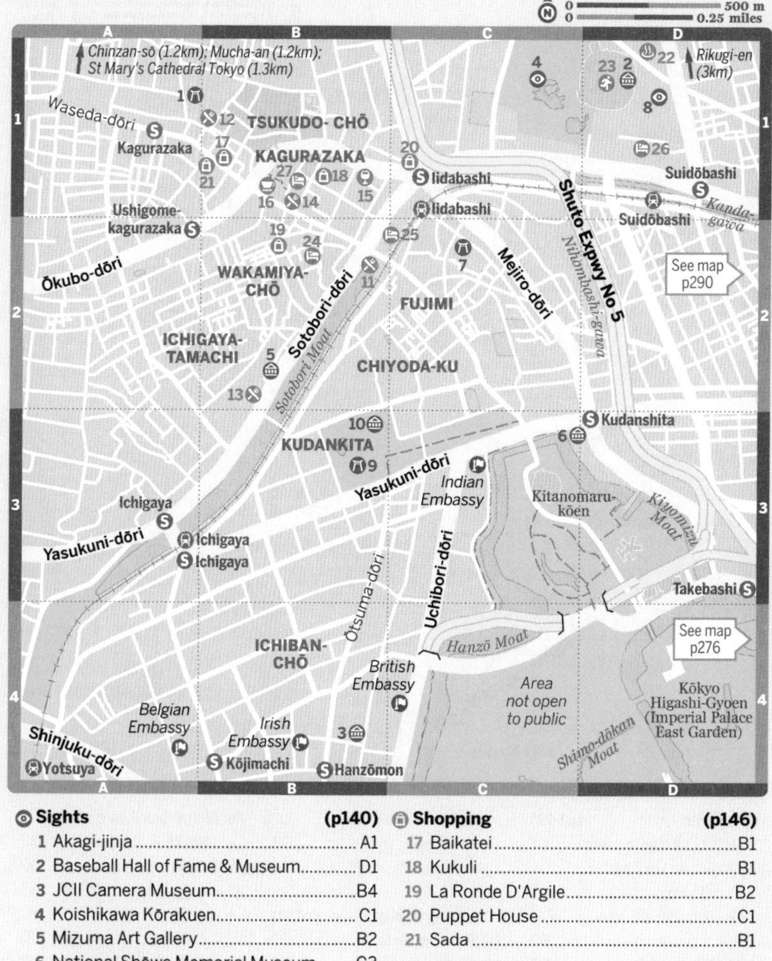

Sights (p140)

1 Akagi-jinja ... A1
2 Baseball Hall of Fame & Museum ... D1
3 JCII Camera Museum ... B4
4 Koishikawa Kōrakuen ... C1
5 Mizuma Art Gallery ... B2
6 National Shōwa Memorial Museum ... C3
7 Tokyo Dai-jingū ... C2
8 Tokyo Dome City Attractions ... D1
9 Yasukuni-jinja ... B3
10 Yūshū-kan ... B3

Eating (p141)

11 Canal Cafe ... B2
12 Kado ... B1
13 Kururi ... B2
14 Le Bretagne ... B1

Drinking & Nightlife (p145)

15 Beer Bar Bitter ... B1
16 Mugimaru 2 ... B1

Shopping (p146)

17 Baikatei ... B1
18 Kukuli ... B1
19 La Ronde D'Argile ... B2
20 Puppet House ... C1
21 Sada ... B1

Sports & Activities (p146)

22 Spa LaQua ... D1
23 Tokyo Dome ... D1

Sleeping (p204)

24 The Agnes Hotel ... B2
25 Tokyo Central Youth Hostel ... C2
26 Tokyo Dome Hotel ... D1
27 Wakana ... B1

Sights (p149)
1 3331 Arts Chiyoda C1
2 Akihabara Electric Town C2
3 Akihabara Radio Center D2
4 Gallery Kura C2
5 Kanda Myōjin (Kanda Shrine) C1
6 Nikolai Cathedral B2
7 Origami Kaikan B1
8 Tokyo Anime Center Akiba Info D2
9 Tokyo Wonder Site Hongo A1
10 Yushima Seidō (Yushima Shrine) C1

Eating (p150)
11 Amanoya C1
12 Botan C3
13 Isegen C2
14 Kanda Yabu Soba C2
15 Kikanbō D3
Komaki Shokudō .... (see 26)

Drinking & Nightlife (p151)
16 @Home Cafe C2
17 AKB48 Cafe D2
Boo .... (see 24)
Cafe Asan .... (see 24)
18 Craft Beer Market Awajichō C3
19 Craft Beer Market Jimbōchō A3
20 Imasa C1
21 Milonga Nueva A3
22 N3331 .... C2

Entertainment (p151)
23 AKB48 Theatre D1

Shopping (p151)
24 2k540 Aki-Oka Artisan D1
25 Akihabara Radio Kaikan D2
26 Chabara D2
27 Jimbōchō Bookstores ... A3
Kayōdō Hobby Lobby .... (see 25)
K-Books .... (see 25)
Komiyama Shoten .... (see 27)
28 mAAch ecute C2
29 Mandarake Complex C1
30 Ohya Shobō B3
31 Technologia D1
32 Yodobashi Akiba D2

Sports & Activities (p152)
33 Super Potato Retro-kan C2

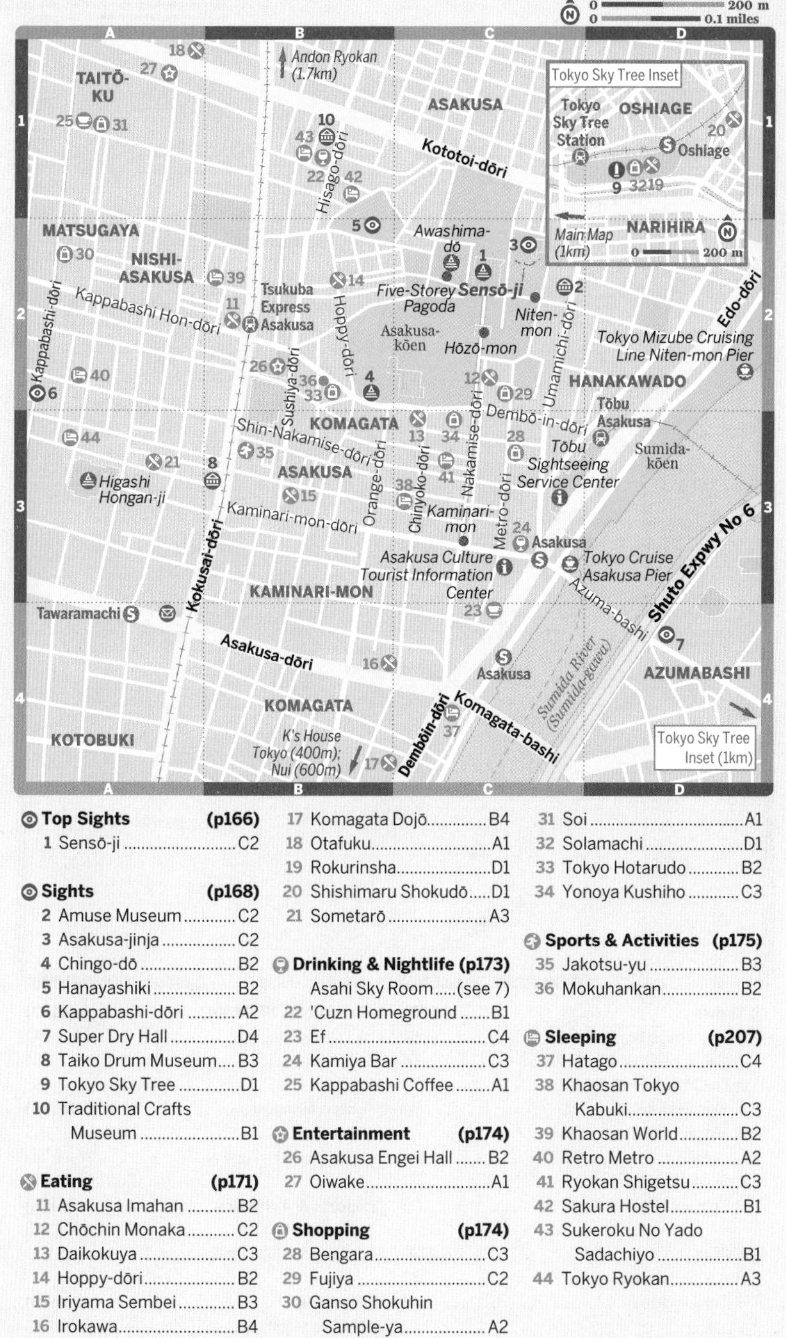

Top Sights (p166)
1 Sensō-ji C2

Sights (p168)
2 Amuse Museum C2
3 Asakusa-jinja C2
4 Chingo-dō B2
5 Hanayashiki B2
6 Kappabashi-dōri A2
7 Super Dry Hall D4
8 Taiko Drum Museum B3
9 Tokyo Sky Tree D1
10 Traditional Crafts Museum B1

Eating (p171)
11 Asakusa Imahan B2
12 Chōchin Monaka C2
13 Daikokuya C3
14 Hoppy-dōri B2
15 Iriyama Sembei B3
16 Irokawa B4
17 Komagata Dojō B4
18 Otafuku A1
19 Rokurinsha D1
20 Shishimaru Shokudō D1
21 Sometarō A3

Drinking & Nightlife (p173)
Asahi Sky Room .... (see 7)
22 'Cuzn Homeground B1
23 Ef C4
24 Kamiya Bar C3
25 Kappabashi Coffee A1

Entertainment (p174)
26 Asakusa Engei Hall B2
27 Oiwake A1

Shopping (p174)
28 Bengara C3
29 Fujiya C2
30 Ganso Shokuhin Sample-ya A2
31 Soi A1
32 Solamachi D1
33 Tokyo Hotarudo B2
34 Yonoya Kushiho C3

Sports & Activities (p175)
35 Jakotsu-yu B3
36 Mokuhankan B2

Sleeping (p207)
37 Hatago C4
38 Khaosan Tokyo Kabuki C3
39 Khaosan World B2
40 Retro Metro A2
41 Ryokan Shigetsu C3
42 Sakura Hostel B1
43 Sukeroku No Yado Sadachiyo B1
44 Tokyo Ryokan A3

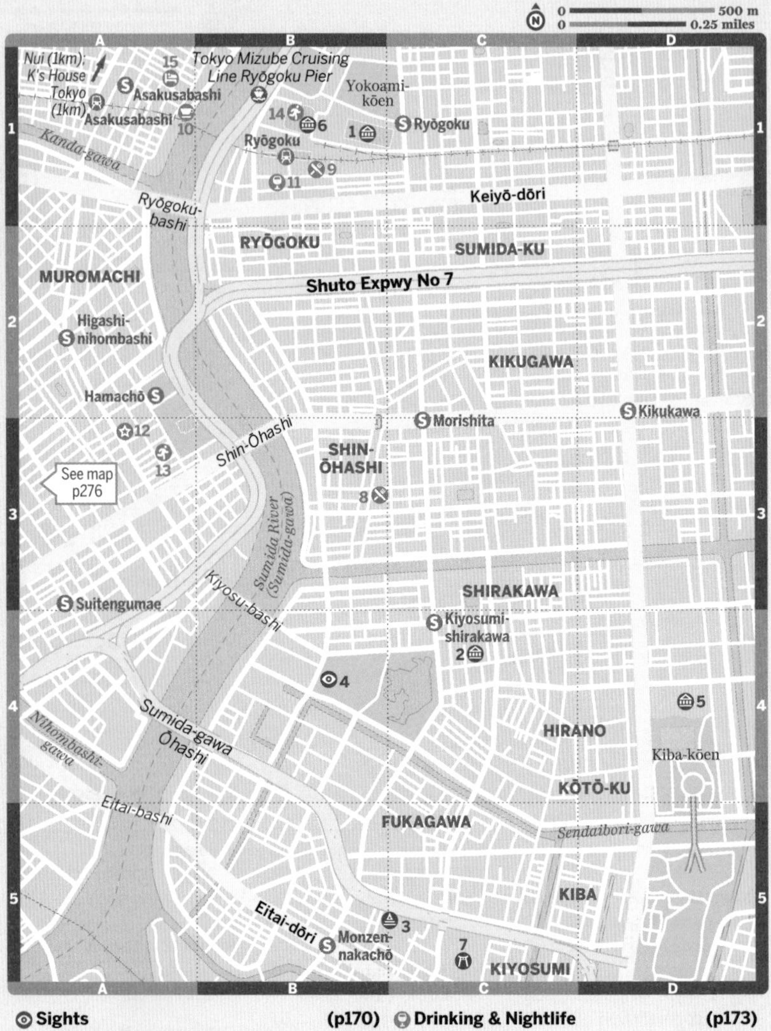

Sights (p170)

1 Edo-Tokyo Museum B1
2 Fukagawa Edo Museum C4
3 Fukagawa Fudō-dō C5
4 Kiyosumi-teien B4
5 Museum of Contemporary Art, Tokyo (MOT) D4
6 Sumo Museum B1
7 Tomioka Hachiman-gū C5

Eating (p172)

8 Kappō Miyako B3
9 Tomoegata B1

Drinking & Nightlife (p173)

10 Lucite Gallery A1
11 Popeye B1

Entertainment (p174)

12 Meiji-za A3
Ryōgoku Kokugikan .... (see 14)

Sports & Activities (p175)

13 Arashio Stable A3
14 Ryōgoku Kokugikan B1

Sleeping (p208)

15 Anne Hostel A1

ODAIBA & TOKYO BAY

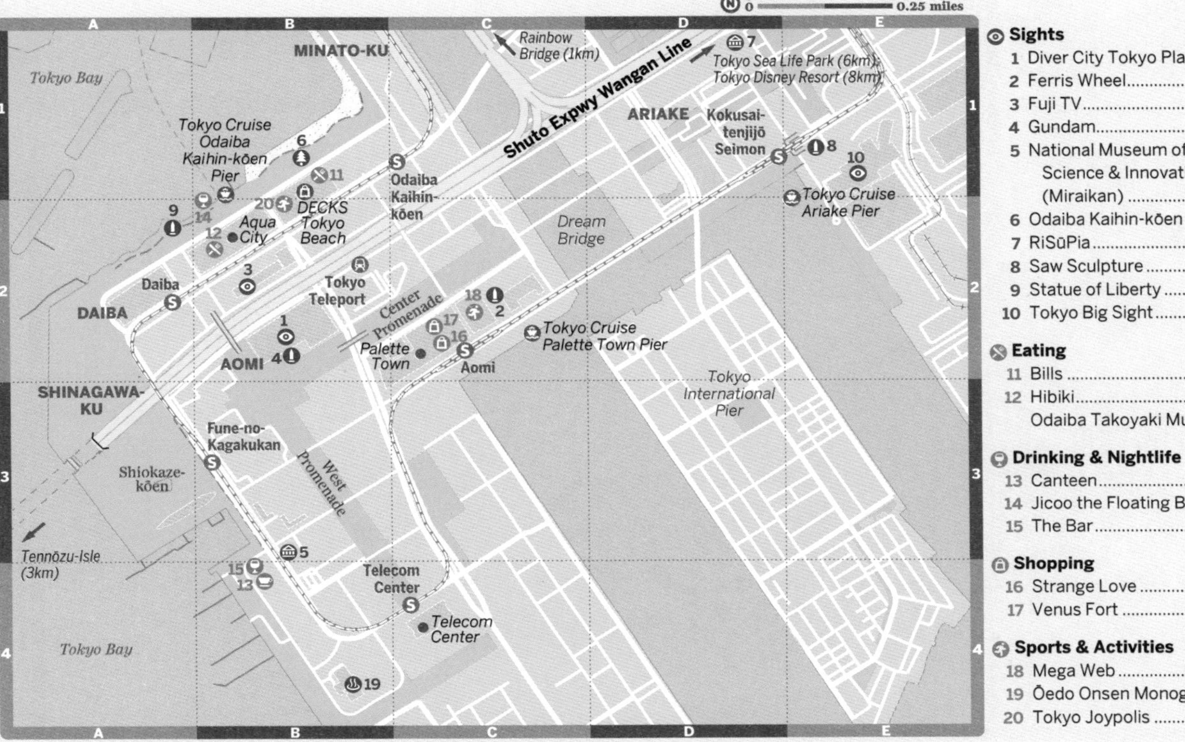

Sights (p178)

1 Diver City Tokyo Plaza B2
2 Ferris Wheel C2
3 Fuji TV B2
4 Gundam B2
5 National Museum of Emerging Science & Innovation (Miraikan) B3
6 Odaiba Kaihin-kōen B1
7 RiSūPia D1
8 Saw Sculpture E1
9 Statue of Liberty A2
10 Tokyo Big Sight E1

Eating (p179)

11 Bills B1
12 Hibiki B2
Odaiba Takoyaki Museum .... (see 11)

Drinking & Nightlife (p180)

13 Canteen B4
14 Jicoo the Floating Bar B2
15 The Bar B4

Shopping (p180)

16 Strange Love C2
17 Venus Fort C2

Sports & Activities (p180)

18 Mega Web C2
19 Ōedo Onsen Monogatari B4
20 Tokyo Joypolis B2

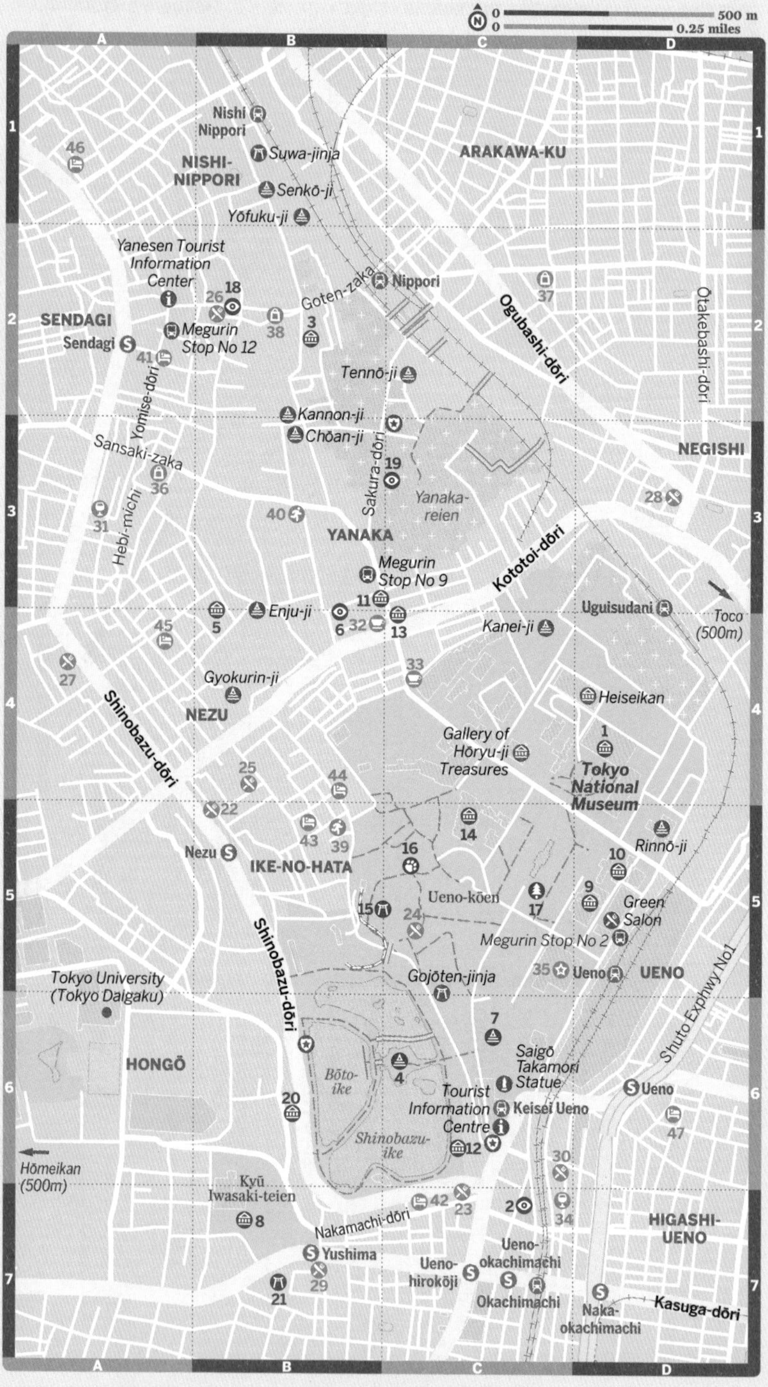

UENO & YANAKA

0 500 m
0 0.25 miles
A B C D
1 2 3 4 5 6 7
Nishi Nippori
NISHI-NIPPORI
Suwa-jinja
Senkō-ji
Yōfuku-ji
ARAKAWA-KU
46
Yanesen Tourist Information Center
26
18
38
3
Goten-zaka
Nippori
37
Ogubashi-dōri
Ōtakebashi-dōri
SENDAGI
Sendagi
Megurin Stop No 12
41
Yomise-dōri
Tennō-ji
Kannon-ji
Chōan-ji
Sansaki-zaka
36
19
Sakura-dōri
Yanaka-reien
NEGISHI
28
31
Hebi-michi
40
YANAKA
Kototoi-dōri
Megurin Stop No 9
11
Enju-ji
6
32
13
5
45
Uguisudani
Toco (500m)
Kanei-ji
27
33
Gyokurin-ji
NEZU
Heiseikan
Shinobazu-dōri
Gallery of Hōryu-ji Treasures
1
Tokyo National Museum
25
44
22
43
39
14
Rinnō-ji
Nezu
IKE-NO-HATA
16
10
9
Ueno-kōen
17
Green Salon
15
24
Megurin Stop No 2
35
Ueno
UENO
Gojōten-jinja
Shuto Expwy No1
Tokyo University (Tokyo Daigaku)
7
HONGŌ
Bōto-ike
4
Saigō Takamori Statue
Tourist Information Centre
Keisei Ueno
Ueno
20
47
Shinobazu-ike
12
Hōmeikan (500m)
30
Kyū Iwasaki-teien
42
23
2
34
8
Nakamachi-dōri
HIGASHI-UENO
Yushima
Ueno-okachimachi
Ueno-hirokōji
29
21
Okachimachi
Naka-okachimachi
Kasuga-dōri

UENO

Top Sights (p155)

1 Tokyo National Museum....D4

Sights (p158)

2 Ameya-yokochō....C7
3 Asakura Chōso Museum....B2
4 Benten-dō....C6
5 Daimyo Clock Museum....B4
6 Edokoro Allan West....B4
7 Kiyōmizu Kannon-dō....C6
8 Kyū Iwasaki-teien....B7
9 National Museum of Western Art....D5
10 National Science Museum....D5
11 SCAI the Bathhouse....B3
12 Shitamachi Museum....C6
13 Shitamachi Museum Annex....C4
14 Tokyo Metropolitan Museum of Art....C5
15 Ueno Tōshō-gū....B5
16 Ueno Zoo....C5
17 Ueno-kōen....C5
18 Yanaka Ginza....B2
19 Yanaka-reien....C3
20 Yokoyama Taikan Memorial Hall....B6
21 Yushima Tenjin....B7

Eating (p161)

22 Hantei....B5
23 Izu-ei Honten....C7
24 Izu-ei Umekawa-tei....C5
25 Kamachiku....B4
26 Nagomi....B2
27 Nezu no Taiyaki....A4
28 Sasa-no-Yuki....D3
29 Shinsuke....B7
30 Yabu Soba....C6

Drinking & Nightlife (p162)

31 Bousingot....A3
32 Kayaba Coffee....B4
33 Torindō....C4
34 Warrior Celt....C7

Entertainment (p163)

35 Tokyo Bunka Kaikan....C5

Shopping (p163)

36 Isetatsu....A3
37 Nippori Fabric Town....C2
38 Yanaka Matsunoya....B2

Sports & Activities (p163)

39 Rokuryu Kōsen....B5
40 Tokyo Bike Gallery....B3

Sleeping (p206)

41 Annex Katsutarō Ryokan....A2
42 Hotel Coco Grand....C7
43 Hotel Graphy....B5
44 Ryokan Katsutarō....B4
45 Sawanoya Ryokan....A4
46 TokHouse....A1
47 Tougenya Hotel....D6

Our Story

A beat-up old car, a few dollars in the pocket and a sense of adventure. In 1972 that's all Tony and Maureen Wheeler needed for the trip of a lifetime – across Europe and Asia overland to Australia. It took several months, and at the end – broke but inspired – they sat at their kitchen table writing and stapling together their first travel guide, *Across Asia on the Cheap*. Within a week they'd sold 1500 copies. Lonely Planet was born.

Today, Lonely Planet has offices in Franklin, London, Melbourne, Oakland, Beijing and Delhi, with more than 600 staff and writers. We share Tony's belief that 'a great guidebook should do three things: inform, educate and amuse'.

Our Writers

Rebecca Milner

Ebisu, Meguro & Around; Shibuya & Shimo-Kitazawa; Harajuku & Aoyama; Shinjuku & West Tokyo; Kōrakuen & Northwest Tokyo; Ueno & Yanaka; Asakusa & Sumida River Rebecca came to Tokyo for 'just one year' in 2002 and still hasn't been able to tear herself away. She's lived west of Shinjuku and east of the Sumida and now shares an apartment in Shibuya (the quiet part) with her husband and cat. Her writing has appeared in the *Guardian*, *Japan Times*, CNN Travel, BBC Travel and Lonely Planet guides to Japan.

Rebecca also wrote the Welcome to Tokyo, Tokyo's Top 16, What's New, Need to Know, Top Itineraries, If You Like..., Month by Month, With Kids, Like a Local, For Free, Eating, Shopping, Neighbourhoods at a Glance, Sleeping, Tokyo Today, History and Arts & Architecture chapters, and the Survival Guide.

Read more about Rebecca at:
lonelyplanet.com/members/rebeccamilner

Simon Richmond

Marunouchi & Nihombashi, Ginza & Tsukiji, Roppongi & Around, Akihabara & Around, Odaiba & Tokyo Bay Travel writer, photographer and videographer Simon Richmond won travel guidebook of the year for his first coauthored guidebook on Japan, published in 1999. He's also written several guidebooks to Tokyo (where he lived and worked as a journalist and editor in the early 1990s) and books on anime and manga. An author with Lonely Planet since 1999, Simon has worked for the company on many titles and features for its website. Read more about Simon's travels at www.simonrichmond.com and on Twitter and Instagram @simonrichmond.

Simon also wrote the Drinking & Nightlife, Entertainment, Day Trips from Tokyo, Sleeping, Pop Culture & Technology and Onsen chapters.

Published by Lonely Planet Publications Pty Ltd
ABN 36 005 607 983
10th edition – Aug 2015
ISBN 978 1 74220 883 1

10 9 8 7 6 5 4 3 2
Printed in China